TEXT, CASES
and
COMMENTARY
on the
HONG KONG
LEGAL SYSTEM

TEXT, CASES and COMMENTARY on the HONG KONG LEGAL SYSTEM

Michael John Fisher

Hong Kong University Press
The University of Hong Kong
Pokfulam Road
Hong Kong
www.hkupress.org

© 2019 Hong Kong University Press

ISBN 978-988-8390-96-0 (*Hardback*)
ISBN 978-988-8390-97-7 (*Paperback*)

All rights reserved. No portion of this publication may be reproduced or transmitted in any form or by any means, electronic or mechanical, including photocopying, recording, or any information storage or retrieval system, without prior permission in writing from the publisher.

The copyright in the Judgments HCMP3908/1997 *Guido Karl Wenk v Alan Lee Goldstein* (16.7.1998) and FACV24/2007 *A Solicitor v The Law Society of Hong Kong* (13.3.2008) are owned by the Government of the Hong Kong Special Administrative Region ("Government"). The Judgments published in *Text, Cases and Commentary on the Hong Kong Legal System* are reproduced from those posted on the Judiciary's website with the permission of the Government. The Government accepts no liability or responsibility for the accuracy or completeness of any of the Judgements being published in *Text, Cases and Commentary on the Hong Kong Legal System*.

British Library Cataloguing-in-Publication Data
A catalogue record for this book is available from the British Library.

10 9 8 7 6 5 4 3 2 1

Printed and bound by Ocean Printing Co. Ltd., Hong Kong, China

Contents

Table of Cases	vi
Table of Legislation	xi
Introduction	xv
1. The Development of the Hong Kong Legal System, 1842–1997	1
2. Sources of Hong Kong Law	59
3. The Hong Kong Court System	129
4. Legislation and the Interpretation of Statutes	173
5. Judicial Precedent and the Doctrine of *Stare Decisis*	236
6. Hong Kong's Professional Judiciary	271
7. The Legal Profession and Legal Education	302
8. Lay Participation in the Hong Kong Legal System	339
9. Legal Aid and Advice and Unmet Legal Need	367
10. Alternative Dispute Resolution	401
11. The HKSAR and PRC Legal Systems Compared	432
12. The Legal Interface between Hong Kong and Mainland China	489
13. Policing and the Decision to Prosecute	528
14. An Introduction to Legal Research in Hong Kong	565
Postscript	588
Illustration Credits/Acknowledgements	593
Index	595

Table of Cases

Hong Kong

Agrila Ltd & Others v Commissioner of Rating & Valuation [2001] HKCFA 42   215

A Solicitor v Law Society of Hong Kong [2006] 2 HKC 429   310, 321

A Solicitor v Law Society of Hong Kong [2008] 2 HKC 1; (2008) HKCFAR 117   46, 48, 50, 102, 105, 109, 121, 131, 132, 239–249, 252, 258–261, 264, 291, 567, 582, 583

A Solicitor v Law Society of Hong Kong and Secretary for Justice [2003] HKCFA 14   108, 136, 324, 446

Aspial Investment Ltd v Mayer Corp [2014] 5 HKC 259   153

Attorney-General v Lui Fuk-yuen (1976) Fct, Crim App No 300 of 1975   218

Bank of China (Hong Kong) Ltd v Fung Chin Kan [2003] 1 HKLRD 181   308

Bank of China (Hong Kong) Ltd v Twin Profit Ltd & Others [2012] 4 HKC 75   153

Bank of China (Hong Kong) Ltd v Wong King Sing & Others [2002] 1 HKC 83   120, 121

Bank of China (Hong Kong) Ltd v Yang Fan [2016] 3 HKLRD 7   495

Beijing Tong Gang Da Sheng Trade Co Ltd v Allen & Overy (A Firm) & Another [2014] 4 HKC 333 (CFI); [2015] HKCA 234   394

Best Sheen Development Ltd v Official receiver and Trustee [2001] 3 HKC 79   89

C & Others v Director of Immigration (2013) 16 HKCFAR 280   149, 386

Calimpex International Co (A Firm) v ENZ Information Systems Ltd [1994] 1 HKC 191   267

CCIC Finance Ltd v Guangdong International Trust & Investment Corporation [2005] 2 HKC 589   516

Chan Kam Nga v Director of Immigration [1999] 1 HKC 347   98, 137, 224, 225

Chan Shun Cho v Chak Hok Ping (Re Chak Chiu Hang) [1925] 20 HKLR 1   4, 5

Chen Li Hung & Another v Ting Lei Mao & Others [2000] 1 HKC 461 (Ku Chia Chun & Others v Ting Lei Miao & Others)   515

Cheung Chi-man v R (1974) FCt, Crim App No 265 of 1974   218

Cheung Lai Wah v Director of Immigration   245

China Field Ltd v Appeal Tribunal (Buildings) (2009) 12 HKCFAR   342

Chiyu Banking Corporation Ltd v Chan Tin Kwun [1996] 2 HKLR 395   492

Chun Sang Plastics v Commissioner of Police [2018] HKCFI 661   218

Commissioner for Television & Entertainment Licensing Authority v Oriental Daily Publisher Ltd & Others (1998) 1 HKCFAR 279   147

Commissioner of Inland Revenue v
  Common Empire Ltd [2004] HKIA 1
  200, 213

Delight World Ltd v The Town Planning
  Appeal Board [1997] HKLRD 1106
  212, 213
Democratic Republic of the Congo v FG
  Hemisphere Associates LLC [2009] 1
  HKLRD 410 (CFI)   229
Democratic Republic of the Congo v FG
  Hemisphere Associates LLC [2010] 2
  HKLRD 66 (CA)   229
Democratic Republic of the Congo v FG
  Hemisphere Associates LLC (2011) 14
  HKCFAR 95   41,97, 228–232, 438
Director of Immigration v Chong Fung Yuen
  [2000] 1 HKC 359   214, 226, 232

Esquire (Electronics) Ltd v HSBC Ltd &
  Another [2006] HKCA 383   276

FB & Others v Director of Immigration
  386
Feerni Development Ltd v Daniel Wong &
  Partners [2001] 1 HKC 373   323
First Laser v Fujian Enterprises (Holdings)
  Company Ltd (2012) 15 HKCFAR 569
  489

GA & Others v Director of Immigration
  387
Guido Karl Wenk v Alan Lee Goldstein
  [1998] HKCFI 252   196–198

Hong Kong Racing Pigeon Association v
  Attorney-General & Another [1995] 2
  HKC 201   213
Hong Kong SAR v Lee York Fai & Others
  CAAR 3/2011   166
Hong Kong SAR v Ma Wai Kwan David
  [1997] 2 HKC 315   25, 34, 100, 241
Hong Kong SAR v Ng Kung Siu [1999] 1
  HKLRD 783   68
Hong Kong SAR v Ngo Van Nam (2016)
  CACC 418/2014   167, 316

Hong Kong SAR v Pan Shenfang & Others
  (No 823 of 2002)   161
Hong Kong SAR v Wan Hon Sik [2001] 3
  HKLRD 283   199, 220
Hong Kong SAR v Yeung May Wan [2004]
  3 HKLRD 797   172
Ho Tsz Tsun v Ho Au Shi & Others [1915]
  10 HKLR 69   4, 5, 116

In the Matter of a Solicitor (1999) CACV
  No 182 of 1999   311
Intelligent House Ltd v Chan Tung Shing &
  Others [2008] 4 HKC 421   143

Joint Official Liquidators of A Co and B Co
  [2014] 4 HKLRD 374   515

Kunming Factory of Prestressed
  Vibrohydropressed Concrete Pipe v
  True Stand Investment Ltd & Another
  [2006] 4 HKLRD   501

Lam Chi Kong v Tai Siu Chin & Another
  [2007] HKCU 975   324
Lam Kin Sum v Hong Kong Housing
  Authority [2004] HKCA 349   214
Lam Kwan-shi v Lam Wan-hing [1967]
  HKLR 616   218
Lau Kong Yung & Others v Director of
  Immigration   171, 225
Lee Fuk Hing v Hong Kong SAR [2004] 7
  HKCFAR 600
Leverson Ltd v Secretary for Transport
  [2003] HKLdT 11   200–202

Man Leung v Man Yuet Kwai [2013] 2
  HKLRD 1122   117
Medical Council of Hong Kong v Chow Siu
  Shek [2000] 2 HKC 428   203

Ng Fung Hong Ltd v ABC [1998] 1 HKC
  291   497
Ng Siu Tung & Others v Director of
  Immigration (2002) 5 HKCFAR   225
Ng Yuen-shiu v Attorney-General [1981]
  HKLR 352   245

Nishimatsu-Costain-China Harbour Joint Venture v Ip Kwan & Co [2000] 2 HKC 445   308

Pepsi-Cola International Ltd v Charles Lee [1974] HKLR 13   566

R v Kwong Kui Wing & Others 1 HKDCLR 15   251
R v Ling Yee Shun [1988] HKCFI 394   220
R v Pang Chun Wai [1993] 1 HKC 233   164
R v Yuen Kuen Chi (1985) Cr App No 52 0f 1985   316
Re C (A Bankrupt) [2006] 4 HKC 582   553
Re Cheng Kai Nam [2002] 2 HKLRD 39   161
Re China Medical Technologies [2014] 2 HKLRD 997   514
Re Insigma Technology Co Ltd [2014] HKCFI 1839   513
Re Irish Shipping Ltd [1985] HKLR 437   513, 514
Re Pioneer Iron & Steel Group Co Ltd [2013] HKCFI 324   514
Re Setaffa Investment Ltd [1998] 3 HKC 342   221
Re The Estate of Ng Shum (No 2) [1990] HKLR 67   117
Re Yung Kee Holdings (2015) 18 HKCFAR 510   514
Re Yung Kwan Lee [1999] 4 HKC 281   37, 38
Ronald Claud Hardwick v Spence Robinson [1975] HKLR 425   323

Secretary for Justice & Others v Chan Wah & Others (2000) 3 HKCFAR 459; [2000] 3 HKLRD 641   88, 223
Secretary for Justice v Wong Sau Fong [1998] 2 HKLRD 254   249
Shandong Textiles Import & Export Corporation v A Hua Non-Ferrous Metals Co Ltd [2002] 2 HKC 122   497

Shenzhen Kai Long Investment & Development Co Ltd v CEC Electrical Manufacturing (International) Co Ltd [2003] 3 HKLRD 774   500
Siegfried Adelbert Unruh v Hans-Joerg Seeberger & Another [2007] HKEC 268   394
Sun Legend Investments Ltd v David Ho [2009] HKCFI 853   303, 304
Susanto-Wing Sun Co Ltd v Yung Chi Hardware Machinery Co Ltd [1989] 2 HKC 504   122
Swire Properties v Secretary for Justice [2003] 3 HKC 347   408–410

Tsang Chin Keung v Employees Compensation Assistance Fund [2003] 2 HKLRD 627   324
Tse Moon-sak v Tse Hung & Others (In Re Tse Lai-chiu deceased) [1969] HKLR 159   6, 115, 116

UBC (Construction) Ltd v Sung Foo Kee Ltd [1993] 2 HKLR 207   254, 568

Vallejos Evangeline Banao v Commissioner of Registration & Another (20013) 16 HKCFAR 45   84, 85, 172, 234, 299
Victor Chandler (International) Ltd v Zhou Chu Jian He [2008] 4 HKC 232   44, 45

Wei Mao International (Hong Kong) Co Ltd v Shanxi Lianli Industrial Co Ltd [2004]   499
Wong Kam Ying & Another v The Estate of Man Hung Pun [[1967] HKLR 201   116, 117
Wright v Hampton, Winter & Glynn (A Firm) [2008] 2 HKLRD 341   309
Yao Yeong Wood & Another v The Standard Oil Co of New York [1907] HKLR 55   114

UK/England and Wales

Allen v Emmerson [1944] KB 362   217
Anderton v Ryan [1985] 2 All ER 355   264, 288
Arthur J S Hall v Simons [2002] 1 AC 615   315, 324

Baker v Jones [1954] 1 WLR 1005   408
Bell v Lever Bros Ltd [1932] AC 181   257
Beswick v Beswick [1966] 3 All ER 1   217
Beswick v Beswick [1968] AC 58; [1967] 2 All ER 1197   204, 217
Black-Clawson International Ltd v Papierwerke Waldhof-Aschafenburg AG [1975] AC 591   203, 204, 209
Bliss v SE Thames RHA [1985] IRLR 308   323

Cambridge Gas Transportation Corporation v Official Committee of Unsecured Creditors of Navigator Holdings plc [2007] 1 AC 508   515, 516
Candler v Crane, Christmas & Co [1951] 2 KB 164   261, 262
Chan Wing-Siu v R [1985] AC 168   267, 268
Cohen v Roche [1927] 1 KB 169   112
Condron v UK [2001] 31 EHRR 1   533

D'Avigdor-Goldsmid v IRC [1953] 1 All ER 403   199
Donoghue (or McAlister) v Stevenson [1932] AC 562   255, 256, 261, 403

Fisher v Bell [1961] 1 QB 394   199, 200, 202, 219
Fothergill v Monarch Airlines [1980] 3 WLR 209   204, 219, 220

Gallie v Lee (*see* Saunders v ABS)
Grey v Pearson (1857) 6 HL Cas 61   201

Hamilton-Jones v David & Snape (A Firm) [2004] 1 All ER 657   323

Harley v McDonald [2001] 2 WLR 1749   324
Hedley Byrne & Co Ltd v Heller & Partners Ltd [1964] AC 465   262, 324
Heydon's Case (1584) 76 ER 637   202
Heywood v Wellers (A Firm) [1976] 1 All ER 300   323

Jones v Padavatton [1969] 1 WLR 328   256

Kleinwort Benson Ltd v Lincoln City Council [1998] 4 All ER 513   104, 107, 289, 290

Lim Chin Aik v R [1963] 2 WLR 42   221, 222
London Tramways Co Ltd v London County Council [1898] AC 375   263

Magor & St Mellons v Newport Corporation [1951] 2 All ER 839   198, 483
Marquis of Camden v Inland Revenue Commissioners [1914] 1 KB 641   220
Maunsell v Olins [1975] AC 373   199
Miller v Jackson [1977] QB 966   112
Moy v Petman Smith & Another [2005] 1 All ER 903   324

Pao On v Lau Yiu Long [1980] AC 614   253
Pepper v Hart [1993] 1 All ER 42   205–216, 576
Powell v Kempton Park Racecourse Co [18989] AC 143   217
Prince Jefri Bolkiah v KPMG (A Firm) [1999] 2 AC 222   308

R v Allen (1877) LR 1 CCR 367   201
R v Ford [1989] 3 All ER 445   348
R v Goodyear [2005] EWCA Crim 888   168
R v Jogee/Ruddock v R [2016] UKSC 8; [2016] UKPC 7   267, 268
R v Secretary of State for the Home Department, ex parte Launder [1997] 3 All ER 961   511

R v Secretary of State for the Home Department, ex parte Launder (No 2) [1998] 3 WLR 221   511
R v Shivpuri [1986] 2 All ER 334   264, 288
R v Turner [1970] 2 QB 321   168, 316
R v Wang [2005] UKHL 9   343
Re Sigsworth [1934] All Er Rep 113   201
Re Singularis Holdings [2014] UKPC 36   515
Rondel v Worsley [1969] 1 AC 191   314, 324
Royal Bank of Scotland v Etridge (No 2) [2001] 4 All ER 449   120, 121, 308
Royscot Trust Ltd v Rogerson [1991] 3 All ER 294   566

Salt v Stratstone Specialists Ltd [2015] EWCA Civ 745   216
Saunders v Anglia Building Society [1970] 3 All ER 961   258
South Caribbean Trading Ltd v Trafigura Beheer [2005] 1 Lloyds Rep 128   254
Stennett v Hancock & Peters [1939] 2 All ER 578   256
Stilk v Myrick (1809) 2 Camp 317; (1809) 6 Esp 129   253, 266, 568
Surrey County Council v Bredero Homes [1993] 3 All ER 705   254
Sussex Peerage Claim (1844) 11Cl & Fin 85   196

Tempest v Kilner (1846) 3 CB 249   219
Trendtex Trading Corp v Central Bank of Nigeria [1977] 1 QB 529   229

Williams v Roffey Bros & Nicholls [1990] 1 All ER 512   253, 254, 266, 568
Witter (Thomas) Ltd v TBP Industries Ltd [1996] 2 All ER 573   216

Wood v Scarth (1855) 8 E & B 815; (1858) 1 F & F 293   111
Wrotham Park Estate Co Ltd v Parkside Homes Ltd [1974] 2 All ER 321
WWF World-Wide Fund for Nature v World Wrestling Federation Entertainment Inc [2007] EWCA Civ 286   254

Young v Bristol Aeroplane Company Ltd [1944] 2 All ER 293   242, 245–247, 249, 250

Other

Brady v US 397 US 742 (1970)   315

Carr v Western Australia [2007] HCA 47   198

Hemofarm DD MAG International Trade Holdings DD, Suram Media Ltd v Jinan Yongning Pharmaceutical Co Ltd [2008] Min Si Ta Zi No 11   501

United States v Lui Kin Hong 110 F 3d 103 (1st Circuit 1997)   512

Xinggang Ouya Technology Co Ltd v Xinjiang Pijiuhua Inc Supreme People's Court Reply to Civil Court Ruling No 48 (2006) (Issued 28 November 2007)   501

Table of Legislation

Hong Kong Legislation

Adaptation of Law (Interpretative Provisions) Ordinance (No 26 of 1998)   40, 41
Administrative Appeals Board Ordinance (Cap 442)   150
Application of English Law Ordinance (Cap 88)   8–10, 44, 45, 63, 65, 105, 114, 176
Arbitration (Amendment) (No 2) Ordinance (64 of 1989)   405
Arbitration (Amendment) Ordinance 2000 (No 2 of 2000)   496
Arbitration Ordinance (Cap 341)   405, 406, 409, 410, 423, 496
Arbitration Ordinance (Cap 609)   406–408, 414, 496, 500, 501
Architects Registration Ordinance (Cap 408)   151

Bill of Rights Ordinance (Cap 383)   *See* Index
Boundary and Election Commission Ordinance (Cap 432)   66
British Nationality (Miscellaneous Provisions) Ordinance (Cap 186)   66
British Nationality Act 1981 (Consequential Amendments) Ordinance (Cap 186)   66
Broadcasting Ordinance (Cap 562)   147
Chinese Extradition Ordinance (Cap 235)   66
Companies Ordinance (Cap 32) [Partially replaced by Companies Ordinance (Cap 622), then re-named Companies (Winding Up and Miscellaneous Provisions) Ordinance   221, 514
Community Service Orders Ordinance (Cap 378)   169
Contract (Rights of Third Parties) Ordinance (Cap 623)   187, 188
Control of Exemption Clauses Ordinance (Cap 71)   63, 119
Control of Obscene and Indecent Articles Ordinance (Cap 390)   146, 147
Conveyancing and Property Ordinance (Cap 219)   10
Crimes (Amendment) Ordinance (No 24 of 1993)   467
Crimes Ordinance (Cap 200)   467
Criminal Procedure Ordinance (Cap 221)   124, 155, 164, 169, 170, 535, 554, 555

Dangerous Drugs Ordinance (Cap 134)   532
Dentists Registration Ordinance (Cap 156)   151

Elections (Corrupt and Illegal Conduct) Ordinance (Cap 554)   549
Electoral Provisions Ordinance (Cap 367)   66
Employment Ordinance (Cap 57)   144, 145
Evidence Ordinance (Cap 8)   517, 518

Film Censorship Ordinance (Cap 392)   147
Foreign Lawyers Registration Rules (Cap 159S)   303

Foreign Marriage Ordinance (Cap 180)   65
Fugitive Offenders Ordinance (Cap 503)
   37, 503, 504, 508

Heung Yee Kuk Ordinance (Cap 1097)   89
Hong Kong Court of Final Appeal
   (Amendment) Ordinance (No 11 of
   2002)   136
Hong Kong Court of Final Appeal
   Ordinance (Cap 484)   45, 60, 134,
   135, 153, 279–282, 335, 336
Hong Kong Reunification Ordinance (Cap
   2601)   31–34, 100

Immigration (Amendment) Ordinance (Ord
   No 23 of 2012)   149
Immigration Ordinance (Cap 115)   67, 148,
   149, 387, 533, 549, 550
Independent Commission Against
   Corruption Ordinance (Cap 204)
   547–549
Independent Police Complaints Council
   Ordinance (Cap 604)   539
Inland Revenue (Amendment) Ordinance
   Ord No 23 of 2012   149
Inland Revenue Ordinance (Cap 112)   149,
   150, 200
Interpretation and General Clauses
   Ordinance (Cap 1)   33, 41, 191–193,
   209–212, 215, 218, 221

Jury (Amendment) Ordinance (No 3 of
   1986)   343
Jury (Amendment) Ordinance (No 72 of
   1997)   345
Jury Ordinance (Cap 3)   344–346, 349,
   350, 355, 359
Juvenile Offenders Ordinance (Cap 226)
   169, 170

Labour Tribunal Ordinance (Cap 25)   144
Land (Compulsory Sale for Redevelopment)
   Ordinance (Cap 545)   143
Landlord and Tenant (Consolidation)
   Ordinance (Cap 7)   142

Lands Tribunal Ordinance (Cap 17)   142,
   427
Legal Aid in Criminal Cases Rules (Cap
   221D)   376
Legal Aid Ordinance (Cap 91)   371, 377,
   379, 380
Legal Aid Services Council Ordinance (Cap
   489)   372
Legal Practitioners Ordinance (Cap 159)
   108, 136, 151, 305, 310, 313, 321, 323,
   332, 333, 352
Legal Practitioners (Amendment) Ordinance
   (No 87 of 2003)   313
Legal Practitioners (Amendment) Ordinance
   2010   320, 336
Legal Services Legislation (Miscellaneous
   Amendments) Ordinance 1997   303
Legislative Council (Electoral Provisions)
   Ordinance (Cap 381)   66
Limitation Ordinance (Cap 347)   323

Magistrates Ordinance (Cap 227)   365,
   366, 563
Mainland Judgments (Reciprocal
   Enforcement) Ordinance (Cap 597)
   493
Mediation Ordinance (Cap 620)   416, 425
Medical Registration Ordinance (Cap 136)
   151, 352
Minor Employment Claims Adjudication
   Board Ordinance (Cap 453)   145
Misdemeanours Punishment Ordinance (No
   1 of 1898)   548
Misrepresentation Ordinance (Cap 284)
   64, 566, 580
Mutual Legal Assistance in Criminal Matters
   Ordinance (Cap 525)   493

New Territories Land (Exemption)
   Ordinance (Cap 452)   92, 93

Offences Against the Person Ordinance (Cap
   212)   467
Official Languages Ordinance (Cap 5)
   160, 193

Table of Legislation xiii

Ombudsman Ordinance (Cap 397)   150, 550, 551
Ordinance No 7 of 1845 (number of jurors)   343
Ordinance No 4 of 1849 (financial eligibility of jurors)   343
Ordinance No 4 of 1851 (character & eligibility of jurors)   344
Ordinance No 11 of 1864 (number of jurors)   343
Ordinance No 37 of 1947 (female jurors)   344
Organised and Serious Crimes Ordinance (Cap 455)   309
Overseas Lawyers (Qualification for Admission) Rules (Cap 159Q)   306

Pension Benefits (Judicial Officers) Ordinance (Cap 401)   285, 286
Personal Data (Privacy) Ordinance (Cap 486)   67, 94
Police Force Ordinance (Cap 232)   532–536
Prevention of Bribery Ordinance (Cap 201)   506, 547, 548
Probation of Offenders Ordinance (Cap 298)   169
Public Order Ordinance (Cap 245)   67
Public Revenue Protection Ordinance (Cap 120)   190

Rating Ordinance (Cap 116)   153
Regulation of Jurors and Juries Ordinance (Ord No 7 of 1845)   340
Rendition of Chinese Criminals Ordinance (No 2 of 1871)   509
Rules of the District Court (Cap 336H)   399
Rules of the High Court (Cap 4A)   323, 399, 400

Sale of Goods Ordinance (Cap 26)   111
Securities and Futures Ordinance (Cap 571)   150, 543, 544
Small Claims Tribunal Ordinance (Cap 338)   146

Societies Ordinance (Cap 151)   67
Solicitors' Accounts Rules (Cap 159F)   311, 321
Solicitors' (Group Practice) Rules Cap 159X   303
Solicitors' Practice Rules (Cap 159H)   307
Solicitors' (Professional Indemnity) Rules (Cap 159M)   311
Stamp Duty Ordinance (Cap 117)   153
Supply of Services (Implied Terms) Ordinance (Cap 457)   323
Supreme Court Ordinance, 1844   7, 8, 64, 113
Supreme Court Ordinance, 1873 [Revised as Supreme Court Ordinance (Cap 4)] (Re-named High Court Ordinance)   6, 8, 34, 116

Telecommunications Ordinance (Cap 106)   147
Theft Ordinance (Cap 210)   535
Trainee Solicitors Rules (Cap 159J)   332
Transfer of Sentenced Persons Ordinance (Cap 513)   38
Trustee Ordinance (Cap 29)   111, 218

Unconscionable Contracts Ordinance (Cap 458)   65

Wills Ordinance (Cap 30)   6, 91

United Kingdom Legislation

Access to Justice Act, 1999   402, 403
Arbitration Act, 1950   405

British Nationality Act, 1981   15, 66

Constitutional Reform Act, 2005   131, 444
Consumer Rights Act, 2015   119
Contracts (Rights of Third Parties) Act, 1999   185
Criminal Attempts Act, 1981   264, 288
Criminal Justice Act, 1988   347
Criminal Justice Act, 2003   356

Criminal Justice and Public Order Act, 1994   533

Finance Act, 1976   205

Human Rights Act, 1998   265, 445, 567

Judicature Acts, 1873–1875   111, 569
Jury Amendment (Northern Ireland) Order SI 1987/1283

Law of Property Act, 1925   10, 217
Law of Property (Miscellaneous Provisions) Act, 1989   10, 65
Law Reform (Miscellaneous Provisions) Act, 1970   10
Legal Aid Act, 1949   371

Misrepresentation Act, 1967   64, 566

Northern Ireland (Emergency Provisions) Act, 1973   356

Occupiers' Liability Act, 1984   65
Offences Against the Person Act, 1861   201

Punishment of Death Act, 1832   465

Restriction of Offences Weapons Act, 1959   199
Restriction of Offences Weapons Act, 1961   199

Sale of Goods Act, 1979   110
Statute of Frauds, 1677   10

Trustee Act, 1925   110

Unfair Contract Terms Act, 1977   63, 119, 574
Unfair Terms in Consumer Contracts Regulations, 1994   119
Unfair Terms in Consumer Contracts Regulations, 1999   119

PRC Legislation

Arbitration Law of the PRC   478, 479, 496, 499, 500

The Basic Law of the Hong Kong Special Administrative Region (SAR) of the People's Republic of China (PRC) *See* Index
Basic Law of the Macau SAR of the PRC   26

Civil Procedure Law of the PRC   480, 481
Constitution of the PRC   69, 70, 122, 434, 441, 447, 451, 452, 459–461, 463, 480
Contract Law (Code) of the PRC   434
Criminal Law (Code) of the PRC   458, 473, 485, 506
Criminal Procedure Law of the PRC   459, 461, 463, 464, 469, 470, 473

Enterprise Insolvency Law (Enterprise Bankruptcy Law) of the PRC   513, 516, 517

The Law on Judges (Judges' Law) of the PRC   452, 453
The Law on Lawyers (Lawyers' Law) of the PRC   470, 475, 476
Legislation Law (Law on Legislation) of the PRC   448, 449, 484, 485

Nationality Law of the PRC   24, 49

People's Mediation Law of the PRC   480

Regulations for the Organisation of People's Mediation Committees   480

Introduction

The parameters of Hong Kong's "legal system" are not clearly defined. I have, broadly, covered those topics encompassed in the syllabus for "Hong Kong Legal System", as required for the pre-PCLL "conversion" examination for this subject. As such, this book should be very useful for those intending to take this examination, especially those preparing via self-study. However, I hope that by including a wide range of learned and thought-provoking readings I have produced a book that will be of interest to those (legal scholars and others) with no "functional" motive. This, I hope, will include those outside Hong Kong since, surely, Hong Kong's current system, influenced by internal and external forces, civil and common law, is unique.

Given that this unique system owes much to a "constitutional" document, Hong Kong's Basic Law, it is inevitable that there is a blurring of the lines between legal system and constitutional law. There is herein, as a result, significant reference to the Basic Law, specifically, and to the Deng Xiaoping-inspired "one country, two systems" doctrine generally. However, I do not claim to be a constitutional law expert and I have made numerous references to the work of such experts which will, hopefully, inspire the reader to look more closely at the constitutional position.

Similarly, while the aforementioned "Hong Kong Legal System" syllabus requires an introductory knowledge of the PRC legal system, I am not an expert thereon and have referred to works by those who are. Students able to read texts in Chinese will have an advantage, in attempts to deepen their PRC law expertise, over the rest of us.

Given the broad scope of this book and the dynamic nature of many of the included topics, the subject is constantly in flux. To take just one example, I mentioned (in my first draft) a relatively minor dispute relating to "anti-hawking" activities in Mong Kok at Chinese New Year, 2015. Twelve months later a similar dispute escalated into a "riot", participants in which have received lengthy prison sentences. This incident and its possible repercussions, given the opportunism of the pro-Beijing camp, threaten the very fabric of "one country, two systems". I have little doubt that, by the date of publication, some of the material herein will be superseded by events. There are times, perhaps, when one envies the scholar of Roman law!

Crucial to Hong Kong's success and well-being is a sustained international recognition of the continuation of the rule of law and an independent judiciary; the cornerstones of "two systems" and, in comparison with the legal system of mainland China, "Hong Kong's difference". Thus far these tenets have been maintained, in the face of enormous political pressure and despite an unsympathetic and increasingly pliant Hong Kong government. Optimism that "two systems" will survive after the 50 years guaranteed by the Basic Law (or even that long) is receding, but Hong Kong has proved its resilience over the years and we can still hope.

MJF

1
The Development of the Hong Kong Legal System, 1842–1997

Overview

When the British first came to Hong Kong they found a territory vastly different from the one we know today. Wesley-Smith[1] writes:

> When Hong Kong was first taken over by the British it was rumoured to be a barren rock with hardly a house upon it. The island's few inhabitants were peasants and fishermen who lived under the rule of Chinese law and custom.[2]

The population of Hong Kong Island in 1841, when the British flag was first raised, was around 5,000.[3] While that small population had previously been subject to the rule of the Chinese emperor, there was no complex, developed legal system in operation. Indeed, Ip writes that there "was not even a civil or military presence there."[4]

The initial approach of the British was to allow Hong Kong's Chinese inhabitants to retain, generally, their previous laws and customs but to impose British law on non-Chinese. This approach gradually gave way to one in which British law would apply unless it ran counter to existing (Chinese) custom and practice. In most situations there was little difference, in practical effect, between the two approaches. This recognition of Chinese customary law became increasingly important with the annexation of the New Territories in 1898, adding around 100,000 largely rural dwellers to Hong Kong's population.

The system whereby English common law operated in Hong Kong unless inapplicable to Hong Kong's situation or specifically amended in Hong Kong remained essentially unchanged until the resumption of sovereignty of Hong Kong by China in 1997. Indeed, to a considerable extent, the system remains today, as a result of the

---

1. Peter Wesley-Smith, *An Introduction to the Hong Kong Legal System* (1st edn, Oxford University Press 1987).
2. Ibid 35. By the 3rd edition Wesley-Smith omits reference to the "barren rock", first attributed to Lord Palmerston, British foreign secretary and later prime minister. The "rock" was indeed barren but this was the result of tree-felling for charcoal rather than soil infertility.
3. The estimate of various historians ranges from 5,000 to 10,000.
4. Eric Ip, *Law and Justice in Hong Kong* (2nd edn, Sweet & Maxwell 2016).

guarantee in the Basic Law of the continuation of the "laws previously in force" for (at least) 50 years from 1997.[5]

1.1 The British occupation of Hong Kong

Writing in 1991, Miners[6] states:

> Hong Kong exists as a separate territorial unit today because of military aggression against the Chinese empire in the nineteenth century.[7]

Curiously, however, the acquisition of Hong Kong was almost accidental, as opposed to part of a planned strategy. At the commencement of the "First Opium War" (1840–1842) Lord Palmerston, British Foreign Secretary, had ordered Rear-Admiral George Elliot and his cousin Captain Charles Elliot to demand restoration of goods (impounded opium), satisfaction for a previous "affront" to Admiral Elliot, security for British traders and payment of debts to British merchants. This was to be either via cession of an island, or through a treaty allowing factories to be set up on the mainland. The aim, as articulated by Lord Palmerston, was "satisfaction for the past and security for the future".[8]

Hong Kong was viewed as an excellent port because of its deep water (far superior to (then Portuguese) Macau) but "a long voyage from Macau and Canton".[9]

Eventually, a somewhat reluctant Captain Elliot,[10] now in charge of the British forces,[11] insisted on the cession of Hong Kong as part of the Convention of Chuenpi[12] (never ratified) in 1841, which followed a successful British expedition to seize the "Bogue forts"[13] on the Pearl River leading to Canton (Guangzhou).

Following further hostilities and several British victories, Hong Kong was ceded to Britain "in perpetuity" under the subsequent Treaty of Nanking, signed in 1842.

Later, after the "Second Opium War", China ceded the Kowloon peninsula to Britain, again "in perpetuity" under the Convention of Peking (Beijing) in 1860.

Finally, in 1898, Britain obtained the New Territories and Outlying Islands, via a further Convention of Peking (also known as the Convention for the Extension of

---

5. This is the combined effect of Articles 8 and 159 of the Basic Law, Hong Kong's post-1997 quasi-constitution.
6. Norman Miners, *The Government and Politics of Hong Kong* (5th edn, Oxford University Press 1991).
7. Ibid 3.
8. Kevin Rafferty, *City on the Rocks* (Viking 1990) 115.
9. See Roger Houghton, 'A People's History 1793–1844 from the Newspapers' <http://www.houghton.hk/> accessed 4 January 2018.
10. Elliot opposed opium use and, in a proclamation of 11 September 1839, stated: "I will not protect opium smugglers. The smugglers have put our lawful trade at risk."
11. His cousin had resigned because of ill health.
12. Signed at Shajiao Fort.
13. A corruption of the Portuguese "Bocca Tigris" (tiger's mouth), itself a translation of the Cantonese "Fu Moon".

Hong Kong) taking advantage of China's defeat in war with Japan. This latter acquisition, however, was, crucially,[14] under a 99-year lease, which expired in 1997.[15]

1.1.1 Captain Elliot's proclamation(s)[16]

Captain Elliot[17] declared British sovereignty over Hong Kong on 26 January 1841 and, six days later, proclaimed that:

> the natives of the Island of Hong Kong and all natives of China thereto resorting, shall be governed according to the laws and customs of China, every description of torture excepted.[18]

The proclamation(s),[19] therefore, envisaged a binary legal system; one law applying (generally) to Chinese citizens and the other to non-Chinese. That this was the effect of the proclamation(s) the Hong Kong courts have endorsed on a number of occasions.[20]

Elliot's declaration, whereby the inhabitants of Hong Kong would have been subject to alternative systems of law dependent on their nationality, the British soon sought to recant,[21] on the basis that Elliot had no authority to make such a proclamation.[22] The editor of the newspaper "Friends of China" stated that:

> we doubt Elliot has authority to found a civil government on Hong Kong or sell any land (as he purported to do). We cannot even say whether the British government will retain the island.[23]

Moreover:

> These two Proclamations were . . . mere interim measures. The Treaty of Nanking, by which Hong Kong was formally ceded to Great Britain, was signed in 1842 and . . . provided that Hong Kong 'was to be governed by such laws . . . as Her Majesty . . . shall see fit to direct.'[24]

---

14. See 1.5 below.
15. Miners (n 6) states that Britain would have preferred an "outright" cession but was hampered by the agreement of leases by the other colonial powers.
16. There were, strictly, two proclamations: one issued to the inhabitants of Hong Kong and the other (not identical) issued generally.
17. Officially "Chief Superintendent of Trade".
18. See GB Endacott, *A History of Hong Kong* (2nd edn, Oxford University Press, Hong Kong 1988) 26.
19. The first proclamation (of 1 February) was issued jointly with Commodore Bremer. The second (2 February) was issued by Elliot alone.
20. See 1.2 below.
21. Though they had always insisted that British in China would not be subject to Chinese law!
22. Elliot's conciliatory approach was viewed by Palmerston as a negation of Britain's military superiority.
23. R Houghton (n 10).
24. PC Woo, moving a resolution in the Legislative Council (LegCo), 7 May 1969.

Elliot was recalled to Britain and replaced by the more bellicose Sir Henry Pottinger.[25] However, despite doubts as to his authority,[26] Elliot's proclamation (or proclamations) remained an important constitutional document, relied on by the courts on numerous occasions.[27]

1.2 The reception of English Law

Wesley-Smith[28] writes:

> Even if the first British officials had bothered to look for it and utilise it, the Chinese legal system as it existed in Hong Kong was scarcely appropriate for the kind of place the colony was destined to become. In any event, the new rulers were intent on establishing a legal system which was familiar to them and which was assumed to be far superior to anything found in the Chinese empire . . .
>
> One of the first things to do, therefore, was to introduce English law into Hong Kong.[29]

The decision to import English law contradicted Captain Elliot's initial proclamation(s) of 1841, when he first took possession of Hong Kong Island. The revised position, following the ratification of the Treaty of Nanking in 1843, was that, instead of Chinese citizens continuing to be subject (in most cases) to Chinese law, English law would operate in Hong Kong *unless* it conflicted with the customs or circumstances of Hong Kong. Wesley-Smith, again, writes:

> From 1846 to 1966, the formula by which English law was received into Hong Kong applied the laws of England which existed on 5 April 1843, the day Hong Kong obtained a local legislature. There was a proviso, however: English law considered not suited to the circumstances of Hong Kong or of its inhabitants was excluded. The intended result was to provide a basic source of legal precepts which, though developed thousands of miles away in response to the notions and traditions of the English people, could be fashioned in accordance with local needs and conditions.[30]

While notionally different, and appearing to involve a different presumption (that English law *would* apply to Hong Kong Chinese citizens "*unless*" . . .) the reception of English law *practically* differed little from Elliot's design in most cases. English law would not apply if contrary to local custom. What would be the major indicator of local custom? In practice, it would be the existence of already established "laws

---

25. Endacott (n 19) states that Pottinger initially supported Elliot's "dual system" approach but later changed his mind. Tsang states that the British Government ordered Pottinger to disavow the dual system: Steve Tsang, *A Modern History of Hong Kong* (Hong Kong University Press 2004) 23.
26. See DME Evans, 'Common Law in a Chinese Setting' (1971) 1 HKLJ 9.
27. See, eg, *Chan Shun Cho v Chak Hok Ping (Re Chak Chiu Hang)* (1925) 20 HKLR 1; *Ho Tsz Tsun v Ho Au Shi & Others* (1915) 10 HKLR 69 discussed below.
28. Note 1.
29. Ibid 38–39.
30. Ibid 35.

and customs of China". The practical continuance of Elliot's "duality" concept may be seen in a number of cases, some of which will now be considered.

In *Ho Tsz Tsun v Ho Au Shi & Others*[31] the Hong Kong Court of Appeal was called upon to determine the application of a Chinese will in Hong Kong and acceded to a request to insert the words "in accordance with Chinese law and custom" after the words "next of kin" in varying a judgment of the Chief Justice. The court president, Havilland De Sausmarez, stated:

> We have in the Colony two systems of distribution, one under the Statute [of Distributions] which has been recognised by the Courts, and the other the Chinese law of inheritance or succession which according to the evidence is and always has been observed by Chinese residents . . .
>
> . . . the practice in the Colony appears to have been to apply Chinese law to the devolution of the personalty of Chinese, and the Statute of Distributions to that of non-Chinese, and unless this is the rule, it is clear there will have to be legislation, as it is manifestly impossible that the legal system of either should apply to the other. But I have come to the conclusion that the practice is in conformity with the law . . .
>
> . . . I have no doubt that the island was, prior to its cession, part of the dominions of the Emperor of China, and that its inhabitants were subject to Chinese law and custom . . . If proof of this were needed . . . we have it in the proclamation of Captain Elliot . . . and a similar proclamation was made in Chinese to the inhabitants . . .
>
> . . . The common law of the Chinese is preserved, torture, which was prevalent, was excepted, and the foreigner is excepted from the common law of China and subjected to 'British law'.[32]

Similarly, in *Chan Chun Cho v Chak Hok Ping*,[33] a case involving an inheritance dispute, Sir Henry Gollan CJ stated:

> Hong Kong is a colony obtained by cession from China and consequently the laws of China as in force in Hong Kong at that time remained operative, except such as were contrary to the fundamental principles of the English law e.g. laws permitting of torture, slavery etc. and subject to the right of the Crown to alter and change those laws . . .
>
> Two proclamations were issued by Captain Elliott [*sic*] . . .
>
> . . . these proclamations recognise a dual prospective system of law in the Colony. So far as British subjects and foreigners are concerned, security and protection according to the principles and practice of the British law are extended to them; whilst in the case of the Chinese the laws and customs of China are reserved in their favour.

---

31. (1915) 10 HKLR 69.
32. Ibid 72–76.
33. (1925) 20 HKLR 1.

> Except, therefore, in so far as the laws and customs of China have been altered by legislation or Orders in Council in the nature of legislation and subject to the conditions above specified, those laws and customs as existing on the dates of Captain Elliott's [*sic*] Proclamations would continue to apply to 'the natives of the Island of Hong Kong and all natives of China thereto resorting.'[34]

This "dual" approach to the "applicable law", based on ethnicity, was not unproblematic. What would be the position, for example, of those with dual ethnicity? Or those Hong Kong Chinese who wished, for example, to adopt the English rules on marriage or inheritance? And, where Chinese law was found to be applicable, should it be that obtaining at the date of Elliot's proclamation, or the date of trial? Some illustration of the difficulties is afforded in the case of *Tse Moon-sak v Tse Hung & Others (In re Tse Lai-chiu, deceased)*[35] involving the validity of a will made, in 1958, by a Chinese resident of Hong Kong. The case concerned an apparent conflict between section 5 of the Supreme Court Ordinance[36] and section 3 of the Wills Ordinance.[37] The former legislation incorporated the principle that English legislation in existence in 1843 (when Hong Kong first obtained a legislature) would apply to Hong Kong unless (locally) inapplicable or locally modified. The latter (Wills) legislation rendered valid wills made according to Chinese law by anyone "native of or domiciled in" Hong Kong or China. The specific issue was whether a testamentary disposition could be valid given the (asserted) rule that Ch'ing law regarded property as belonging to the family rather than an individual.[38]

In reaching its decision the court adopted the principle that English law would apply unless its application would cause "injustice or oppression". Hogan CJ's judgment reveals a subtle reassessment of the significance of Captain Elliot's proclamation. He states:

> The primary question for the court is whether the deceased, who was Chinese by race and domiciled in Hong Kong, was able by this will to exercise a testamentary capacity in accordance with English law. If that question were to be answered in the negative, a further question would arise as to whether the law applicable to the testator's will would be Chinese law as it stood when Hong Kong was ceded or some different or later form of Chinese law and custom . . .
>
> . . . if it had been thought that the relevant English Law was not applicable to the circumstances of those, probably mainly fishermen, who were resident in Hong Kong in 1843 because, for example, of unfamiliarity with the system, would this necessarily mean that sophisticated individuals of the same race now in the Colony, who have long been accustomed to the comparatively cosmopolitan atmosphere which

---

34. Ibid 3–5.
35. [1969] HKLR 159.
36. Cap 4 (and see 1.2.2).
37. Cap 30.
38. A further argument that international law forbade testamentary capacity for Chinese was rejected.

has grown up here and the application of English principles of law and equity in so many matters, should be similarly precluded from the application of English Law?
...
The earlier judgments were clearly influenced . . . by the terms of Captain Elliot's proclamations and they may have tended to impose on the relevant sections of the substantive law an interpretation attuned to giving effect to these proclamations, without making adequate allowance either for the difference in language or for the temporary nature of those parts of the proclamations . . . to making interim arrangements . . . in so doing, they have reversed the approach adopted in the legislation and have virtually assumed that Chinese law and custom should be applied unless found unsuitable whereas the legislation clearly indicates that English law will prevail, unless there are circumstances affecting the inhabitants which make it inapplicable . . .
I cannot think that in the circumstances prevailing in 1960, and indeed for many years before, it could seriously be contended that to permit the deceased to exercise the testamentary capacity . . . could be classified as unjust or oppressive . . . Consequently I think the testamentary capacity of the deceased is to be determined by referring to English law.[39]

This lengthy extract highlights the court's view of changing circumstances. Chinese law, at the time of cession, was the "law of the land" in Hong Kong and would remain in force in the absence of English law rules to the contrary. However, it could not prevail over English law unless the latter operated "unjustly or oppressively". There would now be situations where, far from having English law *imposed*, Hong Kong Chinese citizens might welcome the adoption of English legal rules. Where there was no applicable English law, however, the court accepted that the court would require evidence of relevant Chinese law and custom, leaving vague the question of whether this would be 1843 Chinese law and custom or that of later amendment.

1.2.1 The mechanism for the reception of English law

The constitutional mechanism whereby the new, colonial procedures were implemented involved the introduction of two documents. The first, known as the "Letters Patent",[40] outlined the constitutional structure and conferred powers upon the Governor, while making provision for the assistance of an Executive Council and Legislative Council. The second constitutional document, the "Royal Instructions", set out the rules relating to the composition of the Executive and Legislative Councils and detailed the procedures to be observed in the passing of laws.

After 1843, this constitutional framework allowed laws to be created in Hong Kong. The first significant example was the Supreme Court Ordinance of 1844.

---

39. Ibid 164–193.
40. "Patent" indicated openness, transparency.

1.2.2 The Supreme Court Ordinances

The purpose of the Supreme Court Ordinance 1844 was to incorporate the laws of England into Hong Kong law. English laws were to have effect in the colony except where inapplicable to local circumstances in Hong Kong or its inhabitants. Amendments to the legislation in 1845 and 1846 established that only English laws existing before the institution of a separate Hong Kong legislature in 1843 would automatically apply, *prima facie*, in Hong Kong.

A further Supreme Court Ordinance, of 1873, added the further significant restriction that English laws would not be applicable in Hong Kong where they had been amended by local legislation.

The Supreme Court Ordinances also established the court system of Hong Kong. Although, technically, no distinction was drawn between legislative and common law English rules,[41] in practice English post-1843 *statutory* rules (established by legislation) would not apply in Hong Kong (unless expressly or implicitly intended to have such effect) while *common law* (non-statutory) rules, established by the English courts post-1843, took effect in Hong Kong, unless inapplicable, via the "fiction", known as the "declaratory" theory, whereby decisions of the court are deemed to have "explained" what the common law has always been.[42]

1.3 The Application of English Law Ordinance

Because it became increasingly difficult to determine which laws were in force in England in 1843, and because many of such laws had been superseded by Hong Kong "domestic" legislation, the Application of English Law Ordinance[43] (AELO) of 1966 was passed. The Ordinance:

> ... split English law into two types (enactments, and common law and equity), dealt with each separately, and deleted the [1843] cut-off date.[44]

Section 3 of the Ordinance provides that the common law and the rules of equity[45] shall be in force in Hong Kong:

(a) so far as they are applicable to the circumstances of Hong Kong or its inhabitants;
(b) subject to any modifications as such circumstances may require;
(c) subject to any amendment thereof (whenever made) by:
  (i) any Order in Council which applies to Hong Kong;
  (ii) any Act which applies to Hong Kong;
  (iii) any Ordinance.

---

41. For further discussion of the distinction between statutory and common law rules, see Chapter 2.
42. The declaratory theory has since been declared a myth: see Chapter 2.
43. Cap 88.
44. P Wesley-Smith (n 1) 40.
45. The concepts of common law and equity will be discussed in depth in Chapter 2.

Significantly, the 1843 cut-off date was abolished so that post-1843 common law and equitable developments would be applicable in Hong Kong. As has been noted, this legislative change largely gave force to existing practice whereby post-1843 common law rules continued to be incorporated via the "declaratory" fiction.

Section 4 of AELO stated that Acts of Parliament were to be in force in Hong Kong only if contained in the "schedule" (which contained only pre-1843 legislation) or where they were expressly or implicitly applicable to Hong Kong. The schedule had been drawn up after considerable scrutiny and was limited to those Acts relevant to Hong Kong. The list could be amended by the Legislative Council (LegCo) and, by 1997, was very short. AELO was not adopted as a law of the Hong Kong Special Administrative Region (HKSAR) following the resumption of Chinese sovereignty of Hong Kong on 1 July 1997; so the possibility of subsequent British legislation having effect in Hong Kong ended.

The effect of AELO seems, at first sight, to be relatively straightforward: the English rules of common law and equity would continue to operate in Hong Kong (irrespective of the date of their formation) while post-1843 statutes would apply only if specifically applicable to Hong Kong. The legislation was intended to facilitate considerably the task of legal "research". Legal advisers seeking to determine the applicability of English legislation would only have to look at the schedule and a list of post-1843 legislation specifically stated to apply (or implicitly applicable) to Hong Kong.

The position in relation to common law and equity as developed through case law was, indeed, relatively simple. The cut-off date had largely been ignored anyway via the "declaratory" principle whereby an overruling precedent is "deemed" not to be creating new law but merely "explaining" what the common law always has been! This "fiction", recognised as such and finally abolished by the English courts (post-1997) had the useful function of preventing Hong Kong law being dominated by English rules long considered to have outlived their usefulness.

In respect of statutes, unfortunately, AELO's application in Hong Kong was problematic. A statute passed in the British Parliament might, of course, amend the English common law.[46] The statute would not be listed in the schedule and might not be directly applicable to Hong Kong. However, in so far as the legislation affected the English common law which *was* to be applicable, irrespective of its date of origin, the legislation would appear, *indirectly*, to apply in Hong Kong. The amendment of the English common law by English legislation thus produced a dilemma. If the amended law were to be deemed part of Hong Kong law it would mean that legislation not stated to apply in Hong Kong nor applicable by implication, would still be applicable in Hong Kong as part of the "revised" English common law. But this would negate the apparent legislative purpose of allowing, *prima facie*, common law rules to apply in Hong Kong but not, *prima facie*, legislative ones. Alternatively,

---

46. This would occur, at the latest, as soon as English courts had interpreted and applied the statutory rule.

to preclude the effect of "non-applicable" legislation would mean that Hong Kong would be applying an English common law no longer applicable in England itself.

To take an example, the doctrine of part performance was introduced in equity in response to the rigidity of the Statute of Frauds 1677 requirement that contracts for the disposition of land must be evidenced in writing. Part performance allowed the enforcement of a "land contract" where acts had been done which pointed inevitably to the conclusion that a contract (albeit not one evidenced in writing) had been concluded. The equitable doctrine of part performance was specifically endorsed by Parliamentary enactment of 1925, namely section 40(2) of the Law of Property Act. This subsection was re-enacted in Hong Kong by section 3(1) of the Conveyancing & Property Ordinance (CPO)[47] though, as part of the English common law,[48] it was presumably already part of Hong Kong law (section 3(1) serving merely to consolidate existing rules). The doctrine of part performance was abolished in England by subsequent legislation: the Law of Property (Miscellaneous Provisions) Act 1989. This *statutory* rule, of course, had no direct effect in Hong Kong. Could it take *indirect* effect in Hong Kong as an amendment to the English common law? The answer is no, since it would be inconsistent with Hong Kong legislation (the CPO). Thus, part performance, long-abolished in England whence it originated, remains part of Hong Kong law, post-1997, unless and until repealed in Hong Kong.[49]

But what if the relevant consolidating section of CPO had *not* been enacted? In such circumstances the revised English common law would, indirectly, apply to Hong Kong under section 3 of AELO. By way of a further contract example, the archaic action for breach of promise of marriage was abolished in England in 1970. The relevant statutory rule, section 1 of the Law Reform (Miscellaneous Provisions) Act 1970, had no express or implicit relevance to Hong Kong so was not directly applicable in Hong Kong. Nonetheless, since breach of promise of marriage ceased to be part of the (revised) English common law by virtue of the English statute, it has never been doubted that, by virtue of section 3 of AELO, Hong Kong's common law has been similarly amended, albeit indirectly, by the (legislative) change to the English common law.

Although AELO was "not adopted", post-1997, as part of the law of the Hong Kong SAR, this change was relevant only to the inability of the English Parliament, or courts, to legislate, or establish common law rules, for Hong Kong *post-*1997, since Articles 8 and 18 of the Basic Law maintain (subject to exceptions)[50] the laws "previously in force" in Hong Kong on 1 July 1997. Indeed, under Article 8, the existing rules of common law and equity are *specifically* stated to remain in force (subject to exceptions), unless amended.

---

47. Cap 219.
48. "Common law" here means "non-statutory" law so, confusingly, includes principles of equity (see Chapter 2).
49. Article 8, Basic Law maintains the rules in force on 1 July 1997 (and see Chapter 2).
50. See Chapter 2.

1.4 The Kowloon Walled City phenomenon

In describing the assimilation of English law into colonial Hong Kong, mention must be made of the unique status of the Kowloon Walled City. Whole books could be (and have been) devoted to this historically fascinating entity.

Briefly, the vicinity of the Walled City had been used as a trading outpost by Imperial China since the time of the Song dynasty. China had maintained only a small garrison until Britain's acquisition of Hong Kong under the Treaty of Nanking (Nanjing) in 1842. Then the garrison was rapidly increased and extensive fortifications were added in 1847. In 1854 the Walled City briefly fell to bandits but was retaken within a week. With the acquisition of the New Territories by Britain, under the 99-year lease of 1898, Britain assented to the continuation of Imperial Chinese occupancy (with both sides claiming sovereignty). The wording of the agreement concerning the Walled City was as follows:

> The Chinese officials stationed there shall continue to exercise jurisdiction, except so far as may be inconsistent with the military requirements for the defence of Hong Kong. Within the remainder of the newly-leased territory, Great Britain shall have sole jurisdiction. Chinese officials and people shall be allowed as heretofore to use the road from Kowloon to Hsinan.

When the British asked the officials for help in suppressing a New Territories uprising they decided,[51] instead, that troops sent to put down the uprising were actually there to support it. The British then invaded the Walled City and drove away Imperial troops. In December 1899 an Order in Council provided that henceforth the Walled City would have the same status as the rest of the New Territories. However, this Order was never recognised by the Chinese side. While British troops did briefly occupy the Walled City in 1899,[52] given the sovereignty "stand-off" the area was left largely unattended by both Britain and China.

Before the Second World War, Britain had planned to demolish the area and compensate the few resident inhabitants. Following the Japanese occupation of Hong Kong, however, during which the City's walls were removed and used to enhance the airstrip at Kai Tak, demolition plans were stalled. After the War, large numbers of new immigrants arrived to occupy the "Walled City" which became famous largely for triad-related crime (drug-dealing and prostitution to the fore) and unlicensed doctors and dentists. As a largely unpoliced and "unofficial" area, construction was haphazard, water and electrical supply limited and dangerous.

Despite Britain's claim to sovereignty of the area, law enforcement was kept to a minimum, so as to avoid confrontation with an increasingly powerful China. The lack of proper sanitation and safety procedures in an increasingly modernised Hong

---
51. It is uncertain whether the misunderstanding was genuine or invented.
52. In response to fears that the Viceroy of Canton was using the City to support opposition to the new British rule (discussed briefly in Chapter 2 at 2.4.1).

Kong became an embarrassment and, following the signing of the Joint Declaration (described below) Britain obtained China's support for demolition of the Walled City. All that remained was the difficult job of agreeing compensation for the City's residents and businesses. The City was fully demolished by April 1994 and very rapidly replaced by a park (containing some relics of the City's history).[53]

1.5 The Joint Declaration and the resumption of sovereignty

Irrespective of the legalities of the treaties under which Britain obtained Hong Kong, Kowloon and the New Territories, there is no doubt that the existence of these "unequal treaties" was deeply resented in China. The two "in perpetuity" treaties had been, largely, imposed by a powerful state on a weaker one on which it had just inflicted military defeats. The impropriety of the acquisition was recognised not only by the Chinese. Indeed, the editor of the Canton Register stated:

> Hong Kong is part of China, we cannot just take it . . . We do not have to forcibly take and retain an island—that would be piracy.[54]

Moreover, the 1898 "lease" was imposed by Britain on a China still smarting from defeat at the hands of the Japanese.

The Nationalist "Kuomintang" party had called for the renegotiation of the treaties and the return of the New Territories. Then, during the Second World War, Britain and the United States,

> agreed to the complete abolition of the right of extraterritoriality.[55]

Contingency plans were then made for the return of the New Territories. With the overthrow of the Kuomintang by Communist forces in 1948, the promise of the return of territory was withdrawn and plans were made for the military defence of Hong Kong by the British.

Some idea of the extremity of views held by the "patriotic" group can be seen in the following, polemic description of Hong Kong's colonial position:

> In the mid-19th century, Britain, taking advantage of the corrupt and incompetent Qing government, launched two wars of aggression against this country and forced the Qing government to sign three unequal treaties: the Treaty of Nanking (1842), the Convention of Beijing (1860) and the Convention for the Extension of Hong Kong (1898) . . . In this way, with the help of the three unequal treaties, Britain occupied Hong Kong.

---

53. For further reference on this topic, see E Sinn, 'Kowloon Walled City: Its Origins and Early History', *Journal of the Royal Asiatic Society Hong Kong Branch*, 30–46.
54. R Houghton (n 10).
55. Miners (n 6) 4.

However, the Chinese people have never recognized the three unequal treaties and neither have successive governments since the revolution of 1911.[56]

This "patriotic" view of Hong Kong as a Chinese territory "occupied" by a colonial power against the will of its inhabitants was undoubtedly shared by most Hong Kong residents in the earlier days of occupation. Miners[57] writes:

> There was scant evidence that [British] imperial rule was exercised as a trust for the benefit of the dependent peoples. The loyalties of the Chinese population were directed towards China, not Britain, as was shown by the widespread response in support of the general strikes of 1922 and 1925. Right up to the 1940s governors of Hong Kong feared that any extension of democracy to the Chinese population would produce a majority in favour of the return of the territory to Chinese rule.[58]

However, Miners adds:

> This situation changed completely with the influx of refugees which followed the end of the war with Japan and the victory of the Communists in the Chinese civil war . . .
>
> Instead of being faced with a nationalist movement demanding the end of colonial rule, there was a complete absence of political agitation of any sort and the population showed a clear preference for continued British rule rather than subjection to Communist control . . .
>
> . . . An opinion poll taken in March 1982[59] found that 85% of respondents favoured a continuance of British administration after 1997 and only 4% preferred the return of the colony to China.[60]

Until the 1980s, China's communist government, unlike its Nationalist predecessor, had acquiesced in the continuance of British *de facto* rule, while not formally recognising the "unequal treaties". Tension *did* arise during the 1967 riots in Hong Kong, initially arising from an industrial dispute but soon escalating to political violence and bombings. Such "anti-colonial violence" caused great concern in Hong Kong but had little lasting local support, not least once schoolchildren rather than "colonialists" became targets.[61] The potential for a mainland "takeover" clearly existed at the time, notwithstanding China's internal strife caused by the then ongoing Cultural Revolution. However, those on the "Chinese" side favouring

---

56. *Introduction to the Basic Law of the Hong Kong SAR* (Law Press China 2000) 7–8. It may be noted that: "Publication of this book is sponsored by the Association for Celebration of Reunification of Hong Kong with China Charitable Trust".
57. Note 6.
58. Ibid 15.
59. Carried out by "Survey Research" on behalf of the Hong Kong Reform Club. In fact, 70% favoured continued British rule while 15% preferred "trust territory" status.
60. Miners (n 6) 15–23.
61. "Non-patriotic" schools were a major target of the bombs (only around 15% of which were genuine). Hong Kong inhabitants were also appalled by the targeted assassination of anti-communist radio host, Lam Bun.

diplomacy remained dominant, and local activists were told to end the violence.[62] One significant legacy of the disturbances was a belated recognition by the colonial government of the poor conditions endured by many Hong Kong people, many of them recent escapees from Mao Zedong's China. The result was an improvement in educational provision, strong moves against endemic corruption (with the introduction of the Independent Commission Against Corruption (ICAC)) and, particularly under new Governor MacLehose, a huge expansion in the supply of subsidised public housing. However, a further, less welcome consequence of the "unrest" was the shelving of previous Governor Trench's plan to have a fully elected LegCo. The "non-democratic" legacy remains and all subsequent attempts to introduce a measure of genuine democracy in Hong Kong have been thwarted by the PRC, both before and after 1997. Ip[63] writes:

> [China] always associated democratisation in Hong Kong with eventual independence precluding resumption of Chinese sovereignty.[64]

As we shall see, there has been no development at all in terms of "electing" the Chief Executive by any genuine form of universal suffrage, and while slightly more than half of LegCo seats are filled by elected legislators, the remainder are the province of "functional" (small circle) elections.

Despite the obvious feasibility of a Chinese takeover of Hong Kong by force, considerable advantages accrued from the continuation of the status quo, not least in terms of a huge external trade operating via Hong Kong and significant foreign exchange remitted by Hong Kong citizens to relatives on the Chinese mainland. In pragmatic terms it is clear that "British" Hong Kong served a useful purpose for China since, despite Britain's professed interest in maintaining the security and welfare of Hong Kong, it would have been unable to withstand a serious attempt by China to obtain Hong Kong by force. That such an attempt was never made shows both the value of Hong Kong to China and the greater emphasis placed on first recovering Taiwan.

The position may well have continued unchanged, at least for some time beyond 1997, had it not been for the uncertainty over the New Territories (and Outlying Islands) "lease". While China did not formally recognise the validity of the 99-year lease, Britain did regard it as binding and, having been granted in 1898, it was due to expire in 1997. One school of thought was that Britain and China could have ignored the expiry date and continued as before. Since China had not taken steps to retake Hong Kong thus far despite its clear ability to do so and its (official) rejection of the "unequal treaties", why should the status quo not continue after 1997? The "let it be" approach was given weight by the fact that China, on being offered, in the 1960s,

---

62. While "Red Guards" clearly supported Hong Kong activists, Prime Minister Zhou Enlai reportedly rejected a "non-political" solution to the Hong Kong situation.
63. E. Ip (n 4).
64. Ibid 48.

an earlier resumption of sovereignty in Macau (where Portugal's lease was due to expire in 1999), had rejected the offer lest this led to fears of a similar "premature" reversion of Hong Kong.

The problem with the "passive" approach was that uncertainty and unease were arising as to the validity of leases in the New Territories whose term extended beyond 1997, despite Chinese leader Deng Xiaoping's reassurance to Hong Kong Governor MacLehose, in 1979, that Hong Kong investors should "put their hearts at ease." Britain sought a "formal" assurance of some form of continued British administration in Hong Kong, post-1997, and, in 1982, pressed for formal negotiations to begin. This may well have been a mistake, given the Chinese concept of "face" and the important distinction between "acquiescence" and "formal acceptance" of the status quo. It was one thing for China to "permit" the continuation of British governance of "part of China" as a relic of colonialism and another to give some formal seal of approval to the "unequal treaties". The distinction between acquiescence and formal agreement is illustrated by an editorial in the People's Daily of 8 March 1968 which states that:

> questions like the Hong Kong question and the Macao question are left over from the past and arise from the unequal treaties imposed on China by the imperialist powers . . . We have consistently held that they should be peacefully resolved through negotiations when conditions are ripe and that until that time the status quo should be maintained.[65]

It became apparent that Deng Xiaoping would not agree to the extension of the New Territories lease and that the Chinese position was that the sovereignty of the *whole* of Hong Kong (including Hong Kong Island and Kowloon, previously ceded "in perpetuity") would revert in 1997.

Despite an initially aggressive insistence by British Prime Minister, Margaret Thatcher, as to the validity of the "unequal treaties" and two years of hard bargaining, the result was a foregone conclusion.[66] Even by its own admission, Britain had no "rights" to the New Territories and Outlying Islands, post-1997, and accepted as inevitable that Hong Kong Island and Kowloon were not politically and economically viable on their own. From the British perspective, then, the task was to continue the sound governance of Hong Kong up to 1997, to ensure an orderly transition to Chinese rule in 1997 and to seek the best possible protections for Hong Kong and its people under Chinese rule post-1997. This took the form of the Joint Declaration on the Question of Hong Kong (Joint Declaration), ratified by the British and Chinese governments in May 1985.

---

65. Cited in Law Press China (n 57) 56.
66. Britain's (potentially) main bargaining tool, right of abode for all Hong Kong citizens (free to leave in the case of PRC excesses), had been thrown away by the 1981 British Nationality Act which denied the right of abode in Britain to most Hong Kong citizens.

JOINT DECLARATION
OF THE GOVERNMENT OF THE UNITED KINGDOM OF GREAT BRITAIN AND
NORTHERN IRELAND
AND
THE GOVERNMENT OF THE PEOPLE'S REPUBLIC OF CHINA
ON THE QUESTION OF HONG KONG

The Government of the United Kingdom of Great Britain and Northern Ireland and the Government of the People's Republic of China have reviewed with satisfaction the friendly relations existing between the two Governments and peoples in recent years and agreed that a proper negotiated settlement of the question of Hong Kong, which is left over from the past, is conducive to the maintenance of the prosperity and stability of Hong Kong and to the further strengthening and development of the relations between the two countries on a new basis. To this end, they have, after talks between the delegations of the two Governments, agreed to declare as follows:

1. The Government of the People's Republic of China declares that to recover the Hong Kong area (including Hong Kong Island, Kowloon and the New Territories, hereinafter referred to as Hong Kong) is the common aspiration of the entire Chinese people, and that it has decided to resume the exercise of sovereignty over Hong Kong with effect from 1 July 1997.

2. The Government of the United Kingdom declares that it will restore Hong Kong to the People's Republic of China with effect from 1 July 1997.

3. The Government of the People's Republic of China declares that the basic policies of the People's Republic of China regarding Hong Kong are as follows:

(1) Upholding national unity and territorial integrity and taking account of the history of Hong Kong and its realities, the People's Republic of China has decided to establish, in accordance with the provisions of Article 31 of the Constitution of the People's Republic of China, a Hong Kong Special Administrative Region upon resuming the exercise of sovereignty over Hong Kong.

(2) The Hong Kong Special Administrative Region will be directly under the authority of the Central People's Government of the People's Republic of China. The Hong Kong Special Administrative Region will enjoy a high degree of autonomy, except in foreign and defence affairs which are the responsibilities of the Central People's Government.

(3) The Hong Kong Special Administrative Region will be vested with executive, legislative and independent judicial power, including that of final adjudication. The laws currently in force in Hong Kong will remain basically unchanged.

(4) The Government of the Hong Kong Special Administrative Region will be composed of local inhabitants. The chief executive will be appointed by the Central People's Government on the basis of the results of elections or consultations to be held locally. Principal officials will be nominated by the chief executive of the Hong Kong Special Administrative Region for appointment by the Central People's Government.

Chinese and foreign nationals previously working in the public and police services in the government departments of Hong Kong may remain in employment. British and other foreign nationals may also be employed to serve as advisers or hold certain public posts in government departments of the Hong Kong Special Administrative Region.

(5) The current social and economic systems in Hong Kong will remain unchanged, and so will the life-style. Rights and freedoms, including those of the person, of speech, of the press, of assembly, of association, of travel, of movement, of correspondence, of strike, of choice of occupation, of academic research and of religious belief will be ensured by law in the Hong Kong Special Administrative Region. Private property, ownership of enterprises, legitimate right of inheritance and foreign investment will be protected by law.

(6) The Hong Kong Special Administrative Region will retain the status of a free port and a separate customs territory.

(7) The Hong Kong Special Administrative Region will retain the status of an international financial centre, and its markets for foreign exchange, gold, securities and futures will continue. There will be free flow of capital. The Hong Kong dollar will continue to circulate and remain freely convertible.

(8) The Hong Kong Special Administrative Region will have independent finances. The Central People's Government will not levy taxes on the Hong Kong Special Administrative Region.

(9) The Hong Kong Special Administrative Region may establish mutually beneficial economic relations with the United Kingdom and other countries, whose economic interests in Hong Kong will be given due regard.

(10) Using the name of 'Hong Kong, China', the Hong Kong Special Administrative Region may on its own maintain and develop economic and cultural relations and conclude relevant agreements with states, regions and relevant international organisations. The Government of the Hong Kong Special Administrative Region may on its own issue travel documents for entry into and exit from Hong Kong.

(11) The maintenance of public order in the Hong Kong Special Administrative Region will be the responsibility of the Government of the Hong Kong Special Administrative Region.

(12) The above-stated basic policies of the People's Republic of China regarding Hong Kong and the elaboration of them in Annex I to this Joint Declaration will be stipulated, in a Basic Law of the Hong Kong Special Administrative Region of the People's Republic of China, by the National People's Congress of the People's Republic of China, and they will remain unchanged for 50 years.

4. The Government of the United Kingdom and the Government of the People's Republic of China declare that, during the transitional period between the date of the entry into force of this Joint Declaration and 30 June 1997, the Government of the United Kingdom will be responsible for the administration of Hong Kong with the

> object of maintaining and preserving its economic prosperity and social stability; and that the Government of the People's Republic of China will give its cooperation in this connection.
>
> 5. The Government of the United Kingdom and the Government of the People's Republic of China declare that, in order to ensure a smooth transfer of government in 1997, and with a view to the effective implementation of this Joint Declaration, a Sino-British Joint Liaison Group will be set up when this Joint Declaration enters into force; and that it will be established and will function in accordance with the provisions of Annex II to this Joint Declaration.
>
> 6. The Government of the United Kingdom and the Government of the People's Republic of China declare that land leases in Hong Kong and other related matters will be dealt with in accordance with the provisions of Annex III to this Joint Declaration.
>
> 7. The Government of the United Kingdom and the Government of the People's Republic of China agree to implement the preceding declarations and the Annexes to this Joint Declaration.
>
> 8. This Joint Declaration is subject to ratification and shall enter into force on the date of the exchange of instruments of ratification, which shall take place in Beijing before 30 June 1985. This Joint Declaration and its Annexes shall be equally binding.
>
> Done in duplicate at Beijing on 19 December 1984 in the English and Chinese languages, both texts being equally authentic.
>
> | For the | For the |
> | --- | --- |
> | Government of the United Kingdom | Government of the People's Republic |
> | of Great Britain and Northern Ireland | of China |
> | Margaret Thatcher | Zhao Ziyang |

At no stage were the people of Hong Kong consulted as to their future, nor were they accorded the rights of self-determination guaranteed to all other "post-colonial" peoples.[67] On 8 March 1972, shortly after China's accession to the United Nations, its permanent delegate to the UN had declared that:

> Hong Kong and Macao are parts of the territory of China occupied by the British and Portuguese authorities. The settlement of the Hong Kong and Macau questions is entirely within China's sovereignty and they do not belong at all to the ordinary category of colonial territories covered by the declaration on the granting of independence to colonial countries and people.[68]

---
67. China had insisted that Hong Kong and Macau should be removed from the list of "colonial territories" to be given the right of self-determination by the United Nations, insisting that the fate of Macau and Hong Kong was a purely "internal" matter for China.
68. For an extremely critical view of UN proceedings on the issue, see Nihal Jayawickrama, 'The Right of Self-Determination' in P Wesley-Smith (ed), *Hong Kong's Basic Law: Problems & Prospects*

This view prevailed even though, as Miners writes:

> The British government was well aware that the surrender of 5 million people into the hands of a communist state without their consent was completely contrary to the principles of self-government and self-determination which Britain has followed when granting independence to all other parts of her colonial empire.[69]

That the "surrender" was "without their consent" cannot seriously be doubted. Yahuda,[70] for example, writes that:

> Hong Kong people accepted the colonial administration because it was able to deliver the goods, i.e., it maintained law and order well, guaranteed the freedoms that Hong Kong people treasured, and brought economic development and prosperity to the community. In the opinion surveys in the decade or more before 1997, Hong Kong people consistently showed more trust and support for the colonial administration than for London and Beijing, while the latter usually trailed behind London by a relatively small margin.[71]

In *realpolitik* terms, however, there is much force in the British position, summed up in the UK Government White Paper, issued in November 1984, which re-asserted the two key points that the New Territories (and the Outlying Islands) 99 year lease would expire in 1997 and that (what remained of British Hong Kong) "Hong Island, Kowloon and Stonecutters Island would not be viable alone."[72] As Mushkat has explained:

> it is evident that neither party to the Sino British Joint Declaration has accepted self-determination as a viable option; [and] that no international forum is likely to collectively sanction any 'decolonization' attempt.[73]

As such, the alternatives were to give up Hong Kong as part of an amicable settlement framed in a binding international treaty or "a reversion to China without such arrangements."[74] As the International Commission of Jurists (ICJ)[75] affirmed:

> A strong case can be made for saying that the Joint Declaration represented the best available solution to a complex and very difficult problem. It is, however, impossible

---

(Faculty of Law, University of Hong Kong 1990) 85–98.
69. Miners (n 6) 23.
70. MB Yahuda, 'A British Perspective on Hong Kong: A Decade Later' in JYS Cheng (ed), *The Hong Kong SAR in Its First Decade* (2nd edn, City University of Hong Kong Press 2009).
71. For further information on such polls, see, especially, JYS Cheng, *Hong Kong in Search of a Future* (Oxford University Press 1984).
72. UK Government White Paper, November 1984, para 29.
73. Roda Mushkat, *One Country, Two International Legal Personalities: The Case of Hong Kong* (Hong Kong University Press 1997) 8.
74. UK Government White Paper (n 73). For a very different perspective cf M Roberti, *The Fall of Hong Kong: China's Triumph and Britain's Betrayal* (Wiley 1996) and R McCorquodale, 'Hong Kong and the Right of Self-Determination' (1997) 4 New Law Journal.
75. International Commission of Jurists, 'Countdown to 1997: Report of a Mission to Hong Kong'.

to say that that solution has received the binding and legitimate endorsement of the people of Hong Kong.[76]

That the majority of Hong Kong residents wished the status quo to continue had far less to do with affection for Britain than fear of communist rule (from which much of Hong Kong's population had fairly recently fled). As the ICJ declared:

> Colonial status was acceptable to the people of Hong Kong. Many people had gone to Hong Kong to escape from the People's Republic, and preferred British rule to Chinese.[77]

Such fears proved justified when, in 1989,[78] several thousand[79] unarmed demonstrators were killed by the People's Liberation Army (PLA) in and around[80] Tiananmen Square in Beijing.[81]

Given the military and political reality whereby China could retake Hong Kong "on the basis of a phone call", Britain had a very weak bargaining position. Indeed, one writer spoke of the Joint Declaration as "The Unequal Treaty of 1984".[82] Moreover, by its shameful decision to deny full passport rights to the people of Hong Kong,[83] Britain gave up its only potential leverage: the threat of a mass exodus to Britain of Hong Kong's elite.

In finally yielding all claims to continued sovereignty, and even governance, Britain was able to secure certain assurances that the capitalist way of life in Hong Kong should be maintained, along the lines of the "one country, two systems" doctrine first propounded by Deng Xiaoping as a solution to the "problem" of Hong Kong and Taiwan. That these assurances were reduced to writing appears to have been a considerable achievement on Britain's part. Rafferty wrote that:

> The achievement of British negotiators was to persuade China to commit itself in writing to a series of specific promises on the future shape of Hong Kong. The attitude of the Chinese at the outset was to try to get their promises accepted on trust without being written down and without being too specific.[84]

The assurances were incorporated, initially, into the Joint Declaration, in return for Britain's recognition (in the face of all the evidence) that the return of Hong Kong

---

76. Ibid 2.
77. Ibid 1.
78. The PLA attacks took place on 4 June (though of course many died after that date from wounds).
79. Estimates of deaths caused by the PLA and paramilitary groups vary from a few hundred to several thousand. Amnesty International puts the figure at "up to 1,000".
80. Most of the deaths occurred in the streets surrounding the square which were less publicly visible.
81. Universally described as a "massacre" for many years, the "incident" is now more commonly described as a "crackdown", reflecting the PRC's increased politico-economic influence.
82. See K Rafferty, 'China's Triumph: The Unequal Treaty of 1984' in K Rafferty (n 8) 378.
83. Despite Britain's moral commitment to the people of Hong Kong, "right of abode" was denied to those with British "Hong Kong" passports which became, ultimately, "British National Overseas" passports.
84. K Rafferty (n 8).

"is the common aspiration of the entire Chinese people". The key features of the Joint Declaration are that Britain would "restore" Hong Kong (including Kowloon, the New Territories and the Outlying Islands) on 1 July 1997; that in the period between the application of the Joint Declaration and 1 July 1997, Britain would continue to administer Hong Kong, with the co-operation of the Chinese government; that following the resumption of sovereignty in 1997, Hong Kong would become a "Special Administrative Region" (SAR) of China with a "high degree of autonomy" (except in foreign and defence affairs);[85] that Hong Kong's existing (capitalist) social and economic system would be maintained (for at least 50 years) post-1997; that Hong Kong, post-1997, would be vested with "executive, legislative and independent judicial power, including the right of final adjudication"; that the common law legal system would be maintained post-1997; that the issue of leases spanning 1997 would be addressed; and that Hong Kong's Chief Executive (the successor to the colonial Governor) would be appointed by the Central People's Government and be supported by principal officials appointed by the Chief Executive.

The major areas described were more fully articulated in the three annexes to the Joint Declaration. Annex I explained in detail the key features envisaged for post-1997 Hong Kong and the constitutional relationship of the proposed Special Administrative Region (Hong Kong SAR) with the mainland.

Under Annex II, the task of ensuring the implementation of the Joint Declaration and a smooth transfer of power in 1997 was entrusted to the Sino-British Joint Liaison Group (JLG).

Annex III dealt specifically with the complex issue of providing a legal mechanism for the recognition of leases in Hong Kong intended to span 1997.

1.5.1 The status of the Joint Declaration

The Joint Declaration was an international treaty, signed and ratified by both parties. This would appear to mean that Britain would have *locus standi,* as a party with treaty rights, to complain at any subsequent breaches of the treaty by China (even though any such complaint would have little significance in *realpolitik* terms).[86] However, even this "formal" right has been denied by China, which claims that Hong Kong issues are a "purely domestic" matter, of no concern to Britain. The Chinese view appears to be that the Joint Declaration imposes obligations *solely* for the period from its ratification (recognising Britain's right to administer Hong Kong until 30

---

85. As Ip (n 4) has shown, such "autonomy" was not novel, since by unwritten convention "Whitehall deferred to the Hong Kong Government on how best to administer the Crown Colony", 48.
86. This view was strongly (though of course futilely) espoused by 150 Hong Kong citizens who, in response to the PRC's controversial White Paper on "one country, two systems" (which has been seen as an assault on Hong Kong's promised "high degree of autonomy"), marched to the British Consulate in June 2014 and demanded that Britain take back Hong Kong since the Joint Declaration had not been adhered to!

June 1997) to the resumption of sovereignty on 1 July 1997.[87] Chen Zouer, former deputy director of the Hong Kong and Macau Affairs Office, reportedly asserted that the "theme" of the Joint Declaration had been accomplished in 1997.[88] Thereafter, according to the Chinese view, Hong Kong's constitution becomes the Basic Law, a piece of PRC legislation (indeed a "basic law" of the PRC). Britain has largely acquiesced, ignoring Hong Kong's fate post-Basic Law, due, in no small measure, to a pragmatic perception that good relations with China, politically and economically, are more important than vain attempts to ensure that the PRC complies with the Joint Declaration.[89] The last Hong Kong colonial Governor, (Lord) Chris Patten, has complained that commercial interests have eclipsed Britain's "duty to speak out" on proposed voting reforms but mistakenly implied that the Joint Declaration aspires to election by universal suffrage (such aspiration is limited to the later Basic Law). Moreover, even minor references to Hong Kong by Britain are immediately condemned as "interference with internal PRC affairs".[90] The view that, post-1997, Britain has no *locus standi* in relation to a treaty to which it is a signatory[91] was, sadly, endorsed by Raymond Tam, then Secretary for Constitutional and Mainland Affairs.[92]

1.5.2 The relationship between the Joint Declaration and the Basic Law

The key ingredients of the Joint Declaration described above were ultimately enacted (very fully) under the Basic Law of the Hong Kong Special Administrative Region (Basic Law), Hong Kong's post-1997 constitution.[93] The drafting of the Basic Law (in two languages of course) was an exhaustive (and exhausting) task and the final product contained 160 Articles plus annexes.

Some essential features of the Basic Law, sometimes overlooked, should be stressed. First, and very importantly, it is a piece of *Chinese* legislation, enacted by the National People's Congress of the People's Republic of China, rather than a Hong Kong Ordinance or British enactment. Given China's official stance on the

---

87. See J Crawford, 'Rights in One Country: Hong Kong and China', Hochelaga Lectures 2004 (HKU Faculty of Law, Hong Kong 2005).
88. A Cheung, 'Lone Fight' *South China Morning Post* (Hong Kong, 13 March 2015).
89. See Parker and Sevastopulo, 'Patten Criticises UK over Failure to Act on Hong Kong Reforms' *Financial Times* (London, 2 September 2014).
90. With a British Parliamentary Committee reporting on Hong Kong 30 years post-Joint Declaration, PRC Foreign Ministry spokesman, Hong Lei, was quoted by *China Daily* (26 July 2014) as criticising "an interference of China's domestic affairs". The committee, in fact, was denied entry to Hong Kong ('UK Politicians Refused Entry to Hong Kong' *The Guardian* (London, 30 November 2014).
91. The treaty was lodged with the United Nations.
92. See G Cheng and J Ng, 'Question Hangs Over Pledge of Autonomy' *South China Morning Post* (Hong Kong, 20 December 2014). The same article asserts that China's deputy ambassador to Britain, Ni Jian, announced that the Joint Declaration was now void.
93. Promulgated 4 April 1990 (Decree of the President of the PRC); in force 1 July 1997.

legal status of Hong Kong the Chinese nature of the legislation could hardly be otherwise. This did, however, create the problem of a dissonance between what was agreed in the Joint Declaration, a supposedly binding international treaty, and the final version of the Basic Law, as enacted in Beijing.

While the ultimate form of the Basic Law (which will be considered in more detail in Chapter 2) is largely reflective of the letter and spirit of the Joint Declaration, mention should be made of some areas of divergence, of varying degrees of importance. Much of the divergence arose from serious differences between the British and Chinese "sides" in the 1984–1997 period. The Chinese perspective was that Britain was reneging on its duty to maintain the status quo pending the resumption of sovereignty, while the British view was that changes had been compelled by Britain's responsibility to the people of Hong Kong and the changing scenario produced by the Tiananmen Square massacre and the resulting loss of public confidence in Hong Kong.

Britain's possible unease at leaving the people of Hong Kong to their post-1997 fate, despite professedly seeking to secure their welfare, was much exacerbated by the events in and around Tiananmen Square. Serious concerns about the future were expressed by the people of Hong Kong; there were fears of a mass exodus from Hong Kong and even calls, in Hong Kong, for the abrogation of the Joint Declaration. Britain took a number of steps to try to allay fears, which, while falling short of calls for the right of abode in the UK for all Hong Kong citizens,[94] had a certain stabilising effect. Britain provided for the issue of up to 50,000 full British passports to Hong Kong heads of families from the civil service and professional sectors, who wished to apply, and their families. Britain also promised to speed up the pace of progress towards democracy and to introduce a Bill of Rights. A Bill of Rights Ordinance (BORO) was duly enacted which established, in the form of domestic legislation, many of the rights to which Hong Kong was already notionally committed via its adherence to the International Convention on Civil & Political Rights. These rights were, therefore, reflected in Hong Kong legislation, independent of international treaties and their incumbent uncertainties. Moreover, BORO itself was to have a special status whereby other common law and statutory rules would, if possible, be construed as conforming to it.[95]

To show Britain's continued commitment in Hong Kong up to 1997, and to restore economic confidence, plans were announced to construct a new international airport at Chek Lap Kok, near Lantau, to replace the much-loved but antiquated Kai Tak.

---

94. This denial was essentially racist, given Britain's grant of full citizenship to "white" Gibraltarians and Falklanders in similarly uncertain circumstances, though the desire not to offend China must also have been a factor. See R McKee, 'Doing the Right Thing' (1995) New Law Journal 13 October 1995.
95. But cf 1.7 below.

None of these intended ameliorations were entirely successful and none escaped the disapproval of China, which criticised them as a deviation from the letter and spirit of the Joint Declaration. The issue of passports was seen as a disavowal of China's sovereignty over its own citizens and, in reprisal, China modified the draft Basic Law to drastically reduce, from the original ambit of the Joint Declaration, the number of senior officials and legislators permitted to hold office without being Chinese nationals with no right of abode elsewhere.[96] The extended restrictions run counter to Article 25 of the International Convention on Civil and Political Rights, continued adherence to which is guaranteed by the Joint Declaration[97] and the Basic Law.[98] A spirited (and extensive) defence of the new arrangements can be found in the following text, sponsored by the "Association for Celebration of Reunification of Hong Kong with China Charitable Trust":[99]

> The requirement for 'having no right of abode in any foreign country' in the Basic Law was added by the Drafting Committee for the Basic Law at its Ninth Plenary Meeting, and it was not to be found in the draft of the Basic Law for soliciting opinions promulgated at its Seventh Plenary Meeting, nor in the draft adopted at its Eighth Plenary Meeting. It was added for some objective reasons, especially for the reason that Britain unilaterally decided to change the nationality of part of Hong Kong residents. Since it is a major question on which hinges the stability and prosperity of Hong Kong, we shall discuss it at some length below.
>
> On December 20, 1989, the British Government unilaterally announced that it decided to give 50,000 households of Hong Kong residents the status of complete British citizenship, including the right of abode in the United Kingdom . . .
>
> The nationality of Hong Kong Chinese compatriots should only be determined according to the Nationality Law of the PRC, because it is a matter within the limits of Chinese sovereignty . . .
>
> From this it can be seen that it is very important and necessary for the Drafting Committee of the Basic Law . . . to add the provision of 'having no right of abode in any foreign country' in the relevant articles.[100]

Comment

There is, of course, no reference here to the reason for Britain's action: the justifiable concerns for the future, in Britain and Hong Kong, arising from the Tiananmen massacre which posed the realistic threat of a total exodus of the professional classes from Hong Kong pre-1997.

---

96. See Article 44, Basic Law.
97. Section XIII, Annex 1.
98. Article 39.
99. Law Press China (n 57).
100. Ibid 94–97.

The extremely minor democratic reforms of last Governor Chris Patten[101] (seen as inadequate by the democratic camp!) were condemned by China which, in retaliation, tore up the promises of a "through train" for the Legislative Council members in office on 1 July 1997 and instead set up a Provisional Legislative Council (PLC)[102] to operate pending new elections, post–1 July 1997, under the previous electoral rules.[103]

BORO, while not entirely overturned post-1997, "apparently" lost its special "superior" status[104] (whereby previous inconsistent legislation would be overturned and later legislation would be presumed consistent) which was declared inconsistent with the requirements of the Basic Law.

Finally, even the new airport was not uncontroversial since it and, indeed, all capital expenditure in the transitional period, was viewed with suspicion by China which feared that Britain would exhaust much of Hong Kong's vast monetary reserves in the last days of colonial rule. While the British hoped that the airport would open in 1997, as a fitting epitaph to British rule, the Chinese government was determined that this would not happen and ensured sufficient delays in the supply of finance and labour to ensure a 1998 opening under non-colonial governance.

A significant number of other important differences between the Joint Declaration and the Basic Law have been highlighted by the International Commission of Jurists (ICJ)[105] and should be noted. First, Article 17 of the Basic Law gives the Standing Committee of the National People's Congress (NPC) the power to invalidate any Hong Kong SAR legislation which it considers not to be in conformity with the Basic Law "regarding affairs within the responsibility of the Central Authorities or regarding the relationship between the Central Authorities and the Region". In the view of the ICJ, since the issue involves judicial power, such power should have remained vested in the Court of Final Appeal (introduced post-1997 to replace the Privy Council as the highest court within Hong Kong).[106]

Further, and some would say sinisterly, Article 18 of the Basic Law gives the NPC Standing Committee the power to decide whether the Hong Kong SAR is in a state of emergency such as to justify the application of "national laws" in the SAR.

---

101. Essentially the abolition of appointed LegCo seats and an increase in the number of directly elected seats.
102. While the validity of the "provisional legislature", not provided for in the Joint Declaration, was the subject of subsequent legal challenge, its legality was endorsed by the Court of Appeal in *HKSAR v Ma Wai Kwan, David* [1997] 1 HKLRD 761 and confirmed by the Court of Final Appeal in *Ng Ka Ling (an infant) v Director of Immigration* [1999] 1 HKC 291. The Court of Appeal's acceptance of the PLC's legitimacy was severely criticised by Johannes Chan, in 'A Search for Identity: Legal Development since 1 July 1997', in Gungwu Wang and J Wong (eds), *Hong Kong in China: The Challenges of Transition* (Times Academic Press 1999) 247–250.
103. The PLC began operating (in Shenzhen) in January 1997. One legal objection (that the PLC had "usurped" the role of LegCo in Hong Kong) was rejected on the basis that Shenzhen was not within Hong Kong's jurisdiction. See Chan (ibid) 247.
104. For fuller discussion see 1.8 below.
105. International Commission of Jurists (n 76).
106. Joint Declaration: Section III of Annex I.

This is in clear conflict with the statement in the Joint Declaration that "the maintenance of public order in the SAR will be the responsibility of the Government of the SAR."[107]

Perhaps most controversially of all, Article 23 of the Basic Law requires the Hong Kong SAR to introduce legislation to prevent "subversion", including a prohibition against political organisations establishing ties with foreign political organisations. This, the ICJ pointed out,[108] is contrary to provisions in the International Covenant on Civil and Political Rights, continued adherence to which in the Hong Kong SAR is guaranteed under the Joint Declaration[109] and the Basic Law.[110] Attempts by the then Secretary for Security, Regina Ip, to implement this legislation in 2002–2003 met with huge public opposition,[111] temporary[112] abandonment of the plan and her subsequent resignation.[113]

A further divergence between the Joint Declaration and the Basic Law relates to the position of the Chief Executive, the person filling the role formerly occupied, until 1997, by the Governor. Neither the Joint declaration nor the Basic Law provides for democratic election of the Chief Executive, and on this matter the British side could have few complaints given the "appointed by Britain" nature of all Hong Kong governors.[114] However, on two particular Chief Executive issues the Basic Law is contentious. The first relates to the requirement that the Chief Executive must be a Chinese citizen with no right of abode elsewhere. This requirement is not specified in the Joint Declaration (though de facto the NPC would have been unlikely to appoint otherwise) and is contrary to Article 25 of the ICCPR, a convention stated in the Joint Declaration and the Basic Law to remain in force in Hong Kong. Given that the Central People's Government has, ultimately, total discretion as to the appointment of the Chief Executive, the "single nationality" requirement was hardly necessary.

More significant are the rules in the Basic Law governing the Chief Executive's powers and responsibilities. The Chief Executive is stated, by Article 43 of the Basic Law, to be accountable to, "the Central People's Government and the Hong Kong SAR" whereas the Joint Declaration talks of "executive authorities" being merely "accountable to the legislature". This divergence leads to the issue of the

---

107. Joint Declaration: Section XII of Annex I.
108. ICJ, op cit, 111.
109. Cf. Section XIII.
110. Article 39.
111. More than half a million Hong Kong people marched to protest against the proposed legislation. For further discussion, see Chapter 2 at 2.4.1.
112. "Beijing loyalists" have subsequently called for the reintroduction of the Article 23 legislation following the speedy introduction of the National Security Law in Macau, on the terms previously proposed for Hong Kong, via Macau's own Basic Law. This despite the fact that the PRC "resumption of sovereignty" occurred two years later in Macau than in Hong Kong.
113. While new Chief Executive, Carrie Lam, may wish to avoid the "Article 23 question" its implementation remains a legal duty for Hong Kong; "loyalist" Tsang Yok-sing has implied that if Hong Kong does not act Beijing will impose sedition (etc) laws unilaterally.
114. "The Chief Executive will, in effect, simply be a Governor appointed in Beijing rather than London" (ICJ, n 76, 78).

Chief Executive's relationship with the Legislative Council (LegCo) and his ability to block legislation. The whole thrust of Articles 49–52 of the Basic Law is that, rather than a system of "checks and balances", Hong Kong is to be administered by "executive-led" government. While it is, of course, correct to say that British colonial rule was "executive led", it is also true that 1997 was supposed to mark an improvement, with "Hong Kong people running Hong Kong." It seems somewhat ironic that the only argument in favour of the Chief Executive's extensive powers is that the situation is no worse than in colonial times! The Law Press China text on the Basic Law[115] states:

> The previous governor system of Hong Kong was a political structure characterized by 'domination by the Executive'. The Governor overrides the Executive and Legislative Councils and is in a dominant position in the British Hong Kong Government.
>
> Judged from the relevant provisions in the Basic Law, the political structure of the HKSAR is also one in which 'the executive is dominant'.[116]

In addition to the major *contents* of the Basic Law, there is significance in the *timing* of the legislation. Since it was to represent Hong Kong's post-handover constitution, it need not have been enacted until 1996. The Chinese government, however, decided to enact the legislation in 1990. Why so early? Professor Albert Chen[117] has suggested two possible reasons, one of which may be deemed the "optimistic" explanation and the other the "pessimistic" one. As to the former, Chen explains as follows:

> [the decision] to enact the Basic Law by 1990 can be interpreted as an exercise in giving more legal force to the Joint Declaration, further removing possible uncertainties, and thus inspiring more confidence on the part of the people of Hong Kong in their future.[118]

As to the latter, Chen states:

> the enactment of the Basic Law in 1990 is a means by which the Chinese government can influence constitutional developments in Hong Kong in the transition period between 1990 and 1997. In fact, even before 1990, the fact that the Basic Law was in the process of being drafted was already used in arguments advanced by the Chinese side concerning constitutional changes in the second half of the 1980s.[119]

---

115. Note 57.
116. Ibid 346.
117. Albert Chen, 'Implications for the Transition Period 1990–1997' in Peter Wesley-Smith (ed), *Hong Kong's Basic Law: Problems and Prospects* (University of Hong Kong Faculty of Law 1990).
118. Ibid 23.
119. Ibid 23–24.

1.6 Localisation and adaptation exercises

The expression "localisation" has been used in a variety of contexts in Hong Kong. Notably, for example, it has referred to the localisation of the civil service in Hong Kong, whereby civil service posts, increasingly those at a senior level, have been filled by "local" (effectively local Chinese) staff. The impetus for such reforms was not initially "post-1997" considerations but conformity with the appointment of local staff throughout the British "empire". Miners[120] writes:

> After the last war, Public Service Commissions were set up in all the larger British colonies on instructions from London. The main objectives were to encourage the recruitment of local candidates, and, as far as possible, to insulate the civil service from political interference and patronage as colonies moved towards independence
> ...
> ... Since 1961 it has been government policy that where external recruitment is necessary expatriates shall normally only be engaged on contract terms and shall not be appointed to the permanent establishment unless there appears to be no possibility of Chinese with the appropriate qualifications being available in the next few years.[121]

Long before the "handover factor" the effects of localisation were being felt. By the 1980s Vice-Chancellors of all Hong Kong's major tertiary institutions were ethnically Chinese (though not necessarily "local")[122] and the first Chinese Chief Secretary (head of the civil service), Mrs Anson Chan, was appointed in November 1993.

Some of this localisation process affected the Hong Kong legal system and its administration. The head of the judiciary, the Chief Justice, many senior judges and the head of the Independent Commission Against Corruption (ICAC) were already Chinese long before the Joint Declaration.

However, the Joint Declaration made a hastening of the localisation programme necessary and inevitable for a number of reasons. First, the Joint Declaration, and its (PRC) legislative successor, the Basic Law, required that the head of the executive arm (the Chief Executive) must be Chinese. Thus far, the Chief Executive has been, effectively, selected (rather than "elected") by the PRC via the Beijing-appointed "Election Committee". Even if, eventually, Beijing permits the *election* of the Chief Executive by universal suffrage, which the Basic Law states to be the "ultimate aim", this will only be following *nomination* by a "broadly representative nominating committee"[123] and the actual *appointment* will be by the Central People's

---

120. Note 6.
121. Ibid 93.
122. Surprisingly, and somewhat controversially, the University of Hong Kong appointed an English Vice-Chancellor (from Bristol University) in 2014 (he announced his resignation within 3 years!).
123. The PRC declared in 2014 that any candidate must be "supported" by at least 50% of the nominating committee and the field would be limited to two to three candidates (it has not been made clear how more than one candidate can be supported by at least 50%). Since this "broadly representative"

Government. Moreover, the requirement that the Chief Executive must be Chinese without the right of abode elsewhere will remain.

Second, the Basic Law also requires that "principal officials" must also be Chinese nationals without the right of abode elsewhere (again there is no such stipulation in the Joint Declaration).

Further, and more specific to the legal system, the increasing use of Chinese in the courts has meant that a significant increase in Chinese-speaking judicial officers and legal practitioners became desirable.

The most pressing need, however, in the context of Hong Kong's legal system, was "localisation" of existing laws where required. The Basic Law itself was a localising factor in so far as it gave statutory force, albeit via a PRC statute, to the Joint Declaration, a treaty. Essentially, however, a large amount of existing legislation had to be localised (locally enacted), to ensure compliance with the Basic Law, and many, often substantially unexceptionable, pieces of Hong Kong legislation had to be "adapted" to ensure that their terminology reflected the new legal and political position.

The huge task of overseeing the localisation and adaptation of existing laws was entrusted to the Joint Liaison Group (JLG), consisting of diplomats from the UK and the PRC. The major problem was the existence of a large body of English legislation either expressly or implicitly applicable to Hong Kong before 1997, not having been locally enacted, and obviously not able to continue in force in their present form post-1997. Edwards[124] writing in 1995, states:

> Part of Hong Kong law consists of applied British legislation which cannot survive 1997. If nothing were done to replace this, after 1997 the SAR would suffer from serious gaps in several important areas including civil aviation, merchant shipping, surrender of fugitive offenders, international terrorism and intellectual property. To avoid this, Hong Kong ordinances must be enacted by the territory's legislature to replace the relevant British laws before 1 July 1997.[125]

The JLG managed the localisation of a large number of existing laws via Hong Kong legislation. An even greater number of others were viewed as not requiring localisation and were to lapse after 1 July 1997. While the JLG operated quite amicably for a number of years, relations became more fraught following (the last) Governor Patten's minor moves towards greater democracy in Hong Kong, and the PRC adopted:

---

group (of 1,200) would nominate only pro-Beijing candidates, there would be no "election" in the generally accepted sense of the word. The 2014 reform proposals were rejected by LegCo so that the "Election Committee" (ie, "selection" committee) will remain (indefinitely).

124. DM Edwards, 'China & Hong Kong: The Legal Arrangements After 1997' *Hong Kong Lawyer* (February 1995) 33, 35.
125. Ibid 34.

its new position that adaptation [and presumably also localisation] of laws was a matter of sovereignty; it was 'entirely an internal matter' which should be 'solved by China on its own'.[126]

In addition, much "local" (Hong Kong) legislation had to be "adapted" in order to conform to the Basic Law. This, often, simply required changes of terminology. For example, any reference to "Governor", in Hong Kong legislation, could usually be amended to "Chief Executive". Other issues, however, like nationality and right of abode, involved serious adaptation issues which were not entirely successfully resolved. The British side, for example, pointed out problems with the issue of right of abode for illegitimate children which were ignored by the Chinese side, producing the debacle of the "right of abode" saga. The subsequent (resulting) re-interpretation of the Basic Law by the Standing Committee of the National People's Congress at the request of the Hong Kong government undermined the judicial autonomy of Hong Kong's Court of Final Appeal and called into question the whole concept of "one country, two systems".[127]

However, as Chen[128] states:

> This exercise of adaptation of laws, together with another exercise of localization of laws (i.e. re-enacting in the form of local legislation . . . relevant British legislation originally applicable to Hong Kong directly), have in fact begun in the Legal Department years before the handover. They have generally been regarded as technical, non-political, and uncontroversial in nature.[129]

A major exception identified by Professor Chen related to the concept of "state". The first post-1997 Secretary for Justice, Elsie Leung, referred to the issue in speeches as largely uncontroversial. Thus:

> It was clearly necessary to adapt the reference to 'the Crown'. This was done by substituting the expression the 'State', which is defined as encompassing PRC organs that are the equivalent of the British Crown. The effect is that those State organs are not bound by any local legislation unless it contains an express provision, or a necessary implication, that they are bound.[130]

The significant implications of this adaptation in the context of "act of state" will be considered below.[131]

---

126. Yash Ghai, 'Continuity of Laws and Legal Rights & Obligations in the SAR' (1997) 27 HKLJ 136, 139.
127. For fuller discussion, see Chapter 4.
128. Albert HY Chen, 'Continuity & Change in the Legal System' in LCH Chow and YK Fan (eds), *The Other Hong Kong Report* (Chinese University Press 1998).
129. Ibid 37.
130. Speech by the Secretary for Justice at the 1998 International Dispute Resolution Conference, 11 November 1998.
131. See 1.8 below.

Much of the huge task of the JLG was left unfinished as 1 July 1997 approached, and a significant amount of the essential "tidying up" inherent in the transfer of legal hegemony was effected via the Hong Kong Reunification Ordinance,[132] which came into force on 1 July 1997 but had been enacted well in advance.

1.7 The Hong Kong Reunification Ordinance

The controversy involving the Reunification Ordinance had more to do with the body which enacted it than the substance of the legislation itself. Some consideration of the events surrounding the 1997 resumption of sovereignty is necessary to understand the nature of, and perceived need for, the Ordinance.

In a nutshell, the legislation, and the creation of the "Provisional Legislature" which passed it into law, were the result of increasing mistrust and animosity between the Chinese and British sides in the transitional period between the 1984 Joint Declaration and the 1 July 1997 handover, particularly in the post-Tiananmen period. The initial assumption, post-Joint Declaration, was that Britain would carry on administering Hong Kong, with Beijing's approval, with little significant change, until 1997 and that the Legislative Council (LegCo) in place in 1997 would continue in post; the so-called "through train". The major catalyst for amending these assumptions was the Tiananmen Square massacre and reactions, in Hong Kong and Britain, thereto.

After Tiananmen, there arose a serious threat of a mass exodus of the professional classes from Hong Kong. Many professionals rapidly sought the right of abode in America, Canada, Australia and, to a lesser extent, Britain. Calls were made for Britain to extend the right of abode in Britain for all Hong Kong citizens in accordance with its moral obligations to the people of Hong Kong. Such calls were rejected but, to reassure civil servants and the professional classes, Britain offered 50,000 British passports to selected "heads of households". The rationale was that, free of anxiety as to the post-1997 position, professionals were more likely to remain in Hong Kong rather than leave in panic. Further, at the instigation of the last Governor, Chris Patten, a small measure of increased democratisation was introduced into LegCo, with a small increase in the number of directly elected representatives and a similarly small increase in the number of functional constituencies with an extended electorate.

However, as we have seen, this move caused much official displeasure in the PRC, whose government regarded these moves as an infringement of Chinese sovereignty over its own subjects. The major responses were increasing obstructionism for all capital works whose completion costs would straddle the handover date,[133] the

---

132. Cap 2601.
133. The clearest example of obstructionism was in relation to the new Chek Lap Kok airport, in respect of which the PRC government held up both funding and labour provision to ensure that a pre-handover completion could not be effected before the 1997 handover.

reduction of the number of senior posts which could be held by non-Chinese and, most important in the present context, the derailment of the "through train". The Chinese government made clear that the LegCo elected under the "Patten reforms" would not be permitted to remain in post and new elections under the old (less democratic) rules would be held.

In order to address the problem of a power vacuum immediately post-handover, a "Provisional Legislature" was established by Beijing in advance of the handover. This legislature enacted legislation to deal with the post-handover situation and the intention was that both the Provisional Legislature and the legislation it had already created would take effect immediately on the transfer of sovereignty, with fresh LegCo elections to be held within two years of the handover. On 1 July 1997, while the directly elected LegCo members made their public protest, the new Provisional Legislature took over.

It was essential, of course, if Hong Kong was not to grind to a halt, post-handover, that the functions of government must continue, and with a legal local legislative mandate.

While the Basic Law, PRC legislation applicable to Hong Kong, was clearly binding in the Hong Kong SAR post-handover, it lacked the necessary specific detail required for a smooth transition.

The Reunification Ordinance, already enacted, came into force on 1 July 1997. Its lengthy preamble explains it purposes as follows:

> To confirm bills passed by the Provisional Legislative Council before 1 July 1997, endorse the appointment of judges of the Court of Final Appeal and the Chief Judge of the High Court, assist the interpretation on and after 1 July 1997 of laws previously in force in Hong Kong, continue those laws and confirm certain other laws, establish the High Court, the District Court, magistracies and other courts tribunals and boards, continue legal proceedings, the criminal justice system, the administration of justice and the course of public justice on and after 1 July 1997, continue the public service on and after 1 July 1997, assist the construction of certain documents on and after 1 July 1997, transfer the ownership of certain property and rights and provide for the assumption of certain liabilities on and after 1 July 1997, in consequence of the resumption of the exercise of sovereignty over Hong Kong by the People's Republic of China, and for connected purposes.

Before listing, more specifically, the changes to be made, under nine sections ("Parts"), the Ordinance outlines the politico-historical background to its enactment. Reference is made first to the Joint Declaration, thence to the Basic Law, the establishment of the Provisional Legislative Council by the Hong Kong SAR "Preparatory Committee", (exercising powers "delegated to it by the National People's Congress of the PRC") to, inter alia, consider and pass legislation particularly in anticipation of the reunification and for the proper administration of the Hong Kong SAR including the confirmation of "anticipatory acts". The main purpose of the legislation, therefore, was to resolve which of the previous laws would remain in force and how such laws should be interpreted, and to confirm certain pieces of pre-handover legislation "enacted" by the Provisional Legislature.

Part I of the Ordinance primarily defines key terms such as "Basic Law", "Hong Kong SAR" and "Provisional Legislative Council".

Part II confirms certain enactments of the Provisional Legislature such as the Urban Council (Amendment) Bill, the Regional Council (Amendment) Bill, the National Flag and National Emblem Bill, The Regional Flag and Regional Emblem Bill and the Hong Kong Court of Final Appeal (Amendment) Bill.

Part III provides for the endorsement of key judicial appointments, namely the first Chief Justice of the (new) Court of Final Appeal (CFA), the first three permanent judges of the CFA and the first Chief Judge of the High Court.

Part IV deals with the interpretation of the laws previously in force in Hong Kong. Paragraph 1 makes the general point that such laws will be construed so as not to contravene the Basic Law and to conform to Hong Kong's status as a Special Administrative Region of the PRC. More specifically paragraph 2, inter alia, replaces any reference to rights and privileges of UK forces to reference to rights and privileges of the People's Liberation Army. Further, it amends any legislative reference to the superiority of the English language with recognition that both English *and* Chinese are now official languages.

Most importantly, in accordance with Hong Kong's changed post-1997 status, paragraph 6 provides for the amendment of the Interpretation and General Clauses Ordinance (Cap 1)[134] so that, for example, reference to "the Crown" will now be construed as reference to the PRC government or the Hong Kong SAR government (depending on the context); reference to the "Privy Council", in a judicial context, shall now be construed as a reference to the Court of Final Appeal; reference to a "Royal" government agency shall now be treated as if the word "Royal" were omitted; any reference to the "Colony" of Hong Kong shall be construed as referring to the Hong Kong SAR; and any reference to the "Governor" of Hong Kong shall be construed as referring to its Chief Executive. In accordance with the revised post-1997 structure of the courts in Hong Kong, paragraph 6 adopts the new terminology whereby, for example, the old "High Court" (and "judge of the High Court") becomes "Court of First Instance" (and "judge of the Court of First Instance").[135] There seems to have been little need for these court-related (and somewhat confusing) name changes except an "anti-colonial" agenda. Indeed, Elsie Leung, the first "Secretary for Justice" in the new Hong Kong SAR, stated:

> [apart from the new Court of Final Appeal] the other courts and tribunals that were previously in existence were re-established on 1 July 1997. The only changes that took place were the re-naming of certain of those courts.[136]

---

134. The method employed is to add a Schedule (Schedule 8) to the original legislation.
135. For fuller discussion, see Chapter 4.
136. Speech by the Secretary for Justice at the 1998 International Dispute Resolution Conference.

Paragraph 7 repeats the statement in the Basic Law that "the laws previously in force in Hong Kong" shall continue to apply.[137]

Part V repeals section 3 of the Supreme Court Ordinance[138] and creates a new High Court of the Hong Kong SAR, to include both the Court of First Instance and the Court of Appeal.[139]

Part VI provides for the continuity of proceedings in the Hong Kong courts and the continuing recognition of pre-handover rights of audience. Previous rights to bring proceedings attached to the Crown or Attorney-General will now apply, instead, to the government of the Hong Kong SAR.

Part VII provides for continuity of public service. Public servants shall, therefore, continue in office post-handover and enjoy the same rights and powers. This is subject to the important exception (referred to previously) whereby "principal officials" must, generally, be Chinese Nationals. Where a power was exercised, pre-handover, by virtue of delegation by the Governor, this power will now be delegated by the Chief Executive.

Part VIII provides for the continuing validity of pre-handover documents despite, for example, reference to "The Crown", "The Queen" etc.

Finally Part IX transfers, essentially, the rights and obligations of the Crown, or the pre-handover government of Hong Kong, to the post-1997 Hong Kong government.

Given that the Provisional Legislature is nowhere provided for in the Joint Declaration, its validity and the validity of the rules it enacted have been challenged in the Hong Kong courts. However, the legitimacy of the Provisional Legislature has been judicially upheld.[140]

1.8 Continuation of previous international treaties

In addition to the continuation of Hong Kong's common law system "domestically", the Joint Declaration (and subsequently the Basic Law) guaranteed the continuation of previous international treaties to which Hong Kong had, hitherto, been privy. Article 153 of the Basic Law states:

> The application to the Hong Kong SAR of international agreements to which the PRC is or becomes a party shall be decided by the Central People's Government, in the light of the circumstances and needs of the Region, and after seeking the views of the government of the Region.

And, more importantly,

---

137. For fuller discussion, see Chapter 2.
138. Cap 4.
139. For fuller discussion, see Chapter 4.
140. See, eg, *HKSAR v Ma Wai Kwan David & Others* [1997] 2 HKC 315.

International agreements to which the People's Republic of China is not a party but which are implemented in Hong Kong may continue to be implemented in the Hong Kong Special Administrative Region. The Central People's Government shall, as necessary, authorize or assist the government of the region to make appropriate arrangements for the application to the Region of other relevant international agreements.

Separate provision is made in the Basic Law, under Article 39, for the continuance of certain international covenants, the continuation of which had been a matter of considerable concern and which had been expressly provided for in the Joint Declaration. Article 39 states:

> The provisions of the International Covenant on Civil and Political Rights, the International Covenant on Economic, Social and Cultural Rights, and international labour conventions as applied to Hong Kong shall remain in force and shall be implemented through the laws of the Hong Kong SAR.

The effect of Article 39 is far from as clear as it first appears, especially in respect of the International Covenant on Civil and Political Rights (ICCPR) and the International Covenant on Economic, Social and Cultural Rights (ICESC). The three problem areas are, first, that the ICCPR/ICESC provisions will only continue to apply as they have applied (previously) in Hong Kong; second, that they will apply only in so far as they are enacted in Hong Kong and third, the problem of "reporting". The first problem relates to the limitations, or "reservations", which Britain, the former colonial master, had imposed on the operation of the ICCPR/ICESC in Hong Kong. These reservations related to such things as the segregation of juvenile offenders, deportation of aliens from Hong Kong, equal rights for women, nationality laws, universal and equal suffrage and equal pay rights. Since, under Article 39, the provisions of the various Covenants would remain in force only "as (previously) applied to Hong Kong", no extension of rights, arguably, were to be introduced under the Basic Law.

The second problem is that, since Article 39 talks of the provisions being "implemented through the laws of Hong Kong", they are not to be regarded as automatically applicable but dependent on introduction via Hong Kong legislation. In the Law Press China *Introduction to the Basic Law*,[141] the authors write:

> B. The Two International Covenants Not to Be Directly Applied to Hong Kong.
>
> According to British law, treaties may only be implemented domestically after they are transformed into domestic laws through parliamentary legislation . . .

---

141. Note 57.

From the analysis made above we can see that Britain has made reservations regarding the application in Hong Kong of the provisions of the ICCPR and the ICESC[142] and that the two Covenants are not directly applicable to Hong Kong.[143]

Since this publication is sponsored by the "Association for Celebration of Reunification of Hong Kong with China Charitable Trust" the views expressed may be taken to represent the official PRC government line.

Concern for human rights, post-1997, led to the introduction of the Bill of Rights Ordinance (BORO), which introduced most ICCPR rights in the form of Hong Kong domestic legislation and, in the view of some supporters, attempted to "entrench" such rights. All prior legislation was to be read in the light of, and subordinate to, BORO. Where there was a conflict, the previous legislation was implicitly repealed. However, in the case of subsequent legislation, courts would attempt to construe such in accordance with BORO, but, where this proved impossible, the rules in the subsequent legislation would take effect despite the inconsistency. BORO, in other words, appeared to have no special "entrenched" status as regards subsequent legislation. Professor Yash Ghai[144] has argued that the implementation of BORO could be regarded as the "implementation" of ICCPR "through the laws of Hong Kong" as provided for in Article 39 of the Basic Law.[145] This would have had the result of giving the Covenant's provisions an "entrenched" position via domestic legislation. However, while the Ordinance itself was not abolished post-1997, its elevated and (arguably) entrenched status was held to be incompatible with the Basic Law and was removed. However, despite the primacy of the Basic Law, since Article 39 guarantees the continuation of existing ICCPR protections, and since these are largely reflected in BORO, the rights involved should be maintained.

Cause for optimism is also to be found in China's (eventual) agreement to submit "regular reports" to The United Nations on progress in the area of ICCPR and ICESR rights. This had been an issue of considerable controversy and difficulty, since reporting is to be by "state parties".[146] This would mean that only China (rather than Hong Kong) could be the "reporter" but it had not, by 1 July 1997, signed or ratified the Conventions.[147] The matter was resolved when China agreed to submit reports drafted by the Hong Kong SAR government.

Other than the Covenants expressly provided for by Article 39, there were hundreds of international and bilateral treaties affecting Hong Kong to which the

---

142. The clear implication is that the reservations would continue to apply although some were, ultimately, removed by the PRC.
143. Ibid 335–336.
144. Yash Ghai, 'The Bill of Rights and the Basic Law: Complementary or Inconsistent?' in G Edwards and A Byrnes (eds), *Hong Kong's Bill of Rights: 1991–1994 and Beyond* (HKU Faculty of Law, 1995).
145. Ibid 55–57. Professor Yash Ghai rejects this contention, agreeing that BORO must be subservient to the Basic Law.
146. See Article 40, ICCPR.
147. China has since signed both and ratified the ICESR.

PRC was not privy but which were to continue, post-1997, under Article 153 of the Basic Law. Internationally, for example, Hong Kong, as a financial, transport and logistics hub, needed to continue its international financial, shipping and aviation obligations. Since the continuation of these obligations could not be automatic in a Hong Kong with a new status as an entity formally part of China but guaranteed a "high measure of autonomy", the onerous task of guaranteeing the transition was entrusted, primarily, to the Sino-British Joint Liaison Group. It was eventually accepted that, as regards most of the international treaties to which Hong Kong had been a party, these would continue in force in Hong, despite its new status. To take a few examples: Hong Kong continues to field "international" teams in many sports under the name "Hong Kong, China" and is separately represented at the Olympic Games; Hong Kong remained a member of the World Trade Organization (WTO), even before the PRC acceded to that body; and a whole range of agreements involving international co-operation in the area of criminal law have been maintained, and in some cases extended by local legislation.[148] Brabyn,[149] for example, writes:

> The HKSAR does enjoy a substantial degree of autonomy, both theoretical and real, in its pursuit and granting of international co-operation in criminal matters. In this context the international personality of Hong Kong, the colony, has been passed onto the HKSAR with substantial success.[150]

The question of "bi-lateral" arrangements was particularly problematic and the renewal or continuance of all previous bilateral agreements was not concluded by the time of the 1 July 1997 handover. These bi-lateral agreements usually involved treaties made by Britain, on behalf of Hong Kong, with another state and it was not possible to continue the treaties merely by substituting "PRC" for any reference to the United Kingdom. The process of renewal continued after the handover, which did result in legal challenge to the status of agreements not renewed by 1 July 1997. However, it was normally the case that agreements could continue by virtue of the fact that the relevant bi-lateral treaty had been enacted in Hong Kong via local legislation. In *Re Yung Kwan Lee*,[151] for example, the Court of Final Appeal had to determine the effect of the pre-handover "Anglo-Thai treaty" covering the arrangements for prisoner transfer whereby, for example, Hong Kong citizens convicted in Thailand could serve all or part of their sentence in Hong Kong. The appellants in this case, all Hong Kong permanent residents, had been convicted of drug trafficking in Thailand and served part of their sentence there. They were permitted to return to Hong Kong, before 1997, to serve out their sentences. They subsequently, post-1997, sought to be released on the basis that the Anglo-Thai treaty, and any UK legislation relating thereto, no longer applied in Hong Kong post-handover. The appellants'

---

148. Eg, Fugitive Offenders Ordinance, Cap 503.
149. Janice Brabyn, 'Inter-Jurisdictional Co-operation in Criminal Matters' in R Wacks (ed), *The New Legal Order in Hong Kong* (Hong Kong University Press 1999).
150. Ibid 161.
151. [1999] 4 HKC 281.

claim was rejected on the basis that section 10 of the (local) Transfer of Sentenced Persons Ordinance,[152] enacted in 1997 before the handover, continued to operate in Hong Kong under Article 153 of the Basic Law. Bokhary PJ, with whom the other members of the Court of Final Appeal concurred, stated:

> art 153 of the Basic Law . . . provides that 'International agreements to which the PRC is not a party but which are implemented in Hong Kong may continue to be implemented in the Hong Kong SAR' . . .
>
> . . . The Anglo-Thai treaty is an international agreement to which the PRC is not a party, and it ceased to apply to Hong Kong upon the handover . . . But the Anglo-Thai treaty was being implemented in Hong Kong at the time of the handover. It was being implemented by s 10(1) of the Ordinance. The purpose of that provision is therefore a purpose expressly permitted by art 153 of the Basic Law.[153]

1.9 The application of legislation to "state"

Paragraphs 2 and 3 of Article 19 of the Basic Law state that:

> The courts of the Hong Kong SAR shall have jurisdiction over all cases in the Region, except that the restrictions on their jurisdictions imposed by the legal system and principles previously in force in Hong Kong shall be maintained.
>
> The courts of the Hong Kong SAR shall have no jurisdiction over acts of state such as defence and foreign affairs. The courts of the Region shall obtain a certificate from the Chief Executive on questions of fact concerning acts of state such as defence and foreign affairs whenever such questions arise in the adjudication of cases. This certificate shall be binding on the courts. Before issuing such a certificate, the Chief Executive shall obtain a certifying document from the Central People's Government.[154]

Significant anxiety has arisen concerning the concept of "act of state", involving both the concept's definition and its implications. The definition of "act of state" as described in Article 19 of the Basic Law differs from that agreed under the Joint Declaration in two important respects. First, instead of acts of state being restricted to issues involving defence and foreign affairs only, as stipulated under the Joint declaration, Article 19 describes acts of state as "*such as* [emphasis added] defence and foreign affairs". The effect of this is that defence and foreign affairs now appear to constitute merely two examples of acts of state rather than the totality of the concept. Under Article 19 it appears to be also the case that once the issue of act of state has been raised before a court, that court must obtain a certificate from the Chief Executive on issues of fact that will be conclusive. Further, the Chief Executive must obtain a certifying document from the Central People's Government before issuing

---
152. Cap 513.
153. [1999] 4 HKC 281 at 290.
154. Ibid 290.

his certificate. The net effect of this is that the determination of whether an issue concerns an act of state is to be removed from the courts. No such limitation on the courts' powers is provided for in the Joint Declaration.[155]

Early fears were expressed as to the implications of the wider definition of "act of state", especially in respect of possible state immunity for PRC government-linked companies and the implications for the relationship between Hong Kong and the PRC. In an article appearing in the *South China Morning Post* on 14 June 1995, Martin Lee, barrister, former Basic Law drafter, LegCo member and then chairman of the Democratic Party, posited a bleak scenario. He stated:

> 'Courting disaster'[156]
>
> . . . the Sino-British agreement . . . adopts all the proposals made by the Preliminary Working Committee (PWC). This legitimises a body condemned by Britain and set up as Beijing's shadow government purely to punish [last Governor] Mr Patten for his modest electoral reforms . . .
>
> Britain has accepted the PWC's proposals, including . . . the explicit acceptance of China's faulty definition of acts of state . . .
>
> . . . with the aid of Britain, the Chinese Government has deliberately misinterpreted the common law meaning of acts of state. The Chinese text of the agreement states that the CFA shall have 'no jurisdiction over acts of state, that is, defence and foreign affairs etcetera.' In the common law, "acts of state" refer only to things such as declaring war or making treaties-and the core principle is that it may never be used by the sovereign against its own citizens.
>
> Even Britain agrees that the arrangement opens the door to all politically "sensitive" cases being deemed acts of state by the Beijing central government. The principle of acts of state was so infrequently invoked in Hong Kong that the last [such] case was heard in 1952 . . . it is likely that China will interpret the jurisdiction over acts of state in such a way that Hong Kong people will never be able to challenge the government. This rips the rule of law into shreds since the entire basis for the rule of law is that the Government is subject to the law just as ordinary citizens are. The SAR Government overnight gains a power it never had even under the colonial Government: the power to act with impunity.
>
> Under common law it is an act of state to annex foreign territory in a state of war. But it would not be . . . an act of state for a government to expropriate land that belongs to its citizens or what the court term "friendly aliens". Thus, the defence of acts of state could never properly be used, for instance, to let the People's Liberation Army expropriate property owned by Hong Kong people without compensation. Moreover, since the distinction between politics and business is hazy, a local or international investor could find himself on the wrong side of China's definition of "acts of state" as easily as I could. The "etcetera" in the Chinese text on acts of

---

155. Former Secretary for Justice, Elsie Leung, expressed the view that the word "state" had simply been substituted for the previous "crown" as part of necessary adaptive exercises (Speech by the Secretary for Justice at the 1998 International Dispute Resolution Conference 11 November 1998).
156. Martin Lee SC, *South China Morning Post* (Hong Kong, 14 June 1995).

state is left deliberately vague, so that if you are, say, owed money by a state-owned company or if you want to sue the People's Bank of China, you could be out of luck.

Mr Patten has said that the acts of state definition are "a small hole" in the common law – but can anyone ever be certain that he will not fall into the hole? Indeed, Britain cannot even tell us what China's definition of acts of state may or may not include. A "hole" in our common law today could be a crater tomorrow. If you are in court in Hong Kong after 1997, the bad news is that you will never know whether your opponent has the clout to pull strings in Beijing so that your case will be thrown out.

The Martin Lee prognosis is a bleak one[157] and, thus far, appears overly so. Indeed, Gittings, in a summary of the first 10 years post-1997,[158] stated:

The issue that had most exercised Mr Lee and others back in 1995, an ambiguous definition of the 'acts of state' that lie beyond the jurisdiction of the Hong Kong courts, turned out to be a non-issue. During the first decade of the HKSAR, not a single Chinese state-owned enterprise sought to exploit this ambiguity to escape the jurisdiction of local courts, as Mr Lee and others feared they would.

[However] . . . the Hong Kong branch of Xinhua news agency, which had long served as Beijing's main representative office in Hong Kong, went unpunished in 1998 for a breach of the Personal Data (Privacy) Ordinance.

The Chinese state-owned companies whom Mr Lee and others feared would use 'acts of state' exemption to escape the jurisdiction of the Hong Kong courts would doubtless have been only too happy to try had they been given the green light to do so by Beijing. So too would the People's Liberation Army garrison in Hong Kong, whose legal status was another cause of much pre-handover concern. Instead, in March 2006, the garrison allowed one of its soldiers to be tried and convicted in Tsuen Wan Magistrates' Court after he was caught stealing a key ring at Hong Kong Disneyland.

The Gittings prognosis is far less gloomy than Martin Lee's, though the non-prosecution of Xinhua is a serious issue. Further discussion involving the status of Xinhua and comparable institutions is provided in the following extract from the writings of Professor Albert Chen dealing with post-1997 adaptation of laws.[159]

'Crown', 'State' and Adaptation of Laws

Another highly controversial law passed by the Provisional Legislative Council (PLC) was the Adaptation of Laws (Interpretative Provisions) Ordinance. The Ordinance was one in a series of ordinances enacted for the purpose of making technical changes to the wording of Hong Kong's existing laws so as to adapt them

---

157. Coloured, perhaps, by his work as a Basic Law drafter in which he had been instrumental in avoiding immunity for "all executive acts of the Central People's Government".
158. Danny Gittings, 'Changing Expectations: How the Rule of Law Fared in the First Decade of the Hong Kong SAR' (2007) 7 Hong Kong Journal 2, 5.
159. AYH Chen (n 128) 29–48.

to Hong Kong's post-colonial status . . . They have generally been regarded as technical, non-political, and uncontroversial in nature.

However . . . there was *one* provision in the Adaptation of Laws (Interpretative Provisions) Ordinance 1998 which generated heated debate in the community and intense criticism of the SAR government and the PLC. The provision relates to the adaptation to the post-1997 era of section 66 of the Interpretation and General Clauses Ordinance which reads as follows:

No Ordinance shall in any manner whatsoever affect the right of or be binding on the Crown unless it is therein expressly provided or unless it appears by necessary implication that the Crown is bound thereby.

. . . Section 24 of the Adaptation of Laws (Interpretative Provisions) Ordinance substitutes the word 'State' for the word 'Crown' in section 66 of the Interpretation and General Clauses Ordinance, and the former ordinance also provides an elaborate definition of the new concept of the 'State'. The definition includes the SAR Government, the Central Government in Beijing, as well as subordinate organs of the Central Government that exercise executive functions on its behalf but do not exercise commercial functions. Such subordinate organs would appear to include . . . the Hong Kong branch of the Xinhua News Agency, which has been designated as a work organ authorized to operate in Hong Kong by the Central Government.

Not long before this bill for adaptation of laws was introduced into the PLC, the Department of Justice's decision not to prosecute the Hong Kong branch of the Xinhua News Agency for a possible breach of the Personal Data (Privacy) Ordinance[160] had already attracted much public attention . . .

The main criticism of the adaptative provision substituting 'State' for 'Crown' in section 66 . . . is that it gives institutions like the Xinhua Agency in Hong Kong a special treatment or privileges, inconsistent with Article 22 of the Basic Law which provides that all offices established in Hong Kong by Central Government . . . 'shall abide by the laws of the Region' . . .

. . . Sceptics . . . find in this incident evidence of erosion of the rule of law in Hong Kong under the pressure of 'one country'.[161]

Little has happened since to challenge *overtly* the notion that the concept of "act of state" has been used more sparingly and less controversially than Martin Lee feared. The act of state concept *was* significant in the historic case of *Democratic Republic of the Congo* (DRC) v *FG Hemisphere Associates LLC*, dealt with at length in Chapter 4, but even here the crux of the Court of Final Appeal ruling was that the "act of state" in point, and in respect of which a Standing Committee Basic Law interpretation should be sought, involved the relations between the HKSAR and a foreign government (that of the DRC); hardly supportive of Martin Lee's fears for the immunity of *PRC-related* industries/corporations. In fact, in the case, there *was*

---

160. The alleged breach involved a failure by Xinhua to respond within the statutory time limit to a request for details as to any personal data held as requested by legislator Ms Emily Lau.
161. AYH Chen 37–39.

a quasi-involvement of the "PRC" "commercially",[162] in that extensive funding to the DRC (whose default on sovereign debt had been acquired by the claimants) had been agreed by a consortium of PRC state-connected companies in return for the acquisition of mineral rights and the like. Initial payment of the funding, by "entry fees" from the consortium, was challenged by injunctions from the claimants as the DRC's creditors. The PRC consortium, therefore, had a clear interest in the injunctions *not* being granted. Despite the tangential consequences of *FG Hemisphere* and the specific issues raised by Gittings, the "story so far" is that immunity for PRC state-linked companies in Hong Kong has not been a major issue.

"Act of state" was also at issue in the huge controversy involving the Article 23, dealt with at some length in Chapter 2. One serious concern involved the proposed right of the Secretary for Security to "proscribe" (ban) an organisation in the HKSAR[163] "in the interests of national security or public safety or public order". It was feared that, as an act of state, the proscription would take effect with no possible right of redress in the courts which, under Article 19 of the Basic Law, would "have no jurisdiction". This fear was addressed in a paper issued by the Department of Justice[164] which dismissed the notion that HKSAR courts would be excluded in such circumstances.

> Act of State
>
> This note has been prepared in response to the request of the Panel on Security and the Panel on the Administration of Justice and Legal Services clarifying:
>
> (a) Whether the proscription of a Mainland organisation by the Central Authorities in accordance with national law on national security ground is an act of state as referred to in Article 19 of the Basic Law; and
>
> (b) If so, whether the courts in Hong Kong could deal with appeal concerning the Secretary for Security's decision to proscribe an organisation in Hong Kong which is affiliated with that Mainland organisation.
>
> . . . In the Consultation Document on the Proposals to implement Article 23 of the Basic Law, it is proposed that:
>
> (a) The Secretary for Security be given a discretionary power to proscribe an organisation in the HKSAR if he or she believes that it is necessary in the interests of national security or public safety or public order;
>
> . . .
>
> (f) the decision of the Secretary for Security to proscribe a HKSAR organisation is subject to an appeal procedure. Points of fact may be appealed to an independent tribunal and points of law may be appealed to the courts.

---

162. In fact, a major argument in the case was whether the DRC/PRC consortium arrangements were commercial or "sovereign".
163. The most likely target of a proscription under Article 23 would be the Falun Gong, a religious sect banned in mainland China but legal (though harassed) in Hong Kong.
164. LC Paper No CB (2) 86/02-03(02).

> ... Typical acts of state include the annexation and cession of territory, the declaration of war and peace, the making of treaties, the sending and receiving of diplomatic representatives, and the recognition of foreign states and governments. These acts performed between governments cannot be challenged, controlled or interfered with by the courts, and must be accepted without question.
>
> ... In our view, the question of "act of state" is irrelevant to the proscription mechanism as proposed in the Consultation Document for the following reasons.
>
> ... the proscription of a Mainland organisation is to be made by the Central Authorities in exercise of their power pursuant to national laws ...
>
> ... The decision of the Secretary for Security to proscribe a HKSAR organisation and the decision of the Central Authorities to proscribe a Mainland organisation are two separate and independent decisions, and the decision of the Secretary for Security is reviewable by the HKSAR courts, whether by way of judicial review or the proposed appeal mechanism. Thus there is no question of the doctrine of "act of state" coming into play insofar as the Secretary for Security's decision is concerned.

Comment

While the above debate became temporarily irrelevant with the decision to "postpone" the enactment of Article 23 legislation,[165] similar issues are likely to arise at such time as the Article 23 legislation is, eventually, introduced.[166]

1.10 The impact of Hong Kong's change of sovereignty on its legal system

Article 5 of the Basic Law, Hong Kong's post-1997 constitution, declares that:

> The socialist system and policies shall not be practised in the Hong Kong SAR, and the previous capitalist system and way of life shall remain unchanged for 50 years.

While it might be possible to argue that no time limit is set on the "prohibition of socialism" the essence of Article 5 is an unarguable commitment by the PRC, whose law the Basic Law is, to uphold the principle of "one country, two systems" and to do so for at least 50 years. Further, and specific to the legal system, Article 160 provides for the adoption by the Hong Kong SAR of the laws previously in force in Hong Kong,

> except for those which the Standing Committee of the National People's Congress declares to be in contravention of this [Basic] Law.

Moreover, Article 8 provides for the maintenance of the laws previously in force in Hong Kong (both common law and statutory),

---

165. Following a mass protest demonstration by 500,000 Hong Kong citizens.
166. The eventual introduction of legislation by the HKSAR is mandatory under Article 23 (see Chapter 2 at 2.4.1).

except for any that contravene this [Basic] Law or are subject to amendment by the legislature of the Hong Kong SAR.

In a speech in 1998, then Secretary for Justice, Elsie Leung, stated:

> A central theme of the Joint Declaration and Basic Law is one of continuity. Article 160 of the Basic Law provides that, upon the establishment of the Hong Kong SAR, the laws previously in force in Hong Kong shall be adopted as laws of the Region, except for those which the Standing Committee of the National People's Congress declares to be in contravention of the Basic Law. This means that the common law principles, and nearly all the 600-odd Ordinances, that were previously in force, continue to apply in the Hong Kong SAR.[167]

Nonetheless, the transfer of sovereignty of Hong Kong from Britain to China has obviously had some effects on its legal system, both direct and indirect. Some of these have already been mentioned and others will be dealt with elsewhere, notably in Chapter 2 on "Sources". Briefly, however, the major changes will now be listed.

First, and most obviously, certain laws previously in force have been declared inconsistent with the Basic Law and "not adopted" as part of the laws in force in the Hong Kong SAR post-1997. The documents which formed the constitutional basis for British rule of Hong Kong, the "Letters Patent" and the "Royal Instructions", of course ceased to operate from 1 July 1997. It might be assumed that all "non-adopted" laws would automatically cease to have any significance but in the case of one piece of legislation at least this is not the case. The Application of English Law Ordinance (AELO), which stipulated the extent to which English common law and statutory rules would apply in Hong Kong, was declared inconsistent with the Basic Law and not adopted. While this clearly precludes the application of *new* English statutory rules in Hong Kong, the AELO remains significant in determining which were the laws "previously in force" in Hong Kong on 30 June 1997, which, in turn, will remain in force (subject to exceptions) under the authority of Article 8 of the Basic Law. Wesley-Smith,[168] for example, states:

> The Standing Committee of the National People's Congress announced on 23 February 1997 that 14 ordinances were in contravention of the Basic Law and were not to be adopted as law of the HKSAR. Included was the Application of English Law Ordinance, which, despite being omitted from the statute book, continues to 'count' so far as the legal system is concerned since it identifies what the laws previously in force were.[169]

In *Victor Chandler (International) Ltd v Zhou Chu Jian He*,[170] in the Hong Kong Court of Appeal, Le Pichon JA stated:

---

167. Speech by the Secretary of Justice at the 1998 International Dispute Resolution Conference.
168. Peter Wesley-Smith, 'The Content of the Common Law in Hong Kong' in R Wacks (n 149).
169. Ibid 32.
170. [2008] 4 HKC 232.

it is common ground that the AELO ceased to be part of the laws of Hong Kong as of 1 July 1997 . . .

. . . The non-application of the AELO rendered the imperial Acts inapplicable but left intact the common law. Article 8 of the Basic Law would appear to lend support to this."[171]

The next direct and obvious change relates to the replacement of the Judicial Committee of the Privy Council (Privy Council) by Hong Kong's Court of Final Appeal (CFA) as the final appellate court in respect of Hong Kong legal judgments. Article 81 of the Basic Law specifically states that the Court of Final Appeal "shall be established" and this was effected via the Court of Final Appeal Ordinance.[172] The role and functions of the CFA will be dealt with in Chapter 5. The Basic Law also guarantees that the Hong Kong SAR shall enjoy "independent judicial power, including that of final adjudication".[173]

While some inroads on the CFA's autonomy have been made via the National People's Congress Standing Committee's "interpretation" of the Basic Law, there can be little doubt that the CFA operates as a largely independent court of final adjudication, in Hong Kong, and is a well-respected court which has been far more active in dealing with Hong Kong appeals than was its predecessor in London.

Outside the area of the CFA it is the case that the work and personnel of the Hong Kong courts have remained largely unchanged. Indeed, the Basic Law states that:

The judicial system previously practised in Hong Kong shall be maintained except for those changes consequent upon the establishment of the Court of Final Appeal of the Hong Kong SAR.[174]

However, in a less direct way, change has occurred and will continue, as a result of Hong Kong's new political status. At the time of the handover, a large number of judges were non-Chinese. While most remained in post after the handover, a gradual "localisation" of the judiciary is taking place. This is inevitable and desirable, given that most participants in the civil and criminal justice systems are Chinese, with Cantonese as their first language. The use of interpreters is far from ideal and it is an obvious aspiration that a larger proportion of judges will be Cantonese speakers or, ideally, bilingual. This aspiration is, gradually, being fulfilled.

Localisation can be seen, too, in respect of legal practitioners. Most new recruits to the legal professions are Chinese-speaking. This is inevitable in the case of small to medium sized Hong Kong solicitors' firms and extends also to the bar, where clients are likely to be Chinese and, as importantly, written instructions are likely to be in Chinese.

---

171. Ibid 241–242.
172. Cap 484.
173. Article 2.
174. Article 81.

Nevertheless, the largely unchanged nature of the legal system is very well expressed by the scholar Professor Albert Chen,[175] who writes:

> To what extent has the pre-1997 legal system of Hong Kong been preserved? The answer is that it has been preserved to an extremely large extent, in the sense that more than 99% of the pre-existing laws are still in force, lawyers and judges continue to practise their callings in exactly the same manner as before, the common law approach is still used in deciding cases, and the pre-existing institutions of the legal system have all been maintained, with the exception of appeals to the Privy Council and the establishment of a new Court of Final Appeal . . .
>
> Have the constitutional principles regarding Hong Kong's autonomy enshrined in the Basic Law been upheld in practice? I would give an emphatic 'yes' in answer to this question. The Beijing side has practised utmost self-restraint in exercising its powers under the Basic Law. For example, no Hong Kong law has been invalidated even though the NPCSC has the power to review and invalidate Hong Kong laws under Article 17 of the Basic Law. After 1 July 1997, only one national law has been applied to Hong Kong (under Article 18 of the Basic Law), and it is a law relating to the law of the sea.[176]

In the more than 10 years since Professor Chen wrote these words, they have come to look somewhat over-optimistic. While PRC laws have continued not to be applied to Hong Kong, core Hong Kong values have been under attack; not least the independence of the Hong Kong judiciary, challenged fundamentally by the Central People's Government "White Paper" issued by the State Council in June 2014.

1.11 Continuation and development of the previous legal system post-1997

The general continuation of the pre-1997 legal system in Hong Kong is effected both formally and informally. Formally, as we have seen and will return to in Chapter 2, the continuance of the "laws previously in force" is guaranteed, subject to exceptions, by the Basic Law. The rules of common law and equity and, where appropriate, statutory rules will continue, subject only to their being found inconsistent with the Basic Law or being overturned by subsequent Hong Kong legislation or judicial overruling.[177] The combined effect of Articles 8 (and 18) and 159 is that such continuance will continue for (at least)[178] 50 years from 1 July 1997.[179] Since English

---

175. See AHY Chen, 'The Constitution and the Rule of Law' in SK Lau (ed), *The First Tung Chee-hwa Administration: The First Five Years of the HKSAR* (Chinese University Press 2002).
176. Ibid 83–85.
177. In fact, the Basic Law does not specifically provide for *judicial* change to the laws previously in force but the right of Hong Kong courts to change the pre-1997 laws has not been questioned (see, eg, *A Solicitor v The Law Society of Hong Kong* (2008) 11 HKCFAR 117, [2008] 2 HKC 1 and Chapters 2 & 3).
178. See 1.12 below as to the continuation of the status quo post-2047.
179. Article 8 specifies the continuance of the previous laws; Article 159 precludes amendment of the section within 50 years.

How to determine whether a decisional rule is part of HKSAR law?

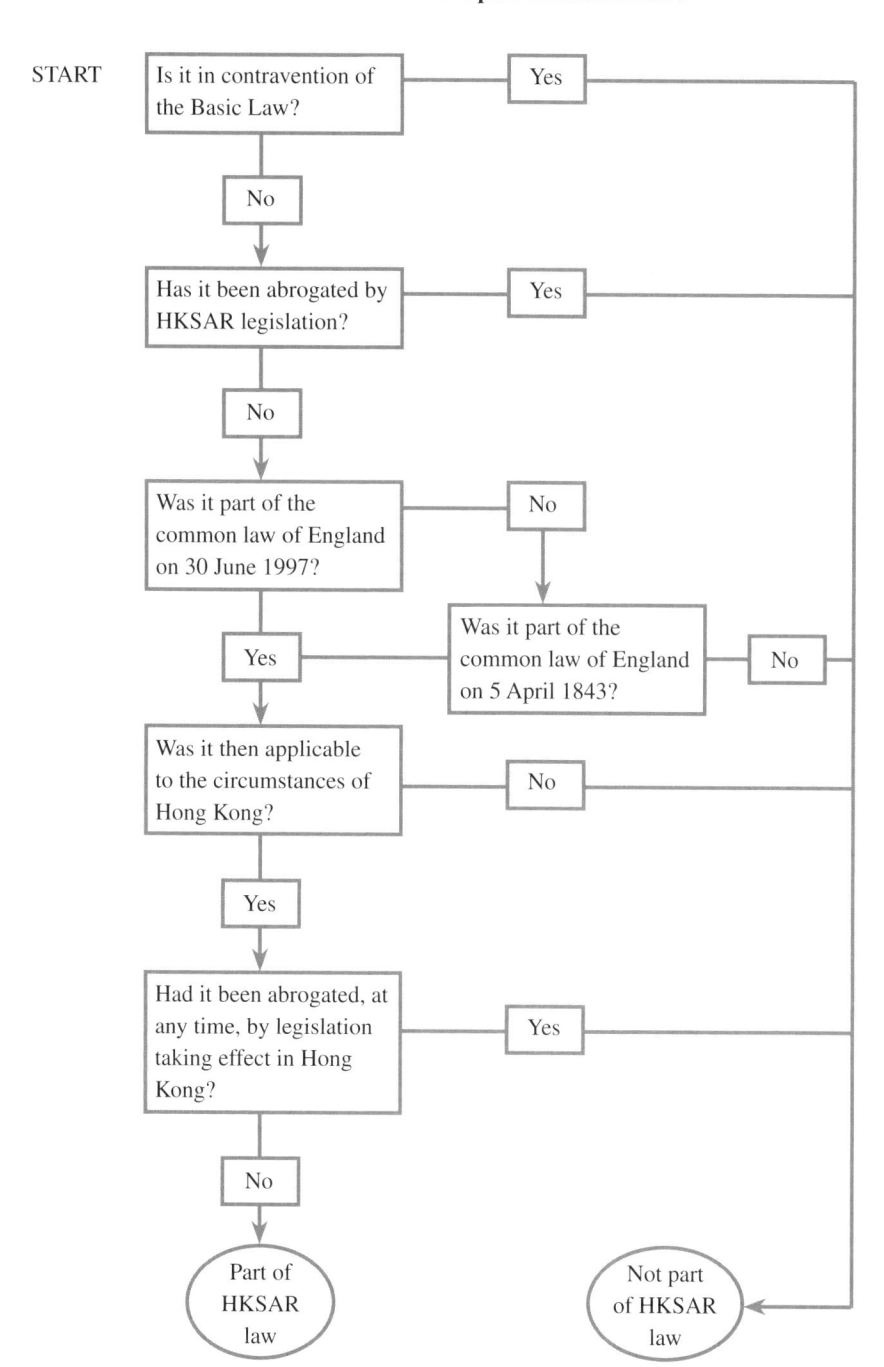

START → Is it in contravention of the Basic Law? → Yes → Not part of HKSAR law

No ↓

Has it been abrogated by HKSAR legislation? → Yes → Not part of HKSAR law

No ↓

Was it part of the common law of England on 30 June 1997? → No → Was it part of the common law of England on 5 April 1843? → No → Not part of HKSAR law

Yes ↓

Was it then applicable to the circumstances of Hong Kong? → No → Not part of HKSAR law

Yes ↓

Had it been abrogated, at any time, by legislation taking effect in Hong Kong? → Yes → Not part of HKSAR law

No ↓

Part of HKSAR law

common law and statutory rules could not apply in Hong Kong if inappropriate to local conditions (which effectively meant if contrary to customary Chinese law) the Basic Law makes additional provision for the continuation of Chinese customary law, where applicable.

Certain less formal factors affect the continuation of the status quo. English judicial statements, post-1997, for example, are given no greater status in the Basic Law than those in other common law jurisdictions; namely that they may be referred to but need not be followed. This "formal" position, however, emphasised by the Chief Justice in *A Solicitor v The Law Society of Hong Kong*,[180] does not reflect the position in practice; that judges tend to give greater weight to English court judgments, even post-1997 ones, than they do to those from other common law jurisdictions. This may be simply because such decisions more readily relate to issues argued before, and established in, the Hong Kong courts pre-1997. It is likely, however, from a "realist" standpoint, that the Anglo-centric nature of the legal education of most Hong Kong judges is a factor.[181]

Ultimately, however, the continuation of the previous legal system will depend on *political* rather than formal legal considerations, since Beijing (particularly in the Xi Jinping era) has shown itself willing to "reinvent" the promises and guarantees of the Joint Declaration and Basic Law via the assertion of "one country" over "two systems". Nowhere has this been more in evidence than the challenge to judicial immunity inherent in the State Council "White Paper" of June 2014.[182] While Article 92 of the Basic Law affirms that judges of the HKSAR may be appointed from elsewhere in the common law world, and while Article 93 asserts the right of pre-1997 judges (including non-Chinese) to remain in post, the White Paper states that:

> V . . . 3. The Hong Kong People Who Govern Hong Kong Should Above All Be Patriotic
>
> . . . Hong Kong must be governed by the Hong Kong people with patriots as the mainstay, as loyalty to one's country is the minimum political ethic for political figures. Under the policy of 'one country, two systems', all those who administrate [*sic*] Hong Kong, including the chief executive, principal officials, members of the Executive Council and Legislative Council, *judges of the courts at different levels and other judicial personnel* [emphasis added] have . . . the responsibility of correctly understanding and implementing the Basic Law . . . In a word, loving the country is the basic political requirement of Hong Kong's administrators.

Leaving aside the controversial epithet "administrator" to include judges, the more chilling element is the elision of loving the country and being "patriotic" with the judicial role. The clear message is that judges are instruments of government who should make "patriotic judgments". While defenders of the White Paper have

---

180. Note 177.
181. See Chapter 6.
182. Central People's Government State Council: White Paper on "The Practice of 'One Country, Two Systems' Policy in the Hong Kong SAR".

suggested that the requirement of "loving the country" may be discharged simply by taking the judicial oath of allegiance,[183] it seems hard to square the requirement of patriotism with the promise of continuing eligibility for non-Chinese judges. It is to be welcomed that Chief Justice Geoffrey Ma, in response, has stated that Hong Kong judges will continue to be guided solely by the law.[184] Similarly, the previous Chief Justice (Andrew Li) has stated that there should be no requirement that judges be patriotic.[185]

As far as *development* of the legal system is concerned, Article 18 of the Basic Law states that:

> The laws in force in the Hong Kong SAR shall be this [Basic] Law, the laws previously in force in Hong Kong as provided for in Article 8 of this Law, and the laws enacted by the legislature of the Region.

In other words, development of the legal system via Hong Kong legislation is *expressly* provided for in Article 18. Further, very limited, development *via PRC legislation* is provided for in Article 18 which adds that national laws shall not be applied in the Hong Kong SAR *except* as provided for by Annex III which deals with such issues as the national flag, emblem, anthem, calendar, capital and territorial waters plus the PRC Nationality Law and rules on Diplomatic Immunity and Privilege. The Basic Law permits development by amendment to the Annex III list but such can only apply to external issues "outside the limits of the autonomy of the Region".[186]

Implicit in the ethos of "one country, two systems", of "Hong Kong people ruling Hong Kong", and of the "right of final adjudication, is the principle that Hong Kong courts may also develop the legal system. The Basic Law can be seen as requiring the continuation of the common law system while permitting its gradual refinement through the courts.[187] While this subject will be explored in more depth in Chapters 2 and 3, suffice to say here that it is clearly recognised that, while only the Court of Final Appeal has power to overturn *pre*-1997 precedents of the House of

---

183. This proposition seems to have been accepted by Lord Neuberger, President of the UK Supreme Court who, apparently, sees nothing sinister in the White Paper's patriotic requirement which he feels is "not-inconsistent" with judicial independence (*South China Morning Post*, 27 August 2014). It is to be welcomed that Hong Kong's senior judicial figures (with more appreciation of the political reality) do not share his view.
184. *South China Morning Post* (Hong Kong, 17 August 2014).
185. *South China Morning Post* (Hong Kong, 15 August 2014). The Hong Kong Bar Association opposed the White Paper, as did the normally more "compliant" Law Society which ousted its Chairman, Ambrose Lam, for his support.
186. Article 18(3).
187. See Chapter 2 on sources of Hong Kong law.

Lords[188] or Privy Council,[189] *all* Hong Kong courts are free to depart from *post*-1997 English (including Privy Council) decisions.[190] Over time, therefore, Hong Kong will establish its own, unique form of common law. This proposition was endorsed by Lord Millett NPJ in the Court of Final Appeal case of *China Field Ltd v Appeal Tribunal (Buildings)*[191] where he stated:

> [the resumption of Chinese sovereignty] should not inhibit the courts of Hong Kong, and in particular this Court which has succeeded the Privy Council as the final appellate court of Hong Kong, from developing the common law in the context of Hong Kong.[192]

The specific issue of law reform in Hong Kong, and the role of the Law Reform Commission of Hong Kong, will be considered in the next chapter.

1.12 The post-2047 position

While the previous section is devoted to "continuation" post-1997, the "guarantees" of the Basic Law are, arguably at least, to remain in force for only 50 years post-1997. Serious doubts, therefore, exist as to Hong Kong's position generally, and the status of the Basic Law particularly, after 2047. Immediately post-1997 the question was rarely raised since 2047 seemed a long way off. It was, then, perceived as a long-term issue and as Keynes once pointed out, "in the long term, we will all be dead". Approaching 20 years from the "handover" however, the 2047 question is being frequently asked; prompted initially, as was the pre-1997 anxiety, by concerns about land-holding in Hong Kong.

Conflicting views are held about 2047. At one extreme, the "optimistic view" is that things will remain largely the same and that the Basic Law will continue (though with greater capacity for amendment). Conversely, the most "pessimistic" view is that both Hong Kong's special "high degree of autonomy" and the Basic Law itself, will cease to exist in 2047. In the first edition of his *Introduction to the Hong Kong Basic Law,* Gittings[193] espoused the optimistic "continuation" line. A somewhat more pessimistic line can be seen in Gittings' second edition, not least following the

---

188. While pre-1997 House of Lords decisions were not technically binding on Hong Kong courts (per Li CJ in *A Solicitor v Law Society of Hong Kong* [n 180]) such House of Lords decisions were the ultimate reflection of the English common law, part of the laws previously in force in 1997 and therefore still applicable pending local abrogation. Such abrogation is likely to occur only via legislation or decision of the Court of Final Appeal.
189. At least as regards Privy Council decisions (technically advice to the Sovereign) on appeal from Hong Kong.
190. See *A Solicitor v The Law Society of Hong Kong* (n 180).
191. [2009] HKCU 1650.
192. At para 78.
193. Danny Gittings, *Introduction to the Hong Kong Basic Law* (Hong Kong University Press 2013), 303–314.

events of the PRC-instigated model for "universal suffrage"[194] (involving the right of all Hong Kong citizens to vote for one or other of Beijing's chosen candidates!),[195] the subsequent acrimonious and lengthy "Occupy Central" opposition, and the rejection of the Beijing model in LegCo. For example, Gittings's final words in his first edition read:

> Although far from certain, it is quite possible that the Hong Kong Basic Law may survive largely in its present form long beyond 30 June 2047.[196]

Conversely, Gittings now states:

> 9.2 What Will Happen after 2047?[197]
>
> ... there can be little doubt that the issue of what will happen to Hong Kong after the end of the 50-year period will need to be resolved long before 2047 ...
>
> One option would be for China to permit 'one country, two systems' to continue largely- or even entirely-unchanged beyond 2047. That would be in keeping with Deng Xiaoping's original version of 'one country, two systems' lasting long beyond its initial 50-year period. It would also be by far the simplest option ... Since the Hong Kong Basic Law contains no expiry date, it could simply remain in force—perhaps with some minor modification to clarify the continuation of the 'one country, two systems' policy ... Chen suggests that this could be accomplished by issuing a separate decision of the National People's Congress on this point ...
>
> In the first edition of this book, [the] 'no change' option was described as one likely path for Hong Kong's future beyond 2047, and one which meant 'the Hong Kong Basic Law may survive largely in its present form long beyond 30 June 2047'. Although that remains a possible outcome, the subsequent emergence of greater antagonism between Hong Kong and the mainland on a number of fronts necessitates some reconsideration of how likely it is that such a relatively benign scenario will prevail beyond 2047 ...
>
> ... Chen notes that the controversy over the 2014 Standing Committee decision on universal suffrage, which precipitated the Umbrella Movement street occupations, has brought to the fore a 'fundamental difference in the understanding of "autonomy" between the Central People's Government and much of civil society in Hong Kong' ...
>
> For the first time, voices have also started to emerge on the mainland suggesting 'one country, two systems' will have outlived its usefulness by 2047 and should be abolished altogether ...

---

194. *Decision of the Standing Committee of the NPC on Issues Relating to the Selection of the Chief Executive of the Hong Kong SAR by Universal Suffrage and on the Method for Forming the Legislative Council of the Hong Kong SAR in the Year 2016*, 31 August 2014.
195. The two to three candidates would be chosen by a Nominating Committee (the previous Election Committee!). Public nomination was specifically rejected. Described as "the moment of truth for 'one country, two systems'" (A Chen, 'The Law & Politics of Constitutional Reform & Democratization in Hong Kong' University of Hong Kong Faculty of Law Research Paper No 2014/035, 30 September 2014).
196. Ibid 314.
197. D Gittings (2nd edn, 2016), 318–321.

> ... [the] argument that a stronger Chinese economy will no longer have any need for 'one country, two systems' harks back to the original rationale for granting a high degree of autonomy to Hong Kong ... the rationale for Hong Kong's autonomy was much more heavily predicated on economic factors. That, of course, makes the argument for continuing that autonomy much weaker if that economic rationale starts to disappear.
>
> ... it seems reasonable to conclude that the chances of Beijing allowing 'one country, two systems' to continue largely unchanged beyond 2047 may have become somewhat lower than they were during the earlier, and relatively calmer, years of the Hong Kong SAR immediately after 1997.

Comment

Three key elements can be identified in Gittings's thesis (as seen in the full text of his Chapter 9, "What Will Happen to 'One Country, Two Systems'?").[198] *The first encompasses "reasons to be optimistic" about continued autonomy. This can be seen in reference to an absence of an "end date" for "one country, two systems"; the "restraint" shown by the PRC in not mobilising the PLA garrison at Tamar during "Occupy Central" (despite its proximity to the demonstration/sit-in); and an almost total restraint on adding National Laws to those applicable to Hong Kong via Annex III of the Basic Law. In particular, Gittings remains optimistic about one area which has concerned some commentators and has echoes of "pre-1997" anxiety: the fate of leases post-2047. He writes:*

> ... Ribeiro and Gilchrist note that while there "is a popular misconception that the arrangements for the Hong Kong SAR, in particular government leases, will come to an end in 2047", in reality "there is no such provision in the Basic Law".
>
> ... concern over the future of land leases in Hong Kong beyond 30 June 1997 was often portrayed as a major driving force behind the Joint Declaration. Britain repeatedly cited its lack of any legal right to issue government land leases over most parts of Hong Kong that expired after that date as one of the main reasons for needing to reach an agreement with China on Hong Kong's future. Annex III of the Joint Declaration resolved that problem by giving Britain the legal authority to issue and renew leases beyond 30 June 1997 – providing that their expiry date was no later than 30 June 2047.
>
> Given this historical background, it is scarcely surprising that similar concerns are now being raised about what will happen to land leases in Hong Kong after 30 June 2047. This is especially so because, ever since Britain's departure on 30 June 1997, the Hong Kong SAR Government has no longer considered it necessary to apply a 30 June 2047 expiry date to the issuance and renewal of land leases. Instead, most leases are now issued or renewed for a period of 50 years, which means large numbers of leases extend beyond 2047. In one well-known example, involving the land used to construct the Hong Kong Disneyland theme park, this includes a right

---

198. 307–321.

to renew the lease for a second 50-year period, a right which (if exercised) would allow this lease to continue until 2100.

...

The power to manage, use and develop that land, including granting land leases, is currently delegated to the Hong Kong SAR Government by the Chinese state ... Even in the most extreme scenario of Hong Kong being abolished as a separate entity after 30 June 2047, and the disappearance of Hong Kong SAR Government that granted those leases, the rights granted under those land leases would not necessarily disappear. Chen (2009) notes that responsibility for any unexpired portion of those land leases would simply pass to the body under whose delegated authority they were originally issued by the Hong Kong SAR Government, namely the Central People's Government.

... Wang Shuwen, a prominent mainland scholar who played an important role in the drafting of the Hong Kong Basic Law, has put it more bluntly. Pointing to the omission of any time limit in Article 123 of the Basic Law, he has dismissed as "groundless and unreasonable" any concern that the Hong Kong SAR Government lacks the legal authority to issue land leases extending beyond 30 June 2047.

The second element of the Gittings analysis involves "reasons to be pessimistic". Here are cited, first, the notorious "White Paper" on the practice of "one country, two systems"[199] which caused serious concerns in Hong Kong, with its firm emphasis on the former at the expense of the latter, its elision of Hong Kong with all other "administrative regions" of China (in contradiction with the special "high degree of autonomy" promised to Hong Kong) and with its call for "loyalty" to Hong Kong's judges (reduced to the status of "administrators"). Also discussed is Beijing's refusal to allow British Parliamentarians to visit Hong Kong on a fact-finding mission on implementation of the Joint Declaration (despite Britain's status as a joint signatory of this Treaty, lodged with the United Nations) and despite Hong Kong's stipulated power (under Article 154(2) of the Basic Law) to regulate the entry and exit of foreign nationals to the HKSAR. Even more worrying was the "mysterious disappearance" of bookseller Lee Bo, almost certainly abducted from Hong Kong to the mainland following the publication and sale of material critical of the senior PRC leadership.[200] Gittings also refers explicitly to the increasing influence of the Liaison Office of the Central People's Government (LO) which he suggests is "likely to continue to grow". An example cited by Gittings is the "apology" made at the Liaison Office by the pro-Beijing LegCo group which "tactically" missed the vote on the government's proposed "universal suffrage" Bill which was thus defeated by a large majority.[201] The pessimistic prediction has been confirmed by overt LO interference in the "election" for Chief Executive (following the decision not to

199. Note 182.
200. The "official" line (that Lee Bo went to the mainland voluntarily to assist with enquiries and somehow evaded the notice of Hong Kong immigration officials) is barely credible.
201. Since this constitutional change required a 75% majority, which was never possible given pan-democratic opposition, there *should* have been a Government majority had not almost all the

seek "re-election" by the hugely unpopular C. Y. Leung) during which pro-Beijing members of the Election Committee[202] were "advised" to vote for Beijing choice Carrie Lam, rather than the more popular John Tsang. Significantly, too, pro-Beijing LegCo member (former DAB president and LegCo President) Tsang Yok-sing stated his view that even if "elected" John Tsang would not be appointed by Beijing.[203]

Most emphatic of all, however, has been the absolute refusal of the Central People's Government to yield an inch on democratic reform in the face of a 79-day "Occupy Central" pro-democracy movement which, after an initially heavy-handed police response, obtained a high measure of popular support and huge international exposure. Depressingly, accounts of "democratic reform" in Hong Kong were almost identical in 2005 as 20 years later![204]

Significantly, while Gittings previously mooted the likelihood of "two systems" operating post-2047, he now, far more conservatively, states that:

> all the evidence still tends to suggest that 'one country, two systems' will survive in some form until [*sic*] the end of the 50-year period guaranteed under the Hong Kong Basic Law, although not necessarily in a form that would be immediately recognisable to anyone who remembered the period of 'maximum autonomy' that Hong Kong enjoyed during the honeymoon years immediately after 1 July 1997.[205]

The third element in the Gittings analysis relates to the "risk" of change before, but particularly after, 2047. There are clearly improvements that could be made from the liberal prospective. Even discounting the unfeasible calls for Hong Kong "independence", post-2047, there are very reasonable improvements that could be made; not least in respect of the indefensible "small house policy" in the New Territories, constantly abused by "indigenous" inhabitants.[206] Abolition has been eschewed by the government, which invariably shirks the task of taking on powerful interest groups (in this case the Heung Yee Kuk). The government's (questionable) justification is that the small house policy is protected by the Basic Law.[207] No such excuse

---

pro-establishment walked out in a vain attempt to stall the vote. The then LegCo President, Tsang Yok-sing, refused to adjourn the vote.

202. While pan-democrats represented just over 300 of the 1,194 Election Committee, the remainder are virtually all representatives of big business and other "special interest" groups with close ties to the Government and Beijing. Given the 777 votes polled by Carrie lam, it is clear that most of the non-democrats toed the Beijing line.

203. It should always be remembered that in the unlikely event of a "non-favoured" candidate being chosen by the Election Committee, Beijing retains an effective veto since the Chief Executive must be "appointed" by the Central People's Government (Article 45, Basic Law).

204. Compare, for example, C Yeung, 'Slow Vote to China' *South China Morning Post* (Hong Kong, 20 October 2005) and S Young, 'Numbers Game' *South China Morning Post* (Hong Kong, 30 April 2015).

205. Gittings (n 197) 314.

206. As a writer on contract law in Hong Kong, the author can attest to the fact that the largest "growth area" in local contract jurisprudence involves "illegal contracts", usually involving abuses of the small house policy.

207. Article 40 guarantees the protection of the "lawful traditional rights and interests of the indigenous inhabitants of the 'New Territories'". Since the small-house policy was introduced by the colonial

for inaction could apply post-2047 but reformers cannot pick and choose, and the reformist agenda is a high-risk one. Scope would then exist for the pro-Beijing camp to introduce its own amendments, notably an attack on the independent judiciary and the presence of "foreign" judges in the Hong Kong courts; both anathema to Hong Kong "loyalists".[208] Thus:

> '... no change beyond 2047' would have its downside as far as Hong Kong is concerned, since it would also freeze in place policies that have become outdated, even where there was general consensus in Hong Kong on the need for a change. But since a 'no change' policy would also protect against any less welcome changes being imposed on Hong Kong by Beijing, that option initially seemed to win support as a safer alternative than trying to rewrite the details of Hong Kong's system after 20147. For instance, Martin Lee, the former leader of the Democratic Party warned in 2009 that 'it would be very foolish of Hong Kong people to say we want to change this and then to keep the rest because the reaction of Beijing would be then we want to change this'.

We may note that even the "less optimistic" revised Gittings prognosis is far removed from the most emphatic and less hopeful forecast exemplified by Robert Morris, writing in support of the proposition that the term of office of a replacement Chief Executive should be the *remaining* portion of the previous incumbent's five-year term. While the *focus* of Morris's article is the term of office issue, almost the whole rationale for his conclusion is that there must be 10 five-year terms of office (from 1997) to coincide with the *automatic* end of the Basic Law and "one country, two systems" in 2047. Thus, Morris writes:

> I must pass for now the interesting and altogether relevant fact (emphasis added) that the Basic Law is a 'temporary law' having a certain sunset date—2047. It is not, like most constitutions, designed to 'endure for ages to come' ...
>
> ... unless the Basic Law were amended, no laws enacted under the Basic Law can surpass or survive the Basic Law, which by its own terms is to have a lifespan of 50 years from 1997 to 2047 ...
>
> Hence, we simply count from 1997 in five-year increments through until 2047-the end of the '50-year' period. All such terms are multiples of fives and 10s. The obvious reason for the selection of these increments is to make the term of the final Chief Executive coterminus [*sic*] with the 2047 end-date of the Basic Law itself ... per Article 5 ...

---

government, it can scarcely be described as "traditional". For an unequivocal rejection of the notion of the policy as constitutionally guaranteed see M Rowse, 'Small-House Policy Overdue for Bulldozing' *South China Morning Post* (Hong Kong, 8 May 2017).

208. The imprisonment of seven police officers captured on film bravely beating up a handcuffed "Occupy Central" demonstrator was a source of major discontent amongst "loyalists" and the fact that the sentencing judge was not Chinese added to their unhappiness. Gittings himself juxtaposes "umbrella movement" calls for post-2047 independence with "loyalist" calls for the abolition of the practice of allowing overseas judges to sit in the Court of Final Appeal.

> . . . My reading of the Basic Law is consistent with both 'one country, two systems' (OCTS) and the Basic Law because the Basic Law enacts OCTS, and because OCTS, like the Basic Law, *must and will end in 2047*. [emphasis added]

This "automatic cessation" view is shared by Pepper who states that:

> Everyone has always accepted that the design had a 50-year shelf-life since the termination date for Hong Kong's 'capitalist system and way of life' was written into Article 5 of the transitional Basic Law constitution. Hence no one has ever argued with the idea that eventually two systems would become one.[209]

Comment

Neither Morris nor Pepper gives much (Basic Law) textual support for their thesis of the automatic cessation of the Basic Law in 2047. Moreover, Pepper's statement that the "termination date" was "written into" the Basic Law is incorrect; given (as Gittings points out) the lack of an explicit statement as to when the 50-year period would commence. Gittings's (even now) far more nuanced arguments appear to have more to commend them than Morris's "five tens are 50" scenario for the abrupt end of "one country, two systems" in 2047 (presumably at 12.00 a.m. on 1 July). Support for the Gittings hypothesis is provided by Chief Justice Geoffrey Ma who has said that nothing in the Basic Law requires convergence of legal systems in 2047.[210]

However, the focus of both of these (Gittings/Morris) projected scenarios is the likelihood (or otherwise) of PRC-imposed "direct rule" (and the triumph of "one country" over "two systems") in Hong Kong, post-2047. Neither extract takes account of the demographic realpolitik. Since 1997, 150 PRC citizens per day have been allowed one-way entry into Hong Kong. That will, by 2047, amount to over 2.5 million citizens; probably more than half of the 2047 electorate[211] (not to mention the large number of "mainlanders" working for PRC banks and businesses). Since Britain acquiesced to the principle that the PRC should determine who was granted such permits,[212] it will be seen as axiomatic that the PRC would select only those in whom it has "political confidence".[213] Moreover, this takes no account of the already large numbers in the pro-Beijing faction before 1997. By 2014, pro-Beijing

---

209. S Pepper, 'Letters from Hong Kong: Waking up to Reality at Last' Archive 10 December 2012. For more detailed discussion, see S Pepper, 'Two Systems Being One: The 2047 Timetable' in MK Chan (ed), *China's Hong Kong* (City University of Hong Kong Press 2008).
210. S Lau, 'Preserve Common Law after 2047: Top Hong Kong Judge' *South China Morning Post* (Hong Kong, 19 March 2014).
211. The average age of the "150-ers" has been put at 33 years by government spokespersons.
212. As evidence of which "side" makes the decisions, the PRC granted "150" status to Shi Junlong, previously convicted of the unlawful killing of two Hong Kong immigration officers.
213. Officially the 150 are said to be selected on the basis of "family reunion" but scant evidence of such exists. While Hong Kong government spokespersons continue to use the "family reunion" descriptor it is difficult to see how they can know this having been excluded from the decision-making process.

personnel held most important political offices (Chief Executive, President of LegCo, etc). It is generally accepted that, despite its caution, Beijing would almost certainly have had a supporter elected in 2017 via genuine universal suffrage, given, not least, the superior organisation and "discipline" of the pro-Beijing faction.[214] *Beijing's influence will only be consolidated over the next 30 years. In short, Hong Kong will be numerically dominated, in 2047, by those with little experience of, or fondness for, the rule of law and judicial independence. Whether rules are determined "locally" or imposed from outside Hong Kong is unlikely to make much difference.*

Hong Kong's special status is under attack in a variety of subtle, and less subtle, ways. The Education Bureau provoked local anger by stating, in January 2014, that Cantonese is not an "official language" (despite its far longer history than Putonghua).[215] *The highly politicised Mass Transit Railway (MTR)*[216] *now issues a constant stream of idiotic announcements to make Hongkongers more compliant (and has relegated the English language to third place after Putonghua). Former Democratic Party Chairman, Martin Lee, talks of Hong Kong being "Tibetified"*[217] *by attempts to introduce "national education" into Hong Kong schools to encourage greater "patriotism". He equates this with the PRC policy of selecting top young pupils in Tibet to be "educated" in Beijing.*[218]

One surprising cause for optimism has arisen from the appalling decision by certain election "returning officers" to bar those advocating Hong Kong independence from standing for LegCo election in 2017.[219] *The rationale (and clearly the officers have not made the banning decisions on their own initiative) is that the Basic Law recognises that Hong Kong is an inalienable part of China.*[220] *Some of those banned have argued that they support independence "post-2047", but the response has been that such a* fundamental *principle cannot be altered even after 2047. Mutatis mutandis, of course, the same argument can be used to support the continuation of other "fundamental" principles including Hong Kong's single most important tenet, the independence of the judiciary.*

---

214. In any event Beijing always has the final weapon of simply not "appointing" a person chosen by the electorate since the Basic Law (Article 45) makes clear that "appointment" is a matter for the Central People's Government.
215. The Cantonese language is, of course, a vital part of Hong Kong's way of life but is at risk. Few would have thought even 20 years ago that Guangzhou (Canton) would now be a Putonghua-speaking city.
216. The Hong Kong Government has the majority shareholding in the MTR which means that the company's constant cost/schedule overruns are subsidised by the Hong Kong taxpayer.
217. With the influx of huge numbers of Han Chinese, Tibetans are now an ethnic minority in Tibet.
218. See also E Luk, 'Fears for HK as Exodus Picks Up Pace amid Mainland Influx' *The Standard* (Hong Kong, 26 September 2014).
219. See S Lau, 'Candidates Jumping Through Hoops' *South China Morning Post* (Hong Kong, 23 July 2016). See also Chapter 2 at 2.4.1.
220. Article 1.

Fundamentally, however, as implied by Gittings, the more realistic cause for optimism stems from possible liberalisation in the PRC itself in the intervening years. In the era of Xi Jinping, prospects for liberalisation appear dim.

2
Sources of Hong Kong Law

Overview

It is impossible to appreciate fully the sources of Hong Kong Law without a firm grasp of Hong Kong's legal history as described in Chapter 1.

Hong Kong's legal sources today encompass elements of colonial, and post-colonial, common law;[1] traditional Chinese law; and both "local" and People's Republic of China (PRC) statutory law.

Given its colonial history and unique post-1997 socio-political position it is not surprising that the sources of Hong Kong law are so diverse. From the early 1840s until 1997 the law of Hong Kong, a British colony, was dominated by the common law of England.[2] Hong Kong's post-colonial "constitution", the Basic Law, guarantees that the common law will continue in force for (at least) 50 years[3] from the reversion of sovereignty of Hong Kong to the People's Republic of China (PRC), in 1997, but it is to be expected that, by a process of divergence, the common law of Hong Kong will become increasingly distinct from the common law of England.

Article 8 of the Basic Law, the constitutional basis for the Hong Kong Special Administrative Region, provides for the continuation of Hong Kong's previously existing laws, including common law, equity, statutory law and customary law, provided they do not contravene the Basic Law and subject to subsequent abolition or amendment. The intention of this Article is that the *general principles* of the common law will continue in force and that the *specific rules* existing before 1997[4] will also do so unless they are amended or found to be contrary to the Basic Law. While this appears to be a simple proposition the operational realities are somewhat more complex.

---

1. As well as (persuasively) "external" common law.
2. While the British generally (very much including the Scots) were involved in Hong Kong's colonial development, it was the "English" common law which was adopted in Hong Kong, Scotland's (civil) legal system being markedly different.
3. Hong Kong's prospects *after* the 50-year period (ie, post-2047) are a matter of increasing concern: see Chapter 1.
4. Although the transfer of sovereignty took place at midnight on 30 June 1997, reference will be to "pre-1997" and "post-1997".

It can be seen from Article 8 that various sources of law in Hong Kong are expressed or implicit. Obviously, the *common law* rules existing on 1 July will generally continue unless and until amended in Hong Kong. Such amendment may be by legislation and, implicitly, by local judicial decision (although there is no provision in the Basic Law for judicial amendment to the common law, this is implicit in the Court of Final Appeal's right of final adjudication).[5]

Previous rules will *not*, however, operate where they contravene the Basic Law, so this crucial constitutional document represents a source of Hong Kong law in itself.

Article 8 also expressly maintains (Chinese) "customary" rules, which were already preserved by the principle that English laws were not effective in Hong Kong if inapplicable to Hong Kong circumstances.[6]

The further intention of the Basic Law is that rules of English common law formulated *post*-1997 will be of no binding effect but merely available for possible guidance in the same way as the rules of any other common law jurisdiction. This is evidenced by the establishment of a Hong Kong Court of Final Appeal with the right of final adjudication[7] and further reference to the fact that this court "may" refer to precedents of other common law jurisdictions.[8] While this may be the theoretical position, in *practice* there is little doubt that post-1997 English court decisions weigh far more heavily with the Hong Kong judiciary than those of other common law jurisdictions.

Finally, though in "hierarchical" terms most importantly, reference must be made to laws passed by the PRC's National People's Congress (NPC) relating to Hong Kong since, although the Hong Kong SAR is guaranteed a "high degree of autonomy" under the Basic Law,[9] Hong Kong is legally part of China under the principle of "one country, two systems", and the NPC has the right to pass legislation affecting Hong Kong.[10] Specifically, the Basic Law, itself a piece of PRC legislation but fundamental for post-1997 Hong Kong, stipulates that certain PRC laws will take effect in Hong Kong (such as laws on the national flag and the Hong Kong PLA garrison).[11] More generally the PRC is responsible for all matters relating to "Acts of State": primarily foreign affairs and national security.[12]

---

5. Subject to exception relating to such matters as national security and foreign affairs.
6. See Chapter 1.
7. Articles 81 and 82, Basic Law. See also the Court of Final Appeal Ordinance (Cap 484).
8. Article 84, Basic Law.
9. Article 2.
10. This right is circumscribed, however, by Article 18 which states that PRC laws are not generally applicable in Hong Kong (see 2.4 below).
11. Listed in Annex III.
12. Discussed in Chapter 1.

2.1 Principal sources of Hong Kong law

On 30 June 1997 the transfer of sovereignty over Hong Kong from the United Kingdom to China marked a significant change in the status of Hong Kong. From its position as a colony of the United Kingdom it has now become a Special Administrative Region (SAR) of the People's Republic of China (PRC). Prior to 1997, Hong Kong's main sources of law were the common law and local legislation. British legislation might also be applicable in Hong Kong (though its influence was declining) and (Chinese) customary law remained of significance, especially in the New Territories.[13]

As noted in Chapter 1, the Joint Declaration on the Question of Hong Kong (Joint Declaration) contains the agreement reached between the People's Republic of China and the United Kingdom concerning Hong Kong's future. The full text of the Joint Declaration, ratified by the respective governments in 1985, is provided in Chapter 1.

In essence, the Joint Declaration provides for the restoration of Hong Kong to the sovereignty of the People's Republic of China as a "Special Administrative Region" enjoying a "high measure of autonomy". Hong Kong is to be largely self-governing and the laws previously in force are to remain unchanged unless they are in conflict with the Basic Law, or unless amended by the Hong Kong SAR legislature. This is in accordance with the so-called "one country, two systems" principle. The broad principles of the Joint Declaration are enshrined in the Basic Law,[14] Hong Kong's "mini-constitution". The Basic Law (a "basic" law of the PRC) is a very extensive piece of (PRC) legislation but the crucial principles, in relation to *sources*, are as follows:

> The Basic Law of the Hong Kong Special Administrative Region of the People's Republic of China
>
> ...
>
> Article 5 The socialist system and policies shall not be practised in the Hong Kong Special Administrative Region, and the previous capitalist system and way of life shall remain unchanged for 50 years.[15]
>
> ...
>
> Article 8 The laws previously in force in Hong Kong, that is, the common law, rules of equity, ordinances, subordinate legislation and customary law shall be maintained, except for any that contravene this Law, and subject to any amendment by the legislature of the Hong Kong Special Administrative Region.

---

13. For the historical background, see Chapter 1.
14. Though, as seen in Chapter 1 there are some specific and significant areas of dissonance.
15. Cf *Comment* below.

> ...
>
> Article 18 The laws in force in the Hong Kong Special Administrative Region shall be this Law, the laws previously in force in Hong Kong as provided for in Article 8 of this Law, and the laws enacted by the legislature of the Region.
>
> National laws shall not be applied in the Hong Kong SAR except for those listed in Annex III to this Law ...
>
> ...
>
> Article 160 Upon the establishment of the Hong Kong Special Administrative Region, the laws previously in force in Hong Kong shall be adopted as laws of the Region except for those which the Standing Committee of the National People's Congress declares to be in contravention of this Law. If any laws are later discovered to be in contravention of this Law, they shall be amended or cease to have force in accordance with the procedure as prescribed by this Law.

Comment

In respect of Article 5, some commentators have made much of the fact that the "50 year rule" only explicitly relates to the "previous capitalist system and way of life". Legalistically, it could be argued that the "non-practising" of socialism is indefinite. By such an interpretation it is possible to argue that capitalism may legally be brought to an end in 2047 but that it cannot be replaced by "socialist systems and policies". In practice, such a scenario is unlikely to outweigh political realities.

In stipulating, in some detail, that the laws previously in force shall include the common law *and* rules of equity, *Article 8 is problematic since it makes a case for the "freezing" of the common law as at 1 July 1997. To the counter-argument, that what is to be preserved is not individual rules but the common law* system, *the obvious rejoinder is that principles of equity would be included within such broader definition of common law. The inclusion of* equity *separately implies the continuation of a common law in the narrow sense of those individual decisions made at common law as opposed to equitable decisions. The probability is that equity (and legislation) were included on a "belt and braces" basis, lest a subsequent attack be made, for example, on the continuation of equitable principles post-1997. A far more detailed debate on this issue is conducted by Wesley-Smith, as outlined below.*

Article 18 is, in essence, little more than a re-formulation of Article 8. Article 8 stipulates the general continuation of the laws previously in force, subject to conformity with the Basic Law and in the absence of subsequent legislative amendment. Article 18 similarly describes Hong Kong's post-1997 laws as deriving from the Basic Law and the laws previously in force with additional reference to the potential for novel *local legislation.*

Article 160 articulates the supremacy of the Basic Law as a Hong Kong legal source. Post-1997, a number of laws "previously in force" have been declared to be in contravention of the Basic Law. Probably the most significant example relates to those parts of the Bill of Rights Ordinance declared to be in contravention of the Basic Law.

The major sources of Hong Kong law today, therefore, are:

(1) Pre-1997 English[16] legislation;
(2) Local (Hong Kong) legislation;
(3) Laws passed by the PRC National People's Congress on SAR matters (including the Basic Law)
(4) Common law (and equity); and
(5) Chinese customary law.

These sources will now be considered in more detail, although the "process" and "interpretation" of legislation will be dealt with separately in Chapter 4.

2.2 English legislation

The status of English statutes, pre-1997 (the so-called "imperial" statutes), was that they were not automatically in force in Hong Kong. Statutes could be stated expressly to apply to Hong Kong, or could do so implicitly, and would then have this effect. Frequently, non-relevant English legislation would be adopted by local, Hong Kong, legislation. The tendency was for British legislation to be adopted in Hong Kong with little amendment, though, in some instances, much later than in England.[17] A residual list of English statutes was listed in the schedule to the Application of English Law Ordinance (AELO).[18] These statutes were to remain in force until removed by the Legislative Council. The list was abolished after 1997 when the AELO was "not adopted" as being contrary to the Basic Law.[19] The effect of this non adoption, as we saw in Chapter 1, is that *post-1997* English legislation can have no effect in Hong Kong while *pre-1997* legislation remains of significance in determining "the laws previously in force in Hong Kong".[20]

Moreover, while English legislation, long before 1997, had largely ceased to have *direct* effect in Hong Kong, it should be noted, as explained in Chapter 1, that where English legislation was viewed as amending the English common law, it could *indirectly* affect pre-1997 Hong Kong, which was generally bound by the English

---

16. The term "English" will be used rather than "British" since it is English rather than British law which was, and to some extent still is, a source of Hong Kong law.
17. The English Unfair Contract Terms Act 1977 was not enacted in Hong Kong (as the Control of Exemption Clauses Ordinance (Cap 71)) until 1989.
18. Cap 88.
19. In any event, few of the remaining statutes were of great significance.
20. And thus to remain in force under Article 8, Basic Law.

common law, *and* post-1997 Hong Kong, as representing the "laws previously in force" which are generally to remain in force.[21]

2.3 Hong Kong legislation

Wesley-Smith[22] writes:

> This (Hong Kong) legislature first provided for the wholesale reception of English law in 1844.[23]

However, since *almost* the very commencement of British imperial rule, Hong Kong was permitted to draft its own legislation.[24] Indeed, Hong Kong was able to enact local legislation suitable to its own conditions with little interference. Given the executive-led nature of Hong Kong government (the Governor was, of course, a British appointment) there was little likelihood of legislation being passed which was against Britain's interests. As the Law Press China "Introduction to the Basic Law of the Hong Kong SAR"[25] emphasises:

> According to the Letters Patent, only the Governor has the power of legislation and the Legislative Council is only an advisory body that assists the Governor in enacting laws. Article vii of the Letters patent stipulates, 'the Governor, by and with the advice and consent of the Legislative Council, may make laws.'[26]

While this may understate the influence of the Legislative Council (LegCo), pre-1997, the executive-led nature of colonial government and legislation cannot be denied.

One consequence of Hong Kong's former colonial status was a tendency to copy English legislation even where this had proved controversial or unsatisfactory. The English Misrepresentation Act 1967, for example, is badly drafted and, in part, difficult to construe. Further, the legislators did not take the opportunity to define the term "misrepresentation" which remains a matter of some difficulty. Hong Kong, however, adopted the Act, via the Misrepresentation Ordinance,[27] with almost no amendment.

Even before 1997, however, there were some signs of an increasing independence in the area of legislation. For example, the English Law of Property (Miscellaneous

---

21. See Article 8, Basic Law and 2.5 below.
22. Peter Wesley-Smith, 'The Reception of English Law in Hong Kong' (paper delivered to the Conference on the Common Law in Asia, The University of Hong Kong, 15–17 December 1986).
23. The Supreme Court Ordinance (No 15 of 1844).
24. Legislative power was entrusted to the governor and Legislative Council by the Royal Charter of 5 April 1843 (and see Chapter 1).
25. *Introduction to the Basic Law of the Hong Kong SAR* (Law Press China 2000), which is prefaced with the following statement: "Publication of this book is sponsored by the Association for Celebration of Reunification of Hong Kong with China Charitable Trust".
26. Ibid 439.
27. Cap 284.

Provisions) Act 1989, which requires that contracts for the sale or other disposition of land must be in writing, was not replicated, by statute, in Hong Kong. The English Occupiers" Liability Act 1984, which extended the duty of care of occupiers of "premises" to trespassers, was, similarly, not mirrored in Hong Kong. Conversely, the Unconscionable Contracts Ordinance,[28] enacted in Hong Kong pre-1997, owes nothing to English influence and is, in fact, modelled on Australian legislation.

Post-1997, Hong Kong's local legislative position is stipulated in Article 66 of the Basic Law which provides:

> The Legislative Council of the Hong Kong Special Administrative region shall be the legislature of the region.

In theory at least, post-colonial LegCo has a more independent legislative function, though the concept of "executive-led"[29] government remains. As will be seen in Chapter 4, most legislation is executive-driven and the Chief Executive can generally count on majority support via the "functional constituency" LegCo members.[30]

There are, too, formal restrictions on the scope of Hong Kong legislation, though these have proved of limited significance, at least so far. Most obviously, Hong Kong has no power to pass legislation which is construed as contrary to the Basic Law. In practice, no post-1997 Hong Kong legislation has been found to be contrary to the Basic Law[31] though some pre-1997 legislation has been so construed. While most Hong Kong Ordinances were adopted without difficulty post-1997, a few pieces of legislation were either, on the grounds of inconsistency with the Basic Law, rejected (not adopted) in full, or not adopted in part or adopted but with adaptation to conform to the new, post-1997, political reality.[32] In the first category (total non-adoption)[33] the most significant pieces of legislation, in addition to AELO, referred to above, were the:

- Trustees (Hong Kong Government Securities) Ordinance (Cap 77)
- Foreign Marriage Ordinance (Cap 180)

---

28. Cap 458.
29. Gittings has queried whether Hong Kong's system is truly "executive-led" and notes that the expression is not used in the Basic Law: Danny Gittings, *Introduction to the Hong Kong Basic Law* (2nd edn, Hong Kong University Press 2016), 101–102. The issue is discussed further in Chapter 4.
30. Traditionally, governor-appointed Members always supported the governor. Majority support for the post-1997 Chief Executive is almost guaranteed by the small circle "functional" seats, the majority of which (representing the government's friends in business) invariable support the government (and see Chapter 4).
31. This is unsurprising, given that, prior to enactment, all Hong Kong legislation must be signed by the Chief Executive, Beijing's appointee.
32. Enacted by "Decision of the Standing Committee of the NPC on Treatment of the Laws Previously in Force in Hong Kong in Accordance with Article 160 of the Basic Law of the Hong Kong SAR of the PRC" (adopted at the 24th Session of the Standing Committee of the 8th National People's Congress on 23 February 1997) (the 23.2.97 Decision).
33. Ibid, Annex 1.

- Chinese Extradition Ordinance (Cap 235)
- British Nationality (Miscellaneous Provisions) Ordinance (Cap 186)
- British Nationality Act 1981 (Consequential Amendments) Ordinance (Cap 373)
- Electoral Provisions Ordinance (Cap 367)
- Legislative Council (Electoral Provisions) Ordinance (Cap 381)
- Boundary and Election Commission Ordinance (Cap 432)

Additionally, certain Ordinances relating to the pre-1997 British armed forces in Hong Kong were not adopted.[34] Much of the above legislation was not adopted, inevitably, because of Hong Kong's new position as part of China, though the non-adoption of the electoral legislation was a result of the PRC's rejection of (last) Governor Patten's minor attempts at electoral reform.

Most notable amongst the legislation rejected *in part*[35] as inconsistent were various sections of the Bill of Rights Ordinance (BORO).[36] The purpose of this legislation, induced by fears for the future of human rights in post-1997 Hong Kong, was to "entrench" in local legislation a range of human rights rules, many of which were already applicable to Hong Kong through its adherence to various international treaties, especially the International Covenant on Civil and Political Rights (ICCPR). The unique status of BORO was that it was to take precedence over other (previous) legislation such that, in the event of inconsistency, the previous legislation could be struck down. Moreover, all subsequent legislation was to be construed, where possible, consistently with the provisions of BORO. While not all of BORO was "unadopted", the Ordinance was amended by the Decision of the Standing Committee of the National People's Congress in accordance with Art 160 of the Basic Law. These amendments repealed the provisions of BORO (ss 2(4), 3 and 4) which enabled the courts to repeal inconsistent pre-existing legislation and to construe legislation subsequent to BORO in a way that is consistent with it. These provisions were repealed on the basis that they were inconsistent with Article 8 of the Basic Law which guarantees the continuation of the laws "previously in force" unless they are inconsistent with the Basic Law or overturned by subsequent Hong Kong legislation. The NPC approach to BORO is explained[37] (rather verbosely) as follows:

> As regards the Hong Kong Bill of Rights Ordinance, it was unilaterally formulated by the British side . . . without consultation and agreement between the two sides. The heart of the matter lies in the fact that the Ordinance has the overriding position over other laws of Hong Kong. According to the Basic Law and the Decision of the NPC Concerning the Basic Law, only the Basic Law has the overriding position

---

34. Ibid.
35. Ibid Annex 2.
36. Cap 383.
37. In Law Press China, op cit ("sponsored by the Association for Celebration of Reunification of Hong Kong with China Charitable Trust").

Sources of Hong Kong Law 67

. . . Such being the case, the Preparatory Committee proposed that the Hong Kong BORO with the provisions for its overriding position not be adopted as a law of the HKSAR. However, on condition that these provisions are annulled, the Hong Kong BORO may still be adopted as a law of the HKSAR.[38]

Other notable "part rejections" relate to definitions of "Hong Kong permanent resident" in the Immigration Ordinance[39] and parts of various electoral Ordinances relating to District Boards, Urban and regional Councils.[40] Parts of the Personal Data (Privacy) Ordinance[41] relating to its "overriding status" were also not adopted (on the same lines as the offending parts of BORO)[42] along with some major amendments to the Societies Ordinance[43] and Public Order Ordinance.[44]

Finally, there is a mass of words, definitions and expressions in prior Hong Kong legislation which had to be amended or adapted to ensure its compliance with the Basic Law and Hong Kong's new political status as an SAR under Chinese sovereignty.[45] Many of these have been dealt with in Chapter 1 and include the deletion of references to "Royal", the amendment of reference to "the Crown", the "colony", the "Governor" and so on.

In addition to the "non-adoptions" of prior Hong Kong laws mentioned above, limitations on Hong Kong's *post-1997* legislative autonomy are imposed by the stipulation that its legislature may not pass legislation affecting defence or foreign affairs ("Acts of State") which are the sole responsibility of the PRC. Article 17 of the Basic Law requires *all* Hong Kong legislation to be reported to the Standing Committee of the National People's Congress (NPC) "for the record". It adds that:

If the Standing Committee of the NPC, after consulting the Committee for the Basic Law of the HKSAR under it, considers that any law enacted by the legislature of the region is not in conformity with the [Basic Law] regarding affairs within the responsibility of the Central Authorities or regarding the relationship between the Central Authorities and the Region, the Standing Committee may return the law in question but shall not amend it. Any law returned . . . shall be immediately invalidated.

Thus far, no post-1997 Hong Kong legislation has been "returned" under Article 17. Gittings[46] points out that this would be "unlikely to prove necessary" given that the Chief Executive would be unlikely to give the necessary approval for the introduction of such a Bill into LegCo.[47]

---

38. Ibid 125.
39. Cap 115.
40. The 23.2.1997 Decision Annex 2.
41. Cap 486.
42. Also via the 23.2.1997 Decision Annex 2.
43. Cap 151.
44. Cap 245.
45. Via 23.2.1997 Decision Annex 3.
46. Note 28.
47. Ibid 74–75.

2.4 Legislation of the People's Republic of China (PRC)

In general, the national laws of the PRC will not apply in Hong Kong. Article 18(2) of the Basic Law states that:

> National laws shall not be applied in the Hong Kong SAR except for those listed in Annex III to this (Basic) Law. The laws listed therein shall be applied locally by way of promulgation or legislation by the Region.

Article 18(3) adds that items may be added or deleted by the Standing Committee of the National People's Congress after consultation with the Committee for the Basic Law of the Hong Kong SAR and the Hong Kong SAR government. The laws currently listed in Annex III include:

- Resolutions/Laws of the PRC on the National Flag, National Day, National Anthem, National Emblem etc
- Regulations of the People's Republic of China concerning Diplomatic/Consular Privileges and Immunities
- Law of the People's Republic of China on the Territorial Sea (and Declaration thereon) and the Contiguous Zone
- Law of the People's Republic of China on the Garrisoning of the Hong Kong Special Administrative Region
- Law of the PRC on the Exclusive Economic Zone and the Continental Shelf
- Law of the PRC on Judicial Immunity from Compulsory Measures Concerning the Property of Foreign Central Banks

The application of the national flag rules of the PRC was a key factor in the decision of the Court of Final Appeal (CFA) in *HKSAR v Ng Kung Siu & Lee Kin Yun*[48] (the flag desecration case). The court was faced with a possible conflict between Article 18(2) which declares the PRC national flag rules as part of Hong Kong's laws and Article 39 which retains ICCPR rights on self-expression as part of Hong Kong's laws post-1997. The CFA determined that the right to freedom of expression is not absolute; that restrictions on freedom of expression must be narrowly interpreted and applied only where necessary and "proportionate"; that restrictions on desecration of the national flag are applied in many states; and that, given the potential for disturbing public order,[49] the national flag rules should be upheld and the illegality of flag-burning upheld. It must be recognised that the decision of the CFA avoided a disastrous political clash in the very early post-1997 situation.[50]

---

48. (1999) 2 HKCFAR 442.
49. Professor Albert Chen, while welcoming the decision, felt that basing it on a potential threat to public order was too narrow an approach ('A Burning Issue' *South China Morning Post* [Hong Kong, 28 March 1999]). However, former Secretary for Justice, Wong Yan Lung, has pointed out that the CFA gave a broad definition of public order, wider than the mere maintenance of law and order (speech by Secretary for Justice to Hong Kong Press Council 21 February 2006).
50. The case also dealt with, as an additional issue, the burning of the *regional* (Hong Kong) flag.

Constitutionally, moreover, other laws of the PRC are, potentially at least, applicable to Hong Kong. In particular, since the PRC is responsible for issues of national (and local) defence, foreign affairs and "other areas outside the limits of the autonomy of the Region", national laws affecting these areas may well have implications for the Hong Kong SAR. For example, national laws may be extended to Hong Kong in emergency situations and at the discretion of the National People's Congress after consultation with the Committee for the Basic Law of the Hong Kong SAR and the Hong Kong SAR government. Zhou-wei also uses the term "implied sources" of post-1997 Hong Kong law to include the PRC Constitution, generally, *interpretations* of the Basic Law by the Standing Committee of the National People's Congress, and international treaties and covenants.[51] It appears that, in light of the recent "co-location" developments, also considered elsewhere,[52] we must now add as a source "statements by the NPCSC" as a direct source of Hong Kong law; to which the requirement of addition to Annex III does not apply. "Co-location" (or collocation) refers to the "decision" that ALL PRC laws would apply at the joint checkpoint area established for the high-speed rail connection between Hong Kong and Guangzhou. There seems to be no reason for such an absolutist position; since the mere application of PRC immigration laws would have sufficed. Any citizen infringing other PRC laws could have been arrested on arrival in Guangzhou. This clear contravention of Article 18 and the avoidance of the proper Annex III procedure is an issue of great concern. Full LegCo discussion has been averted, however; largely because of the reduced LegCo influence of the pan-democratic group whose numbers have been depleted by the "interpretation-inspired" permanent exclusion of six pan-democratic legislators on the grounds of improper oath-taking.[53] Co-location supporters have been unable to produce a consistent justification for the Annex III avoidance. One argument is that NPCSC authorisation for the arrangements constitutes an "Act of State" (the "Article 19" argument; but this results in law by fiat for Hong Kong and totally undermines the apparent legislative intent of Article 18 of the Basic Law. Former Secretary for Justice, Rimsky Yuen suggested that Article 20 of the Basic Law allows the HKSAR to "cede" its jurisdiction in any part of Hong Kong to the PRC. This argument is even less convincing and, again, renders the wording of Article 18 meaningless.

Moreover, and most crucially, the Basic Law, a national law, is a fundamental source of Hong Kong law, providing its constitutional framework and a body of rules with which all (local) Hong Kong legislation must conform.

---

51. Zhou-wei, 'The Sources of Law in the SAR' in P Wesley-Smith (ed), *Hong Kong in Transition: One Country, Two Systems* (Routledge 2003).
52. See Postscript.
53. See 4.4.

2.4.1 The Basic Law

The Basic Law is, essentially, Hong Kong's post-1997 constitution. It provides the structure of relations between the executive, legislative and judicial bodies of the Hong Kong SAR government. The Basic Law was enacted in accordance with Article 31 of the Constitution of the People's Republic of China by the National People's Congress and its purpose is to prescribe the systems to be practised in the Hong Kong SAR, in order to ensure the implementation of the basic policies of the PRC regarding Hong Kong. Constitutionally, the position of the Basic Law has been described as follows:

> The Basic Law is a National Law and provides the basis for legislation of the HKSAR.
>
> The character and position of the Basic Law of the HKSAR are mainly reflected in two aspects. On the one hand, the basic laws enacted by the NPC on the basis of the Constitution are national laws. On the other hand, the Basic Law provides the foundation for legislation of the HKSAR, or the basis for the laws of the region, and no laws formulated by the legislature of the region may contravene the Basic Law.[54]

The provisions of the Basic Law take precedence over other Hong Kong laws in accordance with Articles 8 and 18. Thus, laws that existed before 1997 remain in force (generally) as long as they do not contravene the Basic Law.[55] All new laws enacted by the legislature of the Hong Kong SAR must also conform to the Basic Law and must be "reported" to the NPC Standing Committee.

Much of the content of the Basic Law would be dealt with in far more detail in a work on Hong Kong's constitutional law rather than its legal system. However, given the considerable overlap between what might be viewed as "system" and that regarded as "constitution", an outline of the Basic Law will be attempted here. The extensive contents of the legislation (160 Articles plus annexes) are grouped into nine thematic chapters.

Chapter I (Articles 1–11) establishes certain basic underlying principles, the most crucial of which are that Hong Kong is an inalienable part of the PRC;[56] that the Hong Kong SAR shall exercise a "high degree of autonomy";[57] that the socialist system will not be practised in Hong Kong and the capitalist system shall "remain unchanged" for 50 years;[58] that the laws previously in force will (generally) be maintained;[59] that Chinese and English will constitute official languages;[60] and that no Hong Kong legislation may contravene the Basic Law.[61]

---

54. Law Press China (n 24) 155.
55. It was because it was determined that parts of the Bill of Rights Ordinance were contrary to the requirements of Article 18 that they were "not adopted".
56. Article 1.
57. Article 2.
58. Article 5.
59. Article 8.
60. Article 9.
61. Article 11.

Chapter II (Articles 12–23) determines the relationship between the Central Authorities and the Hong Kong SAR. Notably it stipulates that the SAR should enjoy a "high degree of autonomy" while being under the Central People's Government; that the central government is responsible for foreign affairs but that the SAR may "conduct relevant external affairs on its own"; that the SAR shall be responsible for the maintenance of public order and that the PRC troops stationed in Hong Kong should not interfere in local affairs (unless requested by the Hong Kong government); that the Chief Executive and senior officials shall be appointed by the Central People's Government; that the Hong Kong SAR shall be vested with executive, legislative and independent judicial power; that the laws in force shall be those previously in force, local legislation and the Basic Law, with National laws not normally applied; that local Chinese residents shall elect deputies from Hong Kong to the National People's Congress; that departments of the Central People's Government should not interfere in Hong Kong internal affairs; that (however) the Central People's Government may declare a state of emergency in Hong Kong; and, finally, that (under Article 23) the Hong Kong SAR:

> shall enact laws on its own to prohibit any act of treason, secession, sedition, subversion . . . or theft of State secrets, to prohibit foreign political organizations . . . from conducting political activities in the region and to prohibit [local organizations] from establishing ties with foreign political organizations or bodies.

This last, the so-called "Article 23 legislation" has been extremely controversial, caused large numbers of Hong Kong citizens to take to the streets, and has caused the demise of its main government protagonist.[62] Since the spectre of Article 23 continues to raise its head, a brief history may assist understanding.

Between 1997 and 2002, relatively little activity had taken place in respect of Article 23, save for the occasional calls for speedy implementation from "Beijing loyalists".[63] In 2002, Qian Qichen, Vice Premier of the PRC State Council, called on the Hong Kong government to implement Article 23 speedily. Following a "consultation period" in which the government received over 90,000 submissions,[64] the necessary legislative framework was quickly instituted, though no "White Paper"[65] was issued. A Bill was introduced into LegCo[66] intended, via amendment to existing Ordinances,[67] to implement fully (many would say "too fully") the objectives of Article 23. Since the wording of Article 23 itself had already far exceeded the narrow

---

62. See Chapter 1.
63. The term "loyalist" is used by the pro-Beijing faction in Hong Kong (represented in Hong Kong politics by the Democratic Alliance for the Betterment & Progress of Hong Kong, or "DAB") to refer to loyalty to the Communist government.
64. LegCo response by Secretary for Security, Regina Ip, to question by Martin Lee, 15 January 2003.
65. Most significant legislation in Hong Kong is preceded by a White Paper that facilitates serious discussion of the government's proposals.
66. The National Security (Legislative Provisions) Ordinance.
67. The Crimes Ordinance, the Official Secrets Ordinance and the Societies Ordinance.

scope of what had been agreed in the Joint Declaration, serious concerns were immediately aroused.

Particular fears were engendered by the proposals in respect of secession and sedition. In respect of the offences of secession and incitement thereof, the chief concerns arose in respect of those who, for example, supported independence for Taiwan (or even recognised its current *de facto* independence) or Tibet.

As to "sedition", there was significant concern relating to its definition and, particularly amongst the journalistic ranks, as to the offence of "handling of seditious documents". Moreover, there were realistic fears that the new law would be used as a means of extending PRC suppression of the Falun Gong movement, in China mainland, to the Hong Kong SAR.[68]

A balanced view of the Article 23 legislation, indicating informed concern, is expressed in the following paper from the Hong Kong Bar. The paper is a very long one but the major concerns are encapsulated in the following extract:

> HONG KONG BAR ASSOCIATION'S RESPONSE TO THE CONSULTATION DOCUMENT ON THE PROPOSALS TO IMPLEMENT ARTICLE 23 OF THE BASIC LAW
>
> 1. ... On 24th September 2002, the HKSAR Government ("the Government") published a Consultation Document on "Proposals to Implement Article 23 of the Basic Law" ("the Consultation Document").
>
> 2. Article 23 of the Basic Law provides as follows:–
>
> "The Hong Kong Special Administrative Region shall enact laws on its own to prohibit any act of treason, secession, sedition, subversion against the Central People's Government, or theft of state secrets, to prohibit foreign political organizations or bodies lTom conducting political activities in the Region, and to prohibit political organizations or bodies of the Region lTom establishing ties with foreign political organizations or bodies."
>
> 3. The Bar maintains its position that in most areas, the existing laws of the HKSAR ... are sufficient to prohibit the acts and activities listed in Article 23.
>
> 4. In its Views published on 22nd July 2002, the Bar set out three fundamental principles to be observed when laws are enacted to implement Article 23:–
>
> (1) Firstly, the Government should adopt a minimalist approach, namely, to legislate only when and where it is strictly necessary to do so in order to comply with the requirements of Article 23;
>
> (2) Secondly, the Government should seize upon the opportunity to review and make such changes to our existing laws so as to bring them in line with modern human rights standards while at the same time see to any laws made being consistent with:–

---

68. Especially given then Chief Executive Tung Chee Hwa's description of Falun Gong as an "evil cult".

(a) Minimum standards contained in International Covenant on Civil and Political Rights ("ICCPR");

(b) Minimum standards contained in International Covenant on Economic Social and Cultural Rights ("ICESCR");

(c) Guarantees of fundamental rights of HKSAR residents under Articles 27 to 34 of the Basic Law; and

(d) Johannesburg Principles on National Security, Freedom of Expression and Access to Information ("the Johannesburg Principles").

(3) Thirdly, the drafting in the legislation must be unambiguous, drawn narrowly and with precision.

5. While the Bar appreciates that it is the duty[69] of the HKSAR to enact domestic laws to prohibit the acts and activities listed in Article 23, the Bar does not agree to the legislative proposals as set out in the Consultation Document. In particular, the Bar takes the view that such proposals are not in compliance with the three fundamental principles repeated under paragraph 4 above.

6. While the Government says it has taken into account in framing the proposals contained in the Consultation Document the guiding principle that all offences encompassed by local legislation to implement Article 23 are as clearly and tightly defined as appropriate so as to avoid uncertainty and the infringement of fundamental rights and freedoms guaranteed by the Basic Law, the Government has failed to adhere to such a principle . . . The fact that various government officials[70] have had to come out to make statements about what conduct will not be criminalized demonstrate the vagueness and uncertainties of the limits of the proposed offences. Of course, what government officials say means nothing. It is the wording of the legislation that is paramount and for the courts to interpret.

7. The Bar is of the view that it is difficult to have any meaningful discussion and consultation when the legislative proposals are described in the very broad terms used in the Consultation Document. It is impossible for the public to know precisely with what they are asked to agree or support in the absence of a text setting out the proposals in the form of draft legislation.

III. TREASON

13. Article 23 requires the HKSAR to enact laws on its own to prohibit any act of treason.

. . .

15. The Government presumably intends to enact Article 23 legislation concerning treason by amending the Crimes Ordinance to create new offences and by

---

69. Human Rights Monitor Hong Kong rejected the "duty" on the basis that Article 23 runs counter to the Joint declaration. Such a view is politically untenable.
70. See the Bob Allcock response, below.

repealing certain provisions though this is not made at all clear in the Consultation Document.

...

16. In essence, the Government's proposals are to create the following offences punishable by life imprisonment:

(1) "levying war by joining forces with a foreigner with intent to

(a) overthrow the PRCG or

(b) compel the PRCG by force or constraint to change its policies or measures or

(c) put any force or constraint upon the PRCG or

(d) intimidate or overawe the PRCG."

...

17. The Government also proposes to enact a statutory equivalent of the common law offence of "misprision of treason" punishable by 7 years' imprisonment and unlimited fine being the failure to report to the proper authorities within a reasonable time that another person has committed treason...

18. In addition, the Government proposes to enact legislation dealing with all the inchoate offences of attempting, conspiring, aiding and abetting, counselling and procuring the commission of the substantive offence except incitement which will form the separate offence of sedition and these inchoate offences shall also be punishable by life imprisonment...

19. Finally, the Government proposes to abolish the existing time limit on prosecutions, which requires that all prosecutions for these offences shall be commenced within 3 years of the offence...

20. The offences are to apply to all persons who are voluntarily in the HKSAR and to all Permanent Residents outside HKSAR for their actions outside HKSAR...

21. The proposals depart fundamentally from the requirements of Article 23 by failing to define what are the prohibited acts. Nor has the Government adhered to the guiding principle referred to above. The proposals are not clearly or tightly defined to avoid uncertainty and the infringement of fundamental rights and freedoms...

...

30. The law is to apply to all HKSAR Permanent Residents wherever they may be living.[71] No account is taken of the unique circumstances of Hong Kong and the fact that many who live overseas may have dual nationality or of the fact that many of those who live in HKSAR are not PRC nationals. No special allowance is made for those who owe dual allegiance despite the fact that treason is principally an offence applying to those who have a duty of allegiance to the state of which they are nationals.

---

71. The Department of Justice sought to justify the extra-territorial jurisdiction (see DOJ Paper No 36, May 2003).

31. The proposal to abolish the time limit for commencement of prosecutions is particularly objectionable...

32. The offence of treason should be narrowly defined to specified acts of assisting the enemy where war has been declared by or on the PRC with the intent of assisting the enemy. Those specific acts should be confined to acts involving use of violence such as joining a military force with a foreign State, or provision of weapons to the foreign State knowing that the PRC is at war with that State and with the intent of assisting that enemy.

...

36. The time limit for prosecutions should be retained and the punishments clearly stated to be maximum and not mandatory.

[Similar criticisms/concerns were expressed in relation to planned laws on secession, sedition/seditious publications, subversion, theft of state secrets and support for proscribed organisations. Concern was also voiced as to the proposed concomitant increase in investigative powers. The Bar's paper also drew attention to one area (extra-territoriality) in which the proposed laws were to be more oppressive for Hong Kong citizens than those of the mainland.]

...

38. There is at present no offence termed secession in the HKSAR. The Government proposes to create such law...

...

75. Sedition is an offence that no longer exists in many countries. In those where it is still retained, it is no longer used...

...

The Government proposes to:–

...

(3) Create a separate offence of dealing with seditious publications (etc).

...

93. The Government should remove from the statute book all offences relating to seditious publication and not enact any new and similar offences.

...

98. The Government proposes to:

...Create an offence of subversion to ensure that the HKSAR will not be used as a base for supporting subversive activities in or against the Mainland;

...

106. ... The essence of subversion is to overthrow the Government by force or violence. The offence of subversion should be so defined and confined.

...

117. It is important to ensure that lawful activities in Hong Kong, which may be unlawful or unacceptable in the Mainland, should not be prohibited or suppressed by the subversion offence through the back door . . .

. . .

127. No one should be convicted of an offence of subversion or related inchoate offences solely by reason of affiliation with a Mainland organization that has been proscribed by the CPG on ground of national security.

. . .

128. The underlying basis for legislation for the theft of state secrets is that it should comply with the ICCPR and with all of the Johannesburg Principles . . .

129. The Consultation Document acknowledges that the Official Secrets Ordinance currently protects state secrets . . . The Consultation Document also states that the Government considers that "the existing provisions of the Official Secrets Ordinance already strike an appropriate and delicate balance between the need for open government and for protection of state secrets".

. . .

165. Unless the Government can show that the proposals in the Consultation Document are necessary for the purpose of protecting state secrets under Article 23, all it needs to do to meet the requirement to legislate in this regard is to undertake an extensive review of the Official Secrets Ordinance.

. . .

172. The Government proposes to make it an offence to organize or support the activities of proscribed organizations, or to manage or to act as an "office-bearer" for these organizations. An organisation that has a connection with a proscribed organization might also be declared as unlawful where necessary using standards of the ICCPR . . .

. . .

175. The Bar is of the view that existing mechanism provided under the Societies Ordinance is sufficient to protect the HKSAR from the political activities of FPOs in Hong Kong which may damage national security. A case has not been made out to justify why new laws are needed.

. . .

183. We also are of the view that the power to ban a local organization affiliated with a Mainland organization, which has been proscribed in the Mainland by the Central Authorities, is against the concept of "One Country, Two Systems". Such power also violates freedom of association guaranteed by the Basic Law. The HKSAR government should be allowed to determine which are organizations that may pose a threat to "national security". It is not necessary for the Central Government to determine on our behalf.

Sources of Hong Kong Law

184. It is clear that the concept of "national security" as practised by the Central Authorities is very different from that recognised in the HKSAR and in international standards. Mainland laws on national security are very wide. They include "stability" or "interest" of the government or state. Information relating to economic or health can be said to damage national security. The recent imprisonment of an AIDS activist is a case in point. Should one day the Mainland Authorities proscribe an organisation like the Falun Gong on national security grounds, and go further to notify the HKSAR that a HKSAR Falun Gong body being a cell of and affiliated with such a Mainland Organization has posed a threat to national security, it will be stretching one's imagination to expect the Secretary for Security to say that the HKSAR body should not be so proscribed in the HKSAR.

...

187. ... The Government should drop completely the proposals contained in the Consultation Document for proscription of organizations, which are clearly outside the ambit of Article 23.

...

190. Part III of Chapter 8 proposes to extend ... [investigative] powers.

...

197. The Bar believes that the starting point for any discussion about powers of entry and search is Article 29 Basic Law. It states that: "The homes and other premises of Hong Kong residents shall be inviolable. Arbitrary or unlawful search of, or intrusion into, a resident s home or other premises shall be prohibited".

...

199. ... the Consultation Document fails even to make out a *prima facie* case for creating extraordinary powers of entry, search and seizure in this area ...

207. Government should drop all proposals for adding to the sufficient investigation powers that law enforcement agencies already enjoy ...

...

220. A Hong Kong Permanent Resident with the nationality of another country may actively support his country in levying war against the PRC. Indeed, it may be his legal duty to do so. His actions would not amount to an offence under PRC law because they are lawful under the law of that other country. However, he would be guilty of the offence of treason under HKSAR law according to proposals in the Consultation Document.

...

223. Article 102 covers treason (collusion with foreign states to harm sovereignty). Academic writers in the PRC are of the opinion that only PRC citizens can commit these offences.

...

> 230. The Bar finds nothing in the Consultation Document to persuade it to modify its views expressed earlier on 22nd July 2002 that in most areas, the existing laws of the HKSAR are sufficient to prohibit the acts and activities listed in Article 23[72]...
>
> ...
>
> 236. If the Government's intention to consult the people of HKSAR before enactment of laws implementing Article 23 is no less than genuine, then it must undertake a second round of public consultation on the draft legislative text before it puts a Blue Bill to the Legislative Council for First Reading. The welfare of the HKSAR and the successful implementation of the "One Country, Two Systems" concept demand nothing less.
>
> The Hong Kong Bar Association 9th December 2002

Comment

The Bar's response was certainly very thorough and did include some positive comments on the agreed need to remove or revise some existing legislation. There was also some detailed concern about the meaning and relevance of the term "state" which was shown to be used inconsistently. The "state" argument has been addressed in Chapter 1.

Key to the Bar's concerns was the need to conform with international conventions to which both the PRC and Hong Kong (separately) had previously committed themselves.

While accepting Hong Kong's clearly stated duty *to enact Article 23 legislation, the Bar emphasised that such legislation should be "minimalist", which the Bar believed was certainly not the case in the original discussion document.*

While Security Minister, Regina Ip, was largely dismissive of the Bar's stance,[73] the government did concede/clarify on three issues: that the offence of treason would not apply to foreign nationals; that all provisions must be interpreted in accordance with the ICCPR; and that all offences must be tried by a jury.

The need for "minimalism" was endorsed by the University of Hong Kong Law Faculty's Centre for Comparative and Public Law at a Conference in 2002.[74] Contributor Simon Young[75] stated:

---

72. Human Rights Monitor Hong Kong endorsed this view adding that "the provisions of these [existing] laws are flawed and need to be liberalized, not made worse" (HRMHK, "A Ticking Timebomb? Article 23, Security Law & Human Rights in Hong Kong", August 2001).
73. Stating: "I can understand if individual organizations and individual members of the public have doubts. That doesn't mean the general public has doubts." (Press Statement 14 February 2003.)
74. "Preserving Civil Liberties in Hong Kong: The Potential Impact of Proposals to Implement Article 23 of the Basic Law" (Conference: 23 November 2002).
75. Simon NM Young, (then) assistant professor, HKU.

Sources of Hong Kong Law

> The consultation paper proposes to give the state new extraordinary powers to search premises and to obtain financial information without warrant or prior judicial authorization. The arguments put forward for these new powers are unconvincing, especially since Article 23 itself does not expressly require implementing such powers.[76]

In a similar vein, Fu Hualing stated:

> The two lesser [sedition] offences are broadly drafted and the net is cast too wide. The offences are neither necessary nor proportionate. To punish people for publishing or possessing books can neither enhance the protection of China's national security nor dignify and honour the state. The two lesser offences are awkwardly copied from colonial legislation without careful consideration. They simply cannot be brought to life after their long dormancy. It is time to break away from this draconian colonial tradition.[77]

The Hong Kong government's initial response to the enormous public concern was to "stick to its guns" and assert its Basic Law *duty* to enact the necessary Article 23 legislation. Secretary for Security, Regina Ip, strenuously asserted this duty, emphasising that "shall implement" imposed an obligation. Ip mocked the "quality" of her opponents' arguments and refuted the need for a "white paper" famously stating:

> Are you seriously telling me that taxi drivers, restaurant waiters at McDonald's will want to discuss these proposals with me? A draft bill is for the experts.[78]

Such comments, to the effect that further consultation was unnecessary because the public would not understand the law, offended large numbers of Hong Kong people.

Far more conciliatory was Bob Allcock, Solicitor General, who recognised concerns but sought to allay them in his public utterances. The following is an excellent example:

---

76. SNM Young, 'State Powers of Investigation and Article 23' (HKU Conference 23 November 2002 loc cit).
77. Hualing Fu, 'Past and Future Offences of Sedition in Hong Kong' (23.11.2002 Conference, n 71, 29). The contributions of Fu Hualing and Simon Young were significantly refined and expanded to form the basis of: H Fu, CJ Petersen, and SNM Young, *National Security and Fundamental Freedoms: Hong Kong's Article 23 Under Scrutiny* (Hong Kong University Press 2005)
78. Public statement, 26 September 2002.

Letter to Hong Kong:
"Implementing Article 23 of the Basic Law"
by the Solicitor General, Mr Bob Allcock

1. As you may know, we are nearing the end of the consultation period in respect of the Government's proposals for implementing Article 23 of the Basic Law. Let me try to take stock of the position at this stage.

2. When the proposals were first released in September this year, initial reactions were quite favourable. But, as time has gone by, concern has grown. Having attended many meetings on this subject, I know that some people are sincerely worried. I would like to offer some comments on their worries.

First stage

3. My first comment is that the concerns expressed so far have been noted by the Government. That was the whole point of the consultation exercise – to listen to the views of the community.

4. In several areas, the Government has already said it will review the proposals. For example, concern has been expressed about the offence of possessing seditious publications, about powers of police investigation, and about proposed appeal avenues in respect of any banning of a local organization. The Government has said that it will revisit all those proposals.

...

Second stage

6. My second comment relates to the "devils in the details" argument. Many commentators feel unable to respond fully to the proposals until they see the draft legislation. That is an understandable position to take.

7. However, the opportunity to comment on a Bill will arise early next year – we hope in February. The Bill will be the start of the second stage of this exercise, when everyone – not merely LegCo members – will be encouraged to discuss the fine print.

...

9. Since the proposals were released, Government officials, including myself, have tried to reassure members of the public that many of their fears are groundless. For example, we have pointed out that advocacy of the independence of Taiwan by peaceful means would not be an offence; and that criticism of the Central Government or the Communist Party will remain lawful.

10. Of course, our statements do not have the force of law. But they do indicate what the Government's intentions are. Those intentions can be checked against the wording of the Bill when it is produced, to ensure that assurances are given legal backing.

...

11. The best safeguards against draconian laws are already in place. The Basic Law contains a constitutional guarantee that no law can be validly enacted if it contravenes

international standards of human rights referred to in Article 39. It also ensures that a judicial remedy is available should the Government try to enforce a law in a way that breaches those standards.

12. Our experience during the past five years indicates that the guarantees in the Basic Law are not empty words. They are enforced by the independent Judiciary, which is our ultimate and effective safeguard of human rights.

...

14. No one wants to turn harmless acts of protest into serious crimes against the state. Hong Kong's reputation as a free and tolerant society must not be undermined.

Freedom of expression

15. In particular, Hong Kong's reputation as a place where freedom of speech, and freedom of the press, flourish must be defended at all costs. Some people are concerned that the proposals would undermine those freedoms. Areas of particular concern have been noted – for example, the concern about seditious publications that I mentioned earlier. And the Government will try to address these.

16. I wish to emphasize that the proposals should not have the so-called "chilling effect" that some have alleged. The fact is – only two areas covered by Article 23 relate directly to freedom of expression. They are sedition and the theft of state secrets.

...

18. So far as the theft of state secrets is concerned, broadly speaking the proposal is that we should retain the current law, which is contained in the Official Secrets Ordinance. . . . The fact that a document is classified in the Mainland as "secret" would continue to be irrelevant so far as Hong Kong law is concerned. Mainland laws, and Mainland concepts of state secrets will not be introduced.

...

20. Before the proposals were released, there had been much concern about the need to create new offences of "secession" and "subversion". Those labels seemed very worrying. Many feared that such offences would necessarily crack down on freedom of expression.

...

22. Those new offences could not be committed merely by calling for peaceful change or by criticising the government. Conduct amounting to "levying war, or the use or threat of force, or criminal conduct that is akin to a terrorist act" would have to be proved. The proposed offences are therefore much narrower than many people appreciate.

23. In describing the proposals, I am not claiming that they are perfect . . . But the Department of Justice has advised that they are consistent with the human rights guarantees in the Basic Law and in the International Covenant on Civil and Political Rights. And that view has been endorsed by a leading human rights expert – Mr David Pannick QC.

15 December 2002

Comment

Allcock sought to allay concerns by suggesting that previous draconian laws in this area would be removed and that the new legislation would actually be less repressive than its colonial predecessor. While this may, strictly, have been correct the comment was somewhat disingenuous given that the antiquated colonial laws in this area had scarcely been used in Hong Kong since the 1960s riots. Moreover, the 2002 attempts to enact Article 23 coincided with a campaign of ruthless PRC oppression of Falun Gong which Hong Kong people feared would be repeated in the SAR.

Despite Allcock's assurances and limited government amendments to the originally proposed legislation, public opposition was intensifying rather than abating. LegCo members harried the government and proposed amendments while, on the streets, over 500,000 marchers voiced their discontent in a landmark 1 July 2003 march.[79] On 6 July, then Hong Kong Chief Executive Tung Chee Hwa announced the delay of the second reading of the Article 23 legislation. On 16 July, Regina Ip, Secretary for Security and chief proponent of the legislation, resigned. Eventually, on 5 September, Tung announced the withdrawal of the legislation which was to be reintroduced after public consultation.[80]

Hong Kong has still to "enact on its own" the necessary legislation.[81] However, whenever the debate on electoral reform/universal suffrage becomes heated, a PRC spokesman can be relied upon to make calls for the enactment of Article 23 legislation. In April 2014, despite assurances from then Chief Executive CY Leung and Chief Secretary Carrie Lam[82] that Article 23 legislation was not a priority, Rao Geping, a member of the Basic Law Committee, proposed adopting PRC national security laws in Hong Kong,[83] in clear breach of the Article 23 requirement that Hong Kong should enact such legislation "on its own".[84] To his great credit, LegCo President and former DAB[85] Chairman, Tsang Yok-Sing, responded quickly to Rao's statement, pointing out that the introduction of PRC security laws in Hong Kong

---

79. Regina Ip put the figure at fewer than 60,000!
80. Even after withdrawal of the legislation, Ip was largely unapologetic, blaming "poor timing" (the advent of SARS and economic recession) and the withdrawal of Liberal Party support. She did, however, concede "communication mistakes" (see presentation by Regina Ip, founder of New People's Party, St John's College, University of Hong Kong, 10 October 2011).
81. Though the Macau SAR has already done so. The contrast is well-noted by a disgruntled and impatient Beijing side which has praised Macau for its contribution to national security.
82. Cf Stuart Lau: "Lam said the government 'has had a consistent stance regarding Article 23. That is, this is not a matter for us to handle as a priority'", *South China Morning Post* (Hong Kong, 31 March 2014).
83. Reported in *SCMP*, 7 April 2014.
84. Even Regina Ip has stressed that "on its own" means that mainland laws on national security will not be extended to Hong Kong (St John's College Presentation, loc cit, supra).
85. The DAB, formerly the Democratic Alliance for the Betterment of Hong Kong, now the Democratic Alliance for the Betterment & Progress of Hong Kong, is generally supportive of the Chinese Communist Party.

could not, legally, occur without amendment to the Basic Law.[86] However, in May 2017, Zhang Dejiang, "China's No. 3 state leader", signalled that Beijing's patience on Article 23 was fast running out.[87]

Chapter III (Articles 24–42) is concerned with the "fundamental rights and duties" of Hong Kong residents. The Chapter begins by defining "permanent" and "non-permanent" residents. Thereafter it first (and mainly) emphasises *rights*:[88] stressing that all residents shall be equal before the law; shall have the right to vote and stand for election ("in accordance with the law"); shall have the rights of freedom of speech, association, procession and demonstration as well as the rights to form and join trade unions and to strike. Additional freedoms relate to the right to freedom and privacy of communication, freedom of movement, freedom of conscience and religious belief and the right to engage in academic research. Hong Kong residents are also guaranteed the right to social welfare, freedom of marriage and the right to raise a family. The freedom of the press and publication is specifically guaranteed as is freedom from arbitrary arrest or imprisonment. In relation to "access to law", residents are guaranteed the right to confidential legal advice and judicial remedies, and to the right to take proceedings against the acts of the "executive authorities".

Article 39 specifically preserves in force the provisions of the International Covenant on Civil and Political Rights, the International Covenant on Economic, Social and Cultural Rights and international labour conventions "as [previously] applied to Hong Kong".[89]

Of particular note is the preservation (in Article 40) of the "lawful traditional rights and interests of the indigenous inhabitants of the 'New Territories'".

As regards the rights described above, various comments may be made. First, of course, they emphasise the significance of "one country, two systems", since many such rights are not equally enjoyed elsewhere in the PRC. Obvious examples are the religious freedom denied to the Falun Gong on the China mainland and the denial of the freedom to raise a family implicit in the PRC's "one child" policy.[90]

It should also be noted that the legal existence of "rights" is of little value without mechanisms of *enforcement*. The right to "form and join trade unions" (under Article

---

86. K Ip, 'LegCo Chief Blasts Article 23 Call Again' *The Standard* (Hong Kong, 8 April 2014). This is because not only is such legislation to be made by Hong Kong "on its own" but because only those PRC laws listed in Annex III to the Basic Law can apply in Hong Kong. Pro-Beijing LegCo member Priscilla Leung is said to have argued that Article 18 permits additions to the Annex III list, overlooking that such additions, "shall be confined to those relating to defence and foreign affairs as well as other matters outside the limits of the autonomy of the Region" (Article 18 Basic Law). Since Article 23 specifies Hong Kong's right/duty to enact "on its own" it is clearly *not* a matter outside the limits of its autonomy. Significantly, Tsang Yok-sing, shorn of his LegCo presidency (and no longer required to be neutral) has suggested that China may enforce Article 23 on its own if Hong Kong fails to do so!
87. S Lau, 'Beijing Signals Tighter Grip' *South China Morning Post* (Hong Kong, 28 May 2017).
88. Little is said in Chapter III on *obligations* other than the axiomatic statement in Article 42 that Hong Kong residents and others in Hong Kong have the obligation to abide by the laws in force.
89. See discussion in Chapter 1.
90. Seemingly a "two child policy" from 2016.

27), for example, is more apparent than real where major employers target union members for dismissal, safe in the knowledge that unfair dismissal damages in Hong Kong are woefully inadequate.[91]

The issue of "permanent residency", as defined in Article 24, is of huge constitutional importance, since the broad (over-broad?) definition has caused great concern and has led to a major confrontation between the Hong Kong courts and the government over the interpretation of 22(3) and 22(4) dealt with elsewhere.[92] Whatever the debate about these subsections, however, Article 24(1) appears essentially unambiguous, stating that permanent residents shall be:

> Chinese citizens born in Hong Kong before or after the establishment of the Hong Kong SAR.

A presumably unforeseeable consequence, however, has been the huge influx of PRC "mainland mothers" entering Hong Kong pregnant with the intention of giving birth in Hong Kong and ensuring right of abode for their offspring.[93] The issue became one of great public concern in terms of both the drain on local hospital resources and the potential for excessive population growth. The situation was eased fairly simply by "immigration" health checks to prevent the ingress of pregnant mainland women and, crucially, the tripling of charges for obstetric care for non-Hong Kong residents.[94] The issue of the "status" of those born to such mothers remains, however. Since the Basic Law position is unequivocal, in *common law* interpretation terms, there have been calls for an "interpretation" of Article 24(1) by the NPC Standing Committee. The principal proponent of "interpretation" (yet again) was former Secretary for Justice, Elsie Leung, whose default position is invariably to "leave it to Beijing". Leung called for an interpretation of Article 24(1) in preference to administrative solutions, adding that *amendment* to the Basic Law is not an option. Implicit in Leung's desire for an interpretation (since the Article is unambiguous) is the fact that "interpretation", in the PRC system, is a rather broader concept that at common law.

A different sort of "right of abode" challenge to the status quo was raised in *Vallejos Evangeline Banao v Commissioner of Registration & Another*[95] where a

---

91. Cathay Pacific, for example, remained for years in dispute with a group of dismissed pilots, all of whom were union activists (or, in one unfortunate case, had the same name as an activist!). The compensation awardable at law for the (established) improper dismissal would have been totally inadequate for the dismissed pilots but for the additional, far greater, award made on the basis of Cathay's defamation of the pilots (later reduced on appeal).
92. See below and 3.3.1 and 4.4.
93. Potential right of abode was not the only consideration, with superior medical care and the avoidance of the (then) one-child policy also significant.
94. This dramatic increase of obstetric (and related) care charges was the subject of unsuccessful judicial review challenge on the grounds of *unfair discrimination* by a mainland mother married to a Hong Kong resident (see *Fok Chun Wa & Another v The Hospital Authority & Another* (2010) 15 HKPLR 628).
95. (2013) 16 HKCFAR 45.

Filipina domestic helper, employed for many years in Hong Kong, claimed the right of abode based on seven years' continuous residence in Hong Kong under Article 24(2)(4). The claim failed, essentially, on the ground that Vallejos had not been "ordinarily" resident in Hong Kong as required under the subsection since, as with all domestic helpers, she had been required to return to her country of origin every two years. Unusually, perhaps, the author believes the government's opposition to the Vallejos claim was legally sound, though it is to be regretted that the government demonstrated so little confidence in the local Bar that it chose to "import" David Pannick QC to plead its case.

Further, the theoretical right of permanent residents to "stand for election in accordance with the law" (under Article 26) is hugely circumscribed, in practice, by the fact that, in order to stand for election to the post of Chief Executive, one must be a Chinese citizen at least 40 years old (Article 44); must be "elected" by an Election Committee[96] (Annex 1); and must, finally, be "appointed" by the Central People's Government (Article 45).[97] Even in Legislative Council elections the "right" has been further curtailed by the political screening of candidates by returning officers (guided by the Electoral Affairs Commission, itself almost certainly "externally" encouraged) to exclude those *determined by the returning officers* to be advocates of Hong Kong independence (even post-2047).[98] Even having been elected, the problems for anti-government members are not over, with action now having been taken against those deemed to have taken their oath of office improperly. So far, following yet another NPCSC interpretation (this time on the oath-taking rules) six elected legislators have been disqualified from LegCo membership.[99] The intransigence, generally, of the Central People's Government (CPG) in the face of widespread calls for genuine universal suffrage in Hong Kong was the major factor in the huge (79 days) civil disobedience movement known as "Occupy Central" which attracted huge local support; especially after the initial, heavy-handed, police response, involving excessive use of pepper spray and tear gas. While, in *constitutional law* terms, "Occupy" (and the total refusal of the CPG to offer any democratic concessions) is of huge significance,[100] there will be only limited reference in this *legal system* text.

---

96. The "broadly representative" Election Committee contains fewer than 1,200 members!
97. Article 45 talks of the "ultimate aim" being selection by universal suffrage but only "upon nomination by a broadly representative nominating committee". Under this formula the PRC encouraged, in 2015, a (reformed) system of "universal suffrage" whereby (in 2017) Hong Kong citizens would have been permitted to elect (subject to the CPG "appointment" rule) one from 2 to 3 Chief Executive candidates selected by a "Nominating Committee" (the old Election Committee wearing a different hat). Despite extensive pro-reform propaganda from the Hong Kong government, LegCo rejected this generous offer! The Election Committee thus remains in place. See T Phillips, 'Hong Kong Parliament [*sic*] Defies Beijing's Insistence & Rejects "Democracy" Plan' *The Guardian* (London, 18 June 2015).
98. See C Buddle, 'A Blow to Hong Kong's Clean and Fair Electoral Process—Dealt by Its Own Election Officials' *South China Morning Post* (Hong Kong, 11 August 2016).
99. Evidence that former Chief Executive, CY Leung, himself delivered an improper oath by omitting important words has fallen on deaf ears.
100. Not least for what it tells us about CPG priorities in terms of "internal security" versus "external reputation".

It goes without saying that the "democracy" debate also raises a question mark over the freedom of speech "right" guaranteed under Article 27. Indeed, while freedom of speech, publication and of the press is far better protected in Hong Kong than elsewhere in South-East Asia,[101] there have been worrying developments in the past few years. Moriarty[102] writes that, since 1997, Radio Television Hong Kong (RTHK)

> has been under increasing pressure and even attack, primarily from supporters of Beijing who feel that the problems that undid [first Hong Kong Chief Executive] Tung Chee Hwa stemmed from his administration's inability to sell its policies to the public. They . . . feel that the government needs a mouthpiece, and it should be RTHK.

Since those words were written we have experienced physical attacks on liberal journalists Kevin Lau[103] and Cliff Buddle[104] as well as the abduction to the PRC of "the five booksellers" involved in the distribution of works critical of PRC leaders.[105]

Also of concern is the fact that, while direct censorship is not generally apparent, "self-censorship" appears to be on the rise. In many forums writing about Tibet or Taiwan is particularly circumscribed.[106]

The preservation of New Territories "traditional" rights and interests under Article 40 is also highly significant, reflecting a long history but of crucial current importance. Both the Joint Declaration and the Basic Law provide for such rights and interests to be preserved, despite their archaic and discriminatory nature and the fact that they have been abused for many years to the detriment of the New Territories environment.[107] The "special relationship" between the British government and the traditional New Territories inhabitants arose largely for peace-keeping reasons; the inhabitants had been less amenable to British rule than their counterparts elsewhere

---

101. For example, the Singapore government uses defamation laws to deter critics while journalism in the Philippines is a genuinely dangerous profession.
102. F Moriarty, 'Press Freedom in Hong Kong: The Trend Is Down' (2007) Hong Kong Journal (Summer).
103. Lau, viciously attacked in February 2014, had been the chief editor of *Ming Pao* which had been critical of the wealth accumulated by senior PRC cadres and their families. He had already been controversially transferred from this post.
104. The attack on *SCMP* journalist Buddle (October 2014) while teaching at the University of Hong Kong was written off as the "lone wolf" action of a deranged mainlander. Those familiar with the remote location of the teaching room in question would find this unlikely.
105. While the abductions have never been officially admitted, it is not credible that all five entered China (from Hong Kong, Thailand, etc) willingly and without any record of entry. See O Chou, J Mai, and C Ge, 'Final Chapter for Trade in Banned Books?' *South China Morning Post* (Hong Kong, 5 January 2016).
106. It is sad to note that one of the clearest examples involved the "pulling" of a (human rights activist and barrister) Paul Harris article on Tibet by *Hong Kong Lawyer*, official publication of the Hong Kong Law Society (see T Kellogg, *The Hong Kong Lawyer Controversy and Self-Censorship in Hong Kong*, October 2008).
107. See Tony Kwok, 'End Rural Land Rights Abuse' *South China Morning Post* (Hong Kong, 25 September 2016).

in Hong Kong and more "active" in their opposition. Almost from the first, once Britain had leased the New Territories in 1898, special legislative provision was made[108] since, as Chen Lei writes:

> the Hong Kong colonial administration discovered that the Chinese in the New Territories were very different from the people on Hong Kong Island, both economically and socially.[109]

Trouble had sporadically arisen, from the first days of the 1898 lease. It is recorded that:

> The uprising erupted in 1899 after the British started occupying the area leased to them by China under a 99-year treaty signed on 9 June 1898.
> About 1,000 villagers led by the Tang clan in Kam Tin rose up to resist the British advance.
> Most of the fighting took place around Kam Tin, the home village of the Tangs.
> Outnumbered and outgunned, the villagers lost and the British conquered Kat Hing Wai and Tai Hong Wai.[110]

Traditional land-holding rights in the New Territories (the *t'so* and *t'ong*), though antiquated, have been a largely accepted and uncontroversial feature of the Basic Law's preservation of New Territories rights and interests. The following extract briefly summarises the situation.

> Legal Culture and Legal Transplants
> (Report by Chen Lei: published by International Academy of Comparative Law [Jorge A Sanchez Cordero ed] 2010).[111]
>
> One of the basic principles of customary Chinese law is that of the maintenance and preservation of family property through the male line. An example of this patrilineal system is that of customary trust over land, the *t'so* or *t'ong*. Traditionally, *t'so* was a trust where land was held for the benefit of the clan or the lineage and was created posthumously by the heirs of the deceased landowner for various purposes, particularly ancestral worship. *T'ong* was thought to have been created by the landowner *inter-vivos* with the intention to ensure that the land was held by the clan in perpetuity for such purposes as education, business and social relationships. Therefore, the fundamental purpose of the two types of customary law is to venerate the common ancestor or the family clan. Both customary rules have now been preserved in section 15 of the New Territories Ordinance, which provides:

---

108. The first was Ordinance No 10 of 1899.
109. L Chen, 'Contextualising Legal Transplant: China and Hong Kong", in PG Monateri (ed), *Methods of Comparative Law* (Edward Elgar Publishing 2012) 207.
110. J Law, *The Standard*, 14 June 1997.
111. *Reports to the XVIIIth International Congress of Comparative Law* (Washington DC, USA, 2010), 18–19.

> "Whenever any land is held from the Government under lease or other grant . . . in the name of the clan, family or t'ong . . . or t'ong shall appoint a manager to represent it . . . the said manager . . . has full power to dispose of or in any way deal with the said land as if he were the sole owner thereof, subject to the consent of the Secretary for Home Affairs . . . Every instrument relating to land held by a clan, family or t'ong, which is executed or signed by the registered manager thereof, in the presence of the Secretary for Home Affairs and is attested by him, shall be as effectual for all purposes as if it had been executed or signed by all the members of the said clan, family or t'ong. The Secretary for Home Affairs may on good cause shown cancel the appointment of any manager and select and register a new manager in his place.
>
> If the members of any clan, family or t'ong holding land do not within 3 months after the acquisition of the land make and prove the appointment of a manager, or within 3 months after any change of manager prove the appointment of a new manager, it shall be lawful for the Government to re-enter upon the land held by such clan, family or t'ong, which shall thereupon become forfeited."
>
> It can be seen that *t'sos* and *t'ongs* are not subject to the rule against perpetuities, which has no counterpart in customary Chinese law. Also, the land held by a *t'so* or *t'ong* in customary Chinese law is intended to be inalienable. In practice *t'so* and *t'ong* land may be sold but this only happens under exceptional circumstances for the family clan benefits from the sale, and all members must agree to sell. It is worthwhile noting that the abovementioned customary Chinese law continues to be applied and enforced only in the New Territories. A *t'so* or *t'ong* may hold land in other parts of Hong Kong but customary Chinese law does not apply.

Comment

It is because these customary rules only apply in the New Territories and are clearly long established that they are clearly within the category of traditional rights and interests preserved, largely without controversy, by Article 40.[112]

The "small house" policy,[113] on the other hand, is far from uncontroversial. It provides that a *male* indigenous villager, who can trace his New Territories ancestry back to 1898, has a one-off right to apply to build a small (maximum two storeys in theory) house on agricultural land which he owns. It has resulted in the despoiling of much of the New Territories environment by ugly small houses and their generally

---

112. See 2.7 below. For further discussion of *tsos* and *tongs*, see BSY Wong, 'Chinese Customary Law: An Examination of Tsos and Family Tongs' (1990) 20 HKLJ 13–30.
113. Described by Christine Loh as "an interest of the indigenous inhabitants under Article 40 of the Basic Law" (C Loh, 'Inheritance Rights of Indigenous Women of the New Territories', address to seminar of Centre of Asian Studies, 22 May 2004). This view was supported *obiter* in *Secretary for Justice v Chan Wah* (2000) 3 HKCFAR 459. Cf, however, J Chan, 'Rights of New Territories Indigenous Inhabitants' in Chan and Lim (eds), *Law of the Hong Kong Constitution* (Sweet & Maxwell 2011).

attendant scrap metal for the benefit of male descendants of indigenous inhabitants, usually no longer resident in Hong Kong. The preservation of such rights (or interests), despite their overtly discriminatory nature,[114] owes much to the bargaining power of the Heung Yee Kuk (HYK), a pressure group for the New Territories indigenous inhabitants,[115] long seen as a pro-Beijing "loyalist" institution (and favoured by the Chinese side in pre-1997 negotiations) because of New Territories early resistance to British rule.[116] Ironically, the New Territories resistance had also procured an accommodation with the British since:

> The Government had always wanted to maintain cordial relations with the HYK, probably to maintain social peace and co-operation and in order to resume land in the New Territories for development since the 1960s. The price was to freeze social change among the indigenous villagers.[117]

The small house policy has been subjected to numerous abuses; indeed, small house "scams" have been one of the most common examples of illegal contract in Hong Kong. The following case provides a typical example:

> *Best Sheen Development Ltd v Official Receiver and Trustee*[118]
>
> The plaintiff, a developer, entered into an illegal contract with a New Territories villager. The purpose was that the villager should obtain permission, on behalf of the plaintiff, to build under the New Territories "small house" scheme. In order to obtain the permission, the villager purported to be the legal and beneficial owner. The plaintiff had purchased the land for $250,000 but immediately assigned it to the villager who, in theory, was to pay for it. The court held that in fact this was an illegal "development scheme" and the villager had no interest in the property. On the villager's bankruptcy, the plaintiff successfully sought a declaration that he was the sole beneficial owner. Yuen J stated:
>
> *"... the 'development scheme' was a contract ... which had as its object the deliberate commission of the tort of misrepresentation on the Government as landlord, the misrepresentation being that Lai (the villager) owned the land. A contract to commit a civil wrong is illegal under common law ..."*[119]

---

114. In respect of both women and non-indigenous inhabitants of the New Territories.
115. In the Heung Yee Kuk Ordinance (Cap 1097) the kuk is described as representing (all) "the people of the New Territories". However, its key constituency is the "indigenous inhabitant". The kuk has, more accurately been described as "warlords of power in their individual fiefdoms, eager to hold on to their privileges in times and circumstances that no longer justify their position." (Puja Kapai, 'The Human Rights of Women in the HKSAR' *William & Mary Journal of Women and the Law* 19 February 2013). Described more economically by Philip Bowring as the "feudal kuk" (*South China Morning Post*, 'Backpage', 20 April 2014). Bowring explains that the kuk's already significant influence was increased when former Chief Executive, Donald Tsang, appointed kuk leader Lau Wong-fat to ExCo.
116. See above.
117. C Loh (n 110).
118. [2001] 3 HKC 79.
119. Ibid 87.

Of course, since in normal (non-bankruptcy) circumstances neither party would willingly disclose his part in an illegal contract, this case is likely to be only the tip of a large iceberg.[120] To its shame the Heung Yee Kuk established a legal fighting fund to assist those imprisoned for illegally selling off their right to build to developers.[121]

An alarming, pre-1994, consequence of indigenous male dominance in the New Territories was the fact that women could not inherit land. The (successful) legislative attempt to defeat the discriminatory status quo and the relationship between the amending legislation and the Basic Law (drafted but yet in force at that time) is described in the following.

> Inheritance Rights of Indigenous Women of the New Territories
> By: Christine Loh[122]
>
> Introduction
>
> Ten years have elapsed since the New Territories Land (Exemption) Ordinance (NTL(E)O) 1994 was passed...
>
> ...I hope this paper serves to provide a quick way for people to better understand what happened a decade ago.
>
> Historical Background
>
> Article 40 of the Basic Law (BL) provides that: "The lawful traditional rights and interests of the indigenous inhabitants of the "New Territories" shall be protected by the Hong Kong Special Administrative Region".
>
> ...
>
> British jurisdiction over Hong Kong Island, Kowloon and the New Territories, was acquired through three treaties with China's Qing government between 1842 and 1898...
>
> The New Territories were inherently different since it was leased and not ceded land. However, it suited Britain to administer the whole territory as a colony rather than to regard leased territory as a form of protectorate...
>
> The early policy was to apply customary law by local elders under the supervision of a government officer acting as magistrate. Legislation provided a legal framework for this system, in particular dealings in land. The system had been revised over time but dealings in land remained substantially unchanged until 1994 with the passage of the NTL(E)O.
>
> I. "Lawful traditional rights and interests"
>
> What constitutes "lawful traditional rights" of the inhabitants of the New Territories? The term is not defined in the Basic Law and would need to be discovered by reference to existing law or practice.

---

120. See J Ngo, 'Villagers Alleged to Have Sold Rights to Developers' *South China Morning Post* (Hong Kong, 19 January 2016).
121. KC Ng, 'Rural Leaders Amassing War Chest for Villagers Jailed in Homes Scam' *South China Morning Post* (Hong Kong, 27 December 2015).
122. May 2004, n 110.

In this connection, a key issue for discussion is section 13 of the New Territories Ordinance 1910 (now amended), which provided that:

In any proceedings in the High court or the District Court in relation to land in the New Territories, the Court shall have power to recognise and enforce any Chinese custom or customary right affecting land ...

...

In *Wong Ying Kuen v Wong Yu-shi and others*[123] [the court stated]:

"... the correct law to apply is the Ching law and custom as it existed in 1843 with such modifications in custom and in the interpretation in the laws as have taken place in Hong Kong since that period."

Thus, in summary, Chinese law, custom and customary right to be applied in the New Territories was that which was prevalent in 1843, subject to any changes to its application consequent upon legislative developments in Hong Kong, and further subject to any changes in such custom or its interpretation as may since have become established.

II. New Territories Ordinance (1910) and male succession

The New Territories Ordinance (NTO) of 1910 was a consolidating effort relating to the administration and regulation of the New Territories. Part I contained interpretations and the power of the Governor to appoint administrative officers for the New Territories. Part II contained the substance of regulating land right in the New Territories. The NTO did not restrict its application to Chinese indigenous inhabitants, or even ethnic Chinese Hong Kong resident. The NTO applied to the land itself. Section 7(2) provided for exemption upon application by a landowner to the Governor. This mean that if a New Territories landowner wanted it, and that it was approved by the government, customary law applying to the New Territories could be put aside and the ordinary law of Hong Kong to apply instead.

...

III. Problems Arising

1. Women excluded from land succession in the New Territories

A landowner in the New Territories could of course write a will nevertheless and that a valid will should be able to receive probate under the Wills Ordinance. However, the Probate and Administration Ordinance did not apply to land in the New Territories unless probate could be obtained within three months of death (a near impossibility). As such, the Land Officer could not register a female beneficiary under the will since the officer was bound by customary law to register only male heirs.

...

2. Inequitable law of succession

The law of succession in Hong Kong as a whole was also inequitable as it discriminated against the rights of women when it concerned New Territories land. An

---

123. Miscellaneous Proceedings 19 of 1956.

indigenous landowner with both land on Hong Kong Island and the New Territories would have no problems bequeathing land on the island to a female heir, but even with a properly executed will, the female heir may not be able to succeed to the land in the New Territories, with the result that the land might then devolve to male members of the family . . .

. . .

IV. The Basic Law and its intention

. . . Article 40 protects the rights and interests of the indigenous inhabitants of the New Territories.

Article 40 refers to "lawful traditional rights" and Article 8 states that "customary law" shall be maintained. This means that the Basic Law protects customary rights and not Qing imperial law. It is also important to note the full text of Article 8:

"The laws previously in force in Hong Kong, that is the common law, rules of equity, ordinances, subordinate legislation and customary law shall be maintained, except for any that contravene this Law, and subject to any amendment by the legislature of the Hong Kong Special Administrative Region."

Thus, the question is whether Article 40 and 8 protect Chinese customary, patrilineal succession law.

The argument centred around whether the NTL(E)O passed in 1994 contravened the Basic Law. The effect of this Ordinance is to enable women to succeed to land in the New Territories, thereby putting everyone in the SAR on the same footing legally as far as succession to land goes.

. . .

V. New Territories Land (Exemption) Ordinance 1994

The NTL(E)O divides the land in the New Territories into two categories: rural land and other land. Non-rural land is deemed to have always been exempt from the NTO. The NTL(E)O thereby retrospectively ignores the NTO in the new towns and other developed areas of the New Territories.

Under Section 2, "rural land" means land held under any of several households that as a matter of policy are granted only to indigenous villagers, whether the land is rural in character. Rural land is only exempt from the NTO in respect of disposition of that land following an owner's death, and not in respect of any other matter. The new Ordinance expressly preserves the court's power under the NTO to enforce other land-related customs, such as burial rights. Land held by customary trusts [e.g. *t'so* or *t'ong*] also remained expressly unaffected.

It was argued by the supporters of the NTL(E)O that the Basic Law only protected such traditional right that was lawful, and that a traditional right the infringed the other provisions of the Basic Law was unlawful under the Basic Law, as was made clear by Article 8, and hence not protected by Article 40. The effect of custom on succession discriminated against women, and as such, contravened Article 25 of the Basic Law, which guarantees all Hong Kong residents shall be equal before the law.

> ...
>
> The opponents of that view brought their case to the Preparatory Committee of the SAR, empowered by the NPC to establish the SAR and having the task of recommending whether any existing law contravened the Basic Law. They argued that any discrimination arising from adherence to custom was justifiable because it was necessary to preserve indigenous inhabitants' culture.
>
> ...
>
> It would have been extremely odd for China, who (sic) itself eliminated Chinese customary laws and stresses the upholding of gender equality, to preserve an outdated practice in the SAR when it assumed sovereignty. It should be noted that the NTL(E)O does not nullify traditional culture. It merely makes adherence to customary rights voluntary rather than mandatory. That is, a landowner who wants to restrict inheritance to his male heirs may do so by making a will to that effect. Furthermore, the NTL(E)O also expressly preserves other land-related customs, such as burial rights and customs governing *t'so and t'ong*.
>
> ...

Comment

Certain points should be stressed. The first is that the Exemption Ordinance did not *prevent a New Territories testator from leaving his land to a male or males only. Nor did it interfere with customary* t'so/t'ong *rights. It merely applies "normal" inheritance rules in the absence of such testamentary or customary incidents.*

The second point is that the exemption legislation applies only to rural land since it was "deemed" that the "special indigenous inhabitants" rules had never applied to non-rural land (eg in the numerous New Territories "new towns").

Mention should also be made of the courage displayed by Loh and other supporters of the legislative change who endured serious abuse and physical threats from their opponents.

Chapter IV (Articles 43–104) is largely of a "constitutional" nature, involving Hong Kong's post-1997 "political structure". The first 16 Articles (section 1) deal with the Chief Executive; his appointment and removal and his relationship with the Executive and Legislative Councils. From a legal point of view, the main points to note are that the Chief Executive is responsible for the implementation of the Basic, and other, Laws; that the Chief Executive has the power of appointment and removal of judges at all levels; that the Chief Executive may pardon convicted offenders or commute their sentences; and that the Independent Commission Against Corruption shall be accountable to the Chief Executive.

The next seven Articles (section 2) deal with the executive authorities; their constitution and role. From a legal standpoint the two points most worthy of note are that the Department of Justice (DOJ) shall control criminal prosecutions "free from any interference"[124] and that the Hong Kong government must abide by the law and be accountable to the Legislative Council. The required DOJ independence in respect of the decision to prosecute has been queried, particularly in the early post-1997 period. Few objective observers would accept that the decision not to prosecute Aw Sian (Sally Aw), chair of the group which owned the *Hong Kong Standard* and *Sing Tao Daily* newspapers, for the manipulation of *Hong Kong Standard* (Standard) circulation figures, so as to boost advertising revenue, was "un-political".[125] Gittings[126] also highlights the decisions not to prosecute the Xinhua news agency for breach of the Personal Data (Privacy) Ordinance[127] nor to prosecute former Financial Secretary, Antony Leung, who had resigned following a scandal over his decision to purchase a luxury car just prior to his budget announcement of an additional tax on such purchases. Gittings concludes:

> Ms [Elsie] Leung, who served as Secretary for Justice from 1997 to 2005, repeatedly caused concern by refusing to prosecute in politically sensitive cases.[128]

There is cause for optimism in saying, firstly that most political "pressure" in respect of the decision whether or not to prosecute has come from within Hong Kong (rather than from mainland China)[129] and because, following the replacement of Elsie Leung by the far more able and independent Wong Yan Lung, political interference appears to have declined. It is unfortunate that Wong gave up his post while still young. The tenure of his successor, Rimsky Yuen, was similarly brief. His association with the failed attempt to win Hong Kong people over to Beijing's bogus "universal suffrage" proposals for the 2017 Chief Executive election and "joint checkpoint" co-location plans did little to enhance his reputation or the cause of political independence.[130]

Section 3 (Articles 66–79) deals with the Legislative Council; its composition, constitution and role. Most of the content of section 3 would be regarded as outside the scope of legal system, though the role of the Legislative Council in the introduction and passage of legislation will be outlined in Chapter 4.

Section 4 (Articles 80–96) is extremely important in the legal context since it deals with the judiciary; its composition, role, appointment and removal. Although

---

124. See Chapter 14.
125. For further discussion, see Chapter 14. See also A Chen, 'Continuity and Change in the Legal System' in LCH Chow and YK Fan (eds), *The Other Hong Kong Report 1998* (Chinese University Press 1998).
126. D Gittings, 'Changing Expectations: How the Rule of Law Fared in the First Decade of the Hong Kong SAR' Hong Kong Journal, July 2007.
127. Cap 486.
128. Gittings (n 28) 4 (PDF version).
129. Of course some of the non-prosecution decisions may have been inspired by the desire to please "Beijing" but, for example, even the Sally Aw debacle was described by James Crawford as "a simple local blunder" (J Crawford, Hochelaga Lectures, op cit, 8).
130. Successor Teresa Cheng was mired in controversy even before being confirmed in post; on discovery that she possessed several illegal structures in her (company owned) flat which she was "too busy" to notice.

the judiciary will be dealt with separately in Chapter 6, several key issues should be noted at this stage. First, the section stipulates that the previous judicial system shall operate save for the creation of a (new) Court of Final Appeal, with the right of final adjudication. From a precedent/source standpoint, Article 84 makes the significant point that Hong Kong courts may refer to precedents of other common law jurisdictions. This affirms Hong Kong's continuing membership of the "common law club", while at the same time, implicitly, relegating the English common law to the role of one source amongst many. A similar effect is created by the affirmation, in Article 92, that Hong Kong judges may be recruited from other common law jurisdictions.

Article 85 is important, too, in emphasising the independent power of the Hong Kong courts, free from outside interference, and the immunity from prosecution of judges exercising their judicial functions.

Finally, while section 4 is headed "The Judiciary", it does include two important, though tangential, issues: the preservation of trial by jury[131] and the presumption of innocence.

The remaining parts of Chapter IV, on District Organisations and Public Servants, are of little significance from a legal system viewpoint. The same could be said of most of Chapter V ("The Economy", Articles 105–125). However, Article 105 is of increasingly topical importance. It states:

> The HKSAR shall . . . protect the rights of individuals and legal persons to the acquisition, use, disposal and inheritance of property and the right to compensation for lawful deprivation of their property.

At first sight this appears to ensure maintenance of real property rights[132] and a guarantee of "fair" compensation in the event of deprivation. As so often in Hong Kong, however, the "rules of the game" favour the government's friends in big business. Statutory authority to compulsorily acquire "minority" shareholdings in a (50 years or more old) building (or 30 years if the building is industrial), subject to "fair" compensation, seemed relatively innocuous when the majority shareholding had to be 90%. When the percentage was reduced to 80%, however, the threat became clear. Fun[133] explains as follows:

> *Forcing Sales through Law*
>
> Legislation that calls for the compulsory sale of property is understandably important to a society like Hong Kong because it ensures that whatever space there is in the city is not left to lie derelict . . . Or at least that was how it was argued as developers and

---

131. The jury is dealt with separately in Chapter 8.
132. See also Article 6, Basic Law: "the HKSAR shall protect the rights of private ownership of property in accordance with law".
133. YJ Fun, 'Surreal Estate: Hong Kong's Property Sector and White-Collar Crime Discourse' (HKU Scholar's Hub 2012).

> lawmakers pushed for the passage of the Land (Compulsory Sale for Redevelopment) Ordinance [Cap 545] ...
>
> ... At the time, residents and landowners did not view the law as over-reaching ...
>
> ... it was not until January 2010 that trouble started brewing as the government began to listen to justifications for an amendment to the law in order to make it even easier for developers to buy out individuals and push forward their redevelopment efforts ...
>
> Despite the heavy public opposition, Cap 545A (the 80% legislation) was forced through by the functional constituencies, a body which constitutes half of LegCo and whose sole purpose is to represent the special interests of Hong Kong's many power holders ...
>
> The change of legislation came into effect on April 1, 2010, and less than a month had passed before anecdotal evidence began to surface that developers had been pulling out of negotiations with landowners to force sales at "fairer" prices. Retired civil servant ... Mike Rowse, documented a developer that walked away from their original offer of $17,000 per square foot and, with the blessings of Cap 545A, returned with a compulsory offer of $12,000 per square foot ... the pattern that is emerging ... is one where developers are targeting buildings sitting on the city's premium land while ignoring actually dilapidated areas that have no substantial commercial value.[134]

Comment

It comes as no surprise that this fairly blatant "present" for property developers engineered by the CY Leung administration was, in fact, nothing to do with genuine redevelopment of derelict areas (the alleged purpose of the legislation). Interestingly, in a rare excursion to the "good side", ex-minister Regina Ip opposed the legislative change.

Further, Articles 120–123 deal with land leases and prescribe very detailed rules for the arrangement for leases on a continuing basis, with other specific rules applying to traditional holdings in the New Territories. These arrangements are, historically, of great significance, since it was concern for what would happen to leases in the New Territories once the British "lease" ran out that kick-started negotiations between Britain and China on Hong Kong's post-1997 future.[135]

Chapter VI ("Education, Science, Culture, Sports, Religion, Labour and Social Services") and Chapter VII, which deals with "External Affairs", are of limited importance from the legal system standpoint though, in permitting Hong Kong's

---

134. While the legislative change is recent there is already considerable jurisprudence (see the *Hong Kong Land Law* blog for summaries of important cases since 2011).
135. See Chapter 1.

participation in international agreements and the establishment of foreign consular and other missions to Hong Kong, the latter serves to underline the significant extent of the Hong Kong SAR's autonomy.

Finally, but importantly, Chapter VIII (Articles 158 and 159) determines the right of interpretation and amendment of the Basic Law. These are crucial constitutional articles, which have a direct impact on Hong Kong's legal system and the development thereof. Since the Basic Law is a crucial source of Hong Kong law, its interpretation will be considered briefly here, with far greater detail provided in the "interpretation" section of Chapter 4.

Interpretation is dealt with by Article 158 which makes clear that the power of interpretation of the Basic Law is vested in the Standing Committee of the (PRC's) National People's Congress (NPC). As is well-known to all lawyers, the power to interpret a law is almost as important as the power to create law, since it is the law *as interpreted* which the courts must apply. The issue of interpretation, and the circumstances in which the NPC Standing Committee (NPCSC) will be called upon to interpret the Basic Law, is a thorny one and has called into question the whole issue of the independence of the Hong Kong courts and their right of final adjudication. To understand the controversy, it is necessary to consider the full wording of Article 158 which states:

> "The power of interpretation of this [Basic] Law shall be vested in the Standing Committee of the National People's Congress.
>
> The Standing Committee of the National People's Congress shall authorize the courts of the Hong Kong SAR to interpret on their own, in adjudicating cases, the provisions of this Law which are within the limits of the autonomy of the Region.
>
> The courts of the Hong Kong Special Administrative Region may also interpret other provisions of this Law in adjudicating cases. However, if the courts of the Region, in adjudicating cases, need to interpret the provisions of this Law concerning affairs which are the responsibility of the Central People's Government, or concerning the relationship between the Central Authorities and the Region, and if such interpretation will affect the judgments on the cases, the courts of the Region shall, before making their final judgments which are not appealable, seek an interpretation of the relevant provisions from the Standing Committee of the National People's Congress through the Court of Final Appeal of the Region."[136]

---

136. The Court of Final Appeal (in a majority decision) decided, for the first time, to seek an SCNPC interpretation in *Democratic Republic of the Congo v FG Hemsiphere Associates* (2011) 14 HKCFAR 95. While the request for an interpretation is not, in itself, worrying, opinions are divided as to whether the decision will have an adverse effect on judicial independence. Certainly it is far less objectionable than the Hong Kong government request for interpretation, discussed here. Interpretation and the "Congo case" are discussed more fully in Chapter 4 under the heading "statutory interpretation".

The section goes on to add that no NPCSC interpretation can affect judgments "previously rendered" and that the NPCSC shall consult the Committee for the Basic Law of the Hong Kong SAR before giving its interpretation.

It was generally assumed, or at least hoped, that the Hong Kong courts would be capable of effecting a competent, and uncontentious, interpretation where appropriate and that it would be for the Hong Kong Court of Final Appeal to decide (as the Basic Law stipulates) when a request to the Standing Committee for an interpretation should be made. Events proved otherwise, for which the Hong Kong government must take much of the blame. The landmark cases were *Ng Ka Ling v Director of Immigration*[137] and *Chan Kam Nga v Director of Immigration*,[138] both involving the issue of "right of abode" in Hong Kong. Briefly, the facts were that, under the previous immigration law passed by the controversial Provisional Legislative Council (a body not provided for in the Basic Law but imposed by the PRC in retaliation for (last) Governor Patten's minor attempts at democratic reform in Hong Kong) neither of the claimants were eligible for right of abode in Hong Kong. The claimants were born to Hong Kong permanent residents *on the mainland*. They asserted that the wording of the Basic Law clearly entitled them to right of abode and was, implicitly, in conflict with the earlier Provisional Legislative Council legislation. Although their claims had been rejected by Hong Kong's Court of Appeal, their claim seemed a strong one. Article 24(3) of the Basic Law confers the status of "permanent resident" on those "Chinese citizens" born outside Hong Kong to Chinese citizens who have continuously resided in Hong Kong for seven years or more, as had the claimants' parents. The opposition to the claim was entirely "political"; first an unwillingness on the Chinese side to accept that they had overlooked the consequences of drafting Article 24(3) as they did (and therefore a reluctance to take the appropriate step of Basic Law amendment) and the fear of the Hong Kong government of a wave of "immigrants" from mainland China in the event of the *Ng Ka Ling* and *Chan Kam Nga* appeals being successful.[139] The Court of Final Appeal (CFA) found for the claimants, interpreted Articles 22(4) and 24(2) and (3) without requesting an interpretation by the Standing Committee, and asserted (probably overzealously) the right of the CFA to override PRC legislation where it found this to be inconsistent with the Basic Law.[140] The consequence of the CFA decision was that the Hong Kong government sought an interpretation of the relevant Basic Law Articles by the NPC Standing Committee. Not unsurprisingly the Standing Committee upheld the Hong Kong government's view, "re-interpreted" the right of abode Articles, confirmed that

---

137. [1999] 1 HKC 291.
138. [1999] 1 HKC 347.
139. The government produced some very dubious "research" which predicted an influx of 1.67 million immigrants over 10 years in the event of the appeals being upheld.
140. The CFA did not need to determine this point in order to uphold the appeal, so it may be viewed as unnecessarily provocative. Chen describes the CFA view as "totally unacceptable to Beijing" (A Chen, 'The Constitution & the Rule of Law' in SK Lau (ed), *The First Tung Chee-hwa Administration: The First Five Years of the HKSAR*, Chapter 3,76).

the CFA should have sought an interpretation, and emphasised the position of the Standing Committee of the NPC as the ultimate arbiter on matters of Basic Law interpretation.[141] As Chen[142] states:

> the Hong Kong courts' power to interpret the Basic Law and to determine whether an act of any governmental authority is consistent with the Basic Law, albeit a real and important power, is nevertheless not an absolute one. It is not absolute because it is subject to the overriding power of the NPCSC.[143]

What was so unfortunate about the right of abode saga was the Hong Kong government's eagerness, so soon after 1997, to assume a power of request to the NPC Standing Committee which is *not provided for in the Basic Law*, and which could only have the effect of weakening the autonomy and prestige of the newly-created CFA. It is a matter of relief to note that subsequent interpretations by the Standing Committee have been rare[144] and relatively uncontroversial.[145] However, there remains, at least in theory, the issue of whether private individuals could petition the Standing Committee.[146] Of course the Basic Law makes no provision for this, but neither does it countenance a Hong Kong government petition.

Subsequent interpretations by the NPCSC (on its own initiative or upon request) will be dealt with in Chapter 4.

The power of *amendment* of the Basic Law is vested in the National People's Congress, as made clear in Article 159. Amendment cannot be a speedy process[147] since it involves a proposal to amend from the NPCSC, the State Council or the Hong Kong SAR delegation of the NPC. In the case of an application from the Hong Kong delegation, two-thirds of the local NPC delegates plus two-thirds of LegCo members *and* the Hong Kong SAR Chief Executive must support it. Further, before

---

141. This final point had already been clearly conceded by the CFA in its "clarification" of its earlier judgment at the request of the Hong Kong government.
142. Albert HY Chen, "'One Country, Two Systems' from a Legal Perspective" in YM Yeung (ed), *The First Decade: The Hong Kong SAR in Retrospective and Introspective Perspectives* (Chinese University Press 2007), Chapter 8.
143. Ibid 164–165.
144. Albert Chen had suggested the emergence of a "convention" that the NPCSC would not decide to interpret on its own initiative. Such a convention was short-lived given that the NPCSC *did* interpret on its own initiative in respect of electoral reform (the "second interpretation"): see A Chen, 'The Constitution and the Rule of Law' in *The First Tung Chee-hwa Administration: The First Five Years of the Hong Kong Special Administrative Region* (Chinese University Press 2002) 79.
145. The NPCSC interpreted in re electoral reform (at its own initiative as it is clearly entitled to do) and (at the Hong Kong government's request) as to the term of office of the Chief Executive which *arguably* involved a genuine legislative ambiguity. A more recent interpretation (as to "state immunity") was made at the request of the Court of Final Appeal. There has since been an "own-initiative interpretation" on "improper oath-taking". See also Chapter 4 at 4.4.
146. A fear expressed by then *SCMP* editor Jonathan Fenby (J Fenby, 'Verdict a Dangerous Shift for SAR' *South China Morning Post* [Hong Kong, 6 December 1999]) but so far not materialised.
147. Though this was questioned by Gittings, who quoted a "government spokesman" as saying "we could do it in a day if we liked" (D Gittings, 'Foot-Dragging Led to Abode Row' *South China Morning Post* [Hong Kong, 9 May 1999]).

any proposed amendment is considered by the NPC, the Basic Law Committee of the Hong Kong SAR must study the proposal and give its view. A further very important limitation on amendment is provided for in the brief final paragraph of Article 159:

> No amendment to this [Basic] Law shall contravene the established basic policies of the PRC regarding Hong Kong.[148]

It is via this stipulation that, for example, the guarantee that the "previous capitalist system" shall remain unchanged for 50 years is incapable of amendment. In practice this means that the capitalist system *may* be practised post-2047, unless it is formally abrogated, but that it *must* continue to be practised until that date.

The PRC has been extremely reluctant to amend the Basic Law even where "amendment" would be seen, by many, as a more appropriate action than "interpretation". The administrative difficulties may be one factor but there are also issues of "face" since the responsibility for the final draft of the Basic Law rested with the PRC which would only reluctantly admit that it had (implicitly) "got it wrong".[149] Other polities would be far more sanguine about accepting that unforeseen (post-legislation) social consequences had rendered a piece of legislation in need of reform.[150]

2.5 The "common law"

It has already been observed that under Article 8 of the Basic Law the common law (and rules of equity) previously in force in Hong Kong before 1997 will continue to apply unless amended by legislation. The Hong Kong Reunification Ordinance[151] reaffirms Article 8.[152]

However, while the common law is to be preserved, the determination of what is meant by the expression "common law" is not without difficulty, since it is capable of several meanings depending on the context in which it is used. Common law may mean, for example, "that which is not equity" or "that which is not statutory law" or "that which is not civil law". A further complication is the relationship, post-1997, between the common law of *England* and the common law of *Hong Kong*.

---

148. It has been argued that the NPCSC decision in respect of "universal suffrage" for the 2017 Chief Executive "election" and on the 2016 LegCo election is in conflict with Article 159 since, effectively, it amounts to an *amendment* of the Basic Law and exceeds Article 159 powers (see Surya Deva, 'Standing Committee Decision on Political Reform Is a Violation of the Basic Law' *South China Morning Post* [Hong Kong, 3 September 2014]).
149. Gittings (n 28) footnote 140.
150. As, for example, the influx of "mainland mothers" to Hong Kong to give birth and thereby confer right of abode on their children (see Chapter 4, 4.4).
151. Cap 2601.
152. And see *HKSAR v Ma Wai Kwan David and Others* [1997] 2 HKC 315.

2.5.1 Common law and equity

Common law may be contrasted with equity. In this context common law means the law originating from cases developed by the English common law (Royal) courts as compared with principles of equity developed originally by the Courts of Chancery.

2.5.2 Common law and legislation

Common law may be contrasted with legislation (statutes or Ordinances). In this context common law means law deriving from cases or custom as compared with law made by legislation. Confusingly, in this context equity would be viewed as part of the common law since it is not created by legislation.

2.5.3 Common law and civil law

Common law may also be contrasted with civil law. In this context what are being contrasted are two different types of legal *system*. Common law systems derive primarily from case judgments or "precedents" (amended or expanded by legislation where appropriate). Common law systems include England and Wales, Hong Kong, Malaysia, Singapore, Australia, New Zealand and the United States.[153]

In contrast, civil law legal systems are based on written documents such as constitutions, codes, statutes and regulations. Many continental European countries, Middle Eastern states and countries of South America have civil law legal systems in which, for example, the whole law of contract would be based on a single written code.[154]

To further complicate matters, the expression "civil law" also has a very different meaning when contrasted with criminal law. Civil law would then mean that branch of the law concerned with individual rights and the resolution of private disputes, normally involving compensation to the innocent claimant rather than (criminal law) punishment of the wrongdoer.

2.5.4 Which "common law" is to be preserved?

In the context of that which is to be preserved, post-1997, it is generally assumed that it is the "non-civil law" *system* to which the Basic Law refers; a system based primarily on principles derived from cases as opposed to a civil system based primarily on written codes. This view envisages a common law which may *evolve* over time, through case law (and local legislation) to meet the changing needs of a post-colonial polity.

---

153. With the huge amount of Federal and State "codifying" legislation, some have queried whether the USA remains a common law system.
154. The PRC system is generally regarded as a civil law one, though it retains features of "socialist" legal systems which may be viewed as distinctive (see Chapter 11).

Such a view of the common law is not, however, without difficulty. If, for example, "common law" merely refers to the pre-1997 "system" rather than the particular pre-1997 case law, what need was there in Article 8, Basic Law, to define the "laws previously in force in Hong Kong" (and to be maintained) as including common law, rules of equity, ordinances, subordinate legislation and customary law? It would surely have been enough to assert merely that the previous common law *system* was to be maintained. Including additional elements, such as equity and legislative rules, suggests that it is the *specific laws* themselves which are to be maintained. Such an approach would provide little scope for "evolution" since, although Article 8 makes the preservation of previous laws subject to conformity with the Basic Law and capable of amendment/abolition by local *legislation*, there is no explicit provision for change by local case law.

Such an interpretation of Article 8, though legalistically sound, cannot have been the intention of the Basic Law, since it would have resulted in the preservation of a common law largely "frozen in time" and rendered the Court of Final Appeal's "power of final adjudication", stipulated in Article 82 of the Basic Law, nugatory.

It is most sensible, therefore, to treat the "additional elements" (equity, Ordinances etc) in the Article 8 "laws to be maintained" definition as a "belt and braces" tautology. It is certainly the case that the Hong Kong Court of Final Appeal has no doubt as to its ability to develop the law through local case determinations, unencumbered by pre-1997 baggage.[155]

2.5.5 The common law system

All common law legal systems developed originally from the English legal system. Consequently, it is important to understand some of the history of the English legal system. The English legal system is a common law legal system comprising ancient customs, judicial precedents and enacted laws. It is so called because it was made common to the whole of England and Wales after the Norman Conquest of England in 1066.

As far back as the thirteenth century an action at common law was commenced by issuing a writ. The writ contained a specific complaint (and these covered limited types of complaint). The person making the complaint was called the plaintiff and the other party, the defendant.[156] Certain procedural rules had to be followed and if, for example, the plaintiff's complaint fell outside the strict letter of the writ selected, the action would fail. This system was used for actions in contract (and to a lesser extent tort) primarily for the purposes of claiming damages. While there have been considerable legal refinements regarding this process, it still forms the basis of a civil (non-criminal) action today.

---

155. See, eg, *A Solicitor v Law Society of Hong Kong* [2008] 2 HKC 1.
156. This terminology remains today in Hong Kong, though England has adopted the term "claimant" for the erstwhile plaintiff.

Sources of Hong Kong Law 103

The most important feature of common law systems is their adherence to a principle of "judicial precedent" by which the "decisions" of the higher courts in previous cases are followed in later cases. Crucially, it is not, strictly, the "decision" which is subsequently followed but the legal reason for that decision, the so-called "*ratio decidendi*". The study of any case-law subject (tort, contract, criminal law etc) requires an understanding of the terms "*ratio decidendi*" (the reason for the decision) and "obiter dicta" (things said by the way). These terms are discussed in detail in Chapter 5.

Unless analysis focuses on what has been preserved in terms of a *system*, rather than a collection of rules, difficulties may occur. This is particularly important in light of the fact, alluded to above, that Article 8 of the Basic Law provides for amendment of the "laws previously in force" by Hong Kong SAR *legislation* but *not* by the Hong Kong SAR courts! Given that the Basic Law provides that the Hong Kong SAR courts shall be the "judiciary of the region",[157] and that the Court of Final Appeal shall exercise the right of final adjudication,[158] it is unthinkable that the specific laws existing on 1 July 1997, should be "frozen" unless amended by legislation.

There are, potentially, two ways in which the apparently frozen rules could be "thawed". The first would involve the continuation of the "declaratory theory" of the common law; the second would maintain that the common law system or "process" (including the potential for reform through the courts) is what is retained rather than the individual rules themselves.

2.5.6 *Development via the declaratory theory*

The declaratory theory of common law is that judges do not *make* law; they merely find and apply it. When they state the law they are declaring not merely what it is but what it always has been. According to the theory, even when a court overrules a long-standing precedent, it is not making new law but stating what it always has been; the previous court merely failed to explain the law correctly. It naturally follows from this that, unlike statutory law, case judgments can operate retrospectively. Even where, for example, a company has made commercial decisions based on a House of Lords precedent, such company may be adversely affected by a subsequent overruling by a subsequent House of Lords since, in theory, the company has been acting on the basis of an incorrect assumption as to what the law always has been.

It is clear that the declaratory theory is a "fiction", even if the fiction has been useful in some respects. Most judges today accept that they do, on occasion, change the law or create new law. A cogent renunciation of the declaratory theory is provided in the following words of Lord Reid:

---

157. Article 80.
158. Article 82.

Those with a taste for fairy tales seem to have thought that in some Aladdin's cave there is hidden the Common Law in all its splendour and that on a judge's appointment there descends on him knowledge of the magic words Open Sesame. Bad decisions are given when the judge has muddled the password and the wrong door opens. But we do not believe in fairy tales any more.[159]

The myth of the declaratory theory was officially recognised by the House of Lords in *Kleinwort Benson Ltd v Lincoln City Council*[160] where the court overturned a 200 year old rule that money paid under a mistake of law was irrecoverable. The court expressed the view that courts do indeed change the law on occasion. Nonetheless, the retrospective nature of their judgments was maintained and indeed emphasised by the majority of the court.

While the approach of the House of Lords in *Kleinwort Benson* is clearly realistic, it does produce some difficulties. First, if an "overruling" judgment truly does create new law why should it be allowed to operate retrospectively, given that retrospectively-effective *legislation* is viewed as an anathema in the common law world?[161]

The denial of the declaratory theory also has particular implications for Hong Kong.

2.5.6.1 The declaratory theory and Hong Kong

Were the declaratory theory still to be recognised in Hong Kong it would have considerable theoretical, if not practical, significance. Since the law in force in Hong Kong, post-1997, should be, with some exceptions, that which existed on 30 June 1997, it could be argued "declaratory-wise", that any judicial overruling by the English courts, post-1997, would still be effective in Hong Kong since it would merely "declare" the pre-handover law, albeit retrospectively. While it is true, of course, that *Kleinwort Benson* abandoned the declaratory theory, it is also true that it is a post-1997 case. We are thus faced with a conundrum: if post-handover English judgments have no effect in Hong Kong, *Kleinwort Benson* need not be followed and a declaratory view may be taken, whereby English judgments would still be binding in Hong Kong as a reflection of the true state of the pre-handover law. *However*, if such a declaratory view is embraced, it should follow that *Kleinwort Benson*'s abolition of the declaratory view represents what the law has always been. Declaratory theorists, therefore, should accept that the declaratory view was never part of the English common law (and therefore cannot survive in Hong Kong post-1997).

---

159. Lord Reid, 'The Judge as Law Maker' 12 JSPTL 22 (1972).
160. [1998] 4 All ER 513.
161. Under the UK principle of Parliamentary sovereignty retroactive legislation is possible but unlikely; statutes are presumed not to have retrospective effect. In Hong Kong, retroactive imposition of criminal offences or sanctions is contrary to Article 12 of the Bill of Rights Ordinance (Cap 383).

A further problem is that the Basic Law states that the laws in force on 30 June 1997, will remain in force unless contrary to the Basic Law itself, or overturned by Hong Kong *legislation*. There is, therefore, no express provision for the Hong Kong *courts* to amend the pre-handover laws. This is certainly not the intention of the Basic Law, which establishes a Court of Final Appeal in Hong Kong and declares the right of final adjudication (subject to minor limitations). Nor is it in accord with the general sentiment of the Basic Law that Hong Kong courts *may*, but need not, refer to judgments of other common law jurisdictions. The problem remains, however, that the Basic Law does not, expressly, authorise the Hong Kong courts to amend the laws in force on 30 June 1997. Of course, via a liberal application of the declaratory principle, post-1997 Hong Kong court decisions could be held to reflect the state of Hong Kong law, retrospectively, as at the date of the handover. However, as indicated above, it appears a declaratory approach can no longer be justified. Moreover, even if an argument could be made for preserving the declaratory theory in Hong Kong, post-1997, we would again face the problem that post-1997 English judgments would hold sway since they would effectively *declare* (in theory) the English *pre-handover* law which, in general, was binding in Hong Kong up to 30 June 1997, and the continuation of which is guaranteed by the Basic Law.

In practice, however, we must recognise that no amount of theorising will affect the *political* reality that post-1997 English court judgments will have no binding effect in Hong Kong. A basic tenet of the Basic Law is that Hong Kong courts will generally have the right of final adjudication and that such right can be limited only by the medium of the PRC and *not* by judicial pronouncements in the former colonial power.[162] There would, indeed, be little point in establishing the Hong Kong Court of Final Appeal to replace the Privy Council as the final court of appeal for Hong Kong, nor for the abolition of the Application of English Law Ordinance,[163] were English courts still able to make pronouncements binding in Hong Kong.

2.5.7 *Development via the common law "system"*

While scope for development of a specifically Hong Kong common law cannot be provided, theoretically or politically, via the declaratory theory, such scope does exist by interpreting "the common law", which Article 8 of the Basic Law preserves, as a system or "process". By this interpretation it is not the thousands of individual pre-1997 common law rules which are preserved as much as the process by which such rules came into being. This process, of course, involves the evaluation of previous case precedents by subsequent courts and their possible development, amendment or abolition.

---

162. This view is emphatically underlined by the judgment of the Hong Kong Chief Justice and his colleagues in *A Solicitor v Law Society of Hong Kong* [2008] 2 HKC 1.
163. Cap 88.

While this "broad" interpretation of the term "common law" facilitates the development of a unique Hong Kong common law through the judgments of the Hong Kong courts, it does not fit well with the actual wording of Article 8 which states that the previous laws (including the common law) "shall be maintained", except for "any" that contravene the Basic Law or are amended by the legislature. The implication is that the focus is on individual rules rather than general principles. A highly logical (though politically unacceptable!) analysis of the effect of Article 8 is provided by Professor Peter Wesley-Smith,[164] who illustrates the theoretical difficulty of developing Hong Kong's common law in light of its wording.

The Content of the Common Law in Hong Kong
Peter Wesley-Smith

INTRODUCTION

This essay seeks to explain the content of the common law in the HKSAR. It considers two principal aspects: first whether the common law is frozen in its pre-handover condition...

...

It has been noted that Basic Law Article 8 imposes a new cut-off date on aspects of HKSAR law. The common law, for example, is the common law as it existed in Hong Kong on 30 June 1997. What is the effect of establishing a cut-off date for the common law?

It is arguable that:

1. the view that a cut-off date has no effect on reception of the common law relies upon the declaratory theory (that the common law is immutable, though perceived differently from time to time);

2. the declaratory theory, however, can no longer be accepted;

3. abandonment of the declaratory theory, and recognition that judges make the law, mean that a cut-off date is viable in relation to the common law: it imposes a snapshot or static version of law, solidified in its cut-off day condition;

4. the task of judges in the Hong Kong SAR, therefore, is to determine and apply the law as it stood at midnight on 30 June 1997;

5. no subsequent development of the common law can be permitted, for the only common law received into the SAR is the law previously in force.

All this seems logical enough, but its acceptance would be disastrous for the common law as a dynamic source of law for Hong Kong. The SAR courts have not in fact looked back to the cut-off date when dealing with the common law; this does not

---

164. Peter Wesley-Smith, 'The Content of the Common Law in Hong Kong' in R Wacks (ed), *The New Legal Order in Hong Kong* (Hong Kong University Press 1999) 26.

necessarily mean that the argument is flawed, but it is necessary to examine the steps in the argument to discover whether fallacy can be discovered.

The significance of cut-off dates for the common law has been previously debated in colonial or ex-colonial situations with particular reference to the authority of post-reception decisions of English courts, and the answer was usually determined by each writer's attitude towards the declaratory theory. That theory led Andrew Park, for example, to the view that cut-off dates do not affect the common law: where English law applies it is continually received, with the consequence that judges may be compelled to follow English decisions . . . Tony Allott, rejecting the declaratory theory, took the cut-off date seriously as providing a trunk upon which new growth could be grafted by the local courts. He thus claimed that judges were free to develop the law, and therefore, contrary to Park's assumption, to escape the binding effect of pre-reception decisions.

Cote, adjudicating upon the disagreement between Park and Allan, pointed out that "in practice the courts never apply a cut-off date to the common law"...

. . .

Allot asserted that the declaratory theory "cannot be sustained today by any serious student of the subject," and judges, usually extrajudicially, have often been of the same view. Lord Reid famously described the theory as a fairy tale. The House of Lords has recently emphatically agreed. In *Kleinwort Benson Ltd v Lincoln City Council* each of the five law lords was satisfied that judicial decisions were capable of *changing* common law.

. . .

If the 'realistic' account of the judicial function propounded by the House of Lords is accepted, it would seem that no Hong Kong judge can now develop the common law. The fiction that development does not involve change has been discarded. Therefore any creative act by a judge means amending the common law as it existed on 30 June 1997, and that is not permitted by the Basic Law. Thus, for example, the mistake of law rule must remain part of HKSAR law unless changed by the legislature, and the abrogation of that rule by the House of Lords' decision in *Kleinwort* cannot legitimately be adopted by the Hong Kong courts.

In whatever way that issue is settled, however, Hong Kong judges face an excruciating dilemma: if the common law must be restricted to its pre-handover manifestation it will in time become outdated and out of step with developments elsewhere in the common law world, yet the Basic Law appears to offer no alternative. Judges will have to adjust to the unfamiliar technique of identifying the content of the law at a particular date and suppressing the temptation to tamper with it. The nature of the common law will change and its value to the community will decline.

. . .

Such results are quite unacceptable and no judge is likely to allow them. But how can they be avoided? . . .

> ...
>
> A safer judicial technique, and one occasionally adopted when difficult issues arise, is simply to ignore the problem: carry on as always, modifying and developing the law as is deemed apt. This is the appropriate solution for practical men of affairs. The theoretical consequences can be left for idle academics to debate in common rooms, their abstract speculations unread by lawyers and judges.
>
> ...
>
> Conclusion
>
> Two stubborn facts remain: the common law in the HKSAR is the common law in force on 30 June 1997, and the pure declaratory theory has been unequivocally denounced by the House of Lords though the retroactive effect of judicial decisions was maintained ... Most commentators who attended a seminar in which the static common law thesis was presented strongly preferred the view that the common law is a fertile source of law, not a parcel of petrified precepts. The Basic Law, it was said, does not obviously assume the latter, particularly if the Chinese version of Article 8 of the Basic Law is considered ... Nevertheless, in the search for a solution my own preference is for the fiction or myth of the classical declaratory theory – a desperate recommendation perhaps, but one which is historically respectable and still has much judicial support.

Comment

Despite the academic appeal of Wesley Smith's "frozen in time" thesis, and the argument that Hong Kong judges cannot develop the common law in Hong Kong other than via a discredited declaratory theory, there is little doubt that, in practice, it is the broad "system" approach which courts have adopted in determining the common law which survives post-1997. Previous precedents have generally been followed, because this is the nature of a common law system, but there has been no doubt that, for example, the Court of Final Appeal has the power to amend the existing case law where appropriate. Indeed, the Court of Final Appeal has declared that any restriction on its jurisdiction in Hong Kong is invalid unless specifically provided for in the Basic Law. In A Solicitor v Law Society of Hong Kong and Secretary of Justice,[165] the court held that section 13 of the Legal Practitioners Ordinance (LPO),[166] which stated that the decision of the Court of Appeal was final when hearing an appeal from the Solicitors' Disciplinary Tribunal, was unconstitutional. At first sight, this appears to contradict the principle that legislation takes precedence over case law[167] but the point here was that section 13 of the LPO, in denying the right of final adjudication to the Court of Final Appeal, was found to

---

165. (2003) 6 HKCFAR 570.
166. Cap 159.
167. See Chapter 5.

be contrary to the Basic Law, with which all Hong Kong legislation is required to conform.[168]

Wesley-Smith's support for the declaratory theory, as the only means to allow Hong Kong judges to develop the law, runs up against the unacceptable "political" outcome of post-1997 pronouncements from the English House of Lords representing what the common law was *pre-1997 and, as such, which is to be maintained post-1997. Not only would this be politically unacceptable but it would also run counter to the express views of the Court of Final Appeal as to the status of post-1997 English decisions.*[169]

Of course so much of this debate would have been rendered nugatory by a simple addition to Article 8 of the Basic Law providing for judicial as well as legislative amendment to the laws previously in force.

As yet there are few examples of major departures from the principles of common law that existed pre-1997, but it is envisaged that Hong Kong will gradually develop more localised versions of some of these principles. Local legislation will amend some English-based principles; the Court of Final Appeal will overturn some previously binding English precedents; and English law will develop via cases which may not be followed in Hong Kong. This and increased reference to common law jurisdictions other than the UK will, over time, produce a Hong Kong common law increasingly divergent from that of England.

2.6 Equity as a source of law

The "rules of equity" are specifically listed in Article 8 of the Basic Law as part of the "laws previously in force" and to be maintained post-1997. An understanding of equity and its current significance requires a brief consideration of its historical origins and subsequent development.

The early English common law, administered in the (Royal) common law courts was extremely restrictive and inflexible. Common law courts insisted on the correct "form" of action. A plaintiff must choose the appropriate form of action, the proper "writ", issued in Chancery, or his action would fail. There were other courts or forums administering rules for a particular trade or locality but they were not common to the whole kingdom.

Procedure in the common law courts, which gradually absorbed most of the local or special courts, was complex and slow and the available remedy was usually monetary compensation ("damages"). The complexity, slowness and expense of common law actions meant that many complainants had no effective remedy. The greatest limitation was the rigidity of the writ system. To take a simple example: under the earliest writ procedures a creditor might seek to enforce a debt; however,

---
168. Article 82.
169. See *A Solicitor v Law Society of Hong Kong* [2008] HKC 1.

unless the debt involved was "liquidated" (a fixed amount) a "writ of debt" could not be issued. Moreover, the writ would not extend to a promise to do something followed by non-performance.

Over time, dissatisfaction with the inflexible writ system produced gradual change. The King, unable to deal with all issues personally, delegated the responsibility for reform to his Lord Chancellor. The Lord Chancellor in turn established his own court: the Court of Chancery. Initially one of the Chancellor's chief duties was to supervise the issue of all writs, and eventually this task passed to the Chancery courts and not the common law courts. Over time, these new courts evolved from mere issuers of writs for the royal courts to a forum for providing different forms of remedy for people seeking solutions to their disputes.

The type of justice achieved by these courts became known as equity. Equity, unlike common law, initially had no binding rules and each Chancellor was able to give judgment in an issue in a way that accorded with his own sense of justice. Equity, administered in the Chancellor's courts, became known as a "court of conscience", an expression still used today in the determination of equitable claims. The guiding principle of equity was that there should be "no wrong without a remedy" and a key feature was that equitable remedies were "discretionary", depending on the needs of justice in a particular case.

The most significant of the "creations" of equity was the concept of the *trust*. Indeed, many "equity" or "equity and trusts" courses in the common law world are little more than the study of trusts.

While originally a "supplement" to the common law, "filling in the gaps" and providing remedies, such as specific performance and injunction, unavailable in the common law courts, equity gradually developed, over several hundred years, into what was almost a separate system of law. It established procedures more rigid and time-consuming than those of the common law it had set out to improve[170] and followed its previous precedents every bit as inflexibly as the common law courts.

2.6.1 *The fusion of common law and equity*

Over time equity had become, as indicated, almost an entire system in itself, rather than merely a means of mitigating the rigidity of the common law. Equity had its own courts, rules, procedures and precedents and competed with the common law courts for "business". The word "business" is appropriate since litigants paid a high price for the courts to hear their pleas.

Both common law and equitable principles were adopted in various pieces of legislation. For example, common law rules appear in the English Sale of Goods Act 1979, and equitable principles are embodied in the Trustee Act 1925. The Hong

---

170. Charles Dickens, in *Bleak House*, described a (fictitious) interminable Chancery case, *Jarndyce v Jarndyce*. The lengthy procedures of equity came to be described as "Bleak House Chancery".

Kong equivalents of these two Acts are the Sale of Goods Ordinance[171] and the Trustee Ordinance.[172]

Rivalry between the courts, and the different remedies available in each, was a particular problem for litigants, since not only must they endure the lengthy procedures of one set of courts but they might have, further, to endure the cost and delay of repeat litigation on the same issue in another set of courts! A simple example is provided by the contract case of *Wood v Scarth*.[173] In this case, the defendant offered to let a public house to the plaintiff for £63 per year. The plaintiff accepted after speaking to the defendant's clerk. The defendant intended that an advance payment of £500 should be made but the clerk did not mention this. The defendant then refused to transfer the property on the basis of the "mistake" and the plaintiff sued. His action for specific performance failed in the courts of equity; equitable remedies are discretionary and faced with an obvious mistake, the courts would not exercise their discretion in favour of the plaintiff. However, the mistake was clearly not one which the common law would recognise, since the formal terms of the contract were clear and had made no reference to the additional payment. The plaintiff's subsequent action for damages in the common law courts therefore succeeded. Needless to say the dual litigation involved considerable delay and expense.

It can be seen that the "dual courts" situation which had developed was extremely unsatisfactory and the position was largely resolved by the landmark legislation of the Judicature Acts 1873–1875.

The purpose of the legislation was to merge or "fuse" the two separate systems. This fusion affected both the separate court structures and the rules adopted in each. As a result, a single, unified court system was formed. At its apex was to be the new Court of Appeal, formed from the appellate courts of equity and common law. Below this, the High Court contained, initially, five (later three) divisions; one of them Chancery and the rest based on previous common law courts.

It is a matter of historical note, significant for Hong Kong, that the initial legislative intention was to abolish the judicial function of the House of Lords. This move was resisted by those who felt that the removal of the "judicial" function of the House of Lords might be the "thin end of the wedge" and a precursor to an attack on the "legislative" function of that body. In the event, the judicial function of the House of Lords[174] was retained.[175]

Crucially, not only were the courts merged by the legislation; so were their practices. All courts were now permitted to administer both common law remedies

---

171. Cap 26.
172. Cap 29.
173. (1855) 8 E & B 815; (1858) 1 F & F 293.
174. By evolved convention, though not law, only "Law Lords" and not lay peers dealt with judicial matters.
175. The (Judicial Committee of the) House of Lords remained extant as the final appellate court in Britain until its abolition (and replacement by Britain's Supreme Court) in 2009.

(principally damages) and equitable ones, such as specific performance and injunction.[176] On the (rare) occasion where a rule of the common law was found to be in conflict with a rule of equity, the latter was to prevail.

As a consequence of the legislation, the importance of equity has been diminished but certainly not entirely removed.

2.6.2 The significance of equity today

While both common law and equitable remedies are available in all English (and Hong Kong) courts today, the distinct nature of equity remains of some significance, as recognised by its separate, specific preservation under Article 8 of the Basic Law.

The most important feature of equity today, arising from its historical development as a court of fairness, is that equitable remedies remain *discretionary*, the court deciding whether or not circumstances are appropriate for the award of the remedy sought. This contrasts with the common law remedy of damages which involves an issue of "right". So, for example, if the defendant's activities constitute the tort of "nuisance", the plaintiff is entitled "as of right" to an award of damages. It is, on the other hand, a matter of the court's discretion whether or not to grant an injunction (an order to cease the nuisance) to the plaintiff.[177] Similarly, where the defendant is guilty of a breach of contract, the plaintiff is automatically entitled to an award of damages, in compensation for the breach, but will succeed in an action for "specific performance" (compelling performance) only at the discretion of the court.[178]

The exercise of discretion, again, owes much to equity's historical background. Since equity is a "court of conscience" the exercise is guided by notions of fairness. For example, the previous behaviour of the plaintiff will be significant, and the court will apply the maxim "he who comes to equity must come with clean hands". Thus, if the claimant has acted improperly, albeit lawfully, he may be denied equitable relief. Similarly, applying principles of fairness, "he who seeks equity must do equity" means that in return for the award of an equitable remedy, the court may impose conditions on the claimant to ensure fairness to the other party.

Also deriving from equity's historical development is the continuing principle that equity exists to supplement defects in the common law. Thus, where the common law remedy of damages is adequate, equity will not intervene. Simple breaches of contract or tortious negligence actions can invariably be compensated adequately by an award of damages. Only in special circumstances will monetary compensation be inadequate. The breach of a promise to convey an interest in land may attract the remedy of specific performance, given the unique nature of land, and a continuing nuisance may well be more suitably dealt with by an injunction than damages.

---

176. A typical action today might well seek specific performance or damages "in the alternative".
177. See, eg, *Miller v Jackson* [1977] QB 966.
178. See, eg, *Cohen v Roche* [1927] 1 KB 169.

Finally, it goes almost without saying that the *trust*, equity's major creation, remains of huge significance in all common law systems, including Hong Kong's.

2.7 Customary law

Article 8 of the Basic Law preserves "customary law" as a specific category of the laws "previously in force in Hong Kong", which are to be maintained. The difficulty here is to determine what is meant by "customary law" in this context. The problem is exacerbated by the inconsistent declarations made as to the status of Chinese customary law made after the annexation of Hong Kong by Britain in the 1840s.[179] The first statement of significance was that of Captain Elliot, then Hong Kong plenipotentiary, in January 1841.[180] Elliot proclaimed that:

> pending Her Majesty's further pleasure, the natives of the island of Hong Kong, and all natives of China thereto resorting, shall be governed according to the laws and customs of China, every description of torture excepted.[181]

The legality of Elliot's proclamation(s) is doubtful. First, his authority is questionable; not only was he hastily recalled from Hong Kong by an irate Lord Palmerston,[182] the British Foreign Secretary, who believed Elliot to have been too conciliatory to the Chinese, but the Treaty of Nanking, which formally ceded Hong Kong to Britain, was not ratified until 1843.

Moreover, the "dual" system implemented by Elliot, whereby Chinese were to be subject to a different set of laws from those affecting the European residents of Hong Kong, was fundamentally altered by various pieces of Hong Kong legislation, starting with the Supreme Court Ordinance 1844, which determined that English law would operate in Hong Kong unless "inapplicable" to local circumstances or locally amended. Despite this, Elliot's words have been regularly cited in support of asserted "rights". Miners[183] writes of Elliot's proclamation(s):

> This declaration was promptly disavowed by the British Foreign Secretary, Lord Palmerston, on the grounds that Hong Kong had not yet been formally ceded to Britain. Nevertheless it has been cited by Hong Kong's judges in a number of leading cases as evidence of the intention of the Crown to establish two different systems of law for the colony from its beginning, one for the Chinese and one for the British and other foreigners, even before a Legislative Council was set up and the necessary ordinances passed.[184]

---

179. For fuller discussion, see Chapter 1.
180. The proclamation was issued on 29 January 1841 but dated 2 February 1841.
181. A very similar proclamation, signed by Elliot and Bremer, was dated 1 February 1841.
182. Elliot had, for example, supported Chinese attempts to combat the opium trade stating *inter alia* that it was adversely affecting "legitimate trade" (see Chapter 1).
183. Norman Miners, *The Government and Politics of Hong Kong* (5th edn, Oxford University Press 1991).
184. Ibid 61. For case examples, see Chapter 1.

In theory, at least, the legislative changes represented a significant shift; from declaring that Hong Kong Chinese would not be subject to English law to presuming that they *would be*, "unless". This presumption was continued in subsequent legislation, culminating in the Application of English Law Ordinance (AELO),[185] which stated that:

> the common law and rules of equity shall be in force in Hong Kong, so far as they may be applicable to the circumstances of Hong Kong or its inhabitants and subject to such modifications thereto as such circumstances may require.[186]

In practice the revised principles were difficult to apply. How would a judge know whether the (English) common law was, or was not, "applicable"? In the absence of legislation there could be great difficulties in establishing whether English law was "applicable" and the consequence if not. The Secretary of State had previously alluded to the difficulty, writing that:

> The criterion of applicability to local circumstances is, I apprehend, the only test by which to solve the enquiry, whether any given rule of English Law is, or is not, in force in a British colony. But it is manifestly a most vague and uncertain criterion. The effect of it is to transfer to the Judge a large part of the duties of the Legislature. He must in each successive case determine how far local circumstances admit, or prevent, the application of the law of England.[187]

A rare, but clear, example of the "non-applicability" principle is to be found in *Yau Yeong Wood and Another v The Standard Oil Co of New York*[188] where the Hong Kong Chief Justice stated:

> I think it cannot fail to have struck even the learned Counsel who relied on these (English) cases how very inapplicable many of them seemed to be on the face of them to Chinese contractors. . . .English law is only in force here under the Charter in so far as it may be applicable, and when I come to a series of decisions, the key-note to which is the custom or practice of a certain class of people who enter into contracts in England, I hesitate to apply them as of necessity to the people in Hong Kong.[189]

As Wesley-Smith[190] has pointed out, the approach of the Hong Kong courts has varied:

> Chinese customary law has been held to govern various situations where English rules were considered unsuitable, mostly in the realms of family law or New

---

185. Cap 88.
186. Section 3(1).
187. Cited in P Wesley-Smith, *The Sources of Hong Kong Law* (Hong Kong University Press 1994) 89.
188. [1907] HKLR 55. For a more recent discussion of non-applicability, see *China Field Ltd v Appeal Tribunal (Buildings)* (2009) 12 HKCFAR 342.
189. Ibid 59.
190. P Wesley-Smith, *An Introduction to the Hong Kong Legal System* (1st edn, Oxford University Press 1987).

Territories land law,[191] and modifications ranging from the trivial to the drastic have occasionally been made to the applicable common law.[192]

Nevertheless, the general approach of the courts, pre-1997, was to apply English rules unless they caused "*injustice or oppression*"; the test applied in *Tse Moon-sak v Tse Hung & Others (in re Tse Lai-chiu, deceased)*.[193] In this case the Full Court in chambers had to determine the validity of a will, made, in 1958, by a deceased Chinese, which lacked testamentary power under English law. Hogan CJ stated:

> The primary question for the court is whether the deceased, who was Chinese by race and domiciled in Hong Kong, was able by this will to exercise a testamentary capacity in accordance with English law. If that question were to be answered in the negative, a further question would arise as to whether the law applicable to the testator's will would be Chinese law as it stood when Hong Kong was ceded or some different or later form of Chinese law and custom.[194]
>
> [Having concluded an exhaustive review of (successive) relevant legislation including reference to the two "Elliot Proclamations", Hogan CJ continued:] . . .
>
> It was said of these [Elliot] proclamations . . . that they recognize a 'dual prospective system of law in the colony; so far as British subjects and foreigners were concerned, security and protection according to the principles and practice of the British law were extended to them; whilst in the case of the Chinese 'the laws and customs of China' were reserved in their favour'.
>
> No counsel before us has sought to question the general assumption in Hong Kong that where a Chinese domiciled in Hong Kong dies intestate his property will devolve not in accordance with English law . . . but in accordance with what I will briefly call 'Chinese law'.[195]
>
> [However] . . . I cannot think that in the circumstances prevailing in 1960, and indeed for many years before, it could be seriously contended that to permit the deceased to exercise the testamentary capacity in regard to his property acquired in Hong Kong, which he would have under English law, could be classified as *unjust or oppressive*.[196] [emphasis added]

Having determined that English rules were "inapplicable" (and that there was no relevant "local" (Hong Kong) legislation) the courts would still have the problem of finding and applying the *relevant* (Chinese) customary rules. This was no easy task since, as Chen Lei[197] has said:

---

191. New Territories landholding has been dealt with elsewhere, given the Basic Law's requirement of the protection of the "lawful traditional rights and interests of the indigenous inhabitants of the 'New Territories'": Article 40, Basic Law.
192. Wesley-Smith (n 186) 43.
193. [1969] HKLR 159. Also cited as *re Tse Lai-chiu Deceased*. For further discussion, see Chapter 1, 4–5.
194. [1969] HKLR 159 at 164.
195. Ibid at 166.
196. Ibid at 193.
197. L Chen, 'Contextualising Legal Transplant: China and Hong Kong', op cit, 51.

most of the British expatriate judges were poorly informed on Chinese culture before their arrival in Hong Kong. There were difficulties in translating Chinese technical terms into juristic English. Moreover, judges were inclined to resort to English legal meaning and cultural values when interpreting law and custom.[198]

The general approach was that "Chinese law and custom" applied; namely the Codes of the Qing (or Ch'ing) dynasty and the customary rules accompanying the Codes, which prevailed on 5 April 1843.[199] This would often involve the calling of expert witnesses to determine same. One difficulty, as Wesley-Smith[200] points out, is the dividing line between custom and customary law, since it is only the latter which is preserved under Article 8 of the Basic Law. He cites the example of feng shui, which he argues, has "normative power" in the New Territories but which was not recognised by the courts.[201]

A further anomaly, noted by Wesley-Smith,[202] is that the "Codes" and "accompanying customary rules" are sometimes in conflict, though in practice this seems to have been of little significance.

Moreover, while English law might be inapplicable (such that Qing customary law applied) on the grounds of "hardship or oppression" such hardship or oppression would *not*, it appears, be judged as at 1843 but at any appropriate later date.[203] Should such flexibility also apply to the determination of the date at which to identify Chinese custom, or must the 1843 date be rigidly applied? The issue was addressed in *Wong Kam Ying and Another v The Estate of Man Hung Pun*,[204] a case concerning "dependent" claims (by illegitimate children) for damages[205] following a fatal accident. Huggins J stated:

> First, then, we must seek out the source of the customary law which is applicable. I have already referred briefly to the old s 5 of the Supreme Court Ordinance. In *Ho Tsz-Tsun v Ho Au-shi*[206] the Full Court held that the "applicability" (or not) of the English law must be considered in relation to the local circumstances of the Colony and its inhabitants on 5th April, 1843 . . .
>
> . . . one of the attributes of the English common law is that it does not change although it may develop to meet new circumstances.[207] That remark appears to be equally applicable to the Chinese customary law . . .

---

198. L Chen, op cit, 208.
199. The date of the "reception of English law" by Hong Kong's first legislature.
200. Note 186, 51.
201. P Wesley-Smith, *The Sources of Hong Kong Law* (op cit), 211.
202. Ibid 214–215.
203. Hogan CJ, for example, in *Tse Moon-sak*, seems to have focused on the date of the deceased's death.
204. [1967] HKLR 201.
205. One interesting "aside" in this 1967 case was reference to the recent "outcry in Hong Kong at the cost to parents of school books" (at 223). It seems some things never change!
206. (1915) 10 HKLR 69, 76.
207. An implicit reference to the "declaratory theory" of the common law; see 2.5 supra.

> ... one merely looks to 1843 to ascertain the applicability of the customary law and the basic rules as they then existed and thereafter one applies those rules subject to such developments as may have taken place since that date.[208]

Huggins J's statement draws attention to the considerable difficulty that could arise where a litigant claims that a traditional Chinese customary law had been amended "in China" such that the Codes and accompanying customary rules would be obsolete. In *re the Estate of Ng Shum (No 2)*[209] the Hong Kong High Court upheld the Tsing Imperial Code precluding "vice *tin fong*" wives despite finding that such were "probably" recognised under customary law.

In practice, the difficulty here had normally been resolved by the introduction of relevant local legislation. This is particularly true in the case of family law where, at one time, "customary" laws affected such issues as marriage, divorce and succession to property. In these areas common law was originally felt to be inappropriate for local circumstances. As an example, the customary practice of concubinage, though contrary to common law, was recognised as part of Hong Kong law. Nevertheless, reforming local legislation has eliminated most of the laws covering such customary practices.

Thus, although undeniably a source of Hong Kong law, Chinese law and custom is today of limited application, since local legislation and the rules of common law and equity accommodate most situations. Thus, in *Man Leung v Man Yuet Kwai*,[210] Lam J, in the Court of First Instance, stated that Chinese law and custom is:

> Qing law and custom in force in this part of China in 1843 as varied by local custom.[211]

The impact of the Codes (and accompanying customary rules) is still evident in relation to land-holding in the New Territories, however, and legislative rules, including those in the Basic Law itself, have assisted in determining the nature and status of such customary rules. Article 40 of the Basic Law, for example, states that:

> The lawful traditional rights and interests of the indigenous inhabitants of the 'New Territories' shall be protected by the Hong Kong Special Administrative Region.[212]

Moreover, under Article 122:

> In the case of old schedule lots, village lots, small houses and similar rural holdings, where the property was on 30 June 1984 held by, or, in the case of small houses granted after that date, where the property is granted to, a lessee descended through

---

208. [1967] HKLR 201 at 210–211.
209. [1990] HKLR 67; and see S Yigong, 'The Application of Chinese Law & Custom in Hong Kong' (1999) 29 HKLJ 267.
210. [2013] 2 HKLRD 1122.
211. Ibid 1152.
212. The nature and effect of the traditional rights and interests referred to in Article 40 is dealt with more fully in 2.4.1.

the male line from a person who was in 1898 a resident of an established village in Hong Kong, the previous rent shall remain unchanged so long as the property is held by that lessee or by one of his lawful successors in the male line.

In conclusion we may, in describing the significance of (Chinese) customary law in Hong Kong today, cite the words of Wesley-Smith[213] who writes:

> it is clear that Chinese customary law is, and should be, of little importance to modern Hong Kong. It is largely the law of a peasant community imbued with the culture of a bygone era. Obviously unsuited to urban life, it retains some relevance to parts of the New Territories, but is rapidly declining . . . Chinese customary law remains as part of Hong Kong law, however, and will continue to do so for years to come.[214]

2.8 Non-binding "sources"

In addition to those binding sources of Hong Kong law identified, expressly or implicitly, in the Basic Law, mention should also be made of so-called "persuasive" and "secondary" sources which, while not binding on the Hong Kong courts, are frequently taken into account in the courts' considerations. The most significant are judgments from other common law jurisdictions and various academic sources.

2.8.1 Judgments from other common law jurisdictions

The Basic Law states that Hong Kong courts may refer to ("persuasive") precedents of other common law jurisdictions,[215] though these will not, of course, be binding. We might expect that, given this Basic Law provision, there would be an increase in the number of references to Australian, Canadian and other common law cases, at the expense of English precedents. Although the continuation of the common law post-1997 is enshrined in the Basic Law there was already some slight indication of Hong Kong developing a common law "flavour" of its own, even before 1997. In particular there was a willingness amongst some judges to consider non-English common law decisions; a practice now specifically provided for in the Basic Law.[216] This was, in part, the result of the influence of non-English "overseas" personnel practising in Hong Kong in the legal professions and on the bench.

This divergence from the English common law will inevitably increase in the post-1997 era. Indeed, at first sight it might be thought that such a process would be speedy, given that the new Hong Kong Court of Final Appeal (Hong Kong's highest court) which deals with far more cases than its predecessor, the Privy Council, is dominated by Hong Kong judges. The Basic Law provides that the Court of Final

---

213. Note 186.
214. Ibid 53.
215. Article 84.
216. Article 84.

Appeal may appoint "judges" from other common law jurisdictions to sit as judges of the court where appropriate. It has, however, been decided "extra-judicially" that only one such judge may be appointed at any time. The consequence is that four of the five judges normally sitting will be Hong Kong judges. In practice, however, such judges are predominantly English-trained and steeped in the ways of the English common law, such that increasing divergence is likely to be a slow process.[217]

Ironically, however, the English courts themselves are moving away from the traditions of the common law as a result of the increasing influence of the rules of what was previously known as the European Economic Community and is now called the "European Union". This influence has extended to the English law of contract, especially in areas involving consumer protection. Many European Union rules are directly applicable in England and others have been adopted via domestic legislation. The Unfair Terms in Consumer Contracts Regulations 1994 (and 1999),[218] for example, are a response to a European Union Directive. Having no legal requirement to adopt European legislation, Hong Kong will doubtless eschew such rules, which largely overlap with existing legislation[219] and serve merely to introduce confusion.[220]

English judges, too, are becoming increasingly influenced by "European" considerations. Lord Steyn in the now-abolished House of Lords, for example, was particularly well-versed in the European civil-law tradition and such influences are likely to grow as the English legal professions insist on coverage of European Community law within legal training and as law schools embrace the "European dimension" as a fertile growth area for research.

None of this "Europeanisation" is likely to impact on Hong Kong, since it has nothing to do with the Hong Kong experience, nor with the common law. Indeed, while English commercial rules and factual scenarios become increasingly intertwined with those of Europe (even post-Brexit), the standard Hong Kong experience is likely to revolve around China and the "joint venture" agreement. While the development of the common law is said to depend upon principles rather than factual scenarios, the facts of cases inevitably affect the principles to be applied. This, again, will assist Hong Kong in gradually developing a "common law" of its own. In practice, however, English precedents continue to form the most significant body of law to which Hong Kong judges refer.[221]

---

217. See 2.04.
218. Abolished by the Consumer Rights Act 2015.
219. Most of the Regulations deal with areas already covered by the Unfair Contract Terms Act 1977, and its Hong Kong equivalent, the Control of Exemption Clauses Ordinance (Cap 71).
220. Such overlap and resulting confusion has, indeed, been recognised in England and Wales where consolidating legislation has been introduced in the form of the Consumer Rights Act 2015.
221. See 2.8.3 below.

2.8.2 Academic (secondary) sources

The English common law tradition has always been to treat secondary sources, such as learned textbooks or practitioners' guides with great caution. Indeed, it used to be said that a text could never constitute a "source" until its author was dead![222] Hong Kong courts, at least at the lower level, pay much greater heed to secondary sources. It is not uncommon to find a judgment where no cases appear to have been raised in argument or considered by the judge, and where the sole source has been a practitioner's text. A casual reader might believe, for example, "Chitty on Contract" to be a binding Court of Final Appeal contract case! There is considerable danger in this approach, since judicial precedents may be overruled by higher courts or "distinguished" by lower courts which perceive them as unattractive or out of date. Those dissatisfied with the law as reflected in a precedent may appeal in hopes of it being overturned by a higher court; the opinion of a text book writer, which *is* legally only an opinion, is difficult to appeal against. Given the wealth of judicial authorities from the common law world which the Hong Kong courts are free to consider, it is to be hoped that greater use will be made of primary sources in future.

2.8.3 The continuing influence of English law in practice

While the principle that Hong Kong courts are not bound by post-1997 judgments of the English courts is established by the Basic Law, albeit not unproblematically, in practice the views of the English courts still hold great sway in Hong Kong. This is particularly true in the "common law" subjects of contract and tort where most rules remain grounded in case law rather than statute, and where the pre-handover Hong Kong law showed only minor areas of divergence from that of England. Indeed, were an alien, unfamiliar with Hong Kong's post-1997 legal and constitutional development, to read a typical post-1997 Hong Kong case, he would be hard-pressed to appreciate that things had, supposedly, changed!

Quite simply, Hong Kong judges are referred to, and apply, post-1997 English precedents as a matter of course and the issue of whether such precedents *need* to be followed is rarely raised. A typical example can be seen in *Bank of China (Hong Kong) Ltd v Wong King Sing & Others*,[223] heard in the Court of First Instance before Recorder Geoffrey Ma SC (as he then was).[224] The case involves the area of undue influence and the situation in which a bank, or other lender, should be put on notice as to the possible undue influence of a husband over his wife. The leading case in England is *Royal Bank of Scotland v Etridge (No 2)*[225] which goes on to explain the steps which a bank should take when placed "on notice", including whether to

---

222. On the basis that the author might later change his mind.
223. [2002] 1 HKC 83.
224. Having seen office as Chief Judge of the Hong Kong High Court, Ma was subsequently confirmed as Chief Justice of Hong Kong, succeeding Andrew Li.
225. [2001] 4 All ER 449 and see 11.04.

advise the wife to take independent advice in a private meeting in the absence of her spouse. In the Hong Kong case, Recorder Ma showed exemplary understanding of the complex, and then recent, *Etridge* case, produced an excellent summary thereof, and applied its principles precisely to the case at hand. Nowhere, however, is there any reference to the *status* of *Etridge*, a post-1997 decision; that the decision should be followed is viewed as unproblematic.

What is more, in the secondary sources referred to, text and practitioner books are predominantly English. Where primary and secondary sources are not from England they are generally from Hong Kong relating to areas covered by statutory rules specific to Hong Kong. There is a marked shortage of precedents cited from other common law jurisdictions, despite the apparent aim of the Basic Law to reduce the influence of English precedents vis a vis those of other common law jurisdictions.[226] The pattern has not changed significantly in later years, nor is the ratio noticeably different in respect of those post-1997 cases referred to.[227]

Of course, given that pre-1997 English precedents are usually binding in Hong Kong unless overruled, emphasis on such precedents is unsurprising. What *does* merit consideration is the continued emphasis (over-emphasis?) on *post*-1997 English precedents. One explanation is a "realist" one;[228] Hong Kong's judiciary remains dominated by English or English-trained judges, especially at the senior level.[229] Cases cited to the courts by counsel will still reflect the current background of the Hong Kong bar whose senior members reflect a similar demography. Even junior members of the bar will have been taught, primarily at the University of Hong Kong, in an institution heavily influenced by English teachers and, more important, by English jurisprudence.[230] The current position was predicted, pre-1997, by Wesley-Smith[231] for reasons similar to the above. He added, however, that:

> Legal theory does not require retention of the 'imperial link'. The common law is a historic body of legal principles whose application in particular cases can be misguided and wrong . . . Responsibly and creatively determined, the law of and for Hong Kong can only be strengthened by adoption of a liberal attitude towards the common law of England.[232]

---

226. See Article 84.
227. A noteworthy exception is provided by the case of *A Solicitor v Law Society of Hong Kong* [2008] 2 HKC 1, a case involving the precedent position of Hong Kong's Court of Appeal, in which Chief Justice Li favoured an approach found in Canada and other common law jurisdictions rather than the more restrictive English approach.
228. Ie, put simply, that judicial backgrounds and attitudes affect outcomes (see Chapter 6).
229. See Chapter 6.
230. Reading lists for many "core" legal subjects at the University of Hong Kong remain dominated by English texts.
231. 'The Common Law of England in the SAR' in R Wacks (ed), *Hong Kong, China and 1997: Essays in Legal Theory* (Hong Kong University Press 1993).
232. Ibid 39–40.

2.9 Implied sources

Brief mention may also be made to what Zhou-Wei[233] describes as "implied sources". These are sources not mentioned in Articles 8 and 18 but which "will surely play important roles in the legal system of the HKSAR." Zhou-Wei's list includes the PRC Constitution, Standing Committee Interpretations of the Basic Law, Basic Law interpretations by the Hong Kong courts, Hong Kong subordinate legislation, HKSAR court decisions and, finally, precedents from other common law jurisdictions.

2.10 Hong Kong law as a common law "source"

Thus far we have looked at Hong Kong law as a "recipient" of various sources, with the Hong Kong courts acting as a conduit, leading these sources to where they must be taken up and utilised. Within this framework "local" Hong Kong jurisprudence is regarded as a "source" only domestically. However, it is now being recognised that Hong Kong has, particularly in recent times, begun to develop its own jurisprudence, recognised as a persuasive source of common law elsewhere. Recognition has been slow and, in the case of some academics, grudging but there has been a steady development. There are two main reasons for this. First, the increasing use of the internet has made judges far less insular and there is no longer any reason why, for example, an English court, faced with a novel, undecided point, should not turn to Hong Kong and elsewhere for *persuasive* guidance. Hong Kong has, for example, determined the status of contractual acceptances made by fax before the issue had been adjudicated in the English courts.[234]

The second reason for Hong Kong's expanding influence relates to *personnel*. In the vast majority (over 90%) of Hong Kong Court of Final Appeal contested cases, a Non-Permanent Judge (NPJ) from overseas has been included on the bench. Such NPJs have normally been from either England or Australia. It is to be expected that such a judge, when sitting "at home", would state: "As I said in XYZ in the Hong Kong Court of Final Appeal". Moreover, it would be unusual for the words of such a senior judge not to be accorded serious persuasive weight in his own jurisdiction.

Significant research on Hong Kong as a common law source "elsewhere" has been conducted by Hong Kong barrister and academic, P. Y. Lo. Lo first outlined the theme at a conference on the Court of Final Appeal at the University of Hong Kong[235] and has developed it further as part of the resulting textbook.[236] Lo's analysis considers both the *quantitative* and *qualitative* significance of Hong Kong judgments. Quantitatively, Lo shows that Hong Kong judgments have been cited in the

---
233. Note 50.
234. See *Susanto-Wing Sun Co Ltd v Yung Chi Hardware Machinery Co Ltd* [1989] 2 HKC 504.
235. 'Hong Kong's Court of Final Appeal: The Andrew Li Court 1997–2010' (Conference, The University of Hong Kong, 5–6 March 2010).
236. SNM Young and Y Ghai (eds), *Hong Kong's Court of Final Appeal* (Cambridge University Press 2013).

Judicial Committee of the Privy Council (unsurprisingly); the English House of Lords and Court of Appeal; the United Kingdom Supreme Court; the Scottish Court of Sessions and major courts in Australia (Federal and State), Canada, New Zealand, Malaysia, Singapore, South Africa, the Caribbean, Fiji and Tonga. In addition, there have been numerous references in overseas practitioners' texts, Law Commission reports and journal articles.

Qualitatively, Lo shows that a few cases have been seminal; in particular, the defamation case of *Cheng & Another v Tse Wai Chun* which featured a significant statement by Lord Nicholls on the relationship between the defence of "fair comment" and "malice". Lo quotes leading practitioner text *Gatley on Libel and Slander* as stating:

> It is a fact that the leading authority on malice and fair comment in English law is now a decision of the Hong Kong Court of Final Appeal.[237]

In terms of "explanation" for the "Hong Kong as a source" phenomenon, Lo lists, in particular, the very common practice of having serving British and Australian judges sitting as Non-Permanent Judges of the Court of Final Appeal, and the high quality of Hong Kong's small pool of Permanent and Non-Permanent Court of Final Appeal Justices.[238]

2.11 Law reform in Hong Kong

Law reform in Hong Kong may obviously occur by legislative change or by changes to the common law as described above. These changes themselves may be inspired by a number of factors, including changed political circumstances, changing public opinion and the identification by critics of clear deficiencies in the law. Given Hong Kong's post-1997 status as a former colony, previously dominated by the English common law and now seeking to develop a jurisprudence of its own, one might have expected quite rapid and dramatic law reform. However, the practice of law reform is considerably more restricted in Hong Kong than in England where the Law Commission is, in the words of Professor Peter Wesley-Smith:

> charged with keeping the law under review and attending to its systematic development and reform.[239]

Moreover, law reform in party political Britain is far more politically motivated, since successive governments will seek to utilise legislation to advance their "agenda".

Hong Kong's system for law reform is far more piecemeal, with the Law Reform Commission of Hong Kong (LRC), established in 1982, considering topics referred

---

237. *Gatley on Libel and Slander* (10th edn) vii.
238. See Chapter 6.
239. Note 186, 116.

to it by the Secretary for Justice or the Chief Justice and making recommendations, where appropriate, for reform. Reform via "Member's Bills"[240] is comparatively rare (especially post-1997) so that initiatives for legal change normally originate with the government.

The LRC contains three ex-officio members: the Chief Justice, the Secretary for Justice and the Law Draftsman. Other members are appointed by the Chief Executive on the recommendation of the Secretary for Justice. The membership comprises judges, legal academics, legal practitioners and laymen.

Subjects referred to the Commission are generally considered by a sub-committee whose members, all volunteers, are appointed by the Secretary for Justice.

To date, the LRC has published around 60 reports since its establishment, on diverse and wide-ranging topics. It has produced a similar number of consultation papers. The recommendations in around half of the reports have been implemented in whole or in part. The six most recent reports have been on:

(1) Third Party Funding for Arbitration (2016);
(2) Adverse Possession (2014);
(3) "Excepted Offences" under Schedule 3 to the Criminal Procedure Ordinance (2014);
(4) Charities (2013);
(5) Class Actions (2012);
(6) Double Jeopardy (2012); and

The most recent consultation papers have been on:

(1) Miscellaneous Sexual Offences (2018)
(2) Periodic Payments for Future Pecuniary Loss in Personal Injury cases (2018)
(3) Sexual Offences Involving Children and Persons with mental impairment
(4) Third Party Funding for Arbitration (2015);
(5) "Excepted Offences" (as above) 2013;
(6) Adverse Possession (2012);

Although, as can be seen from the above, consultation papers are often, and unsurprisingly, followed by a report, one striking feature of the more recent reports has been the scarcity of ensuing legislative reform. Even given the time needed for legislative changes to be implemented, it is noteworthy that, since the 1997 "handover", there have been around 25 reports and only seven pieces of resulting "implementing legislation". The speedy response to third party funding proposals is a notable exception. Prior to 1997, the legislative "response rate" to Law Reform Commission proposals was far greater.

---

240. See Chapter 4.

Concerns on this issue have been raised by both academics and practitioners. Solicitor Ludwig Ng has commented:[241]

> ... One area that needs urgent attention is law reform.
>
> ...
>
> Hong Kong's Law Reform Commission was set up in 1980. But it is run quite differently from those in the Commonwealth jurisdictions, and is ill-equipped to take up the task of reform ...
>
> ...
>
> The current commission is made up of brilliant and highly regarded, but part-time members. Its chairman is Justice Secretary Wong Yan-lung.[242] Other members include eminent judges, barristers, solicitors, academics and highly regarded laymen. They are no doubt extremely capable people, but how much time can these part-timers spare for law reform among their various competing duties?
>
> By contrast, the British Law Commission has five full-time commissioners. They are supported by the Commission's Chief Executive and about 20 members of the Government Legal Service, four or five Parliamentary Counsel, some 15 research assistants, a librarian and a corporate services team.
>
> As a result, more than two thirds of the British commission's law reform recommendations have been implemented, according to the UK Law Commission website.
>
> In Hong Kong, by contrast, the commission published 23 reports from 1997–2008, but only two reports, and some recommendations in a third, have been enacted into law.
>
> Our lack of investment in law reform is costing us dearly. Our law is becoming more and more archaic and uncertain. This will no doubt affect our status as a financial and commercial centre.
>
> For example, consultation on reforming the Land Titles Ordinance started more than 20 years ago. The aim was to change Hong Kong's document registration system for landed properties into a much more certain and efficient title registration system. An ordinance was finally enacted in 2004, but the government, Law Society and other interested parties are still haggling over implementation details, and it is still not law today ...

---

241. Ludwig Ng, 'Law for the Times' *South China Morning Post* (Hong Kong, 29 September 2010).
242. No longer in office, having resigned and been replaced by Rimsky Yuen.

Returning to the theme elsewhere,[243] Ng has written:

> ...Hong Kong is unique amongst the major Commonwealth jurisdictions in that the LRC does not have any full-time members... They are no doubt capable people. The question is: how much time can these part-timers spare for law reform among their various, competing duties?
>
> ...The lack of full-time reformers and sufficient support explains the delay of the LRC in publishing its reports. In some cases the delay is truly shocking, particularly in some areas of law which are crying out for reform...

Comment

While one can appreciate the heartfelt frustration of Ng it is far from clear that the lack of legislative action can be (primarily) explained by the part-time nature of the Hong Kong Commissioners. It is true that Ng cited the example of eligibility for jury service being raised in LegCo and a final report only being published in 2010, admittedly unpardonable and especially so given the very limited reforms proposed. However, can legislative inaction really be said to be "as a result" of the Reform Commission's part-time status when, by Ng's own principal exemplar, a law is "enacted" but subsequently haggled over for years?[244] Post-legislative haggling and delay cannot be laid at the door of the Law Reform Commission. It is possible, but unlikely, that a professional commission would command greater respect and prompt LegCo to greater legislative response but legislative inertia in Hong Kong has more to do with political dissension and the lack of legitimacy of the unelected government, from which most attempts at legislation emanate.[245]

The issue of law reform was addressed by then Secretary for Justice, Wong Yan Lung, in his 2011 Address at the Opening of the Legal Year.

Wong said:

> I am grateful to hear from the legal profession their concern about the implementation of the Law Reform Commission's reports. It is of course in the interests of the Commission, the Government and the community that the Commission's hard work come to fruition and that its reports are considered within a reasonable time frame.
>
> As Chairman of the Commission, I have specifically impressed upon bureaux with policy responsibility over the reports the importance of responding to such reports

---

243. 'Reforming Law Reform' *Hong Kong Lawyer* (December 2010).
244. Indeed, Ng himself states, "what is more frustrating is the non-implementation of the recommendations contained in those reports", ibid.
245. See Chapter 4.

and of speeding up their consideration and/or implementation. I will continue to do so. This concern has been duly acknowledged by the responsible bureaux. However, the complexity and scope of the subject-matter of the reports vary greatly and some are likely to require longer than others for bureaux to consider.

Although members of the Commission and its sub-committee members volunteer their services, part-time and unpaid, which means that some Commission projects may take longer to complete, it has the considerable advantage that those projects benefit from the wide range of expertise represented by the Commission and the sub-committee members which might not otherwise be available. Their input to the law reform process is invaluable.

Comment

The last paragraph of this extract implicitly addresses certain criticism of the LRC's position as an "amateur" body. Employing a full-time professional panel might, it is argued, result in quicker reports and greater status for the LRC members. Certainly this appears to be Ludwig Ng's view. In truth, as Wong shows, the LRC Commission and its sub-committees already comprise leaders in the particular area of law under discussion. Bringing in ad hoc *members for specific topics ensures relevant expertise. Moreover, the slowness of reports is secondary in importance to the lack of legislative response. If reports are to remain largely ignored by the executive/legislature, the appointment of a professional LRC would appear to be a pointless expense. What explains the lack of legislative response? While the poor functioning of LegCo, and its largely "obstructive" operations (previously alluded to) have been a factor, the most important blockage has been the opposition of vested interests. For example, the much-needed changes to rules on property descriptions (which had previously permitted the significant exaggeration of floor space) were recommended in 1995, but not (as a result of the property companies' objections) implemented until 2012. Similarly, and largely as the result of the Bar's objections, statutory rules to recognise the benefit of limited use of legislative material to enhance statutory interpretation remains to be enacted, despite the LRC's clear conclusion that legislation would be beneficial.*

In fairness to Wong Yan Lung, it is impossible to say whether his wake-up call to bureaux chiefs had any effect.

Law reform has remained a "hot topic" in Hong Kong with, first, a conference (jointly organised by Ludwin Ng's firm[246] and the University of Hong Kong's Centre for Comparative and Public Law) entitled "Does law reform need reforming in Hong Kong?"[247] and, later, a resulting textbook with a number of eminent contributors.[248]

---

246. ONC Lawyers.
247. At the University of Hong Kong, 17 September 2011.
248. M Tilbury, SNM Young, and L Ng (eds), *Reforming Law Reform: Perspectives from Hong Kong and Beyond* (Hong Kong University Press 2014).

The importance of the topic is stressed by Winn[249] who, in serious vein, states:

> Admittedly, the chaos in LegCo has not helped, but the slowing pace of law reform is going to undermine Hong Kong's rule of law and its claim to being Asia's world city.[250]

---

249. H Winn, 'Impatience over the Slow Pace of Implementing Law Reforms' *South China Morning Post* (Hong Kong, 16 June 2014).
250. See also A Wong, 'Series of Law Reform Ideas Left to Gather Dust' *South China Morning Post* (Hong Kong, 20 December 2010).

3
The Hong Kong Court System

OVERVIEW

The focus of this chapter will be the structure of the Hong Kong courts, their jurisdiction and the appeals process. The nature and composition of the Hong Kong judiciary itself will be dealt with separately in Chapter 6. In order to understand better the nature of the post-1997 reforms in respect of the hierarchy and functions of the Hong Kong courts, the chapter will begin with a brief description of the pre-1997 position. In essence the post-1997 system reflects continuity rather than dramatic amendment, with the replacement of the Judicial Committee of the Privy Council by the Court of Final Appeal (CFA) as Hong Kong's ultimate appellate court, the only significant change.

As with the great majority of legal systems, and with all common law ones, the court structure is divided between those administering *civil* law and those which are *criminal* in jurisdiction. That said, there are a number of courts which exercise both civil and criminal functions. Indeed, like its counterpart in the English system (the Supreme Court), Hong Kong's Court of Final Appeal hears both civil and criminal appeals.

The rationale of the civil justice system differs markedly from that of the criminal one. The essence of civil law is the protection of *private* rights and the enforcement of compensation for their infringement. The two major subdivisions of private law are contract and tort. Contract involves, in theory at least, obligations freely undertaken as part of a contractual agreement, and tort involves, generally, the unlawful infringement of the recognised (non-contractual) interests (personal and proprietary) of others.

The essence of criminal law is the protection of the public generally by the infliction of "punishment" on those who break the criminal law. The underlying intention is that the *public* in general will be protected by this punishment; either because it deters the wrongdoer, and others, from further infringements of the law or, more basically, because the confinement (or death) of the wrongdoer prevents (temporarily or permanently!) re-offending by that individual. Punishment may take various forms, from simple financial penalties (fines) to imprisonment. Hong Kong remains unusual in the common law world in its approach to sentencing in the criminal courts. Sentences in Hong Kong are high by the standards of most common law countries and harsh punishment is generally applauded by the populace. While it is true that capital punishment was abolished in Hong Kong, pre-1997, it is also true that this was contrary to the wishes of the majority of the population and was prompted by fears that capital punishment would be extended to various non-homicide cases, as in the rest of the PRC, with reunification in 1997. This issue is touched on again in Chapter 11, in terms of a comparison between Hong Kong and mainland sentencing practices.

An interesting, and quite topical, issue in Hong Kong involves the "allegedly" very high conviction rate in criminal cases. Controversially, one leading barrister has said that Hong Kong's conviction rate is similar to that in North Korea! Defenders of the system have argued that a high conviction rate may simply signify excellent pre-trial screening, or simply a high incidence of guilty pleas.

"Terminology" also differs in the courts via the civil/criminal dichotomy. While the word "defendant" is used in both the criminal and civil context, cases are waged against the defendant by the "prosecution" in criminal cases as opposed to the "plaintiff" in civil cases.

This chapter will also include a description of the work of "tribunals" of various types. These tribunals differ in some respects from courts proper (though many of them are under the control of the Hong Kong Judiciary Office) and it would be misleading to convey the impression that all judicial work is carried out via the regular courts. Indeed, this phenomenon has become more marked in recent times as parties seek "alternative dispute resolution" through arbitration and mediation, encouraged by reforms to the civil justice system that seek speedier and, arguably, cheaper alternatives to full-blown litigation. In Britain, where such developments preceded those in Hong Kong by some years, there is already lively debate as to whether the alternatives are an extension, or a denial, of justice.[1]

The appeals system is dependent on the court hierarchy since appeals, of course, are made from lower courts to higher ones. The right of appeal is generally, however, not automatic. It may depend on leave being granted and/or whether the reason for the appeal is an issue "of fact" or "of law". Courts, both in Hong Kong and elsewhere in the common law world, are far less likely to grant appeals based merely on dispute as to the facts found by the lower court. Similarly, where the decision of the lower court involves the exercise of judicial discretion, appellate courts will only overturn a decision where the discretion has been exercised improperly.

3.1 The pre-1997 court structure

An outline of the pre-1997 court structure is presented below.

---

1. See the "Woolf/Genn" debate discussed in detail in Chapter 11.

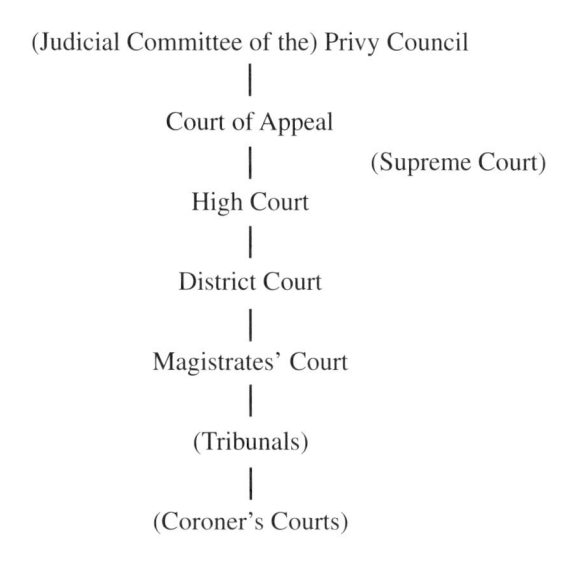

(Judicial Committee of the) Privy Council
|
Court of Appeal
| (Supreme Court)
High Court
|
District Court
|
Magistrates' Court
|
(Tribunals)
|
(Coroner's Courts)

Since most of the above have largely survived the 1997 resumption of sovereignty it is necessary, at this stage, only to comment on those aspects which have been changed. The first court to mention, though it is not listed above, is the (British) Judicial Committee of the House of Lords (House of Lords)[2] since, although it has never been part of the Hong Kong court hierarchy and thus not directly binding on Hong Kong courts, it is significant as a creator of legal rules of relevance to Hong Kong, even today. As was noted in Chapter 2, the law of Hong Kong, pre-1997, was dominated by the common law of England. As the final arbiter of the English common law, the House of Lords rulings, where applicable to and consistent with the Hong Kong local situation, became law in the colony. Even post-1997, since the "laws previously in force" would continue unless amended (or contrary to the Basic Law), *pre-1997* House of Lords judgments may well represent Hong Kong's current legal position. *Post-1997* House of Lords judgments, of course, have no binding force in Hong Kong[3] though, like all judgments from common law jurisdictions, they may be referred to by the Hong Kong courts.[4] Moreover, given that Hong Kong's common law derives greatly from that of England, these judgments will be "treated with great respect".[5]

---

2. The Judicial Committee of the House of Lords has now been replaced by a "Supreme Court" by virtue of the Constitutional Reform Act 2005.
3. A tenuous academic argument could be made for the continuing dominance of the House of Lords via the (now discredited) "declaratory theory".
4. Article 84, Basic Law.
5. Per Li CJ in *A Solicitor v Law Society of Hong Kong* [2008] 2 HKC 1.

The Judicial Committee of the Privy Council (Privy Council) was the final appellate court for Hong Kong pre-1997. As such, its judgments *on appeals from Hong Kong* were binding on the Hong Kong courts, although, couched as "advice to the sovereign", they are only of "persuasive" authority in Britain and elsewhere in the common law world. There was, previously, a general view that Privy Council judgments on "non-Hong Kong" issues were also binding in Hong Kong pre-1997. However, while the issue is largely academic, it has been affirmed that such Privy Council judgments were merely "persuasive" in Hong Kong.[6]

Since, as previously stated, the laws "previously in force" continue *prima facie* to operate in post-1997 Hong Kong, pre-1997 Privy Council judgments continue to bind all Hong Kong courts[7] *except* the newly created Court of Final Appeal (CFA), its successor as final appellate court in Hong Kong. The CFA *may* depart from pre-1997 Privy Council decisions but will do so only "sparingly" and "with great circumspection".[8] *Post-1997* judgments of the Privy Council are in the same position as those of the House of Lords (its personnel are largely the same); that is, they are not binding in Hong Kong,[9] may be referred to, and are likely to be treated with great respect, at least when dealing with Hong Kong–relevant issues.

Other than the two courts mentioned above, little change has been made to the Hong Kong court structure except in terms of terminology. The term "Supreme Court", to encompass the Court of Appeal and High Court, has been replaced by the "High Court" which encompasses the Court of Appeal (unchanged) and the Court of First Instance (replacing the old High Court).

3.2 The present Hong Kong court structure

An outline of the post-1997 Hong Kong court structure is shown below. The role and functions of these courts will be considered in the next section.

---

6. Ibid.
7. Unless amended/revoked by Hong Kong legislation.
8. Per Li CJ in *A Solicitor* (n 5).
9. But cf n 3 above.

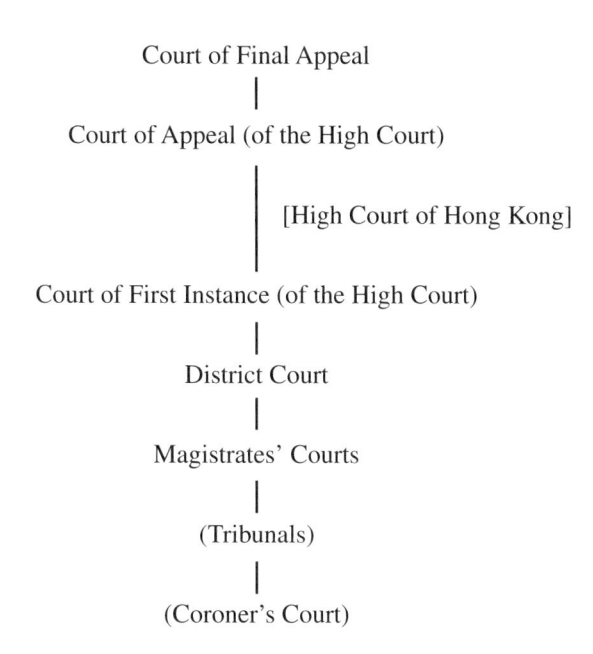

Court of Final Appeal
|
Court of Appeal (of the High Court)
| [High Court of Hong Kong]
Court of First Instance (of the High Court)
|
District Court
|
Magistrates' Courts
|
(Tribunals)
|
(Coroner's Court)

3.3 The role and functions of the Hong Kong courts and tribunals

The majority of the courts in Hong Kong have both a criminal and civil jurisdiction; the major exception relates to the Magistrates' Courts whose function is primarily related to criminal law. The work of tribunals, while differing in some ways from "true courts", will be considered, with emphasis on the more important ones. There will also be discussion of the coroner's courts though these, again, are *sui generis*, fulfilling neither a truly criminal role, nor a classically civil one.

The highest courts (the Court of Final Appeal and the Court of Appeal of the High Court) have only an "appellate" function. Most other courts combine a "first instance" and an appellate role.

3.3.1 The Court of Final Appeal

Until 30 June 1997 the Privy Council, based in London, was the highest appellate court for Hong Kong. The Privy Council hears appeals in civil and criminal matters from some Commonwealth countries and from British colonial territories. However, under Article 19 of the Basic Law, the Hong Kong SAR is vested with independent judicial power, including that of "final adjudication". Hong Kong courts have jurisdiction over all cases in the region except where restrictions are imposed on their jurisdiction under the legal system, including the Basic Law. As such, the Privy Council has been replaced by the Court of Final Appeal (CFA) in the Hong Kong court structure. The court was established by the Hong Kong Court of Final Appeal Ordinance (HKCOFAO). The Ordinance was "gazetted"[10] in 1995 but the court did not sit until 1 July 1997.[11]

> HONG KONG COURT OF FINAL APPEAL ORDINANCE[12] (HKCFAO)
>
> Section 1
>
> (1) This Ordinance may be cited as the Hong Kong Court of Final Appeal Ordinance.
>
> (2) This Ordinance shall not come into operation on or before 30 June 1997 . . .
>
> Section 3
>
> There shall be a Hong Kong Court of Final Appeal (CFA) which shall be a superior court of record . . .
>
> Section 4
>
> (1) The Court shall have no jurisdiction over acts of state such as defence and foreign affairs.
>
> (2) The Court shall obtain a certificate from the Chief Executive on questions of fact concerning acts of state whenever such acts arise in the adjudication of cases, and that certificate shall be binding on the Court.
>
> (3) Before issuing such a certificate the Chief Executive shall obtain a certifying document from the Central People's Government.
>
> Section 5
>
> (1) The following shall be the judges of the Court-
>
> (a) the Chief Justice; and
>
> (b) the permanent judges.
>
> (2) The Court may as required invite non-permanent Hong Kong judges to sit on the Court.
>
> (3) The Court may as required invite judges from other common law jurisdictions to sit on the Court.
>
> (4) . . .
>
> (5) Subject to section 7(2) there shall be not less (sic) than 3 permanent judges
>
> Section 16
>
> (1) Subject to subsection (4), an appeal shall be heard and determined by the Court constituted as follows–
>
> (a) the Chief Justice or a permanent judge designated to sit in his place . . . ;

---

10. ie, formally recognised and published in its final form.
11. The date of the transfer of Hong Kong's sovereignty to the PRC.
12. Cap 484.

> (b) 3 permanent judges nominated by the Chief Justice;
>
> (c) 1 non-permanent Hong Kong judge or 1 judge from another common law jurisdiction selected by the Chief Justice and invited by the Court.
>
> (2) (where) The Chief Justice ... is not available for any
>
> cause to hear an appeal he shall designate a permanent judge to sit in his place and be President
>
> (3) Where pursuant to subsection (2) a judge is sitting in place of the Chief Justice the Court must still consist of 5 judges
>
> (4) Where a sufficient number of permanent judges are not available for any cause to hear an appeal,
>
> the Chief Justice shall nominate a non-permanent Hong Kong judge to sit in place of a permanent judge ...

Comment

Between the gazetting of the Ordinance and its coming into force, a number of changes were made, mainly in relation to eligibility. Requirements as to ethnicity were in retaliation for (last) Governor Patten's very limited attempts at democratic reform. The ethnicity requirements reflect the requirements of the Basic Law which, on this point, is far more restrictive than the Sino-British Joint Declaration.

Even before the HKCFAO had come into force one of its tenets had become eroded via a "backroom" deal of the Joint Liaison Group; namely that the ability to appoint "judges" [sic] from other common law jurisdictions as required was restricted to the right to invite "a judge".[13] *No such interpretation was put on the right to appoint "local" non-permanent judges and, indeed, it is not uncommon for more than one local NPJ to sit.*

The appointment of CFA judges has a clearly "political" aspect, in that appointments are by the Chief Executive (himself a PRC appointee). It should be said, though, that in this regard Hong Kong is not unusual (US Supreme Court Justices, for example, are essentially Presidential appointees; though there are some checks and balances). A crucial factor is that the Hong Kong CFA judges have considerable security of tenure and have been more than prepared to decide against the Government. Judicial autonomy will be considered in more detail in Chapter 6.

The restriction on the CFA's jurisdiction in respect of "acts of state" has been an issue of some concern given the definition of "acts of state" as concerning matters "such as" defence and foreign affairs. This indicates that the two categories are not

---

13. Weng points out that "The Bar Association & LegCo both opposed the agreement but to no avail": BSJ Weng, 'Judicial Independence under the Basic Law' in S Tsang (ed), *Judicial Independence and the Rule of Law in Hong Kong* (Hong Kong University Press 2001).

exhaustive of the definition and appears to leave for scope for other matters to be included.

The CFA constitutes a cornerstone of the "independent judicial power, including that of final adjudication", guaranteed under the Basic Law.[14] It has the power to confirm, reverse or vary the decision of any court from which appeal lies.[15]

In civil cases, leave to appeal, granted by the Court of Appeal or the CFA itself, is required before a case can be heard by the court. There is, however, a right of appeal from the Court of Appeal in civil cases where the amount in dispute is $1,000,000 or more. Other appeals will only be heard on issues of *general or public importance*. Certification of the required importance, from the CFA or the court *from which* the appeal is being made, is necessary.

In the case of criminal appeals, again, leave to appeal is required and this must be granted by the CFA. As with civil cases, certification as to importance is also necessary.

Appeals will normally be from the Court of Appeal though the CFA now has the power to institute "leapfrog" appeals, direct from the Court of First Instance in exceptional cases.[16] The CFA has ruled that any (internal) restriction on its jurisdiction is unconstitutional. In *A Solicitor v Law Society of Hong Kong and Secretary for Justice*,[17] it was held that section 13 of the Legal Practitioners Ordinance,[18] which stated that the decision of the Court of Appeal was final when hearing an appeal from the Solicitors Disciplinary Tribunal, was unconstitutional, since it circumscribed the CFA's right of "final adjudication".

The CFA's power is limited, however, in one important respect, since it has no jurisdiction over "acts of state such as defence and foreign affairs".[19] The court needs to obtain a certificate from the Chief Executive on questions of fact concerning acts of state whenever such questions arise in the adjudication of cases, and that certificate will be binding on the court. "Acts of state" are entirely the province of the People's Republic of China.

The CFA will normally have five members at each sitting consisting of the Chief Justice (or his designated replacement who must be a permanent judge), at least three permanent judges and a non-permanent Hong Kong judge, or judge from another common law jurisdiction, if invited. Since there are currently only three permanent CFA judges, in addition to the Chief Justice, the workload is considerable. This is especially true since, in practice, the CFA has been far more active in hearing Hong Kong appeals than was its predecessor, the Privy Council. Even by 2004, the CFA was dealing with approximately four times the number of appeals that

---

14. Article 19.
15. Section 17(1), HKCFAO.
16. Court of Final Appeal (Amendment) Ordinance (No 11 of 2002).
17. (2003) 6 HKCFAR 570.
18. Cap 159.
19. Article 19, Basic Law: s 4, Hong Kong Court of Final Appeal Ordinance.

the Privy Council had been hearing annually pre-1997. This caseload has continued to increase gradually.

Given Hong Kong's promised "high degree of autonomy" under the Basic Law[20] and the right of "final adjudication" enshrined in Article 19, there were high hopes that the independence of the judiciary, a basic tenet of the common law, would be maintained, free from political interference. Unfortunately, this has proved not the case. By 2004 the Hong Kong government had already twice asked the Standing Committee of the National People's Congress in Beijing to "interpret" the Basic Law so as to avoid or overturn an unwelcome judicial interpretation.[21] In the case of *Ng Ka Ling v Director of Immigration*,[22] the CFA had interpreted the Basic Law in a way which the Hong Kong government argued would have the effect of disastrously increasing Hong Kong's population.[23] The proper course of action would have been to seek to amend the Basic Law but the government, instead, called for an "interpretation" (in fact a re-interpretation) to produce the desired political end. The Standing Committee of the National People's Congress duly obliged, even though the Basic Law makes no provision for a government request for interpretation. With considerable irony, and within five years of the *Ng Ka Ling* case, the then Chief Secretary for Administration, Donald Tsang, called for Hong Kong citizens to produce more children!

The constitutional impact of *Ng Ka Ling* was immense, and prompted the statement that the court was now the "Court of *almost* Final Appeal".[24] An even more extreme example of the government's circumvention of the court was seen in 2005 with the decision to seek an interpretation of the seemingly unambiguous[25] reference in the Basic Law to the Chief Executive's term of office,[26] once it became known that the Central Government favoured a shorter term for whoever was to take office following the premature retirement of Tung Chee Hwa. In this case the decision was to pre-empt any interpretation by the Hong Kong courts and to seek interpretation in advance.

While most common lawyers have found the NPCSC's determination unsustainable, support for the controversial interpretation has been given by Morris[27] who

---

20. Article 2.
21. Since the retirement of Elsie Leung, the first Secretary for Justice of the HKSAR, there have been no further requests (though there have been two subsequent interpretations: see Chapter 4 at 4.4).
22. (1999) 2 HKCFAR 4. See also *Chan Kam Nga v Director of Immigration* (1999) 2 HKCFAR 82.
23. The government had employed highly questionable research methodology to reach this conclusion.
24. Especially after the CFA acquiesced to the government's request that it issue a "clarification" in light of criticism and concerns. The "clarification" in *Ng Ka Ling v Director of Immigration (No 2)* (1999) 2 HKCFAR 141 amounted to a significant climb down by the CFA.
25. The then Secretary for Justice, Elsie Leung, had originally supported the "clear" five-year term but later said that her error was in applying a common law interpretation.
26. 'Interpretation of Paragraph 2, Article 53 of the Basic Law of the HKSAR of the PRC' by the Standing Committee of the National People's Congress.
27. RJ Morris, 'The "Replacement" Chief Executive's Two-Year Term: A Pure and Unambiguous Common Law Analysis' (2005) 35 HKLJ 17.

takes the "purposive" view that it is the intention of the Basic Law to ensure 10 five-year terms since the Basic Law (and Hong Kong's high degree of autonomy and separate Chief Executive) will automatically come to an end after 50 years.[28]

3.3.2 The High Court

Prior to 1997, the highest court in Hong Kong was called the Court of Appeal, from which appeals to the Privy Council could be made. Immediately below the Court of Appeal was the High Court. The term "High Court" now refers to a composite of the Court of Appeal (of the High Court), essentially an appellate court, and the Court of First Instance (of the High Court) which, despite its name, is both a first instance and an appellate court.

3.3.2.1 The Court of Appeal

The Court of Appeal was formerly the highest court situated in Hong Kong but now this role is performed by the Court of Final Appeal. The Court of Appeal is now part of the High Court together with the Court of First Instance and exercises appellate jurisdiction in relation to civil and criminal matters. Appeals are heard from the Court of First Instance, the District Court and various tribunals. Appeals from the Court of First Instance and District Court are normally heard by three judges, known as Justices of Appeal. In the case of criminal appeals, such appeals may be against conviction or sentence (or both). In most cases appeals to the Court of Appeal require leave to appeal (an important exception concerns appeals on a "final matter" from the decision of a Court of First Instance judge). A further appeal to the CFA is also possible, subject to the restrictions described above.[29] An interesting "curb" on criminal appeals to the Court of Appeal is the court's power to *increase* sentence in the case of unsuccessful appeals.

The court may also hear applications from the Secretary for Justice for review of sentences and for rulings on questions of law (known as Secretary for Justice References).

3.3.2.2 The Court of First Instance

The Court of First Instance (CFI) has, in fact, both "original" (first instance) *and* appellate jurisdiction, as well as a "supervisory" role. As part of the High Court, the Court of First Instance deals "originally" with the most serious *criminal* offences as well as having unlimited *civil* jurisdiction. In criminal cases, a Court of First Instance judge will sit with a jury of seven or, on certain occasions, nine. In such

---

28. See discussion in Chapter 1 of Morris's proposition of an automatic end to the Basic Law and its concomitants in 2047.
29. See 3.3.1 above.

cases the role of the judge is to determine issues *of law*, leaving the jury to decide issues *of fact*.

In most civil cases the judge sits alone[30] and is responsible for determining all matters of fact and law.

The CFI's "appellate" role involves dealing with appeals from Magistrates' Courts, the Small Claims Tribunal, the Obscene Articles Tribunal, the Minor Employment Claims Adjudication Board and the Labour Tribunal. Magistrates' Court (criminal) appeals may be lodged by a convicted defendant and may be against conviction and/or sentence. In the case of Tribunal appeals, leave is required; a CFI judge's refusal to grant leave is final.

"Supervisory" jurisdiction relates to the power of the Court of First Instance to regulate the proceedings of inferior courts, administrative and public bodies via the process known as "judicial review". A claimant who feels that a public body has acted improperly, to his detriment, may seek from a variety of remedies ("orders") via judicial review. In all requests for judicial review, action must be taken promptly. There are a number of different orders (sometimes called "prerogative" orders) the most important of which can only be outlined here.[31] First, "*certiorari*", an order which quashes an administrative decision already made, may be claimed. Alternatively, "*mandamus*" may be sought where a body has not acted despite an obligation to do so. The order effectively compels the body to act. The order of "prohibition", on the other hand, orders a body *not* to act (or continue to act) where it has no legal power to do so. It should be noted that a claimant may seek damages *in addition* to one of the orders described but may not seek judicial review solely for the purpose of obtaining damages.

3.3.3 The District Court

The District Court in Hong Kong has both civil and criminal jurisdictions. In criminal cases it tries indictable (serious) offences transferred to it from Magistrates' Courts. However, the most serious indictable offences, such as murder, manslaughter and rape *must* be dealt with by the Court of First Instance. The maximum term of imprisonment in the District Court is seven years.

In the civil arena the District Court hears cases where the amount involved is more than $50,000 but does not exceed $1,000,000. Apart from actions in contract and tort, the District Court may exercise equitable jurisdiction; for example, trusts, administration of estates of deceased persons or mortgages.

Since District Court judges in criminal cases sit alone without a jury there is some concern in respect of its relatively high sentencing powers. If, as its supporters say, the jury is an important constitutional safeguard for those charged with serious

---

30. Most exceptions involve allegations of defamation: see, eg, *Jonathan Lu v Paul Chan & Another* (jury trial, 2014).
31. Judicial review is a major, and expanding, area in its own right.

crime, surely such safeguard should be extended to the District Court. It seems reasonable to assume that the explanation for the denial of jury trial in the District Court involves issues of cost and efficiency rather than matters of principle. However, a (weak) argument for the retention of the status quo can be found in the Basic Law's assertion that the principle of trial by jury "as previously practised in Hong Kong" shall be maintained. The subject of juries will be more closely examined in Chapter 8.

3.3.4 Magistrates' Courts

Magistrates' Courts are essentially criminal courts, though magistrates deal with a wide range of legal matters. Although the criminal jurisdiction of the Magistrates' Court is limited to dealing with the relatively less serious offences, and the power of sentence is in most cases restricted to a maximum of two years' imprisonment[32] and a fine of $100,000,[33] their importance should not be underestimated. The Magistrates' Courts hear over 90 per cent of all criminal cases in Hong Kong and all criminal cases begin before a Magistrate. There are nine magistracies in Hong Kong, and their jurisdiction is outlined below.

(a) The trial of summary offences—those relatively minor criminal offences for which trial by jury is not available, for example, certain motoring offences.
(b) The summary trial of those indictable offences which may be dealt with by the Magistrates' Court—an indictable offence is a more serious crime but some lesser indictable offences, for example theft, may be heard by the Magistrates' Court.
(c) Conduct of committal proceedings—this is a preliminary enquiry to determine whether there is sufficient evidence to warrant the defendant being charged with a serious indictable offence and thus being sent to the District Court or Court of First Instance of the High Court for trial.

Magistrates may issue warrants, for example, for the arrest of a person, and summonses, that is, orders for persons to attend court and give evidence. Although the Magistrates' Court is essentially a criminal court, it also has civil jurisdiction and can make orders for payment of certain civil debts.

Magistrates' Courts are presided over by either permanent, legally trained magistrates or special magistrates who have little legal training and are involved primarily with minor traffic offences.[34] Special magistrates have (fortunately) no power to imprison. There are no juries in Magistrates' Courts.

---

32. This can be extended to three years where there are two or more offences dealt with together, or where statute so specifies.
33. In some cases, where statute so provides, a greater fine may be imposed.
34. For brief further discussion of special magistrates, see Chapter 8.

A significant development in Magistrates' Courts is that cases may be heard in Chinese or English, with the former becoming increasingly the norm.

3.3.4.1 The trial of juveniles

The Juvenile Court, an offshoot of the Magistrates' Courts, has the power to deal with all prosecutions against "juveniles" (those aged between 10 and 16 years),[35] except cases of homicide. The court also has power to grant care and protection orders in respect of young persons under the age of 18.

3.3.5 Hong Kong tribunals

There are four tribunals under the administration of the Hong Kong Judiciary: the Lands Tribunal, the Labour Tribunal, the Small Claims Tribunal and the Obscene Articles Tribunal. Other tribunals operate quasi independently although, in all cases, a right of appeal to the courts "proper" exists. The purpose of tribunals is to provide a speedier, cheaper and more specialised service in specific areas, in contrast to the main courts which offer a generalised service. The Hong Kong tribunals, having been set up in a piecemeal manner by various pieces of legislation, are independent of one another and have differing powers, functions and administrative rules. Each of them, however, serves to divert work from the overburdened court system. The decisions of tribunals are binding on the parties concerned, just as are the decisions of regular courts, subject to any successful appeal. However, since tribunals are not "courts of record", their decisions need not be followed by other courts or tribunals, even when dealing with similar legal issues.[36] While there are some, important, exceptions it is generally the case that legal representation is either not found or is not permitted before tribunals and that procedure, partly as a result, is less formal than before the regular courts. Accordingly, cases tend to be dealt with more cheaply and speedily in tribunals.

3.3.5.1 Lands Tribunal

Given the almost sacred position of land in Hong Kong, it is hardly surprising that the Lands Tribunal, established in 1974, is the most prestigious and formal of Hong Kong's tribunals, presided over by a "President" who is a judge of the Court of First Instance of the High Court (CFI). The Tribunal also comprises two "Presiding Officers", who are District Court judges, and a "Member", who is a land valuation estate surveyor. In practice, however, only one member adjudicates in most cases. The tribunal has the same power to grant remedies as the CFI.

---

35. Those under 10 years of age are deemed to lack criminal capacity.
36. See Chapter 5 for full discussion of the doctrine of precedent.

The Lands Tribunal, created by the Lands Tribunal Ordinance,[37] deals with various types of land-related case including claims for possession of premises by landlords, building management cases, and appeals[38] concerning rates and government rent. The workload of the tribunal is significant, disposing with over 4,000 cases per year. By far the majority of these involve tenancy and building management disputes.[39] Most tenancy cases concern landlords' claims for possession of premises under the Landlord and Tenant (Consolidation) Ordinance,[40] though possession claims arising other than via the Ordinance may be heard.

Very importantly, the tribunal has *unlimited* jurisdiction to determine the amount of compensation payable by the government to the "victim" of a compulsory purchase ("resumption") order or of public development causing a reduction in property value. This aspect of the tribunal's work cannot be over-emphasised. Although compensation cases are only a small percentage of the tribunal's work, they are the most time-consuming. Where major transport-related or public building projects are involved, compensation claims will run to many millions of dollars. Displaced landowners are less likely to challenge the rationale for a project than to complain about the amount of compensation. With a hugely fluctuating property market, ascertaining reasonable compensation is a difficult task. Two examples of compulsory resumption may be noted by way of illustration. The Hong Kong government is currently pushing forward with a controversial, and hugely expensive,[41] rail link to the Guangzhou area.[42] Depending on the finally selected route, large numbers of householders will lose their residences and others will see the value of their property diminish.

A more "historical" example is provided by the decision to demolish the old "Kowloon Walled City",[43] jurisdiction over which, throughout the "colonial" period, was claimed by both Britain and China. The area was known as a largely lawless refuge for illegal immigrants, prostitutes and unlicensed dentists. With the Walled City's demolition came the difficult task of determining the right to and extent of any compensation. Although the compensation issue was not ultimately dealt with by the tribunal, having been determined by a special committee of the Housing Authority, its outcome gives some idea of the scale of compensation, with the government

---

37. Cap 17.
38. It is unusual for a tribunal to exercise an appellate function.
39. Many of these are governed by the Building Management Ordinance (Cap 344).
40. Cap 7.
41. The estimates for the project have already more than doubled before work has begun.
42. Somewhat late in the day the Hong Kong government has admitted that the proposed rail "link" will not actually go to Guangzhou. The work was assigned to the MTR Corporation which, as always, completes late and over-budget. The government has (controversially) now announced plans to allow PRC law to operate at the Hong Kong terminus (the "co-location" arrangement, discussed in chapter 2).
43. See Chapter 1 at 1.4.

finally agreeing to pay over $2.7 billion to local householders and business owners. Even this figure dissatisfied many and evictions were required.[44]

Perhaps the most controversial of the Tribunal's powers, and one that has been dramatically amended in recent times, concerns "compulsory sales" for redevelopment under the Land (Compulsory Sale for Redevelopment) Ordinance.[45] Prior to the Ordinance's commencement, in 1999, compulsory purchase of land was limited to the government which was required to show public need and, of course, to provide adequate compensation (as indicated above). The 1999 legislation meant that, for the first time, private owners of majority shares were able to compel a sale by reluctant tenants. The tribunal would be charged with the task of determining, if no agreement could be reached, the amount of compensation to be paid to the reluctant tenant. This "developers' charter" gave owner/developers the opportunity to force out tenants standing in the way of lucrative redevelopment. There was one important safeguard, however, which was that the agreement of 90% of the tenants was required.[46] Nevertheless, in a blatant sop to the government's tycoon friends, the 90% rule was relaxed in 2010,[47] in respect of buildings over 50 years old, so that only 80% of tenants now need consent to trigger the compulsory sale.[48] Since developers frequently retain 50% of multi-storey buildings, only a relatively few "discreet" purchases are now required to reach the necessary 80%. Of course, the majority *should* seek to purchase all the relevant tenancies[49] but, failing agreement on this, may force the sale. The tribunal is required to ensure adequate compensation, both under the Ordinance and the Basic Law,[50] but this is likely to be based on current value rather than "developed" value and the ensuing windfall for the owner/developer.[51]

Given the scale and importance of the Land Tribunal's work, it is perhaps not surprising that legal representation, via a barrister or solicitor, is permitted before the tribunal. However, since 2009, as part of the new "case management" strategy, "paper directions", avoiding oral hearings, are to be used more often, alongside the "encouragement", in building management cases, of the parties to seek a mediated settlement.

Provision exists to request that the tribunal "review" its decision, as well as the right to appeal to the Court of Appeal.

---

44. The last of these was in 1992, with demolition between 1993 and 1994.
45. Cap 545.
46. Ibid s 3(1).
47. The Order was made by the Chief Executive in Council as permitted by s 3(5) of Cap 545.
48. Land (Compulsory Sale for Redevelopment) (Specification of Lower Percentage) Notice (LN6 of 2010).
49. Cap 545, s 4(2).
50. Article 105 states that "The HKSAR shall . . . protect the right of individuals to . . . compensation for lawful deprivation of property". In *Intelligent House Ltd v Chan Tung Shing & Others* [2008] 4 HKC 421, the tribunal felt that the Article applies only to cases of government acquisition (paras 30–31) but the reasoning was not compelling.
51. Article 105 states that compensation "shall correspond to the real value of the property concerned at the time".

3.3.5.2 Labour Tribunal

The Labour Tribunal, established in 1973,[52] handles disputes between employers and employees. Its procedures are speedy, informal and, as a result, inexpensive. The tribunal may consider any dispute involving a claim for over $8,000; there is no financial limit on its jurisdiction.

The Labour tribunal hears cases involving alleged breaches of employment or apprenticeship contracts lodged by either employers or employees. It also has jurisdiction over employment contracts made in Hong Kong but performed overseas.

Amongst the types of claim made by *employees* are:

- wages due for work done; terminal payments;
- wages in lieu of notice of termination;
- wages deducted contrary to the Employment Ordinance;[53]
- statutory holiday pay;
- annual leave pay;
- sickness allowance;
- maternity leave pay;
- severance pay;
- end of year payments, annual bonuses, commission; and
- long service payments.

The most common actions by *employers* involve claims for payment in lieu of notice on resignation or termination of a contract of employment.

The tribunal has no jurisdiction in tort claims (eg, claims alleging negligence by employer or employee)[54] and generally cannot hear cases involving claims for less than $8,000 (see below).

Jurisdiction is an important issue for the tribunal since, where it *has* jurisdiction, this is "exclusive" in terms of original jurisdiction (appeals elsewhere are possible) such that no other court can hear the commencement of the action. Conversely, the tribunal's jurisdiction is circumscribed, especially by the rule that:

> the Tribunal shall have not have jurisdiction to hear and determine a claim for a sum of money, or otherwise, in respect of a cause of action founded in tort whether arising from a breach of contract or a breach of a duty imposed by a rule of common law or by any enactment[55]

Since the lines between contract and tort are often blurred it has been suggested that the jurisdiction of the tribunal should be more precisely defined. In *Deutsche*

---

52. Under the Labour Tribunal Ordinance (Cap 25).
53. Cap 57.
54. These must be heard in the "regular" courts.
55. Labour Tribunal Ordinance (Cap 25) Schedule para 3.

Bank AG (Hong Kong Branch) v Daniel Mamadou-Blanco,[56] a case involving, inter alia, allegations of breach of confidence, Deputy High Court Judge Lok stated:

> the existing state of law relating to the jurisdiction of the Labour Tribunal is unsatisfactory.[57]

Difficulties may, particularly, be envisaged in relation to certain types of unfair dismissal which may be seen as tortious. Although the tribunal's remit is essentially non-tortious[58] and restricted to monetary claims, its jurisdiction has been extended[59] to improper dismissal under Part VIA of the Employment Ordinance[60] and its remedies include the ordering of reinstatement in such circumstances.[61]

Proceedings in the Labour Tribunal are conducted before a legally qualified "Presiding Officer", generally in Cantonese. Legal representation is not permitted. Appeals by dissatisfied parties may be made *on a point of law* to the Court of First Instance.

3.3.5.2.1 The Minor Employment Claims Adjudication Board (MECAB)

The Minor Employment Claims Adjudication Board (MECAB),[62] as its lengthy title indicates, deals with minor employment-related claims and serves to divert such minor disputes from the Labour Tribunal. The function of MECAB, operated by the Labour Department, is to deal with disputes where the amount (per claimant) claimed is less than $8,000. It has jurisdiction to hear and determine such claims. MECAB is operated by the Labour Department. The major limitations on the Board's jurisdiction are that the dispute must involve not more than 10 claimants and must involve a *contractual* dispute. The Board cannot, for example, deal with tortious claims or those involving insolvency. While all appropriate minor employment claims originate with MECAB, there is provision for transfer to the Labour Tribunal in appropriate cases. Conversely, a claimant is permitted to abandon part of his claim in order to bring it within the jurisdiction of MECAB and benefit from its simplified procedures.[63]

---

56. HCA 1514/2011.
57. Ibid at para 40.
58. To add further uncertainty to the jurisdictional issue, the Judiciary website reference for the Labour Tribunal states the limitation periods in contract *and tort*.
59. 75 of 1997 s 6.
60. Cap 57.
61. Ibid s 32N.
62. Established by the Minor Employment Claims Adjudication Board Ordinance (Cap 453).
63. Having done so, however, the claimant cannot subsequently resume the abandoned claim.

3.3.5.3 Small Claims Tribunal

The Small Claims Tribunal, established in 1976 by the Small Claims Tribunal Ordinance,[64] is intended as a "simple, inexpensive and informal"[65] forum for settling claims for $50,000 or less. Legal representation is not permitted and the parties normally appear in person, though leave to nominate a (non-lawyer) "representative" may be granted.[66] The tribunal deals with claims in contract and most torts.[67]

The types of claim usually pursued in the tribunal include claims relating to debts, the sale and supply of goods or services, arrears of rent and claims arising from minor road accidents.

Proceedings in the tribunal are conducted (generally in Cantonese) before an "adjudicator". A claim for review may be made by a party unhappy with the tribunal's determination, though this is likely to be heard by the original adjudicator. Alternatively, a (more expensive) right of appeal *on a point of law*, to the Court of First Instance, exists.

3.3.5.4 The Obscene Articles Tribunal

The Obscene Articles Tribunal was established following the commencement of the Control of Obscene and Indecent Articles Ordinance (COIAO)[68] in 1987. The tribunal's composition is one magistrate, who acts as chair, and two adjudicators.[69] The tribunal's role is to "classify" articles[70] submitted to it by writers, publishers, distributors, etc, and to make a "determination" in respect of articles referred to it by a civil or criminal court in the course of that court's proceedings. The tribunal's function is to *prohibit* "obscene" articles and to *restrict* indecent ones.

The tribunal, therefore, may declare any article "not indecent or obscene",[71] or "obscene"[72] (in which case distribution will be prohibited), or "indecent"[73] (in which case distribution will be restricted to those over the age of 18). In the case of indecent articles there are further technical restrictions, such as sealed wrapping, warnings etc.

---

64. Cap 338.
65. Hong Kong Judiciary Publication, 2008.
66. The representative must have a close connection to the nominating party and be familiar with the case.
67. The Tribunal does not have jurisdiction in respect of actions in the tort of defamation.
68. Cap 390.
69. Adjudicators are appointed by the Chief Justice.
70. An "article" is "anything consisting of or containing material to be read and/or looked at" (LegCo Secretariat: Information Note IN04/11-12). But cf note on film and television, below.
71. Referred to as "Class I".
72. "Class III".
73. "Class II".

An important limitation on the tribunal's jurisdiction is that COIAO (from which the Tribunal derives its authority) does not apply to films for public exhibition, nor radio and television broadcasts, all of which are governed by separate legislation.[74]

A major criticism of the operation of the tribunal is that it is charged with the dual role of classification *and* determination; it not merely decides as an administrative panel on the indecency/obscenity of an article but also determines the issue judicially.

In terms of classification, the three-person tribunal conducts a hearing in private. It then makes an "interim" classification. If this is not disputed, the classification is final. If there is a dispute, there must be a full hearing, open to the public, in which the magistrate is assisted by four adjudicators. A right of appeal to the Court of First Instance exists but must be exercised within 14 days of the tribunal's classification.

There are no precise legal definitions of "indecent" and "obscene" but the tribunal should take into account such factors as "standards of morality, decency and propriety" as understood by "reasonable members of the community"; the dominant effect of the article as a whole; and the question of whether the article had an "honest purpose".[75]

The tribunal's classifications/determinations are of great significance, since, for example, a person found to have published or imported an "obscene" article is liable to a fine of $1 million and imprisonment for three years. In the case of distribution of an "indecent" article to a minor, the maximum penalty is a fine of $400,000 and 12 months' imprisonment.[76]

Since the tribunal's decisions have implications for free speech, it is not surprising that its work is more often criticised than that of other tribunals. There is some evidence of conflict between the tribunal and the proponents of the Bill of Rights Ordinance and with senior judges.[77] A significant criticism is that the tribunal lacks transparency and does not always deliver reasoned decisions.[78] Since the tribunal has to make determinations about current standards it is important that it is representative of society as a whole, but this seems currently not to be the case.[79] Certainly, the Judiciary has expressed serious concerns: notably in relation to the tribunal's dual function; to the potential for a legally qualified Magistrate to be "outvoted" by

---

74. The Film Censorship Ordinance (Cap 392) governs films. Radio broadcasting is covered by the Telecommunications Ordinance (Cap 106) and television broadcasting by the Broadcasting Ordinance (Cap 562). Both operate via "Codes of Conduct". There is little control of internet obscenity given the difficulty of enforcement. Providers are, however, required to attach warning notices.
75. COIAO s 10.
76. Ibid s 23. Where there is a repeat conviction, the maximum financial penalty is doubled.
77. For an example of unanimous CFA criticism of the tribunal's failure to give "proper" reasons for its findings, see *Oriental Daily Publishing Ltd v Commissioner for Television & Entertainment Licensing Authority* (1998) 1 HKCFAR 279.
78. Ibid.
79. The *South China Morning Post*, in May 2010 (see below), found that 75% of the Tribunal members were over 41 years old and around half were over 50. See also LegCo question from Lau Kong-wah, 10 May 2010.

the lay members; and on the inappropriateness of the Chief Justice selecting panel members representative of society as a whole. Prophetically, the Judiciary's response to the administration's review of the COIAO[80] states:

> The Judiciary notes that in the past, it has made essentially these proposals repeatedly to the Administration.[81]

However, despite an optimistic *South China Morning Post* report in May 2010[82] to the effect that the tribunal's operations would be significantly transformed, as with so many other necessary legal reforms, little has been done[83] and the Judiciary's major proposal that, "the system of OAT adjudicators should be replaced by a jury system, similar to that adopted in the High Court and the Coroner's Court"[84] has yet to be implemented.

3.3.5.5 Competition Tribunal

The Competition Tribunal came into full operation in December 2015. The Tribunal was established under the new Competition Ordinance and its officers are Court of First Instance judges. Given the patent need for a proper competition law in Hong Kong (with its rigged housing, construction and supermarket cartels to name but a few) it is shameful that it has taken so long to enact necessary laws and a supervisory regime. The Tribunal will deal primarily with allegations of competition law contravention brought by the new Competition Commission. It is too early to say what, if any, effect the Tribunal/Commission will have on established practices.

3.3.5.6 Other tribunals

There are many other tribunals in Hong Kong affecting either the public at large or, especially in the case of disciplinary tribunals, limited groups of "members". These will be considered only briefly. The Immigration Tribunal, established under section 53F of the Immigration Ordinance,[85] hears immigration appeals[86] against "removal order" decisions of the Director of Immigration (DOI).[87] Since January 2000, the tribunal also hears appeals against a decision by the DOI not to issue a "Certificate of Entitlement".[88]

---

80. Judiciary Administration, November 2008.
81. Ibid at para 24.
82. J But, 'Moral Guardian Getting a Makeover' *South China Morning Post* (Hong Kong, 9 May 2010).
83. The panel of adjudicators has been enlarged and the maximum term of office is now unlikely to exceed three three-year terms.
84. Judiciary Administration (n 80), para 22.
85. Cap 115.
86. Under s 53A of the Immigration Ordinance.
87. Such decisions may also be made by the Deputy Director or Assistant Director.
88. Under s 2AD of the Immigration Ordinance.

The constitution of the tribunal is that it has a Chief Adjudicator (CA), a Deputy Chief Adjudicator (DCA) and a number of adjudicators. The CA and DCA are retired judges.[89] The tribunal is quorate if two adjudicators are sitting. In determining an appeal against removal, if *either* of the adjudicators accepts the appeal on the facts the appeal is upheld. In practice, successful appeals to the tribunal against removal orders are extremely rare.

An increasingly common objection to removal/deportation involves the allegation that a removed person may be subject to torture once returned to his previous place. As a signatory to the United Nations Convention Against Torture and Other Cruel, Inhuman or Degrading Treatment or Punishment, Hong Kong is obliged to screen torture claimants[90] and not return those who face the threat of torture or the like.[91] Amendments to the Immigration Ordinance[92] permit "torture claimants" to appeal to a Torture Claims Appeal Board, established by virtue of section 37ZQ of the Immigration (Amendment) Ordinance 2012.[93] Appeals may be made by persons dissatisfied with the decision of an immigration officer to reject, or not re-open a torture claim. Given the very recent nature of the legislative amendment, it is too early to comment in detail on the work of this Appeal Board. Screening procedures to date have not kept up with the increase in torture claims[94] and it is essential that the Appeal Board is adequately resourced if appeals are to be dealt with expeditiously.[95] A unified screening mechanism was introduced in February 2014, at considerable expense,[96] in an attempt to speed up torture assessments. However, criticisms remain.[97] "Non-refoulement" claims are rarely successful[98] and, given that Hong Kong does not recognise the principle of asylum, the best that a claimant can hope for is to be transferred to a third party state.

The Inland Revenue Board of Review (IRBR), instituted by section 65 of the Inland Revenue Ordinance,[99] deals with appeals against income tax assessment decisions of the Commissioner for Inland Revenue (CIR). The IRBR consists of a Chairman and Deputy Chairmen with legal experience and a number of Ordinary

---

89. Appointed by the Chief Executive.
90. The Court of Final Appeal, in *C & Others v Director of Immigration* (2013) 16 HKCFAR 280, has stated that this task can no longer be left to the UN High Commissioner for Refugees; not least because that body's decisions could not be the subject of judicial review in Hong Kong.
91. The claims are now categorised as "non-refoulement" claims.
92. Cap 115.
93. Ord No 23 0f 2012.
94. In April 2015, 9,533 applications were outstanding. See J Man, 'Denial of HK's Refugee Past Adds to Blinkered Policy' *South China Morning Post* (Hong Kong, 15 April 2015).
95. There have been complaints about crimes committed by torture claimants and illegal working (torture claimants have no right to work in Hong Kong).
96. See L Wei, 'Government Sets Aside $450 Million to Sponsor Torture Claimants' *South China Morning Post* (Hong Kong, 3 July 2013).
97. See Justice Centre Hong Kong, 'Meeting the Bare Minimum: Hong Kong's New Screening Process', 21 May 2014.
98. "Nearly zero" (J Man, n 94). In fact, since 2009, seven claims have been successful, 3,355 rejected.
99. Cap 112.

Members, all appointed by the Chief Executive. It hears appeals from disputes as to initial income tax assessment and the imposition of additional tax. The appeal must be lodged within one month of the initial assessment or imposition of additional tax. Appeals must enclose the assessment document or claim for additional tax plus the grounds of appeal. The IRBR panel hearing an appeal must consist of at least three members, of whom one must be the Chairman or a Deputy Chairman. All appeals heard by the IRBR shall be heard "*in camera*".[100] At the hearing the appellant is normally required to attend in person or via an authorised representative. The onus of proof is on the appellant to show that the original assessment or imposition of additional tax was incorrect. The IRBR, having heard the appellant's case, delivers a decision (normally in writing). The decision may be to "confirm, reduce, increase or annul" the assessment *or* to remit the case for the CIR's re-assessment. The IRBR has a discretion to order costs against the appellant but will normally do so only where the appeal lacks merit. An appeal, on an issue of *law* only[101] (ie, not on issues of fact) may be made to the Court of First Instance.

Given the increased interface between citizens and the Administration, brief mention should also be made of the Administrative Appeals Board,[102] which as its name indicates, operates as an (independent) tribunal to hear appeals (usually in public) against various administrative decisions. In this context mention should also be made of the work of the "Ombudsman",[103] an officer appointed by the Chief Executive to receive complaints from legislators or the general public[104] relating to administrative actions. The Ombudsman may conduct investigations and make reports/recommendations though not take enforcement action.

Two relatively new tribunals of a specialised nature, very much relevant to the Hong Kong situation, are the Market Misconduct Tribunal,[105] dealing with insider trading investigation and related issues, and the Securities and Futures Appeals Tribunal,[106] presided over by a High Court Judge, dealing with appeals from decisions of financial regulatory commissions such as the Securities and Futures Commission and the Hong Kong Monetary Authority.

In addition to the tribunals described above, which adjudicate on matters of general law affecting the public at large, there are a number of "domestic" tribunals which exercise adjudicatory functions in respect of narrow sections of the community. The best-known examples of such tribunals are disciplinary tribunals established by professional and regulatory organisations, to the jurisdiction of which their

---

100. Ie they are not public hearings.
101. By way of "case stated". Except for appeals on law, "[t]he decision of the Board shall be final": s 69(1), Inland Revenue Ordinance (Cap 112).
102. Established by the Administrative Appeals Board Ordinance (Cap 442) and operating since 1994.
103. Established by the Ombudsman Ordinance (Cap 397) and operating since 1989.
104. Initially, the Ombudsman could only hear complaints brought by legislators.
105. Created by the Securities and Futures Ordinance (Cap 571) and operating since 2003 under the chairmanship of a current or retired High Court judge.
106. Also created under Cap 571 and operating since 2003.

members are subject. Where an association is incorporated by statute or its members are subject to statutory regulation, its disciplinary functions and rules will be stipulated by that statute. Examples include disciplinary tribunals for solicitors and barristers (Legal Practitioners Ordinance (Cap 159)), architects (Architects Registration Ordinance (Cap 408)), doctors (Medical Registration Ordinance (Cap 136)) and dentists (Dentists Registration Ordinance (Cap 156)).

Finally, there are a number of tribunals, normally with disciplinary functions, which regulate the conduct of various professions or associations. Where an association is incorporated by statute or its members are subject to statutory regulation, its disciplinary functions and rules will be stipulated by that statute. Well-known examples include disciplinary tribunals for solicitors and barristers, created by the Legal Practitioners Ordinance[107] and for medical practitioners via the Medical Registration Ordinance.[108] In all cases of "internal" disciplinary procedures there is the right of appeal to the "courts proper" (normally the Court of First Instance) on the basis that the disciplinary proceedings have been conducted contrary to the rules of natural justice[109] or otherwise improperly.

3.4 The Coroner's Court

While the Coroner's Court is described as a "specialised court" and is under the aegis of the Hong Kong Judiciary, Coroner's Courts require separate treatment, since they are neither truly criminal courts, determining guilt or "innocence",[110] nor civil ones, determining compensation. The function of the Coroner's Court is to ascertain the cause of death in cases of "reportable death" in Hong Kong. A Coroner's Court inquiry, an "inquest", must be held whenever there has been a death in custody and may be held in other cases of sudden or suspicious death.[111] Inquests may be held with or without a special Coroner's Court jury.[112] The work of the Coroner's Court Inquest in Hong Kong is relatively small in scale, dealing with around 180 cases per year,[113] and, in keeping with the position elsewhere in the common law world, is significantly circumscribed. The court may make recommendations, for example in cases of death through industrial accident, to attempt to avoid recurrence, but it is

---

107. Cap 159.
108. Cap 136.
109. Essentially that the tribunal was not impartial or that the disciplined person was not given adequate opportunity to state his/her case.
110. Despite the "shorthand", criminal courts do not determine innocence; merely that the prosecution has not established guilt, "beyond all reasonable doubt".
111. Of 10,773 deaths "reported to Coroners" in 2016, only 77 resulted in an inquest (Coroners' Report, 2016, Hong Kong Judiciary).
112. Of the 77 inquests in 2016 (see above) 63 were held with a jury.
113. There is considerable variation since while were 176 inquests in 2013, there were only 108 in 2003 and 77 in 2016 (*Coroners' Report*, 2003–2016).

not able to attribute guilt to any individual.[114] The role of the Coroner's jury, which will also be considered in Chapter 8, is largely symbolic since the jury is expected to conform to the recommendation of the Coroner in respect of verdict.

3.5 The appeals process

Although the appeals system derives from the court hierarchy (obviously appeals are made from lower courts to higher ones) further diagrams are useful to explain the process in the civil and criminal systems. However, since much of the work of the appeal courts has already been described, only a brief outline of the appeals system will be given, highlighting any points of significance.

3.5.1 *The civil appeals system*

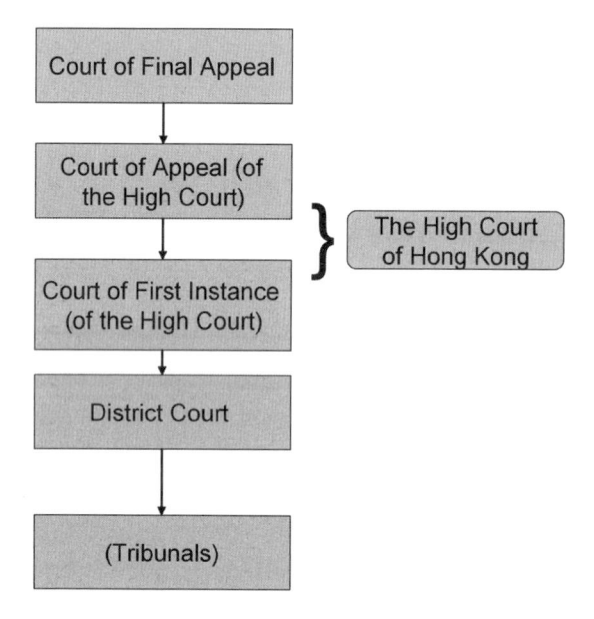

```
Court of Final Appeal
        ↓
Court of Appeal (of
the High Court)          ⎫
        ↓                ⎬  The High Court
Court of First Instance  ⎭  of Hong Kong
(of the High Court)
        ↓
District Court
        ↓
(Tribunals)
```

Starting from the bottom, there is a right of appeal from the various tribunals to the "courts proper". There is a right of appeal, for example, from the Labour Tribunal, the Minor Employment Claims Adjudication Board and the Small Claims Tribunal to the Court of First Instance of the High Court (CFI). The right is essentially restricted to issues of law rather than the tribunals' findings of fact and only around

---

114. The Coroners' Report for 2013, for example, talks of relatives of the dead seeking an inquest "on a common misconception that the purpose of an inquest is to investigate and determine whether the deceased died as a result of medical or surgical mismanagement" (at 18, para 7).

100 appeals are heard in the CFI annually. Appeals from some other tribunals and statutory bodies may be made to the District Court. These include appeals from decisions of bodies created by the Rating Ordinance[115] and the Stamp Duty Ordinance.[116] Appeals from the Lands Tribunal to the CFI must be on a point of law and leave to appeal is required.

From the District Court there is a route of appeal, in civil cases, to the Court of Appeal, again generally on issues of law. Approximately 50 such civil cases are disposed of annually with around 70 others "in progress". For appeals of this nature leave to appeal must be granted.

In addition to those from the District Court, the Court of Appeal also hears civil appeals from the Court of First Instance (CFI). Approximately 300 of such appeals are disposed of annually, with a further 200 "in progress". Where the issue of appeal is a "final matter", CFI appeals to the Court of Appeal are "as of right".[117]

The Court of Final Appeal (CFA) hears appeals from either the Court of Appeal of the High Court or, exceptionally, from the Court of First Instance of the High Court.

Previously, appeals from the Court of Appeal lay, as a *matter of right*,[118] when the matter in dispute concerned a sum of $1,000,000 or more. That automatic right was the subject of much criticism[119] and has now been abolished in relation to Court of Appeal judgments post-23 December 2014.[120] Now, in all cases an appeal from the Court of Appeal may be permitted at the discretion of the CFA *or* the Court of Appeal where it is felt that the issue is one which should be heard by the CFA, usually because of its public or general importance.[121]

The CFA also has an exceptional jurisdiction, at its discretion, to hear appeals in the unlikely event of a Court of First Instance ruling on the eligibility of a candidate for the office of Chief Executive.

Appeals to the CFA from the Court of First Instance (except in respect of a "Chief Executive eligibility" issue, which is unlikely to arise in practice) may be permitted only under the special "leapfrog" procedure. This procedure, introduced in 2002,[122] permits the CFA to grant leave to appeal where the Court of First Instance (CFI) has certified that:

---

115. Cap 116.
116. Cap 117.
117. *Bank of China (Hong Kong) Ltd v Twin Profit Ltd & Others* [2012] 4 HKC 75. There is no right of appeal, unless leave is given, against a CFI decision solely on costs.
118. Hong Kong Court of Final Appeal Ordinance (Cap 484) s 22(1)(a).
119. See, eg, P So, 'Final Appeal Criteria for Civil Appeals: Part ii' *Hong Kong Legal Community* (Hong Kong, 1 December 2010). In *Aspial Investment Ltd v Mayer Corp* [2014] 5 HKC 259, the CFA talked of the "worst excesses caused by the 'as of right' rule".
120. Administration of Justice (Miscellaneous Provisions) Ordinance 2014. This takes the form of the repeal of s 22(1)(a) of the Hong Kong Court of Final Appeal Ordinance.
121. Discretionary leave is possible in other circumstances but is unlikely.
122. See the Hong Kong Court of Final Appeal (Amendment) Ordinance (No 11 of 2002).

1. The issue involves a point of law of great general or public importance, relates wholly or mainly to the interpretation of a statute or the Basic Law and the CFI judge is bound (precedent-wise) by previous decision of the Court of Appeal or CFA;
2. A sufficient case has been made out to justify an application for leave to appeal; and
3. The parties involved consent to the procedure.

Of the total number of civil cases disposed of by the CFA annually (around 40), only a small percentage involve the "leapfrog" procedure.

3.5.2 *The criminal appeals system*

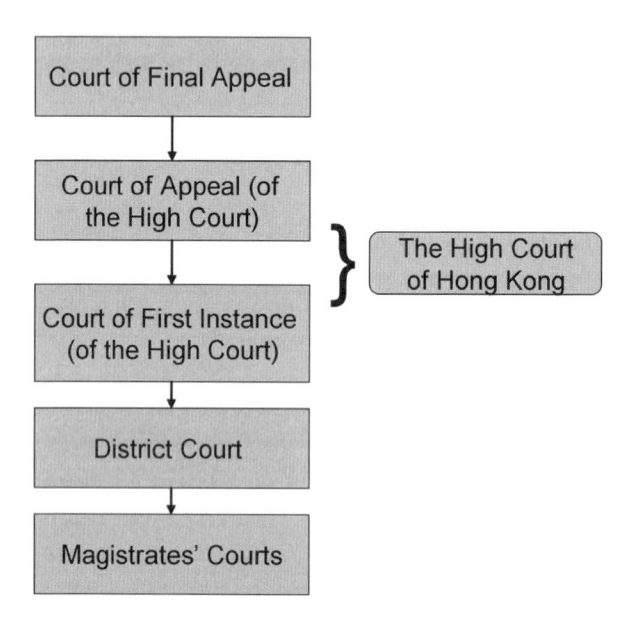

```
        Court of Final Appeal
                 ↓
        Court of Appeal (of
         the High Court)        ⎫
                 ↓              ⎬   The High Court
        Court of First Instance ⎭   of Hong Kong
        (of the High Court)
                 ↓
            District Court
                 ↓
         Magistrates' Courts
```

Starting, again, from the bottom, appeals from Magistrates' Courts lie to the Court of First Instance of the High Court (CFI). These appeals are numerous and rising, with over 1,000 cases disposed of annually. Appeals, which should be lodged within 14 days of the Magistrates' Court decision,[123] may be against conviction or sentence (or both).

From the District Court criminal appeals (against conviction and/or sentence) lie to the Court of Appeal. Approximately 350 such appeals are disposed of each year. Appeals should be lodged within 28 days of the conviction or sentence involved.[124]

---

123. Provision exists for exceptional lodging of appeal "out of time".
124. Provision exists for appeals "out of time" with leave.

From the Court of First Instance, a right of appeal also lies to the Court of Appeal. Approximately 150 criminal appeals of this nature are disposed of annually. In addition, and on a discretionary basis, leave to appeal to the Court of Final Appeal may be granted from a decision of the Court of First Instance where no jury was employed and no right of appeal to the Court of Appeal exists.

From the Court of Appeal (CA), appeals may be made to the Court of Final Appeal (CFA). This is subject to leave being granted by the "Appeal Committee". The Committee comprises the Chief Justice and two Permanent Judges of the CFA (or three Permanent Judges).[125] A large majority of appeals are turned down by the Appeal Committee. A further curb on appeals is provided by Rule 7 of the Hong Kong Court of Final Appeal Rules whereby the Registrar of the CFA may consider that an appeal lacks merit and ask the appellant to "show cause" why the application should not be dismissed. Absent such cause the Appeals Committee may dismiss the appeal. Statistically, most successful criminal appeals are the result of what are seen by the CFA to be prosecution errors, rather than a misunderstanding of law by the Court of Appeal.[126] The biggest cause célèbre has been the "Nancy Kissell" case, in which the defendant's conviction for the murder of her husband was upheld by the Court of Appeal but overturned by the CFA, largely on the basis of improper questioning by the prosecution and the trial judge's misdirection to the jury as to the defendant's plea of self-defence. To the surprise of many, the CFA refused to "apply the proviso" that although a point raised by the defendant might be decided in his/her favour, "no miscarriage of justice actually occurred".[127] On a re-trial, Kissell's conviction was upheld, ultimately by the CFA.

3.5.3 *The significance of appeal decisions in the Court of Final Appeal*

The importance of the CFA's role far exceeds the "mere numbers" of appeals heard and even the "quality" of judgments rendered, since a key task in the post-1997 has been to uphold the promised high degree of autonomy of Hong Kong generally and the Hong Kong courts particularly. In this respect, Hong Kong's first Chief Justice, Andrew Li, was immensely successful despite enormous pressures from those who disdain judicial independence and prefer a more malleable judiciary. Moreover, Li's success was achieved notwithstanding a conspicuous lack of support, at a political level, from Hong Kong's first Chief Executive and first Secretary for Justice.

---

125. In case of unavailability (and the CFA was short of Permanent Judges at the end of the Andrew Li years) a Non-Permanent Judge could be appointed in place of a Permanent Judge.
126. Though the "acceptance" of such errors by the Court of Appeal is an implicit error.
127. Section 83, Criminal Procedure Ordinance (Cap 221).

Such is the importance of the work of the Court of Final Appeal (CFA) that significant research has been done on its role and operation, post-1997.[128]

Some salient features of research on the CFA are that:

1. The CFA has been far more prolific in considering and hearing appeals than its predecessor, the Privy Council. For example, between 1987 and 1997 the Privy Council decided 108 appeals from Hong Kong, while the CFA, between 1997 and 2007, decided 244. In the same periods, the CFA heard at least three times the number of appeal *applications* as its predecessor.
2. The CFA has facilitated the development of a "Hong Kong common law" jurisprudence, via the delivery of a greater diversity of legal opinions. Unlike the single "advices to the sovereign" of the Privy Council, the CFA judges have often delivered separate judgments, even though unanimous as to the "decision", rather than merely "concurring". There has also been greater "dissent" amongst the Hong Kong CFA judges, though this remains quite low, with most cases determined unanimously.[129] Moreover, and to some extent because "overseas" Non-Permanent Judges regularly sit on the CFA bench,[130] Hong Kong is now a source of common law jurisprudence in other jurisdictions.[131]
3. The CFA has also "reversed" decisions of lower courts more readily than did the Privy Council. Between 1987 and 1997 the Privy Council allowed only 40% of appeals while, between 1997 and 2007, the CFA allowed 54% of appeals. It should be remembered that around 85% of applications to appeal are rejected and that it is only from those appeals that "get through the net" that the 54% of appeals are allowed. In other words, the CFA "filtering" system may be more efficient than that of the Privy Council.
4. The type of case heard by the CFA is changing. Increasingly the focus is on public (constitutional) and criminal law issues.
5. Perhaps the most significant of all the statistics, illustrating the crucial independence of the CFA, is that it has found, on appeal, *against* the Hong Kong government in 54% of cases. This compares with the Privy Council's findings against the Hong Kong government, over a similar period, in only 36% of cases.[132]

---

128. See especially, Simon NM Young and A Da Roza, 'Final Appeals Then and Now' in SNM Young and Y Ghai (eds), *Hong Kong's Court of Final Appeal: The Development of the Law in China's Hong Kong* (Cambridge University Press 2014).
129. Bokhary J has been the main "dissenter", while still delivering the largest number of leading (majority) judgments.
130. In fact, there has been an overseas NPJ in over 90% of CFA decisions.
131. See PY Lo, 'Impact of [CFA] Jurisprudence beyond Hong Kong' in Young and Ghai (eds), n 128.
132. This summary of data is derived primarily from Young and Da Roza (n 128).

3.6 The language of the Hong Kong courts

In post-colonial Hong Kong, the language to be used in court has been an issue of considerable debate. Since the issue of language had not been addressed before the 1960s,[133] and had not been seriously considered prior to the 1984 Joint Declaration, Hong Kong had little time to adapt to post-1997 language realities. Writing in December 1997, academic Anne Cheung[134] explained some of the problems:

> Language Rights and the Hong Kong Courts
>
> ...
>
> The buzz-word in the opening ceremony of the legal year of 1997 was "legal bi-lingualism". It was echoed in its various aspects in everyone's speech ...
>
> Hidden behind bi-lingualism is the core issue of language rights. The scope of language rights includes the right to speak and be understood in ... legal, legislative and judicial process ... Broadly speaking, the language of the legal system and courts should reflect to some degree the language used by the population of a state. Failure to do so constitutes discrimination against a segment of the population. The problem was especially serious in Hong Kong before the 1960s.
>
> ... Ever since Hong Kong became a British colony in 1842, English has been the language of the ruling class ... The mother tongue of the majority population is Cantonese, but local subjects who are not proficient in English are in a disadvantaged position in their dealings and communications with the government ...
>
> The tide of events experienced a sudden turn in 1984 when the Sino-British Joint Declaration on the issue of Hong Kong was signed, stipulating that Hong Kong would revert to China in 1997. The increasing significance of the Chinese language was a necessary consequence ... The courts have witnessed an increasing use of Chinese rather than the development of bilingualism and a curious twist of fate nowadays is that English-speaking counsel are forced to use Chinese regardless of their wishes[135]
>
> ...
>
> ... With its recovery by China in sight, [from 1984] Hong Kong experienced a sudden change from an essentially monolingual legal system to a bilingual legal system within a short period of 13 years ...
>
> From 1 July, 1997, the Basic Law became Hong Kong's constitution. Article 9 of the Basic Law states that "in addition to the Chinese language, English may also be used as an official language by the executive authorities, legislature and judiciary [of Hong Kong] ... the fact that English language needs this additional reassurance for its survival as an official language reveals a change in power relations.

---

133. English was the only official language in Hong Kong until 1974.
134. A Cheung, 'Language Rights & the Hong Kong Courts' (1997) 2(2) *Hong Kong Journal of Applied Linguistics* (December 1997).
135. This is not entirely an issue of ethnicity, since a number of ethnically Chinese barristers are more comfortable using English.

... In 1988 a 'Working Party into Greater Use of the Chinese Language in Courts and Court Procedure' was set up to consider the implementation of a bilingual court system in Hong Kong. An ambitious project was recommended ... By 1997 only part of the recommendations had been put into effect but many other issues have been raised and dropped. This is certainly not due to a lack of awareness but due to practical problems. One reason is the difficulty of translating English case law into Chinese. It is hard to envisage that thousands of case materials dating back hundreds of years can be easily expressed in a language other than English. A second reason is the lack of judicial personnel who are proficient in both Chinese and English. A third reason is financial constraints on having documents and reports in both languages ...

It goes without saying that to prepare for a trial, the parties concerned have to understand the notice or the information or the summons issued by the court. If one is unable to read the summons in English, one is hardly aware of the legal problem. A person must be alerted to the problem before he knows how to seek help.

The problem is most acute in criminal cases where an individual's liberty is at stake. The litigant has the right to know exactly what is being alleged against him. Magnet ... argues that in criminal proceedings, the state has an obligation to provide a bilingual forum and not to burden the citizen's right to choose the language by unilingual initiation of the process ...

If the right to use the official language of one's choice has been duly recognized, the next question will be to decide the 'scope' of this right. Does the right to use one's language in court imply the right to have a judge who understands the language spoken? Is the party entitled to have a counsel who speaks and understands his language? ...

In December 1995, Hong Kong had its first High Court case heard in Chinese. The Chief Justice exercised his discretion to use Chinese in the case of *Sun Ey-jo v Lo Ching and others*,[136] where the plaintiff brought an action against her children, claiming that they were holding property on trust for her on the basis of an oral arrangement. The title deeds of the land concerned were all written in Chinese and dated back 30 years. The parties did not know English and were not represented by lawyers ...

The recognition and development of Chinese language in court must go hand in hand with a bilingual law-recording and law-reporting system.

The records of proceedings or transcripts of proceedings are the official records of trials made by judges. They serve two important functions. Judges keep the transcripts to enable them to come to a decision and the transcripts are required for appeals.

The present practice is that judges keep notes of evidence and submissions in English even if the trials are run in Chinese. This happens frequently in the magistrates'

---

136. [1996] 1 HKC 1. The case, before Justice Wally Yeung, was conducted in Chinese as part of a pilot scheme.

courts. This is partly due to the fact that judges receive legal education in English and partly due to the fact that it usually takes longer to write in Chinese than in English. Most magistrates, presiding officers and adjudicators find it difficult to keep records in Chinese.

The problem ensuing from such practice is that error can easily occur. When a judge writes his notes of proceedings in English while the trial is conducted in Chinese, he has to be an interpreter himself. Mistakes or discrepancies in translation will not be immediately known.

In addition, this may prejudice a subsequent appeal case by the defendant when he has to rely on the record of the court proceedings...

... A bilingual law-reporting system is important for the future standardization of legal language, the setting and following of precedents, and for reference in legal education.

The difficulty... is largely the constraints of finance and manpower. First the costs of having law reports in more than one language is high. Secondly, a bilingual reporting system will certainly give rise to disputes as to the meaning of words in the two languages. Lastly, lawyers and judges will be expected to have a good command of both languages before they can fully grasp the intricacies of legal arguments. This indirectly implies reform of the present legal education system. Legal education in the City University and the University of Hong Kong is mainly in English.[137] The development and continuing survival of a bilingual legal system is dependent on future lawyers. Legal education should therefore be geared to language proficiency in both Chinese and English legal language...

Comment

Significant changes have occurred in the 20 years since Cheung's article, especially in relation to bilingual legislation (by May 1997, all existing Hong Kong statutes had been translated) and a great increase in the proportion of bilingual judges. However, the basic premise (that there are huge obstacles in the way of a fully bilingual legal system which guarantees the rights of, generally, Chinese-speaking protagonists in an English-founded legal system) remains sound. Moreover, while, for example, a defendant may request that his trial be heard in Chinese (with a bilingual judge appointed), such application may still be refused; the issue of "language rights" remains.[138]

---

137. Since the article was written, a third law school (at the Chinese University of Hong Kong) has been added. This, too, teaches predominantly in English.
138. See, more recently, SL Ng, 'The Use of Chinese in the Courts in Hong Kong' (2011) Hong Kong Institute of Legal Translation, 3 November 2011. <http://www.hkilt.com/publication_detail.php?nid=117> accessed 4 January 2018.

Legally, then, under the Basic Law, English is retained as an alternative official language[139] and all legislation is now bilingual. Although most people appearing in courts as parties to a civil action, defendants in a criminal case, or witnesses, will have Cantonese as their first language, many of the judges, appointed in the colonial era and permitted to stay on post-1997,[140] are unable to conduct court proceedings other than in English. Traditionally English has been used in the higher courts in Hong Kong with Chinese more frequently used in the Magistrates' Court.[141] Increasingly, proceedings in the District Court and Court of First Instance of the High Court[142] are held in Chinese. Court of Appeal cases are also increasingly conducted in Chinese, though less so in the civil arena. A significant number of cases, however, continue to be held in English[143] and this is likely to continue for some time.[144] Court of Final Appeal cases have been heard almost entirely in English; not least because the great majority of cases feature a non-permanent judge, usually English-speaking.

Indeed, while an application may be made to a listing judge for the trial to be conducted in Chinese before a bilingual judge, the determination as to which of the official languages to use in the trial is a matter for the judge. A crucial legislative provision remains section 5 of the Official Languages Ordinance[145] which states that a judge may use either or both official languages[146] (Chinese and English) and that his decision on the issue is final.[147] Thus, although a defendant (or other party) may elect to use Chinese:

> the constitutional right of a person to use the Chinese language in a court of law in Hong Kong means no more than the right of that person to employ that language, that is, to utilize it, for the purpose of forwarding or protecting his interests. That right . . . does not imply a reciprocal obligation on the part of the court to speak and read that language.[148]

There have, however, been, since January 1998, extensive guidelines, issued by the then Chief Judge of the High Court, as to the exercise of the judge's discretion. Curiously, perhaps, while the two official languages are English and "Chinese", it is not formally determined *which* Chinese language is meant. The judicial approach has been, in general, to adopt Cantonese as the spoken Chinese language. This view

---

139. Article 9, Basic Law
140. Article 93, Basic Law.
141. The replacement of expatriates by local judges will be speedier in the Magistrates' Courts where the retirement age is 60.
142. Court of First Instance criminal trials (with a jury) can now be held in Chinese as a result of the abolition of the English competence requirement for jury eligibility (see Chapter 8).
143. Over 80% of Magistrates' Court cases are now held in Chinese as compared with only around 30% of Court of Appeal civil appeals.
144. Judges in the District Court and above need not retire until they are 65.
145. Cap 5. Enacted in 1974.
146. Ibid s 5(1).
147. Ibid s 5(2).
148. Per Hartmann J, *Re Cheng Kai Nam* [2002] 2 HKLRD 39 at para 19.

was endorsed by Hartman J in *Re Cheng Kai Nam*.[149] However, in October 2002, the Chief Justice announced that the use of oral "Chinese" could include Putonghua.[150]

Concerns have been raised that if the introduction of Chinese into the courts is too rapid, damage may result to the legal system, since while the ranks of English-speaking judges are thinning, the most able local barristers may not wish to join the judicial ranks where this could mean a drop in income.[151] At a more fundamental level, fears have been expressed that a bilingual system may undermine the common law system.[152]

Whatever the language used by the court, witnesses and parties in an action may give evidence in the language of their choice. Given that proceedings may be in either of two languages (or a mixture of both) it is naturally the case that the use of interpreters is considerable in the Hong Kong courts. As a general proposition, when a case goes to appeal, the appeal will be held in the language of the original trial unless the appellant applies for a change (in which case the appellate court may allow or refuse the application for a language change).

Some idea of the shift from English as the language of the courts to the widespread use of Cantonese, especially in the lower courts, can be gleaned from the Judiciary's[153] own figures. What these confirm is that the majority of Hong Kong judges are now bilingual and that, with the retirement of "overseas" judges appointed during the colonial period, this trend will continue.[154]

3.7 Conviction rates in the Hong Kong courts

Enormous controversy was stirred up when, in his preface to the 2010 edition of the widely used *Archbold Hong Kong*, local senior counsel Clive Grossman commented on Hong Kong's high conviction rate which he said was "probably approaching that of North Korea".[155] Grossman added that "an arrested person is almost certain to face imprisonment" as a result.

The then Chief Justice, Andrew Li, described Grossman's remarks as "ill-conceived and intemperate", adding that the criticism was "totally unjustified and

---

149. [2002] 2 HKLRD 39.
150. Press statement, 25 October 2002 (following application for use of Putonghua in case of *HKSAR v Pan Shenfang & Others* (No 823 of 2002)
151. The Basic Law does permit the recruitment of judges from overseas "on the basis of their judicial and professional qualities" (Article 92) but this would be exceptional other than in the CFA.
152. LegCo Secretariat (Research Division), *Use of Chinese in court proceedings* (Information Note IN17/11-12).
153. See eg the Judiciary's Annual Reports 2004–2016.
154. Around 90% of magistrates are now bilingual while in the High Court (CFI and CA) the figure is around 50%.
155. Grossman's comments were enthusiastically, and uncritically, taken up by *The Australian* which produced the headline "The Hong Kong Legal System Takes China's Road to Justice".

wholly misconceived".[156] The then Director of Public Prosecutions, Grenville Cross, felt it "incongruous that comments of this type should have appeared in a preface to a reputable legal textbook". Additionally, the Australian newspaper reported that:

> Long-standing regular orders for copies of the annual Archbold were reported to have been widely cancelled within the legal establishment.[157]

As often is the case, the situation is more complex than simple statistics might show and, as elsewhere, much of the high conviction rate is explained by defendants who "convict themselves" (ie, plead guilty). Some support for Grossman's view *was* provided in data considered by the LegCo Secretariat. These showed that the "overall" conviction rates (including guilty pleas) in the District Court and Court of First Instance for 2008 (the latest figures available at the time) were, indeed, at 92.6% and 94.8%, significantly higher than for the Crown Court in England and Wales and similar courts in Canada and Australia. Guilty pleas in all these courts show a marked similarity but it is the "conviction after trial" statistic which shows the largest disparity. Juries are, of course, used in English Crown Courts and the lower conviction rates there *may*, of course, lend support to criticisms of the gullibility, or even pro-defendant sensibilities on English juries. What is clear is that conviction rates in Hong Kong are, generally, higher in the District Court, where there is no jury, than in the Court of First Instance (CFI), where there is a jury. The LegCo Secretariat has reported that:

> Hong Kong's high conviction rate has . . . raised concern in the legal profession about the lack of jury trials in the District Court. Although the impartiality of judges sitting alone in the District Court has not been questioned, some lawyers in Hong Kong have asked for the extension of the jury system to the District Court.[158]

It must be said, however, that the disparity is a small one,[159] with conviction rates before a Hong Kong jury[160] much higher than for jury trials elsewhere.[161]

Statistics rarely tell the full story and defenders of the Hong Kong system might well argue that Hong Kong has "got it right" and that it is the other jurisdictions which are acquitting too many. Certainly, a high conviction rate *may* indicate

---

156. Support for the Chief Justice's view was supported by a *South China Morning Post* article, IJ Liu and M Ng, 'New Data on HK Convictions Sinks "N Korea" Jibe' *South China Morning Post* (Hong Kong, 31 October 2010).
157. *The Australian*, 26 November 2009.
158. LegCo Secretariat, *Conviction rates in selected places* (Information Note IN19/09-10). The same parsimony which has denied the use of Hong Kong's vast assets to provide adequate legal aid makes the extension of (more expensive) jury trials to the District Court highly unlikely.
159. Indeed, in 2011, the conviction rate was actually slightly higher for jury trials in the CFI than for District Court "judge only" trials (Department of Justice, *Prosecutions in Hong Kong*: 2011 Report).
160. For further discussion of the Hong Kong jury, see Chapter 8.
161. For example, jury conviction rates in Hong Kong between 2006 and 2009 averaged over 20% while, for the same period in the UK, the figure was approximately 8%.

thorough "vetting" of potential cases and pursuance only of those where there is a high probability of guilt. The LegCo Secretariat has stated that:

> The second explanation for the high conviction rates in Hong Kong as suggested by the Hong Kong legal profession is that the Department of Justice prosecutes only with overwhelming evidence, and its rate of success is therefore high.[162]

It is undoubtedly the case, in Hong Kong, that conviction rates are far lower in Magistrates' Courts where, given the less serious nature of charges, pre-trial vetting is likely to have been less exhaustive.[163] This lends support to the argument that "vetting" is the key factor. More worrying, however, is the "first explanation" for generally high conviction rates; namely that the lack of criminal legal aid, leaves some defendants without the opportunity for proper legal representation.[164]

3.8 Sentencing in the Hong Kong courts

Since sentencing is a huge topic in itself, only a brief overview of sentencing in the Hong Kong courts is possible here. As a generalisation, of the four major theoretical models of sentencing—retribution, deterrence (general and individual), prevention and rehabilitation—Hong Kong's practices most closely reflect retributive ideals. Retribution (the theory of "pure punishment") sees punishment as an ideal in itself (irrespective of effectivity), reflecting the degree of public distaste for an activity and insisting that "the punishment must fit the crime".[165] The ideal of retribution has been explained as:

> Punish wrongdoing anyhow. That is your first and simple duty. If incidentally you can make your punishment serve a deterrent or reformatory purpose, well and good.[166]

As a generalisation, and in keeping with retributive notions, it may be said that sentences for convicted defendants in Hong Kong are high by the standards of most common law countries, but not by Asian standards.[167] The relatively high sentences in Hong Kong courts are, it appears, welcomed by Hong Kong's citizens. There is rarely a public outcry about over harsh sentences but the public do decry what they see as over-lenient "rehabilitative" sentences.[168] To take one of the clearest examples, the abolition of the death penalty in Hong Kong was enacted contrary to the wishes

---

162. LegCo Secretariat Information Note (n 158).
163. Former DPP, Grenville Cross, has criticised the lack of proper vetting in Magistrates' Courts.
164. See Chapter 9 for further discussion of legal aid.
165. Of course, the theories are not all mutually exclusive, and a lengthy, retributive sentence may well fulfil deterrent and preventive purposes.
166. W Moberley (Sir), *The Ethics of Punishment* (Archon Books 1968).
167. Moreover, Hong Kong prisons boast far better conditions than most countries in South-East Asia. In Hong Kong offenders go to prison "*as* punishment, not *for* punishment".
168. See discussion of the Amina Bokhary case below.

of the majority of Hong Kong people,[169] as evidenced by numerous polls.[170] The abolition was largely the result of (pre-1997) fears of misuse of the death penalty, post-1997, by a Hong Kong ruled by China (where the death penalty is widely used, including for non-murder offences).[171]

There are maximum sentences laid down by statute in Hong Kong (though, as in Britain, no minimum ones, unlike the American system), but a very large measure of judicial discretion is permitted to the sentencing judge. While guidelines in relation to individual offences may be issued by the appellate courts, there is a less extensive "tariff" system in Hong Kong than in Britain, by which to constrain the sentencing judge.

A very wide array of sentences is available to a court in Hong Kong in dealing with a convicted defendant. The most obvious, of course, is that the convicted person may be sent to prison. As noted, judges have a wide discretion since only the maximum period of imprisonment is stipulated by statute. Such maxima should be applied only in the most extreme cases.[172] Only in the case of murder is the sentence (life imprisonment) mandatory. In exercising his discretion, a judge will take into account mitigating factors: such as previous good conduct, a guilty plea or evidence of remorse; as well as aggravating factors, such as previous convictions and lack of remorse. Sentences of imprisonment may be immediate or "suspended" for a period of time. Where a sentence is suspended the defendant will not go to prison provided that he does not re-offend within the period of suspension. There are some offences which are "excepted",[173] that is, they cannot, because of their seriousness, have any sentence of imprisonment suspended. The Law Reform Commission of Hong Kong has recommended that the list of excepted offences should be abolished,[174] largely because it is felt to interfere unduly with judicial discretion. The Commission indicated that the excepted offences had been introduced as a temporary expedient (40 years previously) in response to an outbreak of violent crime. Moreover, it suggested that it is anomalous to preclude suspended sentences for excepted offences while permitting, for such offences, the imposition of the "arguably lesser penalty" of a

---

169. The public supported the death penalty for murder (Hong Kong had no death penalty for, eg, drug trafficking as exists in Indonesia and Malaysia).
170. Polls, including those conducted by the University of Hong Kong, showed overwhelming support for the death penalty for murder prior to its *de jure* abolition in 1993 (*de facto* all executions were halted from 1966). The Star in 1972 showed 90% support for the death penalty for murder while HKU's poll showed 91% of students (but only 63% of staff) in support.
171. The PRC executes more of its citizens than the whole of the rest of the world. *The Standard* (22 October 2014) reported that, in 2013, China executed 2,400 of its citizens (a drop of 20% from the previous year) as opposed to 778 executions in the rest of the world. For further discussion, see Chapter 11.
172. *R v Pang Chun Wai* [1993] 1 HKC 233.
173. Schedule 3, Criminal Procedure Ordinance (Cap 221). The list includes manslaughter, rape, affray, serious assaults, drug trafficking and firearms offences.
174. The Law Reform Commission of Hong Kong, 'Excepted Offences under schedule 3 of the Criminal Procedure Ordinance', Consultation Paper, June 2013 followed by Report, February 2014. Abolition of the "excepted offences" is supported by both the Bar and the Law Society in Hong Kong.

Community Service Order. The recommendation to abolish the excepted offence Schedule has been supported by the Hong Kong Bar and Law Society. To date, however, there has been no resulting legislation. Given the general tardiness of legislative follow-up to Commission Reports and Consultation Papers, the lack of response to a relatively recent recommendation is hardly surprising.

Maximum sentences in Hong Kong tend to be higher than, for example, Britain, and Hong Kong judges, in general, impose sentences closer to the maximum than they do in Britain. There is rarely a public outcry over "over-harsh" sentences (which enjoy popular support) though in one recent example there at least "appears", ironically, to have been criticism of the (relatively short) prison sentences given to seven police officers caught on film beating up Occupy Central activist Ken Tsang, already handcuffed. The two-year sentences were relatively lenient given the clear abuse of public trust and the helpless nature of the victim, yet many objected. It seems likely that this was, however, an example of the "pro-establishment" camp taking advantage of the fact that the sentencing judge was "foreign"[175] to elide criticism of the independent judiciary with ill-concealed racist calls for the end of "foreign" judges in the Court of Final Appeal (guaranteed in the Basic Law but a sore point amongst the pro-Beijing faction).[176]

Conversely, sentences perceived as over-lenient may be the subject of serious public outrage, especially where the leniency is extended to the rich or famous.[177] Two particular examples are provided by famous young people: Nicholas Tse and Amina Bokhary. Actor Tse was convicted of conspiring to pervert the course of justice with Lau Chi-wai, a policeman. The latter had assisted Tse in "switching" drivers so that Tse would escape penalty for a driving offence. Lau was given a six-month sentence of imprisonment, while Tse received a (240-hour) Community Service Order. The public impression was that Tse was at least as guilty as his co-accused but had been treated more leniently because of his fame and money. Nonetheless, after the trial magistrate refused to alter the original sentence, the Court of Appeal upheld the difference in sentencing approach stressing that the trial judge's/magistrate's determination will only be overturned in exceptional circumstances. Given Tse's previous good conduct, youth, employment record, stable home background and remorse, the sentence was not "manifestly inadequate" or "wrong in principle".[178]

Even more profound was the level of public disquiet over Bokhary's lenient sentence after pleading guilty to charges of careless driving, refusing a breathalyser

---

175. Judge David Dufton. Perhaps significantly, there was far less criticism of the lengthier sentences (imposed by a Chinese judge) for Mong Kok "rioters" who caused only property damage.
176. To her great credit, former Secretary for Justice, Elsie Leung spoke up for the use of overseas judges in Hong Kong (both in the CFA and elsewhere).
177. This is in keeping with a rapidly growing feeling in Hong Kong that there is one law for the rich and another for the poor.
178. Then Director of Public Prosecutions, Grenville Cross, issued a statement of review of sentences (3 December 2002) asserting that community service was not a "soft option" and served both a rehabilitative *and* punitive purpose.

test and assaulting a police officer. Bokhary had twice before been involved in apparently alcohol-inspired incidents. In the first she had been convicted of an assault on a police officer and in the second had pleaded guilty to two assaults; one of them on a taxi driver and the other on a police officer.

Despite her far from unblemished previous record, Bokhary was placed on probation. There was little doubt in the public mind that she had been treated leniently because of her connections with "the great and the good".[179] As with Tse, the Department of Justice (arguably as a result of public concern) sought a review of sentence as it is permitted to do in cases of possible unduly lenient sentences. Nonetheless, having reviewed his original decision, Magistrate Anthony Yuen, did not amend the sentence.[180] The Department of Justice (via the Secretary for Justice) does have a right to ask the Court of Appeal to review sentences but this will be done only exceptionally. In a clear example, *HKSAR v Lee York Fai & Others*[181] the Court of Appeal substituted custody for a suspended sentence in a clear case of attempted "vote-buying" at election time (stressing the crucial importance of "clean" elections).

The difficulty, for the sentencing judge, in finding the appropriate sentence, given often competing sentencing theories, was addressed by (then) Chief Justice, Andrew Li, at the Ceremonial Opening of the Legal Year in January 2008. He said:

> A substantial part of the courts' work consists of the administration of criminal justice. Sentencing is an essential part of this process. It is an exercise of the courts' independent judicial power . . . it is the court's duty to impose a just and appropriate sentence, applying the relevant principles to the circumstances of the crime and those of the offender. Reasons for the sentence are given.
>
> The main objectives of sentencing are retribution, deterrence, prevention and rehabilitation. All of them serve the public interest. Sometimes, seeking to attain one objective may lead to a more severe sentence, while seeking to achieve another end may tend towards a more lenient sentence . . .
>
> . . . For certain types of crime, the Court of Appeal has laid down guidelines for sentencing for the purpose of promoting broad consistency. For example, for the offence of trafficking in dangerous drugs, guidelines have been laid down depending on the type of drug and the quantity involved. They provide guidance to judges in the exercise of their sentencing power.
>
> The courts make sentencing decisions day in and day out in a very large number of cases. The circumstances which arise in the cases are of an infinite variety. Deciding

---

179. Inter alia, one of her uncles was a Permanent Judge of the CFA and another uncle a previous member of the Executive Council.
180. In fairness to Magistrate Yuen, "rehabilitative" sentences, such as probation, are always more appropriate for those with family support and this tends to be more likely in wealthier households.
181. CAAR 3/2011. The defendants had (futilely as it transpired) distributed largesse via a "Welfare Association".

> on a just and appropriate sentence in each case is a challenging and difficult task ... Certainly, there is no mathematical formula for its determination. It is a matter for balanced judgment ...
>
> From time to time, views have been expressed in the public arena that the sentence imposed in a particular case was inappropriate, as either too severe or too lenient ...
>
> In a society which values freedom of speech as a fundamental right, all court decisions, including sentencing decisions, are open to public discussion ... Where the Secretary for Justice considers the sentence in a particular case to be manifestly inadequate or excessive, he may apply to the Court of Appeal for the sentence to be reviewed.

Comment

While the Chief Justice refers to disquiet over over-lenient and over-harsh sentences, in practice public outrage is normally reserved for what is perceived as undue lenience. As indicated this is because, by definition, rehabilitative approaches are "personalised" and emphasise the character of the offender rather than that of the act. As such, like cases are not treated alike and consistency is jettisoned. This can cause public anger, especially since the recipients of "rehabilitative" sentences tend to be those who are seen, already, to have more natural advantages than others.

One of the most controversial sentencing issues in the common law world, very much relevant to Hong Kong, involves plea negotiation or "plea bargaining". Because, as suggested above, a defendant will receive a lower sentence having pleaded guilty that he would receive after conviction at trial, a bargain may be struck whereby the judge, or prosecution, indicates in advance the likely "discount" for a guilty plea (or more emphatically can offer non-imprisonment in return for a guilty plea). There are several advantages to such a bargain. Cost-saving, without lengthy and expensive trials, is an obvious one.[182] Grenville Cross, former Director of Public Prosecutions in Hong Kong has stated:

> guilty pleas lead to fewer time-consuming trials, with a corresponding saving of precious judicial resources and taxpayers' money.[183]

Cross supports the judge playing an active role in such bargaining, adding:

> The duty of a judge, after all, is to manage the case as efficiently as possible from the outset, and this must include being completely frank with the defendant.[184]

---

182. With this in mind, the amount of sentence "discount" for a guilty plea will now depend on how early (or late) the guilty plea comes: see *HKSAR v Ngo Van Nam* (2016) CACC 418/2014.
183. G Cross, 'Let defendants know likely sentence' *South China Morning Post* (Hong Kong, 17 October 2014).
184. Ibid.

Other justifications for plea bargaining are that a guilty plea indicates remorse and that the victim, in rape, sexual assault or other violence cases, is relieved of the burden of giving testimony in court.

Plea bargaining is wholeheartedly endorsed in the United States, where the Supreme Court has described it as "essential" to the administration of justice. Most criminal cases are "negotiated" and trials are very much the exception.[185] Britain, traditionally, was very wary of plea bargaining, especially involving the judge,[186] and Hong Kong has followed the previous British reluctance to bargain. However, in the post-Lord Woolf "judicial case management" era, sentence indications by the judge are no longer frowned upon in Britain.[187]

The essential criticism of plea bargaining, however, is that the main "winner" is the clearly guilty defendant, given a discount merely for saving court time, while the "loser" is the innocent defendant dissuaded from waging his defence by the knowledge that a guilty plea may avoid the sentence of imprisonment which could result from conviction after trial.[188] In their seminal work on plea bargains in Britain, Baldwin and McConville[189] found that a small but significant percentage of defendants asserted that they had pleaded guilty despite their asserted innocence, prompted by the "discount" incentive.[190] Grenville Cross, quoted above, notes the danger but states:

> Of course . . . the defendant must be told that he should not plead guilty unless he accepts his guilt.[191]

Such an observation appears disingenuous.

There exists a wide range of sentencing options other than that of imprisonment and the following lists the major ones.

A convicted person may receive a discharge, either absolute or conditional, where, given the special circumstances involved, it is felt that no punishment is required. The discharge will, however, constitute a criminal conviction. Where a discharge is "conditional", the offender is required to refrain from certain conduct for a fixed period and to lodge a "recognisance" (a sum of money). If the offender

---

185. See AS Blumberg, *Criminal Justice* (Franklin Watts, 1967) in which the author talks of cases being "processed" rather than tried and of the abandonment of the adversary model in favour of "bureaucratic efficiency".
186. Strict restraints on the role of the judge were imposed in *R v Turner* [1970] 2 QB 321.
187. The *R v Turner* restraints were removed for Crown Court judges by *R v Goodyear* [2005] EWCA Crim 888.
188. In principle, one who pleads not guilty cannot be given an increased sentence on conviction. However, since he will lose the almost automatic discount for a guilty plea, this is really a matter of semantics.
189. J Baldwin and M McConville, *Negotiated Justice: Pressures on Defendants to Plead Guilty* (Martin Robertson 1979).
190. Ibid Chapter 4, 59–80.
191. G Cross (n 182).

"misbehaves" during the designated period, he may forfeit the recognisance and can be given a sentence for the original offence.[192]

Community Service Orders (CSOs)[193] require, as the name implies, that the offender, as an alternative to imprisonment, do a certain number of unpaid hours of work for the community,[194] supervised by probation officers. Failure to do the allocated work may result in a custodial penalty for the original offence.

Probation,[195] usually for lesser offences committed by non-habitual offenders, is an order that the offender must be of good behaviour for the period of probation[196] and must report regularly to a probation officer. Failure to comply with the terms of probation may result in a sentence of imprisonment for the original offence. In the Amina Bokhary case, discussed above, the offender's failure to comply with the terms of her probation resulted in the imposition of a six-week term of imprisonment.

Fines are one of the most common sentences and, of course, avoid any custodial element. One complaint about fines for many crimes in Hong Kong is that the maxima are too low and, in any event, are rarely imposed. A major example involves environmental offences whereby it is invariably more profitable for companies to pollute and pay rather than take more expensive measures to control pollution. A further issue of debate is whether the amount of a fine should be adjusted to the assets of the offender, since, obviously, a fine of $1,000 is a far greater punishment for a street sleeper than a rich business man. Differential fines have not been employed in Hong Kong and this is likely to remain the case despite the application of "proportionality" (that the penalty should fit the crime) principles in other contexts.[197]

Compensation Orders are, as the name suggests, an order of the court that the offender, on conviction, should pay a sum of money to a victim who has suffered physical or personal injury as a result of the crime. The order appears to be an example of what noted sociologist, Emile Durkheim, predicted as a gradual move from punitive to restitutionary sanctions. However, since compensation orders normally *accompany* other penalties, the punitive element remains.

Penalty options for *juveniles* differ somewhat from those imposed on adults, though non-custodial orders such as those for community service and probation remain common court choices. Under the Juvenile Offenders Ordinance[198] young offenders over 10 years of age[199] may be subject to special measures. A detention centre order may be imposed where the offender is between 14 and 25 years of age. The regime is "vigorous" and involves strict discipline. Offenders between 14 and

---

192. See ss 107–108, Criminal Procedure Ordinance (Cap 221).
193. See Community Service Orders Ordinance (Cap 378).
194. The maximum number of hours is 240.
195. See Probation of Offenders Ordinance (Cap 298).
196. The maximum period is three years.
197. Thus, an offender's previous good conduct will be relevant in determining the length of sentence, but his "means" will not be taken into account in determining the amount of a fine.
198. Cap 226.
199. Those under 10 years of age cannot be guilty of an offence (s 3, Juvenile Offenders Ordinance).

20 may be sent to a training centre and between 14 and 21 a rehabilitation centre. For offenders between 10 and 14 care orders or reformatory school orders may be imposed. Imprisonment for juveniles (over 14) should be a last resort. No person aged between 10 and 13 may be imprisoned[200] and those aged 14 or 15 can only be imprisoned if there is no reasonable alternative. In the case of those between 16 and 20, too, imprisonment should only be imposed if there is no appropriate alternative,[201] but this does not apply in the case of those "excepted offences" under Schedule 3 of the Criminal Procedure Ordinance (described above).

3.9 Limits on the autonomy of the Hong Kong courts

While Hong Kong is guaranteed a high degree of autonomy under the Basic Law, including the right of final adjudication, some formal limitations do exist (and have been alluded to earlier in the chapter and elsewhere). Most significantly, as already mentioned, Hong Kong courts, including the Court of Final Appeal (CFA), have no jurisdiction over "acts of State such as defence and foreign affairs".[202] Where an issue involving an "act of State" is to be adjudicated, the court must obtain a certificate from the Chief Executive on questions of fact and this certificate shall be binding on the court.[203]

The autonomy of the Hong Kong courts is further limited by the position with respect to interpretation of the Basic Law. Article 158 of the Basic Law states that:

> The power of interpretation of this [Basic] Law shall be vested in the Standing Committee of the National People's Congress.
>
> The Standing Committee . . . shall authorise the courts of the Hong Kong SAR to interpret, on their own, in adjudicating cases, the provisions of this Law which are within the limits of the autonomy of the Region.
>
> The courts of the Hong Kong SAR may also interpret other provisions of this Law in adjudicating cases. However, if the courts of the Region, in adjudicating cases, need to interpret the provisions of this Law, concerning affairs which are the responsibility of the Central People's Government, or concerning the relationship between the Central Authorities and the Region, and if such interpretation will affect the judgments on the cases, the courts of the Region shall, before making their final judgments which are not appealable, seek an interpretation of the relevant provisions from the NPCSC through the Court of Final Appeal of the Region. When the Standing Committee makes an interpretation of the provisions concerned, the courts of the Region, in applying those provisions, shall follow the interpretation of the Standing Committee. However, judgments previously rendered shall not be affected.

---

200. Section 11, Juvenile Offenders Ordinance.
201. Section 109A(1), Criminal Procedure Ordinance.
202. Article 19, Basic Law.
203. Ibid.

The application of Article 158 was crucial in the *Ng Ka Ling*[204] and other "right of abode" cases, discussed more fully in Chapter 4. In determining claims for the right of abode in Hong Kong by a number of claimants born outside Hong Kong to Hong Kong citizens, the Court of Final Appeal initially interpreted Article 24 of the Basic Law in a (literal and sensible) manner unacceptable to the Hong Kong government. The Hong Kong government then asked the Standing Committee of the NPC (NPCSC) to interpret the Article in a more government-friendly way (despite the absence of provision in the Basic Law for such a government request). The Standing Committee duly obliged and the CFA was required to accept the new interpretation in respect of any novel claims.[205] The significance of the "reinterpretation"[206] for the status of the Hong Kong courts was enormous since:

> We can no longer be confident that the final interpretations of the law will be made by the courts.[207]

Since *Ng Ka Ling* and the related right of abode cases there have been four subsequent interpretations of the Basic Law by the NPCSC: one at the request of the Hong Kong government; two at the NPCSC's own initiative; and one at the request of the CFA[208] (as provided for by Article 158). These cases will be dealt with in far more detail in the "interpretation" section of Chapter 4.

Are there *informal* limits on the autonomy of the Hong Kong courts? Has, for example, the loss of "face" occasioned by the, effective, overruling of the Court of Final Appeal by the Standing Committee of the National Peoples' Congress in *Ng Ka King* produced a situation in which Hong Kong courts seek not to upset their constitutional masters in Beijing; a sort of judicial self-censorship? Other than a short-lived "retrenchment" post-*Ng Ka Ling*, in the *Lau Kong Yung* case[209] (where the CFA was criticised for going too far in upholding the NPCSC's *unlimited* power of Basic Law interpretation),[210] there has been little further evidence of "subjugation". The first Chief Justice, Andrew Li, zealously defended the autonomy and impartiality of the Hong Kong courts. Statements from leading mainland figures that the Hong Kong courts should be more accommodating to the executive have been strongly

---

204. *Ng Ka Ling v Director of Immigration* (1999) 2 HKCFAR 4.
205. Article 158 states that "judgments previously rendered" shall not be affected. Bokhary PJ was of the view that those having a "legitimate expectation" as a result of previous judgments should also be unaffected by subsequent interpretation.
206. Then Secretary for Justice, Elsie Leung, insisted that the NPCSC action was an "interpretation" since it was the first interpretation by that body.
207. Yash Ghai, 'Contradiction That Eats at Autonomy' *South China Morning Post* (Hong Kong, 4 December 1999).
208. *DR Congo & others v FG Hemisphere & Associates* (2011) 14 HKCFAR 95.
209. *Lau Kong Yung & Others v Director of Immigration* (1999) 2 HKCFAR 300 (Bokhary J dissenting!). For further discussion, see Chapter 4.
210. Described by Ling as "misguided" (B Ling, 'Subject-Matter Limitation on the NPCSC's Power to Interpret the Basic Law' (2007) 37 HKLJ 619, 633; in which the author argues that the Standing Committee had exceeded its Basic Law powers of interpretation).

rejected. It is also true, however, that Chief Justice Li announced his retirement far sooner than was necessary or anticipated, and there has been no lack of speculation as to the "real reason". On his departure, Li expressed no doubts that his successor would maintain the independence of the Hong Kong judiciary, stating that Geoffrey Ma:

> will be an outstanding successor: he will uphold the rule of law, protect judicial independence and, under his leadership, the Judiciary will continue to safeguard the rights and freedoms of the individual.[211]

Some initial concerns were expressed by Gittings[212] who expresses the fear that a Ma-led CFA may be more conservative, less inclined to "upset Beijing"[213] and less rights-conscious than the Li-led CFA, especially given the (then) imminent prospect of the retirement of Bokhary J (the most pro-rights of the CFA Permanent Judges).

However, all the indications are that, on accession to the post of Chief Justice, Ma has been equally steadfast in defending the independence of the Hong Kong judiciary.[214]

---

211. *The Standard*, 'New Chief Justice Gives Oath on Lawyer Wife' (4 May 2010).
212. D Gittings, 'Hong Kong's Courts Are Learning to Live with China' (Hong Kong Journal, July 2010) <http://www.hkbasiclaw.com/Hong%20Kong%20Journal/Gittings%20on%20Courts%20Learning%20to%20Live%20With%20China.htm> accessed 4 January 2018.
213. Gittings cites the case of *HKSAR v Yeung May Wan* [2004] 3 HKLRD 797 in which Ma J's Court of Appeal was criticised by Li CJ for its delay in upholding the legitimacy of the Falun Gong in Hong Kong.
214. In the *Vallejos* case, for example, involving a claim for permanent residency by a Filipina domestic helper, Ma CJ firmly rejected a request for NPCSC interpretation on the grounds that it was "unnecessary".

4
Legislation and the Interpretation of Statutes

Overview

Despite Hong Kong's status as a "common law" polity (one in which case law is a major source of law and written codes are less significant), legislation remains, as seen in Chapter 2, a very significant source of Hong Kong law. The primary focus of this Chapter will be the creation and "construction" (interpretation) of Hong Kong legislation, though it should be remembered that (pre-1997) British legislation still has a vestigial significance. Moreover, given Hong Kong's "return to China" in 1997, and the limits to Hong Kong's legal autonomy thereby imposed, laws passed by the National People's Congress (NPC) of the People's Republic of China (PRC) can, in limited circumstances, take effect in Hong Kong.[1]

Article 8 of the Basic Law of the Hong Kong Special Administrative Region (the Basic Law) provides for the continuation of Hong Kong's previously existing laws, including statutory laws, provided that they do not contravene the Basic Law and subject to subsequent abolition or amendment. Article 18 of the Basic Law specifically provides that the laws in force in Hong Kong shall be "this [Basic] Law, the laws previously in force in Hong Kong as provided for in Article 8 of this Law, and the *laws enacted by the legislature of the Region*" (emphasis added).

Thus Hong Kong has,[2] as it had during the colonial era, the power to make new laws through the legislature. Yet, while the Basic Law refers to Hong Kong's "high degree of autonomy", this should be put in perspective. Just as the colonial Governor was appointed by Britain, so the Chief Executive of the Hong Kong SAR is a Beijing appointee.[3] Moreover, the Chief Executive's "cabinet", the Executive Council (ExCo) is appointed by the Chief Executive. The nominal legislative body, the Legislative Council (LegCo), remains, as in colonial times, dominated by pro-government legislators. With the final removal of "Governor-appointed" seats in 1995, government majority support has continued to be assured via the "functional"

---

1. For further detail, see Chapter 2.
2. Article 17, Basic Law.
3. Under Article 45 of the Basic Law the Chief Executive shall "be appointed by the Central People's Government". That will remain the case even if (eventually) the Chief Executive is nominated/selected by universal suffrage in Hong Kong.

(generally pro-establishment) constituencies,[4] such that directly elected "opposition" remains a minority.[5] Had there been a successful transition to "universal suffrage"[6] for the election of Chief Executive in 2017, it was intended that all LegCo seats would be directly elected post-2020.[7]

However, as a further confirmation of Hong Kong's "executive-led" government, the Chief Executive has the right to refuse to sign any Bill passed by LegCo.

The intention of Article 8 of the Basic Law is that the legal rules existing before 1997[8] will continue in force unless they are amended or found to be contrary to the Basic Law. Changes to the law will be, largely, the result of local legislation and judicial decision.[9] Since previous rules will not operate where they contravene the Basic Law, this crucial constitutional document represents a source of Hong Kong law in itself. It should be remembered that, while it operates as a *de facto* constitution for Hong Kong, the Basic Law has the legal status of a basic[10] law of the PRC.

The legislative *process* in Hong Kong is a somewhat unsatisfactory one, largely as a result of a political situation which all but guarantees a government majority in LegCo thereby ensuring that the role of government opponents in LegCo is restricted to an obstructive rather than a constructive one. Most legislation in Hong Kong begins with the government and little scope exists for legislation proposed by individual LegCo members. Moreover, government legislation is, generally, enacted with the "opposition's" contribution; at most, the delay of, or minor amendment to, such legislation.

Legislation must, of course, be interpreted (or "construed") before it can be applied and those charged with such interpretation have a crucial role to play. In respect of purely Hong Kong (or pre-1997 British) legislation, the interpretative role is assumed by the Hong Kong Judiciary which is, crucially, independent of the executive and legislative arms of government. The Hong Kong judges, however, have only a circumscribed role to play in the interpretation of the Basic Law, a basic law

---

4. Ghai points out the inherent inequality of the functional constituencies in Yash Ghai, *Hong Kong's New Constitutional Order: The Resumption of Chinese Sovereignty & the Basic Law* (2nd edn, Hong Kong University Press 1999).
5. In addition, the much better financed pro-Beijing party (the "Democratic Alliance for the Betterment and Progress of Hong Kong" [DAB]) enjoys considerable support.
6. While the right for all eligible Hong Kong citizens to vote in such election was conceded by Beijing it insisted that the vote should be for one of two or three hand-picked candidates. Such a proposal was rejected by LegCo so that *LegCo* voting change is now also unlikely; the difficulty remains as to who will be permitted to "stand" for election. Since the CPG always retains the right of "veto" under the Basic Law by refusing to *appoint* an unacceptable candidate, this was an unnecessarily cautious move by Beijing.
7. The rules for the 2012 LegCo election (determined by Amendment to Annex II Basic Law, August 2010) dictated that 35 seats would be "functional" and 35 directly elected. Given the electoral impasse with Beijing, this remained for 2017.
8. Although the transfer of sovereignty took place at midnight on 30 June 1997, reference will be to "pre-1997" and "post-1997".
9. The latter is not expressly stated in the Basic Law but is implicit in, for example, the creation of the Court of Final Appeal in Hong Kong with the right of "final adjudication".
10. In this context "basic" should be with a small b.

of the PRC. The ultimate power to interpret the Basic Law resides with the Standing Committee of the National People's Congress (SCNPC).

In interpreting Hong Kong legislation, Hong Kong judges apply approaches deriving from those of the English courts. These approaches, sometimes referred to, inaccurately, as "rules", are generally complementary, with the ultimate aim said to be the determination of the legislature's true "intention". There are times, however, when conflict arises between those judges who seek to derive intention exclusively from the words used by the legislature and those whose interpretations are based on a wider incorporation of the legislation's social or political "purpose". A particular aspect of this interpretative conflict can be seen in the debate about the extent to which a judge may seek to determine legislative purpose from the pre-enactment debates in the legislature. The relaxation, in British courts, of previous rules precluding all consideration of "Parliamentary debates" in determining Parliament's "intention" has been, broadly, followed in Hong Kong.

An important difference between common law "interpretation", as practised in Hong Kong, and "interpretation" as understood in the People's Republic of China context (where the term encompasses, effectively, the rewriting of rules) has put considerable strain upon the "one country, two systems" relationship in those situations where the Standing Committee of the National People's Congress has been requested to, or has decided to, interpret the Basic Law.

4.1 Applicable legislation in Hong Kong

There are three types of legislative rules which may affect Hong Kong: English legislation, Laws of the People's Republic of China (PRC) and Hong Kong legislation. As regards the latter, which is (numerically and practically) the most significant, such legislation may take the form of primary legislation (Ordinances) or secondary (delegated) legislation.

4.1.1 English legislation

While current legislative rules in Hong Kong emanate almost entirely from the Legislative Council (LegCo),[11] English statutes (at least those in force before 1997) do have a limited effect in Hong Kong.

Before 1997, legislation passed in England could be applicable in Hong Kong.[12] Indeed, up to 1966, British legislation generally *was* applicable in Hong Kong, subject to one important caveat. The position is best summarised by Professor Peter Wesley-Smith[13] who states:

---

11. PRC legislation *may*, exceptionally, be applicable: see 4.1.2.
12. See Chapters 1 and 2.
13. Peter Wesley-Smith, *An Introduction to the Hong Kong Legal System* (3rd edn, Oxford University Press 1998).

From 1846 to 1966, the formula by which English law was received into Hong Kong applied to all the laws of England which existed on 5 April 1843, the day Hong Kong obtained a local legislature. There was a proviso, however: English law considered not suited to the circumstances of Hong Kong or of its inhabitants was excluded. The intended result was to provide a basic source of legal precepts which, though developed thousands of miles away in response to the notions and traditions of the English people, could be fashioned in accordance with local needs and conditions.[14]

The reference to 1966 relates to the Application of English Law Ordinance[15] (AELO) by which, in simple terms, English *common law* rules would continue to operate in Hong Kong (if locally suitable and not locally superseded) while British *legislation* would only operate in Hong Kong if expressly stated so to do. By the time of the transfer of sovereignty in 1997, most English legislation had been superseded by Hong Kong legislation. In any event, AELO was declared inconsistent with the Basic Law so that even the small rump of British "applicable" legislation ceased to operate in Hong Kong. British pre-1997 legislation, therefore, is of (minor) relevance to Hong Kong only in so far as it can be viewed as having amended the English pre-1997 common law which, under the Basic Law, will generally remain in force.[16]

Similarly, existing Hong Kong legislation based on English provisions continues to be valid subject to amendment or cancellation by the Hong Kong SAR legislature or to a declaration of incompatibility with the Basic Law. In the case of such "derivative" legislation, post-1997 amendments to the *English* legislation will be of interest, but will only become law in Hong Kong if LegCo incorporates the changes into new local legislation or the Hong Kong courts choose to incorporate them as elements of the Hong Kong common law.

While pre-1997 British legislation, therefore, has a peripheral claim to be a source of Hong Kong law, it is a clear consequence of the 1997 resumption of sovereignty that *post-1997* British legislation has no applicability in Hong Kong; in formal recognition of same, the Letters Patent and Royal Instructions ceased to have effect on 30 June 1997, such that the United Kingdom can no longer make legislation applying to Hong Kong.[17] English legislation may, of course, remain of some interest from a comparative perspective given the often common legislative history of the two polities. Hong Kong Law Reform Commission reports, for example, often make extensive reference to English legislation relating to the topic in question.

---

14. Ibid 39.
15. Cap 88.
16. Article 8, Basic Law.
17. Article 66 of the Basic Law states that: "The Legislative Council of the [HKSAR] shall be the legislature of the Region."

4.1.2 Legislation of the People's Republic of China (PRC)

With the return of Hong Kong's sovereignty to China, it is clear that the PRC has the power to make legislation affecting Hong Kong, despite (or in a sense because of) the policy of "one country, two systems".

The Basic Law itself, a "basic law" of the PRC, provides Hong Kong's post-1997 constitutional framework. However, the same piece of legislation imposes limits on the extent to which other PRC legislation may operate in Hong Kong. Under Article 18:

> National laws shall not be applied in the Hong Kong SAR except for those listed in Annex III to this Law. The laws listed therein shall be applied locally by way of promulgation or legislation by the Region.

Article 18 goes on to say that the Standing Committee of the National People's Congress (NPC) may add to or delete from the laws listed in Annex III and that the list:

> shall be confined to those relating to defence and foreign affairs *as well as other matters outside the limits of the autonomy of the Region as specified by this law*.[18] [emphasis added]

The list currently includes:

(1) Law of the People's Republic of China on the National Flag;
(2) Regulations of the People's Republic of China concerning Consular Privileges and Immunities;
(3) Law of the People's Republic of China on the National Emblem;
(4) Law of the People's Republic of China on the Territorial Sea and the Contiguous Zone; and
(5) Law of the People's Republic of China on the Garrisoning of the Hong Kong Special Administrative Region.

None of the items on the list are of everyday concern. In practice, therefore, as far as PRC legislation is concerned, those researching Hong Kong's legislative sources needed rarely to look further than the Basic Law. This was, at least, the position until "co-location."[19]

4.1.3 Hong Kong legislation and the Legislative Council

Post-1997, Hong Kong's local legislative position is stipulated in Article 66 of the Basic Law which provides:

---

18. The addition of these rather vague words has caused some concern though, thus far, there has been little indication of PRC legislation limiting Hong Kong's "high degree of autonomy".
19. Discussed at 2.4.

The Legislative Council of the Hong Kong Special Administrative region shall be the legislature of the region.

While, effectively, the powers of the Legislative Council (LegCo) remain circumscribed, it must be recognised that the institution has developed significantly from its humble beginnings. Established in 1843 with only four members (including the Governor), LegCo did not have its first Chinese member until 1884. Even in 1929 there were only three Chinese members. Governor-appointed members existed until 1995 and, even in post-colonial Hong Kong, members chosen by a small circle "Election Committee" continued to be appointed until 2004. The gradual move towards genuine elections, based on voter preference in geographical constituencies, has yet to reach the "ultimate aim" of "the election of all the members of the Legislative Council by universal suffrage" as envisaged by the Basic Law;[20] half of all LegCo seats are still determined, generally,[21] by small "functional constituencies" representing the will of their trade or professional "membership" rather than the electorate at large.

The purpose of the functional constituencies, according to the Hong Kong government, is "to ensure that the economic and professional sectors which are substantial and of importance in the community are represented in the legislature".[22] A less benign description is provided by Van Der Kamp who states:

> The result [of functional constituencies] has been openly declared vote trading that is satisfied only with the award of hugely expensive contracts for public works of dubious value. The corporate beggars get what they want because they maintain the administration's majority in LegCo.[23]

In practice they have continued the old colonial practice of appointed LegCo members by another means. While there have been some relatively "open" functional elections,[24] most seats have been secured on the appointment by a small, closed circle. The *South China Morning Post* has shown, for example, that there are 125 registered electors in the "Finance" constituency, despite the considerable size of the sector in Hong Kong. The "Insurance" constituency contains only 130 electors and the Heung Yee Kuk, claiming to represent the interests of all "indigenous" New Territories citizens, has only 145 electors.[25]

It remains to be seen whether functional constituencies will survive post-2020 in respect of which some indications for change had previously been mooted by the

---

20. Article 68(2).
21. Five of the 35 functional seats are elected by (near) universal suffrage encompassing those not entitled to a functional vote elsewhere.
22. Hong Kong SAR Government, *Administration's Responses to Points Raised on 7 May by Members of the Bills Committee on the LegCo (Amendment) Bill 1999* (21 May 1999), quoted in D Gittings, *Introduction to the Hong Kong Basic Law* (Hong Kong: Hong Kong University Press 2013) 131.
23. J Van Der Kamp, 'Jake's View', *South China Morning Post* (Hong Kong, 9 February 2014).
24. For example, the Legal and Education sectors.
25. T Chong, 'How a Handful of Voters Elect 30 Lawmakers', *South China Morning Post* (Hong Kong, 6 February 2014).

government. However, the total absence of any move towards greater democracy for the 2017 Chief Executive "election" suggests that the pro-government functional constituencies will be retained, despite their patently non-representative nature.

The extensive legislative functions and powers of the Legislative Council (LegCo) are stipulated by Article 73(1) of the Basic Law which states:

> The Legislative Council of the Hong Kong Special Administrative Region shall exercise the following powers and functions:
>
> (1) To enact, amend or repeal laws in accordance with the provisions of this [Basic] Law and legal procedures;
>
> (2) To examine and approve budgets introduced by the government;
>
> (3) To approve taxation and public expenditure;
>
> (4) To receive and debate the policy addresses of the Chief Executive;
>
> (5) To raise questions on the work of the government;
>
> (6) To debate any issue concerning public interests;
>
> (7) To endorse the appointment and removal of the judges of the Court of Final Appeal and the Chief Judge of the High Court;
>
> (8) To receive and handle complaints from Hong Kong residents;
>
> (9) If a motion initiated jointly by one-fourth of all the members of the Legislative Council charges the Chief Executive with serious breach of law or dereliction of duty and if he or she refuses to resign, the Council may, after passing a motion for investigation, give a mandate to the Chief Justice of the Court of Final Appeal to form and chair an independent investigation committee. The committee shall be responsible for carrying out the investigation and reporting its findings to the Council. If the committee considers the evidence sufficient to substantiate such charges, the Council may pass a motion of impeachment by a two-thirds majority of all its members and report it to the Central People's Government for decision; and
>
> (10) To summon, as required when exercising the above-mentioned powers and functions, persons concerned to testify or give evidence.

At first sight this might indicate a powerful, independent legislative body within a system of serious separation of powers. The reality is somewhat different. Since Hong Kong has operated via "executive-led" government from colonial times, the legislative process is now dominated by the Chief Executive (the constitutional successor to the colonial Governor) and his closest advisers, the Executive Council (ExCo). ExCo, whose members are appointed by the Chief Executive, comprises "principal officials of the executive authority, members of LegCo and public figures".[26] The

---

26. Article 55, Basic Law. The "public" figures remain, as they were in colonial times, primarily business ones.

dominance of the executive is guaranteed by the Chief Executive's veto powers over legislation of which he disapproves,[27] his guaranteed LegCo majority via the "functional" members,[28] and the procedural barriers in the way of members instituting non-government Bills. Thus, while legislation may be introduced by government[29] *or* by LegCo members,[30] given the dominance of the executive under Hong Kong's constitution, and the significant restrictions on member's bills, "government bills" are by far the more common method.[31] LegCo retains the ("negative") power to obstruct, or attempt to amend, government bills which has led to an unsatisfactory constitutional situation, based largely on confrontation rather than co-operation. Government machinations in 2017/2018 (described elsewhere) have severely limited the ability of LegCo to "obstruct". Thus, as Tai writes:

> LegCo does not have the capacity to position itself in any significant way other than putting up some form of opposition.[32]

Hong Kong "domestic" legislation consists of "primary" legislation (Ordinances), brought before and approved by LegCo, and subordinate or "delegated" legislation, in which an "enabling" Ordinance outlines the broad purposes of the legislation while leaving it to a subordinate official or body to implement the fine detail within the ambit of the enabling legislation.

4.2 The legislative process in Hong Kong

There are various stages that all bills must go through before being finally enacted and subsequently coming into force. The procedures vary depending on whether the proposed legislation is a government or a member's bill.

4.2.1 Government bills

One of the stated functions of the Hong Kong government is "to draft and introduce bills, motions and subordinate legislation".[33] The government's legislative plans are organised by the Committee on Legislative Priorities, comprising the Chief Secretary for Administration,[34] the Financial Secretary, the Secretary for Justice and the Law Draftsman, whose purpose is to plan the government's legislative strategy for each LegCo session. The political reality is that the government's key legislative intentions

---

27. Even though most legislation emanates from the government.
28. Primarily pro-business and pro-government.
29. Under Basic Law, Article 62(5).
30. Article 74, Basic Law.
31. Only a small minority of Bills are from members and, of these, subsequent enactment is exceptional.
32. Benny Tai, 'Basic Law, Basic Politics: The Constitutional Game of Hong Kong' (2007) 37 HKLJ 503.
33. Basic Law, Article 62(5).
34. Hong Kong's number two post, after that of the Chief Executive.

are rarely thwarted by LegCo but are frequently hindered. This hindrance owes much to Hong Kong's political situation which, effectively, guarantees the government a LegCo majority yet ensures that the largely impotent minority members retain the ability to hold up legislation through lengthy (some would say over-lengthy) debate. "Filibustering", on United States lines, is increasing in Hong Kong's LegCo and it is largely the product of frustration at the slow pace of democratic progress. The consequences are serious since only the government's "priority" legislation is pursued while worthwhile "other business" falls by the wayside. The lack of follow-up on Law Reform Commission recommendations, discussed in Chapter 2, is but one example, of the legislative deficit. However, having (by fair means and foul) reduced the number of opposition legislators (discussed elsewhere) the government and its LegCo supporters are now able to expedite a legislative agenda based primarily on unnecessary, unpopular and always over-budget infrastructure projects.

It is axiomatic that new legislation must have a purpose; either to introduce necessary new rules or to amend existing ones. Before new or amending legislation is introduced in the Legislative Council (LegCo) significant preparatory work must first have been done. The "originator" of the legislation (usually the head of a government department) must first secure the support of the relevant director of bureau. The originator must issue a statement explaining why the proposed legislation is necessary in the public interest. The statement must also explain the major implications, financial and otherwise, of the legislation and, in particular, show that the proposal is in conformity with the Basic Law.

The originator must show that the "views of other parties affected have been considered."[35] As such, before a government bill is introduced into LegCo, it is normal for there to be a "consultation process". It is common for a "consultation paper" or a "white paper" to be published seeking the views of interested parties and the public. Given the imbalance, in practice, between proposed government legislation and that of humble members, it is not surprising that so-called "public consultations" are much criticised, both in terms of irrelevance and flawed methodology. The Hong Kong government's all but guaranteed majority in LegCo,[36] via the so-called "functional constituencies" and the Chief Executive's *de facto* veto powers[37] on legislation, mean that consultation tends to be an issue of form rather than substance. The government's consultation on "reclamation", for example, asks respondents to state their preferred choices for reclamation from a range of selected potential sites, while overlooking public opposition to further reclamation in principle; in short the "government"[38] "sets the agenda". The same is also true of the extensive consultation

---

35. HKSAR General Regulation 451.
36. With only half of LegCo seats elected via geographical constituency it would need all such elected members (or a number of "functional" members) to vote together to defeat the government.
37. The Chief Executive must agree to present the proposed bill to LegCo *and* must give his assent before a bill can become law.
38. Of course, the "government" concerned is not always the Hong Kong one. "Consultations" and debates on infrastructure developments (such as the environmentally disastrous Hong Kong–Zhuhai

on electoral reform[39] which drew attention to the potential for universal suffrage for the 2017 Chief Executive "elections" but made light of the fact that the right to "seek election" would be severely circumscribed.[40] On the deteriorating environment, too, an issue on which Hong Kong people are overwhelmingly unhappy, the government is always more concerned about "progress" than conservation.[41]

The following *South China Morning Post* letter illustrates the deficiencies of the current public consultation methodology:

> I must take issue, however, with [the] statement that the 'proposed development plan underwent extensive public consultation'.
>
> . . . I would like to point out that the extent and quality of such "consultation" exercises in Hong Kong over the last 15 years has been risible.
>
> None of the consultations conducted by Hong Kong's public bodies . . . would be acceptable in Namibia or Malawi, let alone advanced economies like Australia or Canada.
>
> . . . Approaching the public for the first time with proposals that have already been put forward, as the arts hub authority has done, is too late . . .
>
> The consequences of a consultation that is both ineffective and insincere is development that fails to serve the needs of the majority. Whether [this is] due to incompetence, a paucity of skills and knowledge within the government, or, as the Hong Kong public suspects, collusion with big business, is a matter requiring further investigation.[42]

Similar criticisms are voiced by KY Ip who writes:

> Hong Kong's colonial government was good at pitching policy initiatives through public consultations.
>
> After 1997, the city's government simply inherited this legacy, but it has failed to keep up with the times.

---

bridge) are clearly futile when they have already been flagged as part of a PRC three, four or five-year plan. See Peter Kammerer, 'No More No-Brainer Public Consultations in Hong Kong', *South China Morning Post* (Hong Kong, 12 May 2014).

39. In October 2013 the Chief Executive established a three-person "Task Force on Constitutional Development". A 2014 "Public Consultation" followed.
40. The "Occupy Central" movement (ominously described by *China Daily* as an "illegal movement": 10 June 2014) was committed to a campaign of civil disobedience if progress on universal suffrage (including, perhaps, "civil nomination" for Chief Executive in the 2017 election) was not made. Since "civil nomination" is regarded by many (including, naturally, all pro-Beijing and pro-government parties but also, eg, the Hong Kong Bar Association) as contrary to the Basic Law, political and social impasse was almost inevitable.
41. In Donald Tsang's period in office alone, the government increased harbour reclamation and approved the destruction of the Star Ferry Pier and Queen's Pier, all against the clear wishes of most Hong Kong people. "Vanity" projects, such as a "road only" bridge to Macau and Zhuhai, have continued and the government now plots the environmental destruction of Lantau. All such projects are completed late and over-budget.
42. A Morgan, 'Hong Kong's Public Consultations Are Ineffective' *South China Morning Post* (Hong Kong, 4 January 2013).

These days, the government often confuses consultation with promotion, and the majority of the public is increasingly frustrated with the fact that its opinions don't make a difference.[43]

One of the clearest examples of the cynicism involved in "consultation" relates to discussion of retirement benefits. Having foisted the egregious "Mandatory Provident Fund" (which provided serious benefits only to the banks permitted to administer the system) on Hong Kong people,[44] the government has since commenced further consultation on "retirement protection". Thus:

> One of the Hong Kong government's methods to push (or deliberately kill off) a proposed policy is to launch a public consultation. This involves a document that defines the 'problem' as the bureaucrats want us to see it . . .
>
> We normally think of Hong Kong policymakers as hopelessly inept and incompetent. But they are highly skilled at these exercises in cynical manipulation. And they have possible surpassed themselves with the latest—a public engagement on retirement protection. The consultation paper has the tagline 'forging ahead', by which of course they mean 'getting bogged down and not going anywhere'.

Probably the most disingenuous of all so-called "consultations" is that recently involving the "Task Force" on Land Supply. Citizens are asked to give their views on how to improve land supply for Hong Kong people. They are, however, not permitted to advocate any of the three actions which would actually work (limiting land purchases to Hong Kong citizens, prohibiting company purchases and abolishing the small house policy) for fear of alienating the government's friends. Instead they must choose, essentially between yet more reclamation or building on country parks.

As well as public consultation, the original statement of proposals must be sent to the Law Officer (Civil Law) who will advise whether the Secretary for Justice has any objections in principle to the proposed legislation.

After any consultation, the relevant policy bureau issues drafting instructions to the Department of Justice, requesting it to put the proposal into the form of a bill. After drafting by the Law Drafting Division of the Department of Justice (responsible for the drafting of all Government Bills), the bill is submitted for approval to the Executive Council (ExCo), presided over by the Chief Executive who is responsible for the appointment and removal of its members.[45] Under the Basic Law: "The Executive Council of the Hong Kong SAR shall be an organ for assisting the Chief Executive in policy-making".[46] All government bills (and subsidiary legislation) presented to ExCo must contain a memorandum explaining the objective(s) of the legislation.

---

43. KY Ip, 'Public Consultation? In HK It's More Like Promotion' *ejinsight* (Hong Kong, 13 March 2015).
44. Under the Scheme employers were even permitted to claw back their paltry "contributions" from employees' final gratuity.
45. Article 55, Basic Law.
46. Article 54, Basic Law.

If the Chief Executive decides, on the advice of ExCo,[47] to present the Bill to LegCo, a notice is sent to the Clerk to the Legislative Council. The Clerk then arranges for publication of the text of the bill to be published in the "Gazette".[48] A copy of the bill and an explanatory memorandum is then sent to every LegCo member, at which point the bill is deemed to be "presented" to LegCo.

After presentation, all bills must be "read" three times. The First Reading is a formality and involves the short title of the bill being read out to LegCo, by the Clerk to the Legislative Council, and a date for the second reading being fixed. No debate is permitted at this stage. Immediately after the First Reading, the proposer of the bill moves that "the bill be read a second time".[49]

The Second Reading begins with the proposer making a speech explaining the merits and purpose of the proposed legislation. This is normally followed by a brief debate amongst LegCo members on the merits or otherwise of the proposed legislation. After any initial debate the bill may be referred, on adjournment, to the "House Committee.[50] The House Committee may then decide to submit the bill to a bills committee[51] for detailed consideration.[52] Amendments may be suggested which are reported back to the full Council. The second reading will continue and will culminate in a vote. Approval must be by a (simple) LegCo majority, the bill proceeding no further if this is not achieved.

After majority approval at the Second Reading stage, the Bill reaches the Committee Stage. LegCo now sits as a "Committee of the whole Council" where the bill is considered in detail. At this stage, amendments to the bill may be put forward by the Chairman of the Bills Committee or by individual members. If agreed by the government, the amendments will be introduced into the bill.

After the Committee Stage, with or without amendment, the Bill proceeds to the Third Reading stage. A motion is proposed that the third reading be approved and the bill passed. At this stage, members have a final opportunity to propose minor amendments (eg, that there are grammatical errors or omissions) with the permission of the LegCo President. No amendments of substance are permitted. Once the motion for the Third Reading is approved by a majority of the LegCo members,[53] the bill has completed its LegCo passage.

---

47. Under Basic Law Article 56, ExCo must be consulted. If the Chief Executive decides to proceed with a bill contrary to ExCo's advice, he must record his reasons in writing.
48. At this point the final version of the bill is open to public scrutiny.
49. Rules of Procedure of the Legislative Council of the Hong Kong SAR (LegCo Rules) rule 53.
50. LegCo Rules rule 54(4).
51. "In the great majority of cases, the Bill is allocated to a Bills Committee which carries out the detailed examination of the Bill. The drafter of the Bill attends the meetings of the Bills Committee to advise on and answer questions relating to drafting." Law Drafting Division, Department of Justice, *How Legislation Is Made in Hong Kong,* 15–16.
52. LegCo Rules rule 75(4).
53. Government Bills require only a simple majority of the LegCo members present: Basic Law, Annex II.

Two further requirements must be met before the bill becomes formally enacted. First, it requires the Chief Executive's assent.[54] Given that the bill has been introduced by the government, and any amendments have been agreed by it, "assent" is likely to be a formality.[55] The bill is formally "signed and promulgated" (via publication in the Gazette) by the Chief Executive.

Thereafter, the enactment of the bill (as an Ordinance) must be "reported" to the Standing Committee of the National People's Congress (NPC) as a matter of record.[56] This reporting does not prevent the bill/Ordinance coming into force. The Standing Committee has the power to send back the newly created law if it considers that it is incompatible with the Basic Law. This would involve a decision that the law trespassed on issues which are the domain of the Central People's Government (defence, foreign affairs, etc) or that it concerned the relationship between the Hong Kong SAR and the PRC. The Standing Committee has the power to send back legislation but *not* to amend it.[57]

If the Standing Committee returns the Ordinance in question it will be invalidated.

4.2.1.1 Illustration (Privity of Contract Reform)

i. Proposal

Proposals for government legislation may come direct from a government department or follow a Law Reform Commission (of Hong Kong) recommendation. In the case of privity law reform, the impetus had been (in December 2002) a direction from the Secretary for Justice and the Chief Justice that the Law Reform Commission (LRC) should examine the doctrine of privity of contract and make recommendations for reform as necessary. The LRC had issued a Consultation Paper in June 2004. This was followed by a report, published in September 2005, recommending legislation broadly in line with that enacted in English law[58] and elsewhere in the common law world.

A consultation bill was finally issued by the Department of Justice in October 2012 and the views of the legal profession and other interested parties were sought.[59] The LegCo Panel on Administration of Justice and Legal Services also debated the proposals at length.[60]

---

54. Basic Law, Article 76.
55. There is provision, however, for the Chief Executive to "return" a Bill (Basic Law, Article 49). Since this is more likely to apply in respect of "Member's Bills" see 4.2.2 below.
56. Basic Law, Article 17.
57. "No law has been returned by the Standing Committee as at 1 June 2012." Law Drafting Division, Department of Justice, n 50, 18.
58. Contracts (Rights of Third Parties) Act, 1989.
59. See Department of Justice, 'Consultation Paper on Contracts (Rights of Third Parties) Bill 2013'.
60. See, eg, LC Paper No CB(4) 157/13-14(04).

ii. First approval

The proposal is "ranked" by the Committee on Legislative Priorities and included in the government's legislative programme.

iii. Drafting

The proposal is drafted as a "bill" by the Law Drafting Division of the Department of Justice. In the case of this proposal, only minor amendments were made to the original LRC proposals and the bill was drafted as the Contracts (Rights of Third Parties) Bill.

iv. Chief Executive approval

Under the Basic Law, the Chief Executive is required to consult ExCo before approving a bill. The Chief Executive approved the bill and ordered, at an ExCo meeting on 18 February 2014, that it be introduced into LegCo.

v. Publication

After Chief Executive approval, the bill and an explanatory memorandum were published in the Gazette (28 February 2014).

vi. First reading

The short title of the bill was read out by the Clerk to the Legislative Council (26 March 2014). As always, there was no debate at this juncture.

vii. Second reading

The second reading of the bill was moved by the Secretary for Justice, Rimsky Yuen SC, on 26 March, 2014 as follows:

> I move that the Contracts (Rights of Third Parties) Bill be read the second time...
>
> The Administration has consulted the legal profession and other stakeholders[61] on the Bill...
>
> ...The Administration believes that the Bill would enhance Hong Kong's contractual law regime and align it with those of the other major common law jurisdictions.
>
> With these remarks, I would like to appeal to Members to support the Bill.

At this stage there may be brief debate on the merits of the bill which is then referred to the House Committee (all members except the president). The House Committee then determines whether to adopt further scrutiny via a bills committee. In the case of the proposed privity reforms, a bills committee was formed.

---

61. See notes 58 and 59, above.

viii. Resumption

Thereafter, there is a resumption debate on the Second Reading and, if passed, the bill moves to the Committee Stage. The resumption debate, commenced, in the case of privity reform, with a speech in support by the Secretary for Justice (Rimsky Yuen SC) on 26 November 2014:

> Mr President,
>
> The Contracts (Rights of Third Parties) Bill I introduced to this Council in March this year has been examined in detail by the Bills Committee chaired by the Hon Kenneth Leung...
>
> I shall move a couple of Committee Stage Amendments (CSAs) later. The CSAs have all been endorsed by the Bills Committee...
>
> ...the Bill, when enacted, will enhance Hong Kong's contractual law regime. The contents of the Bill will be further improved with our proposed amendments.
>
> With these remarks, I urge Members to support the Second Reading... and endorse the amendments proposed...

ix. Committee stage

At Committee stage, the Bill is subjected to intense scrutiny by the Committee of the Whole Council which considers all provisions of the bill and votes on any proposed amendments. In the case of the privity legislation (relatively uncontentious and already subject to a bills committee vetting) the Committee stage was very quick and no additional amendments were proposed.

x. Third reading

The member in charge of the bill moves that the bill be read for the third time and passed. Debate is limited to any suggested errors which need correcting. There may be no substantial debate nor any further amendments proposed. After the motion is passed, the short title is read out by the Clerk to the Legislative Council who pronounces the Bill passed by LegCo. In the case of the Contracts (Rights of Third Parties) Ordinance, the bill was passed by LegCo on 26 November 2014.

xi. Chief Executive assent/promulgation

The bill is then submitted to the Chief Executive for signature. Thereafter it is "promulgated" by publication in the Gazette.[62] The "privity" Ordinance was Gazetted on 5 December 2014. Only on promulgation does a bill officially become an Ordinance.[63] The privity reforms then became Chapter 623 of the Laws of Hong Kong (Cap 623).

---

62. Under Article 76, Basic Law, a bill may take effect only after Chief Executive signature and promulgation.
63. Prior to "Gazetting" the bill was Ordinance No 17 of 2014.

A date is fixed for the coming into force of the Ordinance, which may be on a stated date or on a date to fixed later. In the case of the "privity" Ordinance, the legislation came into operation on 1 January, 2016 following a Commencement Notice in the Gazette on 5 June 2015.

It is perhaps worthy of note that a relatively uncontentious piece of legislation,[64] with few major objections and building on a large body of experience elsewhere in the common law world, was first referred to the LRC in 2002 and came into force some 14 years later.

xii. Reporting for the record

All legislation enacted in Hong Kong must be reported to the Standing Committee of the National People's Congress for the record. That body *does* have the power to disallow (though not amend) Hong Kong legislation[65] but it has not done so, to date. Since disallowance is permissible in relation to legislation in contravention of the Basic Law, it is common for LegCo Briefing Papers to assert that there is no conflict. This was, indeed, the case with the "privity" reform legislation.[66]

4.2.2 Member's bills

Bills may be introduced into LegCo by individual members or a group of members with a common interest.[67] Member's bills are far less common than government bills[68] and their processes (and likelihood of enactment) are far more greatly circumscribed than bills originating from the government.

Member's bills may be divided into public and private bills. A public bill is one which, if enacted, deals with matters of general law, whereas a private bill is one which affects only certain individuals or persons. Every Ordinance in Hong Kong is referred to as a *public* Ordinance, irrespective of the bill's classification. However, additional restrictions apply in the case of "private" member's bills.

In a typical member's bill scenario, the originating member (or members)[69] will consult those likely to be affected by the bill and to have a "view". Where appropriate there will also be consultation with the appropriate LegCo panel.

The member who intends to introduce a bill is responsible for the drafting of the bill; neither the staff of the Secretariat of the Council nor the Department of Justice will assist in this matter. Since, however, it is a requirement that any member's bill

---

64. Such concerns as had been raised were largely resolved by legislative provision for "opting out".
65. The power is limited to legislation regarded as inconsistent with the Basic Law or affecting issues which are the responsibility of the Central People's Government.
66. See Legislative Council Brief LP 5019/11C.
67. Article 74, Basic Law.
68. Since 1997 the average number of bills introduced by members has been around two per year (with almost none being enacted).
69. Known as the member (or members) in charge of the Bill: LegCo Rules rule 51(8).

Law-Making Process

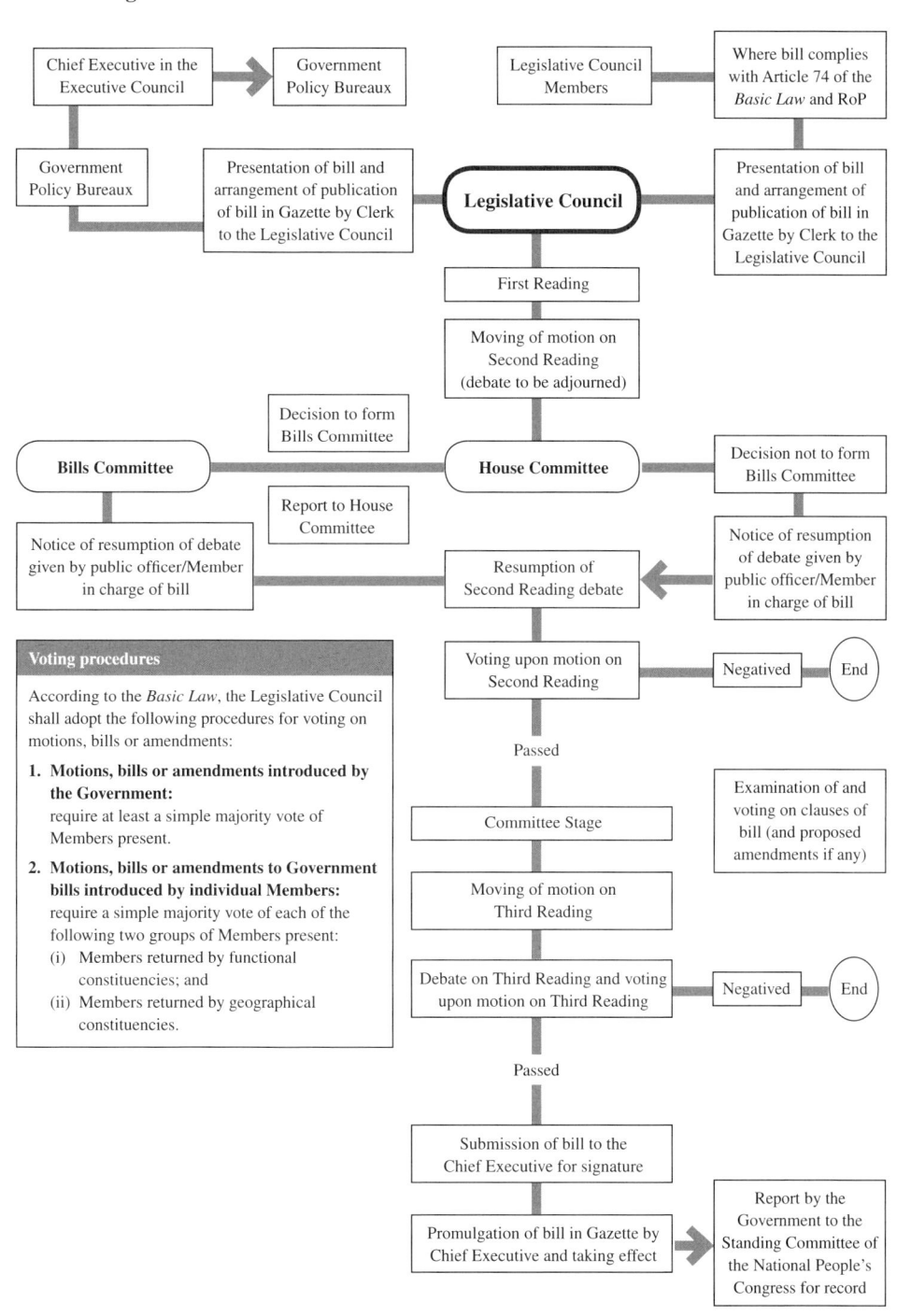

```
Chief Executive in the Executive Council → Government Policy Bureaux
Government Policy Bureaux → Presentation of bill and arrangement of publication of bill in Gazette by Clerk to the Legislative Council → Legislative Council

Legislative Council Members → Where bill complies with Article 74 of the Basic Law and RoP → Presentation of bill and arrangement of publication of bill in Gazette by Clerk to the Legislative Council → Legislative Council
```

Legislative Council flow:
- First Reading
- Moving of motion on Second Reading (debate to be adjourned)
- House Committee
  - Decision to form Bills Committee → Bills Committee → Notice of resumption of debate given by public officer/Member in charge of bill → Report to House Committee
  - Decision not to form Bills Committee → Notice of resumption of debate given by public officer/Member in charge of bill
- Resumption of Second Reading debate
- Voting upon motion on Second Reading → Negatived → End
- Passed ↓
- Committee Stage — Examination of and voting on clauses of bill (and proposed amendments if any)
- Moving of motion on Third Reading
- Debate on Third Reading and voting upon motion on Third Reading → Negatived → End
- Passed ↓
- Submission of bill to the Chief Executive for signature
- Promulgation of bill in Gazette by Chief Executive and taking effect → Report by the Government to the Standing Committee of the National People's Congress for record

Voting procedures

According to the *Basic Law*, the Legislative Council shall adopt the following procedures for voting on motions, bills or amendments:

1. **Motions, bills or amendments introduced by the Government:**
   require at least a simple majority vote of Members present.

2. **Motions, bills or amendments to Government bills introduced by individual Members:**
   require a simple majority vote of each of the following two groups of Members present:
   (i) Members returned by functional constituencies; and
   (ii) Members returned by geographical constituencies.

be in an appropriate form,[70] the member's bill must be accompanied by a certificate issued by the Law Draftsman of the Department of Justice that the bill conforms to the form of bills approved by LegCo Rules of Procedure and the general form of Hong Kong legislation.[71]

Where the member's bill is "private", a further requirement must be met; namely that the member must publish it in two successive publications of the Gazette and the notice of the bill is required to be advertised twice in two daily newspapers published in Hong Kong, one being a Chinese language newspaper and the other an English language one.[72]

The member then sends a notice of his intention to present the bill (whether private or public) to the Clerk to the Council who sends every LegCo member a copy of the bill and its explanatory memorandum. At this point, the bill is deemed to have been *presented* to LegCo. In the case of a public bill the Clerk also causes the text of the bill and its explanatory memorandum to be published in the Gazette.

Since no member is entitled to introduce a "money bill"[73] or one relating to political structure or the operation of the government, the LegCo President must rule as to whether the member's bill infringes this restriction. If the President's decision goes against the introducing member, the bill must be withdrawn. Moreover, the President will also rule on whether the bill relates to government policies. If it is found to do so, the bill may proceed only with the written consent of the Chief Executive.[74] These combined obstacles (especially Article 74 of the Basic Law) have severely curtailed the significance of members' bills.[75]

A crucial barrier to the enactment of legislation unpopular with the government is the requirement that member's bills must be passed by a majority of both the elected *and* the "functional constituency" members. Since the functional constituencies are so constructed as to virtually guarantee a government majority, there is little likelihood of legislation being passed by LegCo of which the government disapproves.

In any event, moreover, a final rein on the enactment of member's bills is provided by Article 49 of the Basic Law. Under this Article, the Chief Executive has the power to return a bill to LegCo, within three months of it being passed, if he is of the view that it is "not compatible with the overall interests" of the Hong Kong SAR. LegCo must then reconsider the bill. If it passes the bill again, unamended, with at least a two-thirds majority, the Chief Executive must sign and promulgate it within

---

70. LegCo Rules rule 50.
71. Ibid rule 51. The "no assistance" rule and the requirement as to form, provides a significant deterrent to members.
72. Ibid Rule 51(6).
73. Money Bills (Revenue Proposals) are also given special treatment whereby "to protect public revenue" the Chief Executive may make a "public revenue protection order" to give money legislation immediate effect (Public Revenue Protection Ordinance, Cap 120).
74. Ibid Rules 51(3) and 51(4) and Basic Law, Article 74.
75. See note 49.

Legislation and the Interpretation of Statutes 191

a month. If he feels unable to do this, and cannot reach agreement after further consultation, the Chief Executive may dissolve LegCo.[76] This "return of bill" process is not, strictly, limited to member's bills but, since government bills will have the implicit approval of the Chief Executive, in practice the process will only operate in respect of member's bills.

Other than the special procedures and restrictions applicable to member's bills, the general procedure, in terms of amendment, voting, "signing and promulgating" is the same for member's bills as for government ones.

The number of successful member's bills in any one year is very small and this is largely the result of Basic Law restrictions.[77] This compares with approximately 25 enacted government bills and roughly 150 pieces of subsidiary legislation per year.

4.2.3 Delegated (subsidiary) legislation

While major reforms and innovations are generally enacted via "primary" legislation ("Ordinances" in Hong Kong), much legislation involves the "delegation" of power to an individual or body to control the detail within the broad principles and purposes described by "enabling" legislation. The sheer volume and detail of modern legislation, coupled with the pressure of time on legislators, means that most modern societies entrust the detailed operation of "delegated legislation" to designated bodies or ministers.

Hong Kong is no exception to this approach and the number of pieces of "subsidiary" legislation, deriving from an "enabling Ordinance", far exceeds that of Ordinances *per se*. LegCo regularly delegates to an individual, or organisation, the power to implement rules within the ambit of the broad framework provided by the "parent" legislation. "Subsidiary legislation" is defined, in Hong Kong, as:

> any proclamation, rule, regulation, order, resolution, notice, rule of court, bylaw or other instrument made under or by virtue of any Ordinance and having legislative effect.[78]

Broadly, therefore, "subsidiary" legislation involves the detailed rules and regulations made by the government and other public bodies to provide the technical and procedural support necessary for the implementation of an Ordinance.[79]

The Interpretation and General Clauses Ordinance[80] specifies two alternative procedures by which subsidiary legislation may be approved by LegCo. First, under

---

76. Basic Law, Article 50.
77. Gittings shows that "in the two years *before* the application of the Basic Law, 50 private [*sic*] Members' Bills were introduced and 22 enacted; while, in the two years post-Basic Law, only two Members' Bills were allowed to go forward" (D Gittings, n 21, 144).
78. Section 3, Interpretation and General Clauses Ordinance (Cap 1).
79. There are, in Hong Kong, approximately 1,450 items of subsidiary legislation compared with almost 700 Ordinances. (Source: Law Drafting Division of the Department of Justice.)
80. Cap 1.

the "negative vetting" procedure,[81] subsidiary legislation may be "laid on the table" of LegCo after it is published in the Gazette. The subsidiary legislation will then take effect on the date of its publication.[82]

After the subsidiary legislation is tabled, it may be amended in LegCo, normally within 28 days. In other words, this type of subordinate legislation takes effect as published *unless* LegCo negatives it.

Under the "positive vetting" procedure, the "enabling" Ordinance provides that the subsidiary legislation will take effect following LegCo approval. A motion, therefore, is required in LegCo that the subsidiary legislation be approved. LegCo may then approve, reject or amend the proposed legislation. This type of subsidiary legislation only takes effect when LegCo approves it.[83]

On those relatively rare occasions when LegCo wishes to consider subsidiary legislation in detail, the normal procedure is to set up "a sub-committee under the House Committee".

Delegated legislation has expanded rapidly in recent years because of certain advantages it enjoys. One such advantage relates to "technicality" of subject matter. Many regulations deal with technical matters which are better dealt with by experts rather than LegCo members and, provided that LegCo retains sufficient powers of "scrutiny", delegated legislation works well. A related advantage is that in emergencies it is often necessary to be able to act quickly, and rules, regulations etc can be made more quickly than Ordinances. A further advantage relates to a lack of legislative time. It is an advantage to the administration that LegCo's precious time, already in short supply, is not given over to legislating minutiae.

There are, however, some disadvantages of delegated legislation. The first concerns the sheer volume of such legislation which may result in a lack of proper public debate on the issues concerned. Further, items of delegated legislation tend to be complex, and the drafting process for delegated rules tends to less satisfactory than would be the case for a bill presented to LegCo. Finally, it could be argued that the time allowed for scrutiny and control of delegated legislation is inadequate; in some cases, regulations become law 14 days after being laid before LegCo unless a motion to amend them is passed. Wesley-Smith[84] summarises the position on delegated legislation thus:

> Only rarely is there consultation with interested groups before it is made; it is not available in draft form prior to becoming law; and LegCo almost never debates it. Thus the safeguards which permit public opinion to be expressed on proposed primary legislation and which try to prevent careless law-making do not apply to delegated legislation. This is law-making by experts and, since it normally involves

---

81. Ibid s 34.
82. Unless another date is stated.
83. Section 35 Interpretation and General Clauses Ordinance (Cap 1).
84. Wesley-Smith, *An Introduction to the Hong Kong Legal System* (n 13).

technical details rather than general principles, there are perhaps fewer reasons for requiring publicity and formal process through the legislature.[85]

The major "theoretical" restraint on delegated legislation is that it must not exceed the bounds of its enabling or "parent" Ordinance. Rules or regulations which exceed the ambit of the enabling legislation may be challenged on the basis of "*ultra vires*" (exceeding [their] power). In practice, enabling Ordinances tend to be drafted quite widely so that *ultra vires* challenge is unusual.[86]

4.2.4 Legislative bilingualism

Throughout most of the colonial period, legislation in Hong Kong was drafted only in English. After the signing of the Joint Declaration in 1984,[87] provision was made for enactment in Chinese. The Official Languages Ordinance[88] of 1987 required that *all* Hong Kong legislation must, henceforth, be bilingual. Under the Interpretation and General Clauses Ordinance[89] both the English and Chinese texts are authentic and are *presumed* to have the same meaning.[90] Where a difference in meaning between the two texts is subsequently discovered, the interpretation most closely in accord with the object and purposes of the legislation will be adopted.[91] All Hong Kong legislation, in English and Chinese, can be accessed via the Bilingual Laws Information System (BLIS), a once essential Hong Kong law research tool soon to be superseded.[92] The establishment of a (bilingual) electronic database of all Hong Kong legislation has been given statutory recognition and is now in operation.[93]

Berry,[94] however, has raised doubts as to the quality of Chinese translations, while conceding that their quality has improved. He cites two main problems: the archaic nature of many of the original English statutes (he favours a two-stage approach of rewriting [and thereby improving] the English versions prior to translation); and the lack of adequate legal language in Chinese which renders accurate translation difficult. It is to be hoped that the improvements which Berry has noted have continued.

---

85. Ibid 90.
86. Miners, in *The Government and Politics of Hong Kong* (5th edn, Oxford University Press 1991), refers to an amusing and embarrassing discovery in 1987 that the Film Censorship Regulations made under the Places of Public Entertainment Ordinance were invalid, such that films had been censored without legal authority for 35 years! (A rectifying Ordinance was hurriedly passed.)
87. See Chapter 1.
88. Cap 5.
89. Cap 1.
90. Ibid s 10B(1).
91. Ibid s 10B(3).
92. See Chapter 14.
93. Legislation Publication Ordinance (Cap 614).
94. D Berry, 'The Effect of Poorly Written Legislation in a Bilingual Legal System' *The Loophole* (Hong Kong, March 2007) 88–92.

4.2.5 The "filibuster" issue

As already noted, LegCo members have little hope of successfully introducing legislation given that "the dice are loaded" in favour of executive legislation. This has caused immense resentment amongst those members who wish to see the introduction of "social" legislation; notably a proper universal pension scheme to safeguard the future for Hong Kong's increasingly ageing population. The Hong Kong government, in contrast, has always favoured infrastructure "vanity" projects over "recurrent" commitments in the form of welfare provision. Previous Chief Executive, Donald Tsang, for example, announced a raft of infrastructure projects all of which are guaranteed to run over budget and all of which will favour big business rather than the average Hong Kong citizen. To take just two examples, the "road only" bridge to Macau and Zhuhai will be an environmental catastrophe, benefiting only those paid to provide the infrastructure and actually contrary to the PRC's "rail over road" strategy. Further, the rail link to "Guangzhou",[95] already highly unpopular,[96] has become far more so with the announcement that it is far behind schedule and will require a far greater budget.[97]

The consequence of the dissonance between government policy and thwarted public opinion has been that radical legislators have attempted to use their only legal power in LegCo, that of obstruction, to hold up proposed government legislation. Huge amounts of proposed amendments and questions have been raised, especially in respect of budget legislation.[98] Ousted legislator Leung Kwok-hung ("Long Hair"), for example, stated that he would continue to "filibuster" until the government introduces a universal pension system for Hong Kong citizens.[99] With the assistance of an NPCSC Basic Law Interpretation, the government has been able to exclude Leung and fellow "trouble-makers" from LegCo.[100]

The previous Secretary for Finance, John Tsang,[101] decried the adverse financial effects of the filibuster on the needy, whose proposed budget provision has been delayed. In fact, the amounts involved are minute in comparison with the huge sums lavished on the aforementioned infrastructure projects. More realistically, however, there *is* a reduction in time available for other, perhaps valuable, legislative projects. The lack of legislative response to proposals from the Hong Kong Law Reform Commission is a case in point.[102]

---

95. In fact, around 30 kilometres from Guangzhou.
96. Mass protests were lodged by New Territories citizens threatened by the project and by those opposing further "integration" with the mainland.
97. LegCo was not officially informed of the delay until long after it was known to be inevitable by the MTR Corporation which had been appointed to deliver on the Hong Kong side.
98. LegCo has the power to "examine and approve" budgets under Article 73, Basic Law.
99. Currently Hong Kong has only the much-derided Mandatory Provident Fund (MPF) Scheme which has certainly not provided a "safety net" for Hong Kong citizens but *has* ensured lucrative profits for the Scheme's administrators. See M De Golyer, 'The MPF System Has Not Produced Returns Able to Support Retirement amid Hong Kong's High Living Costs' *China Daily* (Beijing, 29 May 2014).
100. See 4.4 below.
101. Despite strong competition, almost certainly Hong Kong's most incompetent politician.
102. See Chapter 2 at 2.11.

4.3 The interpretation of statutes

Simplistically it is sometimes said that "common law" (decided via the cases) is judge-made, whereas legislation (statutory law) is made by the legislature. This oversimplification overlooks the fact that, before statutory law can be applied by the courts, it must first be interpreted or "construed".[103] The interpretative function allows judges considerable scope, in practice, to indulge in "creative" solutions to what they may consider poorly drafted legislation which fails to reflect what the judge considers to be the legislature's true intention or "purpose".

Two particular issues add to the complexity of judicial interpretation. The first is that, as Zander points out,

> a legal document speaks not only to the present but is usually intended to cope with the future. That indeed is normally its chief function. But the draftsman's capacity to anticipate the future is necessarily limited.[104]

The second issue is that "context" is all. What may be ambiguous to one in ignorance of a context may be clear with the necessary contextual knowledge. This may mean, where the context is legalistic, that the judge's view of meaning may differ from that of the layman. Spigelman CJ[105] cites the example of the words, "the chicken is ready to eat". *Prima facie* the word "eat" might be used actively or passively, whereas to the reader with knowledge that the chicken is already dead, the meaning is straightforward.

Approaches to statutory interpretation, therefore, tend to vary from a traditionalist view that the words of a statute must be given their strict literal meaning, to more flexible approaches which strive to seek and reflect the legislature's true intent. However, to present literal and purposive approaches as a dichotomy is somewhat misleading, since literalists would argue, given the difficulties already alluded to, that the best gauge of a legislature's intention is the natural meaning of that legislature's words.

4.3.1 General approaches to statutory interpretation

The Hong Kong courts employ a variety of approaches, largely derived from the practices of English judges, in the interpretation of statutes. These approaches are often described as "rules" though they are no such thing, since they may well be in conflict with one another and are not, as a consequence, always applied. Lady Justice Mary Arden has said:

---

103. Although some writers distinguish "construction" and "interpretation", they are used interchangeably in this book in line with the majority approach. Mozely and Whiteley's *Law Dictionary*, for example, defines "construction" as "interpretation".
104. M Zander, *The Law-Making Process* (6th edn, Cambridge University Press 2004) 143.
105. J Spigelman (Chief Justice of New South Wales), 'The Intolerable Wrestle: Developments in Statutory Interpretation' (2010) 84 *Australian Law Journal* 826.

I should say . . . that judges approach the task of interpreting statutes in a variety of ways. There is no single technique which they use or manual which they have. However, there are a number of basic themes.[106]

It is more accurate, therefore, to describe the following "rules" as merely judicial "approaches" to interpretation.

4.3.1.1 The "literal rule" approach

The most traditional of the judicial approaches to interpretation is the so-called "literal rule". This approach is based on the view that it is for the legislature to make laws and for judges merely to "apply" them. Judges should not attempt the ambitious task of seeking the legislature's "true intention" since this is an elusive concept and involves the judge in making his own, subjective, view of what the legislature intended. The rule has been expressed (in the English courts) as follows:

> The only rule for the construction of Acts of Parliament is that they should be construed according to the intent of the Parliament which passed the Act. If the words of the statute are in themselves precise and unambiguous, then no more can be necessary than to expound those words in that natural and ordinary sense.[107] *The words themselves alone do, in such cases, best declare the intention of the law giver.*[108] [emphasis added]

This approach was adopted in the following Hong Kong case.

Guido Karl Wenk v Alan Lee Goldstein [1998] HKCFI 252 (Deputy Judge A Chan)
REASONS FOR JUDGMENT

. . .

4. Mr Kerr for the Defendant contended that the learned Master should have decided in the Defendant's favour because:–

(a) upon a true and proper construction of Ord 71 r 5(4) . . . the Court has jurisdiction pursuant to the Rule to extend the time for applying to set aside the registration notwithstanding the time for doing so has expired;

(b) [assuming his point (a) is accepted] as a matter of discretion, the Court should grant the time extension sought by the Defendant in the circumstances of this case.

. . .

6. Ord 71 r 5(4) reads as follows:–

---

106. M Arden (Lady Justice), 'The Impact of Judicial Interpretation on Legislative Drafting'. Keynote speech at the Commonwealth Association of Legislative Counsel conference (Nairobi, Kenya), September 2007.
107. These words were cited with approval in the Hong Kong case of *Cheung Chun-Man* [1957] HKLR 500 at 503.
108. *Sussex Peerage Claim* (1844) 11 Cl & Fin 85 per Tindall CJ at 143.

"The Court may, on an application made at any time *while it remains competent for any party* to apply to have the registration set aside, extend the period (either as originally fixed or as subsequently extended) within which an application to have the registration set aside may be made." (italics supplied)

7. Mr Kerr submitted that on a true and proper construction of Ord 71 r 5(4), the Court has jurisdiction to extend the time for applying to set aside the registration notwithstanding that time for doing so has expired because:–

...

(b) ... the said words are capable of referring either to the Court or the party making the application. Where the statute in question is capable of two possible constructions, the Court should adopt the one which preserves consistency among related provisions...

(c) there is a presumption that a statute is not intended to oust the existing powers of the Courts or to abrogate the Courts' common law powers, and a construction which preserves the *status quo* should be adopted.

...

(e) to construe Ord 71 r 5(4) [as the other party proposes] ... could create a harsh result and the Court should adopt a construction which will prevent such a result.

(1) Its Plain and Ordinary Meaning

8. The first rule of construction, the so-called "Literal Rule" cannot be better put than in *Craies on Statute Law* (1971) 7th ed,

"The cardinal rule for the construction of Acts of Parliament is that they should be construed according to the intention expressed in the Acts themselves. If the words of the Acts are themselves precise and unambiguous, then no more can be necessary to expound those words in their ordinary and natural sense. The words themselves alone do in such a case best declare the intention of the lawgiver." ...

9. The policy consideration in adhering to this "rule" was stated in Bennion: *Statutory Interpretation* ... :–

"As Sir Rupert Cross put it ...

'The essential rule is that words should generally be given the meaning which the normal speaker of the English language would understand them to bear in their context at the time they were used. It would be difficult to over-estimate the importance of this rule because the vast majority of statutes never come before the courts for interpretation. If it were not a known fact that, in the ordinary case in which the normal user of the English language would have no doubt about the meaning of the statutory words, the courts will give those words their ordinary meaning, it would be impossible for lawyers and other people to act and advise on the statute in question with confidence.'"

...

> 25. As regards Mr Kerr's argument that the construction under the "Literal Rule" may create hardship ... it is not the first time when a statutory provision may potentially create hardship by reason of a prescribed time limit having been imposed by it ... [but] If the rules are certain, it is not for the courts to water them down by ignoring the intention of the legislature as evidenced by the express words. As *Craies* put it:–
>
> "It is not, however, competent for a judge to modify the language of an Act of Parliament in order to bring it into accordance with his own views as to what is right or reasonable."

Comment

The case provides a very clear exposition of, and support for, the literal rule. While other "rules"/presumptions are considered, it is implicit in Chan J's judgment that these should be subservient to the literal rule and should be invoked only in cases, such as ambiguity, where the literal rule cannot provide a clear solution to the construction problem. This would include the situation where a literal approach would, arguably, produce an absurd outcome or would "appear" to thwart the legislature's "true" intention.

To depart from the strict legal meaning of the words in a statute is, to the literalists, a "usurpation of the legislative function".[109] Where the legislature has failed correctly to reflect its intention in a statute, say the literalists, the solution is for the legislation to be amended, *not* for the judges to intervene.[110]

In support of this view it can be argued that a legislature's intent may be difficult to gauge, given the possibly varying views of a statute's proponents and the possibility of compromise and amendment to facilitate a Bill's passage through the legislature. Gleeson CJ has stated:

> That general [purposive] rule of interpretation, however, may be of little assistance where a statutory provision strikes a balance between competing interests, and the problem of interpretation is that there is uncertainty as to how far the provision goes in seeking to achieve the underlying purpose or object of the Act. Legislation rarely pursues a single purpose at all costs. Where the problem is one of doubt about the extent to which the legislation pursues a purpose, stating the purpose is unlikely to solve the problem. For a court to construe the legislation as though it pursued the purpose to the fullest possible extent may be contrary to the manifest intention of the legislation and a purported exercise of judicial power for a legislative purpose.[111]

---

109. See especially the words of Lord Simonds in *Magor & St Mellons v Newport Corporation* [1951] 2 All ER 839 at 841 paras G–H. However, as Burrows (who apparently favours judicial "creativity" for the common good) points out: "There will always be debate about the line between legislation and interpretation" (see J Burrows, 'The Changing Approach to the Interpretation of Statutes' (2002) 33 VUWLR 981, 999 at 999.
110. Ibid.
111. *Carr v Western Australia* [2007] HCA 47.

This Australian example is undoubtedly applicable to the Hong Kong/LegCo experience.

Nonetheless, despite such caveats, it is possible to discover cases where the words of the final legislative draft, *as interpreted by the courts*, has failed to reflect what was almost certainly intended by the legislature.

A classic example of a literal approach, from the English courts, is to be found in the case of *Fisher v Bell*,[112] a criminal case which, nonetheless, has implications for the law of contract. The case involved the display of flick knives in a shop window with a price tag. The relevant statute, the Restriction of Offensive Weapons Act 1959, made it an offence to "offer for sale" various weapons, including flick-knives. The defendant shopkeeper was charged with "offering for sale" a flick-knife.

The prosecution failed on the basis that, in contract law, the display of items in a shop window, even with a price tag, is not an "offer" but merely an "invitation to treat". Thus, a criminal prosecution foundered on the application of a basic contractual principle. One *caveat* to the "literal meaning" approach is implicit in the *Fisher v Bell* decision: namely that "technical" terms are to be given their ordinary *technical* meaning rather than that of the layman.[113]

A similar approach was taken by the Hong Kong Court of First Instance in *HKSAR v Wan Hon Sik*.[114] Here the defendant was, by his own admission, in possession of pirated VCDs and was "introducing them" to potential Japanese customers. He was charged with offering them for sale. The prosecution succeeded in the Magistrate's Court where magistrate Kevin Browne determined that there was no Hong Kong jurisprudential support for *Fisher v Bell* and that English contractual principles were not necessarily applicable to the Hong Kong criminal law. Such an "autonomous" approach[115] was thwarted on appeal where Deputy Judge Longley preferred to follow the English law approach on the basis that, since the relevant legislation referred elsewhere to "exposing" discs for sale, it must have been intended that a mere display would not constitute an "offer for sale".

A very strong case can be made for saying that these decisions contradicted the intention of the respective legislatures. In the case of *Fisher v Bell* such a view is endorsed by the hastily amended legislation which took the form of the Restriction of Offensive Weapons Act 1961, which closed this particular loophole. It should, however, be remembered that there is a further principle of interpretation involved in both cases; namely that, where a *criminal prosecution* is involved, the courts should construe the wording of the relevant statute as narrowly as possible.[116] Only where the wording permits of no other interpretation should a conviction be

---

112. [1961] 1 QB 394.
113. Per Lord Simon of Glaisdale in *Maunsell v Olins* [1975] AC 373 at 391.
114. [2001] 3 HKLRD 283.
115. Described as "an attempt to bring this area of Hong Kong law into the 21st century" (see M Fisher and D Greenwood, *Contract Law in Hong Kong* [3nd edn, Hong Kong University Press 2018] 47).
116. See *D'Avigdor-Goldsmid v IRC* [1953] 1 All ER 403.

upheld. Literal approaches, therefore, are more likely to operate in cases involving a criminal prosecution. In the Hong Kong case of *Commissioner of Inland Revenue v Common Empire Ltd*[117] a similar approach was taken in respect of the interpretation of a taxation statute, the Inland Revenue Ordinance.[118] Deputy High Court Judge To stated:

> Interpretation of a statute is essentially ascertaining the intention of the legislature as expressed by the words used in the statute. [The] purposive approach may only be adopted if the legislative purpose can be clearly discerned. Where, however, the court is unable to find the purpose of an enactment or is doubtful as to its purpose, the literal rule of interpretation prevails . . .
>
> While the court must bear in mind that there is no presumption as to tax when construing a tax statute, it must also bear in mind that there is no equity about a tax. The court must look fairly at the language used and apply the literal interpretation. If applying that rule . . . would produce a result which is absurd and one which is not, the court shall adopt the latter interpretation which would avoid that absurdity. This option is only available if the language admits of such an innocuous interpretation. But if the language does not admit of such an interpretation which could avoid the absurdity, the court simply has no choice. It shall give effect to that literal interpretation however absurd or inequitable it may be.[119]

Qualified support for the literal rule can be seen in the case of *Leverson Ltd v Secretary for Transport* where Deputy Judge Wong stated:

> The object of all interpretation of a statute is to ascertain the intention of the legislature as expressed in the statute, considering it as a whole and in its context, and acting on behalf of the people. The meaning of an enactment that corresponds to this intention is known as the "legal meaning'. The legal meaning may or may not correspond to the grammatical or literal meaning . . . It is the meaning arrived at by applying to the enactment, taken with any other relevant and admissible material, the rules, principles, presumptions and canons which govern statutory interpretation. These may be referred to as the interpretative criteria or guides to legislative intention . . .
>
> There is, however, a plain meaning rule. It is a rule of the common law that where the enactment under inquiry is grammatically capable of one meaning only and, on an informed interpretation of that enactment, the interpretative criteria raise no real doubt as to whether that meaning is the one intended by the legislator, then the legal meaning of the enactment is taken to correspond to that grammatical meaning.[120]

In short the grammatical meaning will be applied "unless". The two most important instances of "unless" arise where the literal/grammatical meaning would

---
117. [2006] 1 HKLRD 942.
118. Cap 112. The case centred, primarily, on s 60.
119. [2006] 1 HKLRD 942 at para 17.
120. [2003] HKLdT 11.

produce an absurd result, or where it appears to run counter to a clearly discoverable legislative intention to the contrary.

4.3.1.2 The "golden rule" approach

The essence of "golden rule" approaches to interpretation is that statutes should be interpreted in such a way as to avoid any absurdity. This approach is generally consistent with the literal rule since it is applied where the literal words have two or more possible meanings. In such a case, the "golden rule" approach is to adopt the most sensible of the meanings. Thus:

> in construing wills . . . statutes, and all written instruments, the grammatical and ordinary sense of the words is to be adhered to, unless that would lead to some absurdity, or some repugnance or inconsistency with the rest of the instrument, in which case the grammatical and ordinary sense of the words may be modified, so as to avoid that absurdity and inconsistency, but no farther.[121]

By way of example, in the English case of *R v Allen*,[122] Allen, who was already married, went through a second ceremony of marriage with another woman. He was charged with the offence of bigamy. The relevant statutory rule[123] stated that "whosoever being married shall marry any other person" during the lifetime of his/her spouse, was guilty of bigamy. Allen's defence was that, since the second marriage was void, he had not "married" any other person! Had this defence been upheld, it would have meant that the statutory rule was completely invalidated since, by definition, any second "marriage" would be void in English law. The court took the view that the word "marry" could mean *either* "legally marry" *or* "go through a ceremony of marriage". Since the latter interpretation produced a sensible result, and did not render the statutory rule meaningless, this was the interpretation which was adopted.

However, there are situations where the literal approach and the golden rule approach are in conflict; namely where there is only one literal interpretation but it produces an absurd result. The court is then compelled to choose between the competing approaches. Such a situation arose in *Re Sigsworth*.[124] Here, a son who had murdered his mother was held not entitled to inherit on her intestacy despite his "entitlement" on the clear wording of section 46 of the Administration of Estates Act 1925. The literal interpretation was not followed because the result would have run counter to a basic principle of the English common law that one should not be permitted to profit from the commission of a crime.

The "golden rule" approach was regarded as a "presumption" in the *Leverson* case[125] where Deputy Judge Wong said:

---

121. Per Lord Wensleydale *Grey v Pearson* (1857) 6 HL Cas 61 at 106.
122. (1872) LR 1 CCR 367.
123. Section 57, Offences Against the Person Act 1861.
124. [1934] All ER Rep 113.
125. Note 118.

There is also a presumption against anomalous or illogical result as aforesaid . . . The Respondent is saying that one can only obtain compensation by proving loss in development potential, but in assessing development potential, the rest of the site is ignored and only that strip of land where the easement is physically located can be counted. The result is that the affected owner can only claim loss of development potential in that part of the land marked on the plan as occupied by the easement, ignoring the fact that his land covers a larger area. It is absurd to suggest that in assessing diminution in value by reason of loss of development potential, the law requires the Tribunal to disregard the whole extent of the claimant's land.

4.3.1.3 The mischief rule

In apparent counterpoint to the literal rule approach are so-called "purposive" approaches via which the judges interpret statutes according to what they perceive to be the legislature's intent. When the literal words of a statute are in accord with the legislative purpose, no conflict arises. However, when a literal approach results in an apparently absurd result, or when it runs counter to the apparent purpose of the legislation, there is a conflict with the "golden rule" and/or the purposive approaches. It could certainly be argued that *Fisher v Bell*[126] produced an outcome that was both absurd and contrary to the legislature's intention.[127] The earliest incarnation of a purposive approach is the so-called "mischief rule", whereby the judge, in interpreting a statute, will take into account the apparent defect in the previous common law or "mischief" which the legislation in question was supposedly seeking to "cure". The mischief approach, sometimes known as the "rule in *Heydon's case*",[128] in deference to the ancient case in which it was first formulated, is of limited application,[129] since it is inapplicable to the situation where legislation is intended to achieve an innovative social purpose rather merely cure a "defect". Moreover, it can be argued that the approach is somewhat obsolete dating, as it does, from a time when (English) statutes had lengthy explanatory "preambles", such that any "mischief" to be cured was inherent in the words of the statute itself.[130]

4.3.1.4 Modern purposive approaches

Given the limitations of the traditional mischief rule approach, it is unsurprising that courts, in England and Hong Kong, have developed a more modern, broader approach to construction/interpretation which stresses the legislative purpose of the enactment in question.

---

126. Note 110.
127. See 4.3.1.1.
128. (1584) 76 ER 637.
129. Though, in theory at least, it has statutory force in Hong Kong (see discussion of IGCO, above and n 150).
130. See J Holland and J Webb, *Learning Legal Rules* (9th edn, Oxford University Press 2016) 268.

A significant illustration of a "purposive" approach to statutory interpretation in Hong Kong is provided by the case of *Medical Council of Hong Kong v Chow Siu Shek*.[131] In this case a doctor, who had been removed from the Register of medical practitioners having been convicted of fraud, applied for what he argued was a right to automatic restoration to the register, once his period of removal had elapsed.

In allowing the Council's appeal, Bokhary J, giving the judgment of the Court of Final Appeal, stated that modern purposive approaches had developed from the mischief rule and added:

> When the true position under a statute is to be ascertained by interpretation, it is necessary to read all of the relevant provisions together and in the context of the whole statute as a purposive unity in its appropriate legal and social setting. Furthermore it is necessary to identify the interpretive considerations involved and then, if they conflict, to weigh and balance them.[132]

This approach is broader than the mischief rule approach since it does not depend on finding a "mischief" which legislation was intended to cure; it seeks the legislature's *purpose* in general.

One obstacle to purposive-based interpretation, however, was the former restriction, in England and Hong Kong, on recourse by the courts to the Parliamentary/LegCo history of the legislation under consideration, notably by reference to Hansard.

The strict principle that courts could not consider legislative history in determining the purpose of a statute was observed until comparatively recently in England. While the "no Hansard" rule seems anomalous in the context of seeking the legislature's "true intent", the rationale for the restrictive principle was based on an avowedly strict adherence to the concept of "separation of powers"; that in effect the courts should not act like the legislature.[133] As Lord Reid said, in the seminal English House of Lords *Black-Clawson*[134] case:

> We often say that we are looking for the intention of Parliament, but that is not quite accurate. We are seeking the meaning of the words which Parliament used. We are seeking not what Parliament meant but the true meaning of what they said.[135]

These words encapsulate much of the ethos of the traditional antagonism amongst judges to the concept of looking beyond the words of a statute themselves and examining their legislative history.

---

131. [2000] 2 HKC 428.
132. Ibid at 438, para G.
133. It was argued for some time that reference by the courts to Hansard would be in breach of the (British) Bill of Rights 1689, on the grounds of "questioning or impeaching" proceedings in Parliament.
134. *Black-Clawson International Ltd v Papierwerke Waldhof-Aschafenburg AG* [1975] AC 591.
135. Ibid at 613.

In addition to objections based on "judicial law-making" there is the further difficulty of the unreliability of inferring legislation's "meaning" from the words of its proponents. Lord Reid expressed this reservation, too, in *Black-Clawson*, stating:

> One might take the views of the promoters of a Bill as an indication of the intention of Parliament but any view the promoters may have had about questions which later come before the court will not often appear in Hansard and often those questions have never occurred to the promoters. At best we might get material from which a more or less dubious inference might be drawn as to what the promoters intended or would have intended if they had thought about the matter, and it would, I think, generally be dangerous to attach weight to what some other members of either House may have said.[136]

A more mundane objection to the use of "extrinsic aids" such as legislative debates involved the cost/time implications. Lord Reid (again) stated in the case of *Beswick v Beswick*:[137]

> For purely practical reasons we do not permit debates in either House to be cited: it would add greatly to the time and expense involved in preparing a case involving the construction of a statute if counsel were expected to read all the debates in Hansard, and it would often be impracticable for counsel to get access to at least the older reports of debates.[138]

A final, and perhaps stronger, argument relies on the legal fiction that all are supposed to know the law and be subject to it; ignorance of the law is no defence in criminal proceedings. It follows that if we *are* (even fictionally) expected to know the law, such law must be readily accessible to the citizen and be comprehensible as it stands, without the further requirement of historical awareness of legislative debate. Lord Diplock summarised the point in *Fothergill v Monarch Airlines*,[139] stating:

> If the meaning of [the] words is clear and unambiguous and does not lead to a result that is manifestly absurd or unreasonable, it would be a confidence trick by Parliament and destructive of all legal certainty if the private citizen could not rely upon that meaning but was required to search through all that had happened before and in the course of the legislative process in order to see whether there was anything to be found from which it could be inferred that Parliament's real intention had not been accurately expressed by the actual words that Parliament had adopted to communicate it to those affected by the legislation . . .
>
> . . . Elementary justice or, to use the concept often cited by the European Court, the need for legal certainty, demands that the rules by which the citizen is to be bound should be ascertainable by him (or more realistically, by a competent lawyer advising him) by reference to identifiable sources that are publically accessible.[140]

---

136. Ibid at 613–615.
137. [1968] AC 58.
138. Ibid at 74A.
139. [1980] 3 WLR 209.
140. Ibid at 221.

Nevertheless, a gradual movement towards more purposive approaches to interpretation almost inevitably required at least a minimal acceptance of the need to consider a statute's legislative history since, as Samuels succinctly put it:

> Those favouring a narrow or literal approach to interpretation tend to wish to exclude extraneous material. Those favouring a wide or liberal or mischief or purposive approach to interpretation tend to wish to admit extraneous material.[141]

Thus, despite the constitutional objections, relaxation of the "no consideration" principle was established in the landmark English case of *Pepper v Hart*.[142] Here the English House of Lords held that the rule prohibiting the courts from referring to parliamentary material as an aid to statutory construction should be relaxed, *in restricted circumstances*, so as to permit reference to parliamentary material (primarily Hansard) in order to assist the determination of Parliament's (the legislature's) intention.

The facts of *Pepper v Hart* involved a series of tax appeals by schoolmasters on the correct basis for valuing benefits in kind, whereby they paid a reduced fee for their own children attending the school at which they were employed. The education of the teachers' children was a taxable benefit under the relevant English tax legislation.[143] It fell to be determined how much the "cash equivalent" of the schooling benefit amounted to in assessing the teachers for income tax. This depended on the interpretation of section 63(1) and (2) of the legislation. The taxpayers claimed that the only expense was the marginal cost to the school of providing food, laundry, stationery etc which was covered by the concessionary fee paid by them anyway. The Inland Revenue claimed that the expense was the provision of education, which was exactly the same as the expense of the other children whose parents were not schoolmasters at the school. Therefore, the expense was a proportionate cost of running the whole school. The dispute between the Inland Revenue and the teachers eventually reached the House of Lords.

Ironically, given subsequent developments, initial arguments before the House of Lords made no reference to relevant Parliamentary debates (as published in Hansard). However, it came to the attention of the court that:

> an examination of the proceedings in Parliament in 1976 which lead to the enactment of section 61 and 63 might give a clear indication which of the two rival contentions represented the intention of Parliament in using the statutory words.

The Law Lords then invited the parties to consider whether they wanted to present further argument on the question of whether it was appropriate to depart from previous authority and, if so, what guidance such material could provide for the purposes of the appeal. The taxpayers took up the offer.

---

141. A. Samuels, *The Interpretation of Statutes* [1980] Stat LR 86 at 99.
142. [1993] 1 All ER 42.
143. Section 61(1), Finance Act 1976.

The Attorney-General submitted that the use of Hansard would breach the privileges of the Houses of Parliament under Article 9 of the Bill of Rights 1688, though he accepted that it was a matter for the courts to decide on the effect of Article 9.

The majority of the Appellate Committee rejected the Attorney-General's submission. Lord Browne-Wilkinson noted that there had been no application by the Attorney-General to adjourn the case to enable the House of Commons to consider its position. He asserted the supremacy of the courts to decide whether a privilege existed and to decide whether such privilege has been infringed. He stressed that the Law Lords were:

> motivated by a desire to carry out the intentions of Parliament in enacting legislation and have no intention or desire to question the processes by which such legislation was enacted or of criticising anything said by anyone in Parliament in the course of enacting it. The purpose is to give effect to, not thwart, the intentions of Parliament.

The House of Lords also rejected the Attorney-General's argument that reference to Hansard by the courts would usurp Parliament's legislative role. The House of Lords thereupon embarked on an extensive examination of the legislative history of the statute in question.

Lord Browne-Wilkinson determined that section 63 of the Finance Act was ambiguous. The "expense incurred in or in connection with" the provision of in-house benefits might be *either* the marginal cost caused by the provision of the benefit in question, as argued by the taxpayers, *or* a proportion of the total cost incurred in providing the service, both for the public and for the employee ("the average cost"), as argued by the revenue. Therefore, if reference to Hansard were permissible, the taxpayers' appeal would be allowed.

The issues that the court had to decide on the question of the admissibility of Hansard are summarised in the following questions put by Lord Browne-Wilkinson:

(1) Should the existing rule prohibiting any reference to Hansard in construing legislation be relaxed, and if so, to what extent?
(2) If so, does this case fall within the category of cases where reference to Parliamentary proceedings should be permitted?
(3) If reference to Parliamentary proceedings is permissible, what is the true construction of the statutory provisions?
(4) If reference to Parliamentary proceedings is not permissible, what is the true construction of the statutory provisions?
(5) If the outcome of this case depends upon whether or not reference is made to Hansard, how should the matter proceed in the face of the warnings of the Attorney-General that such references might constitute a breach of parliamentary privilege?

The court had to decide whether the intention expressed by the Financial Secretary could be said to represent the intention of Parliament as a whole. Lord Browne-Wilkinson decided that it could. He held that the Committee on the Bill:

was repeatedly asking for guidance as to the effect of the legislation once clause 54(4) was abandoned. That Parliament relied on the Ministerial statements is shown by the fact that the matter was never raised again after discussions in Committee, that amendments were consequentially withdrawn and that no relevant amendment was made which could affect the correctness of the minister's statement.

Lord Bridge added, emphatically:

I should find it very difficult in conscience, to reach a conclusion averse to the appellants, on the basis of a technical rule of construction, requiring me to ignore the very material which in this case indicates unequivocally which of the two possible interpretations of section 63(2) of the Act of 1976 was intended by Parliament.

In short, the majority of the House of Lords thought, on balance, that the "legislative history" of a statute could be considered by the courts in seeking to determine the legislature's intention. The arguments in favour of a complete embargo on examining legislative history were found wanting by the majority. Such "historical" consideration should, however be restricted. Lord Browne-Wilkinson suggested that such recourse should be applicable only where:

(a) legislation is ambiguous[144] or obscure, or leads to an absurdity; (b) the material relied upon consists of one or more statements by a minister or other promoter of the Bill together if necessary with such other Parliamentary material as is necessary to understand such statements and their effect; (c) the statements relied upon are clear.[145]

As was so often the case before 1997 (and to some extent still today) Hong Kong jurisprudence took up the baton proffered by the English courts. The Law Reform Commission of Hong Kong issued a major report in 1997 on the use of extrinsic evidence in interpreting statutes. The report focused extensively (though certainly not exclusively) on *Pepper v Hart* and its application in Hong Kong. Since the report runs to over 260 pages, the following extract will focus on the Commission's Report Summary.

> The Law Reform Commission of Hong Kong
>
> Report
>
> Extrinsic Materials as an Aid to
>
> Statutory Interpretation
>
> March 1997
>
> . . .

---

144. In *Pepper v Hart* itself the words in dispute were found to be capable of two differing meanings.
145. [1993] 1 All ER 42 at 69.

Chapter 12

Summary of Report on Extrinsic Materials as an aid to Statutory Interpretation

...

"Should the law governing the use of extrinsic materials in relation to the interpretation of statutes be changed and, if so, in what way?"

What is the importance of statutory interpretation?

12.2 "Legislation constitutes the single most important source of law in our society. There is hardly any aspect of the education, welfare, health, employment, housing, income and public conduct of the citizen that is not regulated by statute". Every day, officials, private individuals, and professional advisers interpret legislation in order to carry out their functions. However, it is only where there is a doubt about the meaning or scope of a statutory provision, or about its relationship with other provisions that recourse to judicial interpretation is made.

12.3 The interpretation of statutes is not only a matter to be considered by reference to the decisions of the courts. A statute is directed according to its subject matter, to audiences of varying extent. The intelligibility of statutes from the point of view of ordinary citizens or their advisers cannot be dissociated from the rules of interpretation followed by the courts, for the ability to understand a statute depends on intelligent anticipation of the way in which it would be interpreted by the courts.

12.4 The United Kingdom Law Commissions in their joint Report stressed the importance of rules of interpretation of legislation being workable rules of communication between the legislator and the legislative audience as a whole. This consideration is particularly important in any assessment of the value of the aids to interpretation extraneous to the statute itself

...

12.6 ... Extrinsic aids have become more important to the interpretation of legislation since the judgment in *Pepper v Hart*, where the House of Lords held that the rules excluding reference to parliamentary materials should be relaxed on certain conditions.

...

12.7 The dynamic between Parliament and the courts in relation to the creation and interpretation of law, and the need for a harmonious balance between them, must always be borne in mind in the debate whether, and to what extent, the courts can look at extrinsic aids. The doctrine of the sovereignty of Parliament has been traditionally understood to include the proposition that the judicial function in relation to legislation is confined to its interpretation and application.

...

12.10 The courts developed various rules for the interpretation of legislation. These were the mischief rule, the literal rule and the golden rule. In Hong Kong, unlike the United Kingdom, the mischief rule, which has been superseded by the term "purposive construction", is incorporated into legislation. Section 19 of the Interpretation and General Clauses Ordinance (Cap 1) states:

> "An Ordinance shall be deemed to be remedial and shall receive such fair, large and liberal construction and interpretation as will best ensure the attainment of the object of the Ordinance according to its true intent, meaning and spirit".

...

12.11 The context for looking at the purpose of extrinsic aids to statutory interpretation has been described thus:–

> "It is self-evident that in order to understand a statute a court has to take into account many matters which are not to be found in the statute itself. Legislation is not made in a vacuum, and a judge in interpreting it is able to take judicial notice of much information relating to legal, social, economic and other aspects of the society in which the statute is to operate".

12.15 Lord Diplock in *Black-Clawson Ltd v Papierwerke Waldhof-Aschaffenberg AG* explained the link between the rules of construction of legislation, and the rule concerning the use of extrinsic aids thus:

> "When it was laid down, the 'mischief' rule did not require the court to travel beyond the actual words of the statute itself... for this would have been stated in the preamble. In construing modern statutes which contain no preambles to serve as aids to the construction of enacting words the 'mischief' rule must be used with caution to justify reference to extraneous documents for this purpose. If the enacting words are plain and unambiguous in themselves there is no need to have recourse to any 'mischief' rule"...

12.17 ...In *R v Warner* it was suggested that there was room for an exception to the rule excluding the use of Hansard, "where examining the proceedings in Parliament would almost certainly settle the matter immediately one way or the other."...

...

12.18 It could be argued that the courts more truly give effect to the intention of Parliament when they adopt a purposive approach. The trend towards a purposive construction, rather than a literal construction, has given an impetus to the courts to use extrinsic aids to resolve a question of ambiguity in the legislation. Indeed, Lord Griffiths, in *Pepper v Hart*, stated "The courts now adopt a purposive approach which seeks to give effect to the true purpose of legislation and are prepared to look at much extraneous material that bears upon the background against which the legislation was enacted."

...

12.20 The new rule of *Pepper v Hart* is outlined in the headnote as follows:

> "Subject to any question of Parliamentary privilege, the rule excluding reference to Parliamentary material as an aid to statutory construction should be relaxed so as to permit such reference where (a) legislation was ambiguous or obscure or led to absurdity, (b) the

material relied upon consisted of one or more statements by a minister or other promoter of the Bill together if necessary with such other Parliamentary material as was necessary to understand such statements and their effect and (c) the statements relied upon were clear".

. . .

Impact of *Pepper v Hart* in Hong Kong

12.24 The courts in Hong Kong have already applied the criteria of *Pepper v Hart*, though only a small number of cases have been reported . . . Despite the differences between the legislative process here and in the United Kingdom, only in *Ngan Chor Ying v Year Trend Development Ltd* was a reservation expressed as to this fact by Findlay J. In *Matheson PFC Limited v Jansen* Penlington J regarded a statement in the explanatory memorandum by the Attorney General as "a clear statement from the equivalent of a Minister . . ."

. . .

[The Law Reform Commission's Report made a number of specific recommendations, most notably that:]

11.53 Having considered all the arguments, the Commission concludes that it would be desirable to codify and modify the common law principles and in the process extend and clarify the position by way of legislation. The proposed legislation could provide comprehensive and easily understood criteria for the use of extrinsic aids.

. . .

11.55 The Commission recommends that it would be more useful to incorporate the criteria for the use of extrinsic aids in legislation by appropriate amendments to the Interpretation and General Clauses Ordinance (Cap 1). It would be most suitably included as section 19A, just after the existing guide to a purposive construction of legislation.[146]

. . .

11.132 The Commission recommends that a Practice Direction governing the production of extrinsic materials before the courts should be introduced in Hong Kong without waiting for legislative reform in this area.

. . .

11.135 . . . On balance, the Commission, having considered the submissions from those consulted, is in favour of legislative reform. The common law position concerning extrinsic aids is complex and not readily understood . . .

---

146. This was indeed the form which the proposed legislation took.

Legislation and the Interpretation of Statutes 211

Comment

One significant point noted in the Report is that Hong Kong courts, unlike their English counterparts, already enjoyed a limited power to interpret "purposively", particularly by virtue of section 19 of the Interpretation and General Clauses Ordinance.[147] *Nonetheless, as will be noted below, it appears that, in cases of reference to extrinsic sources, Hong Kong courts rarely founded such reference on section 19.*

Moreover, as the Report showed, Hong Kong courts had begun following the Pepper v Hart approach some time before the publication of the Report. This was so even though, arguably, differences between the Hong Kong and British legislative systems weaken the "analogy". The report showed that, in practice, there had been little reference by the courts to the significance of the differing legislative processes. However, reference was made to a sole, exceptional, reservation on this basis by Findlay J in Ngan Chor Ying v Year Trend Development Ltd.

Considerable focus in Chapter 10 of the Commission's report was placed on the application of the Bill of Rights Ordinance (BORO) to the issue of interpretation, since that Ordinance required legislation in Hong Kong to be interpreted, if possible, consistently with the Ordinance.[148] *Where prior legislation was found to be incompatible with BORO it should be deemed repealed.*[149] *The relevant section of BORO*[150] *was overturned ("not adopted") in Hong Kong post-1997 having been found inconsistent with the Basic Law. As such, the Commission's discussions on this issue have been omitted. It should be pointed out, however, that BORO largely reflected the impact of international obligations to which Hong Kong remains committed.*[151]

In line with the Law Reform Commission's Report clear recommendation for the introduction of appropriate legislation, a bill was prepared to implement many of the Report's recommendations as early as 1999. However, largely because of objections from the Hong Kong Bar, the proposed legislation was withdrawn and has not been reintroduced. Since, as noted above, Hong Kong courts have been able to develop, and were developing before the report, the common law approach to the traditional "exclusionary rules" it may be that legislation is now deemed unnecessary. It remains, however, a cause for some sadness that an exhaustive (and no doubt exhausting) 260-page report should have produced no legislative response.

One point which should be borne in mind above all, however, is that the relaxation of previous restraints on recourse to "extrinsic materials" (particularly the statute's legislative history) has been strictly limited, both in England and in Hong

---

147. Cap 1. The precise wording is discussed below. The Commission suggested that s 19 had not frequently been expressly cited but had been, more often, *implicitly* taken into account.
148. Section 3(1).
149. Section 3(2).
150. Section 3.
151. In particular, the International Covenant on Civil and Political Rights (ICCPR). See also 4.3.4.

Kong.[152] *The courts wish to ensure that they do not "usurp" the legislature's function and restrict the use of extrinsic materials to situations where there is uncertainty in the words of legislation which legislative "background" may help to resolve.*

An issue which concerned the Commission was the question of Pepper v Hart's "status" in Hong Kong. Is it a binding precedent? The Commission concluded that, as a pre-1997 indication of the common law of England, it did *have binding status subject to subsequent (post-1997) Hong Kong statutory (or judicial) reversal. This view supports the view expressed in Chapters 1, 2 and 4 of this book.*

One issue largely overlooked in the LRC's discussion, is the potential for "selectivity" in Pepper v Hart situations. The judge may *consider legislative history, or not, as he chooses. This differs from the position of "stare decisis" where binding precedents must, in theory at least, be followed.*[153]

A *final difficulty with the application of Pepper v Hart, perhaps unique to Hong Kong, is that, pre-1997, it was not uncommon for Hong Kong to adopt, almost reflexively and with very minor amendment, English legislation, doubtless enacted to fulfil a particular purpose* in England. *The ascription of a legislative* purpose *by a Hong Kong judge in such circumstances is likely to be somewhat artificial.*

There was an attempted (and prompt) legislative response to the Law Reform Commission's Report. The Chief Executive ordered the introduction of the Interpretation and General Clauses (Amendment) Bill 1999 into LegCo. The bill was intended to enact most of the report's recommendations on the basis that "Hong Kong law requires Ordinances to be interpreted purposively".[154] However, at the public consultation stage, objections were received, almost exclusively from the Hong Kong Bar Association. The main objection was that, unlike the situation in the British Parliament, promoters of bills in Hong Kong are "not accountable to the legislature", such that the adoption of *Pepper v Hart* principles was inapplicable to Hong Kong. The Bar felt that "we should wait a few years [sic] to see how the new constitutional arrangements work".[155] The Bar's objections effectively stalled the proposed legislation despite the Department of Justice rejoinder that:

> In fact, the government, as promoter of Bills, is accountable to [LegCo] under Article 64 of the Basic Law, and a majority vote in the legislature legitimises the intention of those who frame Bills. Furthermore, the common law principles of statutory interpretation previously applied in Hong Kong—including those in *Pepper v Hart*—continue to apply in the Hong Kong SAR further to Articles 8, 18 and 160 of the Basic Law. Accordingly there is no reason to delay the Bill.[156]

---

152. See discussion of *Delight World* and *Hong Kong Racing Pigeon* cases below.
153. See J Burrows, 'The Changing Approach to the Interpretation of Statutes' (2002) 33 VUWLR 981–999.
154. Legal Policy Division, Department of Justice, *Legislative Council BRIEF:* LP 5019/6 February 1999 (at para 5).
155. Ibid at para 32.
156. Ibid at para 33.

As the report made clear, Hong Kong courts were already following the *Pepper v Hart* line. The Court of First Instance, for example, noted the case in *Delight World Ltd v Town Planning Appeal Board*,[157] though the strict criteria required to justify the study of legislative history were found to be absent. The trial judge, Keith J, found that the requirement of a *clear* legislative intent was lacking. He stated:

> It may be that if the Legislative Council had addressed the question of whether a judge should be ineligible for membership of the Appeal Board, it would have decided that a judge should be ineligible. But in the absence of a clear statement to that effect, the limitations on the application of the principles in *Pepper v Hart* [1993] AC 593 prevent me from making the leap of faith which Mr Kotewall asks me to.

Implicitly, of course, the judge accepted that, given a clear legislative intent, the *Pepper v Hart* rationale could have been applied. In *Commissioner of Inland Revenue v Common Empire Ltd*,[158] referred to previously,[159] Deputy High Court Judge To appears to have gone one step further in suggesting that the court may even adopt a "strained meaning" in order to apply the legislature's intention if such is clear.[160]

The Court of Appeal, too, considered *Pepper v Hart* in *Hong Kong Racing Pigeon Association v Attorney-General & Another*[161] while again determining that the necessary criteria were lacking. Nazareth V-P stated:

> Mr Hui seeks to bolster his argument by reference to the debates in the Legislative Council in the process of enactment. In *Pepper v Hart* . . . Lord Browne-Wilkinson, with whom Lord Mackay, Lord Keith, Lord Bridge, Lord Griffiths, Lord Ackner, and Lord Oliver all agreed, concluded that the former "exclusionary rule should be relaxed so as to permit reference to Parliamentary materials where (a) legalisation is ambiguous or obscure, or leads to an absurdity; (b) the material relied upon consists of one or more statements by a minister or other promoter of the Bill together if necessary with such other parliamentary material as is necessary to understand such statements and their effect: (c) the statements relied upon are clear.
>
> . . . It will be apparent from what I have already said that in the present context there is simply no ambiguity or obscurity in the definition of "poultry", or the meaning of "pigeon" or indeed in the Ordinance. I have not been able to discern any; nor has anything credible in that way been identified. As to absurdity, the respondents strenuously resist any suggestion of that. They point out that there is no other legislation that deals with the disposal of pigeon waste and they emphasis the flexible provision for exemption. If there is any case that the legislation leads to absurdity, the appellant in my view has not even begun to make it. Plainly the legislation does not lead to absurdity.

---

157. [1997] HKLRD 1106.
158. [2006] 1 HKLRD 942.
159. See 4.3.1.1 above.
160. [2006] 1 HKLRD 942 at para 17.
161. [1995] 2 HKC 201.

> ... In the result, there is neither the need, nor the entitlement to resort to Parliamentary material under *Pepper v Hart*, or indeed to other aids in construction.
>
> However ... the constraints of their Lordships envisaged upon the relaxation of the exclusionary rule in respect of such material is of interest ...
>
> ... Lord Browne-Wilkinson himself at p 1056B said this:
>
> '... reference to Parliamentary material should be permitted as an aid to the construction of legislation which is ambiguous or obscure or the literal meaning of which leads to an absurdity. Even in such cases references in court to Parliamentary material should only be permitted where such material clearly discloses the mischief aimed at or the legislative intention lying behind the ambiguous or obscure words. In the case of statements made in Parliament, as at present advised I cannot foresee that any statement other than the statement of the minister or other promoter of the Bill is likely to meet these criteria.'

A similar reluctance to invoke *Pepper v Hart* was shown by the Hong Kong Court of Appeal in *Lam Kin Sum v Hong Kong Housing Authority*[162] where (then) Chief Judge of the High Court,[163] Geoffrey Ma, stated:

> However ingenious Mr Chan's submissions were, the one point he could not overcome was the presence of the word "Variation". It is difficult to see what other meaning can be given to this term other than to denote an alteration or change to the existing rent. This term admits of no other meaning ...
>
> ... The task of the Court when construing a statute is of course to look for the legislature's intention. This involves, it has to be reiterated, construing the meaning of the actual words found in the statute in the context in which they appear ...
>
> ... Only when the intention of the legislature is obscure, unclear or ambiguous would it assist to look at legislative materials in relation to the provisions in question:– see *Pepper v Hart* ... where Lord Browne-Wilkinson laid down three conditions before resort could be had to legislative materials ...
>
> ... In my view, none of the three conditions in *Pepper v Hart* is satisfied in the present case.[164]

In the Court of Final Appeal case of *Director of Immigration v Chong Fung Yuen*[165] caution was also expressed by (then) Chief Justice Andrew Li, in words echoing the need for public accessibility to the legislation in dispute. The Chief Justice stated:

> The courts' role under the common law in interpreting the Basic Law is to construe the language used in the text of the instrument in order to ascertain *the legislative intent as expressed in the language*. Their task is not to ascertain the intent of the lawmaker on its own. Their duty is to ascertain *what was meant by the language used* and to give effect to *the legislative intent as expressed in the language*. It is the

---

162. [2004] HKCA 349.
163. Now, of course, Chief Justice of the Court of Final Appeal.
164. Ibid at paras 27(1) to 27(4).
165. (2001) 4 HKCFAR 211.

> text of the enactment which is the law and it is regarded as important both that the law should be certain and that it should be ascertainable by the citizen.[166] [emphasis added]

The cases, thus, make clear that, while the Hong Kong courts will adopt the *Pepper v Hart* principles where appropriate, strict criteria need to be applied; such that extrinsic evidence will, in practice, be rarely considered in interpreting statutes.

More recently, Court of Final Appeal support for purposive *"Pepper*-inspired" interpretation can be seen in *Agrila Ltd & Others v Commissioner of Rating & Valuation*[167] where Sir Anthony Mason NPJ stated:

> The rejection of the proposed amendment by the legislature indicates that regulation 2 was understood to mean that even where land subject to a lease is not assessable to rates . . . it would still be assessable for the purpose of Government rent and that it was the *legislature's intention* so to provide. [emphasis added]
>
> . . .
>
> The legislative history strongly confirms the meaning already placed on s 8(2) . . . which is to be discussed shortly. Treating the regulation as ambiguous, it is legitimate to have recourse to the legislative history in conformity with *Pepper v Hart* . . . The statements made by the Secretary who may be regarded as the promoter of the Bill and the regulations are clear.

Various statutory and other developments have assisted the move towards "purposive" interpretation. The Interpretation and General Clauses Ordinance (IGCO),[168] for example, contains definitions of many common words and phrases encountered in legislation which may assist the courts. More notably, section 19 of IGCO provides that, in general:

> an Ordinance shall be decreed to be remedial and shall receive such fair large and liberal construction and interpretation as will best ensure the attainment of the object of the Ordinance according to its true intent, meaning and spirit.

As previously noted, section 19 pre-dated *Pepper v Hart* and may be seen as an example, of Hong Kong being ahead of England in the move towards "purposiveness". However, Wesley-Smith writes that courts had previously not had great recourse to section 19 to justify reference to extrinsic sources.[169] One reason for this, he suggests, is a narrow interpretation of the word "fair" in section 19. The relevant Hong Kong Law Reform Commission (of which Professor Wesley-Smith was a member) report states:

---

166. Ibid at 223 H–J. Of course since the case involved interpretation of the Basic Law, there was a "political" dimension involved: see 4.4 below.
167. [2001] HKCFA 42.
168. Cap 1.
169. P Wesley-Smith, 'Literal or Liberal? The Notorious Section 19' (1982) 12 HKLJ 203. Moreover, the Law Reform Commission of Hong Kong baldly states that "even though section 19 is used in some judgments, it has not been used to admit extrinsic aids" (loc cit, at para 11.46).

Wesley-Smith has noted that the courts have only occasionally referred to section 19. The word 'fair' has been construed as referring not to the result of interpretation but to the interpretation itself[170] so that if the words fairly mean something that may operate unfairly, nevertheless that meaning must be adopted provided it accords with the 'true intent, meaning and spirit' of the provision. [He] indicates that perhaps it is the purposive approach which is to be used in the search for 'true intent, meaning and spirit'. He concludes that it is doubtful whether section 19 has deterred any Hong Kong judge from interpreting ordinances as he pleased. In the vast majority of cases it can safely be ignored . . .

Since Wesley-Smith's article was written in 1982,[171] there has been an increasing trend towards a purposive construction, whether or not section 19 has been relied upon to justify such a construction. There are few cases where the courts have referred to section 19 but those in which they have display a pragmatic approach to carry out the legislative intention.

Within an Ordinance itself assistance on interpretation may be found in:

(i) the long title—purposes and objects;
(ii) the short title—the name of the Ordinance;
(iii) the preamble—the formal explanation of the Ordinance. Although not common in Hong Kong, preambles may outline the mischief which the Ordinance is seeking to remedy;
(iv) headings—the sections and parts of the Ordinance;
(v) Schedules—these are normally found at the back of Ordinances and are used for illustrations, lists, etc;
(vi) Interpretation sections—most Ordinances will contain a section defining terms used in the Ordinance.

All these developments illustrate a growing move towards a less literal, more purposive approach to interpretation whereby the prime focus of the courts should be to discern, as far as "practicable", LegCo's true legislative intent. Since, however, "legislative intent" is not a simple matter, given the differing views of a bill's supporters[172] and compromises made to ensure passage of the legislation (including amendments to a bill), it can be seen that there remains a place for other approaches to statutory interpretation.

---

170. See also P Wesley-Smith, 'Literal or Liberal?' in P Wesley-Smith, *The Sources of Hong Kong Law* (Hong Kong University Press 1994) Chapter 14, 241.
171. P Wesley-Smith (1982) 12 HKLJ 203.
172. For an amusing illustration of the perils of *Pepper v Hart* "purposiveness" see discussion of *Witter (Thomas) Ltd v TBP Industries Ltd* [1996] 2 All ER 573 in *Salt v Stratstone Specialist Ltd* [2015] EWCA Civ 745 at para 15 (per Longmore J).

4.3.2 Specific rules of interpretation

In addition to the generalised approaches outlined above, there are also some specific rules on interpretation which judges must follow where applicable.

4.3.2.1 The statute must be read as a whole

This rule is well-defined by Ingman[173] who writes:

> The words used in a statute must not be interpreted out of their context . . . Each section in a statute must be read subject to every other section, which may explain or modify it. If there is an irreconcilable conflict between two sections in the same statute, or between two subsections within the same section, the correct test to be applied is to determine which is the leading provision and which the subordinate provision.[174]

A good example of the "read as whole" rule is provided in the case of *Beswick v Beswick*, decided in the English Court of Appeal[175] and House of Lords.[176] In the Court of Appeal, Lord Denning MR had tried to use the literal words of section 56 of the Law of Property Act 1925 to circumvent the doctrine of privity of contract (of which he was no supporter!).[177] While Lord Denning's interpretation was clearly a reasonable one, taking account of the words of section 56 in isolation, it was rejected on appeal to the House of Lords, largely because that court was unwilling to accept that (reading the Act as a whole) it could have been intended to sweep away a basic tenet of the English law of contract in a (consolidating) statute of over 200 sections almost entirely concerned with English land law.[178]

4.3.2.2 The *ejusdem generis* rule

The *ejusdem generis* rule, deriving from the principle that a statute should be read as a whole, applies where a list of specific items is followed by general words, in which case those general words should be construed as being of the same "class" or "*genus*" as the specific words. Thus, in a statute applying to any, "*house, office, room or other place*", the word "place" must be viewed as of the same class as the specific words, ie, it must be indoors and enclosed. The word would not include an open, outdoor area.[179] Essentially, the "interpreter" needs to insert the word "such" before

---

173. T Ingman, *The English Legal Process* (13th edn, Oxford University Press 2010) 149.
174. Ibid at p 264.
175. [1966] 3 All ER 1.
176. [1967] 2 All ER 1197.
177. [1966] 3 All ER 1 at 8–9.
178. [1967] 3 All ER 1197 at 1202–1205 (per Lord Reid).
179. See *Powell v Kempton Park Racecourse Co* [1899] AC 143.

the general word(s). In order to establish a *"genus"*, however, it is necessary to have two or more specific words before the general one(s).[180]

The *ejusdem generis* rule was applied in the Hong Kong case of *Lam Kwan-shi v Lam Wan-hing*[181] in interpreting the words, *"solicitor, banker, stockbroker or other person"* in the Trustee Ordinance.[182] The words "other person" were restricted to a class of person of a professional type. Indeed, the (common law) *ejusdem generis* rule has generally been applied by the Hong Kong courts relatively unquestioningly, despite its apparent conflict with the specific (statutory) words of section 3 of the Interpretation and General Clauses Ordinance (IGCO).[183] Section 3 states:

> 'or', 'other', and 'otherwise' shall be construed disjunctively and not as implying similarity, unless the word 'similar' or some other word of like meaning is added.

It would appear that, on any *literal* construction, this section overturns the common law and abolishes the *ejusdem generis* rule for Hong Kong.[184] Of course, were a word such as "similar" to be inserted, there would no need to have recourse to the "labour-saving" *ejusdem generis* approach. Moreover, on a *purposive* basis, there seems to be no other purpose for this section than to remove the application of *ejusdem generis*[185] (it goes without saying that the consequence would not be absurd, so no "golden rule" issue comes into play). Nevertheless, despite some judicial support for "abolition",[186] the *ejusdem generis* rule has been applied in Hong Kong post-IGCO.[187]

4.3.2.3 The *expressio unius* rule

Another specific rule, albeit one of limited scope, is *expressio unius est exclusio alterius*. Literally this means "the reference to one is to the exclusion of another" and, again, it is in keeping with the principle of reading a statute as a whole. The rule is best understood by way of some simple illustrations. If, for example, a statute states that it is illegal to sell alcohol to someone under the age of 18, the obvious interpretation is that it is lawful to sell to others. Equally, where a particular procedure is laid down for obtaining a licence or for the payment of tax, this will be

---

180. See *Allen v Emmerson* [1944] KB 362.
181. [1967] HKLR 616.
182. Cap 29.
183. Cap 1. Section 3 merely restates the words of s 18 of the Interpretation Ordinance (No 24 of 1897).
184. Moreover, s 2(1) of IGCO makes clear that its rules of interpretation should apply to all Ordinances, whether enacted before or after IGCO.
185. Wesley-Smith writes that "In *AG v Lui Fuk-yuen* . . . McMullin J seemed to accept counsel's submission that the real purpose of the 'or' rules was to do away with *ejusdem generis*" (P Wesley-Smith, *The Sources of Hong Kong Law* [n 168], 228). The "or" rule was removed from later versions of Cap 1.
186. See *Cheung Chi-man v R* (1974) FCt, Crim App No 265 of 1974; *AG v Lui Fuk-yuen* (1976) FCt, Crim App No 300 of 1975.
187. For a recent illustration, see the judgment of Seagroat J. in *Chun Sang Plastics v Commissioner of Police* [2018] HKCFI 661. For further discussion, see B Wong and A Ho, *Butterworths Hong Kong Statutory Interpretation Handbook* (part 2) (2nd edn, LexisNexis 2012).

interpreted as precluding *other* methods. So, for example, in *Tempest v Kilner*,[188] it was held that the (old) rule that contracts for "goods, wares or merchandise" were unenforceable unless evidenced in writing did not apply to contracts for the sale of company shares.

A striking example of the non-adoption of this rule is to be found in the "right of abode" cases and the (re-) interpretation of the Basic Law (contrary to the interpretation of Hong Kong's Court of Final Appeal) by the Standing Committee of the National People's Congress at the request of the Hong Kong government.[189] The conclusion to be drawn is that, as a piece of People's Republic of China (PRC) legislation, the Basic Law is not subject to common law interpretative practices.

4.3.2.4 No retrospective criminality under the Bill of Rights Ordinance

While the English common law applies a *presumption* that any statute is not intended to operate retrospectively, the Hong Kong rules are more emphatic since, under the Bill of Rights Ordinance (BORO), no one may be penalised under the criminal law for committing an act which was legal at the time of the commission.[190] Whether, in practice, this represents a "rule" or a "presumption" will be considered below.[191]

4.3.2.5 Penal provisions to be construed narrowly

The long established rule of the English common law is that, in dealing with legislation involving the possible imposition of a penalty, where there is ambiguity it should be resolved in favour of the alleged "offender". It could be argued that the courts were applying this rule in the acquittal of the defendant in *Fisher v Bell*.[192] The "ambiguity" in that case, of course, was between a "technical/literal" construction and a "sensible/purposive" one. The rationale is that since the accused is "deemed" (fictionally, of course) to know the law, and cannot plead ignorance of the relevant criminal law in his defence, he should at least expect that the words of such criminal law will be construed literally and not via an approach based on a legislative history of which he was, almost certainly, unaware. Thus, in *Fothergill v Monarch Airlines*[193] Lord Diplock stated:

> If the meaning . . . is clear and unambiguous and does not lead to a result that is manifestly absurd or unreasonable, it would be a confidence trick by Parliament and destructive of all legal certainty if the private citizen could not rely upon that meaning but was required to search through all that happened before and in the course of the legislative process in order to see whether there was anything to be

---
188. (1846) 3 CB 249.
189. See 4.4, infra.
190. Article 12, Bill of Rights Ordinance.
191. See 4.3.4.
192. Above.
193. [1980] 3 WLR 209.

found from which it could be inferred that Parliament's real intention had not been accurately expressed by the actual words that Parliament had adopted to communicate it to those affected by the legislation.[194]

Ironically, of course, the typical "seller" of flick-knives asked whether he was offering the goods for sale would almost certainly respond (absent the threat of prosecution) "of course". To ascribe to the defendant knowledge of an arcane principle of the law of contract is as fictional as the presumption that the defendant knows the law. However, since "offer for sale" was, presumably, regarded as a technical term (given its particular contract law definition), the court adopted a "technical/literal" approach as defined by Lord Esher in *Marquis of Camden v Inland Revenue Commissioners*:[195]

> If the Act is directed to dealing with matters affecting everybody generally, the words used have the meaning attached to them in the common and ordinary use of language. If the Act is one passed with reference to a particular trade, business or transaction, and the words are used as everybody conversant with that trade, business or transaction knows and understands to have a particular meaning in it, then the words are to be construed as having that particular meaning, though it may differ from the common or ordinary meaning of the words . . .
>
> . . . When it is agreed or contended that statutory words have a technical meaning, evidence with regard to that meaning is unquestionably admissible, and it should generally be preferred to information gleaned from other sources such as dictionaries.[196]

The "technical/literal" approach was applied in Hong Kong (on appeal to the Court of First Instance) in the case of *Hong Kong SAR v Wan Hon Sik*, discussed above.[197] While the defendant in that case was undoubtedly (and by his own admission) in possession of pirated VCD disks and was "introducing" them to potential Japanese clients, he was not "offering them for sale" in the technical sense adopted by the English courts.

The narrow construction of a penal provision was applied in the Hong Kong case of *R v Ling Yee Shun*[198] where the Court of First Instance was called upon, by way of appeal, to construe the meaning of "a constant and adequate supply of clear fresh water"; the key word being "constant". The appellant had initially been convicted on the basis that he had failed to maintain a constant supply based on the Magistrate's interpretation of "constant" to mean "all the time". Hooper J, in setting aside the conviction on this count, stated:

---

194. At 221.
195. [1914] 1 KB 641.
196. Ibid. Cited with approval in the Court of First Instance in *R v Ling Yee Shun* [1988] HKCFI 394.
197. See 4.3.1.1 above.
198. [1988] CFI 394.

This Regulation requires a construction to be put upon the word "constant". No evidence has been led to show that this word has a special meaning in the poultry trade. It must therefore be construed in accordance with section 19 of the Interpretation and General Clauses Ordinance.

. . . The shorter Oxford dictionary defines this word in respect of actions as meaning "continuous", continuous without intermission or "continually recurring". The Magistrate's construction that it means "all the time" was therefore not the only construction open to him on an ordinary use of the word. In my judgment the proper construction to put on this word is "continually recurring" . . . As long as animals have at continually recurring intervals throughout the day an adequate supply, then I cannot see why it would be necessary to require an uninterrupted supply.[199]

4.3.3 Presumptions in interpretation

There are a number of presumptions that the courts may use to assist in interpretation. It is not possible to list them all but the following are the most important:

(1) A presumption that Ordinances do not have *retrospective* effect. The presumption is that legislation (unlike case law) cannot change the law "retrospectively". In *Re Setaffa Investment Ltd*[200] the Hong Kong Court of First Instance had to determine whether s 264A of the Companies Ordinance[201] could adversely affect companies which went into liquidation before the section came into force. The court stated that very clear wording must be used for a statute to operate retrospectively. Le Pichon J concluded:

> In my judgment, s264A operates prospectively only and applies to liquidations that commence after that section came into effect.[202]

In relation to allegations of criminality the presumption has been elevated to a rule under Article 12 of the Bill of Rights Ordinance (BORO) noted above.

(2) A presumption against the imposition of "strict liability" (liability without fault) in the criminal law. There is a general requirement that criminal offences require a "*mens rea*" (guilty mind) and, unless legislation *clearly* envisages liability without fault, it is presumed to require some element of fault (intention, recklessness etc) to constitute guilt. In *Lim Chin Aik v R*[203] the Privy Council, on appeal from Singapore, stated:

> It cannot be inferred that the legislature imposed strict liability merely in order to find a luckless victim . . . the application of the rule [sic] that mens rea is an essential

---

199. Ibid at paras 37 and 38.
200. [1998] 3 HKC 342.
201. Cap 32.
202. At 353 para B.
203. [1963] 2 WLR 42.

ingredient in every offence has not in the present case been ousted by the terms or subject-matter of the Ordinance.[204]

(3) A presumption against the *exclusion of natural justice*. There are two basic aspects of the rules of natural justice: that parties have a right to be heard, and that no one should be "a judge in his own cause". In interpreting any legislation, therefore, the courts will assume that these two principles of fairness have not been ousted.

4.3.4 The impact of the Bill of Rights Ordinance (BORO) on interpretation

The nature of the Bill of Rights Ordinance (BORO) is that it enshrines in statutory form the human rights guarantees of the International Covenant on Civil and Political Rights (ICCPR), to which Hong Kong was already a signatory pre-1997. BORO re-states these rights via "Articles" in Part II. Moreover, in Part I, the Ordinance gives these Articles a special status. The substance of the Articles is outlined in Chapter 2. The historical rationale, of course, was the fear that the post-1997 Hong Kong SAR, under pressure from the People's Republic of China, would roll back the guaranteed ICCPR rights. BORO was introduced hastily in the period before the "resumption of sovereignty" of Hong Kong in 1997.

The special status of the "Articles" listed in Part II involves (previous and subsequent) legislation being interpreted in such a way as to be "consistent" with BORO *and*, in the case of "inconsistent" previous legislation, its repeal.[205] A clear *intention* of the legislation, therefore, is that it should be an aid to statutory interpretation. It is a moot point, however, whether BORO remains of great significance in this context because the "special status" sections of the Ordinance (sections 2(3), 3 and 4) were immediately abolished ("not adopted")[206] post-1997, on the grounds that their special "superior" status was inconsistent with the Basic Law.[207]

Thus, although BORO has not generally been abolished, its use as an interpretative tool is, at the very least, significantly curbed. To take just one example, BORO precludes the retrospective criminalisation of an act which was legal at the time of its performance.[208] Suppose that an Ordinance is later passed that seems to impose retrospective criminality. This will be interpreted, if possible, in such a way as to be consistent with BORO. However, if the Ordinance can only be interpreted as retrospective, BORO cannot be invoked to invalidate the legislation. Moreover, if the "inconsistent" Ordinance was passed *before* BORO, the initially envisaged invalidity

---

204. Ibid at 50–52.
205. Where subsequent legislation cannot be reconciled it takes precedence over the BORO Articles.
206. By virtue of *The Decision of the Standing Committee of the National People's Congress on Handling of the Laws Previously in Force in Hong Kong in accordance with Article 160 of the Basic Law of the Hong Kong SAR of the PRC* made on 23 February 1997.
207. Since the "laws previously in force" (in 1997) shall generally remain in force (Article 8, Basic Law and see Chapter 2).
208. Article 12, BORO.

would not operate because of the "non-adoption" of the relevant sections of BORO. In practice, therefore, there is no more than a "presumption" against retrospectiveness, which already exists at common law. Still, BORO has a limited role in interpretation. It has been successfully invoked in respect of the interpretation of electoral rules in the New Territories which allegedly discriminated against "non-indigenous" inhabitants contrary to its Article 21(a). In the case in question, *Secretary of Justice & Others v Chan Wah & Others*,[209] the Court of Final Appeal upheld the right of non-indigenous villagers to vote, in accordance with Article 21(a), despite the assertion by "indigenous locals" that such an interpretation was contrary to Article 40 of the Basic Law.

4.4 Interpreting the Basic Law

In understanding the special situation regarding interpretation of the Basic Law, it is important to remember that it is a piece of People's Republic of China (PRC) legislation rather than a piece of Hong Kong "domestic" legislation. Moreover, the Basic Law is a "basic law" of the PRC, a superior piece of legislation entailing special "entrenched" status. Further, with clear potential for conflict, "interpretation" has a broader meaning under PRC law than under the common law system.[210]

While *crucially* the Standing Committee of the NPC has the *ultimate/overriding* power to interpret the Basic Law, under Article 158 of that Law, the Hong Kong SAR courts are authorised, *on their own*, to interpret provisions of the Basic Law which are "within the limits of the autonomy of the Region".[211] Essentially, this emphasises that the Hong Kong courts have no jurisdiction over "acts of state"; essentially defence and foreign affairs.

Moreover, Article 158 adds that where the courts of the Hong Kong SAR need to interpret provisions which are the responsibility of the Central People's Government, or concerning the relationship between the Central Authorities and the Hong Kong SAR (the "excluded provisions"), the courts need to seek an *interpretation* from the Standing Committee through the Court of Final Appeal of the Hong Kong SAR, "if such interpretation will affect the judgments on the cases".[212] The Standing Committee will then consult the Committee for the Basic Law of the SAR before giving an interpretation on the law.[213] Provision exists in the Basic Law, therefore, for a request for interpretation from the Hong Kong courts or, implicitly, for

---

209. [2000] 3 HKLRD 641.
210. Discussed further in chapter 11.
211. Article 158, Basic Law.
212. Ibid.
213. Ibid.

a direct interpretation by the Standing Committee on its own initiative.[214] What the Basic Law does *not* provide for is a request for interpretation from any other body.[215]

However, two momentous constitutional cases have determined the issue of interpretation of the Basic Law and, in so doing, have emphasised the primacy of the Standing Committee of the National People's Congress at the expense of the limited autonomy over Basic Law interpretation which *appeared* to have been conferred on the Hong Kong courts by the Basic Law. The two cases are *Ng Ka Ling v Director of Immigration*[216] and *Chan Kam Nga v Director of Immigration*,[217] both involving the "right of abode" in Hong Kong. The applicants were children of Hong Kong permanent residents but born in mainland China *before* either parent had acquired Hong Kong right of abode. Under pre-1997 law such children had no right of abode in Hong Kong but they claimed that Article 24 of the Basic Law, Hong Kong's post-1997 constitution, now gave them that right since they were "born of" permanent residents. Moreover, they argued that, insofar as they conflicted with the Basic Law on this point, Hong Kong's post-1997 immigration laws (passed by the controversial Provisional Legislative Council) were invalid. The legal argument was a strong one since it is clearly accepted that the Basic Law is a "basic law" of the People's Republic of China, having superior force in Hong Kong, such that all local (Hong Kong) legislation must be in conformity.[218] However, the Hong Kong government had campaigned in advance against the arguably clear wording of Article 24,[219] arguing that such an interpretation would lead to a flood of immigrants from the PRC.[220]

In *Ng Ka Ling*, the Court of Final Appeal (CFA) found in favour of the right of abode claimants on the basis that, despite the legality of the Provisional Legislative Council (accepted by the CFA), its legislation on the right of abode issue was not consistent with the (superior) Basic Law. Perhaps over-confrontationally, the CFA added that Hong Kong courts have the right:

> to examine whether any legislative acts of the National People's Congress or its Standing Committee are consistent with the Basic Law and to declare them invalid if found to be inconsistent.[221]

---

214. See Y Ghai, *Hong Kong's New Constitutional Order* (n 4) 197.
215. On an application of the *"expressio unius"* rule, of course, the Hong Kong government's action would not have been permitted (see 4.3.2.3). However, interpretation of the Basic Law is not, it seems, to be based on the common law approach.
216. [1999] 1 HKC 291.
217. [1999] 1 HKC 347.
218. Indeed, the superior position of the Basic Law was the essential rationale for revoking the Bill of Rights Ordinance's "entrenched" power (see 4.3.4).
219. Bokhary PJ found the words of Article 24 to be unambiguous. The author would respectfully (and reluctantly) disagree.
220. The "statistical" evidence on which the government based its case was extremely questionable.
221. [1999] 1 HKC 291 at 323.

Had the CFA merely declared that the Provisional Legislature's legislation was inconsistent it may have avoided subsequent humiliation. In the event, the Hong Kong government asked the CFA for a "clarification" of its judgment in *Ng Ka Ling* and, following the CFA's affirmation of the right of final interpretation of the Basic Law by the Standing Committee of the NPC and the binding nature of any such interpretation, the Hong Kong government then asked the Standing Committee to (re)interpret Articles 22 and 24 of the Basic Law in a way more favourable to its own view. Not surprisingly, the Standing Committee acceded to the Hong Kong government's request [222] and declared that "the interpretation of the Court of Final appeal is not consistent with the legislative intent".[223] Thus, a precedent for a request for interpretation by the Hong Kong government (nowhere provided for in the Basic Law)[224] was established.[225]

Following the "(re)interpretation",[226] in June 1999, which had the effect of "prospectively" reversing[227] the decision in *Chan Kam Nga* and *Ng Ka Ling*, there followed, in December 1999, the Court of Final Appeal's decision in *Lau Kong Yung v Director of Immigration*,[228] where the court ruled that it was bound by the Standing Committee's interpretation and confirmed that the power of interpretation can be exercised on the Standing Committee's *own initiative* without reference to it by the Hong Kong courts. This last point is largely uncontroversial, since if a body has the right of interpretation it is for that body to decide when to exercise it. However, the court (humiliatingly) accepted that the Standing Committee's power to intervene applies *even in* those areas (not involving foreign affairs, defence and so on) previously felt to be within the Hong Kong courts' autonomy.

The most unsatisfactory aspect of the interpretation saga, however, is undoubtedly the potential for the Hong Kong government to ask the Standing Committee to

---

222. Cf *The Interpretation of the Standing Committee of the National People's Congress of Articles 22(4) and 24(2)(3) of the Basic Law of the HKSAR of the PRC* (Adopted at the 10th Session of the Standing Committee of the 9th NPC on 26 June 1999).
223. Ibid.
224. The Hong Kong government argued that the action was justified under Article 48(2) of the Basic Law which makes the Chief Executive responsible for "the implementation of this [Basic] Law and other laws which, in accordance with this Law, apply in the Hong Kong SAR." The argument is tenuous and the consequence (that the government can, effectively, appeal against any judicial ruling of which it disapproves) seriously undermines judicial autonomy.
225. The consequence for "right of abode" claimants was that those who had already succeeded in the courts were unaffected by the interpretation. However, those merely awaiting adjudication *were* affected and were required to leave Hong Kong: *Ng Siu Tung and Others v Director of Immigration* (2002) 5 HKCFAR 1. Bokhary J lodged a fierce dissent, arguing that promises made by Hong Kong officials had given these claimants a legitimate expectation that they would be allowed to stay.
226. Then Secretary for Justice, Elsie Leung, disingenuously argued that there had been no "re-interpretation" since the *NPC Standing Committee* had only interpreted the Articles once. For illustration of a "difference of views" on this issue compare Letter from Margaret Ng (LegCo representative, legal functional constituency) 7 June 1999 and Reply (SJO 5047/2/4C) from Elsie Leung, Secretary for Justice, 14 June 1999.
227. NPCSC Article 158 interpretations cannot affect judgments "previously rendered".
228. [1999] 4 HKC 731.

intervene (potentially) whenever it does not get its own way in the courts. Some cause for optimism can be derived from "post-*Ng Ka Ling*" developments. In *Director of Immigration v Chong Fung Yuen*,[229] (another "abode" case) for example, the Hong Kong government disagreed with the Court of Appeal's ruling, appealed to the Court of Final Appeal (CFA) and argued that the court should seek an interpretation from the Standing Committee. The government, significantly, added that it would not itself seek a Standing Committee interpretation if the Court of Final Appeal rejected its arguments. In the event, the CFA dismissed the government's appeal.

Despite the relative scarcity of post-*Ng Ka Ling* interpretations by the NPC Standing Committee, it is difficult to overestimate the significance of this case and its potential effect on judicial autonomy in the Hong Kong SAR. The essential point of the case was that, for socio-political reasons, the Hong Kong SAR government wanted to restrict the right of abode. In common law systems it is a key tenet of interpretation that the courts interpret without concern for the political effects. If legislation turns out to have a detrimental social effect, the government should seek to amend the legislation. If the Basic Law's meaning had the potential to seriously jeopardise Hong Kong's social fabric, the opportunity to seek amendment of the Basic Law should have been taken. As Professor Johannes Chan has stated:

> A legal decision which produces unpalatable economic or social conditions does not, by itself, suggest it is either 'wrong' or needs to be 'corrected'.[230]

Moreover, as Professor Chan further points out, the case for interpretation by the Standing Committee was a weak one, based on the need for mainland Chinese citizens wishing to enter Hong Kong to "apply for approval", under Article 22 of the Basic Law. This, it was argued by the pro-government camp, was clearly an issue "affecting the relationship between the Central Government and the SAR". Chan emphasises that the *crucial* issue before the CFA was Article 24, the right of abode in Hong Kong; an issue within the autonomy of the Region.[231]

"Politically", therefore, the actions of the Hong Kong government in *Ng Ka Ling* acted as a "warning" to the judiciary that, on important matters, they were determined to have the last word. It went without saying that any request for interpretation by the Hong Kong SAR government would be dealt with favourably by

---

229. [2000] 1 HKC 359.
230. J Chan, 'Judicial Independence: A Reply to the Comments of the Mainland Legal Experts on the Constitutional Jurisdiction of the CFA' in MM Chan, HL Fu, and Y Ghai (eds), *Hong Kong's Constitutional Debate: Conflict over Interpretation* (Hong Kong University Press 2000) 68.
231. Ibid 67–68. A different academic view is expressed by Chan's University of Hong Kong Law Faculty colleague, Professor Albert Chen, who argues that, *legally*, the CFA should have asked for an interpretation (see AHY Chen, 'The Court of Final Appeal's Ruling in the "Illegal Migrant" Children Case' in *Hong Kong's Constitutional Debate*, op cit, supra, 113–142. Senior Counsel Alan Hoo also criticised the CFA ruling, arguing that their approach was not "purposive" given a Joint Liaison Group arrangement of 1993 *and* that amendment of the Basic Law was both unwelcome and unnecessary (see A Hoo, 'Legal Options to Handle the Consequences of the CFA's Right of Abode Ruling' Personal Opinion 13 May 1999).

the Standing Committee. This "warning" was, therefore, a serious erosion of the common law concept of "separation of powers". As Human Rights Watch stated:[232]

> By turning to the NPC to bolster its own case, the [Tung Chee Hwa] Hong Kong government has set a dangerous precedent, effectively giving notice that any time the CFA rules in a way that the executive branch of the SAR finds unacceptable, it will turn to China for assistance.

Fortunately, to date, there have since been only four further "interpretations"[233] under Article 158 of the Basic Law: the first at the initiative of the NPC Standing Committee; the second via reference by the Hong Kong government;[234] the third, constitutionally sanctioned,[235] by the Court of Final Appeal itself and the last (again) at the NPCSC's own initiative. The first involved an interpretation of the rules relating to constitutional/electoral reform (at the NPCSC's own initiative).[236] The second, at the application of the Hong Kong government, involved an interpretation of the rules on the Chief Executive's term of office[237] without any prior court involvement. This unfortunate departure from the concept of "two systems" arose in 2005 in respect of the debate over the length of term of the Chief Executive, given Tung Chee Hwa's mid-term resignation. Since the term is stated, unequivocally, in Article 46 of the Basic Law, to be five years, the Hong Kong government had previously asserted that this would always be the case. However, following "advice from mainland legal experts", the then Hong Kong SAR Secretary for Justice, Elsie Leung, revised her previously clear view. The previous "mistake", she stated, arose because the Hong Kong government had been assuming a common law interpretation. The clear implication is that, henceforth, the Basic Law should no longer be interpreted on a common law basis.[238] Nonetheless, interpretations by the NPCSC have been sufficiently exceptional for Chen[239] to write:

---

232. Quoted by Asian Human Rights Commission 23 August 2001.
233. "Interpretation" is a far broader concept in the PRC: see Chapter 11.
234. As explained previously, such references are legally dubious.
235. See Article 158, Basic Law.
236. *Interpretation by the Standing Committee of the NPC of Article 7 of Annex I and Article III of Annex II to the Basic Law of the Hong Kong SAR of the PRC* (Adopted at the 8th Session of the Standing Committee of the 10th NPC on 6 April 2004). Since the NPCSC has the power of interpretation its exercise of same on its own initiative is relatively uncontentious.
237. *Interpretation of Paragraph 2, Article 53 of the Basic Law of the Hong Kong SAR of the PRC by the Standing Committee of the NPC* (Adopted at the 15th Session of the Standing Committee of the 10th NPC on 27 April 2005).
238. Morris, however, has defended the "two-year" term based on what he describes as, "my reading, as a common law lawyer". See RJ Morris, 'The "Replacement" Chief Executive's Two-Year Term: A Pure and Unambiguous Common Law Analysis' (2005) 35 HKLJ 1728.
239. AHY Chen, '"One Country, Two Systems" from a Legal Perspective' in Y-M Yeung (ed), *The First Decade: The Hong Kong SAR in Retrospective And Introspective Perspective* (Chinese University Press, 2007) Chapter 8.

The NPCSC has practised self-restraint in exercising its power of interpretation of the Basic Law.[240]

Ms Leung's less pro-government successor as Secretary of Justice, Wong Yan Lung,[241] expressed the hope that there will be no further Standing Committee interpretations.[242] Similarly, current Chief Justice Geoffrey Ma has said: "If you use Article 158 to seek an interpretation every time you don't like a court decision, it undermines the authority of the courts."[243] This view, of course, is restricted to interpretations not sought by the Hong Kong Court of Final Appeal (CFA). The Basic Law makes clear provision for the CFA to seek an interpretation where issues not within Hong Kong's autonomy are involved.[244] These include defence, foreign affairs and the relationship of the PRC with other states.

The Court of Final Appeal made its first request for interpretation by the NPC Standing Committee in the case of *The Democratic Republic of the Congo v FG Hemisphere Associates*,[245] the brief facts of which follow. The Democratic Republic of the Congo (DRC) defaulted on repayment obligations to Energoinvest, a company from the (then) Yugoslavia. These defaults were the subject of two arbitration awards, both in favour of Energoinvest. Energoinvest assigned its interest in the awards to the claimants, FG Hemisphere.[246] FG later sought, in the Hong Kong courts, to obtain monies from "Entry Fees" to be paid by the China Railway Group (CRG) to DRC on the basis that, as monies payable to DRC they should be paid to its arbitral creditor (FG). In response, the DRC claimed state immunity in respect of its debt to FG.

The main issue in the case concerned the *scope* of state immunity; since Hong Kong, pre-1997, recognised only "restricted" state immunity (not extending to commercial matters)[247] while the PRC has always accepted the doctrine of "absolute" state immunity. Presciently, Mushkat had previously written:

---

240. Ibid 166.
241. Wong's tenure of office was followed by the short-lived one of Rimsky Yuen; himself succeeded by Teresa Cheng in 2018.
242. So far his hopes have been sustained.
243. S Lau, 'Preserve Common Law after 2047: Top Hong Kong Judge' *South China Morning Post* (Hong Kong, 19 March 2014).
244. Article 158, Basic Law.
245. (2011) 14 HKCFAR 95.
246. Described as a Distressed Debt Fund or "vulture company"; buying up uncertain debts at a discount.
247. It should be noted that the DRC/CRG arrangement was far from a typical "commercial" venture, being more in the nature of a massive PRC provision of infrastructure in return for mining rights in Africa's most prolific source of valuable minerals (see T Carty and O Jones, 'The Congo Case' (2011) *Hong Kong Lawyer* (March 2011) 43–50). Carty and Jones suggest that on balance the DRC/CRG transactions were "sovereign" rather than commercial, endorsing the view of Reyes J in the Court of First Instance.

It may be assumed that the HKSAR judges will continue to follow the "restrictive approach" to state immunity as incorporated in the common law, although this may give rise to some doctrinal conflicts with their mainland counterparts.[248]

Moreover, since China Railway Group was involved, the PRC had a more than ideological "interest" in the outcome of the case.

In the Court of First Instance,[249] before Reyes J, judgment was in favour of DRC on the fairly straightforward basis that DRC enjoyed state immunity as regards any debt to FG and that it had not waived such immunity.

On appeal, a majority of the Court of Appeal (Yeung JA presciently dissenting) found for FG.[250] The court accepted that restrictive immunity had been adopted in Hong Kong before 1997. This had been recognised as pre-1997 common law,[251] had been underlined by the extension of the application of the State Immunity Act 1978 to Hong Kong and, on the cessation of the application of this Act in 1997, had remained the Hong Kong pre-1997 legal position via the resumption of the common law.

The court unanimously accepted that the PRC had always "consistently and unequivocally" recognised absolute immunity. The majority, however, believed that the two conflicting views on immunity (Hong Kong's *restrictive* view and the PRC's *absolute* view) could co-exist within a single state via the "one country, two systems" principle. The majority added that such a dual approach would cause "no prejudice or embarrassment" to the PRC. Yeung JA's dissent noted that:

> [W]hen it comes to foreign affairs of which state immunity is one aspect, there is simply no room for 'two systems' at all . . . Hong Kong SAR courts, having regard to the provisions of the Basic Law should not adopt a legal position concerning state immunity incompatible with the position of the PRC.

The Court of Final Appeal (CFA) found, by a 3–2 majority, for DRC; essentially endorsing the dissent of Yuen JA. It was accepted by the majority that DRC had not waived any immunity; that Hong Kong's pre-1997 position had been to recognise only restricted state immunity; that the PRC had always recognised absolute state immunity; and that it was not possible to adopt conflicting approaches to state immunity within one country (the "one voice" principle). The Hong Kong SAR, while enjoying a large measure of autonomy, did not have authority over matters of state, which encompasses the issue of state immunity. In so stating, the majority rejected the Court of Appeal's statements to the effect that the exercise of a different concept of state immunity within the Hong Kong SAR would not embarrass and prejudice the PRC.

---

248. R Mushkat, *One Country, Two International Legal Personalities: The Case of Hong Kong* (Hong Kong University Press 1997) 167.
249. [2009] 1 HKLRD 410.
250. [2010] 2 HKLRD 66.
251. Cf, eg, *Trendtex Trading Corp v Central Bank of Nigeria* [1977] 1 QB 529.

Having decided that the issue of state immunity was clearly an aspect of "foreign affairs" (for which the Central People's Government (CPG) is responsible under Article 13 of the Basic Law and over which the Hong Kong courts have no jurisdiction under Article 19), the majority ceded to the PRC the decision as to what form of state immunity should be recognised within the "one country".

Having "decided" in favour of DRC, however, the Court of Final Appeal (CFA) decided to refer the interpretation of Articles 13 and 19 of the Basic Law to the NPC Standing Committee (as an issue of foreign affairs which needed to be determined in order to give judgment) under Article 158 of the Basic Law. The initial "decision" of the CFA, therefore, was "provisional" and subject to approval by the Standing Committee (which was asked to respond to a number of questions by the CFA). The Standing Committee, unsurprisingly, confirmed that the state immunity issue was, indeed, a matter of foreign affairs to be determined by the CPG and that the Hong Kong SAR courts were bound to follow the PRC's *absolute* approach to state immunity.

Comment

Essentially, the difference in approach by the two appellate courts came down to the issue of whether absolute immunity, as recognised by the PRC, must now be adopted in the Hong Kong SAR. The majority in the Court of Appeal (and the minority in the CFA) felt that the common law approach to determining immunity should continue to be exercised in Hong Kong (none of the appellate judges had contested that restricted immunity was the pre-1997 rule). The "overruled" judges adopted the principle that the common law should continue in Hong Kong post-1997, as affirmed in, inter alia, Article 8 of the Basic Law; while, perhaps, paying insufficient attention to the limitations imposed on that continuation by the Basic Law and, arguably, to the post-1997 political reality (China Railway Company was effectively a party to proceedings and the PRC's Office of Commissioner of the Ministry for Foreign Affairs had asserted the PRC's "consistent and principled" support for absolute state immunity). In the view of the CFA minority (Bokhary PJ and Mortimer NPJ) the common law position was clear and should be continued. Bokhary, indeed, a lone voice, also supported the view that DRC had waived any immunity by submitting to arbitration. Mortimer NPJ did raise the interesting point that the pre-1997 courts of Hong Kong (as a British colony) had never had the jurisdiction to decide on foreign affairs, yet had frequently determined (uncontentiously) issues of state immunity.

Given the nature and significance of the case it is, perhaps, worthy of note that Chief Justice Geoffrey Ma did not sit in the Court of Final Appeal. This was, in fact, in accord with his previous undertaking not to sit on appeals from the Court of Appeal in which his wife[252] had been a member of the court.

---

252. Maria Yuen JA.

The reference to the Standing Committee by the Court of Final Appeal (CFA), provided for in the Basic Law, is clearly less worrying than a reference by the Hong Kong government for which there is no Basic Law provision. Moreover, in terms of outcome, *one is unlikely to feel sympathy for a "vulture company" losing out on its speculation. The case clearly can be seen in terms of a situation involving the PRC and its relations with foreign governments. However, the case still raises certain concerns. First, some see it is a cession by the CFA of a part of its judicial autonomy and perhaps indicative of a lack of confidence in the majority members (Justice Bokhary, of course, resisted the referral!). Further, the case resonates with fears long ago expressed by Martin Lee that "state" enterprises of the PRC would be able to flout Hong Kong laws with impunity. That fear, which appeared groundless for some time, now appears a genuine prospect.*[253]

From a socio-economic viewpoint, too, the outcome is unfortunate for Hong Kong; since its flagship arbitration system is certain to be adversely affected as commercial "creditor" parties, claiming debts from state enterprises, will simply "cut their losses" rather than have pointless recourse to the Hong Kong court or arbitral system. Likewise more commercial contracts involving "states" will be diverted from Hong Kong.[254]

Academic views on the *Congo* case have been mixed, though generally the CFA's decision has been welcomed as the inevitable outcome, given the political realities. Oliver Jones,[255] writing before the CFA judgment was delivered, clearly favoured adoption of the absolute immunity doctrine for Hong Kong. His basic rationale is that the *common law* doctrine of restricted immunity did *not* revive with the repeal of the State Immunity Act 1978 (expressly in Britain and implicitly in Hong Kong),[256] that the PRC position on absolute immunity is clear, that the "one voice" approach should be followed and that the CFA should have sought a certificate from the PRC/CPG that it was a "persistent objector" to restrictive immunity under Article 19(3) of the Basic Law. In the event of such a certificate being issued, Jones writes, the CFA should have dismissed proceedings.

---

253. See Chapter 1 at 1.9.
254. "[L]ots of contracts which would otherwise have been signed in Hong Kong and subject to Hong Kong law will be signed elsewhere . . . Worse, there are many deals which . . . cannot be signed anywhere but in Hong Kong, so the risks of not being able to get satisfaction from the local courts will add to costs and deter business." (P Bowring, 'Damaging Blow to Our Lifeblood' *South China Morning Post*, "Backpage" [Hong Kong, 4 September 2011]). Conversely, it has been argued that PRC "total" state immunity would apply to contracts made with the PRC *anywhere* (see T Cheng and A Lai, 'Lessons Learned from the FG Hemisphere v DRC and Huatianlong Case' <http://www.arbitration-icca.org/.../media1132342764462706> accessed 4 January 2018.
255. O Jones, 'Let the Mainland Speak: A Positivist Take on the Congo Case' (2011) 41 HKLJ 177–202.
256. Ibid at 177 and 194.

P. J. Yap[257] also believes that the outcome was the right one but argues that a call for interpretation was unnecessary. Yap argues that, as a matter of "comity", the Hong Kong courts and the executive should speak with "one voice" on the issue of state immunity and he criticises the minority judges in the Court of Final Appeal (CFA) for deviating from the principle.[258] Yap states:

> on the facts in *FG Hemisphere*, the Secretary of Justice had intervened on behalf of the Hong Kong government, and had insisted on the application of the doctrine of absolute immunity. If the Hong Kong courts had instead applied the restricted approach to immunity, the 'one voice' principle on foreign affairs would clearly have been violated.[259]

Why, though, does Yap believe that the CFA reference was unnecessary? His view is that "state immunity" falls outside the doctrine of "act of state" as recognised by the common law. He states:

> Assuming that the majority judges in *FG Hemisphere* were indeed applying the common law doctrine of act of state, then they must also accept its parameters, which had always deemed the law on state immunity as falling outside the scope of this doctrine even though it concerned foreign affairs.[260]

Pragmatically, it seems that the majority CFA judges took a sensible course (having decided that the absolute immunity principle must be applied) in seeking a (certain) confirmation by the NPCSC, thus avoiding unnecessary conflict. The alternative view, of course, is that since the CFA majority had reached a decision of which "Beijing" would undoubtedly approve, referral for interpretation was an unnecessary dilution of the court's autonomy.

While reference for interpretation by the Hong Kong courts is seen by some as a cession of Hong Kong's judicial autonomy, it is, at least a willing cession of same. Far more troubling are threats to "seek interpretation" by the government which has no seriously arguable mandate to do so under the Basic Law.

It does not bode well that, faced with (another) scare story as to the influx of pregnant PRC mainland women seeking to give birth in Hong Kong (and thereby conferring right of abode on their children),[261] there were a number of calls for a further interpretation of the Basic Law rules on right of abode[262] by the NPC Standing Committee. Leading the way, and always eager to restrict the autonomy of

---

257. PJ Yap, 'DRC v FG Hemisphere: Why Absolute Immunity Should Apply but a Reference was Unnecessary' (2011) 41(2) HKLJ 393–400.
258. They had "erred" he said in mis-applying a number of cases in which, "the executive never took a contrary stance" (ibid at 397).
259. Ibid.
260. Ibid at 396. This is implicit in the view of Mortimer NPJ noted in *Comment* above.
261. As established by the Court of Final Appeal in *Director of Immigration v Chong Fung Yuen* (2001) 4 HKCFAR 211.
262. Effectively Article 24(2)(1).

the Hong Kong courts, has been former Secretary for Justice, Elsie Leung;[263] once more espousing the view that another interpretation of Article 24 (or an interpretation of the scope of its previous interpretation) by the Standing Committee (at the request of the Chief Executive) was a preferable means to achieving Hong Kong's best interests.[264] In this case, however, the Hong Kong government dealt effectively with the "problem"[265] by relatively straightforward and far preferable administrative means.[266]

Even if the administrative measures had been unsuccessful, the proper solution, where the clear words of (Article 24(1)) of the Basic Law do not accord with Hong Kong's "best interests", is to *amend* the Basic Law. Amendment is permitted under the Basic Law, though not simple. Elsie Leung had described amendment in this case as not feasible and Wang Guangya, Director of the Hong Kong and Macau Affairs Office, described it as "impossible".[267] Both were reflecting the PRC's great reluctance to amend the Basic Law given the potential for criticism of the original drafters. Far better, therefore, for them to suggest, as Leung did, that the Hong Kong courts had "got it wrong".[268]

However, while the actions of the "pro-interpretation" group are of concern, we can perhaps take heart from the immediate response to Leung's calls for interpretation of Carrie Lam, Chief Secretary, who stated that "Hong Kong is a law-abiding community and judicial independence is its core value."[269]

Moreover, even the sometimes cautious Law Society issued a Press Statement proclaiming:

> On the question of Mainland mothers giving birth in Hong Kong, given established legal principles, the Law Society of Hong Kong considers that a referral to the NPCSC to interpret Article 24(2)(1) of the Basic Law will undermine the authority and standing of the Court of Final Appeal and likely damage the rule of law in Hong Kong.[270]

---

263. Secretary for Justice in the Tung Chee Hwa administration. Now Deputy Director of the HKSAR Basic Law Committee.
264. See T Chong and E Tsang, "Beijing Best to End Birth Row, Elsie Leung Says", *South China Morning Post* (Hong Kong, 10 March 2012). To his credit, then Secretary for Justice, Rimsky Yuen, did not share Leung's view.
265. The Hong Kong government view vacillates between obsession with an influx of unwelcome young mainlanders and the "need" to produce more children to address the problem of Hong Kong's ageing population.
266. Even the pro-Beijing DAB party indicated (via its Chairman, Tam Yiu-chung) a preference for "administrative means" (C Chan, 'Beijing Option Kept Open in Baby Crisis' *The Standard* [Hong Kong, 8 March 2012]). Measures taken included targeting "intermediaries", restricting boundary crossing and increasing hospital fees dramatically.
267. C Chan, *The Standard* (quoted above).
268. Indeed, Leung had coupled her preference for an interpretation with a forceful attack on lawyers and judges in Hong Kong who, she stated, lack a proper understanding of the relationship between the CPG and the Hong Kong SAR.
269. *South China Morning Post*, 8 October 2012.
270. The Law Society of Hong Kong: LC paper No CB (4) 192/12-13 (02)10/10/2012.

Further encouragement can be taken from the approach of the CFA in the *Vallejos* case,²⁷¹ in which a Filipina domestic helper, employed in Hong Kong much longer than the normally required seven years, had sought the right of abode in Hong Kong. After a Vallejos "victory" at first instance, there were calls for an interpretation of the scope of Article 158 and a government request for same; in particular, the (binding?) effect of the "ancillary" statement in its previous (1999) interpretation of Article 24. The CFA, in rejecting Vallejos's application, on the simple basis that she had not been "ordinarily resident" in Hong Kong for more than seven years,²⁷² made clear that no further request for interpretation was necessary. Indeed, counsel for the government, David Pannick QC, had conceded that this would no longer be sought if the Government's argument against the right of abode were ultimately successful. Chief Justice Ma stated:

> this Court was asked to seek an interpretation from the Standing Committee . . .
> . . . The necessity condition,²⁷³ however, is not [satisfied]. In the light of the conclusion this Court has reached on the issue of the true construction of Article 24(2)(4) a reference to the Standing Committee is simply unnecessary.²⁷⁴

Unfortunately, the CFA had no scope to assert itself in the most recent interpretation by the NPCSC, undertaken at the latter's own initiative. This involves an interpretation of Article 104 of the Basic Law which states:

> When assuming office . . . members of the Executive Council and of the Legislative Council . . . must, in accordance with law, swear to uphold the Basic Law of the Hong Kong Special Administrative Region of the People's Republic of China and swear allegiance to the Hong Kong SAR of the PRC.

The interpretation²⁷⁵ states that those taking the oath of allegiance must do so "genuinely" and solemnly. The interpretation was used to confirm the exclusion from LegCo of (initially) two elected members from the pan-democratic camp with four more following.²⁷⁶ All had mis-taken the oath in various ways and to a greater or

---

271. *Vallejos Evangeline Banao v Commissioner of Registration & Another* [2013] HKCFA 56.
272. Crucially, Hong Kong domestic helpers may be employed for periods of only two years. Even on re-appointment, they are required to return to their country of origin before recommencing their new contract. Such a requirement (which of course does not apply to other Hong Kong residents) was the main factor convincing the CFA that no domestic helper is "ordinarily resident".
273. The CFA has identified two requirements for referral; the "classification" one (does it relate to issues which are the province of the PRC . . . is it an "excluded" one and the "necessity" one (will referral affect the decision). *Vallejos* lacked the second requirement.
274. Ibid at 24–28.
275. Delivered 7 November 2016.
276. It should be noted that the first two barred oath-takers had been unnecessarily provocative with references to the "Hong Kong Nation" and "Chee-na" (akin to Shina, derogatory name for China). Worse, their actions and those of the other "improper" oath-takers had a disastrous effect on the

lesser degree. The NPCSC interpretation put paid to the possibility of an oath being re-taken (as envisaged by LegCo President Andrew Leung at the time) by inserting into its lengthy interpretation the words:

> If the oath taken is determined as invalid, no arrangement shall be made for retaking the oath.

The effect of the disqualifications, as explained in the footnote, has been momentous; since government supporters have taken the opportunity to amend the LegCo "rule book" to prevent the stalling of unpopular legislation, invariable involving costly and unnecessary capital projects. Far more such projects have already been speedily approved by LegCo post-disqualifications. Debate on the highly contentious "collocation" arrangements (discussed elsewhere) has also been curtailed.

---

pan-democratic cause in LegCo. Currently it had acted as some form of brake on the worst excesses of the CY Leung era via its holding of more than 25% of LegCo seats (preventing constitutional reforms, such as the introduction of "fake democracy", which require a 75% majority). With the removal of the "improper" oath-takers, the power of veto will be lost. True, there is a requirement to hold a by-election BUT there is no time limit. "Loyalists" have acted quickly to change the LegCo rule book in their favour, and we can be sure that the government will not rush by-elections. In a particularly vindictive move, plans were made to bankrupt the barred legislators by seeking repayment of their salaries. This plan has now been abandoned; but not for "compassionate" reasons.

See, for example, R Wong, "Red line drawn with oath ruling" *South China Morning Post* (Hong Kong 28 December 2016); B Haas, "Hong Kong pro-democracy legislators disqualified from parliament" *The Guardian* (London 14 July 2017); P Un, "Off the hook for millions" *The Standard* (Hong Kong 19 April 2018).

5
Judicial Precedent and the Doctrine of *Stare Decisis*

Overview

Courts in most systems will *tend* to follow approaches in previous cases because, in the main, such approaches have been well-considered and reasonable. Arguments found compelling in case A are likely to be found similarly compelling in case B. What characterises the *common law*[1] approach to precedent is the element of *compulsion*; the proposition that in certain circumstances a court is *required* to follow a previous judicial line of reasoning. This binding element is described by the Latin expression "*stare decisis*"; meaning "let the decision stand".

Judicial precedent, therefore, the "custom of the courts", refers to the system, in common law jurisdictions, whereby the decisions of superior courts are followed by lower courts, in subsequent cases dealing with the same legal principle. *Stare decisis*, then, may be described as the system of *binding* precedent. Broadly, this means that the point of law crucial to the decision (the *ratio decidendi*) of a higher court is binding on a subsequent, lower court when dealing with a case involving the same legal principle.

The first essential requirement for a system of binding precedent, is a court "hierarchy". Recognising this hierarchy, the position is that lower courts are bound by the precedents of higher courts and, to some extent, of courts of equal standing. The hierarchy question is more complicated in Hong Kong since attention needs to be focused on both the pre-1997 hierarchy and the (reformed) post-1997 hierarchy. The post-1997 hierarchy is well-established, with the Court of Final Appeal at the pinnacle, binding all lower Hong Kong courts and having the right of final adjudication other than in respect of "acts of state".[2] However, the pre-1997 hierarchy needs also to be appreciated, since (subject to exceptions)[3] the laws previously in force in Hong Kong, as of 1 July 1997, will remain in force unless and until repealed locally. The dominant source of pre-1997 laws had remained the English common law. The

---

1. "Common law" here is used in the jurisdictional sense, so that the binding nature of past judgments would be recognised in, eg, England and Hong Kong.
2. Article 19, Basic Law refers to "acts of State such as defence and foreign affairs".
3. See generally Chapter 2. The major exception relates to (previous) laws which contravene the Basic Law.

dominant pre-1997 precedents, therefore, are those of the (Judicial Committee of the) Privy Council, then the final appellate court in respect of Hong Kong cases; and the (Judicial Committee of the) House of Lords, the then final arbiter of the English common law.

The second essential requirement is a comprehensive and efficient system of law reporting, since if courts are to follow previous precedents these must be accessible and clear. In this respect, though things have improved significantly, Hong Kong still lags behind many other common law jurisdictions.

The operation of judicial precedent "in practice" is much more complex than might at first appear. First, it is not the "decision" of a previous court which must be followed but the *legal reason* for that decision. This involves identifying such legal reason, the "*ratio decidendi*" (*ratio*), and applying it in appropriate cases. Differing judicial opinions as to the true "ratio" of a previous case provide considerable scope for uncertainty. A previous precedent with an apparently wide application may be "narrowed" in a subsequent case by a judge unwilling to apply the wider principle.

A second complication is that courts will only apply previous precedents when they are "relevant". In practice, again, there may be judicial disagreement as to the relevance of a previous precedent. Judges who do not want to apply the previous precedent are more likely to find it inapplicable or "not helpful" to the cases before them. The previous precedent is then said to be "distinguished".

The above complications serve to introduce a high measure of flexibility into the precedent process. While this may be helpful in producing the desired outcome in a particular case, with the judge able to "evade" a previous precedent, the outcome is also a high degree of uncertainty, the consequences of which should not be underestimated.

Certainty means that potential litigants (or their legal advisers) will appreciate in advance the likelihood of success in contemplated litigation and be able to proceed accordingly. Cases with little prospect of success, based on the existing precedents, will not be pursued, to the general benefit of the court system as a whole. Indeed, in areas of law such as contract, parties may regulate their agreements based on the perceived condition of the law as it is understood (from the precedents) at the time. Moreover, those administering a system of legal aid will also be able to gauge the "merit" of a particular case in determining whether or not to grant legal aid in respect of such case.

In addition to *binding* precedents, there are others which, to a greater or lesser extent, may be regarded by later courts as "persuasive". These include judgments of lower courts (or those of equal standing), "minority" judgments in cases involving more than one judge and, in Hong Kong's case, judgments from other common law jurisdictions. Most commonly, however, persuasive precedents are to be found in legal pronouncements which, though perhaps made in higher courts and on matters relevant to the instant, lower court case, were not crucial to the determination of the earlier case. Such pronouncements are described as "*obiter dicta*" (things said by the way) and are not binding on subsequent courts. Apparently binding precedents may well be "distinguished" on the basis that a previous, apparently significant, statement of law was, in fact, "*obiter*". Once again this provides scope for both flexibility and uncertainty.

Finally, and more theoretically, the issue of the judge seeking the desired outcome in a particular case raises the question of the extent to which judges should be active "creators" of legal rules as opposed to passive "appliers" of already established rules. Judicial creativity poses, for example, the question of whether the search for the elusive "just solution" in a particular case should prevail over the notion of treating "like cases alike".

5.1 The meaning and significance of *stare decisis* (binding precedent)

A particular feature of common law jurisdictions is their emphasis on the importance of case decisions and the reasoning therein. This system of "precedent" involves the adoption of the legal principles enunciated in one case by judges in subsequent related cases. Through the steady accretion of precedents, a body of law in a particular area is developed, avoiding the need for general, codified rules. Legislation, in such jurisdictions, is used to "fill gaps" or amend social policy in certain areas, rather than to represent a comprehensive body of law. The law of contract or tort, for example, is predominantly based, in England and Hong Kong, on case law-developed rules rather than statutory ones.[4] The tendency of courts to treat like cases alike is hardly surprising; if a particular line of reasoning appeared appropriate in case A it is likely to be equally appealing in case B. What is peculiar to the common law system, however, is the *requirement*, in appropriate circumstances, that previous precedents be followed; the so-called principle of *stare decisis* (let those things which have been decided stand). The purpose of *stare decisis* (binding precedent) is to introduce an element of certainty into the law so that potential litigants, or more likely their legal advisers, can determine in advance their likelihood of success and proceed accordingly. The requirements of binding precedent are that:

(a) case A must have been decided in a court of higher status than (or sometimes of equivalent status to)[5] the one determining case B;
(b) the legal principle derived from case A is equally applicable to case B;
(c) that principle must have been crucial to the determination of case A.

---

4. The role of statute is, however, increasing in England (and there are calls for a general criminal code). In the United States, legislation is now so important that some deny that it remains a common law jurisdiction.
5. Where a court is required to follow the decisions of a *higher* court this is known as "vertical" stare decisis; where it must follow the decision of a court of *equal* standing this is known as "horizontal" stare decisis.

5.2 The relevance of the court hierarchy to judicial precedent

Requirement (a) above is a relatively straightforward one. It requires, of course, a clear hierarchy of courts as outlined previously.[6] However, given Hong Kong's unique post-colonial status and the general continuation of "pre-1997" rules unless amended, the current hierarchy of the courts does not produce a full picture of the present precedent position. For this reason, consideration must be given to both the pre-1997 and post-1997 court structure.

5.2.1 The pre-1997 hierarchy

The Hong Kong court structure, pre-1997, can be seen in the relevant diagram in Chapter 3.[7] Three crucial precedent points need to be noted from the diagram. The first relates to the role of the (Judicial Committee of the) Privy Council in London. Subject to procedural restraints, appeal from the Hong Kong courts was possible, pre-1997, to the Privy Council, Hong Kong's final court of appeal. Though couched in the form of an advice, the judgment of the Privy Council in respect of the point(s) of law was automatically binding on the Hong Kong courts.[8]

Second, since Hong Kong's law was, generally, the common law of England, Hong Kong courts were *indirectly* bound by the precedents of the (Judicial Committee of the) House of Lords, also sitting in London and, in fact, comprising largely the same type of personnel as would hear a Privy Council appeal. So long as a judgment of the House of Lords was on an issue relevant to, and applicable in, Hong Kong it would take effect in Hong Kong as part of the English common law by which Hong Kong courts were (generally) bound.[9] In other words, a court not strictly part of Hong Kong's court hierarchy nonetheless exercised considerable influence as a source of Hong Kong law.

Finally, and crucially, despite the abolition, in Hong Kong, of the right of appeal to the Privy Council and the replacement of that body by the Court of Final Appeal, pre-1997 judgments of the Privy Council (and the House of Lords) remain highly significant in determining the "laws in force" in Hong Kong on 1 July 1997 and, given the general continuation of such laws, Hong Kong's current law.

5.2.1.1 Modern relevance of pre-1997 hierarchy

Article 8 of the Basic Law states that:

---

6. See Chapter 4.
7. See 3.1 above.
8. That this was the position has since been confirmed by the Court of Final Appeal in *A Solicitor v Law Society of Hong Kong* [2008] 2 HKC 1.
9. See Chapter 2.

> The laws previously in force in Hong Kong, that is, the common law, rules of equity, ordinances, subordinate legislation and customary law shall be maintained, except for any that contravene this Law or are subject to any amendment by the legislature of the Hong Kong SAR.

The basic premise of Article 8 is confirmed by Article 18 which states that:

> The laws in force in the Hong Kong SAR shall be this Law, the laws previously in force in Hong Kong as provided for in Article 8 of this Law, and the laws enacted by the legislature of the region.

Unless previous laws have been overturned or amended in Hong Kong, they will remain in force. Since much of the law in force was the English common law, notice must still be taken of the pre-1997 hierarchies, including that of the English courts. Thus, for example, if a pre-1997 House of Lords judgment was applicable in Hong Kong (not having been superseded by Hong Kong legislation or judicial decision, not being contrary to custom, etc) it would remain law in Hong Kong, post-1997, unless contrary to the Basic Law or locally amended. In the absence of a House of Lords decision on an issue, the common law of England could reside in an English Court of Appeal decision, or even one from the English High Court. None of these decisions (House of Lords, Court of Appeal, etc) were "directly" binding on Hong Kong courts (unlike determinations of the Privy Council on appeal from Hong Kong) *but*, by stating the English common law (which would apply in Hong Kong subject to exceptions) they *indirectly* affected Hong Kong.

Conversely, where an issue had been determined by the Hong Kong courts, pre-1997, the pre-1997 Hong Kong hierarchy would be relevant in determining the "laws in force" as of 1 July 1997. That hierarchy would, of course, have the Privy Council at its pinnacle.[10]

However, while the pre-1997 hierarchy is significant in determining the "laws previously in force" as of 1 July 1997, there remains the question of the power of Hong Kong courts, post-1997, to amend those laws. This question will be dealt with in the following section.

5.2.2 The precedent position of the current Hong Kong courts

The relevant diagram in Chapter 4[11] illustrates the current Hong Kong court structure. It can be seen that, for broadly "political" reasons, some current terminology is somewhat confusing. The pre-1997 structure, for example, contained a Hong Kong "Supreme Court" comprising the Court of Appeal and the High Court. With the abolition of the term "Supreme Court", regarded as politically unacceptable in a

---

10. This relates only to cases of appeal from Hong Kong. Hong Kong courts have never been bound by other Privy Council decisions: see *A Solicitor v Law Society of Hong Kong* [2008] discussed below. Post-1997 Privy Council decisions (obviously never from Hong Kong) are, *a fortiori*, never binding.
11. See 4.2.

Hong Kong SAR now part of China, the functions of the previous Court of Appeal and High Court are now discharged by the Court of Appeal and the Court of First Instance,[12] collectively known as the "High Court".[13] Nonetheless the actual operation of the current hierarchy is relatively straightforward.

Hong Kong's highest court, the Court of Final Appeal (CFA), is bound by no other court.[14] Moreover, a "decision"[15] of the CFA binds all courts below in the structure. The CFA will not, however, regard itself as bound by its own previous decisions. This was made clear in the seminal case[16] of *A Solicitor v Law Society of Hong Kong*[17] which explains very clearly the post-1997 precedent inter-relationship between the Hong Kong courts as well as their precedent relationship with the courts of the United Kingdom.[18] The legal issue in the case involved, primarily the question of standard of proof, need not concern us. The key issues from a precedent point of view were dealt with comprehensively in the judgment of the then Chief Justice, Andrew Li.

> A Solicitor v Law Society of Hong Kong
>
> Chief Justice Li:
>
> 1. I agree with the judgment of Mr Justice Bokhary PJ. The standard of proof for disciplinary proceedings in Hong Kong should be the civil standard. The proper approach to its application is explained in his judgment.
>
> 2. This appeal raises the question of the extent to which the Court of Appeal may depart from its previous decisions. That Court occupies a central position in our judicial system. The question of the extent of its freedom to depart from its previous decisions is an important question relating to the operation of the doctrine of *stare decisis* which is part of the wider doctrine of precedent.
>
> 3. In granting leave to appeal, the Court of Appeal formulated the specific question whether it is:
>
>> "bound by its own decision(s) when that previous decision(s) was influenced or itself bound by a Privy Council decision(s), which has since been either overtaken and/or developed and/or departed from?"

---

12. The latter, confusingly, has both a first instance *and* an appellate function.
13. Article 81, Basic Law.
14. But see discussion of interpretation of the Basic Law above.
15. As explained below, the word "decision" is shorthand for the "legal reason for a decision".
16. Described by solicitor William Clarke as "possibly the most important judgment of a Hong Kong court since *HKSAR v Ma Wai Kwan David & Others*" (WS Clarke, 'Litigation Practice' *Hong Kong Lawyer* (June 2008)) 60.
17. [2008] 2 HKC 1.
18. In this context "United Kingdom" is more appropriate than "England" because we are considering the Judicial Committee of the House of Lords (a United Kingdom court), its successor the Supreme Court of the United Kingdom, and the Judicial Committee of the Privy Council.

4. The question concerning the rule of *stare decisis* arose in the Court of Appeal in relation to the issue of the applicable standard of proof in solicitors disciplinary proceedings. The Chief Judge held that the Court of Appeal was bound to apply the civil standard by its previous decisions pursuant to the rule in *Young v Bristol Aeroplane* [1944] KB 718 which has been adopted in Hong Kong. He also held that even if he were free to depart from them, he would not have done so. Stock JA accepted the civil standard without any discussion of the rule of *stare decisis*. Tang JA (as he then was) held in favour of the criminal standard of proof. He concluded with some hesitation that the Court of Appeal was free to depart from its previous decisions as they had been based on the Privy Council decision in *Bhandari v Advocates Committee* [1956] 1 WLR 1442 which has been departed from by the Privy Council in *Campbell v Hamlet* [2005] 3 All ER 1116 (para 183).

5. The rule of *stare decisis* in relation to the Court of Appeal must be considered in the context of the judicial system as a whole. Before discussing that rule, it is appropriate to address two aspects of the judicial system. First, the binding effect of decisions of the Judicial Committee of the Privy Council ("the Privy Council") in Hong Kong both before and after 1 July 1997. Secondly, the position of the Court of Final Appeal, which replaced the Privy Council as Hong Kong's final appellate court on 1 July 1997, as regards departure from previous decisions.

Privy Council decisions on Hong Kong appeals

6. Prior to 1 July 1997, the Privy Council was the final appellate court of Hong Kong. It also functioned as the final appellate court for many other jurisdictions . . .

7. . . . Before 1 July 1997, when the Privy Council entertained an appeal from Hong Kong, it was functioning solely as the final appellate court in and as part of the Hong Kong judicial system. Its decisions on appeals from Hong Kong were therefore binding on the Court of Appeal and the lower courts in Hong Kong before 1 July 1997.

8. The Basic Law enshrines the theme of continuity of the legal system. Article 8 of the Basic Law provides that the laws previously in force in Hong Kong shall be maintained except for any that contravene the Basic Law and subject to any amendment by the legislature. This is reinforced by Article 18(1). By virtue of these articles, the body of jurisprudence represented by Privy Council decisions on appeal from Hong Kong continues to be binding in Hong Kong after the Basic Law came into effect on 1 July 1997.

Privy Council decisions on non-Hong Kong appeals

9. The position of Privy Council decisions, which were not made on appeals from Hong Kong, is however entirely different . . . In principle, its decisions on non-Hong Kong appeals were not binding on the courts in Hong Kong under the doctrine of precedent prior to 1 July 1997.

10. This conclusion is supported by the view expressed by the Privy Council on an appeal from Hong Kong in *de Lasala v de Lasala* [1980] AC 546. Its judgment

considered the persuasive effect of decisions of the House of Lords in Hong Kong (see para. 15 below). In the course of its judgment, the Privy Council stated that its decisions on appeals from Hong Kong are binding on all Hong Kong courts (at 558 A–B). Although it was not directly focusing on the effect in the Hong Kong courts of decisions of the Privy Council on non-Hong Kong appeals, this statement should be regarded as authoritative.

11. ...

12. A number of statements can be found in judgments of the Court of Appeal and the lower courts in Hong Kong that decisions of the Privy Council were binding on them prior to 1 July 1997, without distinguishing between decisions on appeal from Hong Kong and other decisions. These statements should be read as confined to Privy Council decisions on appeal from Hong Kong.

13. Some judgments have gone further and have stated expressly that Privy Council decisions, including those given on non-Hong Kong appeals, were binding on the courts in Hong Kong before 1 July 1997 ... Having regard to the conclusion reached above on the status of Privy Council decisions on non-Hong Kong appeals under the doctrine of precedent, such statements must be regarded as incorrect.

14. Before 1 July 1997, Privy Council decisions on non-Hong Kong appeals were only persuasive authority. But except where local circumstances were material, their persuasive authority was so great that the courts in Hong Kong virtually invariably followed them before 1 July 1997. The reason was that, unless there were real grounds for distinction, it was unrealistic to expect the Privy Council to take a different view on a Hong Kong appeal from that taken in its earlier decision on a non-Hong Kong appeal, especially where that earlier decision was not an old one. It may be that some of the Hong Kong judicial statements referred to above intended to refer to this realistic position. But to speak of Privy Council decisions on non-Hong Kong appeals as binding in Hong Kong is incorrect and confuses their great persuasive force with what should properly be regarded as binding under the doctrine of precedent.

House of Lords

15. Before 1 July 1997, decisions of the House of Lords stood in a similar position to decisions of the Privy Council on non-Hong Kong appeals. Although they were only persuasive, their authority was very great unless the decision was in a field where local circumstances made it appropriate for Hong Kong to develop along different lines. The House of Lords and the Privy Council essentially share a common membership. Unless local circumstances were material, the Privy Council on an appeal from Hong Kong was unlikely to diverge from a decision its members had reached in a different capacity in the House of Lords ... although the House of Lords decision was persuasive as a matter of juristic theory, it has the same practical effect as if it was strictly binding ...

Overseas jurisprudence after 1 July 1997

16. After 1 July 1997, in the new constitutional order, it is of the greatest importance that the courts in Hong Kong should continue to derive assistance from overseas jurisprudence. This includes the decisions of final appellate courts in various common law jurisdictions as well as decisions of supra-national courts, such as the European Court of Human Rights. Compared to many common law jurisdictions, Hong Kong is a relatively small jurisdiction. It is of great benefit to the Hong Kong courts to examine comparative jurisprudence in seeking the appropriate solution for the problems which come before them. This is underlined in the Basic Law itself. Article 84 expressly provides that the courts in Hong Kong may refer to precedents of other common law jurisdictions.

17. After 1 July 1997, as the Privy Council is no longer Hong Kong's final appellate court, the realistic considerations relating to decisions of the Privy Council and the House of Lords, which prevailed before that date as discussed above (see paras 14 and 15), are no longer relevant. Bearing in mind that historically, Hong Kong's legal system originated from the British legal system, decisions of the Privy Council and the House of Lords should of course be treated with great respect. Their persuasive effect would depend on all relevant circumstances, including in particular, the nature of the issue and the similarity of any relevant statutory or constitutional provision. At the end of the day, the courts in Hong Kong must decide for themselves what is appropriate for our own jurisdiction . . . The question whether the English approach, which has so far been adopted in Hong Kong on the extent to which the intermediate Court of Appeal is bound by its previous decisions, should continue to apply will shortly be examined.

The Court of Final Appeal

18. As from 1 July 1997, with the Court of Final Appeal as Hong Kong's final appellate court, its decisions are of course binding on the Court of Appeal and lower courts. As the final court at the apex of Hong Kong's judicial hierarchy, this Court may depart from previous Privy Council decisions on appeal from Hong Kong and this Court's own previous decisions. This is consistent with the approach adopted by final appellate courts in numerous common law jurisdictions as well as by the Privy Council itself as a final appellate court.

19. The doctrine of precedent is a fundamental feature of our legal system based on the common law. It gives the necessary degree of certainty to the law and provides reasonable predictability and consistency to its application. Such certainty, predictability and consistency provide the foundation for the conduct of activities and the conclusion of business and commercial transactions. But at the same time, a rigid and inflexible adherence by this Court to the previous precedents of Privy Council decisions on appeal from Hong Kong and its own decisions may unduly inhibit the proper development of the law and may cause injustice in individual cases. The great strength of the common law lies in its capacity to develop to meet the changing needs and circumstances of the society in which it functions.

20. Recognising the importance of these considerations, this Court will approach the exercise of its power to depart from any previous decision of the Privy Council on appeal from Hong Kong or any previous decision of the Court with great circumspection. In this connection, the risks of disturbing existing rights would have to be borne in mind. It is a power which will be exercised most sparingly.

The Court of Appeal

21. The Court of Appeal was established in 1976. Prior to its creation, a Full Court consisting of first instance judges was constituted to hear appeals. Apart from the Chief Judge of the High Court, the Court of Appeal at present consists of nine Justices of Appeal. Further, a judge of the Court of First Instance may on the request of the Chief Justice sit as an additional judge of the Court of Appeal ... Adoption of Young v. Bristol Aeroplane

22. In *Ng Yuen-shiu v Attorney General* [1981] HKLR 352, the Court of Appeal decided to adopt the law laid down by the English Court of Appeal in *Young v. Bristol Aeroplane* regarding the circumstances in which it may depart from its previous decisions in civil cases.

...

24. After 1 July 1997, the Court of Appeal confirmed that the rule continues to apply in Hong Kong. *Cheung Lai Wah v The Director of Immigration* [1998] 1 HKLRD 772 at 779H-I, 782J-783C and 787B.

The rule as it has been applied in Hong Kong

25. The rule in *Young v Bristol Aeroplane* as it has been applied in Hong Kong should be stated as follows: The Court of Appeal is bound to follow its own previous decisions subject to the following exceptions:

(1) It is entitled and bound to decide which of two conflicting decisions of its own it will follow. ("the first exception")

(2) It is bound to refuse to follow a decision of its own which, though not expressly overruled, cannot, in its opinion, stand with a subsequent decision of the Privy Council on appeal from Hong Kong or of the Court of Final Appeal. ("the second exception")

(3) It is not bound to follow a decision of its own if it is satisfied that the decision was given *per incuriam*. ("the third exception" or "the *per incuriam* exception")

Of course, under the doctrine of precedent, it is only the *ratio decidendi* of a previous decision which is binding.

26. ...

The question

27. The question in this appeal is whether the rule in *Young v Bristol Aeroplane* should continue to apply to Hong Kong in civil cases. It should be emphasised that the Court is not concerned with the position in criminal cases in the present appeal.

The first and second exceptions

28. In *Young v Bristol Aeroplane*, Lord Greene stated that two of the three exceptions were only apparent exceptions. He was referring to the first and second exceptions. In these two classes of cases, he observed that "it is beyond question that the previous decision is open to examination".

29. In first exception, where there are two previous conflicting decisions of the Court of Appeal, plainly, those decisions cannot both be binding. The Court of Appeal is therefore free to choose which decision to follow. The rule that it is bound to follow its previous decisions cannot apply.

30. In the second exception, where the Court of Appeal reaches the view that its previous decision, though not expressly overruled, cannot stand with a subsequent decision of the final appellate court, it is bound to refuse to follow its previous decision. In this instance, the rule that it is bound to follow its previous decisions also cannot apply. The previous decision cannot be regarded as binding since it is inconsistent with the subsequent decision of the final appellate court which, under the doctrine of precedent, is binding on the Court of Appeal.

The per incuriam exception

31. The third exception that the Court of Appeal is not bound to follow a previous decision if it is satisfied that it was given *per incuriam* (through want of care) represents the only real exception to the rule that the Court of Appeal is bound to follow its previous decisions. The phrase "*per incuriam*" on its own does not give much guidance as to what may be included in this exception.

32. . . . .

33. . . . .

34. . . . .

35. . . . .

36. . . . Lord Neuberger has observed extra-judicially that the effect of recent English decisions is that:

"It is almost as if there is a fourth category, namely that the Court of Appeal is now no longer bound by earlier decisions if it thinks they are wrong."

37. The authorities in Hong Kong have not expanded the *per incuriam* exception in the same way as the English authorities. Where the previous decision did not involve overlooking an inconsistent statutory provision or a binding authority, the Court of Appeal has adopted the test of manifest slip or error test in considering whether it may depart from its previous decision. See *Ho Po Chu v Tung Chee Wah* [2006] 3 HKLRD 553 and *Bowardley Enterprises Ltd v Millennium Group Ltd* [2006] 4 HKC 329.

38. . . . .

39. As discussed above, the first and second exceptions are not on analysis real exceptions to the rule that the Court of Appeal is bound by its previous decisions. To treat

them as exceptions, when they are not in substance exceptions, serves no useful purpose and is not appropriate. Accordingly, they should no longer be regarded as exceptions in Hong Kong.

40. . . . .

The critical question

41. With the treatment of the situations contemplated by the first and second exceptions not as exceptions, the critical question is whether the Court of Appeal should continue to retain the *per incuriam* exception or whether it should be substituted by a different exception.

42. As discussed above when considering the question of the Court of Final Appeal's freedom to depart from previous decisions of the Privy Council on appeal from Hong Kong and its own decisions (para. 19), certainty in the law and predictability and consistency in its application are of great importance. They provide the foundation for the orderly conduct of commercial, business and other activities. When disputes arise, they provide the basis for the negotiation and conclusion of compromises to settle them. On the other hand, too rigid and inflexible an adherence to precedents may impede the proper development of the law and may cause injustice in particular cases. There is thus a tension between the need for certainty, predictability and consistency and the need for adaptability, flexibility and justice. A proper balance has to be struck between these conflicting demands.

43. Plainly, an absolute rule that the Court of Appeal can never depart from its previous precedents would be inappropriate . . . Equally complete flexibility would be unsatisfactory . . . The real question is the degree of flexibility which is suitable for the Court of Appeal as an intermediate appellate court in Hong Kong.

44. In considering the degree of flexibility, the extent of availability of an appeal to the Court of Final Appeal is an important consideration. Since the establishment of this Court on 1 July 1997, much greater use has been made of it, compared to the Privy Council as Hong Kong's final appellate court before the resumption of the exercise of sovereignty. But it has to be recognised that most appeals to the Court of Appeal end there and do not proceed to the Court of Final Appeal . . .

The rule to be adopted

45. Balancing the competing and conflicting demands referred to above, the rule that should be adopted for the Court of Appeal in place of the rule in *Young v Bristol Aeroplane* is that it is bound by its previous decisions but it may depart from a previous decision where it is satisfied that it is plainly wrong.

Plainly wrong

46. Where the arguments whether the previous decision is wrong are finely balanced, the Court of Appeal's mere preference for the view that it is wrong would plainly be insufficient to justify departure from it. Even where the Court of Appeal is satisfied that

the arguments against its previous decision are more substantial and cogent than the contrary arguments in its favour, this would still be insufficient. It is only where the Court of Appeal is convinced that the contentions against its previous decision are so compelling that it can be demonstrated to be plainly wrong that the test is satisfied.

47. Obviously, previous decisions reached in ignorance of an inconsistent statutory provision or a binding authority satisfy the plainly wrong test. Further, decisions which satisfy the manifest slip or error yardstick, which the Court of Appeal has applied in the past also satisfy the plainly wrong test. But the category of decisions which are plainly wrong is not limited to these instances. The reasoning of a decision may be so seriously flawed that it should be regarded as plainly wrong.

48. In examining whether a previous decision is plainly wrong, the Court of Appeal is not confined to a consideration of the matters as they stood at the time the previous decision was made. It may take subsequent developments into account. These include subsequent legal developments, including the enactment of relevant constitutional or statutory provisions and the development in jurisprudence in Hong Kong or elsewhere ...

49. A conclusion by the Court of Appeal, that its previous decision is plainly wrong, does not finally resolve the question whether it should depart from it. The court should take all circumstances into account, before deciding whether to take that course. Such circumstances include the nature of the issue involved, the length of time for which the previous decision has stood, the extent of its application, whether the issue is likely to be before the Court of Final Appeal or the Legislature, whether the matter is best left to this Court or the Legislature, and whether and the extent to which failure to depart from it would occasion injustice in the case in question and similar cases. Where the Court of Appeal is satisfied that its previous decision on a question of statutory interpretation is plainly wrong in failing to ascertain the true intent of the Legislature, it may be more prepared to depart from its previous decision, having regard to the courts' responsibility to give effect to the legislative intent.

50. The Court of Appeal would undoubtedly approach the matter with great caution, having regard to the great importance of the doctrine of *stare decisis* ... The departure from a previous decision in accordance with this test should be wholly exceptional and should only occur very rarely.

51. Applying the plainly wrong test in the present case, the Court of Appeal would not have been justified in departing from its previous decisions establishing the civil standard of proof for solicitors' disciplinary proceedings. Those decisions cannot be considered to be wrong, let alone plainly wrong. Indeed, the civil standard for disciplinary proceedings is the correct one.

The formulated question

52. As has been noted, in granting leave to appeal, the Court of Appeal posed the question whether it is:

> "bound by its own decision(s) when that previous decision(s) was influenced or itself bound by a Privy Council decision(s), which has since been either overtaken and/or developed and/or departed from?"
>
> The point that only Privy Council decisions on appeal from Hong Kong were binding before 1 July 1997 and that they continue to be binding after 1 July 1997 must be reiterated. In the light of the conclusions in this judgment, the answer to this question is that the Court of Appeal is bound by its previous decision unless it concludes, after an examination of legal developments, including subsequent comparative jurisprudence, that its earlier decision should now be regarded as plainly wrong.
>
> *Composition of the Court of Appeal*
>
> ...
>
> 58. A five-judge court does not have any greater power than a three-judge court. See *Young v Bristol Aeroplane* at 725. The decision of the Court of Appeal in *Secretary for Justice v Wong Sau Fong* [1998] 2 HKLRD 254 that only a five-judge court has the power to depart from a decision of a three-judge court is incorrect. But in a case where the departure from previous decisions is likely to arise, it may be appropriate, depending the nature of the issue, for the Court of Appeal to adopt the most exceptional course of constituting a court with five judges. Although a five-judge court has no greater power, its decision, especially if it is unanimous, may carry greater weight. And the risk of another decision taking a different view may be minimised.

Comment

The Chief Justice's comprehensive judgment clarifies the precedent situation in a number of previously uncertain areas.

The CFA itself is bound by no other Hong Kong court but is free to depart from its own previous precedents in exceptional circumstances analogous to those obtaining in the British House of Lords/Supreme Court. There was no doubt in Li CJ's mind that the CFA is entitled to amend the Hong Kong common law, despite a lack of clear authority for such in the Basic Law.

The Hong Kong Court of Appeal is bound by the CFA but binds all lower courts. It may, like the English Court of Appeal, depart from its own decisions in exceptional circumstances. Formally, however, the criteria for such departures have been amended, so that they are no longer synonymous with the criteria to be applied by the English Court of Appeal.

The post-1997 relationship between all the Hong Kong courts and pre-1997 English/United Kingdom judgments is explained; and a key clarification relates to the status of "non-Hong Kong" appeals to the Privy Council which are, states Li CJ, not binding on Hong Kong courts and never were. This latter point was, as Li CJ indicates, previously far from clear.

In relation to pre-1997 *House of Lords judgments Li CJ appears to accept the premise that, while these are technically "persuasive", they are "effectively" binding (provided that they are not inapplicable to Hong Kong conditions) until such time as they are amended by Hong Kong legislation or judicial decision, since they represent the common law of England as on 1 July 1997, which is to remain in force under the conditions of Article 8 of the Basic Law.*[19]

The CFA's, "freedom to depart" from its previous decisions, then, mirrors that established for itself by the English House of Lords via the 1966 "Practice Direction".[20] Like the House of Lords, however, the CFA will be extremely "reluctant"[21] to depart from its previous decisions because of the desirability of certainty in the law. Businessmen and their legal advisers, for example, will base their policies on the law as they understand it. A decision of the CFA will be particularly significant in shaping these policies. Were CFA precedents to be constantly changing, the law would be left in a highly uncertain state. There is one respect, however, in which the CFA is in a different position from that of the House of Lords, in that CFA decisions involving the *interpretation of the Basic Law* may, effectively, be overturned by a (re-) interpretation of the Basic Law by the Standing Committee of the National People's Congress (NPC), which runs counter to the CFA's previous ruling.[22] In such a case the CFA will have no alternative but to overrule its previous decision on the matter. The interpretation of the Basic Law at the request of the Hong Kong government, not provided for by the Basic Law, has been a matter of considerable controversy threatening, as it does, the principle of "final adjudication".[23] Because the CFA is a relatively new court, there are no examples, at this time, of the court departing from its previous decisions other than under "coercion" from the Standing Committee of the NPC.

The Hong Kong Court of Appeal is, of course, bound to follow decisions of the CFA, adopting the hierarchy rules. It is also bound by pre-1997 decisions of the Privy Council in respect of *appeals from Hong Kong*.[24] By the same token, decisions of the Court of Appeal are also binding on all inferior courts, but it is not always bound by its own previous decisions. The Court will, like the Court of Final Appeal, be reluctant to depart from its previous precedents, given the advantages of certainty in the law and *had* previously applied, by analogy, the principles adopted by the English Court of Appeal in the *Young v Bristol Aeroplane* case.[25] In *A Solicitor*,[26] Hong Kong Chief Justice Li, with whom the whole CFA concurred, formulated a

---

19. See Chapter 2.
20. See Judicial Committee of the House of Lords, *Practice Statement (Judicial Precedent)* [1966] 1 WLR 1234.
21. Li CJ said that the power to depart would be used "most sparingly".
22. Article 158, Basic Law.
23. See Chapter 3.
24. But not in re other appeals.
25. *Young v Bristol Aeroplane Company Ltd* [1944] 2 All ER 293, [1944] KB 718.
26. Note 17.

different test for the Hong Kong Court of Appeal, whereby it may depart from its previous decisions where they are "plainly wrong". This "less restrictive" test, said Li CJ, was favoured elsewhere in the common law world. While the move towards greater independence from the former "colonial master" is to be welcomed, it is doubtful, from the examples of "plainly wrong" cited by the Chief Justice, that the new test will produce much difference in practice.

As regards the Court of First Instance (previously the High Court), it is clearly bound by previous decisions of the CFA, the Privy Council (in respect of pre-1997 Hong Kong appeals), and the Hong Kong Court of Appeal. It is generally not bound by its own previous decisions, at least in so far as they are "first instance". Despite its title, however, the Court of First Instance (CFI) has a significant *appellate* jurisdiction and it is suggested (though authority is scant) that appellate decisions of the CFI might be binding in the CFI, at least where the instant case is non-appellate.[27]

District Court judges are bound, of course, by decisions of the CFA, the Privy Council (from Hong Kong pre-1997) and the (Hong Kong) Court of Appeal. They are not, however, bound by other District Court decisions. What remains problematic is the extent to which, if at all, the District Court judges are bound by CFI decisions. Barrister Frederick Chan[28] has made a case for the District Court judges to be bound by CFI decisions, on the basis of the desirability of certainty, while admitting that such judicial authority as exists runs counter to his case. The leading authority is *R v Kwong Kui Wing & Others*,[29] in which District Court Judge Lugar-Mawson declined to follow two previous High Court (the forerunner of the present CFI) authorities. Lugar-Mawson's rationale, it appears, is that no right of appeal lay from the District Court to the High Court (now CFI). This is not to say, of course, that judges will not usually follow previous decisions from courts of equal authority, on the basis of judicial "comity", merely that they are not *required* to do so.[30]

Magistrates' Courts are bound by the decisions of the CFA, the Court of Appeal and the CFI. Magistrates are not, however, required to follow decisions of other Magistrates' Courts or the District Court, since neither has an appellate function (except, in the latter case, in respect of appeals from certain tribunals).

Most cases of authority, therefore, will originate from either the Court of Final Appeal (or its predecessor the Privy Council) or the Hong Kong Court of Appeal. It is possible, in practice (though arguably not in theory) that a court may be faced with two contradictory "binding" precedents. In such an unlikely scenario the court should follow the precedent of the higher of the "binding" courts. Suppose, for

---

27. By analogy a single High Court judge in England is bound by a "Divisional" (full) High Court decision. Conversely, there is no right of appeal from a non-appellate CFI in Hong Kong to an appellate CFI and the lack of an appeal route has been cited as a reason for a court not to be bound (see *R v Kwong Kui Wing* [1996] 1 HKDCLR 15, quoted in FHF Chan article below).
28. See FHF Chan, 'Are Judgments of the CFI Binding on the District Court?' *Hong Kong Lawyer* (April 2008) 45–48.
29. [1996] 1 HKDCLR 15.
30. See discussion of "persuasive" precedents below.

example, that Judge X is sitting in the Court of First Instance and has two apparently binding precedents before him; one from the CFA and the other, contradicting it, from the Court of Appeal. In these circumstances he must follow the CFA precedent. If the Court of Appeal case had come *before* the CFA one, the CFA should be viewed as having (implicitly) overruled the Court of Appeal precedent, even though the CFA has not expressly said so. If the Court of Appeal case came *after* the CFA one, the latter case will be viewed as wrongly decided or *per incuriam*, the Court of Appeal having omitted to follow a binding CFA precedent.

5.2.3 Precedents and "decisions"

Before leaving the issue of how the court hierarchy works it should be pointed out that, for convenience, I have spoken of "decisions" of higher courts being binding on lower courts. It is common to adopt this labour-saving device and, indeed, Li CJ did so throughout his judgment in *A Solicitor*. However, strictly, the "decision" in a case is only binding on the parties to it. The decision (eg, "Judgment for X") may be "reversed" on appeal but such reversal need have no precedent implications (where for example all the previous precedents are upheld but the lower court is held to have mis-applied them). The reversal will affect only the parties in the instant case. Once all avenues of appeal in a case have been exhausted, the matter is *res judicata* (a decided issue). *Prima facie*, a matter *res judicata* cannot be reopened, although most common law systems have provision for a review in exceptional cases, such as the discovery of fresh evidence unavailable at the time of the original trial. Technically, therefore, it is not the "decision" of the higher court which is binding but the legal reason for that decision (the "*ratio decidendi*" discussed below).[31] Conversely, when a previous precedent is "overruled", this may have a profound effect on the precedent position but does *not* affect the parties in the case now determined to have been wrongly decided.[32]

5.3 The applicability of previous precedents

It is, of course, a relatively simple matter to determine whether another court is of higher (or equivalent) standing in the court hierarchy. Far more complex is the issue of whether a previous precedent/principle is "*applicable*". The question for the court is whether the principles of case A are applicable to (the present) case B. In practice, the likelihood is that one of the parties (for whom the application of case A is likely to produce a "good result") will argue the applicability of case A; while the other party (whom case A does not favour) will argue that it is not applicable. This other party might argue that the present case raises a novel point, such that the court

---

31. See 5.4.
32. As explained, those parties are bound by the ultimate decision in their case under the principle of "*res judicata*".

has free rein to determine the appropriate legal principle; or that a more favourable previous precedent is in fact the most apposite.

Students coming to law for the first time tend to imagine that the applicability (or otherwise) of a previous precedent is obvious; litigants or their advisers will know in advance their chances of success and will commence or defend proceedings only in novel situations not previously determined by the courts. In practice it is not so. Consider the following (real) English Court of Appeal contract law scenario (*Williams v Roffey*):[33]

> A (a sub-contractor) owes B (the main contractor) a duty to do certain work for an agreed price. B agrees to pay extra, fearing that A will be unable to do the work on time for the initially agreed price, in which case B will be in breach of the main contract. B subsequently refuses to pay the additional amount, arguing that A was duty bound to do the work for the originally agreed price.

The two major precedents cited to the court are:

(a) A relatively old (non-binding) case (*Stilk v Myrick*) which says that the mere performance of a contractual duty owed by A to B cannot support a claim for an additional promised "bonus";
(b) A more modern but equally non-binding case (*Pao On*) which says that, where A owes a duty to C, the mere performance of the duty *will* support a claim for a promise of reward by B.

The outcome of the case was that A was held entitled to the reward. The court decided not to follow precedent (a) (while refusing to criticise it) and adopted precedent (b) which was actually concerned with a legally distinct principle! Precedent (a) (*Stilk*) is said to be "distinguished" in these circumstances. That is, a distinction is drawn between it and the instant case.[34]

From this simple example we can see how far from certain the legal position really is, especially in Hong Kong. In England, *Roffey* could have been appealed to the House of Lords. A major factor, though, would be the relatively small sums involved, given the huge expense of a House of Lords Appeal. The way lies open, however, for the House of Lords to overrule the *Roffey* precedent in a later case or even for the Court of Appeal itself to depart from its previous precedent. As regards Hong Kong, the *Roffey* decision would have been (indirectly) "binding" before 1997 (representing the English common law position and not being inapplicable to local conditions). Thereafter, being one of the rules in force on 1 July 1997, the judgment remains "binding" unless amended in Hong Kong (or contrary to the Basic Law). If, as has actually happened, a post-1997 *English* case questions the correctness of

---

33. *Williams v Roffey Bros & Nicholls* [1990] 1 All ER 512.
34. The Headnote in "*Roffey*" describes *Stilk v Myrick* as having been "approved" but this is a somewhat liberal use of language.

Roffey,[35] the Hong Kong courts have a free hand as to whether to revise their view of the law in light of the later case. However, a further complication, deriving from *Roffey*, is that a Hong Kong court applied the case fairly unquestioningly,[36] making it more difficult to adapt to any later, post-1997, *Roffey*-critical English decision. And, to add a further complication, the Hong Kong case which readily adopted *Roffey*[37] did so without acknowledging some critical differences between the two cases.[38]

It can be seen then, that despite the system of binding precedent, the common law provides less in the way of certainty than at first appears. Even if a legal point has previously been determined, a higher court has the power to change the law. Moreover, the highest courts—the British House of Lords[39] and Hong Kong's Court of Final Appeal—may depart from their previous decisions. Equally significantly, courts which appear bound by a previous precedent may assert that its principles are not applicable in the instant case and "distinguish" it (as in *Roffey*). The arguments for distinguishing are often far from compelling. To take one example, Ferris J in *Surrey County Council v Bredero Homes*[40] declined to adopt the approach to damages in *Wrotham Park Estate Co Ltd v Parkside Homes Ltd*[41] on the grounds that the former involved "equitable" damages while the claim before him was for "common law" damages. Later (superior) courts felt that this distinction was unnecessary.[42] Essentially, most "distinguishing" reflects a desire by the subsequent court not to follow the prior precedent and an *ex post facto* justification therefor.[43]

5.4 The meaning and significance of *ratio decidendi*

Even if a previous case in a superior court has addressed a legal issue, the hugely important question remains of whether a determination on the issue was *crucial* to the decision in that case. In this context the Latin term "*ratio decidendi*" (the reason for the decision) is used. It is only the *ratio* of a previous case which can be binding on later courts, not the decision itself.[44]

The two key components of *ratio decidendi* (*ratio*) are that:

---

35. See *South Caribbean Trading Ltd v Trafigura Beheer* [2005] 1 Lloyds Rep 128 per Colman J.
36. See *UBC (Construction) Ltd v Sung Foo Kee Ltd* [1993] 2 HKLR 207.
37. Ibid.
38. Crucially, that there was evidence of economic duress (found to be absent in "*Roffey*") in the Hong Kong case.
39. Now the Supreme Court.
40. [1993] 3 All ER 705.
41. [1974] 2 All ER 321.
42. See *WWF World-Wide Fund for Nature v World Wrestling Federation Entertainment Inc* [2007] EWCA Civ 286.
43. Some writers have been highly critical of the lack of clear explanation for the departure from previous precedents (see especially Murphy and Rawlings, 'After the Ancien Regime' (1980) MLR 44).
44. The "decision" in a case affects only the parties to the litigation in question (see final paragraph of 5.2.2).

i. the court has made a determination on a point of law and
ii. that determination was crucial to the decision in the case.

Deciding that a previous court has expressed a view on a point of law is relatively simple. Far more difficult is to determine whether the court's view was crucial to determining *the case before it*. The classic example of the difficulty in determining *ratio* is one case known to all law students, *Donoghue v Stevenson*.[45] In this Scottish case the plaintiff (pursuer) alleged that she had become ill as a result of drinking ginger beer, manufactured by the defendants and bought for her by a friend. The illness, she said, arose because, as she was tipping out the last contents of the ginger beer bottle, the decomposing remains of a snail emerged, causing her shock and illness. As a preliminary point the courts (ultimately the English House of Lords) had to determine whether the defendants owed the plaintiff a duty of care in the tort of negligence. A contractual action, against the seller, was not possible since the plaintiff had not bought the bottle and was therefore not in a contractual relationship with the seller. The action was pursued, therefore, in *tort* against the manufacturer. The preliminary point of law to determine was whether a duty of care *could* be imposed on a manufacturer vis-à-vis the consumer of his product. The House of Lords decided that a duty of care was owed, and the leading judgment was delivered by Lord Atkin. He stated that the manufacturer of a product owed a duty of care to the "*ultimate consumer*" of the product.[46] This determination, that a manufacturer owes a duty of care to the ultimate consumer, is relatively straightforward and relatively limited; it is known as the "narrow rule" of the case. However, Lord Atkin went further and tried to put the manufacturer's duty in a wider context. We all owe a duty in law, he said, not to injure our "*neighbour*" by our careless acts or omissions. Who is our neighbour? Someone, said Lord Atkin, so closely and directly affected by our acts or omissions that we should have them in our contemplation whenever we (carelessly) act or fail to act. This was Lord Atkin's attempt to formulate a general duty of care principle applicable to all situations, without the courts having to determine the existence of a duty of care in every different situation. This wider formulation of "duty of care", though much adapted over subsequent years, has provided a broad framework to assist judges in determining duty of care without having to determine, *ab initio* in each novel fact situation, whether a duty of care should exist.

But, is Lord Atkin's neighbour principle part of the *ratio* of the *Donoghue* case? It is generally felt that only the narrow manufacturer/consumer rule is *ratio* and the wider "neighbour principle" is *obiter dicta* (*obiter*)[47] and merely "persuasive".[48] This is not to say that later courts have not adopted the neighbour principle, indeed many

---

45. [1932] AC 562.
46. This is subject to certain caveats notably that there must not have been opportunity for intermediate inspection.
47. Literally, "something said by the way".
48. See, eg, J Holland and J Webb, *Learning Legal Rules* (9th edn, Oxford University Press, Hong Kong 2016) 194. For further discussion of *obiter*, see 5.5 below.

have,[49] but that they *need not* have done so; the principle is not *ratio* and cannot, therefore, be *binding*.

Assuming, then, that it is the "narrow rule" of *Donoghue* which constitutes the *ratio* of the case, the *ratio* position is still far from clear. A "manufacturer" is liable to the "ultimate consumer" of his product. However, does this apply to manufacturers only of ginger beer (clearly too narrow)? Of "consumable" products, or any products? Could, for example, the *Donoghue* precedent be ignored in respect of the manufacturer of a motor car? And, assuming the acceptance of the rule in respect of all "manufacturers", how is that term to be construed? A layman would have an approximate view of what constitutes manufacture, no doubt, and might be surprised to hear that the term extends to repairers, yet those effecting "major repairs" have been held to be within the category of manufacturers.[50] Again, the term "consumer" would generally be taken to extend only to those willingly partaking of a product yet injury caused by a defectively repaired lorry part to a passing pedestrian was held to be injury to an "ultimate consumer" within the narrow rule.[51]

What *Donoghue* also illustrates is the way in which later courts can use the *ratio* concept to avoid following unwelcome precedents which appear to be binding. This they may do by "narrowing" or "extending" the bounds of an existing precedent, thereby adapting the precedent to fit the courts perception of justice in a particular case. It follows, of course, that the ascertainment of a "just" solution may be at the expense of certainty in the law.

5.4.1 The ratio *in cases of multiple and dissenting judgments*

An additional complication is that in multi-judge cases there may be a dissenting minority and a majority reaching the same conclusion for different reasons! The minority judgments are, of course, not part of the *ratio* but the real complication is that the majority may find for X for differing reasons. Where, as sometimes arise, these reasons conflict, there is a real difficulty in ascertaining the court's *ratio*. A simple example can be found in the English contract case of *Jones v Padavatton*.[52] The case involved a promise by a mother to give her daughter an allowance[53] if she gave up her life in Trinidad and come to England and read for the Bar. The daughter came to England and the agreement was subsequently varied so that, instead of an allowance, the daughter was to live rent free in her mother's house. After five years, with her daughter still not having passed the bar examinations, the mother successfully sued for possession of the house. Two Court of Appeal judges (Fenton Atkinson LJ and Danckwerts LJ) felt that there was no contract here, since there was no inten-

---

49. The principle today has "evolved" to such an extent as to be almost unrecognisable.
50. See *Stennett v Hancock & Peters* [1939] 2 All ER 578.
51. Ibid.
52. [1969] 1 WLR 328, [1969] 2 All ER 616.
53. The parties agreed that an allowance had been promised, though they differed as to the amount.

tion to make a legally binding agreement. The third judge (Salmon LJ) had no doubt that there *was* a contractual intention but that, implicitly, it was to last only for a reasonable period which had now elapsed. Given the view of the majority it can fairly easily be asserted that their view represents the *ratio* of the case. Supposing, however, that one of these two was of the view that there *was* a contract, which remained in place, and found for the daughter? The majority would still support the mother's case and her action would succeed; yet the legal reason would be difficult to ascertain.

The classic case of multiple judgments and difficulty of ascertaining the *ratio* of a case is *Bell v Lever Brothers Ltd*.[54] Here, a High Court in England found in favour of an employer who had mistakenly made an (unnecessary) severance payment to a departing employee and sought to recover it. A *unanimous* Court of Appeal upheld the decision which was, nonetheless, overturned by a bare 3–2 majority in the House of Lords. Confusion was created by the fact that the 3 majority judges gave apparently differing reasons for their decisions and, in at least one case, appeared to make a decision inconsistent with the principle of law which he had enunciated! Ingman[55] writes of this case being "a notorious illustration of the problems involved in seeking to discover what a particular case actually decided" and adds:

> The decision in *Bell v Lever Bros Ltd* has been considered in many subsequent cases but its true meaning is still not clear after 60 years.[56]

The above considerations may lead to the view that multiple judgments only lead to confusion and that a single "leading judgment" delivered by a court would be simpler and create less scope for uncertainty. It has been said that one explanation for the single "advice to the Sovereign" generally delivered by the Judicial Committee of the Privy Council (without dissent or alternative majority view) was the desire to "keep it simple" not only for the Sovereign but also for the relevant courts in "the colony" from which the appeal had been made![57] There appears to be a trend towards the delivery of single "leading judgments" in Britain and, without formal announcement of a policy change, England's Court of Appeal rarely exhibits multiple judgments from the majority today.[58]

One advantage of a reasoned majority judgment (as opposed to a simple "I concur"), however, is the application of justice being "seen to be done". Losing litigants may well be reassured to know that, even if they have lost, the *full* court

---

54. [1932] AC 161.
55. T Ingman, *The English Legal Process* (13th edn, Oxford University Press 2010).
56. Ibid 332.
57. See O Jones, 'A Worthy Predecessor? The Privy Council on Appeal from Hong Kong' in Young and Ghai (eds), *Hong Kong's Court of Final Appeal: The Development of the Law in China's Hong Kong* (Cambridge University Press 2014) 94–118.
58. This could be the effect of the "Europeanisation" of the English system, since dissent is alien to the civil law system. The European Court of Justice features only single judgments and in over 30 cases there has been no "dissent" in the Macau Court of Final Appeal (The TUI); see J Godinho and P Cardinal, 'Macau's Court of Final Appeal' in Young and Ghai (eds), above.

listened to and evaluated their case, rather than having left it to a single member to deal with the case with whom they passively agree. There is also, occasionally, a benefit in terms of division of labour. In the *A Solicitor* case, for example, Li CJ was able to focus almost entirely on the hierarchical/precedent issues, while leaving to Bokhary J the extensive pronouncements on the applicable standard of proof.

There is also a view that multiple judgments (with or without dissent) have an important role to play, preventing, as they do, the view of a single judgment as the ultimate statement of the law, enjoying almost "legislative" status. Lord Reid,[59] in the House of Lords has stated:

> I think that it is desirable to try to extract from the authorities the principles on which most of them are based, when we are trying to do so, my experience has been that there are dangers in there being only one speech in this House. The statements in it have often tended to be treated as definitions and it is not the function of a court or of this House to frame definitions: some latitude should be left for future developments. The true ratio of a decision generally appears more clearly from a comparison of two or more statements in different words which are intended to supplement each other.[60]

It is true to say that alternative majority judgments or dissents are relatively rare in Hong Kong. The Court of Final Appeal (CFA) itself usually involves unanimous decisions and the norm is for a leading judgment to be "agreed" by the other judges or agreed with only minor additions.[61] Nevertheless, the scope for variation, dissent and an element of uncertainty remains. Statistical research[62] has shown that the CFA provides more "multiple" judgments, and dissents, than did its predecessor, the Judicial Committee of the Privy Council. Many would see this as a healthy manifestation of judicial independence.

5.4.2 The status of judgments overruled, disapproved or "not followed"

It is clear that a superior court has the ability to "overrule" a precedent of an inferior court, in which case the inferior court's decision has no further precedent significance. Similarly, when a superior court rejects a point of law in a previous decision not crucial to the outcome of the (previous) case, it may "disapprove" the decision (or the "incorrect" part of it). Again, the disapproved decision (or the relevant part of it) will cease to have precedent significance. One point which remains undetermined,

---

59. See *Saunders v Anglia Building Society* [1970] 3 All ER 961.
60. Ibid at 963. The appeal to the House of Lords was from the Court of Appeal in which the case was reported under the name *Gallie v Lee*.
61. The *A Solicitor* case is a notable exception, with the judgment of Bokhary J focusing on standard of proof with Li CJ "concurring" on this point but providing a detailed examination of Hong Kong's current precedent situation.
62. See SNM Young, 'Final Appeals Then and Now' in Young and Ghai (eds), above.

however, is the status of judgments "not followed". These are, of course, generally regarded as "overruled" and this, in practice, appears to be their status. However, both the English House of Lords in the "Practice Direction" ("Practice Statement) which permitted it to depart from previous decisions, and Hong Kong's Court of Final Appeal (CFA) statement (per Li CJ) in *A Solicitor v Law Society of Hong Kong*, which confirmed the CFA's ability not to follow its own previous decisions, have shied away from using the word "overrule". It may be that this reflects some lingering respect for the "declaratory" theory whereby courts do not amend the common law but merely explain correctly what it has always been.

In the highest court in England, the now-supplanted House of Lords, there is no recorded example of the court departing from a previous decision and subsequently reverting to it. It can reasonably be assumed that the CFA, in Hong Kong, will, similarly, treat the previous (CFA) precedent as overruled, having taken great pains to ensure the correctness of any new approach before "reluctantly" departing from its former approach.

However, this has clearly not been the case in the English Court of Appeal which is permitted to depart from a previous precedent where "two or more" of its previous precedents conflict. Clearly, a case could be made that the *second* precedent (case 2) had overruled the previous one (case 1) with which it is inconsistent. Instead, the Court of Appeal approach is to allow the court in the (third) case to decide which of the previous two conflicting decisions it will follow. Implicitly, therefore, the "not followed" case 1 has not been overruled. It appears, however, that the position in the Hong Kong Court of Appeal is somewhat clearer since it has the power to depart from one of its own previous precedents where it is found to be "plainly wrong". Having determined that a previous decision is "plainly wrong" there seems little doubt that such a precedent will be viewed as "overruled".

5.5 Persuasive precedents

So far we have focused on "binding" precedents; those which, in theory at least, a later (inferior) court is bound to follow. There are, however, many additional sources which, while not binding are, to a greater or lesser extent, "persuasive". Some examples have already been noted, at least implicitly. The CFA, for example, would regard its own previous decisions, while not binding, as "highly persuasive" and depart from them only with great reluctance, mindful of the advantages of certainty in the legal system.[63] To a lesser extent it would regard as persuasive those pre-1997 decisions of the House of Lords (definitive of the English common law and thus, probably, the laws in force on 1 July 1997) and Privy Council (at least in respect of appeals from Hong Kong). The CFA would also, no doubt, attach significant weight

---

63. See *A Solicitor v Law Society of Hong Kong* [2008] 2 HKC 1.

to a *ratio* of the Hong Kong Court of Appeal, especially on an issue never previously aired in the CFA, though clearly not bound to follow it.

Post-1997 *rationes* of English courts (including the Privy Council) would continue to be "persuasive" though not, in theory, more so that those from superior courts in other common law jurisdictions. The "constitutional" background is that while the Basic Law establishes Hong Kong's (large measure of) legal autonomy,[64] the right of "final adjudication"[65] and the principle that post-1997 English legislative and common rules are not binding in Hong Kong,[66] it adds that Hong Kong courts may "refer to precedents of other common law jurisdictions".[67]

These precedents will, of course, only be persuasive ones and, in theory at least, post-1997 English precedents are in the same "persuasive" category as those of other common law jurisdictions. As regards reference to precedents, *post-1997*, we might expect that there would be increasing use of Australian, Canadian and other common law precedents, with a reduced influence of English cases. In *practice*, however, as discussed in Chapter 2, such English precedents tend to be more persuasive than those from elsewhere in the common law world.[68] Typically, even today, when there is no relevant Hong Kong precedent, the first recourse will invariably be to an English source, whether a *primary* case or a *secondary* academic text. Furthermore, the reference to post-1997 English authorities rarely comes with a statement that the authority is not binding and need not be followed. Of course, judicial background may not be the only explanation for the continuing influence of English precedents. If the pre-1997 rules have been based on a line of English cases, it may appear logical to look first at whether these cases have been developed or overruled in England. Similarly, there have been situations where English and Hong Kong law have followed a path which other common law systems have not adopted. The only relevant precedents, therefore, would be from Hong Kong and England. This rationale for the continuing importance of English decisions has been supported by the (then) Hong Kong Chief Justice, Andrew Li who, as noted previously, stated:[69]

> Bearing in mind that, historically, Hong Kong's legal system originated from the British legal system, decisions of the Privy Council and the House of Lords should of course be treated with great respect. Their persuasive effect would depend on all relevant circumstances, including, in particular, the nature of the issue and the similarity of any statutory or constitutional provision.[70]

---

64. Article 2.
65. Article 19.
66. Article 18.
67. Art 84.
68. See 2.2.1.1 above and Chapter 6 below.
69. In *A Solicitor v Law Society of Hong Kong* [2008] 2 HKC 1.
70. Ibid at paras 16–17.

Nevertheless, the English-law background of so many of the Hong Kong judges, including those at the very highest level,[71] is likely to be part of the reason for the continuing influence of English precedents. It is also significant that a majority of the non-permanent CFA judges are English, albeit that there will never be more than one non-permanent judge sitting in that court.[72] We would expect, over time, the relative over-emphasis on English precedents to be gently eroded and there is some evidence of this. In the Court of Final Appeal, for example, Li CJ favoured the adoption of the broader approach of "other" common law jurisdictions rather than the narrower English one, in determining the situations in which the Court of Appeal may depart from its previous decisions.[73]

In addition to non-binding *rationes*, Hong Kong courts would regard as persuasive statements of law by superior courts on issues not crucial to the determination of the superior court; so-called "*obiter*" statements. *Obiter dicta* (things said by the way) comprise all parts of a judgment which are not *ratio*. As such they can, at most, be merely persuasive and can be ignored if the latter, inferior court so wishes. It is common practice for a later, inferior court to restrict or redefine (as *obiter*) a previously accepted *ratio* where the later court wishes not to follow the previous precedent. On the other hand, *obiter* statements may be *extremely* persuasive when they are uttered in a higher court, by a particularly eminent judge and/or are directed at an important issue of law, albeit one not crucial to the decision in the case in which they were voiced. The "neighbour" principle of *Donoghue v Stevenson*,[74] discussed previously, provides a famous illustration of historic "*obiter*" statements. As a Hong Kong example, judges in the District Court would attach great weight to a "non-essential" (*obiter*) statement of law by the Chief Justice in the Court of Final Appeal, even though not *bound* to follow it.

5.5.1 The value of "dissent"

"Dissenting" judgments are, by definition, non-binding precedents. However, later courts may be "persuaded" of the merits of the minority view and choose it over the majority *ratio*. In theory at least, the power to select the minority rather than the majority view can only be reposed in a superior court or, at the very least, a court of equivalent standing. The influence of a dissenting view will depend, in part, on the "status" of the dissenter. One of the most cited, and eventually followed (by a higher court), dissents was that of Lord Denning MR in the *Candler* case.[75] Lord Denning,[76] in fact, has stated that:

---

71. Andrew Li's successor as Chief Justice, Geoffrey Ma, for example, received much of his legal education and training in England (as did Li himself).
72. For further discussion, see Chapter 6.
73. See *A Solicitor v Law Society of Hong Kong* [2008] 2 HKC 1.
74. See 5.4 above.
75. *Candler v Crane, Christmas & Co* [1951] 2 KB 164.
76. Lord Denning, *The Discipline of Law* (Butterworths 1979).

In the Lords it is no good to dissent. In the Court of Appeal it is some good. On occasion a head-note there says 'Lord Denning dissenting' . . . and have led to decisions by the Lords which might never have taken place except for my dissenting from previous precedents; such as *Candler v Crane, Christmas* about negligent statements.[77]

Be that as it may, dissent in the English Court of Appeal is now increasingly rare. Perhaps this is the result of the increased "Europeanisation" of English law, since European, civil law jurisdictions, eschew dissent. Hong Kong courts, led by the Court of Final Appeal, tend not to express dissent and, in the main, proffer unanimous decisions, in the form of a leading judgment and four concurring ones.

As with full concurring judgment, dissenting judgments make clear to those involved that the whole court has focused on the case, rather than leaving the decision almost entirely to the "leading judge". Moreover, there is no doubt that today's "dissenter" may subsequently be viewed as a visionary. Lord Denning MR, despite assumptions to the contrary, did not dissent from his fellow judges that frequently.[78] One of his best-known dissenting judgments in the Court of Appeal, however, in *Candler v Crane Christmas & Co*,[79] involving the duty of care of those making negligent statements causing economic loss, was subsequently hailed by the House of Lords as the correct approach, with the majority view being overruled.[80] While the English courts are moving increasingly towards unified judgments, dissent and conflict are even less pronounced in the Hong Kong appellate courts where alternative majority judgments are relatively rare and dissent even more so. Research has shown that there were only 16 dissenting judgments in the 313 substantive decisions of the CFA for the period 1997–2009. Of these 16, 10 were delivered by Bokhary PJ.[81] Bokhary has espoused the cause of dissent, stating:

> in America, you can see the [Supreme] Court progressing very much by way of a dissenting view becoming the majority view . . . Dissents do not destroy a court, but rather point the way for future decisions. No one should ever, however much they agree with a dissent, regard the dissent as an attack on the Court as an institution, but only as a view of what it is hoped that the Court would do in the future.[82]

With Bokhary now only a Non-Permanent Judge, instances of dissent are likely to become even rarer. Cynics might even see evidence here of the "danger" of dissent, given that Bokhary's tenure as a Permanent Judge was not extended on his reaching retirement age (especially given that his replacement was born in the same year!) despite his willingness to continue.

---

77. Ibid 287.
78. Though he not infrequently sided with the majority on different grounds.
79. [1951] 2 KB 164.
80. See *Hedley Byrne & Co Ltd v Heller & Partners Ltd* [1964] AC 465.
81. See Simon NM Young, 'Final Appeals Then and Now' (n 59).
82. A Mak and M Chien, 'Interview with the Honourable Mr Justice Kemal Bokhary' *Hong Kong Student Law Gazette* (CUHK) Spring 2013.

5.6 The merits of *stare decisis*

Courts in all legal systems are likely to follow a previous approach; if it appeared correct "then", it is likely to be viewed as correct "now". What characterises common law *stare decisis*, in theory at least, is the *binding* nature of past precedents. Thus the major benefit of common law judicial precedent is generally viewed as being the element of certainty. Individuals and businesses need to know their rights and the relevant rules on which their actions should be based. Even more important, since many important commercial decisions will be based on legal advice, legal advisers need to be able to advise on the likely attitude of the courts to a particular course of action. In the event of dispute, legal advisers need to be able to predict the likely outcome of a legal action so that they can advise whether to pursue or defend an action. If every case were simply decided on its merits, without reference to past precedents, this great advantage of certainty would be lost and there would be far more litigation for the already overworked courts.

Of course, if precedent produced total certainty as to the existing state of law, few legal actions would be brought, since the outcome would always be known in advance, except in novel situations not previously considered by the courts. Such a situation would be unduly rigid, however, since it would not permit the law to develop to meet changing circumstances. In practice, the law is far less certain than would at first appear. Courts, as we have seen, have the power to overrule previous precedents of lower courts and, with some restrictions, of courts of equal status. This provides for a considerable measure of flexibility. Similarly, even lower courts have more flexibility than at first appears, since they can "distinguish" an unwelcome precedent of a higher court by finding a "material" difference in facts; such that a different legal principle may be applied in the instant case.

The benefits of precedent, then, may be summarised as sufficient *certainty* to provide guidance to citizens, businesses and legal advisers as to the current state of the law; and sufficient *flexibility* to allow the law to adapt to changing circumstances.

The importance of the balance between certainty and flexibility can be seen with the position of the House of Lords in England.[83] That court had previously been bound by its own previous decisions.[84] This provided great certainty in the law but was over-rigid since, if a House of Lords precedent became outdated, only legislation could change it and legislative time is scarce. Hence, in 1966, the House of Lords issued a Practice Statement[85] which stated that, in future, the court would depart from its previous decisions where it appeared right to do so *but* would do so only rarely and reluctantly given the desirability of certainty in the law. Lord Gardiner LC stated:

---

83. The Supreme Court, Britain's successor to the House of Lords, will adopt the same stance in relation to precedent.
84. *London Tramways Co Ltd v London County Council* [1898] AC 375 (sometimes erroneously described as *London Street [sic] Tramways* etc).
85. *Practice Statement (Judicial Precedent)* [1966] 1 WLR 1234; [1966] 3 All ER 77.

> Their Lordships regard the use of precedent as an indispensable foundation upon which to decide what is the law and its application to individual cases ...
>
> Their Lordships nevertheless recognise that too rigid adherence to precedent may lead to injustice in a particular case and also unduly restrict the proper development of the law. They propose therefore to modify their present practice and, while treating former decisions of this House as normally binding, to depart from a decision when it appears right to do so.
>
> In this connection they will bear in mind the danger of disturbing retrospectively the basis on which contracts, settlements of property and fiscal arrangements have been entered into and also the especial need for certainty as to the criminal law.
>
> This announcement is not intended to affect the use of precedent elsewhere than in this House.

In the 40-plus years since the Practice Direction there have been somewhere between 20 and 30 cases where the House of Lords has departed from its previous decision(s).[86] The use, then, has been sparing and is reserved for situations where it is felt that there is a need for the common law to move in a different direction, rather than simply because the previous decision may have been "wrong". Decisions, it has been suggested, will rarely be departed from where they are based on the interpretation of a statute or where certainty as to the criminal law is involved. However, even here there have been exceptions and none as striking as the pair of cases *Anderton v Ryan*[87] and *R v Shivpuri*.[88] In the former case the House of Lords had adopted an extremely narrow interpretation of the Criminal Attempts Act 1981. That interpretation largely "emasculated"[89] the statute and defeated its objective of clarifying the law as to "attempting the impossible". Following strong criticism from legal academics, notably the incomparable Professor J C Smith, the House of Lords, in *Shivpuri*, overturned their clearly wrong decision in *Anderton v Ryan*. Several points of the "retraction" were significant, notably that: *Anderton v Ryan* had been determined only *months* before; that the case had involved the interpretation of a statute; that such interpretation affected "certainty in the criminal law"; and that one of the judges, Lord Bridge, had sat on the *Anderton* case and admitted his error in *Shivpuri*!

A similar "reluctant to depart" approach has been taken (theoretically) by Hong Kong's Court of Final Appeal, though given its relative youth, this court has yet to depart from a previous decision (except reluctantly under political pressure).[90] As previously quoted, in *A Solicitor v Law Society of Hong Kong*,[91] Li CJ emphasised:

---

86. The figure depends on definition since, although a party must specifically ask the court to exercise its "Practice Statement" power, there have been cases where the House of Lords was able to "distinguish" a previous precedent rather than specifically depart from it: see A Paterson, *The Law Lords* (Oxford University Press 1982).
87. [1985] 2 All ER 355.
88. [1986] 2 All ER 334.
89. The author has "borrowed" this *mot juste* from Professor Michael Zander (see *The Law-Making Process* [6th edn, Cambridge University Press 2004] 200).
90. See Chapter 3 at 3.9.
91. [2008] 2 HKC 1.

Recognising the importance of these [precedent/certainty] considerations, this Court will approach the exercise of its power to depart from . . . any previous decision of the Court with great circumspection. In this connection, the risks of disturbing existing rights would have to be borne in mind. It is a power which will be exercised most sparingly.[92]

5.7 The disadvantages of precedent

The major (theoretical) disadvantage of judicial precedent, especially of the binding variety, is rigidity: *stare decisis* may be seen as unduly fettering the discretion of a judge in reaching the "just" solution in a particular case. In practice, for reasons already outlined, including the mechanisms of overruling and distinguishing, the system is far from rigid.

Ironically, perhaps the biggest potential disadvantage of precedent in action is that it does not produce the "certainty" (or near certainty) which is said to be its major benefit. The sheer volume of cases coming to the courts (or the subject of "alternative dispute resolution") illustrates the lack of certainty in the law, since few of these cases deal with novel, previously undetermined, issues of law. Indeed, one of the major factors detracting from jurisprudential uncertainty is the "cart before the horse" factor; that judges reach their decisions not based on a neutral application of prior principles, but on their own perceptions of the "just" solution in a particular case, subsequently "rationalised" with reference to "sympathetic" precedents and the "distinguishing" of hostile ones. The American "Realist" School emphasised this approach and adopted the position that the most important "predictive" factor of a court's decision would be the politico-economic background of the judges involved in a case rather than analysis of previous precedents.[93]

In a lecture on the Human Rights Act 1998,[94] Lord Browne-Wilkinson made the following "confession":

> The judge looks for what are called 'the merits' and having found them seeks to reach a result, consistent with legal reasoning, whereby the deserving win and the undeserving lose . . . [however] when we get to the judgment, we very seldom find any reference to 'the merits'. The articulated reasoning purports to be based on a process of compelling legal argument leading inexorably to the result achieved . . .
>
> First, the actual decision is primarily based on moral, not legal factors. Second, those moral factors are not normally articulated in the judgment. Third, the morality applied in any given case is the morality of the individual judge: although this will, to an extent, reflect the values of contemporary society.[95]

---

92. Ibid at para 20.
93. For further discussion, see Chapter 7.
94. B Markesinis (ed), *The Impact of the Human Rights Bill on English Law* (Lecture Series) (Oxford University Press 1998).
95. Ibid, pp 22–24 (cited by M Zander, n 86, 303).

Judges, in short, have the opportunity to be "creative" in their interpretation and application of previous precedents and, to a greater or lesser extent, make use of this opportunity.[96]

Uncertainty in Hong Kong, however, is more likely to be engendered by the plethora of precedent "sources" available to the court than any adventurous "creativity" on the part of the judges. Judges will have to determine: the precedential "weight" of pre-1997 English cases; the effect, if any, of English legislation; post-1997 decisions from England and the rest of the common law world; as well as the possible impact of the Basic Law; (perhaps) the Bill of Rights Ordinance; relevant "customary" law; and Hong Kong's own developing jurisprudence. In such circumstances, certainty, for the judges and for litigants and their advisers, may well prove elusive.

5.8 The importance of full and accurate law reporting

Since precedent is based on the application of principles stated in previous cases, it is essential that these principles can be accurately discovered. It is, therefore, crucial that previous precedents can be found and that they are properly recorded. The history of law reporting in England began with reports by individuals in court whose reports were often unsatisfactory. It is sometimes the case, with older English law reports, that different reporters in the court have produced separate reports which differ markedly from each other. In the *Williams v Roffey* case discussed above,[97] for example, considerable difficulty was caused by the fact that a crucial previous precedent, *Stilk v Myrick*, had been reported with significantly different emphasis in two separate law reports,[98] such that each proffered a differing *ratio*.

Modern English reports are far more accurate and based on transcripts signed by the judge involved. These reports are available in hard copy (once printed) but are also available as "neutral citations" very soon after judgment.

In Hong Kong, the Hong Kong Law Reports have been published since 1905 and, since 1997, the Hong Kong Law Reports and Digest has been published monthly. This publication incorporates the official Hong Kong Law Reports and the "Hong Kong Law Digest" which contains case summaries and commentary. The Hong Kong Law Reports are accurate but not very extensive. Over the years many significant cases have remained unreported. A more recent innovation, the Hong Kong Cases, is far more extensive, such that most cases of significance are now reported. However, despite a gradual improvement, some problems remain with the *quality* of the reports produced in this series, since inaccuracies and grammatical errors are not uncommon. It is also the case that *headnotes* do, on occasion, misrepresent the content of the case which they are intended to summarise which may cause

---
96. For further discussion of judicial creativity, see Chapter 6.
97. See 5.3 above.
98. (1809) 2 Camp 317 *and* (1809) 6, esp 129.

confusion.[99] For a clear example of a faulty report (in which an argument rejected by the trial judge was cited in the headnote as part of the *ratio* of the case) see *Calimpex International Co (A Firm) v ENZ Information Systems Ltd (Cheung Chun Hay Samuel, Third Party)*.[100] Law reporting in Hong Kong has an added difficulty given the bilingual nature of court proceedings and the need for accurate reporting in two languages.

As indicated above, however, law reporting in Hong Kong has made great strides in a relatively short time, in terms of both quality and comprehensiveness and this is an essential requirement as Hong Kong proceeds to develop a common law with its own local flavour.[101]

5.9 *Stare decisis, res iudicata,* and the *Jogee* debate

The landmark criminal law cases of *R v Jogee* and *Ruddock v R*,[102] involving joint judgments in the UK Supreme Court and Judicial Committee of the Privy Council,[103] provoked almost immediate debate in Hong Kong as to the potential impact of the decisions in Hong Kong. The cases themselves involved the issue of accomplices and the concept of the "joint enterprise".[104] Briefly, the judgments in the two cases have overturned, in the United Kingdom, 30 years of jurisprudence established in the Privy Council decision in *Chan Wing-Siu v R*,[105] involving an appeal *from Hong Kong*. *Chan Wing-Siu* itself overturned the previous common law position dating back several hundred years. (Very) broadly *Chan Wing-Siu* could be seen as a "policy" decision; making conviction easier in the case of a "joint enterprise" where the precise issue of "who did what" is uncertain. The situation tends to arise where a group jointly decides to commit offence A (eg, a theft) but one of the group "goes further" and commits offence B. Previously, it was necessary to show that an accomplice "aided, abetted, counselled or procured" the offence of the principal offender. Post–*Chan Wing-Siu* it could be enough to show that the secondary party *foresaw* the possibility of the offence being committed. This was especially significant for cases of murder, committed by one of a group, where the principal "actor" could not be identified, but where a jury might readily accept that all of the gang foresaw the possibility of grievous bodily harm being inflicted and could be guilty of murder.[106] In *Jogee* the Supreme Court/Privy Council determined that "we do not consider that the *Chan Wing-Siu* principle can be supported". Instead, the previous

---

99. It is a rule of precedent that headnotes are not regarded as part of the judgment.
100. [1994] 1 HKC 191.
101. For discussion of researching Hong Kong cases, see Chapter 14 at 14.4.2.
102. [2016] UKSC 8, [2016] UKPC 7.
103. The (joint) leading judgment was delivered by Lords Hughes and Toulson.
104. Otherwise known as "parasitic accessory liability", an expression coined by legendary criminal law academic (the late) Professor Sir John Smith.
105. [1985] AC 168.
106. In *Chan Wing-Siu* itself, one of a group of three men (all armed with knives) stabbed and killed the victim. It was uncertain who had made the fatal stab but all were held to have foreseen the

long-standing common law approach was reinstated and, broadly, a requirement of "intent" replaced that of "foresight".

Initial responses by criminal law experts in Hong Kong conveyed an assumption that, given such a high level judgment from both the Privy Council *and* the UK Supreme Court, involving a major review of centuries of jurisprudence, Hong Kong was certain to follow the UK lead and, as such, many prior convictions based on the pre-*Jogee* law were likely to be overturned. The relevant *South China Morning Post* headline[107] read "UK Ruling Could See Hundreds of HK Cases Quashed". The *Post* article stated: "Veteran senior counsel Michael Blanchflower said the cases involved over the past 30 years could potentially run into 'hundreds' and dealing with them would pose an 'immense administrative task' for the judiciary". Blanchflower was quoted as adding that, although the decisions were not binding on Hong Kong courts, "I do not see a Hong Kong court refusing to follow this decision". Similar sentiments were expressed by local solicitor, Colin Cohen, and criminal law academic, Michael Jackson (though the latter did indicate that the issue must be first clarified by the Court of Final Appeal and that *Jogee* is not binding in Hong Kong).[108]

Scant reference was made in the article to the principle of *res judicata*;[109] that *prima facie* once all appeals have been exhausted, a case will not be reopened. True, there may be limited power for the Chief Executive to "pardon" or "commute the sentence" of a convicted person[110] but such an action would be exceptional and would have to involve a miscarriage of justice.[111]

The Court of Appeal could be asked to make a ruling of law, on application from the Secretary for Justice. However, even here, a caveat arises: that *Chan Wing-Siu* is a Privy Council decision *on appeal from Hong Kong*. As Chief Justice Li made clear in *A Solicitor*,[112] such a decision is binding on all Hong Kong courts *except* the Court of Final Appeal which, alone, has the power to overrule it. Such overruling would be made "with reluctance" (and has never yet occurred). As academic Simon Young has said: "To persuade the Court of Final Appeal to overrule itself will always require some effort."[113] Given the CFA decision in *A Solicitor*, the most a reviewing Court of Appeal could have done would be to make the case for consideration of *Jogee* and support any necessary leave to appeal to the CFA.

---

possibility of grievous bodily harm being inflicted. One is guilty of murder, in Hong Kong, if one kills with intent to kill or inflict grievous bodily harm.
107. 24 February 2016.
108. Of course, as explained in Chapter 2 and in this chapter, no post-1997 English/UK decision can have binding force in Hong Kong.
109. See 5.2.3 above.
110. Under Basic Law Article 48(12).
111. It should be borne in mind that in most cases (as in *Jogee* itself) the acquitted "murderer" would be guilty of manslaughter.
112. See 5.2.2 (at length) above.
113. Simon NM Young, 'Landmark UK Ruling Is Not a "Get out of Jail" Card for Hong Kong Felons' *South China Morning Post* (Hong Kong, 9 February 2016).

In short, despite the dramatic tone of the *SCMP* headline, neither the Court of Appeal nor any other court in Hong Kong, except the CFA, has the power to overturn *Chan Wing-Siu*. The CFA *could have done* but, confounding the experts, decided not to do so. It took the view that certainty in the law should not be sacrificed, that those convicted on the basis of joint enterprise were correctly convicted on the basis of the law as it then stood and that different circumstances in Hong Kong mean that it is in the interests of Hong Kong to adopt a different jurisprudence from the UK in this instance.[114] Even if the CFA had supported *Jogee*, this would have affected only later cases as opposed to those already decided (on the basis of *res judicata*). Thus, a later *SCMP* article[115] quoted a "Department of Justice spokeswoman" who opined, quite properly:

> Even upon development of the common law, all earlier decisions made on the basis of the previous law are not automatically invalidated.

That the Court of Final Appeal decided, in *HKSAR v Chan Kam Shing*[116] that *Chan Wing-Siu* was *not* a "wrong turning"[117] and that *Jogee* would not be followed, is a commendable recognition of the CFA as Hong Kong's final arbiter of the common law *in Hong Kong*.

5.10 The future

As the previous illustration implies, it is inevitable that, over time, Hong Kong will develop its own jurisprudence via judicial precedents, particularly those of the CFA. This is particularly likely where, as with *Jogee/Chan Kam Shing*, Hong Kong's socio-economic environment is perceived as different from that of the UK.

Indeed, there is some irony in the fact that Hong Kong courts seem eager to preserve the common law system while the "fount" of the common law becomes increasingly influenced by European civil law concepts (including, for example, proposals for a new criminal "code"). Whether the English trend away from common law will continue "post-Brexit" remains to be seen.

Hong Kong has the ability to develop creatively, since its judges may select from the best of the common law jurisdictions (as permitted by the Basic Law)[118] or go its own way if that appears the better option. The CFA is constantly exposed to non-Hong Kong jurisprudence through the contribution of its overseas Non-

---

114. See F Koo, 'Is Abolishing Joint Enterprise Beneficial for Hong Kong?' *Hong Kong Lawyer* (May 2016).
115. D Lee, 'Convicted Killers Warned UK Ruling Is No Ticket to Freedom' *South China Morning Post* (Hong Kong, 27 March 2016).
116. (2016) 19 HKCFAR 640.
117. M Jackson, 'HKSAR v Chan Kam Shing: CFA Finds "No Wrong Turning"' *Hong Kong Lawyer* (March 2017).
118. Article 84.

Permanent Judges (mainly from Britain or Australia) while at the same time confidence in the competence of Hong Kong's highest courts is shown by the increasing citation of Hong Kong authorities elsewhere in the common law world.[119]

---

119. See PY Lo, 'Impact of [CFA] Jurisprudence beyond Hong Kong' in S Young and Y Ghai (eds), *Hong Kong's Court of Final Appeal: The Development of the Law in China's Hong Kong* (Cambridge University Press 2014).

6
Hong Kong's Professional Judiciary

Overview

While, from a practical point of view, the post-1997 position of the Hong Kong judiciary remains largely unchanged, *constitutionally* there is a fundamental difference. With the 1 July 1997 change of sovereignty, Hong Kong's judges are no longer required (or permitted) to swear allegiance to the old colonial power but to the Hong Kong Special Administrative Region (SAR) of the People's Republic of China. However, the new constitution, the Basic Law, maintains, with some amendment, the existing common law system and, in doing so, expressly states that judges already in post may remain so (on terms no less favourable). As a result, most of the pre-1997 judges remained in office after the handover. The Basic Law imposed ethnic and residential requirements for only a few judicial offices, notably that of Chief Justice, although new appointments are increasingly "local". For the present, the judiciary, at the highest level, remains dominated by those whose legal training was, at least in part, in England. In the Court of Final Appeal this is true not only of "local" Permanent and Non-Permanent Judges but also of the Non-Permanent "overseas" Judges. Given the reality that judges in common law jurisdictions are able to use a considerable amount of "creativity" in finding and applying the law, and that the exercise of such creativity owes much to their background, it is likely that, for some time to come, the common law applied in Hong Kong will continue to be influenced predominantly by the common law of England rather than that of other common law jurisdictions.

While it may be argued that the subject of "judges" should be dealt with in coverage of the courts (to which they are inextricably linked) the focus of this chapter will be on the specific issue of judicial "personnel" as opposed to the court "institutions". In particular, the professional judges serve as a counterpoint to the amateur "players" in the court system: juries and lay prosecutors/magistrates.

6.1 Hong Kong's judicial manpower

There are approximately 190 professional judges in Hong Kong. These comprise the Chief Justice and three Permanent Judges of the Court of Final Appeal (CFA);

16 Non-Permanent Judges of the CFA; the Chief Judge of the High Court and nine Court of Appeal judges; 27 Court of First Instance judges; two High Court Registrars and three Deputy Registrars; 36 District Court judges; the Chief Magistrate and eight Principal Magistrates plus around 80 Magistrates and tribunal members.

This number is felt by many to be insufficient. Concerns as to the judicial "labour shortage"[1] have prompted discussion in LegCo and the production of the following briefing paper.

Legislative Council LC Paper No CB(4) 822/13-14(04)[2]
Panel on Administration of Justice and Legal Services
[for] Meeting on 24 June 2014
Updated background brief prepared on judicial manpower situation at various levels of court

Purpose

This paper provides background information on the judicial manpower situation at various levels of court and a brief account of the relevant discussions at the Panel on Administration of Justice and Legal Service ("the Panel") and the Finance Committee ("FC").

...

Establishment and vacancies

2. As at 1 March 2014, the establishment of Judges and Judicial Officers ("JJOs") at all levels of courts was 193 ...

3. The Judiciary completed the last round of open recruitment exercises for various levels of court in the latter half of 2012 and up to March 2014, a total of 52 judicial appointments have been made.

4. In July 2013, the Judiciary launched another recruitment exercise for the rank of Judge of the Court of First Instance of the High Court ("CFI Judge"). Open recruitment exercises for CFI Judges used to be conducted every three years in the past. To tie in the timing of joining the Bench by interested senior legal professionals in private practice with the recruitment trawl at times, the Chief Justice is of the view that CFI Judge recruitment exercises should henceforth be launched more frequently on a yearly basis. Accordingly, the next CFI Judge recruitment exercise is planned to be launched in the latter half of 2014.

5. ... For the magisterial level, the Judiciary has launched another open recruitment for Permanent Magistrates and Special Magistrates in February 2014 and the recruitment exercises are still in progress.

---

1. See, eg, S Lau, 'Lack of Judges a Threat to Justice' *South China Morning Post* (Hong Kong, 8 March 2012).
2. See also LegCo paper LC Paper No CB (4) 964/14-15 (03) May 2015.

Engagement of temporary judicial manpower

6. According to the Judiciary Administrator ("JA"), the engagement and deployment of temporary judicial manpower has been a long standing practice adopted by the Judiciary to help maintain the level of judicial manpower required, and thereby to help maintain court waiting times at reasonable levels and help reduce such waiting times in some cases. The arrangement also provides opportunities for the deputy JJOs to gain judicial experience at the relevant levels of court.

Retirement age for JJOs

7. The statutory normal retirement age for JJOs is 60 or 65, depending on the level of court. Beyond that, extension of service may be approved up to the age of 70 or 71, depending on the level of court and subject to consideration on a case-by-case basis. According to the Report on Judicial Remuneration Review 2013 published by the Standing Committee on Judicial Salaries and Conditions of Service, retirement is the main source of wastage among JJOs. The anticipated retirement (number) will be 14 (or 8.5% of current strength) in 2013–2014, decreasing to seven (or 4.3% of current strength) in 2014–2015 and going up to 11 (or 6.7% of current strength) in 2015–2016.

Establishment Review in 2013

...

9. The review concludes that additional resources are much needed for the creation of additional judicial (and associated support staff) posts –

(a) For the Court of Appeal of the High Court to enable it to cope with the increased workload; and

(b) At various levels of court to cover the absence of JJOs for dealing with judicial education matters and attending judicial training activities.

...

The Scheme of Judicial Assistants ("the Scheme")

11. In 2010, the Judiciary started the Scheme which sought to provide enhanced support to appellate judges in the discharge of their duties. Under the Scheme, the Judicial Assistants who are fresh and bright law graduates will be recruited normally for a single one-year term and assigned to provide assistance in researching on law points, analyzing and writing memoranda on appeals and applications, drafting memoranda on legal points, assisting with other work of the court and providing direct support to the appellate judges.

...

Judicial manpower situation

15. At the meetings of 16 December 2013 and 31 March 2014, Members were concerned about the persistent shortage of judicial manpower over the past years, particularly in face of increasingly complex cases. Noting that some CFI Judges would

be redeployed as additional judges to hear cases in the Court of Appeal, a Member worried that this arrangement would further affect the resources of CFI, and urged the Judiciary to put in more efforts to solve the overall problem on judicial manpower.

16. JA explained that the Judiciary spared no efforts in conducting recruitment exercises in the past years, but there were fillable vacancies arising from the creation of new judicial posts, elevation of JJOs to higher positions within the Judiciary and retirement to JJOs. Given the increased caseload and the increased number of complex cases, HC remained a pressure area. In this connection, the Judiciary has conducted an establishment review of JJO posts in 2013. This review concluded that additional judicial posts would be needed for HC (in particular for the Court of Appeal) to cope with the increased workload. With the proposed increase in the establishment of the Court of Appeal Judges from 10 to 13, it was expected that much of the judicial resources temporarily redeployed form CFI could be released back to that level of court to hear cases.

17. At the Panel meeting on 27 June 2011, members noted the Hong Kong Bar Association's advice that as the number of legal practitioners who were considered eligible for the posts of judges was small, there would be difficulties in recruiting judges unless the pool of candidates could be further expanded. Members asked whether overseas recruitment was impracticable having regard to the language requirement. JA advised that the Judiciary followed the specific requirements laid down in law in recruiting JJOs. Judges were not necessarily required to be proficient in Chinese and some of the judges recruited in the past were not bilingual. In the previous recruitment exercises, candidates from various backgrounds, including serving JJOs at the lower levels of court, private practitioners and eligible persons in government departments, had applied. The conduct of local open recruitment exercises was considered effective in recruiting suitable candidates to fill vacancies in the Judiciary.

...

21. At the Panel meetings on 26 and 29 May 2008, some members expressed the view that JA should introduce measures to improve the effectiveness of the listing system so that court time and the time and expertise of judges could be utilized in an optimum manner. The listing system should be flexible to ensure that the judges' diaries were utilized as fully as possible and judges had sufficient time to write judgments, especially after the trial of a complicated case.

22. According to JA, the Judiciary was operating an effective listing system in HC and had been making continuous improvements as appropriate. The Chief Judge of HC, assisted by the Listing Judges and a team of listing officers in JA, was responsible for ensuring that judges will have reasonable time to prepare for cases and write judgments, particularly for long and complicated cases.

Impact of statutory and non-statutory appointments of judges on judicial work

23. At the Panel meeting on 13 January 2009, some members expressed concern about the statutory and non-statutory appointments of judges for extra-judiciary

> functions. They considered that careful consideration should be given to the need to appoint serving judges to non-statutory outside offices, in particular those which are non-judicial in nature, and its impact on their judicial duties. Members reiterated this concern at the Panel meeting on 28 May 2012.
>
> ...
>
> *Recent development*
>
> 26. At the special FC meeting on 31 March 2014, JA advised Members that financial resources were sought for the creation of seven additional judicial post at various levels of courts, engagement of a team of 10 legally qualified staff to provide professional support to judicial education, and creation of 59 net additional civil service posts in the Judiciary Administration to meet the needs arising from the increased levels of judicial and registry services. The Judiciary will consult the Panel on its manpower proposals at its meeting on 24 June 2014, before submitting them to the Establishment Subcommittee for endorsement and FC for approval.
>
> ...
>
> <u>Legislative Council Secretariat</u>
> 18 June 2014

The premise of a shortage of judges has been endorsed (tangentially) in an article in the *South China Morning Post*[3] which partially attributes excessive waits for prisoners on remand to judicial manpower shortages. The article quotes Johannes Chan, former Dean of the Law Faculty of the University of Hong Kong, as saying:

> I know of many High Court/Court of Appeal judges who have to use their personal leave and holiday to write judgments simply because the workload is such that they have one case after another.

There is anecdotal evidence that workload can affect the quality of judgments, especially when it results in serious delay. It is not simply that "justice delayed is justice denied" but that delay can produce judicial "forgetfulness". An infamous case, the notoriety of which was commented upon by Britain's *The Times* newspaper,[4] involved Hong Kong (Court of First Instance) Judge Pang. The judge had heard an appeal by a company convicted in the Magistrate's Court. He had indicated, verbally, that he would *allow* the appeal and would present written reasons in due course. Seven and a half months later Judge Pang presented a written judgment stating that the appeal was *dismissed*! On being reminded of his previous assertion that the appeal would be allowed, the judge stated that the version presented was "inaccurate" and

---

3. L Lam, 'Alarm at Time Spent on Remand' *South China Morning Post* (Hong Kong, 14 September 2014).
4. See D Pannick, 'I'll Be the Judge of That and I Reserve the Right to Change My Mind' *The Times* (London, 15 January 2009).

would be amended. A revised version was hurriedly produced which was largely unchanged *except* that the appeal was now stated to be *allowed*. Following appeal to the Court of Final Appeal (CFA), confirmation of the allowing of the appeal was issued together with strong criticism of the judge's mistake and the delay which the CFA believed had contributed to it. Of course it may be that workload did not affect the issue of delay but there have certainly been a number of cases involving similar delays.[5]

A somewhat different view is taken by another University of Hong Kong academic, Malcolm Merry.[6] Writing in his blog, "Not Entirely Legal",[7] Merry writes:

> *No shortage of judges*
>
> For some time now Hong Kong's press has been banging on about a shortage of judges, focusing upon the number of unfilled posts in the magistrates' and the district courts. Journalists have declared a crisis in the judiciary. Lawyers don't want to become judges, has been the refrain, the pay is too low. The refrain is both inaccurate and out-of-date. It is and was inaccurate because the vacancies have not been the consequence of poor pay. On the contrary, the SAR's judges, at all levels, have long been very well rewarded. Also, although there have been vacancies, there have been plenty of judges. They have just not been permanent judges.
>
> *No shortage of money*
>
> By international standards the salary of a district judge, more than HK$200,000 a month, is handsome indeed. That is before you factor in the generous housing and other allowances. But these are not the main attraction, which is the full pension . . .
>
> In the High Court the money is even better . . . Furthermore, their lordships and their honours, unlike other public servants, need fear no pay cut, for reductions in their salary is regarded as an assault on judicial independence (yes, the reasoning escapes me too).
>
> . . .
>
> On top of all that, if you consider the relatively low rate of tax, the take-home pay leaves judges elsewhere floundering in the wake of their SAR brethren.
>
> *The real problem*
>
> The argument, however, has been not that all this money is insufficiently generous by world standards but that it is not enough to attract local practitioners to the Bench because they earn so much as senior counsel or senior partners.
>
> That argument has never been fully convincing . . .

---

5. See, eg, *Esquire (Electronics) Ltd v HSBC Ltd & another* [2006] HKCA 383.
6. Associate Professor and formerly head of the Department of Professional Legal Education, HKU.
7. Part 55.

> The real problem about filling the positions was not that the judicial package was unenticing but that there was a shortage of suitable candidates. They had to be both experienced in law and fluent in written and spoken Chinese as well as English ... The profession began to localize modestly in the 1970s when HKU produced its first batch of law students but there were fewer than 50 a year for the first decade and not all of them went into litigation. In an expanding economy and population, that was not enough to satisfy demand ... By 1997 there were not many who could tick all the boxes.
>
> *Unpromotable*
>
> That is why the judiciary remained disproportionately expatriate at the turn of the century. The courts were kept going by acting appointees ...
>
> *End of an era*
>
> But now the era of the acting appointment is coming to an end. During August [2012] the Judiciary announced no fewer than 23 new judges in the District Court and the magistracy. Most of them came from practice. Shortly more will be announced together with several appointments to the High Court bench. They will include names which might have been thought to be in the too-rich-to-be-tempted category.
>
> Nearly all the new names are or will be Chinese speakers. This feels like a watershed: the full localization of the Hong Kong judiciary. At last.

Comment

The nub of Merry's column (written in 2012) is that LegCo is addressing an issue already largely resolved by the appointment of additional judges. Clearly that argument is not accepted by Johannes Chan who still described the plight of the overworked judge in 2014. Moreover, the Judiciary's Annual Report for 2015 clearly posits "insufficient judicial posts in the High Court, in particular the Court of Appeal" as a reason for the failure to meet all High Court targets.

Merry also describes a situation of "full localization", which appears somewhat premature, especially in the highest courts.

Merry's explanation of the preservation of judicial "terms and conditions", ostensibly to preserve judicial independence, is somewhat disingenuous given the wording of Article 93 of the Basic Law which states that, "Judges ... serving in Hong Kong before the establishment of the HKSAR may all remain in employment and maintain their seniority with pay, allowances, benefits and conditions of service no less favourable than before". Moreover, Article 93 also guarantees the preservation of pensions and other benefits at levels no less favourable than before, "irrespective of their nationality or place of residence". The preservation, therefore, is constitutionally guaranteed.[8]

Merry's argument, that the problems of judicial shortage and overwork have now been addressed, is not shared by (legal functional constituency) legislator, Dennis Kwok, who returns to the theme of overworked judges having to "work through their annual leave". Kwok, writing in September 2013,[9] states:

> The lack of adequate resources and support, coupled with the recent spate of judicial vacancies and imminent retirements, has threatened the judiciary, access to justice and the state of our rule of law.
>
> The average waiting time for cases . . . has increased significantly in recent years. Civil matters in the Court of Appeal now wait an average of 131 days, an increase of 54% since 2008 and in excess of the judiciary's 90-day target. The criminal case list has an average waiting time of 180 days, exceeding the judiciary's 120-day target and an increase of 68% since 2008.
>
> [Also] . . . after queuing for a hearing, litigants also have to wait, sometimes for many months, before judgments can be delivered.
>
> . . . Inevitably, the quality of some judicial decisions suffers as a result of overwork. The heavy workload has also partially contributed to difficulties in the retention and recruitment of judges from the private sector.
>
> Nearly half of the judges in the Court of Final Appeal, Court of Appeal and Court of First Instance are aged over 60 and will reach statutory retirement age within the next five years.
>
> The judiciary administrator . . . has to be ever more responsive to the current difficulties and needs.

While Kwok makes a case for increased expenditure, judicial salary increases are far from being his only suggested improvement. He supports out of hours secretarial support, increased computerisation of court forms, increased vocational training for magistrates and an expansion of the judicial assistants scheme.[10]

6.1.1 The Hong Kong Chief Justice

The Chief Justice of the Court of Final Appeal is the head of the judiciary in Hong Kong. He presides over the Court of Final Appeal. He is required, under the Basic Law[11] to be a Chinese citizen and a permanent resident of the Hong Kong SAR with no right of abode in any foreign country. The appointment of the Chief Justice,

---

8. However, post-1997 "pay cuts" were mooted given the economic downturn and the Standing Committee on Judicial Salaries & Conditions of Service (SCJSCS) opined that such were constitutional as long as salaries were not reduced below pre-1997 levels. The SCJSCS also refuted the notion that pay cuts threatened judicial neutrality (2008 Report).
9. D Kwok, 'Rough Justice' *South China Morning Post* (Insight) (Hong Kong, 13 September 2013).
10. It should be noted, however, that the judicial assistants scheme has raised concerns amongst LegCo members.
11. Article 90.

like all judicial appointments, is to be made by the Chief executive on the recommendation of an independent commission.[12] It must also be approved by LegCo and reported to the Standing Committee of the National People's Congress.[13] Many of these requirements are re-stated in the Hong Kong Court of Final Appeal Ordinance (HKCOFAO)[14] which states:

> Section 6
>
> (1) The Chief Justice shall be appointed by the Chief Executive acting in accordance with the recommendation of the Judicial Officers Recommendation Commission.
>
> (1A) The Chief Justice shall be a Chinese citizen[15] who is a permanent resident of the Region with no right of abode in any foreign country.
>
> (2) The Chief Justice shall be the head of the Judiciary and shall be charged with the administration of the Judiciary and such other functions as may from time to time be lawfully conferred on him.
>
> Section 12
>
> (1) A person shall be eligible to be appointed as the Chief Justice if he is–
>
> (aa)[16] a permanent judge;
>
> (a) The Chief Judge of the High Court, a Justice of Appeal or a judge of the Court of First Instance; or
>
> (b) A barrister who has practised as a barrister or solicitor in Hong Kong for a period of at least 10 years.
>
> Section 14
>
> (1) The Chief Justice and permanent judges shall vacate their offices when they attain the retiring age.
>
> (2) Notwithstanding subsection (1)
>
> (a) subject to paragraph (b) the terms of office of the Chief Justice and of permanent judges may be extended for not more than 2 periods of 3 years by the Chief Executive acting, in the case of the Chief Justice, in accordance with the recommendation of the Judicial Officers Recommendation Commission and, in the case of permanent judges, in accordance with the recommendation of the Chief Justice ...
>
> (b) a person who has attained the age of 65 years may be appointed to be the Chief Justice or to be a permanent judge for a term of 3 years and that term may be extended for one period of 3 years ...

---

12. Article 88, Basic Law and see 6.2.
13. Article 90. Such reporting is also required for the Chief Justice's removal from office.
14. Cap 484.
15. The ethnicity requirement was not part of the Sino-British Joint Declaration (see Chapter 1).
16. Added after original draft.

The administrative role of the Chief Justice, in relation to overseeing the selection, training and operation of the Hong Kong judges, is an extensive one. The first Chief Justice, Andrew Li, remained, however, an active "judicial" member of the Court of Final Appeal over which he presided, in addition to fulfilling his numerous administrative and ceremonial duties. Indeed, Chief Justice Li's workload was prodigious. Between 1997 and 2009, of the 313 cases heard by the CFA, Li CJ sat on 190 cases, wrote 44 majority judgments and seven concurring ones (ie full reasoned judgments). In addition, as one of only three Permanent CFA Judges for much of his period in office, Li CJ had to deal with 177 applications for leave to appeal to the CFA (over a third of all leave applications lodged) and wrote 57 judgments in respect of leave decisions.[17]

Andrew Li's background[18] includes considerable exposure to English education and training. He obtained MA and LLM degrees from the University of Cambridge and was called to the English Bar in 1970, as well as to the Hong Kong Bar in 1973. Li became a Queen's Counsel (senior barrister) in 1988.

The background of Li's successor, Justice Geoffrey Ma (in office from 1 September 2010), is also somewhat "anglocentric". Born in Hong Kong, in 1956, he read law at Birmingham University and was called to the English Bar (as a member of Gray's Inn) in 1978. He was later called to the Hong Kong Bar (1980), became a Queen's Counsel (QC) in 1993 and a High Court Recorder in 2000. Appointed as a Court of First Instance Judge in 2001, his progress thereafter was meteoric; becoming a Justice of Appeal within a year and Chief Judge of the High Court in 2003.

6.1.2 The judges of the Court of Final Appeal

The judges of the Court of Final Appeal may be permanent appointees (from Hong Kong) or non-permanent ones, who may be from Hong Kong or other common law jurisdictions.[19] Amplifying the stipulations in the Basic Law, the Hong Kong Court of Final Appeal Ordinance (HKCOFAO) states:

Section 7

(1) The permanent judges of the Court shall be appointed by the Chief Executive acting in accordance with the recommendation of the Judicial Officers Recommendation Commission...

---

17. See Simon NM Young, 'Role of the Chief Justice' in Young and Ghai (eds), *Hong Kong's Court of Final Appeal: The Development of the Law in China's Hong Kong* (Cambridge University Press 2014).
18. Li retired in September 2010, ahead of his normal retirement date.
19. Article 82, Basic Law. Although Article 82 permits the CFA to "as required invite judges [sic] from other common law jurisdictions to sit" by virtue of a compromise in the Joint Liaison Group, only one overseas judge may sit at any one time. Chief Justices Li and Ma have made maximum use of the overseas NPJs, who have sat on over 90% of all CFA cases since 1997 (see Simon NM Young, above).

Section 8

(1) There shall be a list to be known as the list of non-permanent Hong Kong judges.

(2) The list shall consist of judges appointed by the Chief Executive acting in accordance with the recommendation of the Judicial Officers Recommendation Commission, as non-permanent Hong Kong judges.

Section 9

(1) There shall be a list to be known as the list of judges from other common law jurisdictions.

(2) The list shall consist of judges appointed by the Chief Executive acting in accordance with the recommendation of the Judicial Officers Recommendation Commission.

(1A) A person shall be eligible to be appointed as a permanent judge if he is–

(a) the Chief Judge of the High Court, a Justice of Appeal or a judge of the Court of First Instance; or

(b) a barrister who has practised as a barrister or solicitor in Hong Kong for a period of at least 10 years.

(1) ...

(2) A person shall be eligible to be appointed as a non-permanent Hong Kong judge if he is–

(a) a retired Chief Judge of the High Court;

(b) a retired Chief Justice of the Court;

(c) a retired permanent judge of the Court;

(d) a Justice or retired Justice of Appeal; or

(e) a barrister who has practised as a barrister or solicitor in Hong Kong for a period of at least 10 years.

whether or not he is ordinarily resident in Hong Kong.

(3) A person shall be eligible to be appointed as a judge from another common law jurisdiction if he is–

(a) a judge or retired judge of a court of unlimited jurisdiction in either civil or criminal matters in another common law jurisdiction;

(b) a person who is ordinarily resident outside Hong Kong; and

(c) a person who has never been a judge of the High Court, a District Judge or a permanent magistrate, in Hong Kong.

...

Section 14

(1) There shall be no retiring age for a non-permanent judge ...

> ...
>
> (8) A permanent or non-permanent judge may be removed only by the Chief Executive on the recommendation of a tribunal of judges
>
> Appointed by the Chief Justice...

There are presently three Permanent Judges in addition to the Chief Justice: Ribeiro PJ, Tang PJ and Fok PJ of whom both the latter have been appointed since 2012. All three Permanent Judges have an "anglocentric" background. Ribeiro PJ obtained his LLB from the London School of Economics; Tang PJ, like Ma CJ, obtained his law degree from the University of Birmingham; and "new boy", Joseph Fok, appointed a Permanent Judge in 2013, obtained his LLB at University College, London.

Normally, in a case, there will not be less than three Permanent Judges sitting.[20] Of the Non-Permanent Judges (NPJs), approximately half are from Hong Kong and half from elsewhere.[21] Of the overseas NPJs, those from England predominate and, even from the Hong Kong judges, there are more whose first language is English rather than Chinese. Increasingly localised appointment of judges will eventually affect the latter situation but, given the security of tenure of judges until retirement, change is likely to be slow. At any given time the number of NPJs is around 15 to 20 though up to 30 may be appointed.[22]

One consequence of the previous shortage of Chinese judges was that, as Hong Kong sought to appoint its second Chief Justice, on the retirement of Li CJ, there were few eligible candidates. The only other CFA Permanent Judge eligible (the Basic Law requires a Chinese citizen with no right of abode elsewhere)[23] was Justice Patrick Chan. Since outgoing Chief Justice, Andrew Li, had made it known that he favoured the appointment of a younger man, Chief Judge Ma became an almost certain appointment![24]

A novel issue arose in respect of NPJ appointments made following the announcement by (first) Chief Justice Andrew Li of his resignation in September 2010. Li's stated purpose in taking early retirement was to give his successor some say in the appointment of new CFA judges, given that the CFA was in need of "new blood". At the same time as the appointment, as new Chief Justice, of Geoffrey Ma J (Chief Judge of the High Court for seven years) was confirmed, the appointment of three new "local" Non-Permanent Judges[25] of the CFA (from the Hong Kong Court

---

20. Section 5, Hong Kong Court of Final Appeal Ordinance (Cap 484).
21. Historically two recent appointees are women (Brenda Hale NPJ and Beverley McLachlin NPJ).
22. Section 10, Hong Kong Court of Final Appeal Ordinance.
23. Article 90, Basic Law.
24. Patrick Chan, then PJ, now NPJ, was significantly older.
25. The difficulty in finding suitable new Permanent Judges is reflected in the fact that, to date, only Joseph Fok has been in appointed in the "Ma era".

of Appeal) was recommended.[26] Controversy arose because, as Non-Permanent Judges, the three were to continue as serving Court of Appeal judges. Critics pointed out that, since appeals to the CFA were so significant to Hong Kong, there should be a public "perception" that an appeal from the Court of Appeal went to a truly "different" court. While the critics accepted that the three new Non-Permanent judges would not, of course, hear appeals from their own decisions,[27] the position was not ideal since they would hear appeals from their current Court of Appeal "brethren", *and* their new CFA "brethren" would hear appeals from them. Audrey Eu SC, while accepting that the appointments would be lawful, was quoted as saying:

> This is not an ideal situation in the eyes of the public. It gives the impression that whether you go to the appeal court or the final appeal court, it's still the same pool of judges.[28]

Ms Margaret Ng, then LegCo functional member for the legal profession, added that:

> barristers in civil or criminal cases also feel dual roles for judges lower the chance of a successful appeal because of a lack of new viewpoints.[29]

Ironically, but probably coincidentally, the issue arose very soon afterwards, in stark form, when Hong Kong's newly appointed Chief Justice, Geoffrey Ma, declared that he would not sit on appeals from the Court of Appeal in respect of cases on which his wife (a Court of Appeal judge)[30] had sat.[31]

6.1.3 The Chief Judge of the High Court

Under the Basic Law, the Chief Judge of the High Court is required to be a Chinese citizen permanently resident in Hong Kong with no right of abode in any foreign country.[32] He is subject to the same appointment and removal procedures as the Chief Justice.[33] The Chief Judge is the President of the Court of Appeal and is responsible for the administration of the High Court (which includes the Court of Appeal and the Court of First Instance). The Chief Judge is responsible for the:

---

26. The three were Justice Robert Tang Kwok-ching J (now PJ), Justice Frank Stock, and Justice Michael Hartmann. By the time of publication, it is likely that Justice Tang will again be NPJ, to be replaced as permanent judge by Andrew Cheung CJHC.
27. This is prohibited under s 16(8) HKCFAO.
28. 'Lawmakers Voice Doubts over Dual Role for Judges', *South China Morning Post* (Hong Kong, 5 May 2010).
29. 'Court Picks "Hit Confidence"' *The Standard* (Hong Kong, 5 May 2010).
30. Maria Yuen J.
31. This had the "interesting" result that Ma CJ was unable to sit in the politically important CFA case of *FG Hemisphere v DR Congo* in which a majority of CFA judges endorsed the PRC government's position on sovereign immunity (see Chapter 4).
32. Article 90.
33. See 7.1.

efficient utilisation of judicial resources and court time, and for advising the Chief Justice on matters of policy concerning the operation and development of the High Court.[34]

The two leading contenders for the Chief Judge's position, on the elevation of current CJ, Geoffrey Ma, to the post of Chief Justice, appeared to be Johnson Lam J and e Joseph Fok J. In the event, somewhat surprisingly, the post of Chief Judge went to Andrew Cheung J.[35]

6.1.4 Other Hong Kong judges

In addition to the senior judiciary described above, there are approximately 180 other professional judges, encompassing High Court judges, District Court judges and Magistrates. While there remains a high proportion of non-Chinese amongst these ranks the situation is gradually changing and most new appointments are "local". Such change is inevitable with the increasing use of Chinese in the courts, since few non-locals could conduct a trial in Chinese. Over 75% of cases in Magistrates' Courts are now held in Chinese so, despite Chief Justice Li's commitment to maintain and improve English standards amongst Hong Kong lawyers and judges, the need for more Chinese-speaking judges is clear. A further factor is economic, since successful barristers (from whom the judiciary are largely recruited) may not wish to join the judiciary where this would mean a reduction in remuneration. Since high earnings at the Hong Kong Bar tend to require Chinese language skills, there may be some difficulty in attracting the best Chinese candidates when career prospects at the Bar are good.

6.2 The appointment and removal of judges in Hong Kong

The appointment and removal of members of the judiciary will follow broadly the same system as operated prior to 1997. Those already serving as judges prior to 1997 are permitted, under the Basic Law,[36] to remain in office on terms no less favourable.

Judges of the Hong Kong courts are appointed by the Chief Executive on the recommendation of an *independent commission* composed of local judges, persons from the legal profession and eminent persons from other sectors. The commission consists of three judges (including the Chief Justice); three lawyers (including the Secretary for Justice) and three lay persons unconnected with legal practice. The procedure for appointment is prescribed in the Basic Law.[37] As Chief Justice, Geoffrey Ma, has said:[38]

---
34. Hong Kong Judiciary Annual Report 2008 at 85.
35. In the case of Joseph Fok a consideration may have been his imminent elevation to the CFA.
36. Article 93.
37. Article 88.
38. Chief Justice's speech at Ceremonial Opening of the Legal Year 2014.

Judges are not appointed by the Chief Justice or even by a group of judges. Candidates are considered for appointment by a statutory body known as the Judicial Officers Recommendation Commission set up under the Basic Law: this body's function is to make recommendations to the Chief Executive regarding the appointment of judges at all levels, including the Chief Justice . . . Members of the Commission . . . declare that they will 'freely and without fear or favour, affection or ill-will' give their advice to the Chief Executive.[39]

Almost all new appointments (except to the CFA) are now "local", though the Basic Law permits recruitment from other common law jurisdictions.[40]

In order to ensure the independence of the judges from political, or other social pressure (guaranteed under the Basic Law),[41] judicial tenure of office is largely secure.[42] Judges may only be removed on the grounds of inability to discharge their duties or misbehaviour.[43] The removal shall be by the Chief Executive on the basis of recommendations of a tribunal specially appointed by the Chief Justice. The tribunal shall consist of not fewer than three local judges. The Chief Justice himself can only be removed (again for inability or misbehaviour) by a tribunal appointed by the Chief Executive as provided for in the Basic Law.[44] The tribunal shall consist of at least five local judges. Further security is given to the judges by their immunity from legal action in relation to the performance of their duties.[45] To ensure judicial independence from "influence" from previous judicial colleagues now in legal practice, all judges in the District Courts and above must undertake not to return to legal practice after completing their judicial term of office.

6.3 The retirement of judges

The "normal retirement age" for the Chief Justice, permanent Court of Final Appeal (CFA) judges, High Court[46] and District Court judges is 65.[47] As stated above, the term of office of the Chief Justice and CFA permanent judges may be extended, for a maximum of six years, by the Chief Executive (on advice).[48] In the unlikely (but permissible) event of a Chief Justice or CFA permanent judge being appointed above

---

39. LegCo is empowered to endorse the appointment and removal of CFA judges and the Chief Judge of the High Court (Article 73(7), Basic Law). This "political" power appears not to have been used in practice.
40. Article 92.
41. Article 85.
42. Security of tenure is invaluable in assuring judicial independence. Even in the United States where judicial appointments are "political" (Supreme Court Justices are nominated by the President) security of tenure has permitted appointees to "break ranks" and offer judgment at odds with the judge's supposed political views.
43. Article 89, Basic Law.
44. Ibid.
45. Article 85, Basic Law.
46. This includes High Court Registrars.
47. Pension Benefits (Judicial Officers) Ordinance (Cap 401), s 6(1).
48. Hong Kong Court of Final Appeal Ordinance (Cap 484), s 14(2)(a).

the age of 65, the appointment shall be for three years and may be extended (by the Chief Executive on advice) for one more three-year period only.[49]

There is no retirement age for a non-permanent CFA judge[50] but they are appointed for only three years at a time (renewable by the Chief Executive on the advice of the Chief Justice).[51]

The retirement age for other judicial officers is 60 years.[52] There is provision for extension for a maximum period of five years[53] and, naturally, for a limited extension for judicial officers in order to deliver judgment in a case which goes beyond the judge's retirement age.[54]

6.4 The background of the Hong Kong judiciary

While the demography of the Hong Kong judges, post-1997, is changing, such change is relatively slow given judicial security of tenure and the low turnover of judges.

There are approximately 170 judges. Of these, over 130 are male. This largely reflects the predominance of males at the Hong Kong Bar, from which most judges are recruited.

The overwhelming majority of judges are in the age range 40–59 with well over half above 50 years of age.

Approximately 100 (rather more than half) of the judges are bilingual, in the sense of being able to conduct court proceedings in Chinese as well as English. With the increasing use of Chinese in the Hong Kong courts, it is regarded as a priority to increase the number of bilingual judges. It is clear that lower down the court hierarchy, bilingualism is greater. Over 75% of Magistrates, for example, are bilingual. This means that, as such judges are promoted and more senior judges retire, the percentage of bilingual judges is almost certain to rise.

Most judges in Hong Kong are recruited from the ranks of senior barristers, though some judicial appointments, usually at the lower level, are from amongst solicitors. The almost exclusive recruitment of lawyers as judges is the norm in common law systems but differs from the system in many civil law countries where law graduates choose a career path either as a judge or as a lawyer. The result is that judges in Hong Kong are appointed with no specific judicial training. Training of judges on and after appointment is therefore a priority. The main role of providing judicial training is fulfilled by the Judicial Studies Board (JSB) which was set up in 1988. The JSB comprises judicial representatives from all the courts, appointed by the Chief Justice, as well as the Judiciary Administrator and representatives from the

---

49. Ibid s 14(2)(b).
50. Ibid s 14(3).
51. Ibid s 14(4).
52. Pension Benefits (Judicial Officers) Ordinance, s 6(1).
53. Ibid s 6(3).
54. Ibid s 6(4).

Hong Kong Bar Association, the Law Society of Hong Kong and the Hong Kong law schools.

The terms of reference of the JSB include devising programmes for new judicial appointees; advising the Chief Justice as to matching resources to demand in making judicial appointments; and running training programmes for "Judges and Judicial Officers" (JJOs). Key areas of training are, of course, sentencing guidance and judgment principles. The JSB also sponsors some JJOs to attend part-time courses leading to the award of higher degrees in law. Language training is also a key element of the JSB's role.

As already mentioned, the most senior judges tend to have an English law background, having spent at least part of their academic study period at university and/or the Bar in England.[55] Even those who have been trained exclusively in Hong Kong have been taught almost exclusively in English in a legal educational environment dominated by English law-derived sources.[56] Even as that environment changes over time it will take longer for such changes to be felt amongst first, senior lawyers and, thereafter, the judiciary which recruits almost entirely from the ranks of such lawyers.

6.5 The importance of "the judge"

In all common law systems (and doubtless in many civil law systems) the role of "the judge" rather than mere "judging" is crucial in shaping the development of the law. In Hong Kong, with its tension between the "one country" approach and that of "two systems", a strong, courageous and impartial judiciary is even more crucial to preserve Hong Kong's common law heritage and judicial independence in the face of opposition from those (within and without Hong Kong) who, far from supporting judicial independence, see it as an obstruction to "executive-led" government; to be, at best, reluctantly tolerated.

6.5.1 Judicial "creativity"

Those coming to law (or at least the common law) for the first time are often surprised at the importance of the judge himself in the determination of a case. The "stranger" may believe that all laws are to be found in legal codes which are clear and must simply be applied. Cases would then represent the mere "application" of these codes to the facts of a case to produce a predictable, "correct" outcome. Such an approach may more closely approximate to "codified" civil law jurisdictions but

---

55. Described as "in some sense more English than the English" (see JYS Cheng (ed), *The Other Hong Kong Report* [Chinese University Press 1998] 17).
56. For example, Justice Patrick Chan, previously PJ and now NPJ of the CFA, is an alumnus of the University of Hong Kong as is current Chief Judge of the High Court, Andrew Cheung (additionally educated at Harvard).

is certainly far from the common law truth. Sociologist Max Weber posited an ideal of "rational" law; a bureaucratic system in which an *impartial*, professional arbiter merely "finds and applies" the relevant rules in a totally "disinterested" manner. In a "rational" system, outcomes are predictable and discretion is anathema. Such a view may be stated, formulaically, as:

Facts × Principle = Decision

Fascinated by the relationship between "rational" legal systems and the development of industrial capitalism, Weber initially assumed that there would be a close nexus between rational law and the development of capitalism. Having studied the English legal system, however (having been brought up in Western Europe's civil law tradition) he observed that the world's (then) most advanced industrial nation had a very "non-rational" system, with its highly "interested" magistrates and its "amateur" juries. He abandoned his initial hypothesis in the face of the "England problem"!

It became clear to Weber, as it now is to us, that the common law system allows significant scope for discretion and "choice". As we have already seen,[57] judges are able to be more than mere "finders and appliers" of existing rules and their role involves considerable scope for "creativity". Even accepting the "impartial" criterion,[58] we can see that not *all* facts, from the hundreds existing in any legal dispute, are to be considered "relevant". It is the judge who, to a large extent, determines the *relevance* of facts. Moreover, it is only the "relevant" or "appropriate" legal *principle* which is to be applied and the issue of relevance, again, leaves the judge significant choice. Nor is the scope for choice limited to case law and the doctrine of precedent. Statutory law, too, is less "black and white" than might at first appear and it is the judge who has the task of "interpreting" a statute. If two benches of the Judicial Committee of the House of Lords in England can disagree (within a year!) as to the interpretation of the Criminal Attempts Act 1981,[59] it can be seen that codified law does not necessarily produce certainty.[60]

We may, therefore, agree with the words of Lord Radcliffe who said:

> The legal answer, you may say, is written out in close print or even in archaic language on some distant tablet . . . the judge will read it off and announce to you what is there . . .

---

57. See Chapters 2, 4, and 5.
58. Most common law judges stress the importance of this criterion above all others. It is of some historical interest that juries in England (the "parent" of the common law) were once selected *precisely because of* their knowledge of the accused (and that, even until comparatively recently, English Magistrates were powerful local figures likely to have an "interest" in the outcome of criminal trials).
59. See discussion of *Anderton v Ryan* and *R v Shivpuri* at 5.6.
60. In interpreting the United States Constitution at different times, the Supreme Court has held both constitutional *and* unconstitutional slavery and capital punishment.

> But the essence of that curious activity, the judicial decision, does not consist in that. The law has to be interpreted before it can be applied and interpretation is a creative activity . . .
>
> . . . there was never a more sterile controversy than that upon the question whether a judge makes law. Of course he does. How can he help it? The legislature and the judicial process respectively are two complementary sources of law-making.[61]

The declaratory theory of the common law, based on the proposition that judges do not make the law but merely "discover" it by correctly applying precedents or correctly interpreting legislative rules is now regarded, in England at least, as a myth. In *Kleinwort Benson Ltd v Lincoln City County Council*,[62] Lord Browne-Wilkinson emphatically stated:

> The theoretical position has been that judges do not make or change law: they discover and declare the law which is throughout the same. According to this theory, when an earlier decision is overruled the law is not changed: its true nature is disclosed, having existed in that form all along. This theoretical position is, as Lord Reid said,[63] a fairy tale in which no one any longer believes. In truth, judges make and change the law. The whole of the common law is judge-made and only by judicial change in the law is the common law kept relevant in a changing world. But while the underlying myth has been rejected, its progeny—the retrospective effect of a change made by judicial decision—remains.[64]

One consequence of the abandonment of the declaratory theory is the acceptance of the notion that there is no "right" decision in a case and that judges should seek the "best" solution permitted by the available precedents. The most extreme articulation of this approach is expressed by Schur[65] who writes:

> Judicial precedent and legal doctrine can be found or developed to support almost any outcome. The real decision is made first—on the judge's conceptions of justice, determined partly by his predilections, personal background and so forth—and *then* it is 'rationalized' in the written opinion.[66]

That the declaratory theory was permitted to remain "on the books" for so long, despite its obviously "fictional" character was partly because of its usefulness in

---

61. Lord Radcliffe, *Not in Feather Beds: Some Collected Papers* (Hamish Hamilton London 1968), 213–215.
62. [1998] 4 All ER 513.
63. See Lord Reid, 'The Judge as Law Maker' (1972) 12 JSPTL 22.
64. Ibid 518. It was Lord Browne-Wilkinson's opposition to retrospectiveness that caused him to dissent from the majority and uphold the previous law, even though he thought it should be changed!
65. E Schur, *Law and Society: A Sociological View* (Random House New York 1968).
66. Ibid 43. It should be noted that spirited opposition to this approach has been made by eminent academic, Ronald Dworkin, who believes that there is, invariably a "right" answer for which judges should strive, not least to ensure the certainty; supposedly precedent's great gift: R Dworkin, *Law's Empire* (Fontana London 1986).

permitting judicial "retrospectiveness" (while legislative retrospectiveness is frowned upon or even outlawed). The abandonment of the declaratory theory in England, via the House of Lords decision in *Kleinwort Benson*[67] is not binding in Hong Kong since the case is post-1997. Moreover, even having overturned the theory, the House of Lords in *Kleinwort Benson* preserved the retrospective nature of judicial (case law) decisions.[68] This has practical implications for Hong Kong. The retrospective effect of case law, arguably derived from the declaratory theory, produces an obvious benefit for Hong Kong in that it permits the Hong Kong courts to "develop" the common law remaining in place post-1997. This may seem obvious, given Hong Kong's high measure of judicial autonomy and its right of "final adjudication" under the Basic Law. However, the Basic Law does not expressly provide for amendments to the "laws previously in force" via the Hong Kong courts. Such laws can be changed by local legislation and/or by a declaration that they conflict with the Basic Law. A "declaratory" approach would enable, for example, the CFA to develop Hong Kong's common law by "explaining" what it has always been, thereby avoiding the need for judicial "amendment". The problem with this approach (an insuperable political problem!) is that it would also give scope (were the Hong Kong courts to retain the declaratory view) for post-1997 *English* judicial decisions to be viewed as merely "explaining" what the law was in 1997 and which *prima facie* would now be the law in Hong Kong![69]

In pragmatic, practical and politically realistic fashion, the Hong Kong courts have adopted the common sense view that they may, indeed, by themselves develop Hong Kong's common law and have eschewed any notion of the English courts making law for Hong Kong post-1997. Since the English courts have found no difficulty in reconciling the abandonment of the declaratory theory with the continuance of the retrospective nature of legal judgments, there is no reason why the Hong Kong courts cannot make a similar reconciliation of the two principles.

6.5.2 The potential for "judicial creativity" in Hong Kong

The formal abolition of the declaratory theory in England merely confirmed what had long been recognised: that judges in common law systems do "create" law as well as applying it. This will obviously be the case where a novel point of law arises which has not been the subject of legislation or previous judicial decision. Even outside the area of novel decisions, however, judges will adapt and amend existing rules. This they may do in various ways. Judges in higher courts may *overrule* the precedents of lower courts. The new ruling will make new (albeit retrospective) law. Judges may also be free, in Hong Kong and elsewhere in the common law world, to overrule judgments of previous courts of equal status. This is less common and

---

67. [1998] 3 WLR 1095, [1999] 2 AC 349 and see Chapter 5.
68. Which Lord Browne-Wilkinson deplored.
69. Unless contrary to the Basic Law or overturned by local Hong Kong legislation.

usually may only operate in limited circumstances. The English House of Lords,[70] for example, could (since the 1966 "Practice Statement")[71] depart from its own previous precedents where it appeared right to do so but only exceptionally and with some reluctance, bearing in mind the desirability of certainty in the law. In other words, legal advisers will inform their clients as to their understanding of the law as it stands based on existing rules. If these rules were to be constantly amended, great uncertainty (and arguably injustice) would result.[72] A broadly similar approach, in which the power to depart from its previous precedents would be used only "sparingly", has been adopted by Hong Kong's Court of Final Appeal.[73]

Judges in lower courts, unable to overrule the precedents of higher courts which they now feel to be outdated or inappropriate, may "distinguish" them. Distinguishing involves finding a material point which is different in the previous case, such that it does not have to be followed. Distinguishing should always be on a genuine legal point of difference rather than slight factual differences, since otherwise courts would always be free to ignore previous precedents on frivolous grounds.

The practical operation of precedent has been considered in more detail in Chapter 5. This made clear that the wealth of precedents from which to choose and the capacity to "distinguish" gives judges, in practice, great flexibility in forming their judgments. In this context we talk of judges being "creative" in reaching judgments which accord with their own idea of a "just" solution. Lord Denning[74] has stated:

> [Most judges,] whilst ready to applaud the doctrine of precedent when it leads to a just and fair result . . . become restless under it when they are compelled by it to do what is unjust or unfair. This restlessness leads them to various expedients to get round a previous authority.[75]

A Hong Kong judge is in the position of being able, in the absence of a binding precedent, to *refer to* all common law precedents with a view to choosing the one he feels most suitable.[76] Once he has referred to them, of course, he is free to reject them all if he wishes.

As well as being able to be creative in the selection of judicial precedents, a judge may exercise considerable flexibility in the interpretation of statutes. So, while it may be that the Hong Kong judges must follow legislation, and that legislation

---

70. Replaced by the "Supreme Court" from 2009.
71. See Chapter 5.
72. This is the main reason for the opposition, from Lord Browne-Wilkinson and others, to the retrospective effect of judicial overruling. Their alternative is to change the law if it appears wrong but only "prospectively" (as to the future).
73. See *A Solicitor v Law Society of Hong Kong* [2008] 2 HKC 1 per Li CJ.
74. Former English "Master of the Rolls" (ie, head of the Civil Division of the Court of Appeal).
75. Lord Denning, *The Discipline of Law* (Butterworths London 1979) 285.
76. Article 84, Basic Law.

takes precedence over judicial decisions, the judges have the last word as regards determining the *real meaning* of legislation (except in relation to the Basic Law).[77]

6.5.3 The effect of judicial background on judgments

Having determined that judges can and do make law, an important question is whether their law-making is affected by their "background". Significant studies have been made in the United States by the so-called "legal realist" school[78] on the issue of whether the socio-politico-economic background of the judge affects his judgments. These studies have focused particularly on the Supreme Court and have led to the conclusion by some realists that a detailed study of the background of a court would have greater potential for predicting that court's decision than a detailed study of the judicial precedents and legislation involved.[79] In a well-known English work by Professor J A G Griffith,[80] the author argues that the English judiciary is very homogeneous (like-minded) in being recruited from the male-dominated Bar; being middle-aged or above; being naturally conservative and so on. He argues that in, a number of landmark cases, those characteristics have affected the way the judges have reached their decisions.

While numerous studies have been made of the effect of "judicial background" on judgments in the United States (at least at the appellate level),[81] there is little research on the effect of judicial background on the outcome of cases in Hong Kong, where it could be argued that there is a similar homogeneousness to that described by Griffith, except in relation to ethnicity.

In one respect at least, though, it seems that Hong Kong's judicial background is affecting legal development. This is in relation to the continuing emphasis on recourse to English precedents[82] as opposed to those from other common law jurisdictions.[83] It seems very likely that this has much to do with the educational and professional background of many of the Hong Kong judges, especially at the most senior level.[84]

---

77. The ultimate responsibility for interpreting the Basic Law, of course, resides with the Standing Committee of the NPC.
78. In reality the "School" was far from homogeneous and contained two identifiably different sub-groups ("rule sceptics" and "fact sceptics").
79. This view is associated with the "rule sceptics" who are criticised for focusing on appellate courts, where the "big decisions" are made, at the expense of trial courts, where the bulk of cases are heard.
80. JAG Griffith, *The Politics of the Judiciary* (Fontana/Collins London 1979).
81. Specific focus on the judicial background and its effect on judgments, derives from a "branch" of the realist movement sometimes described as "judicial behaviouralism": see R Cotterrell, *The Sociology of Law: An Introduction* (2nd edn, Oxford University Press 2005), 230–232.
82. See Chapter 2.
83. Even though their "status" is now the same: Article 84 Basic Law.
84. See 6.4. Of course the fact that the Hong Kong courts continue to deal with a common law still dominated by English precedents is likely to be at least as great a reason.

There remains significant scope for "realist" study of the Hong Kong judiciary; in particular of landmark judgments in the Court of Final Appeal (CFA) and the impact of the Non-Permanent Judges (especially from overseas) etc. The beginnings of a "realist" approach can be seen in the statistical studies of the CFA by Professor Simon Young of the University of Hong Kong.[85] These indicate, for example, a more "rebellious" propensity for dissent on the part of Bokhary (then PJ now NPJ) especially in the area of human rights.

Some commentators have also commented on the "more conservative" approach to human rights of (current) CJ, Geoffrey Ma, as opposed to that of previous CJ, Andrew Li. Gittings, for example, draws attention to two cases involving the Falun Gong (banned in mainland China but legal in Hong Kong) in which then Chief Judge Ma's Court of Appeal delivered conservative judgments after serious "procrastination" subsequently overturned by the CFA.[86]

One tangential issue with an arguably "realist" link involves the conviction rate in Hong Kong criminal courts, brought into focus by a controversial introduction to Archbold Hong Kong 2010 by general editor Clive Grossman SC. As discussed in Chapter 3, Grossman compared conviction rates (unfavourably) with those obtaining in North Korea (not known for an advanced, liberal criminal justice system!). He described a situation in which conviction rates are 94.8% in the Court of First Instance (CFI) and 92.6% in the District Court. While Grossman's words[87] have aroused both horror and criticism,[88] and have largely been discounted by more recent, and detailed, statistical information, the view is held, by some at the Bar, that judges with a "public prosecution" background are more "pro-prosecution" than those from a "mixed" career at the private bar. Were this significant, however, one would expect a higher conviction rate in Divisional Court (with no juries) than in the Court of First Instance. Statistics, nevertheless, indicate that, in practice, there is little difference in the rates.[89]

In a far more important "realist" context, however, the homogeneousness of Hong Kong's judges has had a positive impact. Steeped in the common law tradition as they are, Hong Kong judges are a crucial bulwark for the preservation of judicial autonomy and the separation of powers in the developing PRC/Hong Kong SAR relationship under "one country, two systems".

---

85. See Young and Ghai (n 17).
86. See D Gittings, 'Hong Kong's Courts Are Learning to Live with China' (2010) 19 *Hong Kong Journal* and D Gittings, 'Beijing's Nudge' *South China Morning Post* (Hong Kong, 26 July 2010).
87. Grossman has admitted the desire to "start a debate" since his long experience at the criminal bar has led him to conclude that those arrested "are almost certain to face imprisonment".
88. Hong Kong's Chief Justice, Andrew Li, described Grossman's words as "totally unjustified and wholly misconceived". Others drew attention to the fact that Grossman had not taken into account guilty pleas and argued that the figures merely indicated the effective "screening" of prosecutions by the Department of Justice.
89. See Judiciary Annual Reports 2010–2013. In most years, conviction rates have been at least as high in the CFI (where there are juries) than the District Court where there are not. This is unsurprising given that the judge's directions to the jury remain crucial (see also Chapter 8).

6.6 Hong Kong's judges and judicial autonomy

Article 85 of the Basic Law asserts that:

> The courts of the HKSAR shall exercise judicial power independently, free from any interference.

In this final section of the chapter we shall consider the extent to which this crucial requirement of judicial independence has been observed, post-1997.

6.6.1 Judicial autonomy and separation of powers

Most common law systems see the "separation of powers" as an important method of limiting the excessive use of power. The separation is along the lines of the legislature, which creates law; the executive, which puts the laws into operation; and the judiciary, which has the duty to interpret the law and, in some cases, determine whether it complies with any constitutional requirements. Different common law states deal differently with separation of powers but the ideal in each is that there should be a system of "checks and balances". Further discussion of these "checks and balances" will be attempted in the subsequent chapter comparing the Hong Kong SAR and PRC systems.[90] Since the concept of a judiciary free of political interference is the antithesis of the situation in the rest of China, it is important to consider the extent to which judicial autonomy and independence have been preserved in Hong Kong, in the face of an "executive-led" Hong Kong government and pressure from Hong Kong's "Big Brother".

That Hong Kong's governance today remains, as it was in colonial times, "executive-led" is generally accepted. Commentators such as Gittings have posited a separation of powers for Hong Kong, focusing on limits imposed on the Executive by LegCo and the courts. As regards LegCo restraints it must be recognised that, in terms of producing and implementing legislation, the rules are so formed as to ensure that the Chief Executive can normally "get his own way", via a built-in majority of supporters in LegCo. In addition to those pro-government LegCo members elected by popular franchise, the government's domination of LegCo is guaranteed by members elected by "small circle" functional constituencies, some of which have very few voters and most of whom support the government in return for promised benefits to their "members". Most "government bills", therefore, are ultimately passed, though often with amendment. Only where government-friendly members "break ranks" can a government bill be defeated.[91] Moreover, as we saw in Chapter 4, the "private member's bill", originating outside the Executive Committee (ExCo), is now almost entirely defunct.

---

90. See Chapter 11.
91. The best-known example was the defeated Article 23 legislation which was withdrawn only after 500,000 Hong Kong people took to the streets in protest.

The courts in Hong Kong do have a quasi "Supreme Court" role with the right to determine whether a government bill is contrary to the Basic Law, and thereby unconstitutional. However, on the rare occasion that it has been determined by the Court of Final Appeal (CFA) that legislation is contrary to the Basic Law and therefore invalid, the government has been able to "rectify" the CFA's intervention by recourse to a (pro-government) "interpretation" by the Standing Committee of the National People's Congress. Crucially, therefore, the CFA's role in interpreting the Basic Law, and determining "constitutionality, is circumscribed. As Gittings states:

> under any system of separation of powers, interpretation of laws should be a matter for the courts alone. Chan describes this as 'the very root of the common law system'. But Article 158 of the Hong Kong Basic Law modifies this common law position to the extent that the power to interpret the Hong Kong Basic Law is split between the National People's Congress Standing Committee and the Hong Kong courts, *with the former enjoying the ultimate power of interpretation.*[92] [emphasis added]

Further, the Hong Kong courts have had their previous power to declare (prior) legislation invalid if inconsistent with the Bill of Rights Ordinance (BORO)[93] removed.[94]

In so far, therefore, as a separation of powers may be posited for Hong Kong, it is a very circumscribed one. This is not to say, however, that the role of the courts in curbing the power of the Executive (and preserving their own independence) has been insignificant; far from it. The Hong Kong courts, from 1997, have steadfastly preserved their (almost untrammelled) right to adjudicate finally in Hong Kong and have striven to maintain a balance between the rights of the individual and the government. A major plank in the edifice has been the use of "judicial review" a device by which actions of government may be challenged in the courts where they involve the improper or excessive use of power or discretion or where the rules of "natural justice" have been infringed.

That the Hong Kong judges *should* be politically neutral is considered axiomatic by most Hong Kong people. To that end the "Guide to Judicial Conduct" issued by the Chief Justice in 2004 requires that judges refrain from membership in or association with political organisations or activities.[95] The apolitical position of the Hong Kong judges has sometimes been problematic. Judge Pang, as a judge and Chairman of the Electoral Affairs Commission (EAC), until 2009, was accused of

---
92. D Gittings, *Introduction to the Hong Kong Basic Law* (Hong Kong University Press 2013) 158.
93. Cap 383.
94. The special status of BORO, whereby prior inconsistent legislation would be declared invalid, was found to be inconsistent with the Basic Law and the BORO sections conferring such status were "not adopted" as Hong Kong laws in force post-1997.
95. It remains unclear whether lawyers acting as *part-time* judges need similarly refrain (see Editorial, 'Confidence in Judiciary Is Key to Rule of Law' *South China Morning Post* [Hong Kong, 1 June 2006]).

making anti-democratic decisions in his EAC role which called into question his political neutrality.[96] If there was ever any doubt that the EAC plays a political role this has disappeared following the clearly "influenced" decisions to bar "allegedly" pro-independence candidates from the 2016 LegCo elections by EAC officers.

6.6.2 Threats to judicial autonomy

Article 85 of the Basic Law emphasises the principle of judicial autonomy in stating that:

> The courts of the Hong Kong SAR shall exercise judicial power independently, free from any interference. Members of the judiciary shall be immune from legal action in the performance of their judicial functions.

No Article in the Basic Law is more important in ensuring Hong Kong's promised high degree of autonomy and, given the immense difference from the position obtaining in the rest of the PRC (where judges are subservient to the will of the Communist Party), in affirming "one country, two systems". Equally, however, given the huge difference, no Article is so maligned and so constantly under attack by the "Beijing side". Almost from the first, post-1997, the independence of Hong Kong's judges has been assailed, both from within and without Hong Kong. The Hong Kong government's easy recourse to seeking an NPC Standing Committee (re-) interpretation of Articles 22 and 24, given a Court of Final Appeal judgment with which the government disagreed, emphasised the low esteem in which Tung Chee Hwa's government (including its Secretary for Justice) held judicial independence.

It is to the great credit of Hong Kong's judges, and in particular its two post-1997 Chief Justices, that judicial independence has been steadfastly defended. It has been widely asserted (in a story originating with "Wikileaks" it must be admitted) that after the first NPCSC "Interpretation" (following the "right of abode" judgments of the Court of Final Appeal) *all* the members of the CFA considered resigning en bloc. It is further asserted that they decided not to do so because of fear of what might come next (replacement by less experienced, less able and perhaps, given their appointment by a Chief Executive unsympathetic to judicial autonomy (albeit acting on advice) more politically malleable judges). The *South China Morning Post* seems to have accepted that the "Wikileaks" story was probably true, stating, in an editorial,[97] that:

> If true, this means that our city was on the brink of a much deeper crisis than had been appreciated.

---

96. Judge Pang is considered in Chapter 10 in respect of his competence and the suggestion that his multiple duties had affected same.
97. Editorial, 'Judicial Crisis Must Not Happen Again' *South China Morning Post* (Hong Kong, 10 September 2011).

> ... Thankfully, Hong Kong overcame the crisis and moved on. But that would have been much more difficult to achieve if the top five judges had all resigned. The impact would have been devastating. It is to their credit if, as the US cable stated, they ultimately decided not to resign because they considered this to be in Hong Kong's best interests.
>
> The judges concerned went on to apply Beijing's interpretation of the Basic Law. Since then, they and their fellow judges have continued to rule on sensitive cases in accordance with established legal principles. The government has won some and lost some. Confidence in the rule of law has returned.
>
> ... Lessons should be learned from the events of 1999 and every effort made to ensure a crisis of that kind never occurs again.

Alas the "lessons" alluded to have *not* been learned (or have wilfully been ignored) in some quarters. Well-publicised criticism of the judiciary's "failure to understand 'one country, two systems'" by Elsie Leung, Secretary for Justice at the time of the first "interpretation" and now in a more suited role as Deputy Director of the Committee for the Basic Law,[98] bolsters the attacks on judicial independence, as do her ready acceptance of "interpretations" as a cure-all for any difficult socio-political problems. A new "right of abode" scenario involved the influx of pregnant mainland mothers-to-be, attracted by the prospect of conferring Hong Kong right of abode on their offspring. The problem was dealt with effectively by administrative action (improved border screening, etc) but not before Leung had called for yet another "interpretation" of the Basic Law by the NPCSC (despite the unambiguous wording of Article 24(2)(1) on the issue). Suzanne Pepper has summarised the situation very well. She states:

> Leung ... is from a traditional loyalist family, was a founding member of the main pro-Beijing political party in the early 1990s, has remained true to the cause, and controversies about her pro-Beijing bias have continued throughout. Now she is at the centre of another. This latest began with a talk on "Legal Challenges Since Reunification" that she gave at Hong Kong's College of Technology on October 6.
>
> The chief talking point ever since has been her main argument, namely, that Hong Kong judges don't understand the Basic Law or at least Hong Kong's relationship to the central government as spelled out therein. At issue is their disagreement over Beijing's authority to interpret the Basic Law and local judgments. This specific controversy dates back to 1999, when all the judges (of the CFA) considered resigning in protest due to Beijing's decision that overturned one of their judgments. The issue has been revived again by the recommendation she and others have made concerning the Basic Law's Article 24 on birthrights. She argues that the best way to solve the problem of expectant mainland women coming to Hong Kong to give birth is to close the loophole in Article 24 by sending it to Beijing for repairs. This idea flies in the face of what Hong Kong values most, namely, an independent judiciary insulated from Beijing's political interference.

---

98. See J Tam, 'Chief Secretary Carrie Lam Defends Hong Kong's Judicial Independence' *South China Morning Post* (Hong Kong, 10 August 2012).

Moreover, while distancing herself from Leung's criticism of the judges, Chief Secretary for Administration, Carrie Lam, also suggested that an NPCSC interpretation was the "most secure" solution to curbing the influx of mainland mothers.[99]

Ms Leung's criticism of the judges has been widely condemned. Chinese University academic Ma Ngok said:

> What Ms Leung said was shocking. Someone who has been the Secretary for Justice should not have made such a comment on our judicial system. She was putting pressure on our judges.[100]

Justice Bokhary was also, by implication, critical of Leung's statements, saying:

> seeking interpretations or reinterpretations outside the judicial system adversely affects the institutional autonomy, which is an aspect of judicial independence.
> . . .
> It is one thing to say that the Court has made a wrong decision. Anyone is free to say that. But if you say that the Court doesn't understand the relationship between Beijing and Hong Kong, then that sounds like calling for reinterpretation. If this storm breaks it will be of unprecedented ferocity . . . I think it would be more than we have ever experienced in terms of a blow against the rule of law."[101]

Most alarming of the assaults on Hong Kong's judicial independence was the "White Paper" issued by the State Council of the PRC,[102] emphasising the PRC view of "one country, two systems" and describing judges as "administrators", required to be patriotic and "love the motherland" (despite the fact that a significant number of them are not ethnically Chinese!). The White Paper was widely condemned in Hong Kong, especially in legal circles. Unsurprisingly, the Hong Kong Bar criticised the document but, more surprising, Hong Kong's normally conservative solicitors came out in numbers against the Paper. Law Society President, Ambrose Lam, having welcomed the document, was swiftly the victim of a successful "no confidence" vote and resigned.[103] Large numbers of lawyers joined a dignified "silent march" in protest. Previous Chief Justice, Andrew Li, expressed his concern stating that judges should not be required to be "patriotic";[104] while Chief Justice Ma admirably commented, in a conference speech, that judges would continue to act "only on the basis

---

99. Ibid.
100. Ibid.
101. 'Interview with the Honourable Mr Justice Kemal Bokhary', *Hong Kong Student Law Gazette* (Spring 2013). There is some irony in that the "Wikileaks" documents relating to the consideration of resignation by the CFA alludes to Bokhary J's description of Leung as an "unsung hero" in averting even greater interference in Hong Kong's judicial affairs by Beijing officials (see M Benitez, 'Abode Judges Nearly Quit' *The Standard* [Hong Kong, 8 September 2011]).
102. State Council of the Central Government (White Paper), *The Practice of the 'One Country, Two Systems' Policy in the HKSAR* (issued 7 June 2014).
103. His successor, Steven Hung, wisely distanced himself from the debate on taking office, stating, "I am not keen on politics and have no expertise in constitutional law" (J Ng, 'New Law Society Chief Plans to Keep Low Profile' *South China Morning Post* [Hong Kong, 2 September 2014]).
104. 'Comment' *South China Morning Post*, 15 August 2014.

of the law and would not be swayed by any other factor."[105] Outgoing Chairman of the Hong Kong Bar Association, Paul Shieh, stated:[106]

> The sovereign state *should not* purport to impose any ambiguous *political requirements*, such as to be 'patriotic' or to 'safeguard the country's development interests' ... the White Paper sends a wrong message to the people of Hong Kong and the international community as to the role of the judiciary in Hong Kong.[107]

The "liberal" judicial voice is also seen, on occasion, to be under pressure. Bokhary PJ, the most liberal of the CFA judges, was not extended on reaching retirement age and, although he was appointed as a Non-Permanent Judge, it is rumoured that he is kept away from the most politically sensitive cases. Judge Kevin Zervos, formerly Director of Public Prosecutions, was asked by the Department of Justice to "recuse" himself from judging an alleged human trafficking case as he had previously adopted a "positive stance" in addressing exploitation.[108] One might have hoped that opposition to exploitation would be axiomatic.

Indeed, despite constant assaults on their independence and autonomy, from the "right of abode" cases onwards, the story of the Hong Kong judiciary has been one of steadfast resistance to attack, mixed with occasional tactical "retrenchment".[109] Ma CJ's robustness in rebutting an unnecessary[110] government request for "interpretation" of Article 158 by the NPCSC in *Vallejos*,[111] a different type of "right of abode" case involving a claim to permanent residence by a long-standing overseas domestic helper, bodes well for the future.

Statistics indicate that the Hong Kong courts have been extremely even-handed, with slightly over half of all cases waged against the Hong Kong government in the Court of Final Appeal (CFA), since 1997, being successful. This compares with a figure of only 36% of cases against the government being successful before the Privy Council (pre-1997).[112] That this is due to the good offices of the judges, rather than a cipher-like application of "rules" is made clear by a comparison with the

---

105. Conference, University of Cambridge Hong Kong and China Affairs Society, 16 August 2014. Sadly, Lord Neuberger, president of the United Kingdom Supreme Court and Hong Kong NPJ, saw nothing sinister in the labelling of Hong Kong's judges as "administrators" with a "political requirement to love the country". This displays a certain naiveté as to the PRC-Hong Kong relationship.
106. Speech of the Chairman of the Bar Association at the Opening of the Legal Year (12 January 2015).
107. Dean of law at the prestigious Tsinghua University, Wang Zhenmin, suggested that much of the White Paper dispute was the result of errors and omissions in the English version (J Ng, 'Beijing Scholar Admits Error and Omissions in White Paper on Hong Kong' *South China Morning Post* [Hong Kong, 28 August 2014]).
108. L Lam, 'I'm Not Biased: High Court Judge' *South China Morning Post* (Hong Kong, 14 November 2015).
109. "Interpretations" of the Basic Law, by the Standing Committee of the National People's Congress are considered in more detail in Chapter 2.
110. *Practically* "unnecessary" because Ma CJ's CFA reached a decision with which the government would be happy, without any need for referral.
111. *Vallejos Evangeline Banao v Commissioner of Registration & another* (2013) 16 HKCFAR 45.
112. Simon NM Young, 'Final Appeals Then and Now' in Young and Ghai (n 17).

PRC's "other" Special Administrative Region, Macau. In the 10 years since Macau's "resumption of sovereignty, in 1999, and its status as an "SAR", there have been 300 cases in Macau's TUI (Court of Final Appeal). All decisions involving the Macau government, bar 1, have been "pro-government" with only brief judgments and no dissent. Only 3 judges have been used and, despite the power to do so, the court has never appointed "overseas" judges.[113] This comparison illustrates the importance of Hong Kong's well-trained judiciary and the significant role played by "the judge", especially those in the highest courts. It also strongly implies that the presence of "overseas" Non-Permanent Judges in the CFA has been beneficial and speaks for the prescience in the decision of Chief Justices Li and Ma to make as much use of the overseas judges as possible.[114] Once again, however, eternal vigilance is required to preserve this very valuable link to the rest of the common law world, with "mainland scholars" calling for all judges in Hong Kong to be Chinese,[115] in blatant breach of Articles 82 and 92 of the Basic Law. Given that the clear words of Article 82, permitting the invitation of overseas "judges" [*sic*][116] to sit in the Court of Final Appeal, had been undermined by a Joint Liaison Group agreement to limit such invitation to no more than one per case, it is clear that the mainland scholars'/politicians' attacks on the use of overseas judges represent more than an isolated case.

The latest controversy over judicial independence centres on the allegedly "political" decision to seek a review in the Court of Appeal of the previously non-custodial sentences on "Occupy Central" legislators; with the clear aim of rendering them ineligible for LegCo office. While the inspiration for seeking the review was undoubtedly political,[117] critics unfairly targeted the Court of Appeal judges who eventually imposed custodial sentences. While that decision was unfortunate, and clearly furthered the government's interests, it is premature to label this a "political" judgment.[118]

The Court of Final Appeal, in overturning the Court of Appeal's decision,[119] was somewhat critical. Most emphatically, the CFA stated that:

---

113. See J Godinho and P Cardinal, 'Macau's Court of Final Appeal' in Young and Ghai (n 17).
114. There has been an overseas NPJ in over 90% of CFA cases. And see Editorial, 'Foreign Judges Have Crucial Role to Play' *South China Morning Post* (Hong Kong, 7 June 2017). In 2018 Hong Kong appointed its first two female overseas judges as Non-Permanent Justices of the CFA. They are Baroness Hale (UK) and Beverley McLachlin (Canada). Their appointment was confirmed in LegoCo with dissent only from abstainer, Junius Ho, a pro-Establishment figure best-known for his comments that those advocating independence for Hong Kong should be killed.
115. See, eg, Z Xiaoming (deputy head of CPG's Hong Kong and Macau Office), 'Enriching the Practice of One Country, Two Systems' (Essay: reported in *Wen Wei Po*, 22 November 2014).
116. The clear wording of Article 82 was undermined by "private" agreement at the Joint Liaison Group whereby only one overseas judge is permitted (see Chapter 3).
117. See chapter 13.
118. Though the intemperate language of Wally Yeung JA in the Court of Appeal does raise some concern.
119. [2018] HKCFA 4.

In these circumstances, the applications for review of the particular sentences imposed on the appellants should have been refused.[120]

This single statement, of course, is implicitly critical of both the Court of Appeal and the Secretary for Justice. Many of the Court of Appeal's criticisms of the initial sentencing judge were, indeed, rejected and the imposition of a "revised" approach to sentencing for public order offences should not have been applied retrospectively. Yet, while the "political" motivations of Rimsky Yuen SJ are undeniable, the optimistic view of the Court of Appeal's errors is that they resulted from incompetence rather than bias. Given the current make up of that court, this is, unfortunately, likely; and gives cause for serious concern over judicial quality.

---

120. Ibid at para 106.

7
The Legal Profession and Legal Education

Overview

When we talk of the "legal profession" in Hong Kong we think primarily of barristers and solicitors, though the expression also encompasses legal executives and paralegals.[1] Given the restrictions on admission to the legal profession in Hong Kong, and Hong Kong's internationalised operations, legal firms in Hong Kong may also employ professionals from other jurisdictions, especially from mainland China, as legal consultants.

In Hong Kong, as in England, there is a *split* profession. One branch comprises solicitors, who deal directly with clients, and the other consists of barristers, who operate as a "consultancy" branch and are engaged by solicitors on behalf of a client.[2] Barristers tend to practise primarily as court specialists and solicitors in out-of-court work, but this distinction is being eroded somewhat as "higher rights of audience" for solicitors are now granted where appropriate. Perhaps uniquely, and certainly unlike England, Hong Kong maintains a divided profession but little specialised legal education for barristers. All prospective barristers must attend the PCLL programme, which is designed essentially for solicitors, though it does provide some options, particularly in advocacy, geared primarily towards the needs of potential barristers.

There is a small population of lawyers in Hong Kong, relative to the size of the overall population and this means that the cost of legal services is high, particularly since most lawyers operate in the central business district (CBD) of Hong Kong Island where overhead costs are very high. The "clustering" of legal services also means that access to legal advice and assistance in more remote areas is difficult.

Much of the explanation for the small legal population lies in the various artificial barriers which are placed in the way of qualification in Hong Kong, notably the shortage of PCLL places at the relevant Hong Kong law schools.

---

1. There is also an important law-related occupation of "Notary Public" but such practitioners are recruited entirely from the ranks of experienced solicitors (there are approximately 400 solicitors who enjoy Notary status).
2. It is not permitted to practise as a solicitor *and* a barrister, though transfer from one branch of the profession to another is permitted.

7.1 Solicitors

If the legal profession is compared to the medical profession, solicitors may be seen as the "general practitioners" of the legal profession and barristers as the "consultants". Solicitors give legal advice on a wide range of issues; from the formalities necessary to buy and sell property, to the bringing of claims following a road traffic accident. Given the previously lucrative nature of conveyancing, most solicitors, especially those in small local firms, were happy to earn much of their money in this field and to leave court work to barristers. The decrease in conveyancing work post-1997 (and the *de facto* abolition of scale fees which decreased profitability)[3] led to greater calls for rights of audience[4] in courts from solicitors, the far more numerous branch of the profession. The partial success of such calls has meant that the barrister/solicitor division in respect of court and non-court work, or "generalised" and "specialised" work, is increasingly blurred. Many solicitors may specialise in only one or two areas of law[5] and many barristers have general practices in which they do not do much court advocacy.[6] Because of the increasing consonance of the barrister/solicitor roles, there is an ongoing debate about the introduction of a "fused" profession which would see the abolition of the distinction between solicitors and barristers.[7]

A solicitor may work alone or with others in a larger firm known as a partnership. Within a partnership there will be partners, associate partners and assistant solicitors as well as non-admitted staff such as legal executives, paralegals, legal secretaries and office managers. Hong Kong legislation permits the Law Society to approve companies as solicitor corporations.[8] Changes made in 2003[9] now allow solicitors to form "Group Practices"; a number of sole practitioners or small partnerships can group together in order to share operating costs and overheads. The new rules are subject to a number of conditions, notably that there must be no conflict of interest. For example, if one solicitor in a group practice is acting for the plaintiff in litigation, no other solicitor in the group practice can act for the defendant.

Foreign lawyers who wish to practise foreign law in Hong Kong can do so by registering with the Law Society.[10] There are currently around 1200 registered foreign lawyers in Hong Kong (and around 70 foreign law firms). Foreign lawyers

---

3. This trend mirrors that in Britain where the loss of the conveyancing monopoly led to a greater push for rights of audience in the higher courts for some solicitors.
4. Known as "higher rights of audience" since the right to appear in the more senior courts is involved.
5. Some small firms may simply lack expertise in certain areas. Conversely, many large international firms would deal only with corporate clients and have no conveyancing section.
6. This is the so-called "paper practice".
7. See "fusion" debate at 7.6 below.
8. See the Legal Service Legislation (Miscellaneous Amendments) Ordinance 1996.
9. Solicitors (Group Practice) Rules.
10. See the Foreign Lawyers Registration Rules (Cap 159S).

who wish to become eligible to practise as Hong Kong lawyers must pass the appropriate examinations of the Overseas Lawyers Qualification Examination (OLQE).[11]

The solicitor branch of the legal profession in Hong Kong is a relatively youthful one, with over 45% of practising solicitors admitted since 1997. The ranks of partners are dominated by men but, over time, we would expect this to change as over 60% of new entrants to the profession are women.

7.1.1 Type of work

The type of work done by a solicitor depends on the type, size and specialist areas of the particular employing firm. Many solicitors work for the government and also in industry, banking and finance. A solicitor in a small private practice might typically deal with conveyancing work, litigation (civil and criminal), matrimonial and probate matters. In larger firms, solicitors tend to specialise more and such firms often have departments dealing with corporate finance, China law, commercial law, intellectual property and litigation.[12]

In private practice there is a bifurcation between the far more numerous sole proprietor or small/medium firms and the far smaller number of large, generally international firms. Around 45% of solicitor firms in Hong Kong are sole proprietorships. A further 45% have between two and five partners and, of the rest, more than half have fewer than 10 partners. Only 5% of firms in Hong Kong have more than 10 partners (though they are the "big players" in the legal world). This means that the lobbying power of the smaller firms is disproportionate to their earning capacity and ensures that "rank and file" issues (the conveyancing downturn, rights of audience, "numbers" in the profession) tend to dominate Law Society considerations.[13]

For the small, mostly "local" firms, nothing has hit traditional sources of income harder than the downturn in conveyancing. The starting point was a proposal by the (colonial) Attorney-General in 1995 to abolish "scale fees" whereby the fee to be charged by a solicitor for conveyancing was tied to the cost of the property involved rather than the difficulty of the conveyancing task.[14] In *Sun Legend Investments Ltd v David Ho*[15] Saunders J described scale fees thus:

---

11. Depending on their background some common lawyers will be exempt various heads of the OLQE but all will be required to pass the Hong Kong conveyancing examination. When revised rules requiring the study of the Basic Law are introduced this is also likely to be necessary for almost all applicants.
12. The larger international firms would have only corporate clients and may, for example, do no criminal or conveyancing work.
13. Large international firms (often with only corporate clients) are more concerned about the quality of entrants to the profession, enterprise and personal initiative.
14. The move was prompted, especially, by Consumer Council moves for more competition, generally, in Hong Kong. Solicitors may feel they were sacrificial lambs in a Hong Kong which continued, for many years, to permit egregious anti-competitive practices without government intervention.
15. [2009] HKCFI 853.

These proceedings had their genesis in the halcyon days when solicitors were able to charge for conveyancing work in accordance with the Law Society . . . scale of fees. That scale was based principally upon the value of the transaction.[16]

After much initial resistance[17] the Law Society agreed that the old scale fee would remain on an "advisory" basis but that such fee could be amended by negotiation.[18] Given the collapse of the property market between 1997 and 2003,[19] in which private housing prices fell 65%, solicitors felt compelled to indulge in significant reductions to capture such conveyancing business as still remained. With transactions increasing, post-2005, and with property prices continually rising, conveyancing remains reasonable business for most small firms though the "best years" have undoubtedly gone for good. The loss of scale fees has remained a sore topic for many solicitors who see their livelihood threatened[20] but calls for the reintroduction of a similar practice are unlikely to succeed.

A solicitor employed by the Hong Kong government in the Department of Justice (DOJ) will not be involved with corporate clients and may enjoy a less lucrative salary than one employed by a large corporate firm. Conversely, his/her work could be viewed more in terms of "public service" and has the compensation of increased job security and pension rights on retirement. DOJ departments include the civil division; the international law division; the law drafting division; the legal policy division; the administration division and the prosecutions division.[21]

7.1.2 Eligibility to practise

A person who wishes to qualify as a solicitor in Hong Kong must (generally) pass the Postgraduate Certificate in Laws (PCLL) and complete a two-year training contract.[22] A training contract must be carried out within the office of a practising solicitor who must undertake to give experience to the trainee solicitor in a variety of the many fields of legal practice.[23]

---

16. At para 1.
17. It was asserted that "cut-price" conveyancing would lead to an increase in negligent work. The experience from England provided no evidence of same (see LegCo Paper No CB(2) 1164/96-97 [7 January 1997]).
18. This was, essentially, the effect of an amendment to s 56 of the Legal Practitioners Ordinance (Cap 159).
19. The result of three main factors: the Asian financial crisis, SARS in Hong Kong, and (then) Chief Executive Tung Chee Hwa's announcement of a plan to build 85,000 public flats per year.
20. P Kwok, 'The abolition of the conveyancing scale fees in 1997 was . . . a disaster for the solicitors' profession' (Law Society Election Platform 2016).
21. The author is asked to provide a significant number of references for DOJ applications annually and demand for places always exceeds supply.
22. The two-year period can be reduced slightly for those with relevant work experience.
23. At least three distinct areas of practice must be provided during the training contract. Provision exists for a small part of the training contract to be completed in a solicitor's office elsewhere in the common law world.

The majority of entrants to the profession now have a law degree and in the main go straight from this law degree to the PCLL courses which are offered by the Chinese University of Hong Kong, the City University of Hong Kong and the University of Hong Kong. New entrants to the profession (from 2008) must have a (four-year full-time) Hong Kong law degree (LLB), *or* a law degree from a common law jurisdiction, *or* a Juris Doctor (JD)[24] qualification *or* the Common Professional Examination of England and Wales (CPE) qualification. Entry onto the latter two qualifications is open only to those already holding a non-law degree. In all cases eligibility to the PCLL requires completion of 11 "core" subjects,[25] *plus* 3 "top-up" subjects[26] which must be based on Hong Kong law. Law graduates (or JD/CPE holders) without all these core and top-up requirements must "fill any gaps" via the "PCLL conversion" examinations, administered by the Hong Kong legal profession.[27] The PCLL programme then involves a one-year full-time (or two-year part-time) "skills only" course provided at one of the three universities offering PCLL provision.

Those who are qualified as solicitors in other common law jurisdictions may, subject to the relevant admission rules,[28] including length of post-qualification experience,[29] take the Overseas Lawyers Qualification Examination with a view to qualifying for Hong Kong practice.

In addition to the above, newly qualified solicitors have to undertake continuing professional development (CPD). This is to ensure that they keep up to date with current legal developments. Since 1998 the requirement for CPD has been gradually extended to all solicitors. Solicitors can accumulate the required CPD points in the traditional way, by attending short courses or lectures. Alternatively, they may satisfy the requirements by writing articles and law books, giving lectures, writing research dissertations leading to recognised qualifications or by completing distance learning courses.

Finally, in order to practise as a solicitor in Hong Kong a person must have a current practising certificate and must be a member of the Hong Kong Law Society.

---

24. This American-type programme (generally "more breadth, less depth") is now offered by all three law schools.
25. Contract, Tort, Equity & Trusts, Land Law, Criminal Law, Public Law, Business Associations, Evidence, Commercial Law and (bizarrely in a supposedly academic degree programme) Civil Procedure and Criminal Procedure. All these subjects can be studied in any common law jurisdiction, provided that the syllabus involved is acceptable to the legal profession in Hong Kong. The Hong Kong Bar has recommended that Procedure should be taken *only* as part of a Hong Kong legal qualification *or* via "conversion" examinations.
26. Hong Kong Legal System, Hong Kong Land Law, Hong Kong Constitutional Law (but see preceding footnote).
27. All LLB graduates from, eg, Australia or England would be required, as a minimum, to pass the three Hong Kong law "top-up" subjects (and soon, it appears, Hong Kong Civil Procedure and Hong Kong Criminal Procedure).
28. See the Overseas Lawyers (Qualification for Admission) Rules (Cap 159Q).
29. The minimum period is two years' post-admission experience.

7.1.3 Professional qualities (solicitors' "ethics")

All professions which seek to maintain self-regulation are required to impose and maintain complex "ethical" requirements for their members. It goes without saying that lawyers, who handle often large sums of clients' money, and whose competence can affect the very liberty of a client as well as his economic well-being, should seek to maintain the highest ethical standards. The Law Society of Hong Kong is the body charged with the maintenance of professional and ethical standards. Of course all professions are also, as some would describe it, "trade unions in disguise"; seeking to protect the interests of members of the profession. As such the potential for conflict of interest arises and, in the public interest, recourse to the courts must be permitted for disgruntled clients who feel that the profession has not safeguarded their rights.

The following are some of the main ethical requirements of Hong Kong solicitors, as found in the relevant solicitors' codes of conduct and elsewhere. All solicitors in Hong Kong are required to give an undertaking to the Law Society to abide by all practice directions, rules and regulations of the Society. The main source of internal regulation is the Solicitors' Practice Rules.[30]

7.1.3.1 General principles of professional conduct

Under rule 2 of the Solicitors' Practice Rules,[31] a solicitor has a general duty not to do anything which could compromise his independence or integrity, the interests of his client or the court.

A solicitor, unlike a barrister, is not required to accept work. He may refuse "a retainer" because he feels it might involve a potential conflict of interest, or a request to act unethically, or for any other reason.[32] Once a solicitor has accepted a client's retainer, he should not give up the case except for very good reason. Indeed, once the case has gone to court, the solicitor may withdraw only with the consent of the court. Having accepted "instructions", a solicitor should, as a priority, inform the client as to the complexity of the legal issues involved, the likelihood of success and the likely time-scale. He should give as full a picture as possible of the likely cost and advise as to the possibility of legal aid where appropriate. Solicitors' costs cover three, usually distinct areas: "out-of-pocket" expenses, "overheads" and professional charges. Charges are based on "billable hours": the time spent on the client's case. Special charging rules apply in those areas where the profession has imposed "scale fees"[33] or where legal aid work is publicly funded at set rates.

---
30. Cap 159H.
31. Cap 159H.
32. There is, in other words, no "cab rank rule" (see 7.2.4.1 below).
33. Scale fees have been, effectively, abolished for conveyancing work but remain, for example, for legal aid work financed from the public purse.

Since the solicitor owes the client a "fiduciary" duty (a duty of trust) he must avoid any conflict (or potential conflict) of interest. A conflict of interest could arise where the solicitor's "interest" does not coincide with the client's (for example where a client seeks advice as to suing a relative of the solicitor!) *or* where the interests of the client conflict with the interests of another client. A not uncommon scenario, which has occupied the courts over the past 20 years, involves possible "undue influence" (or misrepresentation) by a husband over his wife[34] to induce her to make contracts not in her best interests. In such cases of potential conflict of interest, it is not always essential that a solicitor should refuse to represent both parties. The important undue influence case of *RBS v Etridge (No 2)*[35] in the English House of Lords illustrates the point. It was held here that where a transaction "calls for an explanation" in a "non-commercial" situation (classically a wife pledging her half share of the matrimonial home as surety for her husband's business loan) the lender should be put "on inquiry" and the solicitor should ensure that the wife fully understands the implications of her actions in a meeting at which her husband is not present. The solicitor is not required, however, to refuse to act for both parties since, clearly, separate solicitors would increase costs. The *Etridge* approach has been fully adopted by the Hong Kong courts,[36] including the Court of Final Appeal, and the Law Society of Hong Kong has issued copious guidelines as to the steps which the solicitor must take in such situations.

In similar vein, in *Nishimatsu-Costain-China Harbour Joint Venture v Ip Kwan & Co*[37] an injunction was granted to prevent a solicitor's firm acting for a client in litigation but for its "opponent" in arbitration proceedings involving broadly similar circumstances. In the Court of Appeal Rogers JA stated:[38]

> In my judgment, the plaintiff is entitled to an injunction to restrain the defendant acting as its solicitor in the personal injury litigation during such time as the arbitration proceedings in relation to liability under the [insurance] policy are continuing. It would be wrong for the court to compel a party to be represented in proceedings before it by a solicitor to whom the party involved can point as acting against it in other connected proceedings and the party involved objects.[39]

A key ethical principle is that of "confidentiality". A solicitor must keep absolutely confidential all the details of his clients and ensure that his staff do likewise. The strict rules of confidentiality can only be relaxed where a solicitor is required by a court to divulge information, or where confidential documents are required by

---

34. Despite increased emancipation, such influence is still usually exercised by the male spouse!
35. [2001] 4 All ER 449.
36. See, eg, *Bank of China (Hong Kong) Ltd v Fung Chin Kan* [2003] 1 HKLRD 181 (CFA).
37. [2000] 2 HKC 445.
38. At 466.
39. Rogers JA's view was supported by Leong JA, though Ribeiro JA dissented on this point.

the police (or ICAC) in respect of the investigation of a crime.[40] The most influential case on conflict of interest/confidentiality is that of *Prince Jefri Bolkiah v KPMG (a firm)*[41] (involving the brother of the Sultan of Brunei). Here the English House of Lords made clear that where a firm of solicitors (or similar) has previously represented a party and acquired confidential information (such as the whereabouts of assets) it should not subsequently act against him unless there is no chance that such information will be disclosed to the other party. It is not enough that such disclosure is unlikely; the onus is on the solicitors' firm to show that there is no risk of disclosure. This very strict test has been applied by the Hong Kong courts on several subsequent occasions.[42]

A closely related principle is "legal professional privilege" (LPP). This has a more restricted scope than the general principle of confidentiality *but* can be avoided only in very limited circumstances. LPP only applies to communications between a solicitor (or barrister)[43] and his client for the purpose of giving legal advice *or* in respect of communications with a third party in respect of actual or contemplated legal proceedings. LPP applies to both civil and criminal proceedings but can be more contentious in relation to criminal law. Clearly, if a client is to be assured of a proper defence in a criminal trial he needs to be able to talk frankly with his legal advisers without fear of the consequences, but this consideration may run counter to the desire of criminal investigators to obtain information which may lead to the prevention or detection of crime. In Hong Kong, legal professional privilege is given the highest possible constitutional recognition in that the Basic Law states that "Hong Kong residents shall have the right to confidential legal advice".[44]

Former (and now re-elected) Hong Kong Bar Chairman, Philip Dykes, has drawn attention to the practical difficulties involved in the competing claims of the police and ICAC in the investigation of crime, and the rights of the client to the maintenance of confidentiality. This would arise particularly where the police or ICAC visit a solicitor's office (or barrister's chambers) armed with search warrants to scrutinise documents or computer records.[45]

The scope of LPP is extensive but can be avoided in certain cases. The client may expressly state that he wishes communications to be made public (or at least disclosed to others) or he may do so impliedly (eg, by discussing matters with his solicitor in the presence of others not bound by confidentiality). Disclosure may also be ordered by a court where it is in the interests of a child in a family dispute.

---

40. Anti-money-laundering legislation also requires the solicitor to report any suspicion that his client may be money-laundering (see the Organised and Serious Crimes Ordinance (Cap 455)).
41. [1999] 2 AC 222.
42. See, eg, *Wright v Hampton, Winter & Glynn (a firm)* [2008] 2 HKLRD 341.
43. See 8.2.4.4 below.
44. Article 35.
45. See P Dykes, 'The Practical Protection of Legal Professional Privilege in Hong Kong' Hong Kong Legal Community, 6 May 2009.

In limited circumstances *statute* might compel the disclosure of information otherwise subject to LPP. The statute must clearly provide for the disclosure of such information and, even here, would be subject to dispute on the grounds of incompatibility with the Basic Law. In *A Solicitor v Law Society of Hong Kong*[46] a solicitor had been required by the Hong Kong Law Society to produce documents in respect of an investigation as to whether he was fit to practise. On his refusal, contrary to section 8AA of the Legal Practitioners Ordinance (LPO), he was "charged" with conduct unbefitting a solicitor. A Solicitors Disciplinary Tribunal found him guilty, censured him, fined him $100,000, and suspended him for 4 months (or until he produced the documents). Section 8B(2) of the LPO clearly purports to override LPP on this issue but the solicitor argued that the subsection was in conflict with Article 35 of the Basic Law (which, of course, has superior status).[47] The dispute eventually reached the Court of Final Appeal (CFA) which rejected the solicitor's appeal. Bokhary J (with whom the other four members of the CFA concurred) stated:

> It is obviously conducive to the due administration of justice that clients candidly reveal the unvarnished truth to their lawyers. And of course the law is not so naïve as to imagine that such candour can confidently be expected in practice if disclosure of the contents of client-lawyer communications can be compelled, to a client's prejudice and contrary to his wishes.
>
> [But] . . . privileged documents produced or delivered cannot be used against the client . . . I am prepared to believe that a significant percentage of clients would nevertheless instinctively prefer that nobody sees the documents [and] . . . would in some instances and to some extent inhibit the candour of communications by the client to his solicitor. But I do not think that such instances would be many or such extent large.
>
> It is submitted on the Solicitor's behalf that the client might suffer prejudice even though the documents cannot be used as evidence against him . . . In my view, that is adequately met by the strict confidentiality which the inspectors and all concerned should—and doubtless would—accord to the documents.[48]

The key here is that the information would be used solely in respect of the investigation of the *solicitor*; LPP is intended to protect the *client* and any prejudice to the client here would be minimal and justified by the need to maintain the highest standards in the legal profession.

7.1.3.2 Solicitors' accounts

Given the potential for abuse, since solicitors frequently handle substantial sums of client money, it is clear that stringent rules on the handling of the solicitor's and the

---
46. [2006] 2 HKC 429.
47. See, eg, Chapter 2 on sources of Hong Kong law.
48. [2006] 2 HKC 429 at para 14.

client's money must be observed. Under the Solicitors' Accounts Rules[49] all solicitors are required to keep proper accounts recording any dealings with clients' money. Subject to certain exceptions a solicitor who holds or receives clients' money shall, without delay, pay such money into a client account. A not uncommon cause of the Law Society having to discipline a solicitor is evidence of default or dishonesty in the handling of a client's money.[50]

7.1.3.3 Solicitors' (Professional Indemnity) Rules

Apart from the supervisory function of the Law Society, another form of protection for the client is compulsory indemnity insurance. Under the Solicitors' (Professional Indemnity) Rules[51] all solicitors in practice are required to maintain indemnity insurance. This is to cover liability in law to the solicitor's client for negligence and for other risks such as: failure to account for clients' money; dishonesty or fraud of the solicitor's staff; or loss of documents. The indemnity limit is $10 million for each claim.

In addition, the Law Society is required to maintain an indemnity fund to make good losses of clients' money which has been appropriated and which cannot be recovered from the relevant solicitor.

Concern has been expressed over the financial viability of the indemnity scheme (especially given the termination of a similar scheme in England). The "actuarial" problem is that the amount of contribution to the indemnity fund by solicitors' firms is based, in large part, on a firm's gross fee income. Generally, such incomes are declining while, at the same time, the number of claims by clients against the fund is on the increase. As a result, it is felt that the current scheme is unsustainable in the longer term.[52]

7.1.3.4 Solicitor-advocates

A solicitor in the role of an advocate has similar responsibilities and duties to those which are imposed on barristers.[53] Solicitors owe a duty both to clients *and* the court. This can sometimes produce a tension between what may be seen as in the client's best interests and the duty not to mislead the court. If, for example, a client admits his guilt in a criminal case but insists on a not guilty plea, the solicitor should withdraw from the case.

---

49. Cap 159F.
50. See, eg, *In the Matter of a Solicitor* (1999) CACV No 182 of 1999.
51. Cap 159M.
52. See 'What Went Wrong?' *Hong Kong Lawyer* (President's Message) (March 2014).
53. See 7.2.4 below.

Similarly, in a civil case, via the procedure known as "discovery", a solicitor must make available to "the opposition" all relevant documents, even if they harm his case.

7.2 The barrister

Those who practise at the Hong Kong Bar are known as barristers (or counsel). They are specialists in advocacy and legal advice. The traditional method of qualification as a barrister involves an academic stage of training—a law degree, JD or CPE—followed by a vocational stage—the PCLL. This is followed by a training period known as pupillage (one year) whereby a pupil is attached to a practising barrister and learns the practical skills of working at the Bar. There are, in Hong Kong, just over 1,000 practising barristers whose governing body is the Bar Council of the Hong Kong Bar Association (HKBA). The HKBA Code of Conduct for the Bar of Hong Kong contains the rules of professional conduct and ethics for barristers.

7.2.1 The nature of the barrister's role

Essentially, a barrister practises as a self-employed individual,[54] who shares the expenses of his office by practising with other barristers in "chambers",[55] thus sharing the costs of rent and the services of a clerk.[56] In the main, barristers concentrate on advocacy, for which they are prepared in the vocational stage of training. Barristers are the main practitioners in the Court of First Instance of the High Court and in courts above.

While a barrister's major work involves appearing in court to argue a case, this often includes preparatory work such as drafting pleadings, meeting clients and dealing with solicitors and witnesses. Some barristers choose to concentrate mainly on paperwork by researching and writing opinions on complex points of law.

Barristers of long-standing[57] and good reputation may be awarded the title "senior counsel"[58] in recognition of their achievements. Although there are around 1,000 barristers in practice, only around 85 of these are senior counsel (SC) so the title is a significant one. Almost certainly the engagement of a senior counsel will involve increased expense, not only because of the additional fee which an SC would charge but also because he[59] will be, invariably, supported by "junior counsel". Most judges are appointed from the ranks of senior barristers, though senior solicitors can

---

54. Barristers may not form companies or partnerships (HKBA Code of Conduct para 28).
55. With only limited exception it is not permitted for a barrister to practise other than from recognised chambers (HKBA Code of Conduct para 25).
56. Barristers are not permitted to form partnerships (or companies) and barristers residing in the same chambers may be opponents in court.
57. The minimum period is 10 years.
58. The equivalent, in England, is the "Queen's (or King's) Counsel" commonly known as "silks".
59. The word "he" in this context is appropriate since there are very few female SCs.

also be appointed. In the case of the highest earners at the Hong Kong bar, "elevation" to the judiciary may actually lead to a reduced income (albeit with increased status, and a pension).[60]

A barrister does not enter into a contract with a client (or indeed anyone else) for the provision of his services. Moreover, the barrister is rarely engaged directly by a "client". Instead, the client approaches a solicitor who may, where appropriate, instruct a barrister. A barrister is expected to accept instructions if he is available, unless to do so would involve a conflict of interest.

The barrister's connection to the client will be through a solicitor.[61] The solicitor or a member of his staff will usually accompany the client when he goes to see the barrister.

7.2.2 *Eligibility to practise*

As a result of legislative change in 2003,[62] virtually the only way, currently, that a person may be admitted to the Hong Kong Bar is by passing the PCLL course offered by the Chinese University of Hong Kong, City University of Hong Kong and the University of Hong Kong. Overseas barristers may seek admission to the Hong Kong Bar provided they have at least three years' experience in their jurisdiction of admission and have passed the Barristers' Qualification Examination, the first of which was held in 2004. Very few overseas barristers took the first examination and results were poor. This has continued to be the case and, given increased residency requirements, entry to the Hong Kong Bar is effectively limited to Hong Kong people, such that the PCLL route is the obvious one.

Prior to the 2003 legislation[63] those who had qualified at the English Bar were automatically able to practise in Hong Kong. While the desirability of professional legal education based on *Hong Kong* law seems obvious, the English barristers did have the compensatory factor of having studied on a programme specifically designed for barristers (unlike their PCLL counterparts).

In addition to passing PCLL, intending barristers must also complete one year of pupillage (in which the pupil learns various areas of a barrister's practical legal skills under the guidance of an experienced barrister "pupil master")[64] and *should*, in most cases, fulfil Continuing Professional Development (CPD) requirements. However, these are not compulsory, which is a matter of some concern. The Bar has

---

60. See discussion at 6.1 above.
61. Though, in England, the barrister can be directly liable to the client in the tort of negligence. Similar change in Hong Kong appears imminent.
62. Governed by s 27 of the Legal Practitioners Ordinance (Cap 159) with more detailed rules in s 4(1) of the Barristers (Qualification for Admission and Pupillage) Rules.
63. Via the Legal Practitioners (Amendment) Ordinance (No 87 of 2003).
64. Concerns as to the quality of young barristers and the variable nature of the pupillage experience led the Bar to announce the setting up, in 2010, of a committee to look into the pupillage situation (under the chairmanship of Clive Grossman SC). See 7.6 below.

an Advanced Legal Education scheme but has yet to *require* CPD for its members, despite pressure for such a move. In March, 2013, the *South China Morning Post* looked at calls for Bar CPD and stated:

> Barristers are among the few groups of professional in Hong Kong who are not required to undertake continuing education, which is the norm for peers in many countries including Britain, Canada and Australia.[65]

7.2.3 Engagement of barristers

For the general public, access to barristers is effected through solicitors. Barristers may not, subject to very limited exceptions,[66] provide legal advice or services direct to the public.[67] This mirrors the traditional position in England which Hong Kong practice has tended to emulate. However, recent changes have been made so that, in some instances, barristers may also be instructed by other professionals such as accountants, company secretaries and arbitrators. This is known as *direct professional access* work and is restricted to the taking of instructions from a "recognised professional body".[68] Given the importance of solicitors to the barrister's livelihood there is clearly a danger of "incentives" being offered to solicitors' firms by individual barristers or chambers. Such "touting" is clearly prohibited by the HKBA.[69]

The scope for direct access is significantly less than in Britain, where reforms allow a much greater measure of direct access for clients.

7.2.4 Principles of professional conduct (professional ethics)

As with solicitors, barristers are required to conform to a strict code of conduct. While barristers do not have the same potential for financial irregularity as do solicitors, the potential for harm to a client, especially in respect of negligently performed criminal defence work, is immense. Professional conduct at the Hong Kong bar is regulated by the Bar Council of the Hong Kong Bar Association. Most rules are to be found in the Code of Conduct for the Bar of Hong Kong (CCB), the key aspects of which will now be considered.

First, under CCB paragraph 4, there is a general "aspirational" element:

> Every barrister . . . whether in practice or not, should uphold at all times the standards set out in this Code, the dignity and high standing of the profession of barrister and his own standing as a member of it.

---

65. A Chiu and P Moy, 'Barristers Urged to Raise the Bar' *South China Morning Post* (Hong Kong, 26 March 2013). The article quoted HKU law professor, Simon Young, and (then) DPP, Kevin Zervos, in support of compulsory CPD.
66. Eg, delivering advice free to a friend or relative or, implicitly, via a lecture or textbook.
67. HKBA Code of Conduct para 22.
68. Ibid at para 50(b).
69. HKBA Code of Conduct paras 92–94.

Paragraph 6 imposes on all barristers the duty, *inter alia*, of observing the ethics and etiquette of the bar, of performing all professional functions competently and not to engage in conduct prejudicial to the reputation of the bar.

7.2.4.1 Acceptance of a brief and the "cab rank" rule

A practising barrister must, in principle, accept any brief to appear before a court in the field in which he professes to practise at his usual fee having regard to the type, nature, length and difficulty of the case.[70] Special circumstances such as a conflict of interest or the possession of relevant and confidential information may justify his refusal to accept a particular brief.[71] While this appears to be a strict requirement, barristers can refuse a brief simply on the basis that they are unavailable owing to other work commitments, cannot handle the brief within the time period set, or lack the necessary competence to deal with the brief offered.[72] Senior barristers will, of course, avoid unpopular, less well-paid work simply because their "normal fee" would be out of many clients' price range. The requirement to take a case if the barrister is "available" is known as the "cab rank" rule; the idea is that, like a taxi driver, the barrister cannot refuse work. This is tied to the notion that even an unpopular client (such as one accused of a particularly heinous crime) should have the right to legal representation.[73]

The cab rank rule was previously used as one justification for the immunity of barristers from liability in the tort of negligence on the grounds of "public policy". The argument ran that it would be unfair to allow barristers to be sued for negligence when the cab rank rule required them to take even hopeless cases.[74] The now-discredited argument[75] overlooked the fact that the barrister would only be required to exercise "reasonable skill" and if, in a hopeless situation, the barrister's client lost the case, there would be no reason for a court in a subsequent case to infer negligence from the defeat.

7.2.4.2 Duty to "client" and the court

A barrister, of course, has a duty to represent the client and to exhibit a reasonable standard of expertise and care in so doing. This duty has to be balanced against the barrister's concurrent duty to the court. Specifically, the barrister is under a duty not

---

70. HKBA Code of Conduct para 21.
71. Ibid.
72. HKBA Code of Conduct paras 63–64.
73. The ideal of "representation for all" has been long cherished in the United States and it is a matter of considerable regret that a movement, founded by the daughter of the discredited Dick Cheney, has called for the "naming and shaming" of lawyers prepared to represent those accused of terrorism-related offences.
74. See discussion of *Rondel v Worsley* below.
75. See *Arthur J S Hall v Simons* [2002] 1 AC 615.

to mislead the court. The tension between "duty to the court" and "duty to the client" can produce ethical dilemmas.[76] In civil cases this could arise in respect of pursuing an improper line of questioning in court which might, in fact, assist the client's case. The dilemma may be, however, much greater in the case of criminal trials. Two examples may be mentioned, the first of which involves the situation where the barrister is told explicitly by the client that he (the client) has committed the crime alleged but wishes to run a "not guilty" plea. The correct procedure in such cases of "express admission" is for the barrister to remove himself from the case, even though this may cause prejudice to him and the client. This does not apply, however, merely because the barrister "feels sure" that his client is guilty. There is an entitlement to an "adversarial" trial, in which the barrister pursues instructions to the (legitimate) limit *unless* there has been an actual admission of guilt.

A further dilemma could arise in cases of potential "plea bargain". Plea bargaining describes the situation in which an accused pleads guilty in return for some concession, in the form of reduced charges and/or a reduced sentence. The practice is extremely widespread in the United States and has been endorsed by the Supreme Court.[77] In England and Hong Kong courts have a somewhat more ambivalent attitude and do not actively encourage the practice.[78] Nonetheless both charge and sentence[79] reduction are clearly available to at least some of those who consent to plead guilty, though significant limits have been placed on these practices. The key elements are that the plea is ultimately a matter for the client, that there should be no pressure applied and, in the case of a meeting between barrister and judge, the barrister should not indicate that the judge has suggested a guilty plea.[80] A dilemma will arise if the barrister, knowing that an accused's case is weak and that a guilty plea could lead to a reduced sentence,[81] is nonetheless assured by the client that he is innocent. Here the barrister's duty is to advise the client to plead "not guilty" and strive for acquittal, even though, ultimately, this may not be in the client's best interests.

The duty to the court is also reflected in the statement in the HKBA Code of Conduct that:

---

76. The paramount duty to the court was once a further argument for making barristers immune from negligence liability for work done in court.
77. See *Brady v US* 397 US 742 (1970).
78. One of the first studies of plea bargaining in England was Baldwin and McConville's *Negotiated Justice*. Co-author Professor Mike McConville was later Dean of the Law Faculty at the Chinese University of Hong Kong.
79. This is sometimes put in terms of a show of "remorse" but also, more honestly, recognised as a saving of court time.
80. Nor should the judge indicate that a higher sentence will be imposed if the client refuses to plead guilty (cf the English case of *R v Turner* [1970] 2 QB 321 and the consistent Hong Kong case of *R v Yuen Kuen Chi* (1985) Cr App No 52 of 1985). *Turner* has been superseded in England but remains important in Hong Kong.
81. Significant sentence reduction (by 1/3) is virtually automatic if the defendants pleads guilty "at the first opportunity" (see *HKSAR v Ngo Van Nam* CACC 418/2014).

In a criminal appeal to the Court of Appeal a barrister should not settle grounds of appeal unless he considers that the proposed appeal is properly arguable.[82]

Various less crucial aspects of the duty to the court involve the duty to respect the judge and opposing counsel, to use appropriate language and to appear in court properly attired.

7.2.4.3 Advertising of services

Traditionally the "gentleman's" image of the Bar has militated against the advertising of professional services, which has been seen as lowering the image and status of the Bar as the "consultancy" arm of the legal profession. After debating the issue for many years, the Bar has now relaxed its rules somewhat, so that individual barristers may now "advertise" their expertise publicly. The permitted advertising takes the form of disclosing the barrister's qualifications, expertise and experience. The disclosure must take the form of "passive" provision of information; "touting" is still prohibited.[83] Thus a barrister may not "solicit" work (from a solicitor!) nor provide any gift or payment which might be construed as an inducement to provide work.[84] Nor may barristers publicly declare their charges, lest an unseemly "price-cutting" war break out. More generally, barristers may not issue advertising which is misleading, criticises other lawyers, is "offensive", or is likely to:

> diminish public confidence in the legal profession or the administration of justice or otherwise bring the legal profession or the administration of justice into disrepute.[85]

Merry[86] has pointed out that the relaxation of rules against "self-promotion" is unlikely to make a lot of difference in practice. He writes:

> The irony is that this advertising has made not a jot of difference in reality. Why would it? Barristers' clients are solicitors, a sophisticated and relatively small group well capable of obtaining the information required as to a particular advocate's capabilities. No solicitor would engage counsel simply on the basis of what is contained in an advertisement. But at least freedom of speech has been respected and our new competition commission, assuming we ever get one, will be appeased.[87]

7.2.4.4 Confidentiality and legal professional privilege

Just as a solicitor, a barrister is required to maintain the confidentiality of information passed to him in confidence by the client. Likewise, he must keep confidential

---

82. Paragraph 114, Bar Code of Conduct.
83. As, for example, would be television advertising.
84. HKBA Code of Conduct, para 92.
85. HKBA Code of Conduct, para 101 (2).
86. M Merry, 'Not Entirely Legal' Hong Kong Legal Community, 20 January 2009.
87. Ibid, Part 8: 'Not with a Bang but a Whimper'.

any information about the client brought to his attention by the instructing solicitor. Again, as with a solicitor, the barrister is entitled to break a confidence only under an order of the court or in respect of a requirement of the police or ICAC in the investigation of a crime.

Similarly, just as with solicitors, a barrister's lay or ("direct access") professional client is protected by legal professional privilege (LPP). This applies to all advice from the barrister to the client (or instructing solicitor) and any advice to third parties in respect of actual or contemplated legal proceedings involving the barrister's client.

7.2.4.5 Conflict of interest

Barristers, like, solicitors, must avoid any conflict of interest. This would include, for example, not dealing with a client with whom the barrister had a personal or family antipathy, but the most significant conflict "dilemma" would arise in criminal cases involving joint defendants. While it is possible, and may be convenient and cost-saving, for a barrister to represent joint defendants where their defences are consistent, it would be improper to do so where any defences were in opposition. For example, in cases of several co-accused, it is not uncommon for defendant Z to argue that defendants X and Y were the ringleaders or even that X and Y committed offences with weapons which Z was unaware they were carrying. In such a situation it would be reasonable to assume that the barrister could not defend X and Y to the best of his ability while also putting forward the "extenuation" of Z.[88]

7.2.4.6 Outside practice

Barristers are generally prohibited from engaging in outside practice except in respect of outside work *generally* regarded as appropriate (university teaching or academic writing for example) or work *specifically* sanctioned by the Bar Council on an individual basis.[89]

7.2.5 *Barrister's fees*

The cost of a "private" barrister in Hong Kong is considerable; particularly in the case of high-ranking "Senior Counsel". The high costs are associated, not least, with the location of almost all barristers' chambers in or near the central business district with its associated expensive commercial property rents.

A barrister's fees for courtroom advocacy are itemised in terms of "brief" fee and "refresher" fee. The brief fee covers the cost of studying the "brief" (the legal documents involved in a disputed case) and the first day of appearance in court. The

---

88. HKBA Code of Conduct, paras 57–61.
89. HKBA Code of Conduct, paras 22–23.

refresher fee is the cost for each additional day in court. For court work a barrister is required to state in advance his fee for "attendance" at court.

Since barristers are almost invariably engaged by firms of solicitors, the negotiation of fees is between a solicitor (or legal executive) and the barrister, or, in practice, by the "clerk to chambers" of the barrister.[90] A barrister's clerk (clerk to chambers) is an important figure in most chambers, having the role of negotiating barristers' fees and, in the case of briefs sent to chambers without specifying the barrister sought, arranging the distribution of work.

In addition to court advocacy, barristers are often engaged to write "counsel's opinions" on issues referred to them by solicitors. This may be viewed as analogous to a general practitioner seeking a "specialist's opinion" in a medical case. As private practitioners without the distraction of visiting clients, barristers are regarded as better able to do the researches needed in complex cases. In England, too, they have specialist legal education in areas such as evidence and their advice is sought in particular in such areas.[91] In respect of issues involving "paper practice" (opinion writing etc) the more common practice is for barristers to charge an hourly rate.

Legal aid[92] work in Hong Kong is paid for out of public funds and comes with a "fixed price", significantly lower than that charged for privately funded work.[93] The most senior, well-known, barristers would be unlikely to deal with legal aid work.[94]

7.2.5.1 The recovery of fees

Traditionally a barrister is a "gentleman" who is paid an "honorarium" and is unable to sue for his fees. For some time, such a position was tolerated by barristers since they were unlikely to have difficulty obtaining fees from the solicitors who had engaged them *and* since the lack of a legally recoverable fee rendered barristers immune from actions in breach of contract should they negligently perform their services. However, once it was established that an action in tort could be brought against a negligent barrister for work done in court or its preparation,[95] contractual immunity became less significant. Moreover, while the (albeit lesser) legal aid fee is easily recoverable from the public purse, fees from solicitors are sometimes surprisingly difficult to recover. The problem is less one of non-payment than of late payment, an issue more significant in times of rapid inflation. In cases of non-payment (or seriously late payment) by a solicitor, the barrister's only redress is a

---

90. Negotiation of fee is permitted but once agreed it must be paid. The fee must be agreed *before* the barrister accepts the brief.
91. At present barristers in Hong Kong have little specialised legal education.
92. For coverage of the operation of the legal aid system, see Chapter 9.
93. Especially for criminal legal aid (see U So, 'Lawyers Seek Legal Aid Fee Deal' *The Standard* [Hong Kong, 26 February 2008]).
94. However, over 30% of barristers in practice have been working for fewer than five years and legal aid work is usually important to them.
95. See 7.4.4 below.

complaint to the Law Society which may then take disciplinary proceedings against its errant member.

7.3 "Rights of audience"

The expression "right of audience" is used to describe the right to professionally represent another in a particular court. Thus, for example, Hong Kong practising barristers have full rights of audience in all Hong Kong courts whereas solicitors have full rights of audience in only the lower courts and, currently, limited rights of audience in the higher courts.[96] More fully, the position is that in Magistrates' Courts and District Courts, both solicitors and barristers have rights of audience. In the High Court (Court of First Instance [CFI] and Court of Appeal) and above barristers have a right of audience but solicitors generally do not. In some cases, in the CFI solicitors are permitted to appear (notably in uncontested cases, appeals from the Magistrates' Courts and before a judge in chambers). More generally legislation has now been passed to provide for "higher rights of audience" for solicitors in the High Court (and Court of Final Appeal) on proof of competence.[97] Only a relatively small number of such "solicitor-advocates" have, so far, been granted these increased rights of audience following approval via a Higher Rights Assessment Board. Given the disruption to office procedure, an increase in court appearances will not appeal to many (especially the successful) solicitors' firms.

As regards tribunals, both branches of the profession generally have rights of audience, save for the exception that *no* legal representation is permitted in the Small Claims Tribunal or the Labour Tribunal.

7.4 Professional misconduct

Hong Kong's legal profession is essentially self-regulating, which means the profession administers its own disciplinary code rather than having one imposed externally. Indeed, the continued self-regulation of the legal profession is guaranteed in the Basic Law.[98] This means that both the solicitor branch and the barrister branch of the profession have their own internal disciplinary procedures for members who infringe the professional code of conduct. In addition, it is possible for a "client"[99] to bring an action where loss has been occasioned to him by the legal professional. While disciplinary offences often involve breaches of the civil law (or even criminal

---

96. The rights of audience of "other lawyers" (essentially "legal executives") in Hong Kong is extremely limited.
97. See the Legal Practitioners (Amendment) Ordinance of 2010. This reform is a somewhat milder version of changes introduced in Britain under the Courts and Legal Services Act 1990. See also 7.6.1 below.
98. Article 142.
99. In respect of barristers the word "client" here refers to the person whom the barrister has represented, even though, strictly, barristers' clients are solicitors.

law) there is not a total overlap. Minor instances of professional "misconduct", such as discourtesy to the court or to the opponent's client, may well result in disciplinary offences without rendering the legal practitioner liable for any breach of the civil or criminal law.

7.4.1 Solicitors' disciplinary procedures

Solicitors are subject to professional rules of conduct and practice, including those laid down in the Hong Kong Solicitor's Guide to Professional Conduct (HKSGPC).[100] The Law Society Council has powers under the Legal Practitioners Ordinance[101] to enforce rules of professional conduct and to impose discipline on solicitors.

Complaints about individual solicitors will be dealt with, where necessary, by a Solicitors' Disciplinary Tribunal (SDT). An SDT panel consists of two solicitors and a lay person and has power to inquire into and investigate the conduct of the solicitor who is the subject of the complaint. The Disciplinary Tribunal is not a committee of the Law Society but a separate body with independent statutory existence, though most members of the tribunal are usually senior members of the Law Society. The tribunal has wide powers including the power to strike from the roll of solicitors, suspend, censure, impose conditions on practice, and fine. There is also provision for the Law Society to "intervene" in a solicitor's practice, usually for failure to comply with the Solicitors' Accounts Rules. Additionally, it is now possible to publish the name of a solicitor found guilty of professional misconduct.[102] Appeals from the decision of a Disciplinary Tribunal (generally on the grounds of a breach of natural justice) may be made to the Court of Appeal. The former rule that no further appeal could lie to the Court of Final Appeal (CFA) was abolished by the CFA decision in *A Solicitor v Law Society of Hong Kong and Secretary of Justice*.[103]

The most celebrated solicitor's disciplinary action in Hong Kong, involving "improper" advertising, with the potential to bring the profession into disrepute, involved solicitor and sometime LegCo (functional)[104] member, Paul Tse. "Bringing the profession into disrepute" is an "offence" taken seriously by a profession which, rightly, sets great store by its reputation. The Tse case, *A Solicitor v Law Society of Hong Kong*,[105] is remembered in Hong Kong folklore as one about a solicitor advertising his firm's (legal!) services in his underpants, though rather more was involved. Tse had, indeed, posed in his underpants to demonstrate (he said) that law

---

100. These are produced by the Law Society of Hong Kong.
101. Cap 159.
102. Section 13A, Legal Practitioners Ordinance.
103. [2003] 4 HKC 229.
104. Tse was a member for the tourism functional constituency, on the strength of his travel agent business.
105. [2006] HKCA 267.

should be for all, including the ordinary person.[106] He was (more fully) accused, however, of offering his girlfriend's services as a marriage counsellor (and offering free condoms!), of asserting that his fees were lower than that of other solicitors, of posing for advertising "nude or semi-nude", and, generally, "bringing the solicitor profession into disrepute". The Court of Appeal upheld most of these claims and Tse was finally suspended from practice for 12 months and barred for two years from acting as a sole practitioner.

7.4.2 Solicitors' civil liability to clients

A solicitor owes his client a duty to discharge his professional duties competently in respect of the legal services he provides. The duties must be carried out in a conscientious, diligent, prompt and efficient manner; in short, the solicitor must exercise "reasonable care, honesty and skill".

A solicitor should not attempt to evade his liability for negligence or professional misconduct. Where a client makes a complaint against his solicitor and the solicitor discovers an act or omission which could justify the complaint, the solicitor should inform his client that he should seek independent advice.

Where some aspect of a solicitor's failure to discharge his professional duties in a proper manner (usually involving negligence) has caused a client loss, the client may bring a civil action against the solicitor. This will normally be an action for breach of contract. There is an implied term in any contract with a solicitor that he will exercise reasonable skill in performing his duties. Failure to do so will constitute a breach. Negligence on the part of a solicitor may cause considerable financial loss, especially where it involves failure to make title in a conveyancing transaction which, given Hong Kong's volatile property market, may lose a client millions (especially in the case of a commercial client). It is for this reason that solicitors have to fund a very significant solicitors' indemnity fund[107] and is one argument for excluding non-solicitors from conveyancing work.[108]

Since the client always has a contract with his solicitor, an action for breach is the most likely response to professional negligence. Indeed, at one time it was held that an action could *only* lie in breach and not in tort. This rule was abolished in England some 30 years ago and Hong Kong has followed the same line. Actions may now, alternatively, be brought in the tort of negligence and there are some potential advantages. If, for example, the client suffers "foreseeable" but "improbable" loss as a result of a solicitor's negligence this would be too "remote" in contract but

---

106. Tse's image as "man of the people" was dented somewhat by the fact that he was the sole LegCo member to vote against the introduction of a minimum wage.
107. See 7.1.3.3 above.
108. Solicitors' monopoly in respect of conveyancing was abolished in Britain after a long rearguard action. One argument was that non-solicitors would be less likely to have adequate insurance cover in the event of a conveyancing error (see M Joseph, *The Conveyancing Fraud* [Michael Joseph 1994]).

The Legal Profession and Legal Education 323

not in tort. Moreover, if a client's loss arises more than six years after a solicitor's negligence, it would be "time-barred"[109] in contract but not in tort.[110] An illustrative case is *Feerni Development Ltd v Daniel Wong and Partners*.[111] Here the trial judge, Deputy Judge Gill, found that the defendant solicitors had:

> failed to exercise that reasonable degree of skill and care to be expected of a competent and reasonably experienced solicitor in acting for a client in the purchase of a shop.[112]

The result was that the client was unable to confirm title[113] and lost out on two possible subsequent re-sales. The judge found the defendants liable for breach of contract at common law and under section 5 of the Supply of Services (Implied Terms) Ordinance.[114] In addition, he found them liable in the tort of negligence.

The loss which a client claims against a solicitor will usually be a purely monetary one but it is possible for breach of contract damages to reflect distress or disappointment caused by a solicitor's negligence,[115] where the contract with the client was intended to provide "peace of mind or freedom from distress".[116]

Finally, given the increasing significance of solicitor-advocacy with the onset of higher rights of audience, it should be said that solicitor-advocates are likely to enjoy the same immunity for suit (if any) as that enjoyed by barristers in relation to work done in court and its preparation.[117]

7.4.3 Barristers' disciplinary regulations

The Code of Conduct for the Bar of Hong Kong incorporates relevant rules of practice for barristers deriving from various statutory sources, in particular the Legal Practitioners Ordinance (LPO)[118] and subsidiary legislation, plus the Rules of the High Court[119] and applicable principles of common law. Any serious failure to comply with these rules of practice is viewed as professional misconduct. Where a complaint about a barrister has been received by the Bar Association and it considers that the conduct of the barrister should be looked into, a Barristers' Disciplinary Tribunal (consisting of one senior counsel, one barrister and one lay person) will

---

109. ie, it would be precluded by the Limitation Ordinance (Cap 347).
110. In contract a six-year limitation period runs from the date of the solicitor's breach; in tort the time runs from the date of "loss".
111. [2001] 1 HKC 373.
112. Ibid 391.
113. The defendants finally rectified title but only just before the date of trial.
114. Cap 457.
115. See the English cases of *Heywood v Wellers (a Firm)* [1976] 1 All ER 300 and *Hamilton Jones v David & Snape* [2004] 1 All ER 657.
116. See *Bliss v SE Thames RHA* [1985] IRLR 308; *Ronald Claud Hardwick v Spence Robinson* [1975] HKLR 425.
117. See 7.4.4 below.
118. Cap 159.
119. Cap 4A.

consider the matter. In the event of a finding of "misconduct", the tribunal has the power to censure, suspend, strike off, award compensation to the client, fine, or make any other order it thinks fit. Failure to comply with the rules which does not, in the opinion of the Bar Council, amount to professional misconduct may be viewed as a "breach of proper professional standards". In such circumstances a barrister could be required to report to the Chairman of the Bar Council to be "admonished" or given appropriate advice as to his future conduct.

Appeal from any decision of the tribunal is to the Court of Appeal.[120]

7.4.4 Civil actions against barristers

It was once believed that barristers were largely immune from civil actions by a client owing to the practice that clients could not directly contract with a barrister and that a barrister was engaged by being instructed by a solicitor. There was thus no contract between barrister and client *nor* between barrister and instructing solicitor because of the tradition that a barrister is paid an unenforceable "honorarium" (rather than a fee to which he is legally entitled). The "no contract" immunity was eroded by the extension of *tort* liability for careless advice/statements.[121] However, barristers remained immune, on "*public policy*" grounds, from actions in tort (negligence) for work done in court (and its preparation) under the principle of *Rondel v Worsley*.[122] Although Hong Kong higher courts have not yet had the opportunity to reconsider such issues,[123] House of Lords and Privy Council decisions in England have ruled that there is no longer such an immunity.[124] Although all these cases are post-1997, and therefore not binding on Hong Kong courts, it is more likely than not that the Hong Kong (higher) courts will follow the lead of the English courts on this matter. Tangentially, however, Hong Kong's Court of Appeal has endorsed the principle of "finality" and the notion that the integrity of decisions in cases should not be undermined by "collateral" attacks.[125] Since, particularly in criminal cases, the assertion of defence counsel's incompetence would, indeed, constitute a collateral attack on the integrity of a conviction, there is some support here for the preservation of advocates' immunity from suit.[126]

---

120. A further appeal to the Court of Final appeal is now also possible: *A Solicitor v Law Society of Hong Kong & Secretary for Justice* [2003] 4 HKC 229.
121. Established by the UK House of Lords (albeit *obiter*) in *Hedley Byrne & Co Ltd v Heller & Partners Ltd* [1964] AC 465.
122. [1969] 1 AC 191.
123. Such limited jurisprudence as exists supports the continuance of advocates' immunity in Hong Kong: *Lam Chi Kong v Tai Siu Ching & Another* [2007] HKCU 975; though change appears inevitable.
124. See *Arthur JS Hall & Co v Simons* [2002] 1 AC 615; *Harley v McDonald* [2001] 2 WLR 1749; *Moy v Petman Smith & Another* [2005] 1 All ER 903.
125. See *Tsang Chin Keung v Employees Compensation Assistance Fund* [2003] 2 HKLRD 627.
126. See M Vranken, 'Towards a Hong Kong Law of Tort' in PJ Bokhary, N Sarony, and DK Srivastava (eds), *Tort Law & Practice in Hong Kong* (Sweet & Maxwell Thomson 2007).

7.5 Legal education in Hong Kong[127]

Since most legal practitioners in Hong Kong have had at least some of their legal education in Hong Kong, the quality of such education has a major impact on the quality of legal services in Hong Kong.

There are two ways in which one may qualify as a lawyer in Hong Kong: via the Post-graduate Certificate in Laws (PCLL) followed by a local training contract (solicitors) or pupillage (barristers), or (less commonly) by qualifying fully as a lawyer elsewhere in the common law world and, thereafter, passing the Overseas Lawyers' Qualification Examination (OLQE) to enable qualification as a Hong Kong solicitor.[128]

While legal education at the undergraduate level is of commendable quality in Hong Kong, the same has not always been true of professional legal education. Until recently, legal education was dominated by the University of Hong Kong, with its large Law Faculty comprising a Department of Law and a Department of Professional Legal Education (DOPLE); the latter administering the Post-graduate Certificate in Laws (PCLL) programme which encompasses professional legal education (and training?).[129] A smaller law school at the City University of Hong Kong also administers a law degree and a PCLL programme. Since 2006, a welcome addition to legal education has been a third law school at the Chinese University of Hong Kong.

7.5.1 Concerns over legal education and developments post-2000

In November, 1999, the Hong Kong government formed a steering group to investigate the need to reform Hong Kong legal education and training following concerns raised by the profession and the judiciary about the quality of newly qualified entrants to the profession.[130] As a result, two Australian consultants (Professors Roper and Redmond) were engaged and, in August 2001, they published their report.[131] The key conclusions and recommendations are now summarised.

---

127. "Internal" legal education in Hong Kong is relatively new, with the first law school established only in 1969 (at HKU). Before that legal qualification in Hong Kong depended on the "foreign" (usually English) common law route; studied either overseas or via the University of London (External) LLB programme. See DME Evans, *Taken at the Flood: Hong Kong's First Law School* (Hong Kong University Press, 1989) 10.
128. A similar test exists to cater for potential overseas barristers but it is not commonly pursued.
129. In fact, a key issue for the two "reviewers" of legal education and training (below) was the question of whether PCLL was primarily legal education or training.
130. The two major concerns were the poor standard of English and lack of problem-solving skills (see J Caplan, 'On the Road to Reform' *Hong Kong Lawyer* [November/December 2002]). Fifteen years later the same criticisms are still made by international firms which rarely recruit HK graduates.
131. *Legal Education and Training in Hong Kong: Preliminary Review Steering Committee on the Review of Legal Education and Training in Hong* Kong (Report of the Consultants, August 2001; hereafter "Roper/Redmond Report").

Legal Education and Training in Hong Kong: Preliminary Review

5.9 Conclusions in regard to numbers

... the consultants are reluctant to recommend that there should be any mechanisms along the way in the legal education and training system which artificially control numbers. Rather, what is seen as preferable is one based on merit whereby, through the setting and enforcement of high standards which are appropriate to the ongoing circumstances, some will "fall by the wayside". By this means the numbers in the system will be a reflection of the standards which the profession imposes on itself; in turn a response to the expectations of the Hong Kong legal profession by both Hong Kong society and the international community...

...

6.6 That the process of active learning which, it is recommended be a more dominant aspect of law teaching ... include a strong and rigorous emphasis on the use of English.

...

6.9 It is highly desirable that there be a number of those admitted to practice in Hong Kong who are able to use the Chinese language, where appropriate to their practice, to comparable standards as those in regard to English. Continuing training in the Chinese language should be provided for students and lawyers who have capabilities in the use of Chinese.

7. The academic stage of legal education

...

Briefly stated, the consultants recommend that

... the LLB and the PCLL be restructured so that the treatment of substantive law in the PCLL is transferred to the LLB, mostly as elective subjects, and the professional skills component dealt with in a new legal practice course taught outside the universities ...

...

7.3.1 The study of law as liberal education

... the law degree should be so framed as to meet the needs of students who will go on to professional training in law as well as those who seek an education for its own sake or as preparation for another career.[132]

---

132. This particular suggestion has been consistently opposed by Professor Stephen Nathanson (then of the Department of Professional Legal Education, HKU), who sees the purpose of all legal education as producing good lawyers. In this context Jones describes the issue of whether law schools should, "defer to the demands of the profession . . . or to defend the merits of a traditional legal education": C Jones, 'Legal Education in Hong Kong' in S Steele and K Taylor (eds), *Legal Education in Asia: Globalization, Change & Contexts* (Routledge 2011) 126.

7.4.3 Four-year LLB

... The consultants will recommend that the primary model for the academic stage of legal education in Hong Kong should comprise a four-year degree in the first two or three years of which law and non-law subjects are taken concurrently. Non-law subjects should represent approximately one-quarter of the credit load ... and law subjects three-quarters.

...

7.5.1 That law schools be funded with such additional resources as are necessary to support the adoption of the interactive mode of teaching recommended as the standard mode of teaching and learning. This method requires a lower staff/student ratio than passive modes of instruction based upon large lecture groups.

7.6.5 That at least one of the law schools be permitted, and given the resources to enable it, to offer a true part-time LLB degree that might be undertaken by non-graduates as well as by graduates.

7.9 Achieving balance between the two law schools

...

The present imbalance in student and staff numbers strongly favours the more established school (HKU). Accordingly, the consultants recommend that a conscious decision be taken to strengthen the law student intake and, consequently, staffing levels at CityU so that it achieves the critical mass that is a pre-condition to the healthy competition between two strong, balanced law schools.

...

Benchmark

All those seeking admission to practice in Hong Kong should have undertaken vocational preparation, comprising both institutional training and on-the-job experience and training, which, together with their academic preparation, has provided them with the knowledge, skills and professional values which give them threshold competency to practise law, under appropriate supervision, and to act professionally as a member of the legal profession.

Recommendations

The PCLL

8.1 That the PCLL be discontinued.

Organisational arrangements

That a separate institution be established to conduct a course of practical vocational preparation for law graduates seeking to be admitted as barristers or solicitors in Hong Kong.

Comment

In practice, few of the reviewers' recommendations have been implemented. The one-year PCLL remains (delivered by the universities); lecture-dominated teaching remains the norm at undergraduate level and, although the length of the standard law degree has been increased to four years, this has been to accommodate "rolled back" law subjects from PCLL rather than to include broadening non-law subjects. Indeed, the law schools have asserted that there is no time for non-law subjects; given the need to accommodate an increased number of "core" and elective modules into the law degree (and JD) programmes so as to ensure that the PCLL is a "skills only" programme. The two law schools have not been "equalised", though the advent of a third law school at Chinese University HK may be seen to have obviated the need for such. No genuinely part-time law degree has been introduced at any of the three law schools. The post-review "skills only" PCLL does largely reflect, in part, what the reviewers recommended for professional legal education in Hong Kong, but is far longer in duration from the model envisaged, and is administered by the law schools rather than the legal profession. Thus far, the introduction of an "Academy-led" professional programme has been successfully resisted by Hong Kong's law schools.

In 2015 a further review of legal education was instituted.[133] Many wondered why, given the almost total lack of positive response to the first. Before the second review had published its findings the Law Society announced[134] that, from 2021 (or later), it would administer its own "Common Entrance Examination (CEE)" to ensure maintenance of standards and increase "opportunity". Since the Law Society appears to envisage that only PCLL completers will be permitted to sit the CEE, it is difficult to see any evidence of increased opportunity.[135] The new CEE proposal is discussed below.

On one issue, the need for greater emphasis on active learning,[136] the (2001) reviewers did recognise a major stumbling block; namely that law schools "inherit" students from a Hong Kong school system which places great emphasis on rote and passive learning, at the expense of individual "student-based" learning and analysis. The reviewers quoted a contribution from Professors Yash Ghai and Jill Cottrell (highly experienced [then] Hong Kong University academics) who, while doubting that the problem was Hong Kong specific, stated:

> It is the task of the law faculties to offer the students the chance to learn the law, to stimulate, provoke them, inspire them to take an initiative in doing so. It is

---

133. Under the Chairmanship of Judge Woo with members Professors Julian Webb (Melbourne University) and Tony Smith (Victoria University of Wellington).
134. Law Society of Hong Kong, Press Release, 6 January 2016.
135. In 2015 fewer than 40% of PCLL applicants were accepted on to the programmes.
136. See, eg, D Oliver, 'The Integration of Teaching and Research in the Law Department' (1996) 30 Law Teacher 133, 143 (views endorsed by Roper/Redmond Report at 162).

impossible to deny that we face challenges in terms of achieving these ambitions of inspiring and provoking our students. Most of us feel that the students, while able, lack self-confidence to work on their own, lack experience of doing so, believe that it is the function of the teacher to tell them the answers or how to find the answers ... We may ... face a degree of resistance that is not found in some other countries, resulting from the fact that Hong Kong is a very small place and that the student body is perhaps rather homogenous ... where there is a tradition of bonding and corporate spirit which can very easily be at odds with the objectives of the teachers ... We also know that the students *can* respond and will develop a pride in being able to do things for themselves. Maybe here we are guilty of giving conflicting messages: some courses and teachers giving the impression that passivity is acceptable while others are trying to encourage or even require an active approach.[137]

Hong Kong's education system has been amended to a "3-3-4" system which sees an extra year at university intended to "convert" students to a more active learning curriculum. Ironically, the key review recommendation involving the introduction of a four year LLB degree programme, to accommodate increased legal and non-legal coverage, was only partially met since the additional year allocated has been taken up almost entirely by increased substantive law coverage, to enable PCLL to become a "skills only" programme. The reviewers envisaged the four-year "broadening" LLB programme being followed by a short (around three to four months) professional training programme, offered by a legal profession-run "Academy", to replace the PCLL. The consultants' most emphatic recommendation was for the abolition of the PCLL[138] which they saw as antiquated ("frozen in time") and out of touch with professional legal training elsewhere in the common law world. Roper and Redmond wrote of the PCLL at the University of Hong Kong:

> By world standards, it is incredible that the curriculum could have remained unreformed for almost 30 years – in a time of such rapid and profound change.[139]

While a four-year LLB (with UGC funding) was agreed and commenced in 2004,[140] the University of Hong Kong (HKU), City University of Hong Kong (CityU) and (now) Chinese University of Hong Kong (CUHK) continue to offer a one-year PCLL programme[141] which has been retained as a result of successful lobbying by (primarily) the University of Hong Kong Law Faculty.[142]

---

137. Roper/Redmond Report, 161.
138. Recommendation 76 which recommends tersely: "The PCLL be discontinued."
139. Those familiar with "leadership issues" in the Department of Professional Legal Education at the University of Hong Kong found it less "incredible".
140. The first "four-year" graduates, of course, emerged in 2008.
141. Currently, the University of Hong Kong offers a two-year part-time alternative.
142. The main concern of the then Dean, Professor Albert Chen, was that the loss of one of "his" two departments would threaten the Law School's "Faculty" status. The consultants had anticipated HKU Law Faculty opposition but had reckoned without the "alumni" networking potential of the University of Hong Kong. Former graduates such as Margaret Ng (LegCo representative for the legal functional constituency) immediately condemned the Consultants' Report: M Ng, 'Law Report

The PCLL programmes *have* been reformed so as to make them largely "skills only".[143] As a consequence, since no new substantive law will be taught on the PCLL programmes,[144] a greatly expanded range of "core" PCLL "pre-requisite" subjects has been introduced for PCLL admission from 2008.[145] Thus, as mentioned above, little scope exists for the recommended exposure of students to non-law subjects. Ironically, one effect of the reforms is to make entrance to PCLL far harder for those with common law degrees from outside Hong Kong; despite the fact that a major concern expressed by the consultants was the quality of Hong Kong "local" law graduates.[146] Those graduates (or JD/CPE holders) lacking any of the "core" pre-requisite subjects (usually overseas graduates)[147] must pass public "PCLL Conversion Examinations" in such subjects.[148] The immediate consequence of the reforms was that, in 2008 and 2009, all three Hong Kong law schools were hugely under-subscribed for their PCLL programmes.[149] The "numbers" issue continues to be a major problem since, now, the 2008/2009 shortage of PCLL aspirants has been entirely transformed to a huge over-abundance of eligible PCLL students, many of them unable to obtain a treasured PCLL place.

While the new "skills only" PCLL programmes have produced a significant improvement on the previously obsolete HKU model[150] and while numbers on PCLL programmes have risen to cater, especially, for the graduates of the (now) three JD programmes on offer,[151] two key problems remain. The first is that caps on

---

Fails Grade' *South China Morning Post* (Hong Kong, 15 August 2001); and questioned the reviewers' impartiality. See also A Chen (Dean, HKU Law Faculty, *Third Submission to the Consultants on the Review of Legal Education HK*).

143. No explanation has ever been offered as to why the PCLL programmes need to be one year long, when the consultants believed a programme that lasts three to four months would be adequate.
144. This, at least, is the theory; though subjects such as succession which are not taken on many degree programmes are offered as PCLL options and presumably require substantive coverage.
145. There are 11 "core" subjects, which may be studied in any common law jurisdiction, plus three (but see footnote 25) "top-up" subjects which must be based on Hong Kong law.
146. Most international law firms in Hong Kong recruit primarily from those with common law degrees from outside Hong Kong.
147. All English law graduates, for example, would have to take as a minimum the three Hong Kong law "top-up" papers and, almost certainly, Civil Procedure and Criminal Procedure which are not part of most academic law degrees in Britain. The "almost" in the preceding sentence will, it appears, soon be redundant (see n 25).
148. The examinations are administered by the Hong Kong legal profession via the "PCLL Conversion Examination and Administration Ltd".
149. Given the generally huge demand for PCLL places such under-recruitment was solely the result of the late finalisation and announcement of the changes to PCLL admission rules by the Hong Kong legal profession. Those who had already commenced overseas common law degrees on the assumption that they would be eligible to apply for PCLL on completion discovered only in 2006 that this would not be the case: see L Heron, 'Law Course Hit by Entry-Rule Changes' *South China Morning Post* (Hong Kong, 4 September 2008)].
150. See, eg, S Nathanson, W Chow, and F Chan, 'The University of Hong Kong's New PCLL' (2002) 32/2 HKLJ 381–400.
151. By far the largest of these is the JD at the Chinese University of Hong Kong.

PCLL numbers[152] ensure that Hong Kong retains its low "lawyer to general population" ratio which results in the high cost of legal services and the agglomeration of lawyers in the more expensive central business district (with little local legal service in other areas).[153] The second is that the UGC-funded PCLL remains essentially a programme for intending solicitors, with little specialised legal education for intending barristers.[154] This represents probably the only example in the common law world of a split profession with unified legal education.

"Concerns" about the PCLL "situation" have led to calls for an alternative means to qualification for legal practice in Hong Kong. The concerns reflect two somewhat conflicting views: one that too many students are successfully completing PCLL while lacking the necessary intellectual initiative and independence; the other that there are insufficient PCLL places, causing significant numbers of potentially good lawyers to miss out on a chance to enter the profession.[155] It is certainly the case that almost all accepted students pass PCLL (albeit sometimes after resits).[156] This *could* be explained by pointing out that entry standards are so high that only those good enough to pass are accepted. Nonetheless, anecdotally, there are reports that weak professional students are permitted to pass PCLL. The exceptionally high pass rate does raise concerns, given that the "skills only" PCLL programme differs markedly from the more traditional teaching and learning of the local law degrees, such that one would expect at least some adequate law degree students to be found wanting by the demands of professional legal education.

The PCLL "bottleneck", which prevents many PCLL aspirants from getting a PCLL opportunity, also causes concern; especially amongst parents whose children appear to have done well on overseas law degrees but are denied a PCLL place. One important reason for this is that law schools elsewhere, especially in Britain, treat year one subjects as merely part of a "qualifying year" in which marks do not count towards the final degree classification. Conversely, Hong Kong PCLL providers

---

152. While it is true that the universities have some leeway on numbers via the non-UGC funded, "full cost" route, they have been quite conservative in increasing PCLL opportunities.
153. The Hong Kong situation for prospective solicitors (difficulty in obtaining a PCLL place but excellent job prospects on completion) is the total opposite of that in Britain where finding a Legal Practice Course place is relatively easy but training contracts thereafter are very hard to secure: see, eg, O Bowcott, 'Law Graduates Hit by Stiff Competition, Legal Aid Cuts & Falling Crime' *The Guardian* (London, 29 June 2014).
154. The rationale for this situation is sometimes said to be that it is "too soon" for those just completing their law degree to decide which branch of the profession to join. Apparently, by some osmotic process the decision becomes easier after a year's exposure to a solicitors' professional programme!
155. The sensible view that there should be greater PCLL "opportunity" is espoused by Chan (J Chan, 'Best Practice' *South China Morning Post* [Hong Kong 9 April 2015]) whose arguments are undermined by his wildly inaccurate claim that before 1997 English students could become lawyers in Hong Kong on mere completion of the "Common Professional Examination (CPE)". CPE has never, of itself, produced eligibility to practise.
156. PCLL providers admit, at least privately, that there are almost no failures (post-resits) on PCLL. Given the significant excess of PCLL applicants for available places (allowing providers to be very selective) this is, perhaps, unsurprising.

look at the undergraduate's marks in *all* subjects in determining PCLL admission. A graduate with a 2(1) from a "good" British law school may, therefore, be viewed as undeserving of a PCLL place by PCLL admissions teams, to the great consternation and concern of the applicant (and his/her parents!). This issue is referred to by Malcolm Merry, previous head of DOPLE at the University of Hong Kong, who also refers to the issue of "grade inflation" in overseas law schools.[157]

The "standards/bottleneck" concerns have led, since 2014, to a resurgence of plans to offer an alternative to PCLL, under the aegis of the Hong Kong Law Society, at least in relation to prospective solicitors.[158] This would take the form of a "Common Entry Examination" (CEE), made possible by the provisions in the Legal Practitioners Ordinance (LPO)[159] on qualification for admission as a solicitor. Section 4(1)(a) of the Ordinance states that:

> The Court may, in such manner as may be prescribed by the Chief Justice, admit as a solicitor of the High Court a person who the Court considers is a fit and proper person to be a solicitor and who ... has complied with requirements prescribed by the Council with respect to employment as a trainee solicitor, the passing of examinations and the completion of courses.

The "requirements" described are defined in Rule 7 of the Trainee Solicitors Rules[160] which states that:

> A person may only enter into a trainee solicitor contract if he–
> (a) has passed or received a certificate of completion or certificate of satisfactory completion as the case may be in–
>   (i) the Postgraduate Certificate in Laws and such other examination or course as the Society may require and set or approve; or [emphasis added]
>   (ii) such other examination or course as the Society may require and set or approve

Scope exists, therefore, for the Hong Kong Law Society to extend opportunities for access to the solicitors' branch of the profession in Hong Kong by providing an *alternative* to PCLL *or* to limit numbers still further by requiring the passing of an *additional* test. Indeed, the Law Society has had the Academy/Alternative Route on its official agenda since its "Position Paper",[161] issued very soon after the (2001) review. The paper expressed the view[162] that:

---

157. See M Merry, 'Not Entirely Legal' part 67.
158. The position of the Hong Kong Bar on an alternative to PCLL has not been clarified but it appears to oppose the CEE proposal.
159. Cap 159.
160. Cap 159J.
161. The Law Society of Hong Kong, *Position on Legal Education and Training* (September 2001).
162. Ibid 8. See also Ambrose Lam (then Law Society president) Speech at Ceremonial Opening of the Legal Year, 13 January 2014.

> 2.1 Aim of an LPC course (the PCLL should be discontinued)
>
> A Legal Practice Course (LPC) should orientate students from their academic studies in the law degree to the actual practice of law. It should thus:
>
> (a) prepare students for general practice by equipping them with the basic skills to perform with competence legal work in specific fields; and
>
> (b) provide students with a general foundation for subsequent practice by equipping them with basic skills to develop new competencies in response to employer and client needs.
>
> 2.2 Governance of an LPC course
>
> The LPC should be conducted by a free-standing institution in its own premises established under the Legal Practitioners Ordinance, its own ordinance, as a company or in some other way, and governed by a board which would consist of all stakeholders in legal education (ie the judiciary, government, the universities and the wider community) but with dominant representation by both branches of the profession on an equal basis. Ultimately, the LPC could be conducted by the proposed Academy of Law.

The concerns outlined above have emboldened the Law Society to revisit the issue.[163] However, its current thinking *seems to be* that any new examination would be administered post-PCLL, and be open only to PCLL completers.[164]

The law schools, generally, have been against the introduction of an alternative or profession-led test and have asserted, with some justification, that the legal profession has not formally complained about the standards or delivery of the PCLL, since the first review *and* that all PCLL institutions are subject to External Examiner scrutiny which has not demonstrated serious dissatisfaction. The Bar, too, has opposed the CEE leading to the potentially strange situation of a required additional test for prospective solicitors but *not* aspiring barristers. A temporary hiatus to the Law Society's proposals was produced by the Secretary for Justice's advice that the Law Society should await the publication of the Woo/Rogers Report. The Report has been published and one of its major recommendations is that, "consideration be given to the establishment for Hong Kong of a School of Professional Legal Studies, with a view to preparing candidates for entry to the legal profession and the practice of law."[165] While this may give tacit support to greater involvement in professional legal education for the profession, it is tempered by the recommendation that there should be a "moratorium" to continuation on the "additional examination" (CEE)

---

163. The Law Society issued a consultation paper on CEE in December 2013.
164. Law Society Press Release, *Common Entrance Examination*. It is certain that any test administered by the profession would have a much higher failure rate than PCLL.
165. The key Report concerns are comparability of standards for the three current PCLL providers and equitable "access" to PCLL.

route pending the completion of a "further Benchmarking exercise for PCLL." It is rumoured, however, that the Law Society is determined to press on with CEE.

7.6 The case for fusion

Given the increased blurring of the distinctions between barristers and solicitors (higher rights of audience for some solicitors, a measure of direct access to barristers) and the salient point that barristers have little specialised legal education, there is a strong case for a "fused", unified profession. Nor can this be seen as break with long-established tradition (as in England) given that Hong Kong did, briefly, have a fused legal profession in the nineteenth century.[166]

The notion of a "consultancy" branch of the profession is difficult to make out when both branches of the profession have, broadly, the same legal education and the "consultants" thereafter do only one year of professional training as opposed to the "non-consultants'" two! In the split British profession, where fusion has long been debated, there is at least the counter-argument that barristers have specialised barrister training courses, which focus specifically on the skills needed by a barrister, and seek to attract the best and most highly motivated law graduates. Neither of these arguments applies in Hong Kong where, as reported in the *South China Morning Post*:

> The profession of barrister is now seen as being increasingly polarised between the very best law students, who usually aspire to be barristers, and those students who are not good enough to obtain a training contract at a solicitor's firm.[167]
>
> [Bar Association chairman Russell] Coleman acknowledged that when law firms tightened their budgets for training contracts, inevitably a proportion of law students entered pupillage due to circumstances more than commitment or aspiration.[168]

In the same article the newspaper reported the setting up of a "special committee for pupillage reform" under the chairmanship of Clive Grossman, SC. The objectives of the new committee would be to ensure proper standards of training at the pupillage stage, "which could result in fewer but better barristers who are guaranteed to have met a formal standard". Unfortunately what this proposal does *not* address is the crucial issue that there is no barrister-focused legal education in Hong Kong, without which the case for a separate bar is unconvincing. The reason for this is quite simply economic. Currently the "one size fits all" PCLL is funded largely from the

---

166. See P Wesley Smith, 'Nineteenth Century Fusion of the Legal Profession in Hong Kong' (1992) 22 HKLJ 257–268.
167. This fact has been acknowledged to the author by many senior barristers (on condition of anonymity!). The consequence is an over-supply of barristers such that, "anyone who's less than competent won't survive and should consider changing careers". See P Moy, 'Bar Humbug' *South China Morning Post* (Hong Kong, 11 May 2007). Since then things have got worse!
168. Albert Wong, 'Barrister Training under Review' *South China Morning Post* (Hong Kong, 11 May 2010).

public purse,[169] while separate legal education for barristers would have to be funded by the Hong Kong bar, whose members appear unwilling to pay for such.

A significant argument in favour of fusion is the "cost to client" one. Although the additional cost factor is sometimes exaggerated (solicitors performing the same tasks in Britain usually charge more for them than barristers) the issue of "double-manning" is significant. A solicitor usually needs to be present when a barrister is in court, takes instructions from a client or interviews a witness. This undoubtedly leads to an increase in costs to the client.

One significant argument remains for a split profession with a "consultancy" branch; that barristers (without the distractions of visiting clients) are better able to do research and prepare "counsel's opinions". While this may be true, the importance of such a "paper practice" in Hong Kong is diminishing as solicitors' firms increasing seek expert opinion from barristers (or perhaps tax experts or accountants) outside Hong Kong. This effect of globalisation cannot be restricted (unlike the right to appear in Hong Kong courts which is increasingly denied to overseas barristers).[170]

However, the most compelling reason for the retention of Hong Kong's split profession is that it is constitutionally endorsed by Article 94 of the Basic Law which states that:

> *On the basis of the system previous operating in Hong Kong* [emphasis added] the Government of the HKSAR may make provision for local lawyers and lawyers from outside Hong Kong to work and practise in the Region.

This is hardly an unequivocal assertion of maintaining the divided profession throughout the term of the Basic Law and the same could be said of Article 142(3) which states that:

> The Government of the HKSAR shall continue to recognize the professions and the professional organizations recognised prior to the establishment of the Region, and these organizations may, on their own, assess and confer professional qualifications.

Since the Basic Law refers to, where relevant, the "legal profession" rather than "barristers" or "solicitors" it could certainly be argued that fusion is constitutionally permitted. However, there is more "tangential" support for the divided profession in other legislation. For example, section 12 of the Hong Kong Court of Final Appeal Ordinance enacts that:

---

169. Most PCLL places are subsidised by the University Grants Committee, though (more expensive) self-funded places are also provided.
170. Pre-1997 it was a regular occurrence for British QC's to be briefed to appear in Hong Kong. Given the high cost of "local" Senior Counsel it was often cheaper to import a QC (even allowing for the cost of flights and accommodation!). With post-1997 "protectionism" the use of "imported" barristers is now far less common, though most big trials feature imported British "silks" (Queen's Counsel).

(1) A person shall be eligible to be appointed as the Chief Justice if he is . . .

. . .

(a) a barrister who has practised as a barrister or solicitor in Hong Kong for a period of at least 10 years

and similar wording is used in relation to eligibility to become a Permanent Judge or a Hong Kong Non-Permanent Judge. This provides at least some basis for saying that the Basic Law supports the continuation of a split profession. This was certainly the view taken by (then) Chairman of the Hong Kong Bar Association, Edward Chan SC who, in his 2004 "Opening of the Legal Year" speech, stated that:

> Hong Kong is and has always been one of the few places in the world with a separate and independent referral Bar. The one country two systems enshrined in our Basic Law ensure that our legal system would continue and together with it an independent referral Bar.
>
> An independent referral Bar has been of benefit to Hong Kong. The separation of work between the Barristers and the Solicitors has proved to be efficient and in fact the Hong Kong legal service is renowned for its quality and efficiency. Indeed it is often said that the rule of law and the provision of quality legal services are major factors for Hong Kong's success.
>
> Whatever one may say about the merits of having a fused legal profession few would disagree that an independent bar has been a success. The role of the Bar in safeguarding human rights and the rule of law are obvious for anyone to see.

Chan emphasised in his speech that "the overall paramount consideration must be the question of public interest" and it clear that arguments on both sides appeal to the perceived public interest. Nevertheless, it is inevitable that the Chairman of the Hong Kong Bar is also speaking for his "constituency" just as Presidents of the Law Society have, previously, reflected the interests of their members in calling for a fused profession or in demanding "higher rights of audience".

7.6.1 Higher rights of audience

It is clear that much of the argument for fusion is rendered nugatory by relatively recent developments in the area of higher rights of audience. Prior to these developments, barristers in Hong Kong possessed unlimited rights to appear before all courts while solicitors' rights of audience were far more circumscribed. Solicitors had no rights to appear in the High Court or Court of Final Appeal. Their *de facto* "jurisdiction" was first extended by the significant increase in the District Court's financial limits.[171] Then, via the Legal Practitioners (Amendment) Ordinance of 2010, solicitors were permitted to seek the right to appear in the highest courts. The procedure on application is that the aspirant advocate is assessed by the Higher Rights Assessment

---

171. It was raised to $1 million in 2003, though the limit in cases involving land is $3 million.

Board (HRAB). The applicant must have had at least five years' post-qualification experience, of which at least two years must have been in Hong Kong. The HRAB must be satisfied that the applicant acquired sufficient litigation experience before granting the application. The case for higher rights of audience was a strong one. As Barnes[172] writes:

> It has been apparent for some time that the artificial and illogical restriction on solicitor-advocates appearing in the higher courts is inappropriate and unsustainable ... Ultimately there can be no rational basis for preventing a competent and experienced advocate in his or her area of specialty [sic] appearing in the courts on behalf of a client who wishes the case to be presented by that advocate and no one else ... If anything, the added competition should spur the Bar to strive for higher standards.

In practice, "take up" for higher rights by solicitors has been quite limited. Only those with regular advocacy experience in the lower courts are likely to apply successfully and the numbers are unlikely to be large.

It can be argued that, with an opportunity now being given to enthusiastic and talented solicitors to appear in the higher courts, further moves to fusion are unnecessary. This was certainly the view of outgoing Chief Justice, Andrew Li who said:

> The grant of higher rights of audience for solicitors through an assessment process is a significant development. I think the present structure of the profession has served the public quite well. I do not favour a fused profession.[173]

Nonetheless, rather than require callow PCLL graduates to determine immediately (on the basis of their limited PCLL experience) whether they wish to become solicitors or barristers, it may be more sensible (especially given a unitary PCLL) for all PCLL completers to become solicitor trainees, with a view to them making a decision whether or not to specialise in advocacy/litigation (with or without the epithet "barrister") some years later. This would be more likely to produce "barristers" with a genuine interest, and ability, in advocacy for the benefit of all, including the client.

7.7 The contingency fee/conditional fee debate

Given the high cost of legal services in Hong Kong and the very limited application of publicly-funded legal aid, consideration has been given to the introduction of contingency fees, or conditional fees.

Contingency fees (whereby a lawyer may receive nothing in a lost case but will have a significant "share" in any "winnings") are widely used in the United States. They have the merit of making available the possibility of litigation to those who

---

172. P Barnes, 'Higher Rights of Audience: What Took It So Long' Hong Kong Legal Community, 13 April 2010.
173. 'Chief Justice Andrew Li, "Departing with No Regret"' Hong Kong Legal Community (LexisNexis, Hong Kong, 23 August 2010).

would be unable otherwise to afford the cost. The major concerns over such fees (by which lawyers may recover as much of 50% of a winning client's damages), are that lawyers may cut "ethical" corners and, because of the knowledge that the client will only get a part of the money, that damages awards may be inflated.[174] Because of these concerns, contingency fees are not permitted in England or Hong Kong. English law does now, however, permit "conditional" fees. These permit a "no win, no fee" arrangement in return for an increased fee for the lawyer. The lawyer, therefore, does not get a share of "winnings" but can charge a premium of up to double his normal fee for the work done, in return for remaining unpaid in the event of defeat. Even this limited change to traditional fee arrangements has been resisted in Hong Kong.[175]

7.8 Legal executives

Finally, a brief word on legal executives. These are employed by solicitors to assist them in their professional work. Some firms refer to them as law clerks. While there is sometimes an elision as regards the perception of legal executives and "paralegals" there is a significant distinction in terms of role and status.

The Hong Kong Law Society has introduced benchmarks for the training of legal executives amidst concerns about variable standards. In future, only those who have been educated in a programme validated by the Law Society as fulfilling its benchmarked requirements may use the title "legal executive".[176]

The work of legal executives varies and they are regularly entrusted with work in the office by their principals. It is very common for legal executives to have regular and direct contact with clients.[177] The legal executive is responsible to his principal and the principal is "vicariously" responsible to the client.

While legal executives in Hong Kong do not have the same extensive powers and potential of their British counterparts[178] they do enjoy some special rights of audience. They may appear before a District Judge in Chambers on an uncontested application in a civil matter, or in the Court of First Instance before a Master in Chambers on an uncontested application or on an application listed for a three-minute hearing. In each instance the legal executive must be employed by or under the supervision of a solicitor.

---

174. This is particularly likely in the United States where the use of civil juries remains widespread.
175. See further discussion, including the "maintenance/champerty" issue, in Chapter 9. A further hurdle is that of the insurance required to facilitate such a scheme. It is felt that, in Hong Kong, this may be prohibitively expensive.
176. No such benchmarking exists as to "paralegals", a vague descriptor applied to many non-lawyers working in law firms.
177. Much of the important work of conveyancing is performed by legal executives, albeit under the supervision of a solicitor "principal".
178. There are now a number of partners in British law firms who are legal executives rather than solicitors.

8
Lay Participation in the Hong Kong Legal System

Overview

Laymen play a significant role in the Hong Kong legal system. While most academic attention is focused on the lay jury, Hong Kong has both lay prosecutors and lay ("special") magistrates.

The operation of the jury system arouses great passions throughout the common law world. Some see it as an essential involvement of "the ordinary man" in the administration of justice; a potential check on the power of the state. Others see juries as inefficient, irrational and cumbersome; doing a job which professionals could do much better (and quicker and cheaper). Controversial jury acquittals invariably lead to calls, from the jury's critics, for the abolition or reform of the jury system. This is especially true in those areas where critics see the jury as incapable of understanding complicated evidence, as in the case of complex fraud trials. Conversely, any attempt to erode the use of jury trials tends to be met by fierce resistance from the jury's champions.

The use of the jury in common law systems derives from a very ancient tradition of jury use in England. The introduction of the jury system in Hong Kong is one of the most significant features of the British colonisation of Hong Kong and the continuing use of the jury, post-1997, is specifically stipulated under the Basic Law.[1]

As in Britain (but unlike the United States where the civil jury is not unusual), juries in Hong Kong are used primarily in criminal cases involving crimes of a more serious nature. Indeed, even in relatively serious criminal matters, trial by jury may be denied to a defendant in Hong Kong when his trial takes place in the Magistrates' Court or District Court.

The Hong Kong jury differs in some respects from all its other common law counterparts. For one thing, the importance accorded to jury attendance in terms of "civic duty" is unique, and avoidance of such duty is much harder in Hong Kong than elsewhere. The Hong Kong jury also has fewer members than its counterparts elsewhere and makes greater use of majority verdicts. Most significantly, the recruitment

---

1. Article 86.

of jurors in Hong Kong is from a relatively small pool, given the existing educational requirements, language considerations, and an extensive list of exemptions.

The use of lay prosecutors and special magistrates in Hong Kong has little to commend it other than its cheapness. It really has no place in a modern, developed society. This lay use applies only in respect of less serious criminal offences where it is perceived that a lack of legal training and expertise can do less harm.

8.1 The jury in Hong Kong

While the use of the jury is widespread in the common law world, the Hong Kong jury has its own peculiarities, in terms of numbers of jurors, the system of majority voting and the importance accorded to jury attendance in terms of civic duty. The Hong Kong jury tends to be selected, because of educational and (to a decreasing degree) language requirements, from a fairly small, and some would say unrepresentative, section of society.

While the jury remains a well-respected institution in Hong Kong, analysis of its role and operation is hampered by a lack of contemporary Hong Kong–specific jury research.

8.1.1 The scope of jury use in Hong Kong

The scope of jury use in colonial and post-colonial Hong Kong has always been restricted, partly because of a perceived lack of suitable jurors. The first relevant statute, the Ordinance for the Regulation of Jurors and Juries of 1845,[2] established that, in the Supreme Court, all disputed issues of *fact* should be determined by a jury (of six men). Criminal juries are now relatively rare and civil juries exceptional.

In criminal cases, juries are used only in the most serious cases, such as murder, robbery, rape and serious commercial fraud cases, tried before a judge in the Court of First Instance of the High Court. In overall terms, such jury trials represent only a small proportion of the total number of criminal trials in Hong Kong.[3] In recent times the most celebrated of the criminal jury trials in Hong Kong have been the Kissell "milkshake murder" case and the major corruption case involving former Chief Secretary, Rafael Hui, two of the billionaire Kwok brothers (of Sun Hung Kai Properties) and others.

Juries may also be used in some civil cases but this is exceptional. The use of the civil jury in Hong Kong (as with Britain) has been eroded so that its use is restricted, in practice, only to the occasional defamation case,[4] where one of the parties chooses to have issues of fact determined by a jury *and* that party's request for jury trial is

---

2. Ordinance No 7 of 1845.
3. There were 493 criminal jury cases in Hong Kong in 2015 (Judiciary Annual Report 2015).
4. In statistical terms the civil jury is used in Hong Kong, in fewer than 1% of civil cases and almost only in defamation cases.

upheld on the basis that there are crucial issues of fact to be determined, especially as to the veracity of the parties.

A relatively topical, and well-reported,[5] civil jury case involved Paul Chan, a member of Chief Executive Carrie Lam's administration and previously that of C Y Leung.[6] Chan was sued for libel by Mr Carl Lu and his twin children following an email headed "Head boy cheating", sent by Chan's wife and co-signed by him, stating:

> I've heard through the grapevine that Jonathan and his twin sister were caught cheating at Econ exam but apparently they managed to get away without any consequences and that is because their daddy sits on the board.

The school had investigated the allegations and exonerated the twins but similar subsequent allegations were made by the Chans. The Lus' application for jury trial had been upheld by Poon J and the "seven man"[7] jury subsequently upheld the plaintiffs' case.[8] The Chans were required to pay over $200,000 in damages for injury to the plaintiffs' reputation; doubtless exacerbated by the defendants' affirmation as to Paul Chan's "status", intended to give "weight" to the allegations. The initial verdict was overturned by the Court of Appeal but is currently the subject of a further appeal to the Court of Final Appeal.

This limited use of the criminal and civil jury in Hong Kong endorses the view of Lord Denning, Master of the Rolls, in the English Court of Appeal judgment in *Ward v James*,[9] where he stated (in rejecting the use of a jury in a personal injury case):

> Let it not be supposed that this court is in any way opposed to trial by jury . . . Whenever a man is on trial for serious crime, or when in a civil case a man's honour or integrity is at stake, or when one or other party must be deliberately lying, then trial by jury has no equal.[10]

Juries (of five people) are also used in the Hong Kong Coroner's Court in cases of sudden or suspicious death. These hearings, or "inquests", are relatively brief and the Coroner generally directs the jury as to the verdict they should return. Such inquests are not common and, in the whole of 2015, only 93 jury[11] inquests were held.[12]

---

5. See *The Standard* (Hong Kong, 29 May 2013; 30 May 2013; 5 September 2014; 19 September 2014; 26 September 2014).
6. It would be an understatement to say that Mr Chan is no stranger to controversy.
7. In fact, somewhat curiously, a seven women jury.
8. Despite Chan's earlier claim that the libel case was "far-fetched and desperate"! (*The Standard*, 28 November 2013.)
9. [1966] 1 QB 273.
10. Ibid 295.
11. The Coroner decides whether or not to summon a jury.
12. Hong Kong Judiciary Annual Report 2015.

8.1.2 The function of the Hong Kong jury

In all cases, civil or criminal, the function of the jury is to determine issues of *fact* rather than law. It is the role of the judge to determine issues of law and to advise the jury accordingly. So, for example, a judge in a criminal case may advise the jury that, as a matter of law, if they believe the defendant's defence that he was somewhere else at the time the offence was committed, they must acquit him; but it is for the jury to decide whether they do believe the defendant. Advice on the differing functions of judge and jury should be given by the judge. This will be broadly along the lines (though need not be *verbatim*) of the "model direction" issued by the Judicial Studies Board in England, in 1991, and endorsed by the then Lord Chief Justice:

> It is my job to tell you what the law is and how to apply it to the issues of fact that you have to decide and to remind you of the important evidence on these issues. As to the law, you must accept what I tell you. As to the facts, you alone are the judges. It is for you to decide what evidence you accept and what evidence you reject or of which you are unsure. If I appear to have a view of the evidence or of the facts with which you do not agree, reject my view. If I mention or emphasise evidence that you regard as unimportant, disregard that evidence. If I do not mention what you regard as important, follow your own view and take that evidence into account.

The role of the jury is circumscribed. In criminal cases the jury's function is to determine whether guilt has been established "beyond reasonable doubt". In civil cases, such as defamation or malicious prosecution, the jury has to determine, for example, whether the words alleged had actually been uttered by the defendant. The Hong Kong civil jury, unlike its American counterpart, is not involved in the assessment of damages. Even the role of the Coroner's Jury is restricted, since the jury is expected to adhere to the Coroner's advice in attributing the cause of death. Moreover, the jury is not permitted to assign guilt to an individual via its verdict,[13] or indeed, to indicate civil liability.

While juries are not required to determine issues of law, considerable deference is extended to their findings of fact. It is extremely unusual for appeals to be allowed on the basis that a jury has come to the wrong factual decision; most appeals are on the basis that the judge has made an error of law.[14] The principle is that the jurors have seen and heard the witnesses and the defendant and they, as ordinary laymen, can be trusted to decide who is telling the truth. Only where a jury reaches a decision on the facts which no reasonable jury could reach will their decision be overturned.[15]

---

13. Where it appears to the Coroner that an unlawful homicide has occurred (murder, manslaughter, death by dangerous driving, etc) he must inform the Secretary for Justice and adjourn the inquest until any criminal proceedings are completed.
14. In the famous Nancy Kissell appeal, for example, the grounds were the (alleged) prejudicial nature of part of the trial judge's summing up and the confusion caused by his "verbosity".
15. Given that juries do not give reasons for their verdicts this could hardly be otherwise.

Since a judge determines issues of law he may, having heard the prosecution's case, decide that there is no realistic case for the prosecution (it is for the prosecution to prove guilt and not the defendant to prove innocence). In such a circumstance the judge may direct the jury to acquit. It has long been established that, even in cases of a weak defence, the judge is never entitled to direct a *conviction*. This principle was upheld by the English House of Lords in *R v Wang*[16] where that court stated:

> We would accordingly allow the appeal by saying . . . that there are no circumstances in which a judge is entitled to direct a jury to return a verdict of guilty.[17]

Since the decision reinforces an established principle of the common law by the highest court in England, it is highly likely to be followed in Hong Kong.

8.1.3 Composition and eligibility of the Hong Kong jury

The rules on jury composition and eligibility for jury service have evolved considerably since their inception in 1845.[18] Initially, the jury was to comprise six *men* resident in Hong Kong.[19] The rationale for requiring only six rather than the English norm of 12 was that because of the "smallness of the population [there would be] very great hardship and inconvenience"[20] were there to be a requirement for 12 jurors. Despite the recognised dearth of potential jurors, further restrictions were initially imposed by the financial eligibility rules whereby jurors must either be property holders[21] or have a salary of, initially, $1,000 per year[22] (later reduced to $500 per year to address the difficulty in empanelling sufficient jurors).[23]

Despite the difficulties in finding sufficient eligible jurors, the normal number of jurors was increased from six to seven in 1864.[24] Moreover, judges were empowered, in 1986, to empanel a jury of nine.[25] By 1986, of course, the pool of potential jurors had increased considerably and by increasing the pool the potential existed, especially in lengthy cases, for the jury to remain quorate even where some jurors "fell by the wayside".[26] The Law Reform Commission of Hong Kong[27] quotes research by Duff et al[28] which states that:

---

16. [2005] UKHL 9.
17. Ibid para 18.
18. Ordinance for the Regulation of Jurors and Juries.
19. It appears that the normal principle of interpretation, that the masculine should include the feminine, did not obtain here; since the "jury franchise" was specifically extended to include women in 1947.
20. Ordinance No 7 of 1845, s 1.
21. As owner or tenant of a property with a monthly value of at least $25.
22. Under the 1845 Ordinance.
23. Ordinance No 4 of 1849.
24. Ordinance No 11 of 1864, s 2.
25. Jury (Amendment) Ordinance (No 3 of 1986).
26. A valid jury determination can be made by as few as five jurors.
27. Report on "Eligibility for Jury Service".
28. P Duff, M Findlay, C Howarth, and T-F Chan, *Juries: A Hong Kong Perspective* (Hong Kong University Press 1992).

In anticipation of the forthcoming *Carrian* case, which involved the trial of a complicated commercial fraud, legislation was hurriedly passed to allow the court to increase the size of the Jury to nine.[29]

Further significant developments included the substitution, in 1851, of the property/income qualifications by a vague requirement that a juror must be a "good and sufficient person"[30] and the extension of jury eligibility to women in 1947.[31]

The most important eligibility restriction, however, introduced in 1851[32] in recognition of the fact that English was then the language of the Hong Kong courts, was the disqualification of: "any person ignorant of the English language".[33]

That restriction remained crucial, until comparatively recently, in terms of limiting the pool of potential jurors in Hong Kong *and* in ensuring that the typical defendant was rarely judged by "his peers". Even today, the majority of Court of First Instance (jury) trials are conducted in English.

In respect of current rules, section 4 of the Jury Ordinance[34] (JO) sets out the list of persons who are eligible for jury service. Hong Kong residents aged between 21 and 65, of good character and sound mind, who have sufficient knowledge of the language in which the proceedings are to be conducted, may be selected at random for service. There is, however, a substantial list of exemptions and disqualifications.

The procedure for empanelling the jury is that a jury "pool" (around 20 people) is summoned to appear on a certain date. From this pool, the number may be reduced by a plea of exemption by some of those called and by "challenge" by the defence or "stand by" by the prosecution. The actual jury members for a trial are then selected by ballot in open court. The Hong Kong civil and criminal jury, in the Court of First Instance, normally consists of *seven* members. In appropriate cases, the judge may order that a jury of *nine* members be used. This will normally be in cases which are likely to be lengthy in order to ensure that, in cases of illness or other grounds for withdrawal, the jury will remain "quorate".

A number of exemptions are provided by JO section 5, and this is broader than in most jurisdictions. Some are analogous to those found elsewhere and unexceptional, such as judges, barristers, solicitors, Legislative Council (LegCo) and Executive Council (ExCo) members, police and members of the disciplined services, probation officers, monks, nuns and members of the armed forces. There are also a large number of others, some of them quite curious, such as spouses of judges of the High Court, doctors, pilots and aircraft crew, ships' crews, students, newspaper editors and veterinary surgeons!

---

29. Ibid 38.
30. Ordinance No 4 of 1851, s 2.
31. Ordinance No 37 of 1947.
32. Ordinance No 4 of 1851.
33. Ibid s 2.
34. Cap 3.

The requirement in JO section 4(1) that jurors must also be of "good character" and "of sound mind and not afflicted by blindness, deafness or other disability preventing the person from serving as a juror" further restricts the number of potential jurors, though all these criteria can be seen as sensible. While JO is not explicit as to what constitutes "good character" (the modern successor to a "good and sufficient person"), in practice those with a criminal conviction are excluded. The requirement of a "sound mind" can hardly be questioned and, since jurors are expected to consider the "demeanour" of witnesses and the defendant as well as their words, the blindness and deafness disqualifications are equally sound.

The consequence is that the potential jury pool is significantly reduced. Equally significant, though this will increasingly diminish in importance, is the requirement of understanding the language of the proceedings.

8.1.3.1 The language issue

Until comparatively recently there was a requirement that a Hong Kong juror must be competent in English. The previous version of section 4 of the Jury Ordinance stated that a juror must have "a knowledge of the English language sufficient to enable him to understand the evidence of witnesses, the address of counsel and the Judge's summing up."

Indeed, the first jury trial in Chinese did not take place until July 1997. The result was that the Hong Kong jury comprised, until recently, a disproportionate amount of native English speakers and the local Chinese "elite". In 1992 it was found that the roughly 2% of the population from Europe, Australia and North America constituted over 30% of the jury list.[35] This meant that the jury tended to be a better educated institution than elsewhere in the common law world but at the price of "unrepresentativeness".[36]

Although a formal requirement of English comprehension no longer exists,[37] the fact that a significant number of jury trials are still conducted in English[38] means that many of the summoned pool will not be eligible to sit and the issue of the unrepresentative jury, though diminished in importance, is not altogether a thing of the past. The language issue, and its link to educational requirements, was addressed in a newspaper article by Cliff Buddle who wrote:

> The reason for the educational requirement is that traditionally trials were held in English. But more and more are now being held in Chinese. Opening up the pool

---

35. P Duff, M Findlay, C Howarth and T-F Chan, *Juries: A Hong Kong Perspective* (Hong Kong University Press 1992). The authors also attest that the first Chinese member on the jury list did not feature until 1858.
36. See 8.1.3.3 below.
37. Jury (Amendment) Ordinance (No 72 of 1997).
38. According to the most recent data from the Department of Justice (2012) only 33% of jury cases in the Court of First Instance were conducted in Chinese. That percentage, however, was a considerable increase on that for 2011, so the position seems to be changing quite rapidly.

of jurors to those who cannot speak English would mean a system would have to be devised to tackle the language issue. Should there be a two-tier system, with a separate pool of jurors for Chinese-language trials? Or perhaps interpreters should be used to enable jurors who can speak only Cantonese to sit on English-language trials . . .

Both issues raise difficulties. A two-tier system might be perceived as leading to different standards of justice. The use of interpreters would mean breaking the golden rule that the jury's deliberations . . . must be conducted in secret.[39]

8.1.3.2 Jury challenges and "stand-by"

In common with most common law jurisdictions, Hong Kong allows challenge to potential jurors by the defence and prosecution.

The defendant has a right to challenge up to five potential jurors "peremptorily" (without giving a reason).[40] Where there are multiple defendants they can, potentially, "pool" their challenges by *each* making five peremptory challenges. It is also permissible to challenge "for cause" in the unlikely situation that the defendant can show a likelihood of personal bias against him. Refusal by the court of the defendant's right to challenge will be a ground of appeal and will make the trial a nullity. On the other hand, there is no requirement to inform a defendant of his right to challenge.

The prosecution also has a right to "stand by" potential jurors or to challenge them for cause. "Stand by" as the term suggests, involves requiring the potential juror to go to "the back of the queue" such that he is unlikely to be called on. No reason for "stand by" need be given. If, however, a number of "stand-bys" results in the person previously stood down returning to the head of the queue, the prosecution must now give cause if they wish to remove him (or her). The normal causes for challenge by the prosecution are that the potential juror is disqualified or is in a position where he may be biased in favour of the defendant.

There is a limited right for the judge to depart from the principle of "randomness", either at the request of the parties or on his own volition, in that he can make an order that the jury may be, "composed of men only or of women only".[41]

So, while the jury is "empanelled" on a random basis, its final composition may be less so. However, the use of challenge is not particularly common in Hong Kong, unlike other parts of the common law world. In the United States challenge and the widespread vetting of potential jurors means that the jury system has moved far from the principle of random selection. The use of peremptory challenge in England was

---

39. C Buddle, 'Confidence Ensures the Jury System Will Survive' *Sunday Morning Post* (Hong Kong, 16 March 2003).
40. Section 29, Jury Ordinance.
41. Section 20, Jury Ordinance.

reduced significantly over time[42] and has now been abolished,[43] partly as a result of the perception that multiple defendants were pooling their challenges to produce a jury perceived as being more favourably disposed towards the defendants.[44]

8.1.3.3 Is the jury representative?

The exemptions and disqualifications listed above, serve to reduce the pool, but the educational requirement and that of "language understanding" are more significant, because they may operate against the principal of "representativeness". The colonial requirement that a juror must have "knowledge of the language of proceedings", formerly excluded those who could not well understand English from most cases, given that English was the language of proceedings. Cheung[45] writes:

> The requirement of proficiency of English in Hong Kong, an overwhelmingly ethnic Chinese city, implied that most jury members were well-educated, middle class, professional or business persons. The great majority of the local population, whose native language was Chinese, were ineligible for jury service.[46]

With trials being increasingly conducted in Cantonese, the language issue is losing its importance. However, the typical defendant in a criminal case is still likely to be from a significantly different socio-economic group than most of the jury though the emphasis is increasingly on the difference in educational attainment between the defendant and the typical juror. The requirement, in practice, in respect of educational attainment is, currently, that a juror should have reached at least form 7. The Law Reform Commission report[47] on jury eligibility recommended the retention of the form 7 practice which "should be stipulated in legislation". The Commission recognised, however, that with the (then) impending "3-3-4" educational reforms,[48] the educational requirement would have to be amended.

The joint criteria of language understanding and educational attainment mean that the pool of eligible jurors in Hong Kong is fairly small. Jurors are still, usually, bilingual and middle class and, as such, not typical Hong Kong citizens. The traditional notion that an accused is tried by his peers does not strictly apply. The

---

42. Zander points out that until 1509 it was possible to peremptorily challenge 35 potential jurors! See M Zander, *Cases and Materials on the English Legal System* (10th edn, Cambridge University Press 2007) at page 423.
43. Section 118, Criminal Justice Act, 1988.
44. The Roskill Committee had recommended the abolition of peremptory challenge in fraud trials. However, the Thatcher Conservative government adopted the recommendation in respect of *all* trials on indictment (with a jury). The government was said to have been particularly enraged by the acquittals in the "Cyprus Spy" trial in which the six defendants "pooled" their challenges.
45. A Cheung, 'Language Rights and the Hong Kong Courts' (1997) 2(2) *Hong Kong Journal of Applied Linguistics* 49, 74.
46. Ibid 64.
47. Law Reform Commission of Hong Kong, *Criteria for Service as Jurors* and see 8.1.3.4 below.
48. Essentially Hong Kong pupils/students will spend one fewer year in school and one more at university.

conundrum is that the educational requirement, language considerations, and the culture of "civic duty" make the Hong Kong jury probably more "competent" than juries elsewhere but at the expense of true representativeness. Buddle[49] writes that:

> restricting the pool of jurors to those with a required level of education is controversial. It goes against the principle that defendants, who are often relatively uneducated, should be tried by people from similar backgrounds to themselves.
>
> The result is that Hong Kong jurors are drawn from a more narrow social background than in other parts of the world. They tend to be middle-class and conservative in their outlook and conviction rates are relatively high.[50]

In other jurisdictions, the issue of representativeness has produced extreme difficulties. Should a jury reflect a broad spectrum of society? If so, what society? Given local differences should a jury be representative of the area where the alleged offence was committed? Should the jury be "balanced" in terms of race, gender etc? To take just one example, from Britain, if the alleged offence concerns a black defendant, should the jury be racially mixed? As a general principle the English Court of Appeal has rejected the suggestion and confirmed that juries should be selected "at random". In *R v Ford*,[51] the Court of Appeal rejected the idea that there might be situations where the judge should ensure a "racial mix" amongst the jury. In particular, the court rejected the idea that a randomly selected jury might be incapable of rendering a proper verdict.

Are these sorts of issues applicable to Hong Kong? Hong Kong is a generally more homogeneous society, at least in terms of ethnicity. Moreover, its geographical "compactness" means that jurors are less likely to be out of touch with life experiences in other areas. Nonetheless, Hong Kong does now have sufficiently significant minority populations from Indonesia, the Philippines and South Asia to make ethnicity a potential jury issue.

8.1.3.4 Extending the jury pool

The shortage of potential jurors is one of the reasons that the number of jurors (seven or nine) is lower than in most other jurisdictions and also affects the representativeness of the jury. The increase in the number of trials held in Cantonese is likely to widen the pool of available jurors. Further tentative efforts to expand the jury franchise can be seen in the recommendations of the Law Reform Commission of Hong Kong.[52]

---

49. C Buddle, 'Confidence Ensures the Jury System Will Survive (n 39).
50. Somewhat ironically *The Standard* newspaper reports that some well-educated "overseas" graduates are overlooked under the "form 7" practice, since their qualifications are not on record: N Lau, '"Best Brains" Miss Out On Jury Duty' *The Standard* (Hong Kong, 23 April 2009).
51. [1989] 3 All ER 445.
52. Chaired by Judge Woo.

THE LAW REFORM COMMISSION of HONG KONG
REPORT[53]

Criteria for Service as Jurors

Recommendation 1

We recommend that the existing requirement for jury service that an individual has attained 21 years of age should be retained, but the upper age limit for jury service should be raised from 65 to 70. We also recommend that an individual who has attained 65 years of age should be entitled as of right to exemption from jury service upon his application.

...

Recommendation 2

We recommend that, to be eligible to serve as a juror, a person must have been issued with a Hong Kong identity card three years or more prior to his being issued with a notice of jury service and be resident in Hong Kong at the time the notice is issued.

...

Recommendation 3

We recommend that section 4(1)(b) of the Jury Ordinance (Cap 3) should be replaced by a provision to the effect that a person is not eligible to serve as a juror if he:

(a) has been convicted at any time in Hong Kong or elsewhere of a criminal offence for which he has been sentenced to imprisonment (whether suspended or not) exceeding three months, without the option of a fine;

(b) has been convicted within the previous five years of a criminal offence for which he has been sentenced to imprisonment (whether suspended or not) for three months or less;

(c) is awaiting trial for an indictable offence; or

(d) is remanded in custody pending trial for any offence,

provided that a spent conviction under the rehabilitation of Offenders Ordinance (Cap 297) should not be regarded as a criminal conviction for the purposes of (b).

...

Recommendation 4

We recommend that:

(1) Section 4(1)(c) of the Jury Ordinance (Cap 3) and the existing administrative practice of requiring a potential juror to have attained an education standard of Form 7 (being the minimum entrance requirement for entry to a university in Hong Kong), or an equivalent standard, should be replaced with a statutory requirement that the prospective juror have completed: (a) Form 7; (b) Secondary Six; (c) the IB Diploma;

---

53. Published June 2010.

or (d) such other secondary education as the Registrar of the High Court considers equivalent.

...

Recommendation 5

We recommend that:

(1) Section 4(1)(a) of the Jury Ordinance (Cap 3) concerning disabilities in relation to jury service should be amended to make clear that blindness or deafness should only exclude a person from jury service where it prevents him from fulfilling his duty as a juror. We therefore recommend that section 4(1)(a) should be amended to read:

"(a) the person is of sound mind and not afflicted by:

(i) blindness, or

(ii) deafness, or

(iii) other disability

preventing the person from serving as a juror; and".

(2) The Registrar of the High Court should consider making such changes to the physical configuration of the High Court Building and coroners' courts as would facilitate jury service by those confined to wheelchairs.

...

Recommendation 6

We recommend that the form of jury service should be amended to include:

(a) the principal justifications for excusal from, or deferral of, jury service; and

(b) a box to be marked by the person served with the notice confirming that he has no criminal conviction (and a spent conviction under the Rehabilitation of Offenders Ordinance (Cap 297) is not regarded as a criminal conviction for these purposes), is not awaiting trial for an indictable offence, and is not remanded in custody pending trial for any offence.

The completed form should be returned to the Registrar of the High Court for verification.

...

Recommendation 7

We recommend that the guiding principles for the consideration of applications for excusal from, or deferral of, jury service should be spelt out in the Jury Ordinance to assist the Registrar or the trial judge in determining whether or not to grant such applications. The justifications for excusal or deferral should include:

(a) that substantial inconvenience to the public may result;

(b) that undue hardship or undue inconvenience may be caused to the person or any person under his care or supervision;

(c) that the person is involved in the administration of justice so that bias may result or may be perceived to result;

(d) that jury service is incompatible with the person's tenets or beliefs; or

(e) that it is in the interests of justice to do so.

We also recommend that guidelines should be drawn up for the determination of applications for excusal or deferral, including specific examples of applications that should ordinarily be granted and examples of applications that should ordinarily be rejected.

...

Recommendation 8

We recommend that:

(1) The following categories of persons should be exempt from service as jurors:

(a) members of the Executive or Legislative Council;

(b) any public officer who is:

(i) a member of staff within the Judiciary;

(ii) a legal officer within the meaning of section 2 of the Legal Officers Ordinance (Cap 87);

(iii) serving in the Department of Justice, the Legal Aid Department, the Official Receiver's Office or the Intellectual Property Department;

(iv) a member of the Hong Kong Police Force, the Immigration Service, the Customs and Excise Service or the Fire Services Department including any post specified in the Seventh Schedule to the Fire Services Ordinance (Cap 95);

(v) an officer of the Correctional Services Department;

(vi) a member of the Government Flying Service;

(vii) the Commissioner, Deputy Commissioner or an officer of the Independent Commission Against Corruption;

(viii) carrying out duties in the Hong Kong Police Force, the Immigration Department, the Customs and Excise Department, the Fire Services Department, the Correctional Services Department, the Government Flying Service or the Independent Commission Against Corruption;

(ix) appointed as the principal probation officer, or as a probation officer, under the Probation of Offenders Ordinance (Cap 298);

(x) a social worker employed full-time in any reformatory school established under the Reformatory Schools Ordinance (Cap 225), any place of detention appointed under the Juvenile Offenders Ordinance (Cap 226), or any approved institution within the meaning of the Probation of Offenders Ordinance (Cap 298);

(c) consuls, vice-consuls, and officers of equivalent status, of governments of foreign states and such salaried functionaries of such governments as are nationals of such governments and are not carrying on business in Hong Kong, and the spouses and dependent children of such persons;

(d) barristers-at-law and solicitors in actual practice, and their employees;

(e) persons duly registered as or deemed to be medical practitioners under the Medical Registration Ordinance (Cap 161), persons duly registered as dentists under the Dentists Registration Ordinance (Cap 156), persons duly registered under the Veterinary Surgeons Registration Ordinance (Cap 529), and persons duly registered as Chinese medicine practitioners under the Chinese Medicine Ordinance (Cap 549);

(f) persons duly registered as registered nurses under the Nurses Registration Ordinance (Cap 164) and persons duly enrolled as enrolled nurses under the Nurses Registration Ordinance (Cap 164);

(g) officers employed on full pay in the naval, military or air services of the Hong Kong Garrison, together with the spouses of such officers;

(h) officials or employees of the Central People's Government and their spouses and dependants;

(i) members of the Hong Kong Auxiliary Police Force and persons summoned to act or enrolled or appointed as special constables under any enactment, provided that any person claiming exemption under this paragraph may be required by the Registrar to produce a certificate from the Commissioner of Police in proof of such exemption;

(j) Government chemists and members of the Laboratory Specialist Services Officer Grade serving in the Forensic Science Division of the Government Laboratory;

(k) the Legal Adviser of the Legislative Council Secretariat and any of his assistants who is in the full time employment of the Legislative Council Commission and is a barrister or a solicitor as defined in the Legal Practitioners Ordinance (Cap 159);

(l) investigator appointed by the Securities and Futures Commission and the Ombudsman's office.

(2) Any public officer who is serving as:

(i) a judge, deputy judge, District Judge, deputy District Judge, Registrar, Senior Deputy Registrar, Assistant Registrar, coroner or magistrate; or

(ii) a presiding officer, adjudicator or member of any tribunal established by law,

should be exempt from service as a juror and should continue to be exempt for 10 years after the termination of their judicial office.

(3) The exemption from jury service currently granted to the following categories of persons should be discontinued:

(a) any public officer who is serving in a training or apprentice rank;

(b) editors of daily newspapers in Hong Kong and such members of their staffs in respect of whom the Registrar is satisfied that jury service would disrupt the publication of such newspapers;

(c) registered pharmacists actually carrying on business as such;

(d) clergymen, priests, and ministers of any Christian congregation or Jewish congregation functioning in Hong Kong;

(e) imams of and persons holding similar positions in any Muslim congregation functioning in Hong Kong;

(f) priests of and persons holding similar positions in any Hindu congregation functioning in Hong Kong;

(g) full time students of any school, college, university, polytechnic, technical institute, industrial training centre or other educational (including vocational education) institution;

(h) pilots licensed under the Pilotage Ordinance (Cap 84), and the master and members of the crew of any ship;

(i) pilots, navigator, wireless operators and other full-time members of the crews of passenger or mail or commercial aircraft;

(j) persons who are vowed and full-time members of any religious orders living in monasteries, convents or other such religious communities;

(k) the spouse of:

(i) the Chief Justice;

(ii) a judge of the Court of Final Appeal;

(iii) the Chief Judge;

(iv) a Justice of Appeal;

(v) a judge of the Court of First Instance; and

(vi) a coroner;

(l) justices of the peace.

(4) Subject to and without limiting the general applicability of Recommendation 7, the Registrar or the trial judge, as the case may be, may defer jury service required of the persons listed at Recommendation 8(3) who have been summoned, or excuse them from jury service upon their application, if satisfied with the merits of their applications.

Comment

The recommendations have been limited in scope and, as such, largely uncontentious. Even in those limited cases where the Report calls for the current overall exemption to be relaxed, it is proposed that exemptions can still be claimed for particular cases where there is a risk of prejudice. The Hong Kong Law Society has subsequently made submissions on the LRC's proposals and supports them all except as regards non-practising lawyers who, the Law Society feels, should continue to be excluded. Similarly, the Hong Kong Bar is generally supportive.

It can be seen that the Commission's recommendations represented only a very modest attempt at reform to widen the jury "pool" and are not likely to produce a significant increase in the number of eligible jurors. A call for extending the jury "pool" has also been made by HKU law professor, Simon Young,[54] *who argues that age and educational barriers should be reduced. The latter, of course, may increase jury representativeness at the expense of "efficiency".*

Implementation has been, as so often with the Commission's recommendations,[55] painfully slow. The Commission published a Consultation Paper on these issues in January 2008 and followed this (having received submissions from many stakeholders including the Law Society and the Bar) with its Report in June 2010. Yet, seven years later, despite all stakeholders being broadly in accord, the latest position is that:

> The Department of Justice is preparing a working draft bill, with a view to seeking views of legal professional bodies, the Judiciary and stakeholders in 2017. Subject to the result of the consultation, it is planned that proposed legislation will be introduced into LegCo in 2017/2018 legislative session.[56]

One can only wonder at the "implementation" schedule had the Commission's proposals proved controversial!

8.1.4 Constitutional significance of the jury

In those common law systems where the jury has been retained, it is viewed as a method by which ordinary, non-legal people (laymen) may play a part in the justice system, especially the criminal justice system.

The significance of the jury is well recognised in Hong Kong and the duties of the juror are expected to be taken seriously. All those eligible for jury service asked to attend are expected to do so; deliberate failure, indeed, is an offence under section 32 of the JO.[57] Failure to appear (after attendance) is a criminal contempt of court.[58] Whereas in the English and American systems it is relatively easy to be excused jury service on the grounds of pressure of work or imminent family holidays, in Hong Kong excuses are not readily accepted. Those who *are* excused are expected merely to defer and to serve their jury function at a later date. The Hong Kong Government Guide to Court Services, dealing with the jury, states that:

> Exemptions are not lightly granted. Business commitments are not normally considered to be a sufficient reason to warrant exemption from jury service.

---

54. See E Lee, 'Legal Expert Calls for Increase in City's "Outdated" Jury Pool' *South China Morning Post* (Hong Kong, 10 May 2014).
55. See Chapter 2 at 2.3.
56. Law Reform Commission of Hong Kong website.
57. Subsection (1).
58. Jury Ordinance s 32(3).

Some amelioration of the strict rules on attendance is provided by the statutory requirement that an employer may not discriminate against an employee on the grounds of his/her jury attendance.[59] Indeed, during the trial of former Chief Executive, Donald Tsang, in 2017 the trial judge, Andrew Chan J, made clear that attending jurors must not be required to work on their jury rest days. Employers ignoring his order, he said, would be guilty of contempt.[60] However, the self-employed are in a difficult position given that their business may suffer from their absence and given the relatively small amounts of financial allowance provided to jurors.[61]

The participation of lay people is seen as a safeguard to help ensure that the law does not become inconsistent with the views of ordinary people. The Hong Kong Judiciary website states:

> Trial by jury in fact reflects the principle that a person should be tried by fellow members of [the] community. In this way, the legal system maintains contact with the conscience and attitudes of the community as expressed in the decisions of jurors.

This role can be seen as largely *symbolic*, since the vast majority of cases are not heard by a jury. Most criminal law cases do not go to contested trial since the defendant pleads guilty and the majority of contested criminal cases are heard by a magistrate sitting without a jury in the Magistrate's Court.[62] The "symbol", however, is an important one in terms of participation in the Hong Kong legal system. Constitutionally, what is significant is not the *quantity* of legal work involving juries but the principle of lay people participating in the justice system and its potential restraint on the executive. The safeguards to defendants inherent in the jury system were regarded as sufficiently important, indeed, for the preservation of jury trial to be enshrined in the Basic Law.[63]

The constitutional protection is a valuable one as the history of the jury in the common law world is full of attempts by the executive to restrict jury use. Over time, Britain[64] has severely curtailed the right to jury trial, especially in Northern Ireland, where the use of the civil jury has been abolished[65] as well as the absolute right to a criminal jury in serious cases. Because of fear of threats, bribery and intimidation in

---

59. Jury Ordinance s 33.
60. C Lau, "Judge orders jurors to rest on Saturdays" *South China Morning Post* (Hong Kong, 18 October 2017).
61. Remuneration is provided for under JO s 31 which gives the trial judge or Chief Justice some discretion to increase remuneration in appropriate cases. Broadly, however, it can be said that the attendance allowance is more acceptable to the less wealthy as is the case in most common law jurisdictions.
62. The bulk of the rest are heard by a judge sitting alone in the District Court.
63. Article 86.
64. We should strictly speak here of England, Wales and Northern Ireland, since Scotland has a civil law system and makes far greater use of non-jury trials.
65. For entirely "economic" reasons by the Jury Amendment (Northern Ireland) Order SI 1987/1283.

a very tense "sectarian" political situation,[66] the so-called "Diplock[67] courts"[68] have dispensed justice without the use of a jury in a significant number of serious criminal cases.[69] By way of further escalation, in mainland Britain today, even without the rationale of major civil unrest, juries may now be dispensed with, even in serious criminal cases, where there is reason to believe that threats or inducements may prevent a jury from reaching a proper verdict. The Criminal Justice Act 2003[70] allows for trial without jury in "indictable" cases (where normally the right to jury trial could be claimed) where there is evidence "of a real and present danger that jury tampering would take place."[71]

The (historic) first case in which the "no jury" approach was permitted involved four defendants charged with robbery, possession of a firearm to endanger life and with intent to commit robbery and conspiracy to rob.[72] The "planned" robbery involved the theft of around 10 million pounds in currency. The Lord Chief Justice, Lord Judge, stated that trial by jury was a "hallowed principle" of the common law but that the risk of interference with jurors through their families was too great.[73] Needless to say, there were significantly differing approaches to this historic case from both the (supportive) "crime control" camp and the (opposing) "due process" one. Fears that the first jury-less trial would be the "thin end of the wedge" were raised when two more applications were made in May 2010. *The Independent* newspaper quoted barrister Felicity Gerry as saying: "further applications [for jury-less trials] suggest these may be made more routinely when the legislation says it must be exceptional."[74]

8.1.5 Research on the jury

Somewhat ironically, given the strong emotions roused by the jury system, little research has been done in the common law world on the actual *process* whereby juries reach their decisions. This is particularly true in Hong Kong where scant research exists, and none of it recent. Given the lack of transparency in the system, we have no direct evidence as to the extent or quality of jury deliberations. Much

---

66. Both Catholic and Protestant "sides" in the sectarian divide operated extensive paramilitary groups.
67. Named after Lord Diplock, whose report led to the change in the law.
68. Introduced in 1973 in respect of "scheduled offences" (essentially terrorist-associated) by the Northern Ireland (Emergency Provisions) Act, 1973.
69. Irish (Catholic) Republicans portrayed this as an attack on their cause but the reality was that the main beneficiaries of jury tampering had been Protestant extremists.
70. The Act came into force in 2007.
71. See Criminal Justice Act, 2003, sections 44 and 46.
72. See BBC News, 'First Trial without Jury Approved' (18 June 2009); BBC News, 'Heathrow Robbery Accused Face First Trial without Jury' (12 January 2010) and S Laville, 'Heathrow Robbery Trials Breaks with 400 Year Tradition of Trial by Jury' *The Guardian* (London, 10 January 2010).
73. All four defendants were convicted by the lone judge. It was the fourth trial for the defendants after the three previous (jury) trials were aborted!
74. C Greenwood, 'Two More Suspects May Face Trial without Jury' *The Independent* (London, 6 May 2010).

of our ignorance stems from the secrecy of the jury system; jurors are forbidden to discuss cases with others, except for fellow jury members, and observation of actual jury deliberation is restricted by rules of confidentiality and contempt of court. Moreover, juries are not required (nor permitted) to give reasons for their verdicts. If a jury reached a decision by tossing a coin, we would never know for certain. However, research, especially that involving "shadow juries", tends to support the view that juries reach their decisions rationally, having generally understood the evidence and the judge's directions to them.

Baldwin and McConville[75] made a significant study of the English jury at work in the 1970s. They concluded that there were a significant number of "questionable" decisions; that there were more questionable acquittals than convictions; and that most doubtful acquittals were probably the result of giving great weight to the judge's advice that they must convict *only* where there is no reasonable doubt as to the defendant's guilt. There were a sufficient number of inexplicable decisions for Baldwin and McConville to conclude:

> the evidence that we have presented . . . has shaken our own confidence in the system of trial by jury, though it is not our view that the jury should therefore be abolished.[76]

Baldwin and McConville's research also included the use of a shadow jury which observed actual cases and reached their own "verdicts". They were observed to act rationally, based on the evidence presented in the case and the judge's summing up, and to discuss relevant issues fully and sensibly. Most significantly, there was a high correlation between the "verdicts" of the shadow jury and the actual juries involved in the cases observed. This led to the reasonable inference that the *actual* juries were "generally" behaving appropriately.

Research in Hong Kong has also indicated (cautious) support for the quality of jury verdicts. Duff, Findlay et al[77] state:

> factors external to the evidence do not play a major role . . .
>
> . . . widespread confidence in the jury verdict was expressed by those professionally involved in the administration of criminal justice.[78]

One feature of the jury which appears specific to Hong Kong is a relatively high conviction rate.[79] Research in other common law jurisdictions has found that a judge sitting alone is more likely to convict than a jury (the phenomenon is sometimes referred to as "case-hardening"). The most significant study of the Hong Kong jury

---

75. J Baldwin and M McConville, *Jury Trials* (Clarendon Press 1979).
76. Ibid 132.
77. Note 28.
78. Ibid 100.
79. See debate on conviction rates in Hong Kong triggered by Introduction to *Archbold Hong Kong* (Chapter 3 at 3.7).

concluded that there was little difference between the jury's conviction rate and that of the lone judge.[80]

8.1.6 Jury "equity"

Because a jury contains laymen it is possible that they will give verdicts inconsistent with the evidence where it is felt that the criminal law is a bad one or unduly harsh, or where they feel special sympathy for the accused. In the past, for example, juries have acquitted those they knew to be guilty of theft because it was clear the thief, or his family, were starving. Moreover, where the penalty even for the most minor theft has been extreme, juries have acquitted. In modern times juries have taken pity on, and acquitted, those who have hastened the death of a loved one suffering from a painful, terminal illness. In all these cases the judge will have explained the law in such a way that the legally "correct" verdict would have been conviction.

Such "creativity" by the jury has been termed "jury equity". Supporters of the jury system see such behaviour as a good thing; a sign that lay people can mitigate the effect of harsh or unpopular laws rather than blindly following the advice of the professional judge. Opponents of the jury system regard jury equity as unscientific, or "irrational", making the law imprecise and unpredictable. The sociologist, Max Weber, for example, distinguished "rational law" (characterised by trained professionals applying clear fixed rules to the facts of a case to produce a predictable outcome) from "khadi justice" which involved "decision-making based on subjective reaction to the individual case rather than on the careful application of known legal rules and procedures."[81]

Weber believed that (capitalist) economic development owed much to a system of rational law and had to account for the fact that the most advanced capitalist country of the time (Britain) had a very "non-rational" legal system comprising, in large part, amateur magistrates and jurors. Weber's conclusion was that the "main players" in the British capitalist system enjoyed the benefit of "professional" courts; the poor were denied rational justice. He wrote:

> The first country of modern times to reach a high level of capitalistic development, ie England, thus preserved a less rational and less bureaucratic system. That capitalism could nevertheless make its own way so well in England was largely because the court system and the trial procedure amounted until well into the modern age to a denial of justice to the economically weaker groups.[82]

This analysis was applicable both to the jury system in England and the system of lay magistrates. This "non-rational" criminal justice system remains in Britain

---

80. Duff, Findlay, et al (n 28) 96–100.
81. R Cotterrell, *The Sociology of Law* (Oxford University Press 2005) 169.
82. Translation cited in P Walton, 'Max Weber's Sociology of Law: A Critique' in P Carlen (ed), *The Sociology of Law* (University of Keele 1976) 13.

and even more so in Hong Kong where Weber's words remain apposite as a description of lay participation.

Of course, to those who see the jury in "symbolic" terms, as a guarantee of lay participation and a check on unrepresentative or unwelcome criminal rules, inconsistency and a layman's subjective viewpoint are positively welcome. Baldwin and McConville's criterion for "questionable" jury verdicts was that at least two professionals involved in the case were unhappy with the outcome. But, it can be argued, if lay participation, in the form of the jury, is to be encouraged, it cannot, or should not, be judged by the standard of the expert "professional". Thus:

> Perversity is just a lawyer's word for a jury which applies its own standards instead of those recommended by lawyers . . . The smear of perversity is applied by judges but erased by time. It is not the disobedient jurors whom history has reprobated, but the judges who called them perverse.[83]

Again, the "rational" argument would point to the weakness of the jury system which does not require (or even permit in most common law jurisdictions) the giving of reasons. This criticism was expressed by Professor Christopher Gane, dean of the Law Faculty of the Chinese University of Hong Kong, in an RTHK "Backchat" radio programme.[84]

To those who support "jury equity" on the other hand, it is the freedom from having to give reasons which permits the jury to "ignore" the judge where it feels "justice" so demands.[85] In the same "Backchat" programme in which Professor Gane decried the lack of reasons for the jury decision, Ms Judith Fordham, an Australian academic and practitioner, supported the "irrational" nature of the jury stating that "part of the beauty of the jury system" lay in its ability to give "just" decisions, acting as a buffer between the humble citizen and the "might of the state", which might do "justice" while being legally "incorrect".[86]

8.1.7 Majority verdicts

In Hong Kong, as in England, majority verdicts are permitted after "reasonable consultation" has failed to produce unanimity.[87] The Hong Kong system is more straightforward since, in civil cases, a mere majority of the seven jurors is required and, in criminal cases, a majority of five out of seven (or seven out of nine) is needed. Where, especially in lengthy criminal cases, one or more jurors has become indis-

---

83. These words of Lord Devlin are quoted in H Harman and J Griffith, *Justice Deserted: The Subversion of the Jury* (National Council for Civil Liberties 1979) 10.
84. 30 May 2014.
85. The acquittal of civil servant "whistle blower" Clive Ponting by an English jury was generally seen as completely counter to the judge's summing up.
86. Ms Fordham gave the example of possible jury compassion in the case of a loving euthanasia termination of life which might be, legalistically, murder.
87. Jury Ordinance (Cap 3), section 24.

posed, provision exists for a legitimate verdict to be delivered by a quorum of not fewer than five jurors.[88] Of course, in criminal cases, there is an argument that if two of the jurors vote for acquittal, there cannot be guilt "beyond a reasonable doubt" as the law requires.[89] Nonetheless majority verdicts are well established and the main argument in their favour is that they make tampering with jurors (by threat or bribery) much less likely since it will be impossible to know whether the *approached* juror has done what he was told to do or not. The majority verdict position is unlikely to change; indeed, it could be argued that any change would be unconstitutional since the Basic Law requires that "[t]he principle of trial by jury previously practised in Hong Kong shall be maintained."[90]

However, the better opinion is that it is only the principle of jury trial which must be maintained and that minor changes to the *operation* of such system would be constitutionally permissible.[91]

8.1.8 Criticisms of the jury system

Many of the criticisms of the jury in Hong Kong are equally applicable elsewhere. Juries, for example, are seen as expensive and inefficient. The use of juries in addition to the judge obviously does increase expenditure since, even though juries are not paid a *wage*, they are reimbursed for expenses and have to be paid a daily allowance. Supporters of the jury system would argue that jury expenditure is money well spent.

There has been a great amount of research on questionable or "perverse" jury verdicts, especially in England and the United States. In general, the conclusions reached are that there are more questionable acquittals than questionable convictions and that, generally, the questionable verdicts can be justified on the basis of giving the defendant the benefit of any doubt, as the law requires. Since juries are told to convict *only* when they are satisfied of guilt beyond any reasonable doubt, it should not be surprising that, on occasion, the defendant is given the benefit of what may appear a very small doubt.

As already stated,[92] critics dislike the fact that juries have, historically, acquitted people who have surely committed the crime of which they are accused; where, for example, the jury disapproves of the law in question, feels it is too harsh, or feel

---

88. In criminal cases. where a seven-man jury has been reduced to six (or five) a verdict may be delivered by five (out of six) or five (unanimously) respectively: Cap 3, s 24. In a civil case a simple majority will suffice. In no case may there be fewer than five jurors (ibid s 25).
89. See G Maher, 'Jury Verdicts and the Presumption of Innocence' (1983) Legal Studies 146.
90. Article 86.
91. To interpret Article 86, Basic Law, as not allowing any change to the *operation* of the system would be an abuse of language (but no more so than the so-called "Interpretation" of the Basic Law by the NPCSC in the "right of abode" cases; see especially Chapters 3 and 4).
92. See 8.1.6.

particular sympathy towards the defendant.[93] Conversely, such "jury equity", evinced by lay participants, is viewed as a strength by those who support the institution.[94]

Since juries are generally inexperienced, critics argue that they are far more likely to accept an implausible defence than a judge who will have heard such stories many times before. Again, the supporters of the jury system argue that the "case-hardening" of the professional judge is a greater problem than the gullible jury.

Since intelligence is not a criterion for selection, critics argue that the jury is likely to be swayed by an eloquent defending counsel and to be incapable of understanding the prosecution's case, especially in complicated fraud cases. Nonetheless, the generally bilingual Hong Kong juror, with at least form 7, *tends* to be of above average intelligence and, certainly, to be more educated than his typical counterpart in England or America.

It has even been argued that jurors whose income is likely to suffer because of jury service, or who resent giving up their time, may be tempted to reach hasty decisions in order to minimise their loss or "get things finished".[95] The potential risk has been described by Buddle who states:

> no judge wants to have an unhappy juror. A fair trial depends on jurors paying attention to the evidence. If a juror is sick, stressed about being absent from work or seething because he had to give up a dream holiday, it is better to find another one without such distractions.[96]

This, like many of the arguments for and against juries, is difficult to assess given that the deliberations of the jury are confidential so that research is difficult. Such research as does exist, via the use of "shadow juries",[97] tentatively suggests that juries do *generally* take their duties seriously and attempt to reach sound verdicts based on the evidence.

Two more recent concerns involve the "CSI effect" whereby it is believed that jurors increasingly accept forensic evidence as unimpeachable, and cases of jurors doing their own "research" online instead of basing their decisions entirely on the evidence before them.[98]

---

93. See TA Green, *Verdict According to Conscience, 1200–1800* (University of Chicago Press 1985).
94. See 8.1.6.
95. See P Darbyshire, 'Notes of a Lawyer Juror' (1990) New Law Journal 14.9.1990, 1264–1267.
96. C Buddle, 'Rafael Hui Trial Highlights the Importance of Jury Service' *South China Morning Post* (Hong Kong, 28 May 2014). Buddle's article was inspired by the discharge of a numerically depleted jury before the (first) trial of former Chief Secretary for Administration, Rafael Hui, had even commenced.
97. See 8.1.5.
98. See S Tse, 'For and Against: Hong Kong Juries on Trial' *South China Morning Post* (Hong Kong, 27 October 2009).

8.1.9 Should jury use in Hong Kong be extended?

Despite the criticisms of the jury system described, there is an argument not merely for the maintenance of the jury system (which is constitutionally guaranteed)[99] but for its extension in criminal cases. The argument is that if jury trial is regarded as an important safeguard of the common law system, it should be available in *all* serious criminal cases. Similar arguments have been used in Britain when, for example, the abolition of juries for "minor theft" has been mooted.[100] In Hong Kong, *a fortiori*, the argument for extension is raised because the right to jury trial is denied in the District Court, even though judges in that court have *significant* sentencing powers. The initial rejection of jury trials in the District Court is said to have been based on the once very small "pool" of potential jury members, deriving from previous educational and language requirements.[101]

On 11 November 2009, Ms Margaret Ng[102] asked the following question in LegCo:

> Recently, there have been views that the jury system is a good tradition of common law, and as the maximum imprisonment term that may be imposed by the District Court in criminal cases is 7 years, which is by no means light, the ideal arrangement is for juries to be formed to try cases in the District Court. Such views have also pointed out that as English was the official language used in court in the past, the number of the public eligible for serving as jurors was just sufficient for trying cases in the High Court . . . However, since the use of Chinese as an official language in court, the number of members of public [*sic*] eligible for serving as jurors has grown significantly and hence the jury system should be extended to the District Court.

Ms Ng went on to ask, formally, whether the government would consider implementing the jury system in the District Court and what resource implications there would be. The (then) Secretary for Justice (SJ), Mr Wong Yan Lung, replied that:

> The government has no current plan to introduce juries for criminal trials in the District Court.

He added (somewhat defensively) that a defendant would be:

> equally assured of a fair trial by a judge alone in the District Court, in a trial in which the judge is required to give a fully reasoned judgment, which may then be scrutinised on appeal.

The SJ added that the issue had previously been raised in 1997 and that the administration was "not convinced" that a re-examination was warranted. The SJ added, somewhat confusingly, that:

---

99. Article 86, Basic Law.
100. Arguments against abolition in such cases have focused on the social stigma and employment implications involved in even a minor theft trial.
101. See 8.1.3.
102. (Then) member representing the legal functional constituency.

The number of criminal cases tried in Chinese in the District Court has shown a steady increase in recent years, while the number of those in the Court of First Instance (CFI) has shown no comparable increase. Since 2007, the availability of an increased pool of Chinese speaking jurors has not led to an increase in jury trials in Chinese in the CFI.[103] It appears unlikely therefore that the introduction of jury trials in the District Court would lead to an increased use of Chinese in that Court.

With respect to the then SJ, this part of his reply seems both evasive and unconvincing. Since he *did* accept that the use of Chinese in the District Court had already increased, all that matters (aside from "logistical" considerations) surely, *if* the use of juries is seen as being of merit, is that a sufficient pool of jurors now exists to meet District Court needs.

What was more significant in the SJ's response, however, was the *implication* that extended use of juries might be "unconstitutional", since his reply refers to Article 81 of the Basic Law's commitment to "maintain" the judicial system previously practised and Article 86's commitment to "maintain" the principle of trial by jury previously practised. The implication is that any "tinkering" with the system may be in breach of the Basic Law, but this seems hardly justified by the wording of Article 86 which seeks to maintain the "principle" of jury trial, not to set in stone the 1997 "operation" of the system for all time.

The SJ's reply went on to note the "considerable" extra manpower that would be needed to extend jury trial to the District Court and the "resource implications" of refitting courts to accommodate juries. This fails to address the fundamental issue of why, if the jury system is an important plank of the common law, significant enough to be specifically retained by the Basic Law, it should be available for *very serious* criminal trials but not for merely *serious* ones.

Following (failed) attempts[104] by Ms Lily Chiang[105] (charged with company law offences) to assert her "right" to a jury trial, controversy over jury use was rekindled. The LegCo Panel on Administration of Justice and Legal Services[106] specifically addressed the issue of whether there is a common law "right to jury trial"; a point clearly rejected by courts in the Lily Chiang case. The LegCo discussion paper stated:

> Article 10 of the Hong Kong Bill of Rights guarantees the right to a fair and public hearing by an independent and impartial tribunal . . . It does not confer the right to trial by jury in either civil or criminal cases.[107]

---

103. While this may have been correct, in 2009, Department of Justice figures since 2010 show a steady increase in Chinese language trials in the CFI.
104. N Lau, 'Chiang Loses Bid for Trial by Jury in Fraud Case' *The Standard* (Hong Kong, 10 February 2009).
105. See also Chapter 13 on the role of the prosecutor.
106. LegCo discussion paper (of submission from Department of Justice June 2015), "Reform of the Current System to Determine Whether an Offence Is to Be Tried by Judge and Jury or by Judge Alone', LC Paper No CB(4)1168/14-15(03) (22 June 2015).
107. Ibid para 3.

Comment

Given the preponderance of non-jury trials in Hong Kong (and in Britain the fount of the common law) the LegCo conclusion is hardly surprising. Indeed, the argument that there is no need to extend jury use and that there is confidence in the ability of District Court judges to ensure fair trials is well-rehearsed. However, if jury trial is such a fundamental good (sufficiently important to warrant specific preservation, post-1997, by Article 86 of the Basic Law), it is difficult to see how, other than for financial reasons, its denial to those, like Ms Chiang, charged with serious offences, can be justified. The LegCo paper did discount the argument (tentatively suggested by previous Secretary for Justice, Wong Yan Lung)[108] that the Basic Law (Article 86) guarantee of the maintenance of the jury system precluded its extension.

It is noteworthy that, while the extension of jury use in Hong Kong seems to have been ruled out, some (very limited) use of juries has been mooted, surprisingly, in civil law mainland China. *The Standard* newspaper reported in February 2015:

> Shenzhen authorities have decided to mirror Hong Kong's financial success by adopting a judicial system with Hong Kong nationals serving as jurors in the special economic district of Qianhai.
>
> A local expert said the decision to copy Hong Kong's jury system is intended to build confidence among investors and businessmen to set up businesses in Qianhai.
>
> There was a primitive form of jury system in rural China after the Communist Party came into power in 1949, but this came to a halt during the Cultural Revolution.
> . . .
> Ye Qing, the leading judge of foreign-related trials in the Shenzhen Intermediate People's Court, said the innovative system of court management, trial and services will be explored . . .
>
> Ye said members of the jury will be chosen from Hong Kong nationals [*sic*] . . .
>
> Ye said the court will explore expanding the applicability of Hong Kong law in certain cases.

The story appears significant at first sight but is likely to be far less so in practice. The article goes on to say that, "the court will only handle civil and commercial disputes. Criminal trials will still be based on the mainland legal system." Moreover, it adds that the "question of which legal system to be used in a trial will depend on whether the case involves commercial contracts signed in Hong Kong or in the mainland." In short, it appears that what is being described is a limited opportunity for disputes over cross-boundary contracts, signed in Hong Kong, to be resolved in Qianhai courts. It also appears that the jury, while comprising Hong Kong citizens (wrongly described as "nationals" in the article) will differ significantly from the Hong Kong jury since the criteria for jury suitability will "probably include a knowledge of law".

---

108. See Chapter 13 at 13.2.2.

8.2 Lay prosecution

Lay prosecution is an anachronism whereby the right to prosecute before a magistrate in Hong Kong is delegated to people without legal qualification. The relevant statutory rule is section 13 of the Magistrates Ordinance.[109] The current version of the section reads:

> The Secretary for Justice may appoint any public officer or class of public officers to act as public prosecutor or prosecutors and to conduct generally on his behalf any prosecution before a magistrate or any specified classes of prosecutions or any particular case. Any public prosecutor so appointed may without any written authority appear and plead before a magistrate any case of which he has charge which is being inquired into, tried or reviewed.

Significantly, given the quite wide jurisdiction of magistrates in Hong Kong, the "lay" prosecutors described may prosecute in relation to offences which are imprisonable.

The system of lay prosecution has been trenchantly criticised by Philip Dykes, SC, former Chairman of the Bar Association (and recently re-elected). In his 2007 address at the Opening of the Legal Year,[110] Dykes said:

> the concept of 'lay prosecution' remains, in my view, oxymoronic though it is, admittedly, a less frightening concept than 'lay dentistry' or 'lay surgery'.

In more serious vein, Dykes added:

> I submit that employing unqualified persons to prosecute contentious serious offences, ie imprisonable offences where people can and do go to prison for up to three years, and where professional judgment is called for during a trial, may indeed be good value for money by the bureaucratic standards of the civil service auditor, but it is not really acceptable in this day and age.

Dykes, further, went on to question whether the continued use of lay prosecutors was consistent with Hong Kong's international commitments saying:

> Employing unqualified persons to prosecute is, in any event, on the face of it, inconsistent with the UN Guidelines on the Role of Prosecutors adopted in 1990 which lays down minimum standards for prosecutors, which standards include adherence to a code of professional conduct. The Bar's Code of Conduct, which applies to barristers when they defend or prosecute, is such a code. The Law Society also has its own code. Unqualified persons providing legal services are, by definition, not bound by any professional code.

While the Bar does, of course, have an "interest" in the issue of laymen performing tasks which barristers feel should be performed by members of their profession,

---

109. Cap 227.
110. 8 January 2007.

Mr Dykes' words highlight an area in which Hong Kong's legal development has not kept pace with its social development.

8.3 Special magistrates

The use of unqualified, "special magistrates" may be seen as an unjustifiable relic of the former colonial power, harking back to a legal system little changed from that of Victorian England where criminal justice was dispensed "to the masses" by those without legal qualification.

The statutory basis for the appointment of special magistrates is section 5(1) of the Magistrates Ordinance.[111] Special magistrates (generally Cantonese speakers) are recruited largely from lay persons with some courtroom experience, such as lay prosecutors and court interpreters, but without legal qualification. Their use is explicable only in terms of their cheapness. The quality of legal adjudication by special magistrates is extremely poor. The author has experienced pronouncements that a defendant representing himself was not permitted to read his notes in court and, even more bizarrely, that a civil servant was not entitled to question the veracity of police testimony! While it is true that the limited jurisdiction of special magistrates[112] limits the amount of damage they can do (they deal mainly with alleged motoring and hawking offences and generally do not impose custodial sentences), they do have the power to imprison and to impose significant fines. Moreover, for many Hong Kong citizens, trial by a special magistrate may represent their first and only encounter with the Hong Kong criminal justice system. An illustrative example is provided in the case of Baldwin Lam, convicted of careless driving by a special magistrate Hau Cheuk-man. In quashing the conviction, High Court Judge Woo said that Hau's judgment was "riddled with holes" and so poorly written that "it could weaken public confidence in judicial officers".[113]

At first sight, Hong Kong special magistrates may seem analogous to the unpaid magistrates ("Justices of the Peace")[114] of modern Britain. The analogy, however, is a false one, since the role of the lay magistrate in Britain is to adjudicate on issues of fact, and to be guided on all issues of law by a legally qualified clerk. This is not the case with Hong Kong's special magistrates, who make legal determinations in spite of their lack of legal training.

---

111. Cap 227.
112. See Magistrates Ordinance ss 91, 94 and 97.
113. E Luk, 'Magistrate Slammed as Judge Clears Driver' *The Standard* (Hong Kong, 11 March 2014).
114. Hong Kong, too, has Justices of the Peace but they no longer have a judicial function.

9
Legal Aid and Advice and Unmet Legal Need

Overview

Publicly-funded legal aid and advice is only one aspect of a broader consideration; that of "access to justice". Legal aid in Hong Kong has, as in so many areas, broadly followed the English position, whereby legal aid has been made available in an attempt to provide access to justice for the poorest members of society but with significant restraints on calls on the public purse. The result is that, as it is often said, "only the poor or the rich can afford to go to law". The plight of the middle classes (the so-called "sandwich class") is that they are generally excluded from public funding, at least in cases of civil dispute, even where their cause is a justifiable and justiciable one. Conversely, given the high cost of legal services in Hong Kong, they are often unable to fund, without assistance, their contemplated litigation. The main deficiency in the provision of legal aid in Hong Kong is the lack of public funding and the resulting "means testing" for legal aid claimants. As financial limits for access to legal aid, especially in civil cases, have failed to keep up with increasing Hong Kong incomes, there are now large numbers of would-be litigants who are by no means wealthy yet fail to qualify for legal aid. In the roughly 40 years since a fairly comprehensive system of legal aid and advice was introduced in Hong Kong, for those of limited financial means, the percentage of the population eligible to receive full, or partial, legal aid has declined significantly. Partly, and here Hong Kong again echoes the British position, this is because criminal legal aid is given priority. Since a person's liberty may well be at stake in a criminal case, it is unarguable that priority should be given to the criminal area. Civil litigants, it could be said, are "volunteers" whereas the defendant has no choice as to whether to go to court *and* has more to lose. While this is true, there are many cases in which the civil litigant "needs his day in court" almost as much as the defendant in a criminal case. Moreover, if the sanctity of contracts is to be preserved, if employers' safety obligations to employees are to be upheld, if intellectual property rights are to be defended, etc, worthy civil actions should not be discontinued merely through lack of financial resources.

Broadly, the provision of standard legal aid in Hong Kong is of three types: "normal" legal aid in civil cases, supplementary legal aid and criminal legal aid.

The Legal Aid Department (LAD) provides legal representation in civil and criminal cases whenever an applicant has satisfied a financial eligibility test (means test) and the Department is satisfied that there is a clear justification for legal representation (merits test). Once granted legal aid, a case will be assigned to a member of the LAD's Litigation Division or to a lawyer in private practice who does this type of work.

The major restriction on the availability of legal aid arises from the "means-testing" of the claimant's resources. This is done by ascertaining his so-called "disposable" resources (capital or income). Those over a certain level of disposable income or capital will be denied legal aid (though these upper limits can be waived by the Director of Legal Aid in exceptional cases). The impact of wage inflation, and the failure of the financial limits to keep up with such, have meant that many are not eligible for legal aid, despite being far from wealthy. The problem of access is further compounded by Hong Kong's relatively small number of lawyers (especially outside the main urban "high rent" areas) particularly in certain specialised but important areas of expertise, such as family law. The consequence is that many are not merely denied legal aid but are then faced with the prospect of very expensive private legal services. As if the means-testing rules were not enough, applicants for legal aid also have to pass a so-called "merits test", in respect of which a strong case can be made that the rules are being applied unduly restrictively in Hong Kong.

The limitations on the availability of legal aid "proper" have led to the introduction of some additional schemes, such as those for free legal advice and duty lawyer provision as well as encouraging alternatives to litigation in the civil arena.

Of course legal aid, funded by the state, is not the only possible solution to the problem of funding litigation. In the United States an alternative to legal aid is widely employed, namely "contingency fees". In the contingency system, those with a reasonable prospect of litigation success but without the means to fund an action, may be represented on a "no win, no fee" basis by a lawyer who will get nothing in the event of failed litigation, but who will receive a generous share of any winnings.[1] The introduction of contingency fees has been rejected in the English and the Hong Kong systems. The arguments are complex but the most significant arguments against lawyers obtaining a share of the "spoils" are the fear that unprofessional, unethical tactics might be employed to "win at all costs" and to inflate the amount of compensation claimed.[2] A variation on contingency funding, the "conditional fee", has been introduced in Britain and, in many cases, has supplanted legal aid as the means whereby those unable to afford the full cost of legal representation may be assisted on a "no win, no fee" basis. The difference between contingency and conditional funding is that, in the latter case, the lawyer gets no share of the winnings *but*

---

1. The lawyer's share is agreed contractually in advance and can be as much as 50% if the case is finally determined in court (as opposed to via settlement).
2. This appears to be particularly likely in the United States where civil juries are widely used and determine the amount of damages which a plaintiff will be awarded.

is permitted to charge a premium on normal charging rates.[3] Even the more limited conditional fee innovation has been rejected in Hong Kong, such that those unable to afford the cost of legal services but ineligible for legal aid are forced to drop contemplated litigation *or* represent themselves. Hong Kong, indeed, has a high level of "litigants in person". This may be viewed differently depending on one's perspective. The litigant in person can be seen as an independent person utilising independence and self-help, evidencing what is sometimes called "the Hong Kong spirit". More realistically, these litigants are pursuing their legal actions in the only way (financially) open to them; out of desperation rather than enthusiasm. The pursuit of a legal claim by those without legal expertise or training is rarely satisfactory. Judges and other legal experts find it far more difficult to deal with "amateurs" who are unversed in the techniques of court, the rules of evidence etc. Judges have a duty to assist unrepresented litigants, "up to a point", without presenting their case for them; a delicate balancing act. Proceedings, in general, take longer when litigants in person are involved, which counters, to some extent, the savings to the public purse in limiting legal aid. While it is true that Hong Kong provides reasonable support for unrepresented litigants, with advice centres available to assist them, this should be viewed as "second best" provision. It is axiomatic that if society is to spend large sums of money on the education and training of lawyers, it is on the assumption that lawyers bring "added value". It necessarily follows that those unable to make use of legal professionals are at a disadvantage. Litigation in person should, ideally, be limited to those who feel strongly that they wish to bring or defend their own case and feel confident in their ability to do so.

A further alternative to publicly-funded *litigation* is via "diversion" from the adversarial position to other means of settlement; so-called "alternative dispute resolution" (ADR). Hong Kong has seen a phenomenal growth in ADR in the past 10 to 15 years and sees itself as a potential regional hub for ADR provision. The subject of ADR will be dealt with separately in the next chapter.

"*Pro bono*" work (from the Latin "*pro bono publico*"; for the public good) presents a further potential amelioration of the lack of legal aid funding. *Pro bono* work involves law firms taking on deserving cases free as part of their contribution to public service. While laudable in itself and reasonably extensive in Hong Kong, *pro bono* work suffers from the problem that unpopular causes are unlikely to be adopted. Why take on free work if the public, far from lauding your public-spiritedness, regard you as the firm that "assists trouble-makers" or "helps wife-beaters"? The problem is even greater in the "political" domain where, for example, large international firms privately admit that they would refuse *pro bono* work for someone regarded as "unpopular with China". The provision of *pro bono* work (or lack thereof) is a subject dear to the heart of former Chief Justice, Andrew Li, who decided to look closely at the situation as his first "post-retirement" project.

---

3. The maximum increase is 100% (ie, the lawyer can charge double his/her normal fee for the work done).

9.1 "Access to justice" in principle

Articles 10 and 11 of Hong Kong's Bill of Rights, to be found in the Bill of Rights Ordinance,[4] enshrine the principle of "equality before the courts and the right to a fair public hearing".[5] There are also "constitutional" access rights prescribed in the Basic Law, in particular under Article 35 which guarantees:

> the right to confidential legal advice, access to the courts, choice of lawyers for timely protection of lawful rights and interests or for representation in the courts, and to judicial remedies.

It can hardly be doubted that "equality" is an elusive (and perhaps illusory) concept, given the superior position of the party with more money, power, influence and access to the best legal advice. However, it is generally accepted, in advanced societies, that the state has a duty to attempt, at least, to redress the balance and provide support for its weaker members. Publicly-funded legal aid and advice is, obviously, one way in which the state can help and it will be the prime focus of this chapter. There are, however, various alternative ways of improving "access to justice": helping the weak to help themselves; "diverting" apparently "legal/lawyer work" to other spheres; the "donation" of free expertise by legal experts; and improving/simplifying procedures, such that access to experts becomes less time-consuming and, as a result, more affordable. A limited (possible) improvement, where large numbers of potential claimants are involved, is provision for "class actions". This was the subject of a Hong Kong Law Reform Commission Report[6] in 2012 which recommended the institution of a regime for instituting class actions (starting with those involving consumer issues) mindful of the danger of encouraging "unmeritorious claims". It does not seem likely that such a development (even if followed by legislation)[7] would have a major impact on access to justice.

9.2 Legal aid

Most "developed" states recognise the importance of access to the law for all sectors of the community and the need for "the state"[8] to assist. Zander[9] writes:

---

4. Cap 383.
5. The Articles reflect the provisions of Article 14 of the International Convention on Civil and Political Rights, to which Hong Kong remains a party.
6. Published 28 May 2012.
7. In a typical Hong Kong scenario, a "Working Party" has been set up. It has met 13 times between February 2013 and April 2016. There has been no resulting legislation.
8. Given Hong Kong's unique constitutional position, the word "state" is of course not strictly accurate in the local context.
9. M Zander, *Cases and Materials on the English Legal System* (10th edn, Cambridge University Press 2007).

Legal Aid and Advice and Unmet Legal Need

It has been recognised in most civilised countries that there is a significant denial of justice if the state does not assist poor persons to meet the cost of lawyers. In England this recognition goes back decades.[10]

The first legal aid legislation in Britain, the Legal Aid Act 1949, was enacted by Britain's Labour Party (then a socialist party) as part of its wide-ranging social reforms which included the National Health Service and the nationalisation of many key British industries. Unsurprisingly, given the United States "anathema" view of socialism, no civil legal aid is available in America other than through voluntary "pro bono" work. Given the fierce resistance even to the concept of universal health care in that country, state assistance to those who "choose" to go to law would be unthinkable in the United States. Those embroiled in the criminal justice system, however, do have available publicly-funded "public defenders".

It might be thought that Hong Kong, espousing a far more "self-reliance"-based doctrine than Britain, might similarly shy away from state-funded legal aid. Raffell,[11] for example, writes:

> In a society like Hong Kong, based as it is on the doctrine of free enterprise, of people earning and paying their own way in life, it may well be that the idea of legal aid and the provision of free or state subsidised legal services is anathema to the majority of the population and is regarded as an alien socialist doctrine.[12]

However, in this context, Hong Kong has followed the lead of the "colonial master" and first instituted a system of civil legal aid in 1966.[13] Cynics have argued that the influential legal profession has an interest in the provision of legal aid which, while not paying as well as privately funded legal advice and representation, is a means of obtaining legal work which would otherwise not exist. As Wesley-Smith[14] states:

> various schemes exist to help those who cannot afford lawyers (and, it must be admitted, to help lawyers who might otherwise have few clients).[15]

Moreover, the provision of publicly-funded legal aid and advice seems to have generated little public opposition in principle, at least provided that the recipient of the funding is seen as "deserving".

---

10. Ibid 585.
11. A Raffell, 'Legal Aid and the Provision of Legal Services in Hong Kong' Law Lectures for Practitioners 1989.
12. Ibid 77.
13. The original Legal Aid Ordinance was introduced in that year. Legal Aid in the criminal sphere had been introduced on a gradual, piecemeal basis some time earlier.
14. P Wesley-Smith, *An Introduction to the Hong Kong Legal System* (3rd edn, Oxford University Press 1998).
15. Ibid 114. In *The Sources of Hong Kong Law* (Hong Kong University Press 1994), Wesley-Smith suggests that the English "pauper's petition" was received as part of the law of Hong Kong (see Chapter 2). It is not clear, however, whether recourse was ever had.

In Hong Kong, as in Britain and elsewhere, the key considerations in the operation of a legal aid system are: the need to give access to law to those with deserving cases who could not otherwise pursue them; to ensure that those who can pay for (all or part of) the legal services obtained do so; to discourage frivolous or undeserving claims; and to balance the interests of would-be litigants with those of the tax-payers who fund the system. Given the high cost of legal services in Hong Kong, the low ceiling on full or partial legal aid eligibility, and the high level of financial reserves available to the government, it can be said that legal aid provision in Hong Kong is not generous.[16] Nonetheless:

> The policy objective of legal aid is to ensure that no one with reasonable grounds for pursuing or defending a legal action is denied access to justice because of a lack of means.[17]

9.2.1 The administration of legal aid in Hong Kong

The regulatory system for administration of the legal aid scheme is also an issue of some concern, not least because one area of litigation concerns actions against the Hong Kong government, especially in the form of actions for judicial review. In such cases there is clearly a case for oversight independent of government. However, although a monitoring and advisory function is assumed by the independent[18] Legal Aid Services Council (LASC), established in 1996,[19] that body:

> was created as a stop-gap measure to secure operational independence, as a palliative for the lack of institutional independence . . . [it] has no legally trained or independent research staff . . . the advisory/supervisory system does not function as hoped. LASC cannot manage the LAD adequately and properly because it is the HAB [Home Affairs Bureau] which appoints and promotes.[20]

Thus, the actual administration of legal aid remains the province of the Legal Aid Department (LAD), a government agency.[21] This fact has been, and remains, an issue of some concern since it has been said that:

---

16. Eligibility limits were raised quite significantly under former Secretary for Justice Wong Yan Lung. Many middle-class litigants, however, remain ineligible or are required to pay significant contributions.
17. Legislative Council Panel on Administration of Justice and Legal Services January 2015, 'For discussion on 26 January 2015'.
18. Though its (non-lawyer) chair and its members are appointed by the Chief Executive. Responsibility for this rests with the colonial government which conferred the power of appointment on the governor.
19. By the Legal Aid Services Council Ordinance (Cap 489).
20. Statement by the Hong Kong Bar Association, 26 September 2012.
21. The current director of legal aid is Thomas Kwong.

If rule of law[22] objectives are to be met, it is important that legal aid be administered independently of the executive government, particularly as some recipients of legal aid are involved in legal action against government officials.[23]

The "ideal" as proposed by Wesley-Smith has not been realised and the reality remains as described by Raffell[24] some time ago:

> it must be remembered that the Legal Aid Department is a government department . . . Under these circumstances, political pressure is sometimes bound to be exerted on the Legal Aid Department and the Duty Lawyer Scheme (see below).[25]

It *is* within the remit of the LASC to "advise" on the establishment of an independent administration of legal aid, and the "separation of powers" view was (initially) endorsed by the LASC which advocated in its own publication:[26]

> Doubts about independence in the operation of the LAD undermine public confidence and often leads to the Government, even with the best of intentions, being suspected of and criticised for influencing the decisions of the LAD, whether it has done so or not. Job security of staff of the LAD as civil servants could not be the foundation for operational independence . . . An independent legal aid authority . . . would recognise and give expression to institutional protection for operational independence through clear separation of the powers to make legal aid policies on the one hand and to operate legal aid services on the other.[27]

Calls for an independent Legal Aid Authority have also been made by both branches of the legal profession[28] and questions have been asked in the Legislative Council (LegCo). On 27 February 2013, Dennis Kwok asked the following question in LegCo:

> Establishment of an Independent Legal Aid Authority
>
> President . . . There have been long-standing calls from both members of this Council and the two legal professional bodies . . . for the setting up of an independent legal aid authority (ILAA) to administer the provision of legal aid services in place of the LAD. Moreover . . . in 1998, the Legal Aid Services Council (LASC) recommended that an ILAA should be established . . . For this purpose, the LASC commissioned a consulting firm in October 2011 to conduct a study on the same topic.

---

22. For further discussion of the rule of law, see Chapter 12.
23. P Wesley-Smith, *An Introduction to the Hong Kong Legal System* (3rd edn, Oxford University Press 1998) 114.
24. A Raffell, 'Legal Assistance' in Gaylord and Travers (eds), *Introduction to the Hong Kong Criminal Justice System* (Hong Kong University Press 1994).
25. Ibid 118.
26. Legal Aid Services Council, *Legal Aid in Hong Kong*.
27. Ibid 233.
28. See Hong Kong Bar Association, 'Statement . . . on the Desirability of an Independent Legal Aid Authority—the Current Situation Is an Impediment to Access to Justice for Persons of Limited Means and "the Sandwich Class"' (26 September 2012).

Kwok went on to ask when the draft report would be submitted, whether it would be published and whether there was a timetable for implementation. His clear optimism, based on the LASC's previous view, was unfounded. As is so often the case in Hong Kong, the "consultancy route" had been used as an alternative to action and to diffuse criticism of unpopular (in)action. The LASC, within a few years, had, seemingly, changed its mind about the desirability of independent supervision and, now,[29] reported that:

> As recommended by the consultant, the LAD should be retained as a government department because it is considered that the degree of independence upheld and exercised by LAD is sufficient . . . The Council agrees with the consultant that there is no immediate need to establish an independent legal aid authority . . . we also maintain the view that it would be worthwhile to revisit the independence issue from time to time.

Thus, the views of the legal profession, expressed over 25 years, as well as the LASC's own previously consistent view, are overridden by the advice of consultants "Deloitte Consulting". As so often, the lesson to be learned is that if the message is unwelcome to the Hong Kong government, the messenger is changed. To her credit, one member of the LASC, barrister Josephine Pinto dissented and stated that the Council should provide strong reasons for its change of position.[30]

Administration of legal aid, then, is to remain in the hands of the Legal Aid Department, a government department despite the clear scope for conflict of interest in government-related litigation and the subjective element involved in "merits test" determinations. The only change of note recommended by LASC, following the consultancy report, is that the LAD should report to the Chief Secretary for Administration, rather than the HAB. It is unsurprising that the government announced[31] that, "after careful assessment of LASC's recommendations", it would accept these in principle including, notably, that "there is no immediate need to establish an ILAA" and that "LAD should remain a government department, as the degree of independence upheld and exercised by LAD is considered sufficient."[32]

9.2.2 Legal aid in criminal cases

While criminal legal aid has been available for longer than its civil counterpart, its provision was initially very limited and has developed gradually. Up to 1962, legal aid was only available in the old "Supreme Court"[33] and only on a limited

---

29. Legal Aid Services Council letter to Chief Executive, 30 April 2013.
30. See *South China Morning Post*, 'No Need for Independent Legal Aid Service, Say Advisers in U-Turn' (13 May 2013).
31. Legislative Council Panel on Administration of Justice and Legal Services: LC Paper No CB (4) 822/13-14(05).
32. Ibid para 4(a).
33. See Chapter 4.

basis.[34] Following various pieces of piecemeal development, criminal legal aid is now "potentially" available for cases heard in the District Court, the Court of First Instance, the Court of Appeal and the Court of Final Appeal. It is also available in the Magistrates' Courts for "committal" proceedings (a determination whether there is a sufficient case to be heard in the Court of First Instance) in respect of serious criminal charges.

Criminal legal aid "proper" is *not* available for other Magistrates' Court cases. However, even here, an impecunious (without sufficient means) applicant may apply for help under the duty lawyer scheme,[35] now expanded to cover all cases where "the interests of justice" require assistance for the applicant.

Where an applicant is appealing against conviction for murder, the grant of legal aid is mandatory, subject to a financial means test. In all other cases the Director of Legal Aid must consider all the surrounding circumstances in determining whether the granting of legal aid is in the interests of justice.

In 2016, 3,567 applications for legal aid in criminal trials were made, of which 2,657 were granted.[36] The key considerations are the means of the defendant and the merits of his defence.

Applications for criminal legal aid are to be made in person to the Legal Aid Department's offices if the applicant is on bail (or not in custody).[37] If the applicant is in custody, the application should be made through the Correctional Services Department.

9.2.2.1 The means test

Criminal legal aid (for proceedings other than in Magistrates' Courts) is generally available to any person in Hong Kong (resident or non-resident) who satisfies a financial eligibility test. This means test is carried out by the Legal Aid Department on behalf of the Director of Legal Aid. Legal Aid can be granted where an applicant's financial resources do not exceed the prescribed limits. This does not apply, however, to trials in the Magistrates' Courts, where legal aid is available only in respect of committal proceedings. Beyond the upper limit, legal aid can be granted only exceptionally where the Director of Legal Aid decides it is "in the interests of justice". The most recent figures (still operative in 2017) require that the upper limit for financial eligibility is $302,000. This follows a significant increase in 2012 and smaller ones in 2013 and 2015.[38] The figure is not gross, however, and requires some explanation.

---

34. Capital cases, cases referred to the court for consideration by the Full Court, and cases where the Full Court chose to exercise its discretion.
35. See 9.4.1 below.
36. Legal Aid Department Annual Report 2015.
37. Provision also exists for a preliminary application online where no hearing date has been fixed (via Legal Aid Electronic Services Portal [LAESP]).
38. The cut-off figure, which had not kept pace with inflation, was increased by approximately 50% from May 2011 and increased slightly, to its current level, from 17 July 2015.

The upper limit figure is a person's monthly "disposable" income (× 12) plus his/her "disposable" capital. In calculating disposable income deductions are made for rent and rates plus the applicant's "personal allowances" which vary according to his family position. A single applicant, for example, will have only $6,220 per month as a personal allowance, while an applicant with six or more dependents will have an allowance of $27,950.[39]

In assessing "disposable" capital, the applicant's cash, bank account, jewellery, stocks, shares, valuables and property held as an investment will be counted. *Not* included are the value of the house in which the applicant resides, plus items such as furniture, clothes and "tools of trade".[40] Even with the improved eligibility rules introduced from 2012 and subsequently, much of the "sandwich class" will be denied criminal legal aid. Moreover, even in cases where the applicant is judged eligible to receive *some* criminal legal aid, he is likely to have to make a financial "contribution". Unless the applicant's total disposable income and capital is $37,750 or less, a contribution will have to be made. The contribution figure ranges from $755 to $75,500. There is provision, under the Legal Aid in Criminal Cases Rules,[41] for the Director of Legal Aid to exercise his discretion to grant legal aid in criminal cases even if an applicant's financial resources exceed the $302,000 limit, provided he is satisfied that it is in the interests of justice.[42] Here, however, the applicant's contribution will rise, on a sliding scale, and will range from 30% to as much as 67% of the applicant's assets.[43]

Where criminal legal aid is granted, the applicant may request that a specific lawyer from the Legal Aid Panel be appointed. Such a request will be noted. The final allocation, however, is made by the Director of Legal Aid from whose decision there is no right of appeal.[44] Similarly, there is generally no right of appeal against the refusal of legal aid.[45]

---

39. A spouse's income (and capital) will be taken into account unless the spouses are separated or involved on opposite sides of a dispute.
40. Additional capital allowance is also permitted for those over 60 years of age.
41. Cap 221D.
42. Ibid rule 15(2). In 2015, legal aid was granted in 30 cases in which the applicant exceeded the means limit.
43. The means test may be waived in cases of murder (or, more theoretically than practically, treason or piracy with violence) on the application of the defendant.
44. The distribution of legal aid to those on "The Panel" of Legal Aid Practitioners shows that most work goes to lawyers with more than 10 years of practice experience with the number of "distributions" ranging from 10 to 50 per year.
45. An exception exists in relation to appeals to the Court of Final Appeal where an appeal against refusal may be made to a Review Committee.

9.2.2.2 The merits test

Although, generally, those who are *financially* eligible will obtain criminal legal aid (at least at first instance),[46] there is also a "merits" test which may be applied, in that the award should be "in the interests of justice". This merit criterion is generally assumed to be satisfied in cases of first instance trials in the District Court and Court of First Instance. Refusal on merit only is almost unknown in the Court of First Instance. In those relatively few cases in which legal aid is refused on merits the applicant may ask the judge to grant legal aid provided that the means test has been satisfied.[47] In relation to appeals, the "interests of justice" criterion is augmented by the requirement that the appeal must be based on "reasonable grounds" and here the grant of legal aid is far more restrictive. The merits test restrictions do not apply, however, in the most serious cases such as murder,[48] where the judge also has the right to waive the means test contribution rules.

9.2.3 Legal aid in civil cases

The regulations governing the granting of civil legal aid are to be found in the Legal Aid Ordinance.[49] Application is made directly to the Legal Aid Department offices. An appointment is made and a statement about the case is made. This statement is then passed on to a lawyer to evaluate. Alternatively, an application can be made online through the Legal Aid Electronic Services Portal (LAESP). As with criminal legal aid, the granting of civil legal aid is subject to both a "means" and "merit" test.

Prima facie, "ordinary" civil legal aid (under the Ordinary Legal Aid Scheme) is available in respect of all civil proceedings; subject to "means" and "merit" tests, as with the criminal situation. However, important exceptions apply in respect of defamation actions, Small Claims Tribunal and Labour Tribunals matters and actions involving derivatives, securities or futures. As to the latter, the total exclusion of legal aid has been removed and applications may be approved where fraud, misrepresentation or deception are alleged in respect of the sale of such financial products.[50] Most of these are uncontentious: the tribunals involved wish to encourage resolution of disputes without lawyers and those dealing in derivatives can be taken to have willingly consented to run high risks. The defamation bar, however, is controversial (though it merely follows the English practice). The argument seems to be that a plaintiff who pursues a defamation action is seeking to preserve or protect

---

46. It is relatively unusual for an applicant who "passes" the means test to be refused criminal legal aid on merits.
47. There were eight successful applications in 2014.
48. The same applies to treason or piracy with violence which are virtually obsolete (but note "Article 23" debate in respect of treason: see Chapter 2).
49. Cap 91.
50. Amendment to Schedule 2 of the Legal Aid Ordinance (Cap 91) (LAO). By Resolution of the Legislative Council, under s 7(b) of the LAO, passed 17 July 2012 (effective 30 November 2012).

something less valuable than his physical or financial well-being (his reputation) and, in so doing, is seeking to reduce freedom of expression. This may be true but hardly explains why legal aid should be denied to a defamation *defendant* especially where, as in England, the onus of proof rules favour the interests of the "claimant" (plaintiff) as opposed to the ideal of freedom of speech.[51] The unassisted defendant's position becomes even more hazardous where a jury trial is permitted, with resulting increased costs for the loser.[52]

9.2.3.1 The means test

Means testing is conducted in the same way as for criminal legal aid (see above), *except* that an applicant who exceeds the financial limits will automatically be precluded from receiving any legal aid; the Director of Legal Aid has no discretion to waive the upper limit in civil cases *except* in "meritorious" cases involving a possible breach of the Bill of Rights Ordinance (BORO) or the International Covenant on Civil and Political Rights (which is given local statutory force via BORO). The Social Welfare Department will normally compile the necessary report on the financial status of the applicant, though this can be carried out by the Legal Aid Department itself in cases of urgency.[53]

In 2016 there were 14,733 applications for legal aid in civil cases,[54] of which 59% were granted.[55] The downward trend of applications (reflecting, perhaps, the financial ineligibility of much of the Hong Kong populace and the recognition of the futility of an application in such cases temporarily reversed in 2014, has reappeared. The Legal Aid Department (LAD) has commented (in 2013) on the perceived ineligibility of much of the "sandwich class" stating:

> It is possible that a person with reasonably large income or capital asset can be eligible for legal aid. Records kept by the Department show that applicants with income of about $58,000 and capital of $1.3 million qualified for legal aid under OLAS[56] and SLAS[57] respectively.[58]

---

51. English law (unlike, eg, the USA's) put the onus on the defendant to prove his statement was true (rather than requiring the claimant to prove untruthfulness). London had become internationally notorious for "libel-shopping". Reforms under the Defamation Act 2013 have largely eliminated the "shopping" phenomenon and the defence of "honest opinion" also redresses the pro-claimant situation.
52. Jury trials are unusual for defamation in Hong Kong but not unknown (see Chapter 8).
53. Where the financial status of the applicant improves (or where it becomes clear that his financial position was not accurately stated) there is provision for the Director to revoke legal aid.
54. Around 90% of applications involve personal injury claims or matrimonial disputes.
55. Legal Aid Department Annual Report 2016. The approximately 60% rate of successful applications has remained stable for some years.
56. The Ordinary Legal Aid Scheme.
57. The Supplementary Legal Aid Scheme.
58. Legal Aid Department ("Legal Aid News"), 'Common Misconceptions about Legal Aid Services'.

This does indicate that extension to the allowances, introduced from 2011 onwards, has improved eligibility; though the statement does not make clear that many of those eligible as a result of the improvements may still be required to make hefty contributions. Those, for example, of the means quoted by the LAD would be making contributions close to the maximum of $75,500. Applicants seem to be reasonably accurate in predicting their financial eligibility status, in that only 5% of the total refusal rate (of 41%) was based on means in 2016.[59]

9.2.3.2 The merits test

The merits test is far more significant in the civil than in the criminal sphere (since generally it will be regarded as "in the interests of justice" for a criminal defendant to be legally represented). With civil legal aid the Director of Legal Aid needs to be satisfied that the applicant has reasonable grounds for bringing or defending the case and that there is a reasonable prospect of success or at least a reasonable chance of deriving some tangible benefits from being provided with legal representation.[60] Given the "tangible benefits" approach even a potentially winning case may be refused legal aid if the amount likely to be recovered is disproportionately small. However, there is scope for the Director to take into account non-monetary considerations where, for example, an important point of principle is involved.[61] However, serious concern exists in respect of the merits test since it has been pointed out, by academic Professor Michael Davis,[62] that, on top of the normal merit and means test, the Hong Kong authorities have been adopting a further (unlawful?) restriction by granting legal aid only where the case has more than a 50% chance of success. Such a test appears more restrictive than the "reasonable prospect of success" provided for in the regulations, and case law endorses this view. The *South China Morning Post*,[63] referring to Davis's criticism, has stated that:

> The Legal Aid Department has repeatedly used the wrong test to assess whether or not to fund civil cases, raising concerns that the poor have been denied access to justice.
>
> A recent High Court judgment showed the department had required a case to show a more than 50% chance of success to qualify for legal aid, rather than a 'reasonable chance of success', as written in the Legal Aid Ordinance.

---

59. Legal Aid Department Annual Report 2016.
60. In some cases (especially those involving constitutional issues/judicial review applications), the director may consult experts from private practice.
61. Legal aid granted on this basis may be "discharged" where it becomes clear that there is no longer merit in proceeding.
62. Recently, and reluctantly, retired from the University of Hong Kong.
63. A Chiu, 'Legal Aid Error May Have Denied Justice to Poor' *South China Morning Post* (Hong Kong, 13 January 2014) and A Chiu, 'Harsh Government Test Denying Needy Legal Aid' *South China Morning Post* (Hong Kong, 7 April 2014).

The incorrect test was adopted despite at least two earlier judgments ruling that the over-50% threshold was wrong—one in 2012 and one as far back as 1999 . . .

The error came to light in the case of Chung Yuk-ying . . .

Chung [denied legal aid] appealed to a High Court master . . . and argued that the department . . . used the wrong test.

The master dismissed Chung's appeal, but the High Court papers . . . show that a legal aid department lawyer had referred to a handbook used in England to argue a 'reasonable chance' meant a chance higher than 50% . . .

Chung has now been granted permission [by Queeny Au-Yeung J] to lodge a judicial review of the master's decision.

The issue has been swiftly taken up by the Hong Kong Bar Association, who issued a statement in 2014:

> Views of the Hong Kong Bar Association on Merits Test for Legal Aid
>
> 1. Section 10(3) of the Legal Aid Ordinance (Cap 91) requires the Applicant to show "reasonable grounds for taking legal action." This has been translated into the "Merits Test" for the purpose of legal aid applications. However, this statutory Merits Test does *not* require the Applicant to *prove a chance of success, or prospect of success*. It is NOT confined to a narrow debate on the percentage chance of success.
>
> . . .
>
> 4. The cases such as *Nguyen Trong Son v DLA* . . . and now *Chung Yuk Ying v DLA* . . . demonstrate that it is wrong to require the Applicant to prove a "*greater than even chance*" of success . . . There may have been uncertainty and confusion in the past and there is now a need for clarification of and amendment to the internal guidelines of the . . . LAD so as to properly apply s 10(3) of the Ordinance.
>
> . . .
>
> 7. As a matter of principle, on a proper construction of the Merits Test . . . "*reasonable grounds to take legal action*" may be established even in cases where the "*chance*" or "*prospect*" of success is thought to be less than 50%. In short, if, on a qualitative assessment, the Applicant has reasonable prospects, the Merits Test is satisfied. That is all the Applicant has to show in order to be entitled to legal aid.
>
> . . .
>
> 11. In their reply to the *South China Morning Post*, LAD still persists in using the UK Legal Aid Handbook 1997 to interpret the Hong Kong case of *Nguyen Trong Son*, with the expression "*reasonable . . . chance*" as meaning higher than 50% chance. However, this approach has been rejected by the Court in *Chung Yuk Ying*. This again reveals a pressing need to review and revise the relevant Departmental Circulars and manuals on the Merits Test in line with the decision in *Chung Yuk Ying*.
>
> . . .
>
> 14. The *Chung Yuk Ying* case is an interesting example of how vigilant one needs to be in protecting access to legal aid. All counsel need to be informed by the Bar

> Association of this pitfall arising from the erroneous interpretation or application of the Merits Test.
>
> 15. It is also advisable that LASC should take notice of the error revealed in this case and to ensure that LAD revise the internal guidelines forthwith to ensure proper assessment of legal aid applications in future.
>
> ...
>
> 21.2.2014

Comment

It is not uncommon practice for Hong Kong government departments to adopt internal "practices" which conflict with legislative rules and to give precedence to the practice over the rules. This being the case it is all the more important that the "watchdog" should, as indicated previously,[64] be independent of government.

Appeals against the refusal of civil legal aid may be made to the Registrar of the High Court, or, in Court of Final Appeal cases, to a Committee of Review. The decisions of both these bodies are final. Despite the improper interpretation of the merits test criteria by LAD as described, the success rate of such appeals (at 4% in 2015/2016) is low.

9.2.3.3 Funding via the "Director's Charge"

When a legally aided litigant loses a case (even the restricted merits test does not guarantee success!) he is required to make no further contributions other than those determined by the means test. This will, of course, represent a loss to the Legal Aid Scheme. However, this situation is redressed by the fact that those legally-aided litigants who *win* will be confronted by the Director of Legal Aid's First Charge which is used to make good any cost incurred in supporting the assisted litigant from money or property obtained from the loser. Thus, for example, there will be a first charge on damages obtained by the assisted litigant to cover the cost of support to that litigant *minus* any sums already contributed by him and minus any costs obtained from the losing opponent.

9.3 The "Supplementary Legal Aid" Scheme

Where a person's resources exceed the financial limit under the standard legal aid scheme, but that person cannot afford the high costs of litigation, a system of Supplementary Legal Aid (SLA), which has been in existence since 1984, can be used. The object of this scheme is to assist those members of the "sandwich class"

---

64. See 9.2.1 above.

(middle-class) who exceed the still modest limits for legal aid proper but who are far from wealthy and would generally struggle to pursue or defend any but the most straightforward action. Under the SLA scheme a form of assistance can be given to applicants whose disposable financial resources exceed the $302,000 limit for ordinary legal aid but do not exceed $1,509,980.[65] Crucially, the scheme is essentially self-funding. Thus:

> The costs of SLAS are met from the Supplementary Legal Aid Fund (SLAF), which is financed by the applicants' contributions and damages or compensation recovered.

The applicant must pay a non-refundable $1,000[66] deposit and, if granted SLA, must pay a further $72,595 interim contribution. This will be a contribution to costs and will only be recoverable (in part or in full) if there is a surplus after payment of costs. In addition, if an action is successful, the applicant has to pay 10%[67] of the damages recovered back to the Scheme.[68] The applicant is also liable to pay the costs of the action expended on his behalf from any damages recovered *subject to* credit being given for his application fee and interim contribution. The Scheme is only available in actions to recover monetary compensation in the Court of First Instance, Court of Appeal or District Court (generally where the claim exceeds $60,000). The scheme is limited to cases of personal injury and death, employee compensation claims (irrespective of the amount claimed) and negligence claims against lawyers, doctors, dentists and, now, other professionals such as accountants, surveyors and architects.[69]

There is a "merit" test, in that there should be "reasonable grounds" for taking proceedings and this, given that the scheme must be self-funding, is quite strictly applied. However, given that the applicant will have to pay a significant part of any winnings to the Scheme, s/he is unlikely to take on proceedings lightly.

In 2016 there were 225 applications for Supplementary Legal Aid, of which 164 were granted.[70]

---

65. The more generous figures now in place were announced by then Secretary for Justice, Wong Yan Lung (Concluding Address by Secretary for Justice at Conference on Civil Justice Reform, 17 April 2010). A large increase, to $1,300,000, was introduced in 2011 and raised to the current level in 2015.
66. $5,000 in the case of medical and professional negligence claims.
67. The figure is 20% in cases of medical/professional negligence.
68. The figure is 6% if the case is settled before a barrister is instructed (15% in the case of medical professional negligence cases).
69. The extensions to possible claims against various professions by legislative amendment in 2012 necessitated an increase in contributions since the SLAF must be self-funding.
70. Supplementary Legal Aid Fund Annual Report 2016.

9.4 The Duty Lawyer Service

The Duty Lawyer Service, initiated in 1978,[71] is funded entirely by the government. It operates the Duty Lawyer Scheme, the Free Legal Advice Scheme, the Tel-Law Scheme and the Convention against Torture Scheme. The Service, though government subvented, is incorporated as a company limited by guarantee and managed jointly by the Hong Kong Bar Association and the Hong Kong Law Society under the aegis of a Council.

9.4.1 Duty Lawyer Scheme

The Duty Lawyer Scheme is a scheme of free legal representation for defendants in criminal cases. The Scheme has gradually developed and expanded its scope.[72] Originally limited, on a pilot basis, to defendants charged with six scheduled offences in three Magistrates' Courts, the Scheme was later extended to cover nine scheduled offences in all Magistrates' Courts.[73] Later still, following the enactment of the Bill of Rights Ordinance (BORO)[74] the Scheme was expanded to offer representation to defendants in the Magistrates' Courts[75] in almost all cases. The crucial provision involves the right:

> to have legal assistance assigned to him, in any case where the interests of justice require, and without payment by him in any such case if he does not have sufficient means to pay for it.[76]

Essentially, subject to means-testing,[77] the Scheme is available for all "Standard List Offences". This list (of over 300 offences) covers almost all offences except hawking offences,[78] traffic summonses and other "regulatory" offences. All defendants are permitted to approach the Liaison Office for the Magistrates' Court in which they are due to appear. In the case of defendants remanded in custody, Court Liaison Office staff will automatically contact them to offer the service of the Duty Lawyer Scheme on the date of their first appearance in court. Committal proceedings in Magistrates Courts are not included in the Scheme, since they are governed by ordinary legal aid.

The Scheme also extends to all defendants charged in Juvenile Courts (except by Summons) and to those who are the subject of Care and Protection Proceedings.[79]

---

71. The Service was known as the Law Society Legal Advice and Duty Lawyer Schemes until renamed in 1993.
72. The Scheme dealt with 25,096 defendants in 2016: Duty Lawyer Scheme, Annual Report 2016.
73. There was a discretion for a Magistrate to refer cases outside the nine scheduled offences list.
74. Cap 383. Section 8 of the Ordinance introduces the Bill of Rights itself (listed as "Articles").
75. The Duty Lawyer Scheme is represented (by a Court Liaison Office) in every Magistrates' Court.
76. Bill of Rights (under s 8 of BORO) Article 11(2)(d).
77. There is no means test for a first appearance in court.
78. Though is does extend to appeals against the refusal of a hawker licence.
79. Juveniles are not means tested but must pay a small ($570) handling charge.

Further extensions cover assistance to those threatened with extradition proceedings and those appealing against the refusal to issue a hawker's licence.

The Scheme has also been available, since July 2000, in respect of Coroners' Courts proceedings where a party is at risk of criminal prosecution as a result of giving evidence at a Coroner's Inquest. The Duty Lawyer Scheme fulfils, obviously, a vital role in "filling the gap" in criminal legal aid "proper" whereby there is no provision for legal aid in Magistrates' Courts, other than in respect of committal proceedings.[80] In the early days of the Duty Lawyer Scheme, barrister and law teacher Andrew Raffell[81] wrote:

> unrepresented defendants are likely to suffer injustice and unfairness and are likely to be treated less favourably in court than represented defendants. If the lack of representation is the exercise of freedom of choice by the individual, then that is a situation which society cannot and should not do anything about. On the other hand, if the lack of representation is because the individual cannot afford to pay for it, then that is unjust and destroys the whole concept of equality before the law . . .
>
> In my opinion this [Duty Lawyer] scheme is excellent, both in conception and operation . . . it is vital that it is retained in some form or another.[82]

9.4.1.1 Means test

There is no means testing for those charged with one from the "Standard List of Offences" *on their first court appearance*. Thereafter, assistance under the Scheme is dependent on simple means testing, conducted by the Court Liaison Office. To be financially eligible the claimant must have a "gross annual income" of not more than $193,750.[83] If the applicants "passes" the means test, he/she will be required to make a one-off handling charge of $540[84] but *no other charge*, irrespective of the length of trial.

9.4.1.2 Merits test

In addition to the financial means test criteria, the Duty Lawyer Service must also determine that it is in the interests of justice to allow the claimant access to the Scheme.

The Service[85] has confirmed that:

---

80. See 9.2.2.1 above.
81. A Raffell, 'Legal Aid & Provision of Legal Services in Hong Kong' (n 11).
82. Ibid 79–84.
83. The administrator of the Scheme has a discretion to grant legal representation to defendants where the gross annual income exceeds the normal upper limit.
84. This can be waived at the Administrator's discretion.
85. See, eg, Duty Lawyer Service Annual Report 2016.

The merits test adopted by the Scheme is based on the criteria set out by the Widgery Committee in 1966.[86] The Committee stated that the proper scope of an adequate scheme of legal assistance is 'to secure that injustice does not arise through an accused person being prevented by lack of means from bringing effectively before the court matters which may constitute a defence to the charge or mitigate the gravity of the offence.'[87]

In determining whether it is in the interests of justice to grant access to the Scheme the Duty Lawyer Service will adopt the "Widgery Criteria" as follows:

(i) that the charge is a grave one in the sense that the accused is in real jeopardy of losing his liberty or suffering serious damage to his reputation;
(ii) that the charge raises a substantial question of law;
(iii) that the accused is unable to follow the proceedings and state his own case because of his inadequate knowledge of English, mental illness or other mental or physical disability;
(iv) that the nature of the defence involves the tracing and interviewing of witnesses or expert cross-examination of a witness for the prosecution; or
(v) that legal representation is desirable in the interest of someone other than the accused as, for example, in the case of sexual offences against young children where it is undesirable that the accused should cross-examine the witness in person.[88]

9.4.2 The Free Legal Advice Scheme

This scheme provides free "preliminary" legal advice (without means testing) for those who need it.[89] The advice is given by "volunteer lawyers" at nine designated District Offices throughout Hong Kong. Most of these operate only once a week,[90] but have the merit of operating outside the central business district (unlike most solicitors' offices). Clients who wish to see a volunteer lawyer have a preliminary interview with clerical staff who summarise the nature of the legal problem in preparation for the volunteer lawyer.[91] Over 1,100 lawyers (about an equal number of solicitors and barristers) donate their services to the Scheme on a "*pro bono*" basis.[92]

---

86. The Widgery Committee established the criteria for the granting of criminal legal aid in England and Wales.
87. Widgery Criteria, para 56.
88. Ibid.
89. Although there is no means testing the free advice will be refused to "inappropriate" cases (such as those already in receipt of legal aid, those involved in building management disputes and those already legally represented).
90. The Central and Western District Office is open twice a week and the Wanchai Office three times.
91. The volunteer lawyers deal with five cases on each evening they participate.
92. There is also additional provision for volunteer assistance by University of Hong Kong law students. Additionally, there is a "hotline" set up by the Hong Kong Federation and a, very limited, access provision for female sex workers seeking (legal) advice.

In 2016, 8,248 cases were handled by the Scheme. The largest number of cases remains "matrimonial" despite the growth in family mediation since, from 2010, the Scheme has subsumed the "Free Legal Consultation" established by the Family Welfare Society's Mediation centre which, itself, is supported by 45 volunteer lawyers. A related scheme has been operated, since 2010, by the Professional Legal Education Department of the University of Hong Kong, with the applicant members of the public being interviewed by students who prepare notes for the volunteer lawyers/legal academics who will give advice.

It should be emphasised that the free Scheme is intended to give only basic information as to a "client's" legal position. No actual case preparation or representation is provided.

9.4.3 Tel-Law Scheme

This scheme, introduced in 1984, provides legal information over the telephone. It is a fully computerised 24-hour automatic answering service. Eighty tapes are available on topics divided into eight groups (family law; landlord and tenant/land law; criminal law; employment law; commercial and banking law; constitutional and administrative law; tort law and the environment; and "general information").

The tapes are available in Cantonese, English and Putonghua and provide a very useful "first stop" service. During 2017, 17,738 telephone calls to the Scheme were recorded. This indicates a gradual decline in telephone calls *but* this is explained by the fact that the Tel-Law Scheme is increasingly accessed online. The Scheme's website recorded a huge 566,556 "hits" in 2017.

9.4.4 The Convention Against Torture (CAT) Scheme

At the end of 2009 an assistance Scheme was introduced on a pilot basis to assist those claiming to be the victims of torture contrary to the United Nations Convention Against Torture and Other Cruel, Human or Degrading Treatment or Punishment. The genesis of the Convention Against Torture (CAT) Scheme seems to have been court criticism of the screening process, adopted by the Department of Immigration, in *FB & Others v Director of Immigration and Secretary for Security*.[93] The Court of First Instance in *FB* had particularly criticised the refusal to allow legal representation at screening interviews and the failure to publicly fund representation for claimants who are generally impecunious. Further, and more emphatically, the Court of Final Appeal, in *C & Others v Director of Immigration*,[94] stated that the Director of Immigration must *independently* investigate whether a well-founded fear of persecution has been established (rather than leaving this to the United Nations High Commission for Refugees). The CAT Scheme, originally restricted to "torture" cases

---

93. [2009] 2 HKLRD 346, [2009] 1 HKC 133.
94. (2013) 16 HKCFAR 280, [2013] 4 HKC 563.

was extended, in 2014,[95] to cover assistance in all "non-refoulement" claims under the new "Unified Screening Mechanism"[96] process. The new screening system, introduced in March 2014, is administered by the Hong Kong government and is intended to work more quickly and efficiently than the previous screening by the United Nations High Commission for Refugees (UNHCR). Essentially, "claimants", though not having the right to enter and remain in Hong Kong,[97] assert that their removal to a particular "Risk Country" would expose them to the risk of:

1. "Torture" as defined under Part VIIC of the Immigration Ordinance;[98]
2. "Torture or cruel, inhuman or degrading treatment or punishment" under Article 3 of section 8 of the Hong Kong Bill of Rights Ordinance;[99] and/or
3. "Persecution" as recognised under Article 33 of the 1951 Convention Relating to the Status of Refugees.

Screening is by the Immigration Department but appeals against the decision may be made to the Torture Claims Appeal Board whose role has been extended to cover all "non-refoulement" appeals under the new, unified system. In those (rare) cases where a "non-refoulement" claim is successful, Hong Kong merely agrees not to deport to the "risk state"; it does *not* accept the principle of political "asylum".[100] The percentage of non-refoulement claims upheld is *very* low (approximately 1%), prompting assertions of "fake" claims. Previous Hong Kong Chief Executive C Y Leung (controversially) asserted that Hong Kong may leave the United Nations Convention "when necessary".[101] Ironically, the refugee union has supported such a departure, on the grounds that the current "unified screening" scheme (with a 99% rejection rate) is a "fake".[102] In addition to the low "success" rate of applications, there is also concern as to the rule whereby claimants cannot, generally, work while their cases are being investigated (often a long time). With subsistence allowance to claimants very low there is a likelihood of claimants turning to crime.[103]

The Duty Lawyer assistance in these CAT Scheme cases extends to full legal representation in the first and second stages of the screening process. The service is

---

95. Without, its critics say, adequate consultation: see M Daly, 'Refugee & Non-Refoulement Law in Hong Kong: The Introduction of the USM' *Hong Kong Lawyer* (October 2014).
96. More formally the "Unified Screening Mechanism for Claims for Non-Refoulement Protection".
97. Hong Kong does not recognise the principle of "asylum": see Immigration Department (April 2014), *Notice to Persons Making a Non-refoulement Claim*, para 66.
98. Cap 115.
99. Cap 383.
100. Space does not permit extensive coverage of this area including two main concerns: the lack of specialised training for screeners given their new, expanded role, and the overlap between claims *commenced* under the UNHCR and transferred to the HKSAR authorities.
101. News Conference (post-2016 Policy Address, 13 January 2016). The PRC is a signatory to the UN Convention.
102. Refugee Union, 'Refugee Union Supports Withdrawal from UN Torture Convention' (Hong Kong, 1 February 2016).
103. The refusal to allow claimants to work has been legally challenged: *GA & Others v Director of Immigration* (2014) 17 HKCFAR 60, [2014] 3 HKC 11.

free but the claimant must declare that s/he is financially unable to pay for the cost of legal representation. The scale of the Duty Lawyer Service task is clearly expanding in this area: up to 2013, 5,599 CAT Scheme referral cases taken up by the Service; by 2015, that figure had reached 10,147.

9.5 The Bar Free Legal Service Scheme

Since June 2000, the Bar Association has offered a free legal advice service.[104] The Scheme is not publicly funded and, as a result, is not intended to provide the services of a barrister over a lengthy period or to handle complicated cases in their entirety. The nature of the service is that a panel of barristers from private practice, with wide-ranging experience, volunteer their services such that they provide three days (or 20 hours) of free legal service per year. The volunteer barrister may either give free written or oral advice or represent the applicant free in court. The Scheme is managed by a Management Committee of the Bar Association and has a part-time co-ordinator. More than 100 barristers volunteer their services to the Scheme.

Since the object of the Scheme is to provide assistance only to those who lack means and cannot obtain assistance elsewhere,[105] there is a vetting procedure which examines both the merits of the applicant's case and his means. Most applications for assistance are made on a walk-in basis and around half of the 300 plus applications made annually[106] are screened out on a "merits" basis (the rest receiving some form of assistance).[107] The Management Committee has an absolute discretion whether or not to provide the free service and no right of appeal against refusal exists.

9.6 Helping the unassisted litigant

Given the significant number of litigants in Hong Kong who represent themselves, public assistance has been somewhat tardy. A Resource Centre for Unrepresented Litigants commenced its operations in December 2003 following a report, in 2002, by the Steering Committee[108] appointed by the Chief Justice to advise on the establishment and operation of such a Resource Centre for potential civil litigants.[109]

The Resource Centre, after some years in operation, provides significant advice to lay litigants, bringing or defending actions in the District or High Court, as to the "practices" of the courts. This is in keeping with the stated purpose of the Centre

---

104. Information from the Hong Kong Bar Association website stresses that the barrister's "advice and assistance" is free but that expenses such as court fees must be met by the applicant.
105. "Those who fall through the cracks", as they are described in the Report of the Steering Committee on Resource Centre for Unrepresented Litigants.
106. Most of these involve criminal law.
107. The key criteria are whether the applicant has a good case, whether he needs free help or can afford to pay, and whether the services of a barrister are the most appropriate for the applicant's problem.
108. Steering Committee on Resource Centre for Unrepresented Litigants.
109. The (then) Chief Justice had announced his intention to institute such a centre in his speech of January 2002 at the Opening of the Legal Year.

which is "to provide facilities to enable unrepresented litigants to deal with the court rules and procedures in the conduct of their cases".[110]

Clearly, familiarity with the arcane procedures of the courts is important. One of the difficulties with unrepresented litigants, recognised by courts throughout the common law world, is their inability to "play by the rules" (to ask leading questions, to neglect court etiquette, etc).[111] In implicit recognition of the problem, the Steering Committee Report states that:

> They [unrepresented litigants] represent a significant demand on judicial time and resources . . .
>
> The increasing number of unrepresented litigants poses challenges for the courts.[112]

The problem has become exacerbated by the significant changes to civil procedure introduced as a result of the Civil Justice Reforms of 2009.[113] The problem is implicitly recognised by the innovation of the pilot scheme (see below) abbreviated, by the Home Affairs Bureau, as the "Procedural Advice Scheme".

What the Resource Centre addresses less well, is the problem of the lack of "legal knowledge" on the part of the unrepresented litigant. Indeed, it is a principle of the Resource Centre that staff will not give legal advice or make any comments on the merits of a case, in order to maintain the principle of judicial impartiality. It is difficult to see how a "typical" unrepresented litigant can compete equally with a legally represented adversary; indeed if s/he *were* able to do so it would reflect badly on the quality of legal education and training in Hong Kong. The dilemma, then, for the judge, is how far to assist the unrepresented litigant. If he helps too much he may be viewed as "favouring" the litigant in person, while if he fails to assist he may be criticised for being unfair to him.

A somewhat expanded scheme for advice for litigants in person was introduced in 2013 as a two-year pilot scheme.[114] It provides for short meetings[115] with "Resident Lawyers" of the Scheme or volunteer "Community Lawyers". It extends to actions in the Court of Final Appeal but, again, does not extend to advice on the merits of a case or detailed preparation of such. Crucially, this Scheme is means-tested, broadly as for civil legal aid, such that those failing the legal aid means test are unlikely to be eligible. It does have the potential, however, to assist those denied legal aid on a merits basis who, nonetheless wish to proceed.[116]

---

110. See para 1.5 of the Steering Committee's report.
111. "Professionals" in the criminal justice system take a similarly dim view of the defendant who chooses to defend himself.
112. Ibid at paras 1.2 and 1.4.
113. See 9.10 below.
114. Pilot Scheme to Provide Legal Advice for Litigants in Person.
115. The maximum period is 45 minutes but there may be up to five sessions.
116. From 2017 the scheme became a regular government programme, was expanded somewhat and was re-named the "Legal Advice Scheme for Unrepresented Litigants on Civil Procedures".

This raises the question of *why* a litigant would choose to represent himself. It could be that the litigant has an inflated opinion of his own legal expertise (or a poor opinion of the level of expertise of lawyers) but, more likely, as the Steering Committee suggested, the key factors are the level of legal fees, the current economic climate, and the increased use of Chinese in the courts. Indeed, the Steering Committee referred to a survey conducted by the Judiciary Administration which found that 63% of litigants in person represented themselves because of financial constraints, while 7% felt a "lawyer was not necessary".[117] All of these factors ultimately boil down to the issue of cost. The "economic climate" simply means that the client has less to spend on (expensive) legal services and even the use of Chinese, which may prompt the litigant in person to feel more confident in handling his own case, would not be a determining factor if the litigant could readily afford skilled legal help.

Given that, according to the data, 70% of litigants in person cited economic constraints (and presumably had applied unsuccessfully for legal aid or did not even think it worth trying) what is indicated is a difference in perception between the litigant and "the State". Assuming denial of legal aid on "merits" grounds, the litigant pressing on regardless evidently did not share the LAD's perception of the weakness of the case. Conversely, if the denial was based on "means" grounds, the implicit assumption that the litigant could afford to pay for legal representation appears not to have been shared by those litigants deciding to represent themselves. However, it is too early to say whether the enhanced financial eligibility rules for legal aid have reduced the amount of litigation in person.[118]

In short, litigation "in person" will generally be inferior litigation. Ideally, the litigant with a good case, financially unable to pay for private legal representation, should be assisted by the public purse. If the litigant is forced to proceed unaided, a "Resource Centre" is better than nothing. It should be recognised, however, as a poor substitute for adequate provision of "proper" legal aid.

9.7 Contingency fee and conditional fee systems

Since increased calls on the public purse are always strenuously opposed by those with money, power and, above all, "influence" (who espoused the view that $28 an hour was a proper minimum wage!) an alternative could lie in the American approach of funding legal expertise on a "no win, no fee" basis. The so-called "contingency" fee system has long flourished in the United States. Lawyers do very well from the system but, it must be said, litigants in America, who would never be able to afford a lawyer in Hong Kong, are able to pursue claims, with excellent legal advice and representation. The contingency fee system works on the basis that the lawyer does

---

117. Report of the Steering Committee on Resource Centre for Unrepresented Litigants, Appendix 1.
118. Certainly, up to the time of the improved financial eligibility rules, there had been a fairly consistent number of applications for legal aid annually, and a similarly consistent percentage of refusals.

not get paid if the case is lost *but* does very well if the case is successful. Practice varies but, typically, a law firm might obtain 30% of an early settlement, 40% of a "mid-trial" settlement and 50% of any damages awarded after a full trial. The obvious argument against the system is that the plaintiff does not receive full compensation (though this is also true in legal aid systems where significant charges are levied)[119] but the rejoinder to this argument is that "something is better than nothing" and without this system the litigant would be "lawyer-less". One obvious danger of a contingency system is that lawyers will not take on cases with little chance of success. Against this is the point that hopeless cases should, in any event, be discouraged and that the legal expert is best placed to judge whether a case has merit. The fundamental "ethical" argument, that lawyers should not have a vested interest in the outcome of a case, will be dealt with after consideration of the "conditional" fee alternative.

While, during the major reconsideration of the civil justice system in Britain, the use of contingency fees was rejected, the alternative of "conditional" fees was adopted. Conditional fees, like contingency ones, operate on a "no win, no fee" basis *but*, instead of allowing the lawyer a share of any "winnings", merely allow him to charge a "premium" over normal rates. The maximum of the premium is 100%. To take a simple example, if a solicitor's fee for handling a case would normally be £10,000, he would be entitled, on a conditional fee basis, to charge up to £20,000.[120]

The main reason that contingency fees were not adopted in Britain is the ethical fear that the lawyer who is to receive a share of damages will "exceed the limits" (bearing in mind that he owes a duty to the court as well as his client) and not merely seek to "win at all costs" but also to obtain the highest amount of "compensation" possible from the other side. In America, where juries are widely used in civil cases (and where they have a role in determining the amount of damages as well as the issue of liability), there is little doubt that damages are inflated to take account of the fact that the client will only get part of the award. Moreover, "punitive" (non-compensatory) damages are much more likely to be sought by lawyers in America.[121]

The possible introduction of conditional fees in Hong Kong was considered by the Law Reform Commission of Hong Kong in 2007. However, as the following press release makes clear, the Commission decided that the time was not right for the introduction of conditional fees, despite the strong arguments in favour of extending access to legal services via this route.

---

119. See 9.2.3.3 above.
120. Early experience of conditional fees in Britain was that they had increased rather than decreased cost: see C Buddle, 'Britain Offers Key to Legal Reform' "Legal Focus", *South China Morning Post* (Hong Kong, 27 July 2001)].
121. It is true that contingency fees are likely to have an "inflationary" effect. However, in the true spirit of "adversarialism" (which the common law traditionally espouses) contingency lawyers can be relied on to do their best for their clients.

Release of report on conditional fees[122]

The Law Reform Commission (LRC) today (July 9) released a report on conditional fees which advises that conditions at this time are not appropriate for the introduction of conditional fees – a form of "no-win, no-fee" arrangement.

Professor Edward K Y Chen, chairman of the LRC's Conditional Fees sub-committee, explained that although conditional fees could enhance access to justice for a significant proportion of the community who are currently neither eligible for legal aid nor able to fund litigation themselves, a successful conditional fees regime requires the long term availability of affordable insurance (called "after-the-event" insurance) to cover the opponent's legal costs if the legal action fails.

However, responses from the insurance industry to an earlier consultation paper issued by the sub-committee suggested that this was unlikely to be the case in Hong Kong, he noted.

"In the absence of "after-the-event" insurance, we do not recommend the introduction of conditional fees because those in the middle income group might not be able to absorb the other side's costs, and might face financial ruin if required to pay those costs," Professor Chen said.

On the other hand, given the widespread support for the consultation paper's proposal to expand the existing Supplementary Legal Aid Scheme administered by the Legal Aid Department, the report recommends that the Government should increase the financial eligibility limits of the Supplementary Legal Aid Scheme, as well as expanding the types of cases covered by the scheme.

As an alternative to the existing legal aid schemes, the report further recommends the setting up of a Conditional Legal Aid Fund ("CLAF") to screen applications for the use of conditional fees, brief out cases to private lawyers, finance the litigation, and pay the opponent's legal costs should the litigation prove unsuccessful.

Comment

Historically, as the Law Reform Commission noted, the issue of contingency funding is tied to the ancient offences[123] of "maintenance" and "champerty". Maintenance is the improper encouragement of litigation which "increases strife" by giving aid to one party to bring or defend a legal action without just cause. Champerty is a variation on maintenance in which the party "encouraging" the unjust cause does so for a share of the "proceeds". It can be seen, of course, that contingency fees conflict with anti-champerty rules, while conditional fees may be reconciled with them.[124]

---

122. Press Release, 9 July 2007.
123. Both criminal and tortious.
124. The point is moot, since the lawyer has an "interest" in winning but not in how much is won.

Though of ancient origin, maintenance and champerty remain outlawed in Hong Kong on the grounds of "public policy". Indeed, champerty is a "live" issue in Hong Kong, as evidenced by the following questions raised in the Legislative Council (LegCo).

> Legislative Council 26 March, 2014
>
> Official Record of Proceedings
>
> ...
>
> Improvement to the Legal Aid System
>
> 1. Mr Frankie Yik (in Cantonese):
>
> *President... Given that the LAD generally assigns, according to the wishes of legally aided persons, the solicitors or counsel nominated by them to be their representatives, and legal aid cases are assigned mainly to a small number of lawyers at present, some members of the taxi and public light bus trades are worried that the legal aid system is susceptible to abuse. For instance, law-breakers may engage in champerty and abet the injured in traffic accidents to exaggerate the degree of their injuries sustained in order to make fraudulent insurance claims. Due to the increase in the amount of compensation payout, insurance companies raise the insurance premiums for vehicles, resulting in an increase in the operating expenditure of the trades. In this connection, will the Government inform this Council:*
>
> (1)...
>
> (2)...
>
> (3) *whether it will invite the Corruption Prevention Department of the Independent Commission Against Corruption (ICAC) to give advice on the existing procedure for assigning legal aid lawyers, so as to ensure that the procedure is fair and transparent; if it will, of the details; if not, the reasons for that?*
>
> SECRETARY FOR HOME AFFAIRS (in Cantonese): President, the Government's policy objective of legal aid is to ensure that no one with reasonable grounds for taking or defending a legal action is denied access to justice because of a lack of means...
>
> As regards the three parts of Mr YICK's question, the answer is as follows:
>
> (1)...
>
> (2) Under the common law, maintenance and champerty are criminal offences, and are prohibited under the code of professional conduct of The Law Society of Hong Kong and the Hong Kong Bar Association. Notices are displayed at the LAD offices to remind the public of the risk of engaging recovery agents and of the prohibition of improper touting activities by law firms within the LAD premises. If a nominated lawyer is found to have engaged in any improper conduct, the LAD will impose appropriate sanctions on the lawyer concerned and refer the case to the Hong Kong Bar Association or The Law Society of Hong Kong for follow-up action.
>
> To address the public concern on improper touting or champerty activities, the LAD has introduced a "Declaration System" for legal aid cases in September 2013 after

> consulting the Legal Aid Services Council and the two legal professional bodies. The system seeks to ensure that the aided person's choice of lawyer is not affected by the champerty or improper touting activities on the part of the lawyer concerned. A nominated lawyer who is unable to accept the above declaration condition will not be allowed to take up assignment to handle the case.
>
> Meanwhile, the LAD also noted that there were Panel Lawyers who had been assigned with a relatively larger number of cases. Such situations may not necessarily be related to improper touting or champerty activities. The LAD will consider enhancing liaison with the two legal professional bodies to combat improper touting, and imposing appropriate sanctions on law firms that have acted unreasonably or have no handled claims properly.
>
> (3) A Department Monitoring Committee (DMC) chaired by the Director is established to evaluate the performance of assigned lawyers in handling legal aid cases and the number of legal aid cases assigned. In the past, a representative of the ICAC had attended DMC meetings as an observer.
>
> To enhance the transparency and fairness in the assignments of lawyers, the LAD and ICAC have formed a Corruption Prevention Group to discuss issues relating to prevention of corruption and bribery. We understand that the Group has agreed to commence a review of the lawyer assignment procedures in the middle of this year. The Home Affairs Bureau will closely monitor the situation.

Despite the traditional bar on champerty, however, in the case of *Siegfried Adalbert Unruh v Hans-Joerg Seeberger & Another*,[125] the Court of Final Appeal (CFA) indicated a softening of attitude based on developing public policy considerations. In particular the CFA stressed that the law would not be enforced against those who have a "common interest" in the outcome of litigation, nor in cases where there are "access to justice" considerations and the assisted party would not have been able to bring a (legitimate) legal action without the support.[126] However, despite the public policy considerations of *Siegfried Adelbert Unruh*, champerty remains an offence in Hong Kong and champertous claims will be rejected. This was made clear in *Beijing Tong Gang Da Sheng Trade Co Ltd v Allen & Overy (A Firm) & Another*, where a finding of champerty by Le Pichon J in the Court of First Instance[127] was upheld by the Court of Appeal.[128] The main criterion was a lack of a genuine "common interest" on the part of the "funder". A "Focus" article in the *South China Morning Post*[129] attributed some doubts as to the desirability of retaining champerty to Court

---

125. [2007] HKEC 268.
126. The CFA concluded that maintenance and champerty should not be used as "too blunt an instrument" (Herbert Smith [Solicitors] Hong Kong, *Litigation Briefing*, March 2007).
127. [2014] 4 HKC 333.
128. [2015] HKCA 234.
129. P Moy and S Lau, 'A Crime That Doesn't Pay' *Sunday Morning Post*, "Focus" (Hong Kong, 7 April 2013).

of Final Appeal Permanent Judge Ribeiro, given abolition in Britain. However, the same article indicated support for the retention of the crime of champerty from former Director of Public Prosecutions, Kevin Zervos, who states:

> The idea of lawyers or agents taking a certain percentage of the compensatory monies ... is generally viewed unfavourably and it is considered that it may be open to abuse ... we are not the UK, we are not America, we are Hong Kong, we have our own local issues and should make sure our law suits our purposes.

Zervos had particularly in mind the prevalence of dubious "recovery agents"; a particularly Hong Kong phenomenon. Indeed, the Legal Aid Department has issued a specific "flyer" on the issue headed "Protect Your Legal Interest" and warning "Beware of the Touting Activities of Claims Recovery Agents".

9.8 Reducing the cost of lawyers

A recurrent theme of studies concerning "access to justice" is the cost of professional legal assistance. In Hong Kong, particularly, the high level of lawyers' fees is a constant refrain. A number of examples were cited in the Civil Justice Reform Interim Report.[130] One relates that:

> In March 2000, Mr Mark Bradley, a solicitor and Council Member of the Hong Kong Law Society, launched an attack on the level of barristers' fees on the basis of his experience in the Law Society's Claims Committee, alleging that local counsel most in demand 'are now charging something like four times as much as their equivalents in the UK'.[131]

The second noteworthy reference in the Interim Report concerns an article in the *South China Morning Post* which refers to parties being prepared to:

> fly a barrister out first-class from London, put him up at the Mandarin for a few weeks and fork out $8,000 an hour rather than hire a [more] 'costly' Hong Kong counterpart.[132]

Finally, lest it be thought that the criticisms were solely about over-expensive *barristers*, the Interim Report refers to an internet comment that:

> the average solicitor in Hong Kong charges more in two hours than the average worker earns in a month. In three hours, legal advice can cost as much as a month's salary of a well-paid university graduate – who still has to live with his parents in order to make ends meet.[133]

---

130. The report was prepared by the 'Working Party on Civil Justice Reform', appointed by the Chief Justice in February 2000.
131. Para 40.1(a) of the Interim Report.
132. Ibid para 40.1(d). The use of overseas barristers is now less common but only because it is now more difficult to get approval to brief outside Hong Kong.
133. Ibid para 40.2.

While the *de facto* abolition of scale fees[134] for solicitors'[135] conveyancing work and the possible over-manning at the lower levels at the Bar (an increasingly "young" profession) has led to some reduction in the cost of legal services, Hong Kong remains an expensive place in which to hire a private lawyer. The two main problems remain the relative shortage of lawyers and the congregation of lawyers in the expensive central business district, where overheads are inevitably very high. Like all good "trade unions", the legal profession exhorts us to believe that there are "too many lawyers" while the three main indices of "over-manning" (lawyer unemployment, reduced fees as a result of competition, and "migration" to cheaper accommodation) are all notably lacking.[136] The need for increased legal aid proper would be ameliorated were there to be more PCLL places,[137] more lawyers and more competition in Hong Kong.

Of course one of the major reasons that lawyers are so thin on the ground in areas such as Mong Kok is that local residents have less money, and "demand" for legal services tends to be related to income level. If we think of obvious "law jobs" such as conveyancing, it is clear that such work is less in demand in poorer, mostly rental areas. However, the real issue is not the demand for legal services but the demand for *well-paid* legal services. We know it is untrue that there are no crimes in Mong Kok, or no matrimonial disputes, or no landlord and tenant issues; what is lacking are rich individuals or businesses able to pay high legal fees to resolve their legal problems. A classic Hong Kong example is provided by family law, where problems of divorce, separation, custody are widespread and, not uncommonly, of cross-border concern. Very little law degree or professional legal education has been provided in family law in all the years that Hong Kong law-based degrees and the PCLL programme has been offered.[138] Why not? Because family law has traditionally been seen as low-paid work.[139] As a result, few Hong Kong lawyers have family law expertise, except those who have studied for overseas law degrees.

Lawyers, of course, have the ability to "create" law work by designating potentially lucrative tasks as "legal". The classic example is conveyancing, in respect of which lawyers have managed to convince the populace that the assistance of a lawyer is essential to the transfer of title to real property (a view not endorsed in the lawyers' Utopia of the United States!). Joseph[140] has shown that the two rationales for the need for lawyers in respect of conveyancing (would you ask a lawyer to sell

---

134. See Chapter 7.
135. In reality this work is generally performed by a clerk/legal executive "under supervision".
136. Try, as the author has, a simple internet search for a solicitor's office in Mong Kok and you will find only a very small selection.
137. See Chapter 7.
138. Even after the legal education reforms referred to in the previous chapter, family law receives scant undergraduate and PCLL coverage.
139. Ironically those few practitioners with expertise in family law have carved out a lucrative niche market.
140. See M Joseph, *The Conveyancing Fraud* (Michael Joseph 1994).

Legal Aid and Advice and Unmet Legal Need   397

your car?)—"professional expertise" and "someone to sue if it all goes wrong"—are both wildly exaggerated. First (as a previously successful solicitor with a wealth of conveyancing experience), Joseph shows that most conveyancing work is done by legal executives with minimal supervision. His (simple) evidence was to highlight "trade" advertisements for clerks/legal executives "able to do conveyancing with minimal supervision". Second, Joseph explains that the solution, if something goes wrong, is to have recourse to compulsory insurance. While Joseph's work was undoubtedly unpopular with fellow lawyers,[141] it is significant that the solicitor's monopoly over paid[142] conveyances has since been abolished in England and Wales (though not in Hong Kong).[143]

9.9 *"Pro bono"* work

Clearly one way to alleviate the problem of meritorious litigants being unable to afford high legal fees, or to qualify for legal aid, is via the provision of free assistance donated by volunteer professionals. This work is known as *"pro bono"* (short for *pro bono publico*; for the public good). Contributions of this kind by legal professionals in Hong Kong are to be welcomed and are not insignificant, especially given the separate Hong Kong Bar "Free Legal Service" (dealt with above)[144] also involving volunteers. Nonetheless, the extent of *pro bono* work is not huge and is offered, primarily, by large or medium-sized solicitors' firms. Not surprisingly, small firms have greater difficulty in sparing the time and manpower for the provision of a free service. The problem with leaving things to the bigger firms is that they tend to be "commercial-client" focused and less able, perhaps, to provide free services to those most in need. Moreover, these large firms, generally involved in the PRC legal market (or aspiring to be), will be unwilling to handle cases which might be perceived as in any way politically sensitive.[145]

The Report of the Steering Committee on Resource Centre for Unrepresented Litigants noted the (largely unpublicised) contributions of solicitors' firms in respect of *pro bono* work, as well as the value of the Bar Free Legal Service Scheme. The Report recommended consideration of an "annual goal" for a set amount of *pro bono* work[146] as well as the provision of legal advice at a "minimal charge".[147]

---

141. Since finding a publisher was difficult, Joseph decided to publish himself, so beginning a flourishing "second career".
142. English law always permitted a person to do his own conveyancing despite the supposed high risk involved!
143. "Licensed conveyancers" (fully insured) now operate in Britain and conveyancing has become much cheaper (though abolition of "scale fees" is a more significant reason for this).
144. See 9.5.
145. The Hong Kong Bar has been far more prepared to "offend China" in defence of rights than has the solicitors' branch of the profession.
146. As in the United States experience.
147. Steering Committee Report, paras 3.54 and 3.55.

Greater focus on *pro bono* work is now likely since the announcement by former Chief Justice, Andrew Li, of his intention, to study the provision of *pro bono* services as his first "post-retirement" project.

9.10 Civil Justice Reforms in Hong Kong

In addition to extending legal aid availability, an obvious strategy to extend access to justice is to simplify and speed up the process, especially in the area of civil justice where litigants, to some extent, have a choice as to whether to fight in court and to be legally represented.

In February 2000, the (then) Chief Justice set up a working party to review the operation of civil justice in Hong Kong and to recommend any necessary reforms, "with a view to ensuring and improving access to justice at reasonable cost and speed". The working party's Final Report was released in 2004. The report rejected the idea of an entirely new code of civil procedure, as had been introduced in England with the Civil Procedure Rules (CPR) of 1998,[148] and recommended instead selective amendments to the existing rules,[149] taking into account Hong Kong's special circumstances.[150] Hong Kong's Civil Justice Reforms (CJR) are, therefore, an adaptation but certainly not a replication of Britain's CPR. Lord Woolf himself supported the idea of Hong Kong learning from the British experience, saying:

> I urge you to look at what we are doing to see if there are any lessons for Hong Kong.[151]

While a detailed treatment of the Civil Justice Reforms (CJR), introduced in 2009,[152] is not possible here, the most important features may be noted. These may be subsumed under the heading of "underlying objectives" as stipulated under Order 1A, rule 1 of the Rules of the High Court (RHC). These underlying objectives are:

(i) To increase the cost-effectiveness of any practice and procedure to be followed in relation to proceedings before the Court;
(ii) to ensure that a case is dealt with as expeditiously as practicable;
(iii) to promote a sense of reasonable proportion and procedural economy in the conduct of proceedings;
(iv) to ensure fairness between the parties;
(v) to facilitate settlement of disputes; and

---

148. The so-called "Woolf Reforms".
149. Primarily the Rules of the High Court (RHC) and the Rules of the District Court (RDC).
150. The rejection of a wholesale adoption of the Woolf Reforms has been welcomed by experts on the grounds that Hong Kong can learn from Britain's experience: see WS Clarke, 'Civil Justice Reform—The New "Underlying Objectives"' in *Law Lecturers for Practitioners* (Hong Kong Law Journal Ltd 2008), 1–16.
151. Quoted in C Buddle, *South China Morning Post*, "Legal Focus", 27 July 2001. One lesson learned appears to be that conditional fees were not a success and should not be adopted in Hong Kong.
152. Effective 2 April 2009.

(vi) to ensure that resources of the court are distributed fairly.

The key to fulfilling most of these objectives is effective "case management" by the judge in a civil case. This marks something of a departure from the common law tradition of the judge being not merely a "neutral umpire" but also a "passive" umpire, not intervening unless lawyers (or litigants in person) transgress. Lord Woolf, himself, has described case management as the key, stating:

> I am afraid you have got to give new powers to the judges ... They have got to get their jackets off and get down to the job of managing cases. It can make a huge difference.[153]

Case management in relation to "cost effectiveness" involves, particularly, "encouraging"[154] the parties to consider alternative dispute resolution (ADR).[155] In respect of "expeditiousness", a particular aspect of case management is the power of the judge to impose "milestone" dates for the completion of various stages of pre-trial procedure. The purpose, of course, is to eliminate unnecessary delay. Moreover, there are now increased opportunities to make "admissions" in respect of monetary claims so that "quantum" issues not in dispute can be expeditiously concluded.[156] "Proportionality" refers to the need to ensure that additional proceedings (interlocutory issues, appeals, etc) do not have the result of making the costs of a case out of all proportion to the amount involved. Of course amount ("quantum") will not always be the only consideration and the court will still be able to take into account issues of principle in determining the issue of proportionality. The "fairness" objective (an adaptation of the English "equal footing" objective) might involve a party appealing against the refusal of legal aid (on a "merits" basis) where his opponent is legally represented.[157] What it will *not* do is ensure that each party has a legal representative of equal expertise and experience. "Facilitating settlement" has, as solicitor[158] William Clarke suggests, always been a feature of the British and Hong Kong system in which costs "normally follow the action". In other words, the fear of losing, and therefore having to pay the opponent's costs, has always been a factor which encourages settlement. Unless, says Clarke, the judge himself is to be involved in settlement discussions (both unlikely and unwelcome) it is not clear what this "new"

---

153. Ibid.
154. In Britain those "unreasonably" refusing mediation, for example, may be penalised in respect of costs. Hong Kong has not (yet) adopted similarly punitive methods of encouraging ADR. Previous Secretary for Justice, Wong Yan Lung, has said: "Court ordered mediation ... does not form part of our CJR" (concluding address at Conference on Civil Justice Reform, 16 April 2010). However, in most cases, parties may be required to confirm whether they have considered mediation (Practice Direction 31).
155. The *Guide to General Civil Proceedings in High Court and District Court* for unassisted litigants states in its introduction that: "Court action should be your last resort." For a fuller consideration of ADR, see Chapter 10.
156. Under Order 13A, Rules of the High Court (Cap 4A) and Rules of the District Court (Cap 336H).
157. See WS Clarke (m 151) 5.
158. And former University of Hong Kong legal academic.

objective adds to previous court practice.[159] Finally, the objective of "fair distribution of resources" involves the need to balance the requirements for court time of "bigger", more technical and complex cases with the needs of other litigation to be heard reasonably expeditiously.

Significantly the Hong Kong CJR "objectives" involve not only the judge, since all parties are required to assist in attempts to fulfil them. Quicker, cheaper, more efficient and transparent court procedures will clearly assist in improving access to justice but this should be seen as "complementary" to the provision of adequate legal aid, rather than as a substitute.

9.11 The future

Given the Hong Kong government's reluctance to spend money on "welfare-related" issues (as opposed to new roads) it is unlikely that publicly funded legal aid will become much more widely available. The extended financial eligibility rules of late 2012 and beyond were an important improvement but it is essential that such improvements are regularly reviewed so as to keep them in line with inflation.

Meanwhile, despite improvements, legal aid remains beyond the reach of many in the sandwich class. *Pro bono* work may ameliorate the situation, as may improvements to the efficiency and expeditiousness of court procedures. However, short of increased (genuine) competition in the legal marketplace, legal costs will remain high and, for many, constitutional guarantees of a right to legal representation are somewhat illusory. For this reason, and because of civil justice reform initiatives, we are likely to see an increase in the move away from traditional litigation to various "alternative" methods of resolving disputes. Such alternatives will be discussed in the next chapter.

---

159. Though in more specific terms the new rules on "sanctioned offers" and "sanctioned payments" provide financial "disincentives" for those who reject opportunities to conclude reasonable settlements before conclusion of a trial (see, eg, Order 22, Rules of the High Court).

10
Alternative Dispute Resolution

Overview

The traditional way of resolving disputes in common law jurisdictions has been by trial before a judge. Over recent years, however, and following its success in the United States, alternative dispute resolution (ADR) is becoming increasingly popular, especially in commercial cases. Alternatives to litigation are important today, for a variety of reasons; the most important being cost, speed and jurisdictional concerns. The best-known form of ADR is arbitration but mediation (and conciliation) are more recent and fast-growing variations. Clearly there are areas of nexus between this chapter and the last, since the move towards ADR and away from court litigation is, *in part*, the result of inadequate access to affordable legal services and the relative unavailability of legal aid in Hong Kong.

It can be argued that ADR is counter to the common law tradition of "adversarial" justice, in which two competing "rivals" (or their legal advisers) battle for a "win" on an "all-or-nothing" basis. ADR, indeed, seems to have more in common with civil law notions of an "active", interventionist judge and is more consistent with traditional Chinese notions of compromise and the avoidance of conflict. In simplistic terms, most ADR "events" involve neither side getting exactly what it wants but neither being an absolute loser. Given the Chinese emphasis on "face", a system which produces no outright winners and losers will, of course, have its attractions in Hong Kong.

There is no doubt that "cost", especially cost to the public purse, is a factor in the development of ADR. The limitations on the availability of civil legal aid, outlined in the previous chapter, mean that many potential litigants are financially unable to fight trials in the traditional way. However, cost is far from the only factor in the move to ADR and even in commercial cases where the parties have the ability to "fight" it is common to resort to ADR or to undertake, contractually, in advance, that some form of ADR will be attempted instead of, or before, recourse to the courts.

10.1 Reasons for the growth of ADR

Various factors have prompted the development of different forms of ADR. The most important is that an increase in the workload of the "regular" courts has caused a backlog and inevitable delays in the conclusion of litigation. This means that getting a case to court can be a very lengthy procedure. Moreover, appeals from court decisions are much more likely to be made (and approved) than those from an ADR forum. While reform of the civil justice system has been introduced (in 2009) in Hong Kong, via a somewhat diluted version of the English civil justice "Woolf reforms",[1] delay remains a problem and ADR appears to offer a speedier alternative.

Moreover, once a litigated case reaches court, the trial process itself often seems excessively long and unduly complex, as existing rules of procedure and evidence have to be strictly adhered to. Improved case management may help over time, but the trial proper is still seen today, by many, as unnecessarily formal and lengthy. Some media reports of judgments "reserved" by a judge for many months have caused some loss of confidence in the efficacy of the legal process, especially since such delays seem to have *reduced* rather than increased the quality of judgments.[2] Such disquiet further encourages alternatives to courtroom litigation.

Since the length of proceedings obviously affects costs, there are strong financial reasons for seeking alternatives to litigation. In the recent economic downturn particularly, Hong Kong clients were increasingly *settling* legal actions or looking at ADR alternatives. Legal costs have tended to be relatively high in Hong Kong, largely because of a lack of competition in the legal market place, the relatively small number of lawyers in Hong Kong and, of course, the significant overheads for lawyers,[3] especially commercial rents for a profession largely based in the central business district and unwilling to practise elsewhere.[4]

---

1. In Britain, Lord Woolf MR advocated a number of measures to improve the civil justice system, including the extension of judicial case-management and the encouragement of ADR. His recommendations were largely adopted by legislation in the form of the Access to Justice Act 1999.
2. The most infamous case involved Judge Pang who, having reserved written judgment in a criminal case for eight months (after stating in court that he would allow an appeal and quash conviction) subsequently "upheld" the conviction in writing having apparently forgotten his original decision! On being informed of his previous statement he changed his mind again! In severely criticising Judge Pang (by implication) the Chief Justice indicated his distaste for judges holding non-judicial offices. Judge Pang's array of "other jobs", it may be inferred, had adversely affected his judicial role.
3. Dame Professor Hazel Genn shows that demonising "fat cat" lawyers has been a way for the British government to justify the abandonment of civil trials: H Genn, *Judging Civil Justice* (Hamlyn Lectures 2008) (Cambridge University Press 2009) 44.
4. Wesley-Smith, writing in 1998, cited a 1985 survey which found that 75% of law offices were on Hong Kong Island, 13% in Kowloon and only 9% in the New Territories. He concluded that little had changed. See P Wesley-Smith, *An Introduction to the Hong Kong Legal System* (3rd edn, Oxford University Press 1998) 121. The position remains similar today but *may* be changing due to extremely high rents in Central. Famous law firm Freshfields Bruckhaus Deringer has announced plans to move out to Quarry Bay: Y Kriegler, 'Freshfields to Move Out of Hong Kong Central District' *Hong Kong Lawyer* (Hong Kong, 27 January 2017).

In the UK, following the so-called "Woolf reforms" and the Access to Justice Act 1999, significant savings have been made to the public purse by reducing the amount of litigation and by "diversion" to ADR. Critics, notably Professors Zander[5] and Genn,[6] have viewed the development unfavourably, suggesting that important legal principles *affecting not just the parties to an action* should be litigated, with appropriate legal precedents set in open court rather than the confidentiality of ADR. Genn[7] states:

> those cases that do proceed to litigation provide the material for the elaboration of the common law and provide a useful social function in giving the courts the opportunity to restate or develop the law.[8]

The move to ADR, inspired by government and courts, is essentially viewed, by critics, as cost-cutting in the civil law sector to fund the ever-burgeoning criminal "system" costs.[9] Dame Professor Hazel Genn has stated:

> In England, we are witnessing the decline of civil justice, the degradation of court facilities and the diversion of civil cases to private dispute resolution—accompanied by an anti-court, anti-adjudication rhetoric that interprets these developments as socially positive.[10]

Indeed, an example of the "rhetoric" to which Genn refers is provided by Lord Woolf who states:

> Litigation is the most inefficient means of resolving disputes. Taking cases to court tended to drive those involved apart, instead of bringing them together. It was so easy under our (pre-reform) system to find situations where, as a result of litigation, both sides had lost and no one had benefited.[11]

Lord Woolf's strictures on the defects of litigation are, of course, appropriate to matrimonial/family disputes where there is merit in limiting conflict between the parties. The same may be true of long-time contracting parties who wish to continue, post-resolution. Such strictures might seem less appropriate to the victim of a serious defamation or the grieving relative seeking to affix responsibility for medical negligence.

---

5. See M Zander, *The State of Justice* (Hamlyn Lectures 1999) (Cambridge University Press 2000).
6. See H Genn, *Judging Civil Justice* (n 3).
7. Op cit.
8. Ibid 21. Genn later argues that the landmark *Donoghue v Stevenson* case would not have been litigated today.
9. Lord Woolf has insisted that judges have consistently opposed *government-led* cuts to the funding of the civil system to make it self-financing: see F Gibb, 'Woolf v Genn: The Decline of Civil Justice' *Timesonline*, 23 June 2009).
10. Genn (n 3). See also Genn, 'Civil Justice Reform and ADR', Civil Justice Conference, Hong Kong (April 2010).
11. Lord Woolf, 'Access: The Future of Law' (speech to symposium: British Council, 24 July 2001).

Moreover, the UK experience involves "pressure" on litigants to adopt ADR via cost penalties for those unwilling to drop even winning litigation. So far, while encouraging the growth of ADR, the Hong Kong government and courts have not exerted pressure on litigants in this way. Indeed, the position in Hong Kong is described as:

> more moderate, less ambitious and more sceptical towards moving towards activist courts.[12]

A further significant factor in the move from litigation in Hong Kong has been the unavailability of legal aid for the middle classes in Hong Kong because of the financial eligibility rules.[13] Many may be, in the words of Professor Peter Wesley-Smith, "too poor to hire lawyers for themselves, yet too wealthy to qualify for legal aid".[14] The "perception", at least, is that ADR is a cheaper alternative. While it is generally so, in respect of the "public purse", it is not necessarily so for the parties.[15]

Apart from financial constraints it is also the case that litigation can be extremely stressful both before the trial as well as during the trial itself so that any alternative appears attractive. This may be made worse by the fact that litigants often feel intimidated, bewildered and frustrated by the legal *formality* of courtroom procedure and their lack of control over the proceedings. The stress involved may also increase because most trials take place in open court; it can come as a shock to the litigants that private matters are so publicly aired. ADR, in the form of family mediation, for example, may well avoid the public airing of private conflicts. Moreover, many business-based ADR's are benefited by the lack of publicity involved.

Much of what has been said so far espouses ADR in a "negative" sense (defects in the trial system) but, in many areas, a case can be made for the preferability of skilled, specialist arbitrators or mediators with particular expertise in a specific legal area, or even with primarily social work-type skills as opposed to legal ones. Former Chief Justice, Andrew Li, emphasised that the courts are able to handle the amount of work coming to them and that ADR should be used where it is a preferable means of settling disputes rather than as a means to lighten the courts' caseload. Potentially, the value of ADR lies in the fact that there is a whole spectrum of dispute resolution mechanisms available and the appropriate one for the particular subject matter, parties and context can be chosen. What is unarguable is that arbitration and mediation have enjoyed a meteoric rise in many jurisdictions, particularly in Hong Kong whose "special relationship" with the rest of China is seen as giving it a unique potential as a regional ADR hub.

---

12. Genn (n 3) 60.
13. See Chapter 9.
14. P Wesley-Smith, *An Introduction to the Hong Kong Legal System* (n 4), 114.
15. See comments of M Merry, 10.3 below.

10.2 Arbitration

Arbitration is a method for the private resolution of a civil dispute, by a neutral and independent person (often appointed by the parties to the dispute), as an alternative to litigation in the courts. It has a considerable history, though its "traditional" use was limited in scope. Ip[16] writes that:

> Arbitration is as old as the Crown Colony itself . . . Hong Kong Island was little more than a collection of self-administering fishing villages before British rule, disregarded by imperial mandarins across the harbour. Most disputes in such a society were resolved by overlapping structures of informal power, from clans and village elders to guilds and secret societies.[17]

Arbitration has now become so well established, in Hong Kong as elsewhere, that many do not consider it any longer "alternative". This is primarily because of its increasingly formal nature and because it is the mandatory form of dispute resolution for many disputes involving parties who would contract only on the basis of a mandatory "arbitration clause". Arbitration, as is implicit in the last statement, may be, and most often is, adopted where *prior contractual agreement* to arbitrate is involved. It is, however, open to parties to agree mutually to submit to arbitration even after formal litigation has commenced but only if *both* parties agree. In such cases, of course, the litigation will be stayed pending the outcome of arbitration.

10.2.1 Dual or unitary system?

When arbitration was first introduced into Hong Kong,[18] via the Arbitration Ordinance,[19] it was based on English arbitration rules.[20] The Ordinance provided for a unitary system for both domestic and international arbitrations. Following recommendations of the Law Reform Commission of Hong Kong, in 1987,[21] and resulting legislative reform,[22] it was decided that *international* arbitration rules for Hong Kong should reflect those of the "model law" of the United Nations Commission on International Trade Law (UNCITRAL) while those for *domestic* arbitrations should remain largely unchanged. The result was an international/domestic arbitration procedure dichotomy. Further debate and a Consultation Paper by the Department of Justice[23] engendered a proposal for consolidation of the two approaches. In his

---

16. Eric Ip, *Law and Justice in Hong Kong* (2nd edn, Sweet & Maxwell 2016).
17. Ibid 329.
18. In 1963.
19. Cap 341.
20. Initially the Arbitration Act, 1950.
21. Law Reform Commission of Hong Kong Report, 'The Adoption of the UNCITRAL Model Law of Arbitration'.
22. Enacted as Arbitration (Amendment) (No 2) Ordinance (64 of 1989); amending Arbitration Ordinance (Cap 314).
23. Published 31 December 2007.

speech at the 2010 Opening of the Legal Year, the Secretary for Justice, Wong Yan Lung, stated:

> Expansion of Hong Kong's capacity as an international arbitration centre continues to be a prime policy objective. The Arbitration Bill, aiming at bringing the domestic arbitration regime in line with the (UNCITRAL) model law . . . is now before a Bills Committee of LegCo. New UNCITRAL initiatives to be implemented include conferring on the Hong Kong courts the power to recognise and enforce interim measures ordered by an arbitration tribunal sitting outside Hong Kong.

The proposed new legislation was duly adopted and the former (Cap 341) Arbitration Ordinance was, in 2010, repealed[24] and replaced by a new (Cap 609) Arbitration Ordinance,[25] which reintroduces a unitary system.

10.2.2 The perceived advantages (and disadvantages) of arbitration

In addition to the general trend towards ADR outlined above, arbitration *per se* may be preferable to litigation for a number of reasons. Speaking in early 2014, former Hong Kong Secretary for Justice, Rimsky Yuen,[26] summarised the advantages of arbitration (in the international business arena) as follows:

> Businessmen normally do not prefer to litigate, still less to litigate in a foreign place and subject to a foreign legal system. International arbitration is the natural substitute. Besides, confidentiality, cost-effectiveness, choice of venue, choice of expert arbitrators, flexibility of the arbitral process and ease of enforcement of arbitral awards also explain the growing popularity of international arbitration.

The first *apparent* advantage of arbitration is said to be "flexibility". The principle of so-called "party autonomy" means that the parties are free to make choices on such matters as the identity, number and qualifications of arbitrators, the applicable procedural law and the procedures to be adopted. This freedom might, in practice, be restricted by, for example, a contractual undertaking to adopt particular model rules for arbitration but, essentially, there is an element of choice for the parties, whereas court procedure is externally determined. Two types of arbitration are generally recognised: "ad hoc" where the parties to a particular dispute determine their own procedures; and "institutional", where the parties agree to follow the prescribed rules of an institution such as the Hong Kong International Arbitration Centre (HKIAC). The "flexibility" advantage of arbitration is likely to be eroded as increased professionalisation and standardisation reflect Hong Kong's aspirations to be a regional hub

---

24. This repeal had been recommended in a report by a prestigious "Committee on Hong Kong Arbitration Law" in 2003!
25. Cap 609 was enacted by LegCo on 10 November 2010 and came into force on 1 June 2011.
26. Speech on 'Hong Kong: An International Hub for Legal and Arbitration Services' (Phnom Penh, 21 February 2014).

for top-quality alternative dispute resolution, and "ad hoc" arrangements become less common. Moreover, as litigation itself becomes more flexible, with increased "case management" and other changes introduced by the Civil Justice Reforms, the rigidity/flexibility contrast is likely to become less marked.

A second advantage is that the arbitrator (or arbitrators) is/are likely to be *experts* in the specialised area with which the dispute is concerned. This may be seen as a significant advantage in niche areas such as maritime or construction law cases where knowledge of what actually happens in practice (rather than theory) may be welcomed by the parties. If the parties are in agreement, the choice of arbitrator can lie with them;[27] litigators, of course, cannot select their judge.

A further "advantage" relates to the *privacy* of arbitration procedures. Allegations and evidence arising via an arbitration will not be reported in the press and arbitration awards are, with few exceptions, not reported. There may, of course, be further "disclosures" where a case is appealed to the courts from arbitration but, in comparison with open court trials, confidentiality is much greater in arbitrations. This factor is a major consideration in many commercial disputes where, for example, a company may not wish to acknowledge publicly its processes or procedures, or even to publicise a dispute with a regular trading partner. The Department of Justice, which actively seeks to promote Hong Kong as a forum for arbitration, states that:

> A major feature of the Ordinance (Cap 609) is the provisions on the protection of confidentiality in arbitration proceedings. To enhance confidentiality for international arbitration, the Ordinance provides that as a starting point, court proceedings relating to arbitration are not to be heard in open court. Such proceedings will be held in open court only if any party so applying can satisfy the court that for good reasons the proceedings ought to be held in open court.
>
> The Ordinance also provides that unless otherwise agreed by the parties or under any exceptions as provided for in the Ordinance, no party may publish, disclose or communicate any information relating to arbitral proceedings and awards. The Ordinance adheres to the international practice that arbitral awards should only be made public with the consent of the parties concerned, having regard to the private and confidential nature of arbitration. This provision seeks to strike a proper balance between safeguarding the confidentiality in arbitration and the need for parties in the arbitral proceedings to protect or pursue their legal rights or for them to enforce or challenge an arbitral award.[28]

As regards the "public interest", however, secrecy may be seen in a less favourable light.

It is also the case that, from the perspective of "finality", arbitration awards are usually final, with only limited grounds for challenge. Parties to an arbitration often agree contractually that they will be bound by the outcome and not seek further

---

27. In cases of *appointed* arbitrators, a disgruntled arbitratee may "challenge" the appointment under s 26 (Cap 609) which applies Article 13 of the UNCITRAL model law.
28. Department of Justice Website, *Arbitration*.

proceedings in court. Where an arbitration award has been made, only *very limited* grounds exist in Hong Kong for an arbitral award to be set aside.[29] With the adoption of the UNCITRAL system (by Cap 609), the grounds for setting aside an award,[30] in *all* cases, are:

- incapacity of any party to the proceedings or invalidity of the arbitration agreement;
- no proper notice of appointment of arbitrator or commencement of proceedings;
- the award is outside the scope of the arbitration agreement;
- the arbitration tribunal was improperly constituted;
- the subject-matter of the award was not capable of resolution by arbitration;
- the award was contrary to public policy.[31]

The Hong Kong courts have emphasised their desire to uphold arbitral awards wherever possible and to "deter" unreasonable "public policy" objections by penalisation on costs. In *A v R*,[32] for example, the Court of First Instance emphasised that it was actually in accordance with public policy that arbitral awards should be generally final and that disappointed arbitrates should not use "public policy" claims to have a "second chance" having previously agreed to the finality of the arbitration. However, an agreement to exclude the courts is not of total effect, since, generally, courts in common law jurisdictions always reserve the right to intervene if, for example, due process (in the form of the rules of "natural justice") has not been complied with. Indeed, an agreement to exclude totally the jurisdiction of the courts in this regard would be struck down as contrary to public policy.[33] There is also limited scope for appeal *with leave granted* on an assertion of material irregularity by virtue of section 4 of Schedule 2 and on a point of law in Hong Kong by virtue of section 5 of Schedule 2 of the Arbitration Ordinance.[34]

These additional grounds, however, are subject to the parties having "opted in" to Schedule 2 and require that all appropriate measures to seek correction, variation and additions to the original award have been exhausted under section 69 of the new Ordinance.

An illustrative example of the restrictive approach of the courts is provided by the case of *Swire Properties Ltd v Secretary for Justice*.[35] The case concerned a dispute between Swire Properties and the Hong Kong government over the

---

29. In some countries *no* court interference is permitted in respect of an arbitral award.
30. By the High Court of Hong Kong.
31. Section 81, Arbitration Ordinance (Cap 609), implementing Article 34 of the UNCITRAL model law.
32. [2010] 3 HKC 67. The CFI added that, since, such unmeritorious appeals ran counter to the newly adopted Civil Justice Reforms, costs should be awarded against the appellant.
33. See, eg, *Baker v Jones* [1954] 1 WLR 1005. Procedural irregularity is also a ground of appeal under (former) s 25(2) of the Arbitration Ordinance (Cap 341); now s 81 (Cap 609).
34. Cap 609.
35. [2003] 3 HKC 347 (based on Cap 341 but still pertinent).

implementation of a redevelopment project and the permitted gross floor area (gfa). The parties agreed by deed to refer their dispute to arbitration and "an eminent retired judge of the English Court of Appeal" was appointed arbitrator. He found for the government and Swire sought to appeal on a "point of law" as permitted by section 23 of the Arbitration Ordinance.[36] They argued that the arbitrator had erred in law. Leave to appeal was refused by the Court of First Instance and the Court of Appeal upheld such refusal. However, it granted leave to appeal to the Court of Final Appeal (CFA) on the issue on the basis of "very exceptional circumstances"; namely that the appellants stood to lose a great deal of money. In rejecting the appellants' appeal, the CFA made a number of points of general application, which emphasise the limited circumstances in which an appeal from an arbitrator's award will be upheld in the absence of a breach of the rules of natural justice.[37] The CFA held that the contractual provisions in this case were "one-off" and had no general interest either for the commercial fraternity or the development of the law generally. In such a case intervention would only occur where the arbitrator was "obviously wrong". In this case the arbitrator had weighed the evidence and reached a decision which he was entitled to reach. Bokhary PJ added that, since arbitration is aimed at speedy and final adjudications, a decision to refuse leave to appeal should not be lightly overturned.[38]

An additional "bonus" of arbitration awards is that they may be *enforced*, within Hong Kong, as easily as court judgments.[39] As regards enforcement elsewhere it may well be easier to enforce an arbitral award "overseas"[40] than a judgment of a Hong Kong court. Any Hong Kong arbitral award may be enforced relatively simply in any state which, like Hong Kong, is a signatory to the New York Convention (NYC).[41] Although, initially, some doubt on this issue may have been raised arising from the "1997 situation" of Hong Kong's reversion to China (and an arguable loss of its treaty-accession capacity), the latter's accession to the Convention has settled the problem of enforcement in all New York Convention states.[42] In respect of international arbitration awards affecting "non-New York" parties, these may also be enforced in Hong Kong under section 2GG(2)[43] of the Arbitration Ordinance.[44] It

---

36. Cap 341. Now s 5, Schedule 2, Cap 609.
37. In brief, a breach of natural justice would arise in cases of "forum" bias or a failure to hear both parties.
38. Bokhary PJ added that reasons should be given for a refusal to grant leave to appeal to comply with Article 10 of the Bill of Rights (instituted under s 8 of the Bill of Rights Ordinance (Cap 383)) but these need only be brief.
39. See s 2GC, Arbitration Ordinance.
40. Enforcement of Hong Kong arbitral awards in mainland China will be dealt with in Chapter 12.
41. The New York Convention on the Recognition and Enforcement of Foreign Arbitral Awards (1958).
42. The continuing "problem" of enforcing Hong Kong arbitral awards in mainland China will be dealt with in Chapter 12.
43. Introduced as an amendment to the original legislation.
44. Cap 341.

is very difficult to resist enforcement of a "New York Convention" (NYC) award in Hong Kong. Anthony Chiu writes:[45]

> There are only a few circumstances as set out in art V of the NYC where recognition or enforcement of the award may be refused . . . and Part IV of the Arbitration Ordinance[46] implements and repeats the said art V . . . The starting point for one to understand the (HK) courts' approach is to examine s 44(1) of the Arbitration Ordinance which provides that: 'Enforcement of a convention award shall not be refused except in cases mentioned in this section'. The import of the words 'shall not' stipulates that enforcement shall always be allowed save in certain situations. From the wording . . . alone one may naturally deduce that once an exception is found and established, the Convention shall then not be enforceable. However, this is not the case when one then reads the subsection in conjunction with s 44(2), which says that enforcement of a Convention award 'may' only be refused if one of the six situations is found. Even if one of the situations is fulfilled, the enforcing court is given residual discretion to enforce a Convention award. This explains the *pro-enforcement bias of the Hong Kong courts.* [emphasis added]

Cost may also be a factor in parties deciding on arbitration rather than court proceedings but this is not inevitable. Ip[47] writes:

> complex arbitrations tend to resemble the due process of law, with the full panoply of pleadings and discovery—not much faster, more informal, or more flexible than civil litigation.[48]

Arbitrators charge for their services, of course, and may well be expensive. Lawyers are not precluded from arbitration proceedings and their costs, too, need to be met. The arbitration venue, too, will normally have to be paid for; in litigation both the judge and the courtroom are free.[49] In the *Swire Properties* case considered above, it is reasonable to assume that a retired Court of Appeal judge would not have come cheap. Moreover, the parties involved were likely to have regarded speed (and perhaps a lack of publicity) as more important than cost. However, given that "time is money" and that arbitration is usually quicker overall, it is probably true to say that arbitration will generally be cheaper than litigation. Two particular factors assist in making arbitration generally quicker than litigation. The first, already mentioned, is that only limited scope for appeals from arbitration decisions exists.[50] The second

---

45. A Chiu, 'Enforcement of New York Convention Awards in Hong Kong: Is It Possible to Resist Enforcement? (Part 1)' *Hong Kong Lawyer* (July 2004).
46. Cap 341.
47. Eric Ip (n 16).
48. Ibid 334.
49. See Merry's comments referred to at 10.3.
50. See *Swire Properties* case, above.

is the relative simplicity of commencing arbitration proceedings, especially against those based outside Hong Kong. Cheung Kwok Kit[51] writes:

> Unlike litigation, no special procedure is necessary for overseas service of the notice of arbitration on a foreign party. Simplicity and informality are two distinct advantages of using arbitration as a means to resolve disputes. It can cost considerable time and money to effect service of a Writ overseas. For arbitration proceedings, it is sufficient to fax the notice unless the arbitration agreement provides otherwise.[52]

A final *potential* advantage for arbitration may, before too long,[53] emerge in the form of "third party funding"; whereby those, perhaps without the means of funding an arbitration, may be supported by third party finance.[54] For genuine litigation, third party funding is all but impossible because of the laws on maintenance and champerty.[55] It has never been clear whether the Hong Kong champerty rules extend to arbitration.[56] A Law Reform Commission of Hong Kong (LRC) consultation paper,[57] in October 2015, sets out the case for Hong Kong to permit third party funding of arbitration.[58] Following an LRC report,[59] legislation has now been passed in the form of the Arbitration and Mediation Legislation (Third Party Funding) (Amendment) Ordinance of 2017.[60] This represents a very speedy response to LRC recommendations despite a slight delay caused by a surprise proposal for amendment to exclude application to legal practitioners. This at a time when the courts have repeated the rejection of third party "assistance in respect of actual *litigation*.[61]

The most obvious disadvantage of arbitration as against litigation is the absence of a strict doctrine of precedent (and its accompanying hierarchy of courts) so that decisions may be more variable and inconsistent. No qualitative distinction is made between the decision of an experienced arbitrator, with previous judicial experience, chosen by both parties for his relevant expertise, and that of a far more "junior" arbitrator, appointed by the Hong Kong International Arbitration Centre on the parties' failure to agree on their own appointment of an arbitrator. In the case of appeal,

---

51. Cheung Kwok Kit, 'A Simple Guide to Arbitration in Hong Kong and Mainland China' (Deacons, Hong Kong, April 2007).
52. Ibid 2.
53. In Hong Kong "before too long" is a relative concept (see Chapter 2 at 2.3).
54. The funder would normally be motivated by the promise of a share of "winnings" rather than altruism.
55. See Chapter 9.
56. In *Cannonway Consultants Ltd v Kenworth Engineering Ltd* [1995] 2 HKLR 475, [1995] 1 HKC 179 the Hong Kong High Court held that the champerty rules do not apply to arbitrations. The Court of Final Appeal subsequently accepted that champerty would not be applied where an arbitration award had been made in a state which did not recognise champerty; the question of whether it would apply to third party funding of purely Hong Kong arbitrations was left open: *Unruh v Seeberger* (2007) 10 HKCFAR 31.
57. Third Party Funding for Arbitration Sub-committee (LRC) 19 October 2015.
58. A major consideration was the enhancement of Hong Kong as an international arbitration hub. The Law Society supported the proposal in a Submission on 5 January 2016.
59. October 2016.
60. 6 of 2017 (June 2017).
61. See *HKSAR v Mui Kwok Keung* [2014] 1 HKLRD 116.

a "finding of fact" by any arbitrator is most unlikely to be overturned. Given the "finality" of most arbitral decisions, arbitration lacks the guidance of, for example, the Court of Final Appeal in shaping best practice, unlike the position with litigation proper.[62]

10.2.3 A brief outline of procedure

Most arbitrations start as a result of a dispute between parties subject to an arbitration clause in their contract. Where this is the case and one party wishes to go to arbitration the other can refuse only in very limited circumstances, whereby that other party can go to litigation instead. Normally, when the "non-arbitratee" commences litigation proceedings, the "arbitratee" can stay proceedings pending the outcome of arbitration. A court will refuse to stay proceedings only where there is some defect in the form or substance of the arbitration agreement.[63] A typical arbitration clause in a Hong Kong international contract, providing for Hong Kong International Arbitration Centre (HKIAC) administered arbitration in Hong Kong, will say:

> Any dispute, controversy, difference or claim arising out of or in connection with this contract, including the existence, validity, interpretation, performance, breach or termination thereof or any dispute regarding non-contractual obligations arising out of or relating to it shall be referred to and finally resolved by arbitration administered by the HKIAC under the UNCITRAL Arbitration Rules in force when the Notice of Arbitration is submitted, as modified by the HKIAC Procedures for the Administration of International Arbitration.[64]

A variation on such clause can be used where the parties have agreed to an HKIAC-administered (non-UNCITRAL) arbitration. A similar clause, not specifying HKIAC supervision, may be adopted for "ad hoc" arbitrations. These, again, may be subject to UNCITRAL procedures or may adopt the "Domestic Arbitration Rules" as stipulated by HKIAC.[65] Of course, the parties are free to choose their own form of words but adoption of one of the suggested forms is common.

A particular feature of the revised (2014) model forms is the stipulation as to the law of the "arbitration clause" since, while it is very common to stipulate the law governing the main contract in dispute, parties have, traditionally, failed to specify the law of the arbitration clause itself.

If there is no "arbitration clause" the parties may, nonetheless, willingly agree to arbitrate instead of proceeding to court litigation.

To commence arbitration proceedings, the normal procedure is that one party gives written notice to the other of the substance of its complaint/dispute. Less

---

62. Of course, where appeals *are* heard by the Hong Kong courts, their decisions are binding in subsequent Hong Kong arbitration proceedings.
63. Litigation proceedings may also proceed if the nominal defendant has begun a formal court defence.
64. HKIAC, *Model Clauses*.
65. The latest version was adopted in 2014.

formality is required in outlining the complaint but sufficient detail should be included to ensure that the arbitrator can deal with all disputed issues.

The identity of the arbitrator (and even the number of arbitrators) can be determined by the parties if they can agree. The "complainant" may suggest an arbitrator (or arbitrators)[66] and the respondent can either agree or nominate an alternative (or alternatives). If the parties fail to agree, normal Hong Kong procedure now is that an arbitrator can be appointed by the HKIAC,[67] which has the means to appoint an arbitrator with the necessary expertise to handle the issues in dispute. The HKIAC may also determine the number of arbitrators, absent agreement by the parties.

The arbitrator may determine procedures but, again, these may have been preselected by the parties.[68] There will normally be a preliminary hearing, at which the arbitrator will explain the timetable for hearing the dispute. The arbitrator will fix a date for the full hearing, before which most documentary evidence will have been submitted and examined. It is possible to have a "document only" arbitration, by agreement, without the need for a hearing and attendance by the parties.

Once the arbitrator has heard all the evidence he[69] will make his decision. This may be with or without reasons[70] and, in complex cases, may often be reserved. It is possible for the arbitrator to determine the "win/lose" decision but to reserve judgment on "quantum" (amount to be paid by the loser). The arbitrator will normally make an award of costs (including the cost of his own professional charges)[71] to the winner.

While procedures may vary considerably from one arbitration to another, especially in respect of "ad hoc" arbitrations, there are said to be two *essential* underlying principles: "due process and a fair hearing" and "the impartiality and independence of the arbitrator".[72]

10.2.4 Arbitration schemes in Hong Kong

There are a number of well-recognised and well-used schemes/centres of arbitration in Hong Kong reflecting its ambition to be a regional and, indeed, world hub of ADR. One of the best-known is that obtaining in the construction industry. So well-used is arbitration in the Hong Kong construction industry, indeed, that it is common to talk of "construction law and arbitration" as a single subject with its own literature. The industry has its own Hong Kong Construction Arbitration Centre

---

66. It is common to have only one but three is far more usual than two.
67. The parties may have agreed on an alternative method of selection in the event of a failure to agree. This will almost certainly involve insistence on a specified level of relevant expertise and qualification.
68. They may, for example, have selected the Domestic Arbitration Rules of the HKIAC.
69. Where three arbitrators are used the decision is based on the majority view.
70. Reasons should be given unless the parties have agreed otherwise.
71. Merry's note that the judge is free but mediators charge (see 10.3 below) is also applicable to arbitrators, of course.
72. Described as the "magna carta of arbitration": J Lew, L Mistelis, and S Kroll, *Comparative International Commercial Arbitration* (Kluwer Law International 2003).

(established in 2006) with its own standard arbitration (and mediation) procedures. The Centre makes use of experts with many years of both construction and legal experience and both trains and accredits new members. Recognising the unique position of arbitration in the construction industry, special provision was made in the (Cap 609) Arbitration Ordinance for an automatic "opt-in" to the Schedule 2 appeals procedures.

Other important schemes relate to maritime arbitration (with a Maritime Arbitration Group, established in 2000 as a branch of the HKIAC). The HKIAC will lend its logistical support (venues, staff, etc) to assist (maritime) arbitrations whether these adopt HKIAC standard rules, UNCITRAL rules, London Maritime Arbitrators Association (LMAA) rules or "ad hoc" procedure.

Other important arbitration areas dealt with in Hong Kong include commercial arbitration generally and insurance arbitration. The growth of arbitration in Hong Kong has been rapid and impressive. Hong Kong has the largest "branch" membership of the Chartered Institute of Arbitrators, based in London, and Hong Kong members hold senior positions. With the adoption of a *unitary* (UNCITRAL-based) arbitration system and the apparent resolution of the problem of enforcement in the burgeoning mainland China market, Hong Kong has become a big ADR "player". Although the total of arbitration cases before the HKIAC declined between 2009 and 2012, that decline has been reversed. Not only was there an increase in new arbitrations from 2013, but the percentage fully administered by HKIAC rose to over 30% (with a total amount in dispute of US$2 billion).

One recent development which will be mentioned only briefly is the introduction, into Hong Kong, of a forum for the settling of "investor-state" disputes under the auspices of the Permanent Court of Arbitration (PCA) in The Hague. Amidst some fanfare, former Secretary of Justice, Rimsky Yuen, announced, on 3 March 2015:[73]

> the promotion of Hong Kong as a leading centre for international legal and dispute resolution services in the Asia Pacific Region is one of the key policy areas of the Government . . .
>
> One of the various developments we have been closely monitoring is investor-state disputes. In recent years, we have seen a growing number of investor-state disputes in Asia, involving either Asian claimants or Asian respondents . . .
>
> It is against this background that the Department of Justice decided to enhance Hong Kong's capacity and infrastructure to offer first class services for handling investor-state disputes. Accordingly, with the support of the Central People's Government (CPG) (especially the Ministry of Foreign Affairs . . .) the CPG signed with the PCA a host country agreement in January this year on the conduct of dispute settlement proceedings in Hong Kong.

---

73. Seminar on Investor-State Dispute Resolution, 3 March 2015. See also Hong Kong Government Press Release, 'Permanent Court of Arbitration Provides Arbitration Services in Hong Kong', 4 January 2015).

Yuen went on describe Hong Kong's "competitive advantages" in the ADR field: including its respected judiciary, established support for, and expertise in, ADR, and a "modern and robust" legal system.

There is some irony in the support of the PRC for this development which depends, of course, on states giving their consent to the arbitration of investor-state disputes. The PRC's absolutist views on state immunity would appear to preclude them from participation in such a scheme. Perhaps, moreover, there is good reason for states not to consent to such investor-state arbitrations. An article in Britain's The Economist[74] was highly critical of investor-state arbitration schemes, stating:

> If you wanted to convince the public that international trade agreements are a way to let multinational companies get rich at the expense of ordinary people, this is what you would do: give foreign firms a special right to apply to a secretive tribunal[75] of highly paid corporate lawyers for compensation whenever a government passes a law to, say, discourage smoking, protect the environment or prevent a nuclear catastrophe. Yet that is precisely what thousands of trade and investment treaties over the past half century have done, through a process known as "investor-state dispute settlement" or ISDS.

The article goes on to say that Brazil has refused to enter ISDS agreements (but still receives much foreign investment) and adds that other states are beginning to follow Brazil's lead. Given the Hong Kong government's predilection for putting the interests of big business over those of ordinary people, it is perhaps unsurprising that ISDS arbitration is being welcomed so warmly at the highest level in the SAR.

10.2.5 The role of the Hong Kong International Arbitration Centre

The Hong Kong International Arbitration Centre (HKIAC), which was established in 1985, plays an important role in the administration and development of arbitration in Hong Kong.[76] Although it receives funding from both the Hong Kong government and the business community, it is an independent body.

The HKIAC has increased the level of standardisation for domestic and international arbitration proceedings in Hong Kong by providing its own standard "model" procedures as indicated above. It is also authorised to appoint arbitrators to hear a dispute where the parties to such a dispute are unable to reach consensus on the appointment of an arbitrator. The HKIAC will offer its services (arbitration staff and facilities) *whether or not* the arbitration is to be conducted according to its model procedures.

---

74. 'Investor-State Dispute Settlement: The Arbitration Game', *The Economist* (London, 11 October 2014).
75. UNCITRAL does provide Rules on Transparency for ISDS Arbitrations but there are numerous exceptions.
76. Two other important "players" operating in Hong Kong are the Chartered Institute of Arbitrators and the International Court of Arbitration.

10.2.6 The training and "benchmarking" of arbitrators

While, in theory, parties are free to choose their own arbitrators, arbitration requires certain generic skills in addition to the subject-specific expertise which the arbitrator is likely, already, to possess. Just as judicial training has been increasingly recognised as a vital and continuing process so, too, has the training of arbitrators and (as we will note later) mediators.

The major "benchmarkers" of arbitrators in Hong Kong are the Hong Kong Institute of Arbitrators (HKIArb) and the Chartered Institute of Arbitrators (CIArb). Both provide training courses and examinations incorporating legal and practical aspects of arbitration. Recognition takes the form of "associate membership" (for those with professional expertise and limited arbitration experience) and "fellowship" for those with both professional expertise *and* considerable working experience in the arbitration field.

A number of educational establishments in Hong Kong, including the three major law schools,[77] offer general or specialised arbitration programmes at the diploma, post-graduate diploma and master's level. These may provide limited recognition or exemption from some modules of the two Institutes' fellowship requirements.

Arbitration qualifications are increasingly sought by "re-training" lawyers but appeal to many in those specialised areas where arbitration is a common method of settling disputes.

10.3 Mediation and conciliation

Mediation, or "conciliation",[78] may be described as an "assisted negotiation". The definition under section 4(1) of the Mediation Ordinance[79] is as follows:

> (1) For the purposes of this Ordinance, mediation is a structured process comprising one or more sessions in which one or more impartial individuals, without adjudicating a dispute or any aspect of it, assist the parties to the dispute to do any or all of the following:–
>
> identify the issues in dispute;
> explore and generate options;
> communicate with one another;
> reach an agreement regarding the resolution of the whole, or part, of the dispute.

Mediation, then, involves procedures whereby an independent, impartial person (or persons) assists the parties to reach an agreed settlement of their dispute.

---

77. At the Chinese University of Hong Kong, The University of Hong Kong, and the City University of Hong Kong.
78. Strictly conciliation should "reconcile" the parties' differences while mediation accepts the differences but seeks to find a "middle way" acceptable to both. In practice (in Hong Kong at least) the terms appear to be used interchangeably, though "mediation" is now the expression most commonly favoured.
79. Cap 620.

Mediation differs from true litigation in that the mediator (conciliator) may *suggest* a solution which the parties are free to accept or reject. Two key elements are that the outcome is not "zero sum" and that the process should be "non-adversarial". This being the case, the question may come to be asked as to why the process should be (as it is currently) dominated by lawyers.[80] The process is extra-judicial and in the main voluntary. But, if the parties do reach such a settlement and the settlement is embodied in written form, it is a contract which is enforceable between them. The main limitation, given the general principle of "voluntariness", is that there is generally no compulsion to participate, so that if one party to a dispute refuses mediation, the result is either that the legal dispute must be halted or formal litigation must be pursued. Moreover, even if the parties have a "mediation clause" in their contract, either may reject the proposed settlement having gone through the mediation process.

Nevertheless, mediation is undoubtedly a growth area in Hong Kong. Its proponents include previous Chief Justice, Andrew Li (who referred to the merits of mediation in several important speeches, including two Openings of the Legal Year) and his successor, Geoffrey Ma CJ. At the 2008 Opening of the Legal Year, the Chief Justice stated:

> Mediation is an alternative method of dispute resolution which is complementary to that of litigation. Its promotion is plainly in the public interest. As an alternative to adversarial litigation, its benefits are well known. For the parties, with settlement at a relatively early stage of their dispute, the reduction in stress, the saving of time and costs and the achievement of a satisfactory solution, including the maintenance of a continuing relationship. And for society, the economic and social benefits of alleviating conflict and achieving harmony . . .
>
> Mediation is being encouraged not because the courts cannot cope with the caseload but because of its benefits . . .
>
> The benefits of mediation have been increasingly recognised in Hong Kong. The governing bodies of both branches of the legal profession fully understand its importance and are committed to its development. The promotion of mediation is now a matter of Government policy . . .
>
> . . . we have already achieved considerable success in encouraging mediation in family disputes and also in construction disputes.
>
> It is important that legal aid funds should be available to cover the costs of mediation where the legally aided person wishes to attempt it . . . Further it is likely to result in savings for the public purse."[81]

It is this final aspect, the "cost-saving", which critics see as the real attraction to those in various common law jurisdictions charged with the task of managing the trial system. This consideration is seen by such critics as operating at the expense

---

80. See n 104.
81. Nearly three years later, having left office, Andrew Li continued to extol the virtues of mediation: 'Chief Justice Andrew Li: Departing with No Regrets' Hong Kong Legal Community, 23 August 2010.

of "proper" litigation and constitutes a denial of justice or, at least, the imposition of second-best justice at the expense of properly funded, legally aided court trials. The Woolf/Genn debate referred to previously illustrates the divergent opinions on civil justice reform in Britain and the resulting increase of ADR at the expense of court trials. The "doubters'" view in Hong Kong is well expressed by barrister and academic Malcolm Merry who writes:[82]

> The vogue for mediation, or to be more accurate the promotion of mediation, shows no sign of abating. The Chief Justice is all for mediation. The Secretary for Justice thinks we should have more of it. The Law Society arranges courses on it, as does the Bar. Commercial organisations charge handsome fees for transforming lawyers into mediators[83] ...
>
> Mediation is part of the procedure in the Family Court and in the Lands Tribunal. Judges elsewhere are suggesting at every opportunity that litigants try it ...
>
> I find this enthusiasm rather curious. Resolution of disputes through an intermediary must have been around for as long as there have been disputes. The courts and lawyers are there to provide services when that or a similar means of settlement ... break down. By saying to parties 'why don't you try mediation?' those courts and lawyers are in effect saying 'please don't use our services, they're no good'.
>
> Well of course litigation is no good in the sense that it's expensive and leaves a bitter taste at the end. But you might expect disputants to know this before they resort to legal proceedings. You might also expect them to have considered trying to settle the dispute before starting proceedings and to have concluded that this will not work. I cannot imagine they are likely to change their minds when they learn that a mediator will cost them thousands of dollars an hour while a judge comes free ...
>
> Another thing about mediation is that it requires the parties to be genuinely willing to compromise their differences. No sane litigant would declare an unwillingness to settle, so may readily go through the motions of mediation. However at the initial stages of a case when parties say that they are willing to settle, they usually mean that they are willing to settle on their terms, which is hardly the correct spirit in which to agree to mediation.[84]

---

82. M Merry, 'Not Entirely Legal—Part 8' Hong Kong Legal Community, 20 August 2009.
83. In fact, most lawyers who have considered mediating have now "trained up" and mediation training courses now comprise more non-lawyers than lawyers.
84. The Secretary for Justice has recognised: "There are bound to be practitioners who remain sceptical about mediation. I have come across one or two who frankly admit they don't believe in mediation at all and fear that it might undermine the quality of justice in individual cases and in the long run." (Wong Yan Lung SJ, Concluding Address at Conference on Civil Justice Reform, 16 April 2010). Presumably he had talked to Malcolm Merry! Current Chief Justice Ma has suggested that lawyers are becoming more supportive of mediation: Moy, Ng, and Chiu, 'Chief Justice Praises Mediation' *South China Morning Post* (Hong Kong, 11 January 2011). This was in reference to the CJ's speech at the Opening of Legal Year 2011.

Comment

Two significant points emerge from Merry's comments: that mediation (and other forms of ADR) are not necessarily cheaper for the protagonists (though there may be a saving to the public purse), and that some types of dispute lend themselves better to mediation than others. As to the latter point we may concede, for example, that in matrimonial disputes a mediated "amicable division of assets and child arrangements would be a better outcome than an acrimonious "battle". Conversely, where, for example, a claimant is asserting the wrongful infringement of his intellectual property by another, it is difficult to see that he can be accommodated other than through "zero sum" litigation.[85]

The key to the success of mediation appears to be "voluntarism". Genn,[86] essentially, identifies two categories of "mediatees": those who want a mediated settlement, and those pressured into it by the threat of financial penalty for refusing mediation. She concludes:

> Why do litigants accept the opportunity to mediate once they have commenced court proceedings? It seems that the principal motivation for mediating is to avoid the anticipated cost, delay and discomfort of trial . . . It is because parties have been told and believe that mediating is a quicker and cheaper way of achieving some sort of remedy. More recently an important motivating factor seems to have been the concern to avoid the risk of . . . cost penalties.
>
> As far as customer satisfaction is concerned, evaluation of court-annexed mediation schemes shows high levels of satisfaction amongst those who *volunteer* to enter the process.[87] [emphasis added]

It is to be hoped that Hong Kong will learn from the UK experience and "encourage" rather than compel mediation. Initially this appeared to be the case. Then Secretary for Justice, Wong Yan Lun, stated, in 2010: "Court-ordered mediation does not form part of our CJR."[88]

That sentiment was echoed by incoming Chief Justice, Geoffrey Ma, who stated in his Opening of the Legal Year speech in 2011 that "the courts would not force parties to use the alternative mechanism [mediation]."

However, given the cost penalty which can now be imposed on those "unreasonably" refusing mediation, these "voluntarist" statements appear somewhat disingenuous. The Judiciary website, for example, expands upon the "voluntary" adjective as follows:

---

85. Moreover, the establishment of such rights in an open court (of record), as opposed to a private tribunal, should be seen as in the public interest.
86. H Genn (n 3).
87. Ibid 111.
88. Wong Yan Lung, Concluding Address (n 84).

the mediation process is entirely voluntary. *However* [emphasis added] if the dispute is or will be subject to Court proceedings, the Court will take into account all relevant circumstances, including whether a party has unreasonably refused to take part in mediation, in exercising its discretion to award costs. You may face an enhanced costs order if the Court finds that you refused an offer to mediate unreasonably.[89]

More emphatically, the following Practice Direction, which came into force on 1 November 2014,[90] specifies the effect of refusing mediation.[91]

PRACTICE DIRECTION – 31

MEDIATION

Part A

1. An underlying objective of the Rules of the High Court and the District Court is to facilitate the settlement of disputes. The Court has the duty as part of active case management to further that objective by encouraging the parties to use an alternative dispute resolution procedure ("ADR") if the Court considers that appropriate and facilitating its use ("the duty in question"). The Court also has the duty of helping the parties to settle their case. The parties and their legal representatives have the duty of assisting the Court to discharge the duty in question

2. The aim of this Practice Direction ("PD") is to assist the Court to discharge the duty in question. It applies to all civil proceedings in the Court of First Instance and the District Court which have been begun by writ except the proceedings set out in Appendix A.

3. ADR means a process whereby the parties agree to appoint a third party to assist them to settle or resolve their dispute. Settlement negotiations between the parties do not amount to ADR. A common mode of ADR is mediation. This PD applies to mediation. Where the parties are engaged in arbitration proceedings, the court proceedings would be stayed and this PD would not apply to such proceedings.

4. In exercising its discretion on costs, the Court takes into account all relevant circumstances. These would include any unreasonable failure of a party to engage in mediation where this can be established by admissible materials. Legal representatives should advise their clients of the possibility of the Court making an adverse costs order where a party unreasonably fails to engage in mediation.

5. The Court will not make any adverse costs order against a party on the ground of unreasonable failure to engage in mediation where:

---

89. Judiciary website, 'FAQs on Mediation', A 15.
90. It replaced a previous Practice Direction 31 of 2009.
91. A similar Direction had already come into force covering specifically Family Mediation (Practice Direction 15.10, in force 2 May 2012).

> (1) The party has engaged in mediation to the minimum level of participation agreed to by the parties or as directed by the Court prior to the mediation in accordance with paragraph 13 of this PD.
>
> (2) A party has a reasonable explanation for not engaging in mediation. The fact that active without prejudice settlement negotiations between the parties are progressing is likely to provide such a reasonable explanation. However, where such negotiations have broken down, the basis for such explanation will have gone and the parties should then consider the appropriateness of mediation. The fact that the parties are actively engaged in some other form of ADR to settle the dispute may also provide a reasonable explanation for not engaging in mediation in the meantime.

In short, mediation remains, nominally, voluntary. Non-volunteers, however, may be subject to financial penalty.

10.3.1 *The scope of mediation in Hong Kong*

Mediation may operate on a statutory basis in certain areas such as matrimonial disputes. It may also arise voluntarily, via parties agreeing in advance that, in case of dispute, attempts would first be made to arrange a mediated settlement, with recourse to court litigation arising only on the failure of mediation. While "mediation", in an informal way, has always been possible, as Merry suggests, the focus today is on skilled, trained mediators. Qualification of mediators is highly organised via courses which invariably require at least one actual (supervised) or simulated mediation. There is a strong focus on the "ethical" aspects of mediation, involving, of course, a required absence of partiality and the key concept that mediators are "facilitators" who assist parties to resolve their differences but do *not* make decisions.

A key to the expansion of mediation is an increase in public awareness. The government has introduced a Mediation Information Office[92] whose principal function is to help potential mediates to understand the process and what help is available.[93] Moreover, legal practitioners are now required to explain to clients the alternative (to litigation) of mediation.

The Hong Kong Mediation Council (HKMC), which is part of Hong Kong International Arbitration Centre (HKIAC), exists to promote the resolution of disputes through mediation and other forms of ADR. The HKMC is particularly active in promoting the use of mediation in commercial, insurance, construction, community and family disputes. It has promulgated general Mediation Rules, a General Ethical Code and Guidelines for Professional Practice of Mediators in family mediations. It

---

92. Opened 4 January 2010.
93. Public service videos frequently portray a client going to a lawyer and seeking litigation; unaware that there is an alternative "solution".

also trains and accredits mediators for listing on HKIAC's panel of mediators and on panels in overseas jurisdictions, such as Australia.

An example of modern mediation procedure applicable in Hong Kong is provided by the Hong Kong International Arbitration Centre's (HKIAC's) Mediation Rules. These closely follow the Hong Kong government's own mediation rules (also administered by the HKIAC) and are published in consultation with the Hong Kong Mediation Council (HKMC). Access to the rules may be via a contractual mediation clause (a form of which is indicated by the HKIAC) or by mutual agreement. The "Suggested Mediation Clause" is as follows:

> Any dispute or difference arising out of or in connection with this contract shall first be referred to mediation at HKIAC and in accordance with its then current Mediation Rules. If the mediation is abandoned by the mediator or is otherwise concluded without the dispute or difference being resolved, then such a dispute or difference shall be referred to and determined by arbitration at HKIAC and in accordance with its Domestic Arbitration Rules".

The key features of the Rules are confidentiality, voluntariness and non-binding assistance to seek a negotiated settlement. A proposal by one party to mediate must be agreed by the other within 14 days or regarded as rejected. The parties may choose a mediator or, failing agreement, have one appointed by the HKIAC. The mediator, of course, must be a person without "interest" in the outcome of the mediation. The duration of the mediation should not exceed six weeks and a mediator cannot continue beyond three months without the written agreement of both parties. The control of procedure is a matter for the mediator who should be prompted by the best interests of the parties. Legal representation is not barred *but* the cost must be borne by the represented party. The costs of the mediation are borne by the parties equally and the mediation will terminate with the signing of a settlement agreement *or* at the request of either party or determination by the mediator himself that a continuation is futile. The parties must agree that the mediator is immune from any action arising from the discharge of his duties.

The growing trend towards mediation in Hong Kong has been extended to the courts. Under the Civil Justice Reform introduced in 2009, the court is required to promote the use of ADR (initially mediation) as a procedure which could be used in lieu of or in parallel with litigation, for example in family disputes. Judges are now encouraged, under the new civil justice rules, to undertake more case management as part of their role in proceedings. Thus, Practice Direction 31 states:

> 1. An underlying objective of the Rules of the High Court and the District Court is to facilitate the settlement of disputes. The Court has the duty as part of active case management to further that objective by encouraging the parties to use an alternative dispute resolution procedure (ADR) if the Court considers that appropriate ... The

> parties and their legal representatives have the duty of assisting the Court to discharge the duty in question.
>
> ...
>
> 4. In exercising its discretion on costs, the Court takes into account all relevant circumstances. These would include any unreasonable failure of a party to engage in mediation ...

The Arbitration Ordinance[94] empowers the Court of the First Instance, in default of appointment by the parties, to appoint a conciliator where parties give consent in writing or provision for this is contained in an arbitration agreement.[95] Furthermore, where a reference to arbitration has been settled through conciliation or mediation, the terms of the parties' settlement agreement may be enforced summarily in the same manner as an arbitral award. This obviates the need to bring proceedings in contract to enforce the agreement because it will be treated as a judgment of the court.

10.3.1.1 Family mediation

A family mediation service is available via the Hong Kong Judiciary's Family Mediation Co-ordinator's Office (FMCO), situated in the Family Court. The service originated as a pilot scheme but has since been extended. Family mediation is also available via the Hong Kong Marriage Advisory Council as well as other voluntary agencies. Family mediation (though not information sessions) may involve the expense of a private mediator or a subsidised or even free service from some voluntary organisations. The norm is that the "parties" are advised to attend an information session held by the FMCO. If they wish to commence mediation they are first interviewed to ascertain whether their circumstances are suitable for mediation. Where parties have already been to seek legal advice, a solicitor is expected to advise on the possibility of seeking a mediated settlement where appropriate. The mediation process itself may last as little as two to three sessions (of two hours) and in all cases is likely to be much shorter than protracted litigation. The average duration for family mediation in 2012, apparently the later figures available to the Judiciary (between appointment of mediator and completion of the mediation) was 91 days but the average hours spent reaching a full settlement[96] (the "easier" cases) was four hours. The average cost per mediation was a modest $12,900 per case for a full settlement.[97]

---

94. Cap 341.
95. Ibid s 2A(1).
96. For generally more difficult partial settlements the figure was seven hours (Judiciary, 'Mediation Figures and Statistics').
97. The figure for partial settlements was $14,500 per case (Judiciary, ibid).

Family law, especially relating to matrimonial disputes, is especially appropriate to mediation, since the litigation "win-lose" approach will invariably make the possibility of reconciliation difficult if not impossible.[98] Conversely, it is often in cases of matrimonial dispute that attitudes towards the other party are most hostile (more so than in commercial cases) such that the skills of the negotiator are crucial. To take two examples, parties in a contract/commercial dispute may accept that there is potential for future collaboration which should not be jeopardised *and* that litigation is only worthwhile if it is "profitable"; matrimonial disputants, on the other hand, may wish to have no future "collaboration" and may be prepared to suffer loss provided that the other party suffers more! In such situations a key mediating focus is on "the future rather than the past".[99]

Moreover, a key function of the mediator is to encourage the parties to focus on the (perhaps poor) alternatives to accepting a mediated solution.[100] A further key function of the mediator involves focus on "perspective and communication"; if the "ex" spouse is seen solely in that role, antipathy is likely to remain. Those who have benefited from family mediation (where they have children) tend to stress recognition of their former partner as the mother/father of the couple's children rather than a "failed" partner.

The key focus is that the mediator is a "facilitator" but that it is the parties themselves who provide the final agreement; the mediator doing no more than suggesting possibilities. A typical "Agreement to Mediate" will commence with an agreement by both parties to make use of the agreed mediator who will act as a "neutral facilitator". The mediator agrees *not* to make decisions about "right or wrong", nor to *tell* the parties what to do. The mediator does not give legal advice (the task of a solicitor)[101] nor give counselling or therapy.

Family mediators are well-trained and usually recruited from the ranks of lawyers, social workers or social psychologists. Their role is to gain the trust of the parties, to be scrupulously impartial, and to *assist* the parties to reach (their own) settlement. Since full and honest disclosure is expected of the parties the mediator agrees to maintain absolute confidentiality with regard to all matters disclosed in the mediation process. Indeed, the maintenance of confidentiality and the "privilege" of communications is a major plank of the Mediation Ordinance[102] which came into force in January 2013.

---

98. Mediation theorists refer to the distinction between "distributive" (win/lose) and "integrative" (win/win) bargaining.
99. See Hon Chi Yi Ludwig, 'The Common Problems and Suggested Solutions of Mediation in the Construction Industry in Hong Kong' (2006) 15(4) *Surveyors Times* (Hong Kong Institute of Surveyors, Surveying Practice).
100. See Maurice WM Lee, 'Essential Dispute Resolution and Mediation Principles in a Nutshell for Lawyers' *Hong Kong Lawyer* (August 2000).
101. Parties are permitted to seek the advice of a solicitor throughout to ensure that their legal rights are not compromised.
102. Cap 620.

Alternative Dispute Resolution   425

Where a mediation agreement has, eventually, been drawn up with the mediator's guidance, a party may seek to make it enforceable by virtue of a court order. It is not, otherwise, contractually enforceable as is an arbitral award.

Mediation is not always appropriate and indeed, in some cases, is refused where, for example, there are allegations of spousal or child abuse. Moreover, those commencing mediation may regret this and parties are free to start at any time (irrespective of whether divorce proceedings have been commenced)[103] *and* to cease mediation at any time. Unless both parties wish to continue, a mediation must cease.

Given the clear benefits of mediation in *most* family disputes it is unsurprising that one of the first "persuasive" Practice Directions,[104] permitting a costs penalty against a party "unreasonably" refusing mediation, related to family mediation. The Practice Direction does not apply in unsuitable mediation situations, as indicated above, such as allegations of child abuse or domestic violence.

10.3.1.2 Labour relations mediation

The Labour Relations Department (LRD) offers a "conciliation" service to employers and employees to assist in the speedy settlement of conflicts. The conciliation may be "ordinary" or "special"; the latter involving the Commissioner for Labour appointing a special conciliator. The Labour Relations Ordinance[105] also authorises the Commissioner to appoint a mediator or a board of mediation to mediate the dispute. As with mediation generally, the service is a voluntary one in that any recommendations of the mediator need not be accepted by the parties. The success of the conciliation efforts of the LRD officials depends very much on the goodwill and consent of the parties to co-operate and compromise at conciliation meetings in which the conciliation officers act as neutral intermediaries, assisting the parties in dispute to resolve their differences. If the parties are to have confidence in the conciliation/mediation officer, he must, of course, be above suspicion of bias or prejudice and be seen to be maintaining his impartial stance at all times. The strenuous training of LRD officers focuses on the ethical issues of objectivity as well as the non-interventionist position of the conciliator/mediator; someone present to assist the parties in reaching their own "solution" but not himself making a "decision".

10.3.1.3 Government contracts

It is the case that all standard form contracts made by or with the Hong Kong government contain a provision for mediation. In the huge (mainly pre-handover) Airport Core Programme contracts, involving infrastructure works on the Chek Lap Kok airport, opened in 1998, it was compulsory procedure to submit to mediation (or

---
103. Where mediation is commenced any litigation is automatically stayed.
104. Practice Direction 15.10 (Family Mediation) Per Ma CJ, 28 March 2012.
105. Cap 55.

ADR "Adjudication")[106] before the commencement of any arbitration proceedings. A likely difficulty with submission to mediation in respect of government contracts, at least those of a minor nature, is that the government representative may not have authority to act "outside the box" and agree to proposed settlements and/or that the representative is an unwilling participant.

10.3.1.4 Construction contracts

Mediation clauses are standard in many Hong Kong construction contracts. The most recent version of the standard form, the Standard Form of Building Contract 2005 (SFBC), arising under the 2005 "Conditions of Contract", stipulates that, in relation to the settlement of disputes:

> if the dispute is not resolved by the Designated Representatives within 28 days of the dispute being referred to them by the Architect, either party may give a notice to the other party, by special delivery, to refer the dispute to mediation.[107]

As with mediation generally, of course, this applies only where the parties have agreed, contractually, to adopt the "Conditions of Contract". Where they have done so, negotiation via the "Designated Representatives" becomes the first step. In the absence of a successful resolution by this means within 28 days, however, mediation *precedes arbitration* as the next step.[108]

One clear concern, as mentioned above, is that mediation in respect of government construction contracts may be conducted by someone with little permitted flexibility to agree a settlement and with little enthusiasm for the mediation task.

A clear advantage of mediation (or other forms of ADR) arises in respect of situations where parties have an ongoing relationship, such that a litigation "win" might involve a Pyrrhic victory whereby the loser no longer wishes to do business in the future. A compromise, even of a potentially winning cause, has a greater potential to encourage further collaborations. Such considerations are particularly applicable in large-scale, and potentially on-going, construction collaborations. As such, the enormous trend towards mediation began a little earlier in the construction area than more generally. Indeed, as Justice Fung has said:

> You may be pleased to know that mediation which the construction industry has pioneered is now an integral part of our legal system ... most of the disputes in the construction of the new airport were resolved by mediation.[109]

---

106. See 10.4 below.
107. Clause 41, 'Agreement and Schedule of Conditions of Building Contracts for Use in the Hong Kong SAR' (2005 edition).
108. This is the recommended practice under the Hong Kong Construction Arbitration Centre Mediation Rules (2009).
109. Speech at conference on 'Practical Approach to Resolving Disputes in the Construction Industry' (11 April 2014).

Alternative Dispute Resolution

It is of note that while mediation was initially fostered in the construction industry, it may be supplanted in that industry, before too long, by statutory adjudication (see below).

> Practice Direction 6.1 (Construction and Arbitration List)[110] provides:
>
> F Voluntary Mediation
>
> General
>
> 20. Parties in construction cases are encouraged to attempt mediation as a possible cost-effective means of resolving disputes.
>
> 21. To promote the use of mediation, the Court may impose cost sanctions where a party unreasonably refuses to attempt mediation.
>
> ...
>
> (4)
>
> 41. Where a Mediation Notice has been served, an unreasonable refusal or failure to attempt mediation may expose a party to an adverse costs order.
>
> Once again the "voluntary" nature of the mediation is emphasised while, in practice, the threat of sanctions provides a strong "inducement" to volunteer. This Practice Direction came into effect on April 2, 2009; earlier than the (original) more general Mediation Practice Direction 31.[111]

Similar "encouragement" to use mediation exists in the case of building management disputes[112] and disputes over compulsory sales.[113] In respect of building management disputes, a survey on satisfaction with the mediation system, for the period 2008–2010,[114] showed that over 80% of interviewees felt that the mediation had saved time, while 79% felt it had saved money.

10.3.1.5 The training and "benchmarking" of mediators

Despite suggestions for a unified accreditation system for mediators,[115] none such (quite) yet exists. However, the "benchmarking" of mediators is taken very seriously by the various regulating bodies. To a considerable extent the training, benchmarking

---

110. The "non-exhaustive" list of matters under the List is lengthy and includes claims against builders, engineers, architects, surveyors and other professionals relating to the construction industry.
111. In force 1 January 2010.
112. Direction Issued by the President of the Lands Tribunal Pursuant to s 10(5)(a) of the Lands Tribunal Ordinance (Cap 17), LTPD: BM No 1/2009 (in force 1 July 2009).
113. Direction Issued by the President of the Lands Tribunal pursuant to s 10(5)(a) of the Lands Tribunal Ordinance (Cap 17), LTPD: CS No 1/2011 (in force 15 February 2011).
114. Building Management Mediation Co-ordinator's Office (The Judiciary), 'Evaluation Report on Mediation for Building Management Cases in the Lands Tribunal of the Judiciary' (September 2011).
115. See 10.3.1.7 below.

and use of mediators overlaps with that of arbitrators. The HKIAC has a "Mediator Accreditation Committee" and, for qualified solicitors, the Hong Kong Law Society runs training schemes and accords recognition as appropriate. Mediation qualifications may be general or specific and, in such areas as family mediation, expertise in the specific area of family law (as well as a sufficient general law background) is required. It is generally accepted that, while mediation in *most* areas is a generic, transferable skill, family mediation requires special, distinctive skills and should be separately accredited.

Numerous academic courses are offered by tertiary institutions in Hong Kong, catering for general and specialised mediation. These courses may afford exemption or accelerated qualification as a recognised "mediator". While mediation is currently dominated by members of the legal profession,[116] new courses increasingly focus on those with other professional backgrounds appropriate for specialised mediation. Importantly, especially for non-lawyers, some mediation courses are now being delivered in Chinese,[117] which mirrors the increasing use of Chinese in the courts proper.

With the recognition of the desirability of unified benchmarking, steps towards such "unification" have been made. The Working Group on Mediation (WGM) promulgated a "Mediation Code" in 2010, intended to provide a common standard amongst mediators. Moreover, the WGM expressed the view that a there should be a single "industry-led" accreditation body. Following that recommendation there is now a *de facto* overarching accreditation body, the Hong Kong Mediator Accreditation Association Ltd (HKMAAL), co-founded by the two branches of the Hong Kong legal profession, the Hong Kong International Arbitration Centre and the Hong Kong Mediation Centre. It will be increasingly the norm that intending (or existing) mediators will seek the imprimatur of the HKMAAL. The stated aims of the HKMAAL are:

- to set standards for accredited mediators (and others involved in mediation);
- to set standards for mediation training courses;
- to promote a culture of best practice and professionalism.

10.3.1.6 The future of mediation in Hong Kong

There is no doubt, as Merry[118] avers, that mediation is currently "flavour of the month" in Hong Kong. The Working Group on Mediation (WGM), supported by

---

116. Some doubts have been expressed as to the desirability of lawyer domination: see LegCo question from Albert Ho and written reply from Secretary for Justice, Rimsky Yuen, 24 April 2013. There is also a need for a change of mindset for lawyers from an adversarial tradition: see GF Relyea, 'From Gladiator to Mediator: The Challenges for Lawyers Who Become Mediators' *Hong Kong Lawyer* (October 2010).
117. With, for example, role-playing exercises in Chinese.
118. Note 82.

the Hong Kong government and under the aegis of the Department of Justice, was chaired by no less a figure than the Secretary for Justice himself. Its report, published in February 2010, recommends greater "public education and publicity" in respect of mediation, via such means as an "umbrella mediation awareness programme", the teaching of mediation in schools and universities, "continuing professional development" (CPD) for the legal profession (and mediators), and public interest announcements on radio and television.[119] Indeed, were such proposals made from within mainland China, they would surely be resisted as an attempt to erode Hong Kong's common law adversarial system well before its guaranteed 50 year time span! Companies have jumped on the bandwagon and, in May 2009, 64 major Hong Kong companies signed a "Mediate First" pledge. Of course signing a pledge may provide good publicity; it may also serve to "divert" customers away from more business-harmful litigation, especially given the guarantee of privilege and confidentiality obtaining in mediation settlements. There is little to be lost in signing a pledge to mediate of course. While there is some debate about the enforceability of a promise (contractual or otherwise) to mediate, the argument is largely moot since a basic tenet of mediation is that either party may terminate the process at any time.

Moreover, the WGM recommends the consideration of the introduction of mediation pilot schemes beyond areas such as matrimonial and construction disputes (where mediation is appropriate, is widely used, and works effectively) to areas such as intellectual property and medical malpractice,[120] where litigation (with proper funding in the latter case) appears more appropriate. Given the serious abuses of intellectual property in Hong Kong, and especially in mainland China, *litigation*, and the proper enforcement of judgments, should surely be the aspiration, rather than a mediated "settlement". Similarly, in cases of medical malpractice, victims want adequate compensation or, just as commonly, an acceptance of "fault"; precisely the two things that mediation will avoid.

It is, of course, often stated that mediation is voluntary and that no one is required to seek mediation instead of litigation. Moreover, a party embarking on mediation may cease the procedure at any time. However, although mediation is said not to be "compulsory", the costs sanctions for those "unreasonably" refusing mediation make a refusal to mediate (or a decision to abandon mediation) a risky financial prospect. Moreover, a party determined to litigate who wishes to circumvent the "mediate first" costs sanction is likely to fall foul of rules to avoid "box-ticking". For example, during his speech at the 2011 Opening of the Legal Year, then Secretary for justice, Wong Yan Lung, stated:

> Practice Direction 31 on Mediation came into operation on January 1, 2010, but we already have heard of suspected abuses where mediation was reduced to a 'tick-box'

---

119. WGM recommendations 3, 4, 8, 17, 18, 19, 20, 21, and 24.
120. Recommendation 9.

and a motion to go through. The question of quality control of mediation and mediators has become more pressing.

Following the . . . Report of the Working Group on Mediation . . . [there] was a strong call to put in place a system of single accreditation of mediators much earlier than recommended [in the report].

It is clear that there is a determination that parties should be encouraged to "mediate first" in substance rather than merely in form.

Indeed, even though the Working Party on Mediation did not recommend "compulsory" mediation (as some critics would argue has occurred in Britain) it did add the words "at this stage, but the issue should be revisited when mediation in Hong Kong is more developed."[121]

Irrespective of the merits of the march to mediation, there can be no doubting its expansion, with costs sanctions now the general rule, both branches of the profession "signed" up to an agreement to bring the option of mediation to the attention of their clients and large swathes of "issues" in the "mediate first" camp. Despite this, however, the figures for 2014 show that generally, after mediation, 35% of cases had still failed to reach a settlement. Nor, surprisingly, was the settlement figure much different for, specifically, family mediation.

10.4 Contractual and statutory "adjudication"

A much less well-known form of ADR is so-called contractual "adjudication". This is a somewhat misleading title since it is not the same as adjudication by a court. In the present context "adjudication" refers to a *binding* form of ADR determined by an expert Adjudicator or Panel of Adjudicators,[122] which provides speedy, enforceable determinations while allowing "ex post facto" final resolution. Adjudication follows either contractual agreement by the parties to submit or an offer of adjudication to a party in dispute agreed by the other. The parties may agree to accept the adjudication in final settlement but more normally it serves as an interim measure pending the outcome of more formal (and lengthier) arbitration.

Adjudication is not widely used in Hong Kong and almost exclusively in the construction arena. However, adjudication, via a panel of experts, was particularly useful during the massive (and massively complex) Chek Lap Kok Airport processes. The Airport Authority used a dispute review panel of experts to vet disputes. When such arose, one of the panel members would be chosen by the parties to the dispute who could make a binding decision such that work could continue speedily. The decision could be appealed to arbitration but only *after completion* of the works. In the context of the need to build a new airport with as little delay as possible, the "adjudication" process was particularly appropriate.

---

121. Recommendation 45.
122. There is currently no statutory benchmarking as long as *both* parties find the adjudicator acceptable.

To date, adjudication has been *contractual* (requiring both parties' consent). However, Hong Kong's construction industry has proposed "Security of Payment" legislation, involving statutory *compulsory* adjudication from which those in the industry will not be able to opt out. Statutory adjudication is seen as a valuable innovation; especially in cases where one of the parties has cash flow problems which would make lengthy mediation or arbitration procedures problematic. Given the overwhelming support in the construction industry for this form of compulsory adjudication, and its successful operation in the UK, it seems likely that the necessary legislation will be passed relatively speedily and is likely to supplant construction arbitration in most cases.

10.5 Conclusion

Alternative dispute resolution (ADR) is undoubtedly expanding in Hong Kong and is set to continue to do so, at least in the short to medium term. The reasons are partly "user-oriented" (more specialisation, less confrontation, greater speed and flexibility, reduced publicity, reduced formality and the saving of cost and "face") and, at least equally, inspired by government and the desire to control cost to the public purse.

Given the tradition in China of reaching "peaceful settlement" and the desire to avoid public discontent, the extension of ADR in the Hong Kong SAR and the rest of China may be seen as an early move towards harmonisation of the common law and civil law systems of the respective jurisdictions.

11
The HKSAR and PRC Legal Systems Compared

Overview

It is clear that, in a work of this kind, consideration of the vast and complex area of the comparison between the legal systems of the Hong Kong SAR and the (mainland) People's Republic of China (PRC) needs to focus on "macro" issues. This chapter will consider the *core features* of Hong Kong's common law system and contrast these with the situation obtaining in the PRC.[1]

The key, broad focus will be the "rule of law" in Hong Kong; what it means and the extent to which it is to be found in the PRC's rapidly developing legal system. In so far as consideration is given to specific "micro" issues, these will be by way of illustration of more general principles rather than as part of a detailed study of the PRC legal system, for the study of which students should refer to texts dedicated to this subject.[2]

While the PRC, in the past 30 or so years, has made enormous and rapid strides towards the development of a modern legal system, with a huge expansion of courts, judges, lawyers, legal assistance and alternative dispute resolution, a key consideration is the extent to which law in *practice* reflects the legal *form* in the PRC (what socio-legal writers describe as the "law in action/law in books" dichotomy) given, especially, the vastness of China and the practical problem of efficiently delivering centrally introduced reforms to the provinces.

11.1 The "two systems" aspect of "one country, two systems"

It is accepted, and indeed affirmed in the Basic Law, that Hong Kong's is a "common law" system.[3] While, as has been noted, that expression is capable of differing meanings, in this context it refers to a system of law deriving initially from the

---

1. In adopting a "generalist" approach, this chapter reflects the approach of the syllabus for Hong Kong Legal System, as approved for the PCLL "conversion examination"; namely that the focus should be on the "essential differences" between the two systems.
2. A particularly recommended text is Professor Albert Chen, *An Introduction to the Legal System of the PRC* (4th edn, LexisNexis 2011).
3. See especially Articles 8, 18, and 84 of the Basic Law.

English courts and adopted subsequently in various jurisdictions, *usually* having colonial links with Britain.[4]

A general characteristic of common law systems is their emphasis on "judge-made" law, law which derives *primarily* from cases, amended and supplemented as these may be by legislation.[5]

But if Hong Kong's system is uncontroversially a common law one, what of the PRC system? It is most commonly described as a "civil law" one; that is, a system deriving from the "codification of law" approach of the Roman Empire subsequently adopted and spread, particularly by Napoleonic and post-Napoleonic France. But the ascription "civil law" is not uncontentious. Indeed, the first point to stress is that the whole concept of law and any sort of legal system has only recently re-emerged in the PRC. Chen,[6] in describing "The Legal History of Modern China",[7] notes that the first "belated efforts" to modernise the Chinese legal system were not made until the early part of the twentieth century and adds that: "The Qing empire was overthrown in 1911 before it began to implement the new laws which had been drafted."[8]

Chen goes on to state that:

> In the period 1928–1935, a series of comprehensive codes of law were promulgated. They were partly based on the European (civil) continental model (such as the laws of Germany, Japan and Switzerland), partly on the Anglo-American model, and also to some extent on the existing traditions of the late Qing and warlord periods.[9]

Most significantly, however, *all* this extensive legal development was swept away during the Cultural Revolution in which:

> The demise of the legal system . . . was not merely an incidental side-effect of the fanatic and violent political campaign . . . The legal system was one of the targets of deliberate attacks by the radicals. The very idea of law was discredited and held in contempt . . . legal institutions were attacked and paralysed or dismantled. Law schools were closed down. Members of the legal community were persecuted or forced to shift to other kinds of work. In short, law neither existed as an academic discipline nor as a rational mechanism of social control . . . It was not until 1972 that the court system was gradually re-established. The procuratorates [prosecuting departments] . . . were not resurrected until 1978.[10]

---

4. Occasionally, for political reasons, a jurisdiction may adopt the "common law" as a deliberate rejection of a "civil law" legacy: this appears to have occurred, to some extent, in Rwanda whose Tutsi government blame civil law France for assisting previous Hutu oppression of the Tutsi.
5. See in particular Chapters 2 and 4.
6. A Chen, *An Introduction to the Legal System of the PRC* (n 2).
7. Ibid Chapter 3.
8. Ibid 23.
9. Ibid.
10. Ibid 32–33.

The Mao era has been described by Cheng Li[11] as one of "legal nihilism". Li adds, strikingly, that:

> the neglect [in Mao's China] of even a basic legal consciousness accounted for the fact that, from 1949 to 1978, the PRC promulgated only two laws, one being the constitution itself and the other being the marriage law.[12]

The importance of law was recognised by the post-Mao PRC leaders, none more so than Deng Xioaping, twice "purged" in the turmoils of the Mao Zedong "lawless" era.[13] The absence of a proper, developed legal system was seen as one reason for the emergence of the radical, "anti-rights" forces of the Mao era. The effective construction of a post-Mao legal system (involving the creation of thousands of courts and procuratorates, extension of judicial training, codification of laws and the development of alternative dispute resolution) has been effected with incredible speed for a country as large as China.

What has emerged, in this very short time, is a rapidly developing, rapidly evolving system,[14] which is part codified civil law[15] and part "socialist" law (the latter with its emphasis on the primacy of the political; the supremacy of the Communist Party). Indeed, even the common law has significance in the modern PRC system since, for example, the Contract Law Code draws heavily on concepts well understood by common lawyers,[16] and the criminal procedure rules are argued to be moving from a civil law "investigating judge" tradition to a more "adversarial" common law-type procedure,[17] at least in theory. Even the common law "bedrock" principle of "judicial precedent" has attained some significance in the PRC with the Detailed Rules on Implementing Guiding Cases introduced by the Supreme People's Court in 2015.

Given such a rapid development of the PRC legal system it is perhaps inevitable that there will be, occasionally, government nervousness and "retrenchment".

---

11. C Li, 'The Rise of the Legal Profession in the Chinese Leadership' *China Leadership Monitor*, No 42.
12. Ibid 12.
13. It has been suggested that Deng's fateful "Tiananmen" decision was influenced by his fear of student-led terror, experienced at first hand during the "Red Guard" era.
14. Between 1979 and 2006 the number of cases filed in PRC courts increased from 520,000 per year to 7.89 million! The increase continues though the rate is slowing. A major impetus was China's entry into the World Trade Organization in 2001.
15. The major influences have been the German civil code and Japanese law (itself influenced by German law).
16. "PRC's contract law presents a hybrid version with key concepts from both Common law tradition and the Civil law tradition": G Li, 'The PRC Contract Law and Its Unique Notion of Subrogation' (2009) 4.1 Journal of International Commercial Law and Technology 12, 21.
17. See G Zheng, 'Towards an Adversarial System of Criminal Justice?', University of Hong Kong/National University of Singapore Law Symposium: 'The Common Law in the Asian Century', HKU Faculty of Law, 11–12 December 2006.

11.2 The rule of law: Meaning[18]

During the turmoil of "Occupy Central", no phrase was used more widely (and to mean more different things!) than "rule of law". Part of the problem with any definition is that the expression has no succinct and definitive meaning; that the expression may be used to accord with the writer's "interest" in an issue; and that the expression may change over time. The problem is exacerbated by a recognition by some writers of a broad definition of rule of law ("thick" rule of law) encompassing such concepts as human rights[19] which contrasts with a minimalist "thin" approach which recognises the impermanence and historical/geographical variation of human rights and seeks to restrict the rule of law to fewer, generally agreed, precepts.[20]

The following[21] well summarises the difficulties:

> The 'rule of law' represents a symbolic ideal against which proponents of widely divergent political persuasions measure and criticise the shortcomings of contemporary State practice. This varied recourse to the rule of law is, of course, only possible because of the lack of precision in the actual meaning of the concept; its meaning tends to change over time and . . . to change in direct correspondence with the beliefs of those who claim its support and claim, in turn, to support it.[22]

Nowhere was this statement more accurate than during the "Occupy Central" controversy of 2014. Opponents of the Occupy movement indicated that since the occupation was illegal, it undermined, *per se*, the rule of law. The assertion was manifestly absurd, in the same way as it would be absurd to suggest that (illegal) theft undermines the rule of law. The rule of law *would*, however, be at risk were there to be, as alleged, "selective" enforcement of laws; prosecuting Occupy supporters with vigour, for example, while ignoring police use of excessive force. The clearly fallacious use of the expression by opponents of Occupy was highlighted by Paul Shieh SC, outgoing Chairman of the Hong Kong Bar Association in his farewell speech at the 2015 Opening of the Legal Year.[23] Shieh said:

> According to a report by the Hong Kong Examinations and Assessment Authority published last November, many secondary school students [*sic*] misunderstood the concept of 'Rule of Law' as merely meaning executing or obeying the law. The report recommended that students should enhance their understanding of the concept . . .
>
> In a speech I delivered [last year] . . . I said the following:–

---

18. For the views of a former Hong Kong Chief Justice, see A Li, 'The Rule of Law' (2013) 43(3) HKLJ 43.
19. See T Bingham (Lord Bingham), *The Rule of Law* (Penguin Books 2011).
20. See, eg, J Raz, *The Authority of Law: Essays on Law and Morality* (Clarendon Press 1979).
21. In G Slapper and D Kelly, *The English Legal System* (14th edn, Routledge London and New York 2013–14).
22. Ibid 23.
23. 12 January 2015.

> "There is no universal definition of 'Rule of Law'. Many countries ... claim to practise the Rule of Law but in fact what they practise is not 'Rule of Law' as we understand the concept but, at most, Rule by Law or a very rudimentary form of Rule of Law namely that there shall be laws to regulate the conduct of individuals and that they should obey the laws made by the sovereign.
>
> ... Comical as it may sound, the Government in Hong Kong has become accustomed in recent years to preface almost every description of what it does by the phrase 'doing so according to law' ... Everything is done according to law.
>
> ... in my view and in the view of the Hong Kong Bar, ironically that could have the opposite effect of misleading the public as to the meaning of the Rule of Law.
>
> First, as we all know, Rule of Law means far more than just blind adherence to laws—respect for an independent judiciary, the need to ensure minimum contents of laws in terms of human rights protection, respect for the rights and liberty of the individual when law enforcers exercise their discretionary powers are examples of requirements of Rule of Law which go beyond just obeying the law. In fact it can be said that over-emphasis of the 'obey the law' aspect of 'Rule of Law' is the hallmark of a regime which is keen on using the law to constrain the governed, rather than as a means to constrain the way it governs."
>
> ...
>
> In particular, in a system without a truly independent judiciary and where laws are arbitrarily enforced, the judiciary and the executive 'co-operate' to ensure that laws are interpreted in a way preferred by the executive and are used to suppress persons or entities who do not find favour with the Government. This is often dressed up as 'Rule of Law', but is in fact 'Rule by Law'. 'Do things according to law' means 'do things according to our will'.

All the leading speakers at the 2015 Opening of the Legal Year gave prominence to the "rule of law"; particularly pertinent with the "Occupy Central" movement still to the fore. The stance of Secretary for Justice, Rimsky Yuen, however, leant more towards what Shieh would have described as "rule *by* law" or "obedience to law", stating: "the law remains the law and is there to be obeyed."

Ip[24] describes this approach as one of "mere legality" ("*yifa*"); a concept that "falls noticeably short of the rule of law standard" and talks of an "alarming" increase in the use of this limited definition of "rule of law" by Hong Kong public officials.

This rather narrow approach to rule of law is perhaps to be expected of a member of the government and is far less objectionable than the risible views of a previous Law Society president, Ambrose Lee, expressed some months later. The latter managed to depict a connection between the "Occupy" protests and the subsequent robbery and kidnapping (for ransom) of the granddaughter of Bossini founder, Law Ting-pong. The kidnapping, apparently perpetrated by mainland criminals, was evidence to Lee of a "reduced fear of the law", inspired by "Occupy".

The Chief Justice, Geoffrey Ma, in his Legal Year Opening speech, emphasised three features of the rule of law: "equality, fidelity to the law and its spirit, and

---
24. Eric Ip, *Law and Justice in Hong Kong* (2nd edn, Sweet & Maxwell 2016) 129.

judicial independence". The political neutrality of the judiciary he saw as epitomised by equal treatment for all "parties" in the Occupy scenario.

Despite the difficulty of a definitive definition there are, as Shieh implies, certain features of a "rule of law" society which would distinguish it from others. "Primacy" of law is one such, as is "equality" before the law. An independent judiciary is essential in this context, since equality requires the protection, by the courts, of the individual from the excesses of the more powerful state. It is also implicit in Shieh's statement that, despite its claim to a "rule of law", the PRC (unlike Hong Kong) practises rule "by law" rather than rule "of law". Indeed, as we shall see, the PRC leadership explicitly rejects certain tenets of the liberal-democratic concept of "rule of law" as examples of Western *erroneous thought*".

Before moving on to individual features of the rule of law, as enjoyed in Hong Kong, it should be noted that "rule of law" is, everywhere, an "ideal" form. All polities claiming to be guided by the rule will fall short of this ideal on occasion. No one, for example, could seriously claim that rich and poor are treated alike in the criminal justice system of the United States.[25] Likewise, it could hardly be argued that the litigant in person (unable to afford private legal representation but denied legal aid on financial grounds) has equal access to the law as the rich (or legally aided) litigant. The key point is whether deviation from the ideal is regarded as malign and deserving of improvement.

11.2.1 The rule of law: The "primacy" of Law

A key feature of the rule of law is the primacy of law. This means that law takes effect over and above political considerations; it is not secondary to them. Of course it may be that common law systems fall short of their ideals in *practice*, and permit political considerations to impinge on judicial decisions, but this will be exceptional rather than normal practice and deserving of criticism.

It can be asserted with some confidence that the Hong Kong courts have generally given their judgments without thought for the political implications. In his speech at the Opening of the Legal Year 2015, Chief Justice Geoffrey Ma asserted:

> the administration of justice by the courts is not, nor can it be, influenced in the slightest by extraneous factors such as politics or political considerations. The courts and our judges apply only the law. The constitutional role of judges is to adjudicate on legal disputes between parties. It is no part of the courts' function to solve political questions, but only to determine legal questions even though the reason for bringing legal proceedings may be a political one.
>
> . . .

---

25. A simple example can be seen from the disparity in capital sentencing between the rich and the poor. Some would see the disparity in purely racial terms, but it could hardly be argued that the black (but wealthy) OJ Simpson was dealt with unfairly by the criminal justice system.

The constitutional role of judges to apply only the law is reflected in those provisions of the Basic Law dealing with the exercise of judicial power. Article 84 of the Basic Law states simply that judges shall adjudicate cases in accordance with the law. The Judicial Oath taken by all judges requires adherence to the law and the safeguarding of the law without fear or favour.

Certainly there were political "implications" in the *Democratic Republic of the Congo (DRC)*[26] case (dealt with elsewhere) where it fell to be determined whether Hong Kong courts should apply the more common "limited state immunity" doctrine rather than the "full state immunity" doctrine as recognised in the PRC. There was a political dimension to the case since the PRC government (or a satellite thereof) was involved in massive infrastructure work in the DRC and clearly had an interest in the DRC's successful plea of state immunity against the ("vulture company") plaintiff. However, despite some criticism on "legal autonomy" grounds, a strong case can be made for saying that Hong Kong's Court of Final Appeal merely followed the clear requirements of the Basic Law in seeking an interpretation of that law by the NPC Standing Committee under Article 158.

Hong Kong, then, *may* sometimes fall short of its primacy ideals, but they remain ideals to which it seeks to aspire. A strong contrast can be drawn with the position in the PRC where law is always secondary to the rule of the Communist Party. Indeed, it is part of Marxist ideology that law is *always* subservient to the will of the dominant class; all that differs is the identity of the "dominant". In capitalist systems, runs the theory, law always supports the interests of the capitalist class. Those legal innovations (case decisions, legislation) which *appear* adverse to the capitalist cause are mere ideological tools to convince the oppressed that the law is even-handed and to keep them from the path of revolution. In this context, E P Thompson's celebrated postscript to his work "Whigs and Hunters" has been of great academic interest, positing as it does the "relative autonomy" of law and its capacity not merely to "appear" to support the underdog but (sometimes) actually to do so.[27]

While the PRC has made great strides towards an increased emphasis on "legalism" and a rudimentary "rule of law", it has yet to recognise the primacy of law over political considerations. Politicians still describe the PRC legal system as "socialist" and consider that its essential function is to "serve the Party". Professor Albert Chen[28] describes the:

> dominance of the Party apparatus over the state, and the Party's unwillingness to subject itself to the supremacy and autonomy of the law.[29]

---

26. *Democratic Republic of the Congo v FG Hemisphere Associates* (2011) 14 HKCFAR 95.
27. Contrast, for example, George Jackson's *Soledad Brother*, and the author's notion of the capitalist benefits of a move from "chattel" slavery to economic "wage" slavery, with Sian Rees's *Sweet Water and Bitter*, detailing the clear financial loss and huge loss of (seamen's) lives resulting from Britain's determination to end the slave trade.
28. A Chen, *An Introduction to the Legal System of the PRC* (n 2).
29. Ibid 37.

Chen, however, adds optimistically that:

> the supremacy of law rather than policy has not only won acceptance by constitutional theory but is also gaining ground in practice as the Chinese legal system evolves. A dynamic approach to the study of this system would recognise the increasing authority of legal norms as distinguished from mere policy documents issued by party and governmental authorities.[30]

Despite this progress, Chen, elsewhere, notes:

> attempts by the ruling party to prevent the logic of the Rule of Law . . . from threatening the political supremacy of the Chinese Communist Party, and to draw a distinction between the kind of Rule of Law that is being promoted in China from the Rule of Law as it is understood and practised in Western liberal democracies.[31]

11.2.1.1 Equality before the law

A specific aspect of "primacy" is the ideal of "equality before the law". This means that all citizens (high or low) should be subject to the *same* law and treated alike, irrespective of wealth and position. The principle that "all Hong Kong residents shall be equal before the law" is enshrined in Article 25 of the Basic Law.

In his speech at the 2015 Opening of the Legal Year, noted above, Chief Justice Ma spoke of the importance of recognising and enforcing human rights. He asked:

> How is this achieved in reality? The starting point is an acceptance that everyone is equal before the law. This includes everyone: the Government, the authorities, members of the public. No person, group of persons or organisation can claim to be above the law nor to enjoy any preferential treatment by the courts. This is key to the notion of respect for the rights of other persons.

There are really two aspects to this: that even the most humble enjoy basic rights, and even the powerful (including the government) are subject to the law. This ideal is often found wanting in the common law world but it is at least espoused as an "ideal". A clear departure from the ideal clearly arises in relation to access to justice since it can be seen that the rich enjoy better legal representation than the poor.[32] America's criminal justice system, for example, provides many examples of the rich being treated more leniently and the poor being much more likely to be convicted and, if convicted, to be more harshly punished.[33] Again, though, this can be seen as the system falling short of its ideals rather than abandoning the ideals entirely.

---

30. Ibid 96.
31. Ibid 59.
32. Sarony writes that that a "squeeze" on legal aid funding means that Hongkongers are not equal before the law: N Sarony, 'The Silk Purse' *South China Morning Post* (Hong Kong, 29 April 2011). This remains a problem even though financial eligibility rules have been relaxed since his article.
33. See 11.4 below.

Hong Kong, too, has fallen short of the ideal of equal treatment for all, though such "lapses" have frequently been "extra-judicial". The most shocking case was the decision of the then Secretary for Justice, Elsie Leung, not to prosecute Sally Aw, the chairman of Sing Tao Publishing Group (at the time, owners of the *Hong Kong Standard* newspaper). The Group had deliberately exaggerated circulation figures to encourage advertisers but, even though senior staff of the *Hong Kong Standard* were prosecuted for conspiring with Aw to defraud advertisers, the Department of Justice decided to take no action against Aw herself. The ostensible reason was that a prosecution was "not in the public interest". There was little doubt that Aw's position as a "friend to Beijing" as well as to then Chief Executive, Tung Chee Hwa, was the determining factor. Indeed, Leung's absurd explanation that a prosecution might ruin the newspaper and cause the loss of jobs (itself a departure from equality before the law) was further undermined by the newspaper ceasing publication soon afterwards.[34] Some 15 years later, Grenville Cross, Director of Public Prosecutions at the time of the Aw case, asserted, in the *South China Morning Post*, that he had disagreed with Secretary for Justice Leung over the issue at the time.[35] Moreover, in the same article, former government lawyer Andrew Bruce SC is quoted as saying that prosecuting Aw "would have sent out a message that no one is above the law".[36]

Thankfully, departures from the principle of equality have been relatively rare since the departure of Tung Chee Hwa and Elsie Leung.[37] Serious disquiet *was* raised, at the time, over the allegedly over-lenient judicial treatment of Amina Bokhary; convicted of assaulting the police (not for the first time) and refusing to take a "breathalyser" test, but given a non-custodial sentence. The leniency was based on Bokhary's known mental health problems and her "good family" background. Bokhary is related both to (uncle) Kemal, then a Permanent Judge of the Court of Final Appeal, and Ronald Arculli, a previous ExCo member. Criticism of "unequal" treatment came, in this case, mainly from the pro-establishment camp, eager for an opportunity to attack a relative of Hong Kong's most liberal judge.[38]

Inequality, if it did arise in the Bokhary case, was in the form of greater lenience for someone "from a good background". This is quite common (and logical) in influencing a sentencing court to move in the direction of "rehabilitation" rather than "retribution".[39] However, since the recipients of rehabilitative sentences tend to be

---

34. It should be noted that there is now, again, a *Standard* in Hong Kong but it is under new management.
35. C Buddle, 'Ex DPP Tells of Split over News Tycoon Prosecution' *Sunday Morning Post* (Hong Kong, 17 November 2013).
36. Ibid.
37. Other notable "non-prosecutions" in the Tung-Leung era included the decision not to prosecute disgraced ex-financial secretary, Anthony Leung (who resigned having been found to have bought a luxury car with notice of an impending tax hike announcement) nor Xinhua News Agency (Beijing's unofficial pre-1997 "consulate") for breach of personal data rules.
38. Bokhary was, at the time, a Permanent Judge of the Court of Final Appeal and regarded as its most independent member.
39. Those seen as having less family support tend to be perceived as less likely to respond to rehabilitative approaches. "Stable home background" was also a factor in the Nicholas Tse case, discussed in

those who have already had more advantages in life, inequality (of opportunity) may be seen to be the precursor of further inequality (of treatment in the criminal justice system).[40] "Equal treatment", especially with regard to sentencing, is an elusive concept. Is, for example, a person with a "good background" likely to suffer more in prison than others? If so, should that justify a shorter custodial sentence? Would that apply to convicted policemen, or even foreigners?[41]

Worrying echoes of the Leung/Aw scenario have resounded with the tardiness in prosecuting policemen recorded on camera beating up an arrested and defenceless "Occupy" demonstrator. The policemen involved were identified sufficiently clearly to be immediately suspended from duty, yet a decision to prosecute was reached very slowly and only after significant public criticism.[42]

While the PRC still refuses to recognise the "equality" of the citizen with the State/CCP, it has begun to act against "personal" inequality[43] in the legal sphere; not least because this may become a locus for civil unrest. To take one example, it was reported[44] that in Qinyang those "outsiders" who invested more than $6 million were given the status of "honorary citizen" which would ensure discounted medical treatment, priority schooling *and* exemption from minor traffic laws! The scheme, it was reported, was halted by Central Government following local complaints.

A public perception of the law favouring "the rich" clearly has implications for social cohesion. Writing of the Hong Kong experience, Liu and Kuan[45] write:

> Legal cynicism, as measured by the belief that the rich were given favourable treatment by the court, was connected with a pessimistic view of the future condition of the Hong Kong people, a defeatist view of long-term planning, and an inclination to adopt a passive attitude toward [*sic*] the future.[46]

Recognising the potential for social unrest, former paramount leader Deng Xiaoping had said:

Chapter 3.
40. In the Court of Appeal (CA), Stock VP said it was "unfortunate" that sentencing magistrate Anthony Yuen had referred to Bokhary's "good background" but felt it had not affected the decision to impose a non-custodial sentence (which the CA endorsed). Eventually, having broken the terms of her probation order, Bokhary did serve a short prison sentence.
41. See SNM Young, 'Justifying Sentencing Discounts for Foreigners' (2002) 31(3) HKLJ 369.
42. As evidence of the increasing polarisation in Hong Kong society, the sentences given to the convicted policemen, while on the low side by Hong Kong standards were seriously criticised by the pro-establishment camp which seems to see nothing wrong with overt police brutality. In a rare Hong Kong example of criticism of an over-harsh sentence, there were numerous personal attacks on the "foreign" sentencing judge, Dufton J.
43. Article 33(2) of the PRC Constitution states: "All citizens of the People's Republic of China are equal before the law".
44. D Harris, 'Chinese Law Makes Some More Equal than Others' Harris & Moure pllc, 27 May 2007.
45. Z Liu and H-C Kuan, *The Ethos of the Hong Kong Chinese* (Chinese University Press 1988).
46. Ibid 128.

Crimes committed by the children of high-ranking officials and celebrities need to be treated urgently, for their bigger social impact and higher hazard.[47]

With the increasing economic inequalities in modern, post-Deng China, considerable public disquiet had been voiced about the actions of cadres (and their families), seemingly able to break the law with impunity. Huge publicity was given to the eventual arrest, trial and conviction (for rape) of Li Tianyi, the son of two famous cadres.[48] Li, who like Ms Bokhary had been in trouble before, was convicted as the prime mover in a gang rape of a woman the group had met in a bar.[49] Li was sentenced to 10 years imprisonment which, in the PRC, is a very low sentence for such an offence. Again, the rationale was Li's (youth and) good background, making rehabilitation more likely. The Australian Broadcasting Company (ABC)[50] reported that:

> In China the children of high-level Communist Party officials are seen by many as being spoilt and above the law.
> Li has become the most prominent target of these complaints.

The judgment of the court appears to have much to commend it. Li was not only convicted, despite his parents' eminence, but the court emphasised, for the victim's sake, that the case was one of "rape and not solicitation of prostitution".[51] Less laudable, given the public interest element, was the decision not to hold an open trial,[52] though this is often the case when juvenile defendants are on trial. There is little doubt that there was government determination to have Li convicted, as evidence of "equality before the law", once public concern, and dislike of favouritism, had been aroused. It is to be regretted that the prosecution case was not particularly compelling[53] and was presented behind closed doors.[54]

11.2.2 *The rule of law: Separation of powers*

Perhaps the greatest tension, in terms of the primacy of law, involves the question of the independence and autonomy of the judiciary, an aspect of the so-called

---

47. Deng Xiaoping, *Selected Works of Deng* (People's Publishing House 1993). Historically, this approach has not always been the norm in China (in Qing law, for example, status affected penalties).
48. Li's father is a PLA general and his mother a famous PLA singer.
49. While Li's co-defendants pleaded guilty, Li lodged a defence based on the "consensual prostitution" nature of the sex (which he also claimed to have been too drunk to remember!). The defence was given some succour by the assertion by Tsinghua University Professor, Yi Yanyou, that "raping a chaste woman is more harmful than raping a bar girl": J Kaiman, 'Chinese General's Son in Gang-Rape Trial' *The Guardian* (London, 28 August 2013). Yi later apologised for his comments.
50. S McDonnell, 'China Jails Famous Couple's Son Li Tianyi for Gang Rape in "Second Generation Rich" Case' (ABC/Reuters, 26 September 2013).
51. Li's co-defendants admitted that the victim had been unwilling to remove her clothes.
52. See 11.2.4 below.
53. Forensic evidence of sexual relations against Li was non-existent, for example.
54. For further discussion of "closed trials", see 11.2.4 below.

"separation of powers". This cornerstone of United States and (to a lesser extent) British constitutional law is deserving of discrete discussion.

"Separation of powers", in its purest sense, involves the recognition of three pillars of a constitution: the "executive", the "legislature" and the "judiciary"; each, ideally, separate from, and independent of, the others and all acting as a system of "checks and balances".[55] The "ideal" concept of separation of powers is of ancient origin, owing much to the work of Locke and Montesquieu around 300 years ago.[56]

It is worth noting, before considering the extent to which the PRC and the Hong Kong SAR conform to the ideal of separation of powers, that the "ideal" is just that. In practice no constitutional system has a perfect separation of the three "pillars" and foolproof checks and balances do not exist. Indeed, it has been suggested that the British system which Montesquieu used as his exemplar fell far short of his "separation" ideal since:

> [the] formulation by . . . Montesquieu, was based on an analysis of the English constitution of the early eighteenth century but an idealised rather than a real English constitution . . . No writer of repute would claim that it is a central feature of the modern British constitution.[57]

To look, first, at the United States system; it is clear that the legislature (Congress) has a "checking" function on the executive arm. Classic examples are to be found in the failed attempt of the Clinton administration to introduce universal, affordable health care (introduced by President Obama and enacted only after intense debate and opposition). In extreme circumstances Congress may even remove an errant President, via the "impeachment" procedure.[58] The President, via his power of veto, may curb the power of the legislature. Even in the case of agreement between executive and legislature, the judiciary, in the form of the Supreme Court, has the power to overturn legislation; *not* on the grounds of unpopularity but on the basis of its "unconstitutionality".

However, two examples may be used to show that even the United States system does not correspond to the "ideal" form. First, judges in America are not entirely apolitical. Locally, they are elected and run for election on overtly political grounds. Moreover, judges who make unpopular decisions may well forfeit re-election.[59] In the highest court of all, the Supreme Court, vacancies are filled by judges *nominated by* the President (though Congress may reject the nomination). The "legal realist"

---

55. Writers have questioned whether "checks and balances" are integral to the British constitutional system but they are certainly a pillar of the United States one.
56. See J Locke, *Second Treatise of Civil Government* (written in 1690, available widely in e-form) and Montesquieu, *The Spirit of Law* (written in 1748 [Batoche Books Canada 2001]).
57. S De Smith and R Brazier, *Constitutional and Administrative Law* (revised 7th edn, Penguin 1999).
58. This almost happened to Presidents Andrew Johnson and Bill Clinton (both impeached but acquitted) and would have happened to President Richard Nixon but for his resignation.
59. Questioning the legality/constitutionality of the death penalty is a definite "vote-loser" in most US states (not least Texas: see 11.7 below).

school of socio-legal researchers has, indeed, focused on the politico-economic background of Supreme Court judges and asserted a correlation between the "world view" of a particular Supreme Court bench and the outcome of the case before it. One important postscript should be added, however, since it is relevant to a consideration of the PRC situation: Supreme Court judges are "permanent appointments" and can only be removed on the grounds of gross misbehaviour.[60] This has led even clear political appointees to abandon, on principle, the anticipated wishes of their "patrons" free from concern as to the (employment) consequences.

A second, distinct "special case" is the wealth of "emergency" power that the President possesses and, in the Bush (younger) years, exercised, leading to complaints of an increasingly executive-led government. Under the Trump administration such complaints have increased.

To consider the British situation, there have been notable deviations from the ideal of separation, though some have been (belatedly) rectified. The (executive) Prime Minister is also a Member of Parliament (the legislature) as are members of his Cabinet. The (judges of the) House of Lords exercised, for hundreds of years, both a legislative function (as members of the "Upper House") and, of course, a judicial one. Indeed, at one time *all* members of the House of Lords were free to exercise a judicial function, though few non-judicial Lords did so in practice. The Head of the House of Lords, the Lord Chancellor, even donned three hats since he was, in addition to being head of the House of Lords and the Judiciary, *also* a member of the Cabinet. The Lord Chancellor and Law Lords anomaly, indeed, was the chief cause of the abolition of the House of Lords' judicial role and its replacement by the Supreme Court.[61] Mention should also be made of the "political" nature of judicial appointments in Britain since, traditionally, judicial appointments have been made either by, or on the advice of, the Lord Chancellor (a member of the cabinet) or the Prime Minister. Indeed, Griffith's[62] conclusion is that:

> The most remarkable fact about the appointment of judges [in Britain] is that it is wholly in the hands of politicians.[63]

However, while in *theory* judicial appointments in Britain are still by the sovereign on advice from the Lord Chancellor[64] or Prime Minister, in *practice* the determination is made by a Judicial Appointments Commission (JAC) (established in 2005) except for appointment to the Supreme Court.[65] Indeed, the Prime Minister

---

60. They are said to be appointed "*dum bene gesserunt*" (as long as they behave well).
61. As a result of the Constitutional Reform Act, 2005.
62. JAG Griffith, *The Politics of the Judiciary* (Manchester University Press 1977).
63. Ibid 17. A notable example was Prime Minister Thatcher's insistence on the appointment of Sir John Donaldson as Master of the Rolls.
64. The Lord Chancellor's role has also been significantly modified since, while he may also hold the position of Secretary of State for Justice, he is no longer the senior member of the judiciary nor is he the Speaker (Head) of the House of Lords (see Constitutional Reform Act 2005).
65. New appointments to the Supreme Court (the original Justices being the former 'Law Lords') are nominated by a differently constituted Committee, reflecting the United Kingdom (rather than English) dimension of the Supreme Court's work.

is required to put forward to the sovereign the candidate nominated by the JAC. The JAC is required to appoint solely on merit.[66]

As to "checks and balances" in the British system, many political commentators have lamented the erosion of Parliament's authority in the "Blair years", with an almost total absence of debate in the House of Commons particularly. "Prime Minister's Question Time" has been particularly affected, with the event now largely a stage-managed selection of pre-approved questions. Post-Blair his legacy remains and serious Parliamentary debate remains rare.

Moreover, the British judiciary lacks the power, existing in the United States, to overturn legislation on the basis of its unconstitutionality. The rationale has always been that Parliament is "sovereign" and may enact laws as it sees fit. The role of the judiciary is merely to interpret and apply the legislation that has been enacted. It is true that, with Britain's membership of the European Union (formerly European Community) "sovereignty" has been eroded (or, it could be argued, at least indefinitely suspended) given that senior judges may now declare domestic legislation to be incompatible with EU law. Moreover, the judiciary does have the power to declare legislation incompatible with the Human Rights Act 1998. However, it is perhaps still too early to talk of the British judiciary as a significant "check" on the legislature. What *is* shared with its American Supreme Court counterparts is the British judiciary's "security of tenure", which goes some way to ensuring that political considerations do not need to weigh heavily on the judges when they make their judgments.

Turning now to the Hong Kong situation, it is clearly recognised that its politico-legal system is, and always has been, "executive-led". The British colonialists ruled Hong Kong largely via the Executive Council (ExCo) which comprised hand-picked, largely pro-government figures, generally representing big business and other vested interests. While "opposition" figures might be co-opted, this was never such as to prevent the enactment of legislation which the colonial government (directly or "on orders from London") wished to introduce. The less powerful Legislative Council (LegCo) was dominated by appointed officials and the representatives of the so-called "functional" constituencies; again predominantly pro-business. The small measures to extend the functional franchise and increase the number of directly elected LegCo seats, introduced by last Governor Patten, were *immediately* nullified on 1 July 1997. While, therefore, it is possible to identify three distinct branches in Hong Kong's constitutional set up, it can scarcely be claimed that they are of equal "counterbalancing" force. Virtually all legislation in Hong Kong emanates from the executive and "member's legislation" is almost unknown, especially post-1997.[67] LegCo, it is true, has a limited power to slow down the executive's legislative proposals but, even here, controversial legislative moves, such as the arrangements for

---

66. Though it should "have regard" to the need to encourage diversity.
67. See Chapter 4.

the exorbitant and dubiously necessary "runway three",[68] are taken via the procedure of the Chief Executive in Council, ousting LegCo's oversight role. Moreover, given the guaranteed majority of the pro-government forces, most "government" legislation is, in practice, enacted eventually irrespective of opposition voices.[69] Only in respect of matters involving major constitutional change is LegCo able to hamper government initiatives, since these require a two-thirds LegCo majority.[70]

Similarly, while the Hong Kong Judiciary is appointed apolitically[71] and has 'security of tenure' (like its English counterparts),[72] it has limited power to overturn legislation on the basis of unconstitutionality generally. In this respect Hong Kong's judges are in a position more akin to their brethren in Britain than those in the United States. It was, formerly, intended that the Bill of Rights Ordinance (BORO) would give the Hong Kong judges a limited power of oversight in respect of legislation, since they had the right to construe prior legislation in a manner compatible with BORO. Moreover, in the absence of compatibility, such legislation could be struck down. This "superior" status of BORO was abolished on the grounds of inconsistency with the Basic Law.[73] More important, at least in theory, is the Hong Kong judiciary's power to declare legislation inconsistent with the Basic Law itself. The superior status of the Basic Law, unlike that of BORO, is of course uncontentious. However, the unfortunate experience of the Hong Kong judges in attempting to strike down the "right of abode" legislation, enacted by the Provisional Legislative Council, on the basis of its inconsistency with the Basic Law,[74] indicates that further declarations of "unconstitutionality" by the Hong Kong courts (as opposed to the Standing Committee of the National People's Congress) will be adopted with caution. The Court of Final Appeal has made such decisions, though, without controversy in such areas as declaring unconstitutional (as contrary to the Basic Law) legislation restricting the court's "right of final adjudication".[75]

---

68. The third airport runway proposal has huge environmental costs and there is clear evidence that the current runways are not being operated to capacity and that nearby competition is rapidly increasing.
69. Only "people power" (as with mass opposition to government-proposed Article 23 legislation) has been able to halt the government juggernaut.
70. Democrats were able to prevent the passage of the government's so-called "reform package" which was to give everyone in Hong Kong a right to vote for one from two to three candidates selected by a hand-picked 1,200 strong "nominating committee". Even such limited obstructive power has now been reduced following the disqualification of six elected pan-democratic legislators (discussed at 4.4).
71. Article 92 of the Basic Law requires that judges be appointed (solely) on the basis of their "judicial and professional qualities". The only, very limited, exception to the principle of appointment on merit is the nationality requirement for the Chief Justice and the Chief Judge of the High Court (see Chapter 6).
72. See Chapter 6.
73. Exercising the power conferred by Article 160 of the Basic Law, the Standing Committee of the NPC abolished ss 2(3), 3 and 4 as incompatible with Article 8 of the Basic Law.
74. See Chapter 4.
75. See *A Solicitor v Law Society of Hong Kong & Secretary for Justice* [2003] HKCFA 14, discussed in Chapter 3.

In serious contrast, the concept of "separation of powers" is not recognised in the PRC's civil/socialist legal system; or at least it is felt, by the PRC leadership, inappropriate to such a system. Indeed, in its official statement of February 2015,[76] the PRC Supreme People's Court stressed that:

> [the country] must preserve the judicial system of socialism with Chinese characteristics . . . [rejecting] Western judicial independence and the separation of powers.[77]

The PRC Constitution emphasises the leadership of the Chinese Communist Party, to which law, and legality, are formally subject. Moreover, the line separating the "executive" and "legislative" organs of government is blurred. Nor, in relation to "primacy", is there provision for the courts to strike down legislation on the grounds that it offends the Constitution. Indeed, the PRC Constitution makes clear that the role of interpreting and enforcing the Constitution is that of the NPC Standing Committee *not* the courts. A single, "lowly", attempt to overturn local legislation on the grounds of its conflict with national legislation was attempted by (the now famous) Judge Li Huijuan. While determining a contract dispute over the quantum of damages in a dispute over the (non) delivery of seeds,[78] the judge stated, in Luoyang Municipal Intermediate People's Court (Henan Province), that the *local* mechanism for assessing seed price must be rejected as in conflict with the *national* seed law. It was reported that:[79]

> Judge Li defended her decision by citing Article 64 of China's Law on Legislation which provides that 'where a national law or administrative regulation enacted by the state has come into force, any provision in the local decree which contravenes it shall be invalid.'

At the insistence of an angry Henan Province People's Congress, Judge Li was initially removed from office; though later reinstated following significant public concern. PRC constitutional lawyers have, generally, opined that Judge Li's action was improper, since the right to review constitutionality resides solely with the NPC Standing Committee. Nonetheless, some sympathy was expressed given the difficulty and delay involved in seeking the Standing Committee's intervention.[80] It appears that the more common, and less controversial, approach to these conflicts is for the court to apply the higher statutory authority and simply ignore (rather than

---

76. Supreme People's Court (Party Leadership Group), 10 February 2015.
77. The two concepts were described as examples of "the West's erroneous thought and mistaken viewpoints".
78. For further discussion, see M Zhang, *Contract Law: Theory and Practice* (Martinus Nijhoff 2006) 15–24.
79. China Law & Governance Review, Luoyang City 'Seed Case Highlights Chinese Courts Lack of Authority to Declare Laws Invalid' (2004) Case Files No 2 June 2004.
80. A judge should first refer the matter to the Supreme People's Court (Article 90, Law on Legislation). That court *may* then refer any conflict to the NPC Standing Committee which has the power to annul local laws under Article 67 of the PRC Constitution. In practice referrals to the Standing Committee are rare and resulting action rarer.

reject) the lower one.[81] The "Judge Li" case, while of humble origins, gained great notoriety, not least amongst opponents of the PRC system. The *New York Times* feted Judge Li (and her "rags to riches" ascent to the bench) and described the case as one of "youthful ideals meet reality".[82] It continued:

> 'The authority of the National People's Congress is not to be challenged' said Mao Yinduan, head of the legal office, in an interview. 'The judge . . . had every right to choose which law to use. But courts have no right in a verdict to say which law is valid.'
>
> . . . [yet] China's Law on Legislation stated that local laws that conflicted with national laws should be abolished. [Li] thought including this point in her opinion was within her judicial purview.

The swift reinstatement of Judge Li illustrated considerable sympathy for her plight, not least amongst legal academics in China. Balme and Lihua write:[83]

> the affair attracted important controversies about the constitutional status of the law referred to [the Law on Legislation][84] and about the procedure.

Essentially, however, the issue was one of procedure rather than substance: the role of the PRC judge in civil cases is to adjudicate as between the parties, *not* to determine the constitutionality of legal rules. Judge Li was entitled to follow the correct legislative rule. She was *not*, however, free to criticise the incorrect rule, since that is a matter solely for the Standing Committee.

The role of the PRC courts remains similarly circumscribed even 10 years after the Judge Li case. Moreover, even within the limits prescribed, and despite rapid moves to provide judges with greater freedom from political interference, such freedom remains significantly limited.

11.2.3 The rule of law: Judicial independence and autonomy

A specific aspect of separation of powers, important enough to warrant separate consideration, is the issue of judicial independence and autonomy. Tsang[85] writes:

> What sets [Hong Kong] apart from the PRC more than anything else is the existence of the rule of law and an independent judiciary.[86]

---

81. This was indeed the practice adopted by the Henan High Court which reheard the case.
82. Yardley J, 'A Judge Tests China's Courts, Making History' *New York Times* (28 November 2005).
83. R Balme and Y Lihua, 'The Politics of Constitutional Reform in China: Rule of Law as a Condition of or as a Substitute for Democracy?' in F Grotz and T Toonen (eds), *Crossing Borders: Constitutional Development & Internationalisation* (De Gruyter Berlin 2007) 170.
84. Especially Article 64 thereof.
85. S Tsang, 'Commitment to the Rule of Law & Judicial Independence' in S Tsang (ed), *Judicial Independence & the Rule of Law in Hong Kong* (Hong Kong University Press 2001).
86. Ibid 1.

In Britain this is underpinned by the "security of tenure" of judges, who may act without fear of the political and employment consequences and give judgment "according to law". As we have seen, similar security of tenure is enjoyed by the Justices of the United States Supreme Court. Security of tenure comes, of course, at a price. It is difficult to remove a judge from office on the grounds of incompetence (as opposed to venality) and both in England and Hong Kong there have been examples of judicial incompetence in respect of which formal sanctions are almost non-existent. Zander[87] talks of the Lord Chancellor (now President of the Supreme Court) having a "quiet word" with judges who act incompetently and there is little doubt that an "interview" with former Hong Kong Chief Justice, Andrew Li, would have been an unpleasant experience for a judge felt not to have acted with due care and attention.[88] Nonetheless, security of tenure for the (untypically) incompetent is felt to be a reasonable price to pay to ensure judicial integrity and impartiality. As Zander[89] writes:

> Calls for the judge's dismissal are wide of the mark. A judge cannot, and should not, be at risk of dismissal for incorrect decisions. That would threaten the essence of the independent judiciary.[90]

Judges in Hong Kong enjoy a similar security of tenure to their British counterparts. A key component of the general continuation of Hong Kong's existing legal system, post-1997 (prescribed by the Basic Law), was that:

> The courts of the Hong Kong SAR shall exercise judicial power independently, free from any interference. Members of the judiciary shall be immune from legal action in the performance of their judicial functions.[91]

Moreover, judges then in post would be permitted to continue "post-1997" (irrespective of their nationality),[92] their conditions would be "no less favourable",[93] and the removal of judges (other than via retirement or resignation) would be exceptional and effected only by special procedures.[94] While the judicial system in Hong Kong has not been immune to "political" considerations, there has been no indication of any member of the judiciary being swayed by threat or inducement.[95] It is true that the recent sentences of imprisonment on pro-democracy legislators (with its resultant tipping of the LegCo balance of power) produced a "pro-government" outcome.

---

87. M Zander, *A Matter of Justice* (Oxford University Press 1989).
88. This was undoubtedly the case for Judge Pang, the "judge who changed his mind" (see Chapter 10 at 10.1).
89. *A Matter of Justice* (n 87).
90. Ibid 130.
91. Article 85, Basic Law.
92. Article 93, Basic Law.
93. Ibid.
94. Articles 89 and 90, Basic Law.
95. A greater threat has been "political" considerations in determining whether or not to prosecute; as in the infamous "Sally Aw" case (see Chapter 13).

This does not mean, however, despite international concern to the contrary, that Hong Kong's judiciary has become politicised.[96] In the Court of Final Appeal, which has been the subject of significant judicial-political analysis,[97] statistics[98] have shown clearly that the court has been more than prepared to make decisions unpopular to the Hong Kong government.[99] Gittings[100] states that:

> Where the critics were right is in forecasting that Beijing would have difficulty learning to live with a court that—unlike its counterparts on the mainland—takes seriously the concept of judicial independence ... [however ...] The lack of reaction to the CFA's more recent rulings suggests a recognition that, like it or not, Beijing has learned to live with the reality of an independent judiciary in Hong Kong.[101]

Implicit in Gittings' statement, however, is the lack of full independence for the judiciary in the PRC. Chinese political leaders frequently praise the more accommodating approach of the Macau judges and their co-operation with the executive, as opposed to the "difficult" judges of the Hong Kong SAR (especially those of the Court of Final Appeal). The conceptual difference in perception of the judge's role, as between Hong Kong and the mainland, is exemplified in the furore surrounding the publication, by the PRC State Council, of a "White Paper" on "One Country, Two Systems". The description of judges as "administrators", who should be "patriotic", seemed uncontentious to the PRC "side" yet was regarded as highly sinister by many in Hong Kong. Outgoing Hong Kong Bar Chairman, Paul Shieh, stated:[102]

> I now address the publication of the White Paper by the State Council in June 2014. A lot of controversies focused on whether judges were correctly characterized as "administrators" of Hong Kong. The matter was blamed on translation. However, the real problem with the relevant part of the White Paper is that irrespective of translation, judges perform judicial tasks independently. The sovereign state should not purport to impose any ambiguous political requirements, such as to be "patriotic"[103] or to "safeguard the country's development interests".

---

96. See K Macdonald, 'Legality Is Vital to Upholding the Rule of Law' *South China Morning Post* (Hong Kong, 5 September 2017); C Buddle, 'Shock and Law' *South China Morning Post* (Hong Kong, 27 August 2017); C Lau and J Hollingsworth, 'Judiciary in the Dock' *South China Morning Post* (Hong Kong, 25 August 2017).
97. Much of this was presented at a conference entitled 'Hong Kong's Court of Final Appeal: The Andrew Li Court 1997–2010' at the University of Hong Kong, 5–6 March 2010; later published as Young and Ghai (eds), *Hong Kong's Court of Final Appeal: The Development of the Law in China's Hong Kong* (Cambridge University Press 2014).
98. Especially those provided by Professor Simon Young. See SNM Young, 'Final Appeals Then and Now' in Young and Ghai (eds) (ibid).
99. According to Young, op cit, roughly half of appeals involving the Hong Kong government have been determined against it. The record of the Macau CFA has been far more "subservient"; cf Godinho and Cardinal, 'Macau's Court of Final Appeal' in Young and Ghai (eds) (n 96).
100. D Gittings, 'Changing Expectations: How the Rule of Law Fared in the First decade of the Hong Kong SAR' *Hong Kong Journal*, 1 July 2007.
101. Ibid 3.
102. Speech of Chairman of the Hong Kong Bar Association at the Opening of the Legal Year 2015.
103. Especially since Hong Kong's judges need not be Chinese (see Chapter 6).

> ... the White Paper sends a wrong message to the people of Hong Kong and the international community as to the role of the judiciary in Hong Kong. It also shows a gap in mindset. In systems subscribing to our concept of Rule of Law, the Government does not paternalistically issue edicts for judges to perform political tasks. This mentality may be commonplace on the Mainland, but it is inappropriate here.

Indeed, while PRC leaders may, reluctantly, accept the independence of the judiciary for Hong Kong, they are far from accepting it as a proposition for the PRC.[104] In the first place, implementation of a truly independent judiciary in the PRC is hampered by constitutional restraints since, while Article 126 of the PRC Constitution provides that courts:

> exercise judicial power independently, in accordance with the provisions of the law, and are not subject to interference by any administrative organ, public organisation or individual.

This is subject to Article 128 which states that:

> The Supreme People's Court is responsible to the National People's Congress and its Standing Committee. Local People's Courts at various levels are responsible to the organs of state power, which created them.

While, following the Law on Judges (2000),[105] the judiciary is viewed as a separate organ, with separate rights and obligations from other state organs, and while improvements to qualification and training are integral to the developing judiciary, the subservient position of the courts is constitutionally maintained. One of the criteria for judicial office is that the judge "supports the Constitution of the People's Republic of China";[106] which includes, of course, reference to, "the leadership of the Communist Party of China" and adherence to "the socialist road". Senior judges are appointed by the People's Congress[107] (or the Standing Committee thereof)[108] or, in the case of local People's Courts, by local People's Congresses on the advice of the local President of the Court. Even though new appointments to the judiciary are now recruited "on merit"[109] via a standard, unified public examination (the State Judicial Examination, introduced in 2002)[110] their numbers are still relatively small in comparison with those recruited previously, often with little legal expertise or training.

---

104. Article 126 affirms: "The People's Courts shall, in accordance with the law, exercise judicial power independently." However, the "removability" of judges, performance assessment and remuneration/promotion processes create significant indirect pressures (see J Cohen [n 111]).
105. Or Judges Law, depending on translation.
106. Article 9, Law on Judges.
107. In the case of the President of the Supreme People's Court (SPC).
108. On the recommendation of the President of the SPC.
109. This criterion, however, encompasses both "ability and political integrity".
110. Article 12, Law on Judges.

Moreover, in the context of judicial autonomy, the process of appointment is less significant than the rules on *removal*. Removal may be, at the local level, by local People's Congresses and, at the State level, by the National People's Congress (NPC). Judges may be removed for "incompetence", failure to perform judicial duties, lack of qualification, absenteeism and refusal to accept a transfer.[111] Moreover, "promotion and rewards" are dependent on *annual* "performance reviews". It is clear that the potential to remove, or at least deny promotion to, a judge on political grounds is a real one. The problem is far more acute at the local level of which Cohen,[112] writing in 2006, said:

> Judges are hired, paid, promoted and fired by local officials . . . increasing numbers are now fresh out of law school and inexperienced in both law and life. Usually decisions in nonroutine [*sic*] cases are made by administrative superiors within the court rather than the customary panel of three judges who hear the case . . . Outside agencies . . . frequently influence rulings behind the scenes.[113]

Indeed, then, true judicial autonomy, as understood in the common law world, is not even an "ideal" in the PRC system (much less a reality). Article 5 of the Law on Judges explains that the function of a judge includes "to take part in a trial as a member of a collegial panel". Moreover, under Article 7(7) there is a duty to "accept legal supervision and supervision by the masses." The PRC Constitution itself proclaims that:

> The Supreme People's Court is responsible to the National People's Congress and its Standing Committee. Local People's Courts at different levels are responsible to the organs of state power which created them.

In short, judicial independence and autonomy exist *currently* neither in theory nor in practice. Nonetheless, as with all issues of law and legalism in the PRC, things are changing fast. The "professionalism" of judges, a key component of respect for, and the autonomy of, the judiciary, has been rapidly enhanced. The first step towards professionalisation, the Law on Judges, was not enacted until 1995 and before that "judges in mainland China were treated as cadres of the state".[114]

In the relatively few years since the Law on Judges, the status of judges has changed so that they are regarded as "separate" from other state officers; rules on qualification and training have been introduced; and, crucially, protections have been introduced to defend judges from political interference and to guarantee their security of tenure. With the increasing proportion of judges appointed via an open, unified and competitive examination system (with the establishment of a Commission for Examination and Assessment of Judges charged with the training and assessment of

---

111. Article 40, Law on Judges.
112. J Cohen, 'China's Legal Reform at the Crossroads' *Far Eastern Economic Review* (Hong Kong, March 2006).
113. Ibid.
114. Chen (n 2) 135.

judges) and with increasing moves towards central control of judicial appointments, there is room for cautious optimism. The advantage of having discontent vented in court rather than on the streets is obvious in a country as vast and disparate as China and this fact alone is likely to produce improvements in the quality of judicial selection, training and adjudication.[115] Clear examples of the will to change and improve can be seen in the introduction of a Second Five Year Reform Programme for the People's Courts (introduced by the Supreme People's Court in 2004) and by the introduction of extensive programmes aimed at improving the professionalisation of the Chinese judiciary.[116] Most recently, in July 2014, the Supreme People's Court announced a (fourth) Five-Year Reform Plan to Enhance Judicial Independence. The Plan seeks (*inter alia*) to improve selection processes for judges; to restrict the influence of local governments; to enhance judicial transparency; and to improve the administration of the courts. Among the more specific proposals,[117] it is suggested that cases involving local environmental issues be held in superior courts or those outside the affected area; that circuit judges be appointed to assist local judges in difficult cases; that judicial performance be better monitored; that illegally obtained evidence be excluded; and that information on hearings be made available in advance to allow public attendance. The Economist[118] describes an increasingly professionalised system in which well-qualified judges will receive substantial pay increases while the "old guard" judges (without qualifications) will be downgraded.

The power of the State, under President Xi Jinping, is being brought to bear against corruption, and it is clear that attempts to "influence" judges for corrupt motives are frowned upon. In *that* sense efforts are being made to increase the "independence" of the judges. At the same time, a full separation of powers is not to be contemplated. The dilemma faced by the PRC leadership is summarised in the *New York Times* article inspired by the "Judge Li case".[119] It notes:

> Faced with the complex demands of governing a chaotic, modernizing country, China's leaders have embraced the rule of law as the most efficient means of regulating society. But a central requirement in fulfilling that promise lies unresolved—whether the governing Communist Party intends to allow an independent judiciary.[120]

Ten years later that theme is repeated by Cary Huang, writing in the *South China Morning Post*.[121] He says:

---

115. Well-reported cases in 2010 of attacks on judges have illustrated the connection between respect for the judiciary and social stability.
116. Eg, the Judicial Studies Training Programme (JSP) involving a collaboration between Britain and the Supreme People's Court and similar collaborative schemes to improve judicial management.
117. There are 45 proposals in all.
118. *The Economist*, 'Judging Judges' (London, 26 September 2015).
119. See 11.2.2 above.
120. J Yardley, *New York Times* (n 82).
121. C Huang, 'Party Faces Catch 22 with Attempts at Judicial Reform' *South China Morning Post*, 'What the Mainland Media Say' (Hong Kong, 5 April 2015).

In an effort to implement the legal reforms announced at last October's party plenum, the central government has published new measures under which all officials who interfere in judicial cases will be publicly named.

Officials will be seen to have broken the rules if they tell judges how to handle a particular case, or ask court officials to meet litigants or defendants privately.

While hailing this development as a step forward in promoting the rule by law, [*sic*] state media have also cast doubt about how feasible it will be to implement within the existing legal system.

... the Legal Daily said it was time to draw a red line so people knew interference would no longer be tolerated and also make clear the division between executive power and the judiciary.

China's legal system is known to have been dogged by a lack of transparency, weak enforcement and allegations of rampant corruption. At the centre of the problem is the lack of 'judicial independence' ...

... President Xi Jinping has put legal reform at the top of his agenda, including finding ways to reduce local governments' direct control over the courts and prosecutors.

Yet the concept of 'judicial independence' has also come under fire during Xi's leadership ...

Currently China's judiciary is subject to a variety of internal and external controls that greatly limit the ability of the courts to make independent decisions.

At the moment, local courts and prosecutors are considered part of the civil service and are financed and administered by local governments. This means local governments often try to interfere in court cases.

...

The party wants to give judges and prosecutors greater independence ... while not wanting to see the kind of separation of powers between the party and judiciary that has the potential of challenging the party's absolute grip on power.

Comment

Herein lies the dilemma for the PRC leadership. "Corrupt" attempts to influence judges are not to be tolerated and the "independence" of an increasingly professional judiciary willl be maintained, except in the case of politically sensitive cases (a minority) where influence aimed at maintaining the primacy of the Chinese Communist Party (CCP) must continue to be brought to bear. However, since most local government "influencers" are also CCP members, the distinction between acceptable and unjustified interference is difficult to ascertain.

The judicial independence/CCP supremacy dichotomy is reflected in competing messages from the higher echelons. The Supreme People's Court, in October 2013, issued a paper stating that the PRC must "rid its courts of corruption and stop officials interfering in decisions" yet, little more than a year later, Chief Judge Zhou

Chiang, delivering the Court's report to the annual plenum meeting of the National People's Congress,[122] asserted that:

> We must unify the three tasks of maintaining the leadership of the party, treating the people as masters and ruling the country according to law, unswervingly walking the path of socialist rule of law with Chinese characteristics.

He went on to add that the PRC must: "Reject Western notions of 'judicial independence' and 'separation of powers' [indicative of] the West's erroneous thought."

Zhou emphatically repeated these sentiments in a speech to provincial judges on 14 January 2017.[123]

The concept of a fully "independent" judiciary in the Western sense remains, therefore, far away. However, the more optimistic view is that, leaving aside the rhetoric, substantive moves are being made to improve the quality and independence of the judiciary.[124] It remains to be seen whether significant action results from these proposals. Indeed, pessimists would point to indications that, under the presidency of the reactionary Xi Jinping, the move towards judicial independence, in the "separation of powers" sense, has stalled or even gone into reverse. In this vein, Qian Gang[125] writes:

> Following the recent Fourth Plenum on rule of law (or, as some would prefer, rule by law) the crux of official 'interpretations' loudly promoted in Party media was the Party's leadership of so-called rule of law . . . 'constitutionalism' was roundly attacked, so too was 'judicial independence' . . . in the wake of the Fourth Plenum, a gnawing fear of constitutionalism, of the checking of power . . . seems to have gripped China . . . as the gloves come off, as 'judicial independence' becomes the target of open hostility, the Party's declarations about 'the independent and fair exercise of the powers of trial and prosecution' can only become naked falsehoods. And all efforts at judicial reform in China can only become wasted energy.

Comment

While the Qian Gang "pessimistic" view appears to reflect the current mainland situation, more worrying for Hong Kong is the current emphasis, by PRC spokesmen, on the "subservience" of the Hong Kong courts to a Chief Executive holding a position "transcending" the executive, legislature and judiciary in an "executive-led"

---

122. Concluding remarks, 15 March 2015. Prompting S Lubman, 'Questions Loom over China's Legal Reform Drive' *Chinarealtime* (17 March 2015).
123. See C-y Choi, 'Chief Justice Unleashes Legal Storm' *South China Morning Post* (Hong Kong, 18 January 2017).
124. Kuhn, for example, emphasises improvements in the financing of the judiciary and the judicial appointments system: RL Kuhn, 'How US Critics Misread China' *South China Morning Post* (Hong Kong, 4 October 2015).
125. Qian Gang, 'Who Gave "Judicial Independence" a Death Sentence?' China Media Project (Hong Kong, 14 January 2015).

system.[126] *Some of the most emphatic statements in this context have been made by Zhang Xiaoming, head of the highly influential CPG's Hong Kong Liaison Office. It is reassuring that current Chief Justice, Geoffrey Ma, while of course not entering into political "debate", has emphasised the Basic Law's endorsement of an independent judiciary and equality of all before the law.*[127]

11.2.4 The rule of law: Right to a fair trial

The right to a fair trial involves basic issues of natural justice; in particular, that an accused has the right to be heard[128] (and generally to be legally represented) and that the adjudicator should have no "interest" in the outcome (the "neutrality" principle). The right to be heard, of course, means that both parties to a civil action have a right to fully present their case to the court. More significantly, perhaps, in any criminal case (or disciplinary proceedings) the "defendant" should have the right to know precisely the nature of the offence with which he is charged and to present his defence, personally or via his legal representative. If the accused is convicted, this should be on the basis of the *evidence* produced in court, rather than on his "character". Any sentence, of course, should be based on a penalty *prescribed in advance* for the offence in question. These principles have developed with the evolution of the common law and, although they have not always been recognised, they are of significant longevity within the common law world.[129] The "interest" rule, that "no one should be a judge in his own cause", would require, for example, a judge who is related to the accused (or who has reason to dislike him) to stand down.[130] The "interest" rule is important, too, in relation to the decision to prosecute. In most cases,[131] the Hong Kong decision to prosecute is taken independently[132] by the Department of Justice (DOJ). An important contrast can be seen with approaches to corruption where Hong Kong has investigation by the independent ICAC, followed by a further filter of the DOJ's decision as to prosecution.[133] The PRC battle against corruption is, conversely, often seen as "selective" and a tool to bring down politi-

---

126. See G Cheung, 'Why Beijing Is Laying Down the Law' *South China Morning Post* (Hong Kong, 16 September 2015) and S Lau and J Ngo, 'Authority of HK Chief Is Above All: Beijing' *South China Morning Post* (Hong Kong, 13 September 2015).
127. J Ng, 'Hong Kong Chief Justice Geoffrey Ma Transcends Political Debate but Stands up for Separation of Powers' *South China Morning Post* (Hong Kong, 21 September 2015).
128. Sometimes described by the Latin maxim "*audi alteram partem*".
129. To take two examples: the "right of silence" derived from the old English common law rule that the accused was not *permitted* to speak in his own defence; further, the ancient English jury was selected precisely *because* it knew the defendant and could base its verdict on his known character.
130. Standing down is known as "recusal". The most spectacular example of the wrongful failure of a judge to recuse himself involves Lord Hoffmann (*Re Pinochet* [1999] UKHL 52).
131. The Securities and Futures Commission's power to investigate *and* prosecute has been criticised as an anomaly.
132. Though the "independence" of Secretary for Justice, Rimsky Yuen, on political issues in which he has a clear "interest" has been called into question (see Postscript).
133. Not to mention external scrutiny by no fewer than four independent advisory committees!

cal enemies.[134] However, the NPC Standing Committee has recently announced the imminent establishment of a new, independent body, incorporating under one roof the various current anti-corruption bodies in the PRC.[135]

In actions brought against the government, of course, the independence *and neutrality* of the judiciary are crucial to a fair trial. Hong Kong's record on political neutrality is excellent. Research by Professor Simon Young and others,[136] for example, shows that the Court of Final Appeal has decided *against* the government, in judicial review cases, slightly more often than *in its favour*. So great is the difference between the Hong Kong and PRC systems that this statistic would not even be regarded as laudable in the latter jurisdiction, where judicial review is in its infancy, is more restricted, and rarely involves criticism of government. Further, by way of local contrast with Hong Kong, Macau's far more pliant Court of Final Appeal (the Tribunal de Ultima Instancia (TUI)) has been far more reluctant to decide against the government.[137]

In general, the right to a fair trial seems well adhered to in Hong Kong and there is transparency by virtue of the fact that trials are open to the public (subject to space restraints)[138] with reporting restrictions only such as to ensure a fair trial. There are, however, occasional allusions to the "pro-prosecution" tendencies of the criminal courts. Certainly the existence of "special" magistrates (with no proper legal expertise) is a departure from international best practice (as is the system of lay prosecution) but their utilisation only in respect of the least serious (regulatory) offences vitiates this deficiency. There remains, unfortunately, an over-representation of former prosecutors in the ranks of District Court judges, giving some force to the "pro-prosecution" argument. Former Chairman of the Hong Kong Bar Association, Clive Grossman, has alluded (highly controversially) to the conviction rate in Hong Kong criminal cases being on a par with those in North Korea (a state not famed for its enlightened jurisprudence).[139] Defenders of the system, however, have suggested that Grossman's figures included guilty pleas and argue that the rate, in *contested* cases, is not excessive.[140] In answer to criticisms of "pro-prosecution" District Court

---

134. There have been calls for a PRC ICAC to be established; the obstacle to such a move is similar to that involving moves to "genuine" judicial independence.
135. See T Kwok, 'Best Practices' *South China Morning Post* (Hong Kong, 27 January 2017).
136. See SNM Young, 'Final Appeals Then and Now' (n 97).
137. See J Godinho and P Cardinal, 'Macau's Court of Final Appeal' (n 98).
138. In "causes célèbres" such as the Nancy Kissell and Rafael Hui cases some "spectators" have been disappointed.
139. 'Introduction to Archbold Hong Kong (2010). The Chief Justice criticised Grossman's comments as "ill-considered and intemperate".
140. Moreover, high conviction rates could merely reflect excellent pre-trial screening. This is the view supported by a Hong Kong Law Society (comparative) submission. However, the *South China Morning Post* reports that "lawyers disagreed" and quoted solicitor Michael Vidler as saying: "Among criminal defence lawyers, both solicitors and barristers, there's a general view that conviction rates are high": J Man, 'Conviction Rates Not Too High, Law Society Finds' *South China Morning Post* (Hong Kong, 20 July 2010).

judges, it should be noted that conviction rates in the Court of First Instance (with a jury) are very similar to those in the District Court.[141]

One difficulty for defendants in the Hong Kong process remains the issue of legal representation, since appointed legal aid personnel are likely to be of variable quality and many defendants are unable to afford their own (privately engaged) legal advisers, given the great cost of legal expertise in Hong Kong.[142] Nonetheless, defendants are able to know the nature of the charges against them, to wage their own defence or engage the services of a legal professional who can defend their case without fear of political repercussions. Moreover, in accordance with the maxim that justice should "be seen to be done", Hong Kong adheres to the common law principle of openness in its courts.[143]

Two particular tenets of the right to a fair trial are the "presumption of innocence"[144] and the "presumption of legality". These two presumptions are generally pervasive in common law systems. The presumption of innocence involves the proposition that, in a criminal case, it is for the prosecution to prove guilt and not the accused to prove his innocence. Indeed, in many common law jurisdictions, the defendant is within his rights to remain silent,[145] refuse to answer questions (without disparagement) and insist on the prosecution proving his guilt. In the English system (today) judges and/or juries are permitted to draw adverse inferences from an accused's silence in certain circumstances, but the general proposition that it is for the prosecution to prove guilt remains a constant.[146] Moreover the "standard of proof" which the prosecution must reach is that of "beyond reasonable doubt" or some similar formulation.[147] Inherent in the presumption of innocence is the proposition that, *prima facie*, the unconvicted person should remain free. This "presumption of bail" (in most advanced civil and common law jurisdictions) is, of course, subject to the right to refuse "bail" where a defendant is a potential danger to the community or likely to abscond. Those refused bail and "remanded" are, of course, detained without trial and this should be for the minimum possible amount of time.

---

141. See Chapters 6 and 8.
142. Driven by the high operating costs associated with expensive business property and the shortage of lawyers in Hong Kong relative to its population.
143. Arbitral/mediation tribunals may be different but openness is primarily of concern in criminal cases.
144. Guaranteed in Hong Kong by Bill of Rights Article 11(1).
145. Ditto, Article 11(2).
146. Wong writes that "PRC criminal codes ... do not provide for who bears the burden of proof with clarity and certitude ... [and] unlike in the west ... The defense [sic] has a duty to co-operate with a criminal investigation, including the volunteering of information, production of evidence, answering of pertinent questions, and submitting to examination" See KC Wong, 'Understanding PRC Criminal Justice Process: Anatomy of the "Big Spender" Case' (paper delivered at PRC-HK Law Seminar on "Legal Issues in Cross-Border Crimes: Looking into the Future", 27 November 1998, 69). See also J Low, 'The Presumption of Innocence in Singapore and Hong Kong: The Privilege against Self-Incrimination and Associated Rights' *Columbia East Asia Review* (Spring 2013).
147. It has been argued that majority verdicts in criminal cases (as permitted in Britain and Hong Kong) run counter to the "beyond reasonable doubt" criterion (see G Maher, 'Jury Verdicts and the Presumption of Innocence' (1983) *Legal Studies* 146).

Concern has been raised, in Hong Kong, at the significant increase in time spend on remand.[148] There is some irony in the fact that the PRC's legal system probably outperforms Hong Kong in the speed in which it brings defendants to trial.

The presumption of legality reflects the rule of law concept that what is not prohibited is permitted and lawful. This contrasts with the approach in totalitarian states that what is not specifically permitted is presumed to be *unlawful*. There is no serious departure from the presumption of legality in Hong Kong.[149] The situation in the PRC is somewhat different, however. The PRC Constitution itself is vague on the issue, although the nebulous nature of certain citizen's "obligations" provides significant scope for "catch all" criminality. Article 51, for example, states that in exercising their rights citizens "may not infringe upon the interests of the state, of society or of the collective, or upon the lawful freedoms and rights of other citizens". Article 53, in addition to imposing a duty to uphold the Constitution and the law, requires that citizens "respect social ethics". On 10 March 2010, Li Fei, deputy director of the Legal Affairs Commission of the NPC, stated that: "In civil law, if the law does not forbid something then it is not illegal. But in public law if the law does not authorise something then it is forbidden."[150]

There is considerable irony in the postscript to Li's "explanation", since he was referring to his view that the resignation of five pro-democracy activists, in order to force a by-election, was unlawful. In response, ex-Secretary for Justice, Elsie Leung, supported the view that the so-called "referendum" caused by the resignations had no legal validity.[151] Leung added that there was no need, at this stage for (yet another) NPC interpretation[152] of the Basic Law while adding that the Hong Kong government could initiate one. Since, presumably, interpretation of the Basic Law is a public law issue, and since there is no provision in the Basic Law for the Hong Kong government to seek an interpretation, both Li and Leung (applying Li's logic) should have viewed such requests as unlawful!

While Hong Kong largely maintains the right to a fair trial, this is clearly not always the case in the PRC. In this regard we encounter the greatest dissonance between the "form" of the criminal law and procedure and its "substance". The PRC Constitution, for example, stipulates the right to a proper defence.[153] The Criminal Procedure Law of the PRC[154] more specifically enacts that the courts have a duty to ensure that the accused obtains a defence and states that the accused has the right

---

148. See D Lee, 'Remand Times an "Alarming Blight"' *South China Morning Post* (Hong Kong, 5 June 2016) (quoting former DPP, Grenville Cross).
149. Newcomers to Hong Kong, however, are often bemused by the fact that street parking is illegal even in areas not designated "no parking".
150. Reported in *South China Morning Post*, 11 March 2010.
151. It is a matter of some doubt as to whether Leung has ever disagreed with a Beijing spokesman.
152. See Chapter 5.
153. Article 125, PRC Constitution.
154. Article 26.

either to defend himself or to appoint others to do so.[155] However, in high-profile cases, defence lawyers have complained that they are denied sufficient time to prepare a defence and are often given only partial, or late, access to the material on which the charges are based.[156] Nor is a spirited defence without its dangers, since lawyers acting for defendants, especially in rights-type cases, run the risk of themselves being punished. To take just one example, Gao Zhisheng, previously voted as one of China's top 10 lawyers, has been subjected to detention and torture for his support for oppressed[157] Falun Gong practitioners.[158] On 17 March 2010, *The Standard* newspaper reported that:

> Foreign Minister Yang Jiechi has added to the mystery over missing [for over a year] lawyer, Gao Zhisheng, saying he has been sentenced on subversion charges but offering no details of his status or whereabouts.[159]

Far from improving, things appear to have got worse for civil rights lawyers. As part of the "709 crackdown" many rights lawyers have been imprisoned including Zhou Shifeng (for seven and a half years!); a lawyer who *inter alia* assisted victims of the (melamine) contaminated milk scandal.[160]

The PRC Constitution provides that trials should be "open" *unless* otherwise provided for by law.[161] "Open" means that the entire process should be open to the public and the press. In open cases the court should announce in advance the name of the case, the defendant's name and the time and place of the trial. However, a very big exception to the "open trial" rule is the fact that it is not applicable to cases involving personal privacy, or minors, nor, most importantly, to cases involving "state secrets". The classification of a huge raft of "offences" as involving "state secrets" represents the biggest departure from due process in the PRC. Routinely, for example, those who report on natural disasters or industrial accidents are tried for compromising "state secrets".[162] Most disconcertingly, the status of a particular issue may change from "reportable" to "state secret" merely because of external responses to the reporting. To give one example, a report of a strike involving 500 workers was held to be a state secret, justifying the incarceration of reporter Zheng Enchong, even though the strike was widely known locally and despite PRC con-

---

155. See 11.4 below.
156. A further problem is that prosecution "witnesses" rarely appear; with written statements the norm and cross-examination therefore impossible: see G Cross, 'Witnesses Must Be Questioned in Chinese Courts' *South China Morning Post* (Hong Kong, 13 April 2017).
157. Despite the PRC Constitution's guarantees of religious freedom (Article 36) state-sanctioned oppression of practitioners is "justified" on the basis that Falun Gong is a "cult".
158. For a fuller report and further examples, see J Cohen and E Pils, 'The Fate of China's Human Rights Lawyers' *Far Eastern Economic Review* (Hong Kong, 4 December 2009). See also 11.4 below.
159. 'Activist Mystery Deepens' *The Standard* (Hong Kong, 17 March 2010).
160. See Z Pinghui and N Gan, 'Four Faces of the Rights Movement' *South China Morning Post* (Hong Kong, 6 August 2016).
161. Article 125.
162. Clearly this represents a significant exception to the rights of freedom of speech and freedom of the press guaranteed by Article 35 of the PRC Constitution.

stitutional "guarantees" of "freedom of the press".[163] It appears that Zheng's real "crime" was defending the rights of those unlawfully evicted to assist development projects.[164] Other "state secrets" include reports of medical epidemics, the extent of AIDS in China, and the extent to which capital punishment is being implemented in the PRC.[165] Rosenzweig (for the Dui Hua Foundation)[166] writes:

> One of the limitations to public trials allowed under the ICCPR is on grounds of 'national security', and Article 152 of the CPL[167] requires Chinese courts to close court proceedings in cases 'involving state secrets'. The reasonableness of this limitation is, of course, dependent on the legitimacy of the standards used to classify state secrets. China's use of vague and flexible standards of classification with respect to secrecy is a major impediment to the transparency of the entire criminal justice system. In particular, the broad range of topics subject to secrecy classification in China serves to restrict access by the public to court proceedings and, therefore, threatens defendants' right to a fair trial.
>
> If the limitation in the CPL is interpreted to mean that criminal proceedings in which state secrets may be introduced as evidence, then it would be reasonable for courts to restrict public access to those proceedings. However, current practice allows for an 'all or nothing' decision in which entire trials are either public or closed.

In conclusion, there is a huge distinction between the often secret nature of criminal trials in the PRC and the (Hong Kong) common law notion that "justice should be seen to be done". While the lack of openness may be seen as evidence of "something to hide", it may be, sometimes, that the "something" is inefficiency rather than malfeasance. Zou[168] writes:

> Recently[169] open trials and hearings, except for those involving privacy, minors or state secrets, have been undertaken in big cities such as Beijing . . . Open trial is a principle of litigation that attempts to maximise the fairness and transparency of the judicial system . . .
>
> . . . However, the biggest problem in open trial, as Xiao Yang, president of the Supreme People's Court, once admitted, is the quality of judges.[170]

---

163. Article 35, PRC Constitution.
164. Asian Human Rights Commission, 5 December 2003.
165. Dui Hua Foundation, 'Submission for the Universal Periodic Review of the PRC' (Convened by United Nations Human Rights Council), February 2009.
166. JD Rosenzweig, 'Public Access and the Right to a Fair Trial in China', Du Hua Foundation Issue 28 (2 August 2007).
167. Criminal Procedure Law.
168. Keyuan Zou, *China's Legal Reform: Towards the Rule of Law* (Martinus Nijhof Leiden Boston 1 January 2006; Brill Academic Publishers 10 January 2010).
169. In fact, Zou's book was first published in 2006.
170. Keyuan Zou (n 167) 157.

It appears that there are increasing moves towards openness in trials proceedings, perhaps in an effort to increase public awareness of the drive against corruption. Professor Zhao Zhengqun[171] states that:

> Solving social conflict through judicial procedure will win more support and understanding from the public.
> . . .
> Justice must be done, and it must be seen to be done.
> . . . these case [such as that of Bo Xilai] demonstrate the pursuit of real justice and a special focus on procedural justice, with an essential premise of openness and transparency.

Xinhua Insight[172] quotes Ma Huaide, vice-president of China University of Political Science and Law as saying:

> Justice calls for a just and rational hearing, as well as independent and impersonal judgement. Only openness and transparency can ensure the justice of trials and sentences while consolidating the authority of law and the credibility of the judiciary.

Xinhua Insight[173] goes on to add:

> Signalling openness and transparency as major goals for the judiciary, the Supreme People's Court in July urged courts at all levels to shake off the 'mysticism' of justice and promote judicial openness, instructing them to carry out live broadcasts of trials and upload judgment documents online.

The most famous example of the policy of increasing openness involves the trial for corruption of Bo Xilai, former Communist Party chairman in Chongqing and political "rising star". Media access to the trial was restricted but the court published lengthy transcript extracts throughout the five days of Bo's trial. Ironically, China's critics were able to criticise the procedure both for insufficient openness (there were significant omissions in the transcripts released) *and* for reintroducing the "show trial" in China. The *New York Times* reported[174] that:

> political analysts and party insiders say a guilty verdict for Mr Bo has almost certainly been predetermined.
> Even legal scholars who applauded the new style evident in Mr Bo's trial recognise that it was an exception and not necessarily a model. Given Mr Bo's popularity among ordinary Chinese . . . leaders no doubt felt compelled to allow Mr Bo his say, within narrow parameters.
> . . .

---

171. 'Open Trials, Sentences Showcase China's Volition in Rule of Law' *Xinhua Insight* (Beijing, 28 September 2013).
172. Ibid.
173. Ibid.
174. E Wong, 'China Debates Effect of Trial's Rare Transparency' *New York Times* (New York, 2 September 2013).

Mr Bo was given leeway to speak in court but there were obvious limits . . . According to unofficial written records from a court observer, he spoke of rivalry for top positions [etc] . . . but those remarks were kept out of the official transcripts, as were instances when he talked about specific threats made by investigators.

Chinarealtime reported[175] that:

Public confessions and sentencing proceedings for criminal defendants that are televised or otherwise public are stages for admissions of guilt and remorse. These will continue, regardless of any incremental reforms. They are not 'open trials' as that term is used in the West or even in the Chinese Constitution, which states (Art 125) that 'Open' means the entire process should be open to public auditing and to the press.

A more optimistic interpretation of the Bo events was expressed in VOA News which quoted Professor Jacques Delisle as saying:

The Bo case was, it appears, an attempt to confirm that we are not back in the old Mao days or Stalin style political trials, that he had a chance to present a defence.[176]

The trend towards openness (at least in high-profile corruption trials) appeared, for a time, to be continuing with *China Daily*[177] reporting that:

China will hold an 'open trial' for the country's former chief of security Zhou Yongkang, the president of China's Supreme People's Court said . . .
Asked whether the trial of Zhou . . . would be open, Chief Justice Zhou Qiang answered that it would be 'open in accordance with the law'.
. . .
Sensitive cases are normally held in camera.

However, by adding a charge of "disclosing state secrets" to the corruption charges, the prosecution was able to justify a secret trial[178] and Zhou was convicted (and sentenced to life imprisonnment) surprisingly quickly. The *Wall Street Journal* reported that:

The party took no chances in prosecuting Mr Zhou, once the man who controlled China's police forces and the state-security apparatus . . .
The tight control on information about the trial indicates unusual efforts by the party to limit the likelihood events could go off script.[179]

A further element of secrecy applied in Zhou's case; namely that he had been detained (as is permitted in cases involving state security) in a secret location before

---

175. Chinarealtime, 'Why Maoist Show Trials in China Aren't Going Away Any Time Soon' (10 September 2014).
176. Professor of Law, University of Pennsylvania.
177. *China Daily Asia*, 'Open Trial for Zhou Yongkang: Chief Justice' (13 March 2015).
178. Via Article 152 Criminal Procedure Law.
179. JT Areddy, 'China's Former Security Chief Zhou Yongkang Sentenced to Life Imprisonment' *Wall Street Journal* (New York, 11 June 2015).

trial. Commentators noted a marked physical deterioration in Zhou's physical condition, post-detention.

Philosophically, a major difference between Hong Kong and PRC criminal trials can be viewed in terms of the application of a more "due process" approach in Hong Kong and a determinedly "crime control" model in the PRC. Wong, writing about the "Big Spender" trial in the PRC states:

> Lastly and more fundamentally, as this anatomy of Cheung's case clearly revealed, the PRC judicial authority is less concerned with "technical application" of the rule of law, i.e. attaining due process, than the "correct realization" of the purposes behind law, i.e. attaining substantive justice. In this way, it can be argued that the PRC authority is more interested in the "spirit" of the law (punishing the guilty) than the "letter" of the law (following the rules).[180]

One specific feature of most common law jurisdictions is the use of juries as a constitutional safeguard; giving lay people a participating and "oversight" role in the administration of criminal justice. The extent of jury use varies considerably worldwide and there are many democratic "due process" states which eschew jury use. In Britain all (serious) "indictable" offences are at least potentially triable by a jury at the defendant's behest.[181] Juries in civil cases are rare. The United States (which initially derived much of its criminal justice system from England) has, in theory, the greatest respect for the jury and makes it available for all serious crimes and in many civil cases. However, the use of juries in *practice* is much reduced by the constitutionally approved system of "plea bargaining", whereby defendants are given charging and sentencing discounts in return for their agreement to plead guilty to lesser charges and avoid trial altogether. The jury in the Hong Kong SAR is used in the Court of First Instance and is a generally respected institution. Historically, the Hong Kong jury has been middle class and unrepresentative, given the previous requirement that juries must have proficiency in the English language. This led to a situation in which the pool of potential jurors was relatively small. This is one possible explanation for the non-use of juries in the District Court, even though District Court judges have significant sentencing powers. While the preservation of the jury system in Hong Kong is guaranteed by the Basic Law, there is an argument that *reform*, such as extending the jury franchise to the District Court, could be contested on the grounds of conflict with the Basic Law.

In the PRC the jury is not used. Nor is there any likelihood of its introduction, given the more "civil law" nature of the PRC's legal development. Juries are inconsistent with the Eurocentric civil law tradition, and run counter to Weber's

---

180. KC Wong, 'Understanding PRC Criminal Justice Process: Anatomy of the "Big Spender" Case', op cit, 73.
181. There is now a minor, controversial, exception whereby a judge can dispense with a jury trial where, for example, there is a likelihood of threats to jurors by organised criminals (see Chapter 8).

ideal of "rational" law, administered by disinterested professionals. However, it was reported, in 2014,[182] that:

> Shenzhen authorities have decided to mirror Hong Kong's financial success by adopting a judicial system with Hong Kong nationals serving as jurors in the special economic district of Qianhai.
>
> . . .
>
> There was a primitive form of jury system in rural China after the Communist Party came into power in 1949, but this came to a halt during the Cultural Revolution.

In fact, the proposal was rather more limited than at first appeared since, as the same article later stated:

> The court will only handle civil and commercial lawsuits. Criminal trials will still be based on the mainland's legal system.

Moreover, it appears that even this limited role was to be further restricted by its application only to "commercial contracts signed in Hong Kong".[183]

11.3 The severity of punishment in the criminal justice system

The severity of criminal sanctions is an area in which the systems of Hong Kong and the PRC diverge widely. To some extent this represents the differing stage of socio-economic development of the two societies. Durkheim posited that harsher penalties tend to be associated with "undeveloped" societies in which there is more "sameness", conformity and a more clearly identifiable "collective conscience". As societies become economically more developed, they are characterised by differentiation, interdependence and a focus on the individual. This focus on the individual provides the impetus to punish those who hurt other individuals *but*, at the same time, restrains the severity of punishment of the transgressor, himself an individual.

In historical terms, Britain's move away from capital punishment is relatively recent, with executions still relatively common into the nineteenth century.[184] Nor has the transition to abolition followed a smooth historical progression. Thus:

> By the end of the fifteenth century, English law recognised eight major capital crimes . . . Under the Tudors and Stuarts, many more crimes entered this category. By 1688 there were nearly fifty. During the reign of George II, nearly three dozen more were added, and under George III the total was increased by sixty. The highpoint was

---

182. Q Luo and E Luk, "'HK Jury' Blueprint for Qianhai Cases' *The Standard* (Hong Kong, 1 August 2014).
183. Ibid.
184. Before abolition (introduced on a trial basis in 1965 and subsequently made permanent) various pieces of legislation had reduced the number of capital offences and the mode of execution. The most significant was the Punishment of Death etc Act 1832 (full title: "An Act for abolishing the punishment of death in certain cases and substituting a lesser punishment in lieu thereof").

reached shortly after 1800. One estimate put the number of capital crimes at 223 as late as 1819.[185]

Moreover, while a majority of Members of Parliament, in a "free vote", have supported abolition, opinion polls indicate majority support, within the population as a whole, for the return of capital punishment, at least for some types of homicide.

The retention of capital punishment in much of the (economically developed) United States, with public support, runs counter to Durkheim's hypothesis. Moreover, while Durkheim recognised a second variable, "absolutist government", which might restrict the effect of economic development, the "retentionist" United States is democratic *as well as* economically developed. In practice, indeed, given attitudes to capital punishment in most of Asia and the United States, abolitionism might more accurately be viewed as largely Eurocentric.

Certainly, Hong Kong's approach to crime and punishment is difficult to define in Durkheimian developmental terms. In the latter years of colonial rule, a very rapid shift occurred from rurality to urbanisation and industrial development. Despite this, the Hong Kong SAR imposes relatively harsh criminal sanctions, in comparison with other common law jurisdictions. It would be tempting to ascribe this to the imposition of harsh punishments by a colonial power to maintain order amongst a recalcitrant populace. In reality, however, harsh punishment seems to reflect public sentiment in Hong Kong.[186] When capital punishment for murder was abolished in Britain, for example, this took place in the face of only a narrow majority opposed to the change. Abolition in Hong Kong (*de jure* from 1993 but *de facto*, in line with the approach of the colonial power, since 1966)[187] on the other hand, flew in the face of overwhelming support, in principle, for capital punishment for murder.[188] In June 1976, the Chairman of the Kai Fong Association of Hong Kong and Kowloon districts visited England to lobby for the restoration of the death penalty, arguing that abolition was counter to local custom and tradition and that 99% of Hong Kong people favoured immediate reintroduction of capital punishment. On 26 June 1991, Kingsley Sit moved a motion in the Legislative Council (LegCo) that:

> in view of the increasing concern caused by the present law and order situation, this Council urges the Government to resume immediately the carrying out of the death penalty . . .

---

185. JA McCafferty, *Capital Punishment* (Routledge 2017) 8.
186. The colonial power, for example, did not introduce capital punishment into Hong Kong, but merely changed its *form* from beheading to hanging.
187. Death sentences continued to be handed down by the courts (as statute required) but were routinely commuted by the Governor of the day.
188. In 1972 The Star reported that 90% of those polled supported capital punishment for murderers, while a study at the University of Hong Kong (by Professor Harris) found that 91% of students and 67% of staff supported capital punishment for "deliberate murder".

... it is clearly stated in the law[189] that convicted murderers should be sentenced to death ...

... the Security Branch published an information paper this April. It was revealed that the majority of Hong Kong citizens agree to have capital punsihment resumed. But owing to the constitutional position of Hong Kong vis a vis the United Kingdom, death penalty has not been carried out ...

... a total of 243 convicted murderers' death sentence has been commuted by the Governor in Council since 1966 ...

... in our society, we are not abusing the death penalty but rather the Governor in Council is in abuse by commuting the death sentence.

The Legislative Council did not support the restoration but, instead, favoured a (fundamental) amendment moved by Martin Lee, to replace the death penalty with one of life imprisonment.

The ensuing *de jure* abolition, in April 1993,[190] took place, despite the lack of public support, because of fears of the consequences should capital punishment have remained "on the books" post-1997; not least because capital punishment on the mainland was inflicted for many offences other than murder. A *South China Morning Post* editorial of the time[191] stated:

After 27 years as a legal fiction the death penalty has finally been given the coup de grace. Forty one convicted murderers held in Stanley Prison's Condemned Block will be moved and their sentences commuted to life imprisonment ...

No one has been hanged in Hong Kong since the death penalty was abolished in Britain in 1966. However, because the penalty was retained here, more than 300 people have been condemned to death in that time ...

This anomaly has long been in need of reform ... After the enactment of the Bill of Rights, it became even more unlikely that Hong Kong would bring back the rope ...

... The extra factor which has produced the change, so that the law matches legal practice, has been the approach of 1997. The fear that the future SAR government might be less inclined to leave the death penalty in abeyance left no room for complacency.

In the PRC, only now "catching up" with its own, even more rapid, economic development, harsh penalties remain the norm. The PRC executes far more of its citizens than any other state (indeed as many as the rest of the world combined);[192] nor are these executions for murder alone. There remain dozens of capital offences

---

189. The sentence was mandatory for *murder* (s 2, Offences Against the Person Ordinance (Cap 212)), *treason* (s 2(2), Crimes Ordinance (Cap 200)) and *piracy* (s 19, Crimes Ordinance (Cap 200)).
190. By the Crimes (Amendment) Ordinance [No 24 of 1993].
191. 'Law Matches Reality', *South China Morning Post*, Editorial (Hong Kong, 23 April 1993).
192. Cornell University Law School (CULS) estimates (the precise figure is a "state secret") that there were 3,000 executions in the PRC in 2013: CULS, 'Death Penalty Worldwide: China' (10 April 2014). The Dui Hua Foundation puts the estimated figure for 2013 as 2,400. *The Standard* (Hong Kong, 22 October 2014) reported that executions had fallen to 2,400.

in the PRC[193] and, while some are rarely invoked, others remain actively utilised. The execution level has fallen in the past few years as there is extended provision of legal aid, the recording of interrogations and a mandatory review of sentence procedure. The number of executions remains, however, very high in China by world standards.

Nevertheless, it must be said that, as in Hong Kong, there is significant public support for capital punishment in the PRC; at least for murder. A survey conducted by the Max Plank Institute in 2007/8[194] found that 54% of the population opposed abolition of the death penalty, while only 19.7% supported it. Moreover, for murder, there was 76% support for continuation of the death penalty.

Capital punishment, moreover, is far from being the only harsh "physical" punishment in the PRC. The most notable example was "reform through labour" (used mainly against political dissidents) whereby the convicted person is subject to a harsh physical regime while in prison. The practice of reform through labour was officially abolished in 2013 by a Decision of the Standing Committee of the National People's Congress.[195] However, there is much anecdotal evidence that physical punishment is still inflicted on prisoners, especially followers of the Falun Gong religion. Such practice contrasts with Durkheim's notion of "pure punishment" (the simple removal of liberty) and the modern view in capitalist societies that people go to prison "as punishment" rather than "for punishment". Hong Kong, in principle at least, adopts the "pure punishment" approach. The Correctional Services Department's mission statement talks of:

> [detaining people in] a decent and healthy environment, and providing comprehensive rehabilitative services in a secure, safe, humane and cost-effective manner, so as to enhance the physical and psychological health of prisoners, protect the public, and help reduce crime.[196]

The image of the PRC criminal justice system as an entirely punitive one has been challenged by academics Ng and Xe[197] who write that:

> The emergence of reconciliation in the criminal justice system of China . . . defies the popular perception of the system as a draconian and repressive one that still relies on stiff punishment to achieve deterrence. Chinese-style criminal reconciliation is a highly 'transactional' process that epitomizes the role of money as a form of cure-all compensation.

---

193. The number was reduced, in 2011, from 68 to 55.
194. D Oberwitter and Q Shenghui, *Public Opinion on the Death Penalty in China* (Max Planck Institute for Foreign and International Criminal Law 2009).
195. K Zhui, 'China's Labour Camp System Officially Abolished' *South China Morning Post* (Hong Kong, 29 September 2013).
196. Cited in C Jones and J Vagg, *Criminal Justice in Hong Kong* (Routledge-Cavendish 2007) 596.
197. K Ng and X He, 'The Limits of Legal Commensuration: Blood Money and Negotiated Justice in China', City University of Hong Kong conference paper.

It is, of course, obviously the case that although some of the "compensation" cases cited by the authors were serious (including rape and serious assault) they were offences against fellow citizens, rather than the state.

11.4 Access to justice

It is accepted that a "proper" legal system requires adequate "access". This involves not merely the "right" to legal representation, but the ability to avail oneself of that right in practice. In this regard, the key issues in Hong Kong are seen to be the availability of affordable legal services or, at least, adequate provision of legal aid.

Legal services in Hong Kong are accepted to be expensive. If a client is to be represented by a barrister in court, this is particularly expensive, since the client must first engage the services of a solicitor and *then* pay high charges for the services of an independent barrister. Two factors add to the cost problem: the shortage of lawyers in Hong Kong, especially outside the central business district (CBD) and the high property rentals in the CBD which add hugely to the overheads of solicitors' firms or Bar chambers.

Publicly-funded legal aid is subject to such stringent means-testing[198] that the so-called "sandwich class" are excluded from its ambit in respect of civil disputes or, at the very least, have to pay daunting levels of contribution. The consequence is that most civil litigation is waged by the very rich or the indigent.[199]

In the criminal arena legal aid is available where "in the interests of justice" though significant contributions may be required. However, in Hong Kong's defence, there is significant scrutiny of the legal aid "list" of eligible practitioners, such that legally aided defendants are likely to be represented by competent lawyers. This contrasts markedly with, for example, the United States system: where those represented by "public defenders" are far more likely to be convicted, to strike worse "plea bargains"[200] and to receive the death penalty than their rich, privately represented counterparts.[201]

The cost, as well as the availability, of legal representation, remains problematic in the PRC despite significant moves to improve access to justice in both the civil and criminal law sphere. Private lawyers are expensive in terms of earnings for the majority of PRC citizens and it can still be difficult to engage a lawyer in politically sensitive cases. State-funded legal aid, however, has expanded considerably in recent times. The decision to construct a legal aid system was first made in 1994 and this was followed, in 1996, by two pieces of legislation: the Revised Criminal

---

198. See Chapter 9 for detailed coverage of the legal aid eligibility criteria.
199. N Sarony, 'The Silk Purse' *South China Morning Post* (Hong Kong, 29 April 2011).
200. See, eg, Blumberg, *Criminal Justice* (New Viewpoints 1974).
201. A disproportionate percentage of the black population is incarcerated in America and the death penalty is reserved largely for the poor (see, eg, Amnesty International, *Death by Discrimination–The Continuing Role of Race in Capital Cases* (2003); Human Rights Watch, *Blacks Hit Hardest by Incarceration Policy* (5 May 2008).

Procedure Law of the PRC and the Law on Lawyers which made provision for the provision of, and funding for, limited legal aid/legal assistance. In 2003 the first Regulations on Legal Aid came into force. Currently, legal assistance is administered via a four-tier structure (the vastness of China so often requires both state-wide and local administration). In the smaller "counties" and districts, legal aid centres may be set up. Where this is not practicable legal aid is the responsibility of local "Judicial Bureaux". In "prefectures" and cities legal aid centres are responsible both for the administration and the implementation of legal aid. On a more "centralised" basis, there are legal aid centres in all "provinces" which supervise the administration of legal aid within their jurisdiction. Finally at the over-arching National level, the Ministry of Justice administers a "Centre for Legal Assistance" which supervises the operation of legal aid throughout the whole of China. The basic requirements of legal aid are that it should be available to those who are able to prove they need assistance to safeguard their legal rights and interests and who cannot afford to pay their legal fees. More specifically, in the criminal law sphere,[202] Article 34 of the (revised) Criminal Procedure Law of the PRC[203] states that:

> For public-prosecuted cases, the court can designate a lawyer who provides legal assistance to defend the accused if the accused fails to appoint a defence attorney for economic or other reasons. If the accused fails to appoint a defence attorney because s/he is blind, deaf, mute or a minor, the court should designate a lawyer who provides legal aid to defend the accused. If the accused receives a death penalty, but fails to appoint a defence attorney, the court should designate a lawyer who provides legal aid to defend the accused.

Moreover, the Law on Lawyers[204] states that:

> Citizens who need legal assistance but cannot afford to pay for lawyers' fees may, in accordance with state regulations, seek legal assistance in such matters as supporting the elderly, workplace injuries, criminal lawsuits, state compensation and the granting of pensions for the disabled or survivors of an accident. Lawyers should assume the responsibility of legal assistance and dutifully help those in need in accordance with state regulations.[205]

By 2009, there were more than 3,200 government legal aid institutions throughout the PRC, handling around 500,000 legal aid cases per year.[206] Particular efforts have been made to assist disadvantaged groups, with around 50% of the annual legal aid cases involving farmers and migrant workers. The extension of legal access provision continues apace. In June 2015, *China Daily* reported that, under a new policy

---

202. In this context the PRC has international obligations since it is a signatory to the International Covenant on Civil and Political Rights (ICCPR) which stipulates that anyone charged with a criminal offence has the right to defend himself in person or through a lawyer.
203. Enacted 17 March 1996.
204. Enacted 15 May 1996 but revised 2007 and 2012.
205. Law on Lawyers, Chapter 6.
206. PRC Ministry of Justice, *Legal Aid in China* (2009).

in respect of the filing of complaints, 30% more lawsuits had been filed in May of that year than 12 months previously. Sun Jungong, spokesman for the Supreme People's Court, was quoted as saying that the new policy was to "protect litigation rights of individuals". He added:

> as of May 1, courts at all levels are strictly prohibited from declining to take a case when the action meets legal criteria.
> ... The court has to give the plaintiff a proper cause if it decides not to file the case.[207]

The new policy not only relaxes the rules on filing but also requires that all complaints must be recorded and a receipt issued. This is clearly aimed, in part, at preventing the corrupt refusal to endorse unpopular complaints. Even the rapid expansion of legal aid is seen to be, still, not meeting demand and on July 2 the Ministry of Justice announced a further expansion to support "vulnerable groups".[208] In addition, Vice-Minister Zhao Dacheng announced (in a news briefing):

> Apart from the vulnerable groups, free legal aid will be extended to those involved in civil disputes and criminal cases involving people's livelihoods, such as marriage and family, food safety, education and healthcare.[209]

The provision of legal aid/assistance is financed either by public funds, charitable donations or the rapidly increasing amount of lawyers' "pro bono" work. By way of example, a fund to provide legal aid for senior citizens, announced in June 2006, involved the use of over 2 million yuan raised by public donation,[210] while a free legal aid service for migrant workers, launched in 2007, was the result of a joint collaboration between the United Nations Development Programme, the All China Lawyers' Association and the China International Centre of Economic and Technical Exchange.[211] One problem with the small, local nature of much legal aid is inconsistency of approach. *China Daily* reported in July 2015 that 9% of counties still made no local government provision for legal aid.

The "formal" limitations on legal aid (financial and otherwise) are, however, only part of the problem of legal assistance in the PRC. Further problems arise with regard to the *quality* and *independence* of PRC lawyers.

"Quality" remains an issue not least because the "rebirth" of a legal profession in China is quire recent, post-Mao development. Lawyers, like, judges, had been almost entirely purged in the Mao era and only a handful of lawyers still survived by the mid-1970s. Peng Xuefeng[212] has stated, baldly, that:

---

207. Y Zhang, 'Lawsuits Spike after Rules Eased' *China Daily* (Beijing, 10 June 2015).
208. "Migrant workers, the elderly, women, minors and the disabled" [Y Zhang, 'Vulnerable Groups to Get Free Legal Aid' *China Daily Asia* (Beijing, 3 July 2015)].
209. Reported in *China Daily*, 3 July 2015.
210. Reported by Xinhua News Agency, 30 June 2006.
211. United Nations Development Programme (press release, 4 February 2007).
212. Founder of Dacheng Law Offices, China's largest law firm.

The legal profession was abolished by the government of the PRC in 1957–58, with many lawyers subsequently sent to jail or re-education camps. The government reintroduced the profession in 1979, the same year China established diplomatic relations with the United States. At that time there were only 212 lawyers in the country.[213]

The re-emergence of a legal profession began after the foundation of the Ministry of Justice in 1979 and development, especially in more recent times, has been rapid.[214] A key development has been the professionalisation of lawyers, with a rigorous examinations stage to be completed[215] as well as professional training prior to practice. Numbers have increased dramatically and the "status" of lawyers has been elevated as more high-ranking government officials come with a law background.[216] Nonetheless, it is the civil/commercial side of law which attracts most new entrants for both financial and "other" reasons. Peng Xuefeng[217] states that:

> When [I began my] law firm, lawyers handled primarily criminal and civil litigation. Today, however, the majority of Chinese firms are large, multiservice partnership firms that principally practise corporate law, with specialised practice groups in such areas as corporate finance, international trade and banking.

While, clearly, financial reward is a major attraction of the civil/commercial side of law, such practice is also less troublesome and even, simply, "safer" in an environment where those representing alleged criminals or "enemies of the state" are far from secure from government reprisal. Chen Youxi writes:[218]

> ... depending on their area of practice, lawyers can suffer great constraints in what they can realistically achieve and in the exercise of their rights. This is gradually leading to a bifurcation within the system; between lawyers dealing mostly with civil and commercial matters who benefit from both an increasing ability to exercise their rights and from growing financial rewards; and lawyers who deal with more sensitive administrative and criminal cases, who face often insurmountable challenges, and as a consequence, tend to be much less successful financially and enjoy a much lower status within the legal profession as a whole.

---

213. UCLA Centre for Chinese Studies, 'Modern Legal Profession in China Is Only 35 Years Old' (Los Angeles, 28 January 2014).
214. Between 1997 and 2013 the number of PRC lawyers more than doubled.
215. The China Bar examination (now replaced by the National Judicial Examination) is notoriously difficult with a very low pass rate. There is now only very limited scope to qualify other than via the examination so that overall quality is improving quickly.
216. See C Li, 'The Rise of the Legal Profession in the Chinese Leadership' (2013) 42 China Leadership Monitor 1, 26.
217. Note 212.
218. C Youxi, 'A Tale of Two Cities: The Legal Profession in China' International Bar Association's Human Rights Institute, March 2013.

In other words, while legal practitioners may be part of the same bar association and work within the same city, they are actually living and working in two separate and different worlds, depending on the nature of their practice. The outcome is that the brightest and most capable lawyers tend to refrain from handling precisely those types of cases where a lawyer can make a difference in the protection of fundamental rights . . .

. . . criminal cases and administrative litigation cases to a large extent remain less rewarding financially and are more risky from a professional point of view, and thus they fail to appeal to many successful and capable lawyers.

Overall, the role of defence lawyers at pre-trial stage is essentially a passive one. There is little they can do before the case goes to trial . . .

. . . The collection of evidence remains one of the most (and potentially dangerous) aspects of the defence counsel's work. This is due to two main reasons. First, the police and the prosecutors tend to consider the collection of evidence by lawyers more as a 'nuisance' than as a statutory right of the lawyer, and therefore might create obstacles. Secondly, and more importantly, the lawyer's right to collect evidence and testimonies is subject to the important limitations set out under Article 42 of the Criminal Procedure Law and Articles 306 and 307 of the Criminal Code of the PRC (the 'Criminal Code').

Article 306 . . . punishes a legal defender for 'helping others' to destroy or forge evidence . . .

Article 307 punishes anyone who . . . obstructs a witness from giving testimony, but also anyone who 'instigates another person to give false testimony' . . .

These provisions seem, on the face of it, to be just and fair . . . but the crucial fact is that these provisions have been misused in China, to the point of becoming prejudicial to the defence counsel's ability to build and argue a case.

. . . the defence lawyer may be in a difficult position of knowing that . . . producing a witness statement that differs from what was said to the police or the prosecutor may mean that a lawyer is held liable under Article 306 . . . Li Zhuang, a top criminal defence lawyer, was disbarred and imprisoned for a year and a half for allegedly advising his client . . . to challenge prosecution evidence . . .

'Weiquan' lawyers . . . is a term used to identify a group of practitioners who have developed profiles as 'human rights' or 'public interest' lawyers . . .

. . . weiquan lawyers tend to be seen by the state at best as a nuisance; and at worst, as a threat in cases where the particular group the lawyer is defending has been labelled an 'enemy of the state', or is being accused of other crimes such as 'subversion of state power' or 'revealing state secrets'. In these cases, the weiquan lawyer treads a dangerous path, one where the mere decision of defending such a case . . . may put him on the receiving end of sanctions such as disbarment, or failure to renew the licence.[219]

---

219. Ibid, 3–18.

Comment

Youxi's article highlights the differences between form and substance in the PRC criminal justice system. There is a "right" to legal representation but it is, practically, circumscribed. While China possesses lawyers of ability, many of these steer away from representing those disapproved of by the state, because it doesn't pay and it is risky.

The risks should not be underestimated. In December 2009, the *Far Eastern Economic Review* featured a harrowing account of the treatment (including arrest, torture and "disappearance") of PRC human rights lawyers such as Chen Guancheng, Gao Zhisheng, and Hu Jia.[220] At around the same time, Amnesty International took up the case of Huang Qi, imprisoned for "unlawfully holding state secrets" after his legal support for victims of the 2008 Sichuan earthquake.[221] More recently, in 2011, the *South China Morning Post (SCMP)*[222] reported an increase in the repression of dissidents and their legal advisers. The *SCMP* article reported on the fate of "respected legal advocate", Fan Yafeng. It stated that:

> He was tortured for nine days and threatened with 20 years in prison for allegedly engaging in ilegal business practices and subversion.
>
> Released almost two weeks later, the normally fearless legal expert was a broken man . . .
>
> One expert on human rights said the frightened lawyer was number 1 on a list of some 20 lawyers and countless activists who were targeted . . .
>
> Apart from going silent, some lawyers have started to turn down cases.

More recently still, in 2015, *The Guardian* newspaper reported that:

> On 9 July Chinese security services launched what observers describe as an unprecedented offensive against the country's outspoken 'rights defence' movement, a network of lawyers known for taking on politically sensitive cases.
>
> Scores of lawyers and their associates were detained or interrogated in what activists believe is a co-ordinated attempt to stamp out opposition to the Communist Party.
>
> Many were subsequently released after being warned not to speak out, but more than 20 activists, lawyers and legal staff remain in detention, with some being held in undisclosed locations.[223]

---

220. See J Cohen and E Pils, 'The Fate of China's Rights Lawyers' *Far Eastern Economic Review* (Hong Kong, 4 December 2009). See also T Branigan, 'China Accused of "All Out Attack" on Lawyers' *The Guardian* (London, 8 June 2009).
221. Amnesty International, 'China Must Free Activist Who Defended Earthquake Victims', 23 November 2009.
222. P Mooney, 'Silence of the Dissidents' *South China Morning Post* (Hong Kong, 4 July 2011).
223. T Phillips, 'Families of China's "Disappeared" Say Country Is a Place of Fear and Panic' *The Guardian* (London, 31 August 2015). The story was a follow-up to a previous Phillips article, 'At Least Six Missing after Clampdown on Human Rights Lawyers in China' *The Guardian* (London, 21 July 2015).

Lawyers, moreover, may feel that the risk involved in defending unpopular causes is not justified given little likelihood of success. A stark example is provided by Zhang Sizhi, a retired defence lawyer, who spent 25 years defending accused persons . . . and never won a case![224]

"Independence" is a serious issue in respect of the legal profession, with both direct and indirect restraints. Obviously the threats already referred to discourage the vigorous support of "unpopular" causes. There are, though, also formal constraints on lawyers' independence. Although, once obtained, a practising certificate permits practice anywhere within the PRC, it is subject to annual review. The decision whether or not to renew is made by the local bureau of justice and not the bar association so, while the 2008 Lawyers Law requires that lawyers 'safeguard the legal rights and interests of their clients', the threat of licence revocation might well evoke caution. Moreover, since lawyers are required to practise within a firm (rather than solely) there is a further restraint in that firms are subject to an annual registration renewal system. Tania Branigan[225] illustrates the problem in writing that:

> [In 2009 . . .] At least 17 rights defence lawyers did not receive the new licences they needed at the end of last month, in effect disbarring them. Three firms were also denied approval, affecting more lawyers.

Moves towards greater independence for lawyers have been slow, despite the increasing representation of those with a law background within the PRC government. Li[226] writes:

> Critics of China's legal development are cynical about the growing numbers of legal professionals in the CCP leadership . . . because the new leadership has neither loosened party control over the legal profession nor pursued judicial independence[227] . . .
>
> The paradoxical relationship between the demands of advanced legal reform and continued CCP interference in the legal system—the growing representation of law degree holders and the regime's harsh treatment of independent lawyers and NGO activists—is a defining characteristic of present-day Chinese politics. China's future will hinge, to a large degree, on whether the continued development of legal professionalism and constitutionalism can resolve this impasse.[228]

Li appears rather pessimistic on the issue of lawyers' independence and such pessimism is endorsed by Chen Youxi,[229] who writes that:

---

224. See M O'Neill, 'Losing Hope: The Defence Lawyer Who Always Loses' *South China Morning Post* (London, 28 February 2010).
225. T Branigan, 'China Accused of "All Out Attack" on Lawyers' *The Guardian* (London, 8 June 2009).
226. C Li, 'The Rise of the Legal Profession in the Chinese Leadership', China Leadership Monitor No 42.
227. Ibid 12.
228. Ibid 23.
229. C Youxi, 'A Tale of Two Cities: The Legal Profession in China' (n 217).

some of the signals in recent years seem to point to a ... direction ... in which lawyers will continue to be seen as having first and foremost an obligation to serve the interest of the state ... the system has still not found viable ways to resolve the conflict between the role of the lawyer depicted in the Lawyers Law and the need to achieve overarching objectives like social stability, fighting crime and protecting the 'socialist legal system'.[230]

Professional independence now appears to be on the back foot, as plans are announced to introduce "political commissars" into all "professional groups" (including lawyers) in Tianjin, apparently as a pilot scheme. The commissars will reportedly act as "idealogical supervisors".[231] Moreover, as recently as 2012, the PRC Ministry of Justice introduced a pre-admission oath for entry to the legal profession which described "the sacred duties of a legal worker for socialism with Chinese characteristics".

Most chilling of all, under the increasingly draconian rule of Xi Jinping, is the charge of "subversion of state power" (the maximum sentence for which is life imprisonment) levelled against a group of human rights lawyers in January 2016.[232] Even more recently, *The Guardian*[233] has drawn attention to the immense physical changes in the physical appearance of human rights lawyer Li Heping after two years in custody during which he was tried in secret (for "subversion of state power") and given a "suspended sentence".[234]

11.4.1 Alternatives to litigation

Given the supposed Confucian preference for compromise rather than the "zero sum" conflict of the common law "adversarial" system,[235] it might be thought that China could lead the field in arbitration and other forms of alternative dispute resolution in the civil law[236] area. In reality the Confucian/adversarial dichotomy is over-simplistic, since movements towards civil justice reform in Britain and, later, Hong Kong have eroded the adversarial nature of litigation while, at the same time, some writers have expressed doubt as to the Chinese dislike of legal conflict.[237] Nevertheless, in

---

230. Ibid 19.
231. See C-y Yuk and E Li, 'Lawyers Latest Front in Ideological War' *South China Morning Post* (Hong Kong, 19 May 2017).
232. Reported in *The Guardian* (London, 14 January 2016).
233. T Phillips, '"Emaciated, Unrecognisable": China Releases Human Rights Lawyer from Custody' *The Guardian* (London, 10 May 2017).
234. The very high level of continuing "supervision" for Li makes the suspended sentence a very different concept from, for example, its British variant.
235. In theoretical terms this would align with the "relational" view of contract as opposed to the adversarial one: see D Campbell (ed), *The Relational Theory of Contract: Selected Works of Ian Macneil* (Sweet & Maxwell 2001). Put simply, parties (especially long-standing ones) would rather get along and solve problems amicably than begin an acrimonious dispute.
236. Ie, non-criminal law.
237. See Fu Hualing reference at footnote 241. It is suggested that an increasing preference for litigation is the product of the transition from rural to urban society, whereby local community connections

both Hong Kong and the PRC there has been significant development in the area of "alternative dispute resolution" (ADR) which encompasses, chiefly, arbitration and mediation.[238] There are two somewhat conflicting views of ADR; one that it provides an alternative to formal litigation to those who might prefer ADR's less formal procedures, more specialised adjudicators, speedier processes, etc, and the other that it is mere cost-cutting, providing a second-best system for those "denied justice" by the lack of formal legal aid. In Britain there has been a fierce dispute between the judicial champion of civil justice reform, Lord Woolf, and Professor Hazel Genn; the latter concluding that "diversion" from formal legal procedures frequently constitutes a denial of justice.[239] Interestingly, that theme has been taken up *in relation to China* by Pissler.[240]

In Hong Kong, ADR is a significant "growth area"[241] with the purported aim of making Hong Kong a regional hub for arbitration in particular, and with a greatly increased focus on the training and benchmarking of arbitrators and mediators. First Chief Justice Andrew Li lauded the development of mediation in several speeches at the Opening of the Hong Kong Legal Year and elsewhere. Li's views were endorsed by then Secretary for Justice, Wong Yung Lan, and funding was made available (and has continued to be available) for mediation, especially in the area of family law. Andrew Li's successor as Chief Justice, Geoffrey Ma, has continued the support for mediation at the highest level. Of course cynics might argue, along "Genn" lines, that the real agenda is cost-cutting, with ADR replacing more time-consuming and expensive trial court time and deflecting attention from Hong Kong's deficiencies in the administration of legal aid and affordable private legal services. The funding of centres to assist "litigants in person" may also be seen in this light, since the growth of litigation in person in Hong Kong is undoubtedly the result of the inability of the "sandwich class" to afford to pay for professional legal representation.

ADR in the PRC is said to have a significant cultural basis so that, while current rules and procedures provide for formalised ADR structures, such approaches are deeply rooted in Chinese history.[242] Former Secretary for Justice, Wong Yan Lung, described a move (back) to mediation in Hong Kong as "distinctly Asian" and "a process of cultural awakening". Chen[243] posits the two competing forms of social regulation in Chinese feudal society: "Legalism" and Confucianism. Legalism advocated the widespread use of formal laws ("*fa*") to regulate behaviour; Confucianism,

---

are weakened.
238. For a more detailed consideration, see Chapter 10.
239. H Genn, *Judging Civil Justice* (Cambridge 2010) (60th Hamlyn Lectures 2008). See also M Zander, *The State of Justice* (51st Hamlyn Lectures, 1999).
240. KB Pissler, *Mediation in China: Threat to the Rule of Law?* (Oxford University Press, Oxford, 2012).
241. See Chapter 10.
242. Fu Hualing, however, has questioned the "popular belief" in English literature that the Chinese are "generally non-litigious people": Fu Hualing, 'Understanding People's Mediation in Post-Mao China' 6(2) *Journal of Asian Law* (Spring 1993).
243. A Chen, *An Introduction to the Legal System of the PRC* (n 2).

on the other hand, emphasised "education, persuasion and moral example" ("*li*").[244] Indeed, thought the Confucians, an over-emphasis on formality would erode the moral basis of social regulation. Some echoes of this approach can be seen in the views, many years later, of Gramsci[245] and the "hegemonic" theorists, who saw the function of law as *primarily* one of ideological education. Be that as it may, Chen[246] states that:

> Confucianism did triumph over Legalism in the sense that it was officially accepted as the state philosophy ... and remained the dominant ideology in Chinese society until the fall of the Qing dynasty in this century.[247]

Moreover, while under the Cultural Revolution period of Chairman Mao, Confucianism was reviled as "revisionist", Chen adds that:

> [the] paternalistic image of the ruler or the government [in Confucianism] provides a key to understanding not only political phenomena in traditional China but also developments in modern China.[248]

Far from being perceived as "revisionist" by current PRC leaders, Confucianism, as Chen implies, is now fully "rehabilitated". Indeed, it is not uncommon for senior Communist Party officials to decry the confrontational tactics of Hong Kong democrats and lament their departure from traditional Confucian conformism.

Modern ADR in the PRC is regulated by various pieces of legislation. The Arbitration Law of the PRC, 1995, has produced a "unified" system of arbitration throughout China. It is, in form at least, in conformity with international standards. The system is a voluntary one, with arbitration committees having no power to hear disputes unless at least one party makes an application. Moreover, while the "system" (procedure) of arbitration is intended to be unified, the individual arbitration agencies should operate independently of one another and be free of government pressure. Further, the arbitration agencies are separate from the formal court structure, though courts retain a supervisory jurisdiction. Just as in the (soon to change) Hong Kong system, procedure in the PRC differs as between domestic and "foreign" arbitrations, with the former having a greater potential for "variation" by the PRC courts. The involvement of the courts is problematic; foreign businesses have far greater confidence in arbitrations conducted under CIETAC[249] rules than litigation in the "variable" PRC court system. The clear benefits, at least at this stage in China's legal development, of having clear, consistent rules, justify the refusal of the PRC to allow internal "ad hoc" arbitrations.[250] This fact, however, is one of the

---

244. Ibid 8.
245. See, eg, A Gramsci, *Prison Notebooks Volumes 1 & 2* (Columbia University Press 2010 and 2011).
246. *An Introduction to the Legal System of the PRC* (n 2).
247. Ibid 11.
248. Ibid.
249. China International Economic and Trade Arbitration Commission (CIETAC).
250. See Chapter 10 for explanation.

main reasons for the confusion over the enforceability of Hong Kong arbitration in the PRC, especially those of an "ad hoc" nature.[251] Generally, however, "foreign" arbitrations (ie where one party is from outside the PRC) are both enforceable and, increasingly, enforced in China. With the introduction of the Civil Procedure Law, in 2012, courts should no longer refuse enforcement based on "insufficient evidence" or "misapplication of the law" and should intervene only in cases of malfeasance on the part of parties or arbitrator. The assurance of a proper system of arbitration (as CIETAC rules ensure) and adequate enforcement (by the PRC courts if necessary) is vital to ensure China's commercial development.

Arbitration in China has grown enormously in a short time:

> The People's Republic of China (PRC) now conducts more arbitrations than any other country and has become one of the most important places for commercial arbitrations in the world . . . The . . . China International Economic and Trade Arbitration Commission (CIETAC) . . . is the world's leading arbitration institution in terms of the number of cases handled; in 2008 alone, CIETAC accepted 1,230 cases for arbitration.[252]

It is clear that the variable quality of the PRC courts "proper" is a factor in the rapid development of arbitration in China, as well as other forms of ADR. The increasing importance of arbitration in China has led, however, to one unfortunate development; the CIETAC "schism". The reason for the schism was dissatisfaction in two "sub-commission" areas (Shenzhen and Shanghai) with new CIETAC rules introduced in 2012.[253] These rules stipulate that *unless* an arbitration agreement specifies one of the sub-commissions as the arbitration administrator, administration would be by CIETAC Beijing. Previously, a claimant was entitled to submit a dispute to Beijing *or* one of the two sub-commissions. The likely loss of arbitration business irked Shenzhen and Shanghai which broke away to form, respectively, the Shenzhen Court of International Arbitration (SCIA)[254] and the Shanghai International Arbitration Centre (SHIAC).[255] Since CIETAC (Beijing) does not recognise the "breakaway" sub-commissions,[256] a period of uncertainty has arisen which can only hinder China's aim of extending the use of arbitration. New CIETAC rules of 2015 offer something of a compromise in permitting the hearing of arbitrations in Shenzhen and Shanghai by newly constituted CIETAC sub-commissions *but* do not recognise the two breakaway centres. It appears that arbitrations heard in

---

251. As a "New York Convention" signatory, the PRC has enforced "foreign" ad hoc arbitrations. Confusion remained because of the "special relationship" between Hong Kong and the PRC. The matter now appears to be resolved (see further discussion in Chapter 12).
252. RT Tung, *International Arbitration, Litigation and Dispute Resolution* (Mayer Brown 2010).
253. Effective from 1 May 2012.
254. More fully the South China International Economic and Trade Arbitration Commission.
255. More fully the Shanghai International Economic and Trade Arbitration Commission.
256. It does not recognise their right to accept and *administer* CIETAC arbitrations though the two locations can be the "geographic venue" for an arbitration.

the two centres will be recognised *locally* but not necessarily elsewhere; a far from satisfactory situation.

Given the uncertainties in respect of recognition and enforcement, China remains, it is fair to say, an unpopular venue for arbitration, at least for non-PRC parties. China's increasing economic "muscle" means, however, that more parties agree to Chinese mediation, albeit reluctantly.[257] In short, therefore, the growth of arbitration is supported by government and the judicial system in both the PRC and Hong Kong but the latter remains a more popular forum where parties have a genuine choice.

Mediation, the "encouragement" of parties to reach a settlement, has a lengthy history in China but is now expanding in scope. Mediation is, in fact, in its various forms, somewhat more developed in the PRC than in Hong Kong and has clear judicial *and* political support. The Second Amendment of the Civil Procedure Law specifically encourages the principle of "mediation first".[258] However, some types of "mediation" in the PRC would not be recognised as such in the common law world. Of these types, a number are governed by statutory rules.

The first type of mediation, and that with the longest history, is "civil mediation" (People's mediation"); originating in ancient China, at its peak in the 1930s, and resurrected with the accession to power of the Chinese Communist Party in the 1950s. The PRC Constitution states that:

> People's Mediation Committees are working committees under grassroots autonomous organisations—Residents Committees, Villagers Committees—whose mission is to mediate civil disputes.[259]

These committees act as a supplement to, and often a substitute for, the formal judicial system; encouraging citizens to resolve their own disputes without recourse to the courts. Yet, while the resolution of a private dispute is "personal" in nature, mediation also serves what Tappan describes as the "educative-moralizing function of law",[260] since Article 5 of the Regulations for the Organisation of People's Mediation Committees states that:

> The mission of People's Mediation Committees is to mediate civil disputes and, through such mediation, publicise laws, regulations, rules and policies and educate citizens to abide by laws and respect universally accepted morals.

It is clear that the People's Mediation Committees are seen as having the potential to "divert" cases from the formal court system but also to "defuse" disputes which would otherwise have the potential to create civil unrest at a local level. Indeed, the Committees are instructed, as part of their mission, *not* to be passive but actively to

---

257. D Harrison, 'Arbitration in China: Get Used to It' (Harris and Moure blog, 22 September 2011).
258. Article 122.
259. Article 111. In 2010 the People's Mediation Law was enacted.
260. In P Tappan, *Crime Justice and Correction* (McGraw-Hill New York 1960) 247.

seek to reduce the scale of disputes and to prevent them from "escalating". However, as with ADR in general, the principle is that of "voluntariness"; if a party wishes to have his "day in court" he cannot be forced into mediation instead.

It can be seen that the role of People's Mediator is an important one. The Mediator is expected to be familiar with legal and "policy" issues and, above all, to be impartial. The Mediator is assisted by a "Judicial Assistant", working for the local "grassroots" court, who may assist the training of the Mediator and broaden his expertise by, for example, inviting him to sit on cases involving "in-court mediation".

The second, and more formal, type of mediation is "judicial mediation". Here the rules are governed primarily by the Law on Civil Procedures of the PRC (CPL). Under Article 86 of the legislation, mediating courts are to be presided over by a single judge or a mediating panel. Essentially, mediation should be the first "port of call" and only in the absence of mediated agreement should the court move into "trial" mode. The CPL states that:

> When handling civil cases, courts of law should, based on consent of the litigants, mediate the cases on the merits of the cases themselves.[261]

The mediation should, as far as possible, take place in court. In addition to the parties and listed witnesses, the court may (under Article 87) invite other parties to assist. Article 88 emphasises that any mediation agreement must be consented to by both parties and may not be imposed by the court. Where a mutual agreement has been reached this should be reflected in a "mediation document", signed by the judge and the clerk and bearing the court's official seal. The document should briefly explain the nature of the dispute and the result of the mediation.[262] In exceptional circumstances,[263] the mediation document may be dispensed with.[264] Once the parties have agreed the mediation, normally by signing the mediation document delivered to them, it is binding and can be challenged only by proof that the agreement was not voluntarily consented to or is illegal.

Judicial mediation differs from common law principles in that the judge "undertakes the role of mediator and ultimate adjudicator"[265] in the same dispute. While, in theory, the outcome is based on the parties' consent, the alternative (that parties may have to litigate before the same judge)[266] "encourages" such consent.

A third type of mediation in the PRC is "Administrative mediation". Such mediation involves "out of court" mediation conducted in lower-level governments

---

261. Article 35.
262. Article 89.
263. Eg, where a divorce petition has been made but "reunion" has been achieved via mediation.
264. Article 90.
265. M Tai and D McDonald, 'Judicial Mediation in China Explained' (Herbert Smith Freehills, 30 July 2012).
266. Article 91 of the Civil Procedure Law states that a court should "adjudicate in a timely fashion" if mediation fails.

(villages, townships) or by government departments. These usually involve economic or labour disputes.

Finally, the PRC recognises mediation via mediation centres to which parties have voluntarily brought their dispute, or "Arbitration mediation", whereby parties agree to mediate and recourse to a full-blown arbitration only occurs where the mediation fails.[267]

It can be seen that mediation is well-recognised in the PRC and in many ways better established than in Hong Kong. It has become an almost inevitable consequence of the rapidly escalating number of legal disputes in China, much of it the result of rapid economic development.[268] It also takes more different forms though, as stated above, some of these would not be recognisable as mediation in the common law world.

11.5 The interpretation of legislation

In the area of statutory interpretation there are significant differences between the rules and procedures of Hong Kong's common law system and that of the PRC. It is axiomatic in most common law jurisdictions that the "interpretation" (as opposed to the enactment) of legislation is a job for the judiciary. Indeed, interpretation by the courts may be seen as a facet of the separation of powers.[269] In adopting interpretative techniques the common law courts must endeavour to do no more than "interpret" and to leave the function of "enactment" to the legislature.[270] This is sometimes easier said than done and judicial approaches vary. Some traditionalists insist on not going outside "the text"; a strict application of the words used. Even here, however, there is room for "context" since it is a principle of interpretation that a statute must be read as a whole and words should not be given a meaning incompatible with the statute as a whole. To take a simple example, the (singular) word "he" will generally be taken to include the feminine (*and* the plural). This is true, though, unless the *context* otherwise requires. Some sexual offences, for example, have been viewed as capable of commission only by a man against a woman;[271] conspiracies may only be committed by more than one person, etc.

More "liberal" judges may give greater emphasis to the apparent "purpose" of an enactment and its legislative history. The starting point, however, for most common law judges, is the *wording* of a statute. Where this is clear and capable of only one meaning, the statute will be so construed. In cases of ambiguity, courts may look at

---

267. See CIETAC Arbitration Rules Article 45: Combination of Conciliation with Arbitration.
268. There are around nine million "people's mediation" cases per year (96% of them settled) and 10 million "judicial mediations" (two million of them settled).
269. See 11.2.2.
270. For much fuller discussion, see Chapter 4.
271. In Hong Kong "rape" can only be committed by a man against a woman (though reform is under consideration). In England recognition of "rape" of a man is comparatively recent. Moreover, given an extended definition of rape, commission of rape by a *woman* is also possible in Irish law.

finding the more "sensible" meaning or the one which appears most to conform to the *purpose* of the legislation. Very exceptionally, a court may decline to follow the most obvious meaning when the result would be absurd, or where the result appears to run counter to the legislature's intention. Even here, the court will strive to find a possible, albeit unlikely, construction more in keeping with the sense or purpose of the legislation. Re-wording legislation, or "filling in gaps" to produce a result more in keeping with the legislature's perceived "intention", is generally frowned upon.[272]

Statutory interpretation in the PRC context is very different. Indeed:

> Under Chinese law, there is no firm distinction between interpretation and amendment of laws.[273]

Goodstadt[274] excellently summarises the position with reference to the "right of abode" interpretation. Chinese officials, he said, focusing on the socio-political implications of the CFA interpretation:

> had failed to comprehend that, in Hong Kong, the rule of law was expected to protect the individual's rights regardless of the administration's priorities or the community's convenience.[275]

No common lawyer, reading the latest NPC Standing Committee (NPCSC) "interpretation" of the Basic Law (on oath-taking)[276] would recognise it as such. Former HKU Dean of Law, Professor Johannes Chan,[277] described the NPCSC "interpretation" as "making a new law, which the Standing Committee cannot do."[278]

First and foremost, interpretation is a "political" function. Essentially, while rules and practices are complex, the basic proposition is that it is the body which *creates* a law in the PRC which has the ultimate power to *interpret* it. To be more specific, firstly, by legislation (the "Resolution"), in 1989:

> In cases where the limits of articles of laws and decrees need to be further defined or additional stipulations need to be made, the Standing Committee of the National

---

272. Lord Denning spoke of "filling in the gaps" to make better sense of legislation in his Court of Appeal minority judgment in *Magor v St Mellons and Newport Corporation* [1950] 2 All ER 1226. He was rebuked for this by Lord Simonds in the House of Lords in the same case [1951] 2 All ER 839. Simonds described filling in the gaps as a "naked usurpation of the legislative function under the thin guise of interpretation".
273. C Lai and C Lo, *From Nowhere to Nowhere: Constitutional Development Hong Kong (1997–2007)* (Civic Exchange 2007) 29.
274. LF Goodstadt, 'Prospects for the Rule of Law: The Political Dimension' in S Tsang (ed), *Judicial Independence and the Rule of Law in Hong Kong* (Hong Kong University Press 2001).
275. Ibid 194.
276. For further discussion, see Chapter 4.
277. Chan is unpopular with the pro-establishment camp and his "alleged" support for "Occupy Central" led to the rejection of his expected pro-vice chancellorship by HKU's Council.
278. J Ng, 'Detailed Beijing Ruling Amounts to a New Law' *South China Morning Post* (Hong Kong, 6 November 2016).

People's Congress shall provide interpretations or make stipulations by means of decrees.[279]

However, the Supreme People's Court has the power to interpret laws where their specific application is relevant to court trials. Moreover, the Supreme People's Procuratorate (Prosecution Department) has the power of interpretation in respect of laws relating specifically to the work of the Procuratorate.

Further, the State Council may interpret points of law relevant to its work of an administrative (rather than judicial or prosecution) nature.

Finally, at a local level, the Standing Committee of the Local People's Congress may interpret provisions in local statutory rules enacted by it, where clarification or addition is required.[280]

The key agents of interpretation, therefore, are the Standing Committee of the NPC, the Supreme People's Court and the Supreme People's Procuratorate. From the perspective of the Hong Kong SAR it is the role of the Standing Committee of the NPC which is crucial since it has the ultimate power of interpretation of Hong Kong's Basic Law (a "basic law" of the PRC).[281]

These rules on interpretation are now supplemented by provisions in the Legislation Law of the PRC, enacted in 2000. This emphasises the primacy of the NPC Standing Committee[282] by stating that:

> The power to interpret a national law shall vest in the Standing Committee of the NPC.[283]
>
> ... Legislative interpretation issued by the Standing Committee of the NPC shall have the same force as national law.[284]

Under Article 43 of the Legislation Law a long list of those bodies entitled to ask for an interpretation by the Standing Committee of the NPC is stipulated. These include the State Council, the Central Military Committee, the Supreme People's Court, the Supreme People's Procuratorate, special committees of the Standing Committee of the NPC, and various local Standing Committees of the People's Congress. It appears that the emphasis on the primacy of the Standing Committee of the NPC has not abolished the right of interpretation enjoyed by the various bodies stipulated in the 1981 "Resolution".[285]

Just as important as the *power* of interpretation of PRC legislation is the *nature* of the "interpretative" function in the PRC. This is clearly far broader than in the

---

279. NPC Standing Committee's Resolution on Strengthening the Work of Interpretation of Laws.
280. For further detail, see A Chen, *An Introduction to the Legal System of the PRC* (n 2) 119.
281. Indeed, a disproportionate amount of the Standing Committee's interpretative time has been spent on interpreting the Basic Laws of Hong Kong and Macau.
282. Chen (n 2) states that there was debate as to whether interpretative functions should be transferred to the courts.
283. Article 42.
284. Article 47.
285. See Chen (n 2) 123.

Hong Kong SAR and elsewhere in the common law world. As has been suggested, the common law approach is to interpret but not to augment a statutory text. The 1981 "Resolution" clearly permits the NPC Standing Committee to "supplement" existing legislation where necessary. Under the Legislation Law there is no reference to supplementing legislation. Article 42 refers to the Standing Committee making an interpretation if:

(1) the specific meaning of a provision needs to be further defined; or
(2) after its enactment, new developments make it necessary to define the basis on which to apply the law.

In practice, though, the NPC Standing Committee has continued to make interpretations which are "supplemental" in nature. Certainly "interpretations" of the Hong Kong Basic Law have included "additions", as have interpretations of the PRC Criminal Code. To take just one example, that of the duration of the term of office of Hong Kong's Chief Executive, the Basic Law *appears* clear. Article 46 states that:

> The term of office of the Chief Executive of the Hong Kong SAR shall be five years. He or she may serve for not more than two consecutive terms.

On the resignation of first Chief Executive, Tung Chee Hwa, following massive street protests against his administration,[286] it fell to be determined how long his successor, Donald Tsang, could remain in office. The words of Article 46 appear clear; the maximum term would be 10 years from his appointment. An alternative suggestion, that his first term would be constituted by his completing Tung's (second) term of office, was initially rejected by then Secretary for Justice, Elsie Leung, on the basis that the words were clear. However, following publicly expressed views to the contrary by "mainland legal scholars",[287] Tsang's government asked the NPC Standing Committee to interpret Article 46. The Standing Committee of the NPC (SCNPC) made an "interpretation" which elided Articles 46 and 53 (concerned with the situation where the Chief Executive's functions are temporarily fulfilled by a deputy (the Chief Secretary, Financial Secretary etc) or, in the case of longer absence, pending the appointment of a new Chief Executive) and defined Tsang's first term as that necessary to complete Tung's term. The NPCSC stated:

> in the event that the office of Chief Executive becomes vacant as he (she) fails to serve the full term of office of five years as prescribed by Article 46 of the Basic Law . . . the term of office of the new Chief Executive shall be the remainder of the previous Chief Executive . . .

---

286. Tung pleaded ill health but very soon made a full recovery.
287. The assumption is that, given Tsang's previous allegiance to the colonial administration, a "trial period" was preferred by Beijing.

The interpretation is hardly convincing to a common lawyer, running together disparate rules on the term of office and method of election of the Chief Executive.[288] The rationale, as espoused by an apologetic Elsie Leung, was that this was a civil law "purposive" interpretation deriving from a PRC system which recognises specified "term lengths". An alternative "purposive" explanation for the SCNPC interpretation has been offered by Suzanne Pepper who has always maintained that the Basic Law is intended to run for 50 years *and no more*. This, therefore, in the Pepper view, must tie in exactly with 10 five-year Chief Executive terms of office.[289] There may have been other considerations in limiting the length of Tsang's (first) term; as with all issues of interpretation in the PRC, one needs to recognise the "political" element and the basic premise that there is no "primacy of law" in the Chinese legal system.[290]

11.6 The citizen and the "state"

Citizens in Hong Kong have guaranteed rights to bring legal actions against the government where their rights have been infringed. The Basic Law not merely guarantees a great number of rights to its citizens but provides for those citizens a right of redress against the Hong Kong government should such rights be infringed. In addition to the general proposition that:

> In civil or criminal proceedings in the Hong Kong SAR, the principles previously applied in Hong Kong and the rights previously enjoyed by parties to proceedings shall be maintained.[291]

Specific reference is made, in Article 35 of the Basic Law, to the fact that:

> Hong Kong residents shall have the right to institute legal proceedings in the courts against the acts of the executive authorities and their personnel.

This right, exercised against the government via "judicial review", is a very real one. Hong Kong judges are certainly not "rubber stampers" and have taken a genuinely impartial line in respect of cases brought by individuals against the Hong Kong government.[292]

Limited power for individuals to bring action against the state now exists in the PRC but it is circumscribed, in practice if not in theory. Commentators have seen the extension of citizens' rights against the state largely in "symbolic" terms; seeking to provide a forum for the airing of grievances as a "safer" alternative to more radical

---
288. The latter provided for in Annex 1 of the Basic Law.
289. See Chapter 1 at 1.12 for fuller discussion of the Pepper (and Morris) view.
290. An obvious explanation is that the PRC leaders did not want 10 years of Tsang. That view may have been shared by Hong Kong citizens until the succession of the immensely unpopular CY Leung.
291. Article 87, Basic Law.
292. See statistical information on the Court of Final Appeal compiled by Professor Simon Young, in Young and Ghai (eds), *Hong Kong's Court of Final Appeal: The Development of the Law in China's Hong Kong* (Cambridge University Press 2014), also referred to in Chapters 4 and 7.

opposition but generally ineffective in protecting the individual against government impropriety. Palmer[293] describes the legislative reform of the introduction of the Administrative Litigation Law (ALL) and other innovations to provide "government according to law" but concludes that:

> The People's Republic in the post-Mao era has revived and developed a broad range of systems for controlling and making accountable administrative conduct. Overall, however, they have been of limited effectiveness in challenging the conduct of the State—which, in China, has long been seen as entitled to enjoy strong powers in administering the country.[294]

He further points out that judicial practice in administrative proceedings has increasingly "diverted" procedure from confrontation to *de facto* judicial mediation, with the avowed goal of a "harmonious society".[295] He concludes, however, that: "social control has been a significant dimension of China's transformation."[296]

11.7 Intellectual property rights

An area in which the PRC differs markedly from Hong Kong is the recognition of intellectual property (IP) rights. There *are* legal protections but they are ignored more frequently in China than elsewhere. Friedmann[297] advises that "your intellectual property is a high risk factor in China". He adds that, with the exception of copyright, "If you do not register your intellectual property rights . . . in China, you are unprotected and it makes it near impossible to stop counterfeiters." Friedmann advises registration of all IP rights (including copyright), the establishment of clear contractual duties to observe IP rights, and the setting aside of sufficient company funds to "protect and enforce" IP rights. While similarly pessimistic views have been expressed elsewhere in the past,[298] there is a sense that things are improving since China's entry into the WTO and as the PRC becomes increasingly innovative, with a greater incentive to recognise, assert and enforce IP rights. Perkowski,[299] for example, while recognising that continued risk to IP rights remains the biggest

---

293. M Palmer, 'Controlling the State? Mediation in Administrative Litigation in the PRC' (2006) 16 *Transnational Law & Contemporary Problems* 165–187.
294. Ibid 186.
295. Palmer describes the post-Tiananmen goal of "a socialist harmonious society in which there is only limited, incremental political change . . . and only limited room for the autonomy of the courts" See M Palmer, 'Compromising Courts and Harmonizing Ideologies: Mediation in the Administrative Chambers of the People's Courts in the PRC' in A Harding and P Nicholson (eds), *New Courts in Asia*, (Chapter 12).
296. Ibid 187.
297. D Friemann, 'How to Prevent and Act upon Intellectual Property Rights Infringement in China' ipdragonimport, 5 May 2008.
298. See FL Frankie Leung, 'Tradition of Copying in China Fuels the Piracy of Intellectual Property' *LA Times* (Los Angeles, 5 March 1995).
299. J Perkowski, 'Protecting Intellectual Property Rights in China' *Forbes* (New Jersey, 18 April 2012).

concern for US firms entering the China market, notes that "the country's goal was to transform itself from a 'made in China' to a 'designed in China' market."

Perkowski adds that "applications from China's patent office have risen . . . from 171,000 in 2006 to nearly 314,000 in 2010." Even more recently and emphatically, Fry[300] writes that,

> They don't want to be the low-cost manufacturer of other countries' inventions; competing on low-wage labour. They want to be the innovative country. To do that, you need to respect IP rights. This is a matter of national self-interest for them.

Caution remains, however, and as recently as January 2017 New[301] quotes US Trade Department concerns[302] over significant, and continuing, IP rights abuses.

11.8 Conclusion

It is clear that enormous differences remain as between the Hong Kong SAR common law and the PRC civil/socialist legal systems. Greater consonance is likely to be achieved in the years up to 2047, as Hong Kong in some areas (such as the growth of ADR) abandons its common law adversarial tradition while the PRC adopts certain traits generally associated with the common law. Nevertheless many of the differences will remain, at least while Hong Kong enjoys its guarantee of the continuation of the common law system (until 2047).[303] Moreover, the key distinction lies not in the common law/civil law dichotomy but in the "status" of the law in each system; with Hong Kong recognising the primacy of law to which *all* are subject and the PRC system emphasising the supremacy of the state and the Communist Party. It is this "Western" understanding of "rule of law" which remains Hong Kong's competitive advantage in the legal market place.

A major task, as Hong Kong's economic and political future becomes increasingly entwined with that of mainland China, is to ensure co-operation between both "parties" while maintaining their distinct legal systems. This "interface" will be the subject of the next chapter.

---

300. E Fry, 'IP Protection in China Is Finally Changing. Or So It Seems' *Fortune MPW* (New York, 18 October 2016).
301. W New, 'After 15 Years in WTO, China Still Weak on Many IP Rights Rules, US Says' *Intellectual Property Watch* (Geneva, 10 January 2017).
302. US Trade Representative's 2016 Report to Congress 2016.
303. This date is the "minimum" of the guarantee. For discussion as to the post-2047 situation see Chapter 1 at 1.12 and Postscript.

12
The Legal Interface between Hong Kong and Mainland China

Overview

The interface between the Hong Kong and mainland China (PRC) systems reflects a dichotomy resulting from the "one country, two systems" formula initiated by Deng Xiaoping and reflected in the Joint Declaration and the Basic Law. On the one hand, "one country" envisages collaboration between the Special Administrative Region and its "big brother"; while, on the other hand, "two systems" reflects the acute differences between Hong Kong's common law system and the civil law/socialist law system of the PRC.

In the field of criminal law there is an obvious and understandable reluctance on the part of Hong Kong courts to surrender criminal suspects to a system in which trials are not conducted by an independent judiciary and in which the harshest sentences, including regular use of the death penalty, are meted out. It is this reluctance, on the part of the Hong Kong courts and its people, which has prevented the introduction of a "rendition" agreement between Hong Kong and the PRC. Nonetheless, cross-border (now "cross-boundary") co-operation in the criminal law field, already commenced in the pre-1997 era, has further developed in the areas of cross-border policing and investigation.

In the civil sphere, moreover, there is increasing co-operation. Even before the transfer of sovereignty in 1997, Hong Kong had a number of mutual recognition agreements with the PRC and with other states via bi-lateral international treaties involving Britain, the colonial power. While the *international* agreements could continue, post-1997, with the PRC's blessing, the new political order (with Hong Kong a part of China) made legally impossible any "international" treaty between Hong Kong and the PRC.[1] Increased co-operation has been created, therefore, by joint agreements and mutually agreed legislation, the "inspiration" for which is to be found in Article 95 of the Basic Law.[2]

---

1. The problem had been belatedly recognised and a "Working Party on Legal and Procedural Arrangements between Hong Kong and China in Civil and Commercial Matters" established by the then Attorney-General, Jeremy Matthews, under the chairmanship of David Edwards.
2. See 12.1 below.

In the spirit of Article 95, mutual co-operation has been developed and strengthened in the areas of mutual recognition and enforcement of civil judgments, the service of judicial documents and mutual recognition and enforcement of arbitral awards (although some difficulties remain in the latter area). Cross-border insolvency remains an area in which recognition in the PRC has sometimes been found wanting; though here the problem is less to do with the non-international relationship between Hong Kong and the PRC than with the generally undeveloped and parochial nature of the PRC's insolvency procedures.

12.1 Concurrent jurisdictions

The key to the operation of "one country, two systems" is that each "party" nurtures a very different legal system. This was succinctly stated in the Court of Final Appeal[3] by Lord Collins who said:

> Although the Hong Kong SAR and the mainland PRC are part of one country, for the purposes of the conflict of laws they are separate law districts.[4]

The common law system in Hong Kong, developed since 1841, is guaranteed, by the Basic Law, to continue until at least 2047.[5] The "laws previously in force" in Hong Kong before 1997 shall continue in force subject only to limited, specific exceptions.[6] While it is clearly beneficial, as Hong Kong's social and economic future becomes more closely intertwined with that of the PRC, to collaborate as far as possible with the PRC on legal issues, this must not be at the expense of Hong Kong's "high degree of autonomy".[7] More specifically, the Basic Law stipulates that "national laws" are not applicable in Hong Kong (except those, mainly dealing with foreign affairs and defence, listed in Annex III)[8] and that Hong Kong laws are not applicable in the PRC. The Hong Kong courts have the right of "final adjudication"[9] and, while there are some limitations on this, they are of a political rather than a judicial nature.[10] There is no right of appeal from any Hong Kong court to a mainland (PRC) court and, precedent-wise, PRC court decisions are not binding in Hong Kong. In short, as Fu[11] writes:

---

3. *First Laser Ltd v Fujian Enterprises (Holdings) Company Ltd* (2012) 15 HKCFAR 569, [2013] 2 HKC 459.
4. Ibid at para 43.
5. The combined effect of Articles 8 and 159, Basic Law.
6. Article 8, Basic Law.
7. As guaranteed by Article 2, Basic Law.
8. Article 18, Basic Law.
9. Article 19, Basic Law.
10. See Chapter 4.
11. Fu Hualing, 'One Country and Two Systems: Will Hong Kong and the Mainland Reach an Agreement on Rendition?' *Hong Kong Lawyer* (January 1999) 51–53.

The Basic Law protects Hong Kong's legal system from any possible Mainland intrusion by conferring upon it an equal status to that of the Mainland, no less and no more. Importantly, it does not confer any primary rights on either system. The 'One Country, Two Systems' doctrine separates the jurisdictions, while still allowing them to negotiate on how they should interact. This arrangement does not create any positive or affirmative powers on one system as opposed to the other. It simply recognises their equal status without depriving either system of its jurisdiction according to its own law.[12]

It should further be remembered that the Basic Law is a National Law of the PRC and that it has the status of a "basic law" (lower case!) enacted by the full National People's Congress (NPC) as opposed to the (lesser) laws passed by the Standing Committee of the NPC.

However, despite the concurrent nature of the PRC and Hong Kong SAR jurisdictions, and the relative autonomy of the latter, there are good reasons for adopting as much co-operation as is possible, given Hong Kong's increasing integration with China mainland. As Fung[13] has said:

> Quarantining Hong Kong's legal and judicial systems from those of the Chinese mainland does not mean that no interface may exist at all between the two systems.[14]

The legislative "encouragement" for such interface is provided by Article 95 of the Basic Law which provides that:

> The Hong Kong SAR may, through consultations and in accordance with law, maintain juridical relations with the judicial organs of other parts of the country, and they may render assistance to each other.

Since 1997, the two jurisdictions have increased interface, through both formal and informal means. Exchanges have been common and, to take just one example, there have been training schemes, since 1999, to train PRC judges in the common law; evidencing the PRC's willingness to understand Hong Kong's legal system.[15] Via "attachment" schemes, such learning has been a two-way effort; with Hong Kong judges receiving training as to the PRC system.

---

12. Ibid 51.
13. Daniel R Fung, 'Hong Kong's Unique Constitutional Odyssey and Its Implications for China' (1997) 24 *Asian Affairs: An American Review* 199, 210.
14. Ibid 206.
15. See Hong Kong Department of Justice: 'Training Scheme in Common Law for Mainland Legal Officials'.

12.2 Mutual legal (judicial)[16] assistance

In the years since 1997, consistent with the aims of Article 95 of the Basic Law, legal co-operation between the Hong Kong SAR and the PRC has developed significantly, especially in relation to mutual enforcement of civil judgments, recognition of arbitral awards and the service of judicial documents.

In the criminal sphere, however, progress on mutual assistance has been slow. This is despite the fact that, via the Mutual Legal Assistance in Criminal Matters Ordinance,[17] Hong Kong has instituted a large number of bilateral agreements with overseas courts.[18] The Ordinance specifically states that it refers to arrangements between Hong Kong and a place outside Hong Kong "other than any other part of the People's Republic of China".[19] Thus, as has been the case in a number of instances, it has proved easier to deal, in terms of mutual legal assistance, with clearly "foreign" jurisdictions than with the mainland. One reason could be that the "parties" do not feel constrained to act by Article 95 (Basic Law) which provides for the arrangement of mutual "juridical relations" rather than legal assistance generally and may interpret such narrowly. However, Fu[20] has written:

> neither 'juridical relations' nor 'judicial organs' in Article 95 have a precise meaning, and the terms are used very loosely. It is submitted that Article 95 covers all mutual legal assistance, including extradition.[21]

12.2.1 Enforcement of judgments

Prior to legislation in 2007, mutual enforcement of judgments between Hong Kong and the PRC was fraught with difficulties. While legislation had provided for some mutual enforcement with designated "foreign" jurisdictions on the basis of "registration",[22] such procedure was impossible vis-à-vis the Hong Kong/PRC relationship which cannot, for obvious political reasons, be regarded as an "international" one. A very limited scope existed to enforce mainland judgments in Hong Kong on a common law basis, but this involved lengthy and costly procedures.[23] Enforcement of Hong Kong judgments in the PRC was simply not provided for,

---

16. The syllabus for the PCLL conversion examinations refers to mutual "judicial" assistance though it is more common to use the wider term "legal" assistance.
17. Cap 525.
18. There have been over 30 such bilateral agreements.
19. Section 2(1), Mutual Legal Assistance in Criminal Matters Ordinance. See also section 3.
20. HL Fu, 'The Form and Substance of Legal Interaction between Hong Kong and Mainland China: Towards Hong Kong's New Legal Sovereignty' in Wacks (ed), *The New Legal Order in Hong Kong* (Hong Kong University Press 1999).
21. Ibid 101.
22. See the Foreign Judgments (Reciprocal Enforcement) Ordinance (Cap 319).
23. See, eg, *Chiyu Banking Corporation Ltd v Chan Tin Kwun* [1996] 2 HKLR 395.

according to most PRC courts, except via the institution of fresh, PRC, proceedings.[24] However, influenced by the "legislative intent" in Article 95 of the Basic Law, both "sides" sought to introduce measures to improve mutual enforcement, at least in areas of civil law where the parties were agreeable and there was mutual confidence, in Hong Kong and the PRC, as to each other's procedures.

A ground-breaking "Arrangement" was entered into between Hong Kong and the PRC in 2007. Its full title is "Arrangement on Reciprocal Recognition and Enforcement of Judgments in Civil and Commercial Matters by the Courts of the Mainland and of the Hong Kong SAR Pursuant to Choice of Court Agreements between Parties Concerned"(!). The required legislative rules to reflect the Agreement have now been enacted on both sides. In Hong Kong the relevant legislation is the Mainland Judgments (Reciprocal Enforcement) Ordinance,[25] which came into force on 1 August 2008. In the PRC, the Supreme People's Court has promulgated a Supreme People's Court Interpretation of the Arrangement, also taking effect on 1 August, 2008. The main features of the legislation are that, in Hong Kong, a mainland judgment may be enforced provided that:

(i) it has been delivered by a "designated" court on or after 1 August 2008;
(ii) the judgment is final and conclusive;
(iii) it is enforceable on the mainland;
(iv) it involves the payment of money in respect of a commercial agreement;
(v) the parties have entered into a "choice of mainland court agreement" on or after 1 August 2008.

In mainland courts, a Hong Kong judgment can be enforced provided that:

(i) it has been delivered by the Court of Final Appeal, the High Court or the District Court on or after 1 August 2008;
(ii) the judgment is final and conclusive;
(iii) it is enforceable in Hong Kong;
(iv) it involves the payment of money in respect of a commercial agreement;
(v) The parties have entered into a "choice of Hong Kong court" agreement on or after 1 August 2008.

---

24. While the enforcement of some "foreign" judgments was possible on the Mainland, it was contentious whether this could apply to Hong Kong and Macau. Moreover, even for "foreign" judgments, enforcement in the PRC courts is rare (the first enforcement of a foreign (Singapore) judgment on the basis of "reciprocity" involved the Nanjing Intermediate People's Court in December 2016).
25. Cap 597.

12.2.1.1 Limitations on mutual enforceability

The first obvious limitation on enforcement via the new legislation is temporal; the new rules apply only to judgments delivered after 1 August 2008 *and* only where the parties have made the relevant choice of law on or after that date.[26]

A second limitation on enforcement relates to the legal *scope* of the Arrangement. The mutual recognition/enforcement encompassed by the Agreement and subsequent legislation applies only to "money judgments" arising from commercial contracts. Private and employment contracts are excluded, as are agreements concerning non-monetary issues, such as disputes over land. The term "money judgment" refers to damages or action for an agreed sum, and any equitable remedies are outside the scope of the legislation.

Next, as is clearly stated, there is a requirement, under the Arrangement, for a "choice of law". A "choice of Hong Kong law" agreement may be enforced in the mainland courts and vice versa. As a result, there is some indication that parties may be reluctant to designate Hong Kong under a choice of law clause as a result of fears as to the competence of mainland (as opposed to Hong Kong) courts. There are clearly, still, some concerns as to the quality of the civil judicial system on the mainland.[27] As Zhang and Smart write:[28]

> Regardless of legal terms and technical grounds, the real concern behind all the worries expressed seems to be the concern with the quality and competence of the judiciary of the Mainland . . .
>
> On the other side, the judiciary of the Mainland and their work needs to be further improved. For a long time, wrongly decided cases caused by lack of training, corruption, local protectionism, political or command influence have made headlines from time to time both in and outside the Mainland. In a recent report of the Standing Committee of the NPC on examination of the implementation of the Judges' Law and Prosecutors' Law, it was openly pointed out that judicial incompetence, corruption and lack of professional ethics of certain judges and prosecutors were major concerns of the people in mainland China.[29]

It has, of course, already been noted that judicial professionalism and competence have been strengthened in the years since Zhang and Smart made these observations.

Since the Arrangement relates only to judgments which are "final and conclusive", it is restricted in application to "designated courts". In Hong Kong this means

---

26. Macau and the PRC entered into a similar (2006) arrangement post-reunification in 1999. However, the Macau agreement provides for enforcement of judgments delivered between 1999 and the date of the new arrangement.
27. See Chapter 11.
28. X Zhang and P Smart, 'Development of Regional Conflict of Laws: On the Arrangement of Mutual Recognition & Enforcement of Judgments in Civil & Commercial Matters between Mainland China and Hong Kong SAR' (2006) 36 HKLJ 553–584.
29. Ibid 577–578.

the Court of Final Appeal, the Court of Appeal and Court of First Instance of the High Court and the District Court. For the mainland, however, there is a very exhaustive list of "designated" courts. The Supreme People's Court, the Higher People's Court and the Intermediate People's Courts are all listed, as are around 50 designated "Basic People's Courts". The key factor is "finality". While this is obvious in the case of the Supreme People's Court (PRC) or the Court of Final Appeal (Hong Kong) the finality criterion may also be fulfilled in respect of lower courts where the time limit for appeal has expired. A further factor regarding "finality" is the "protest regime"; whereby the PRC Procuratorate exercises a supervisory role over judgments. In *Bank of China Ltd v Yang Fan*,[30] To J held that despite substantive changes to the relevant PRC rules:

> whether a PRC judgment is rendered not final and conclusive by reason of the regime of protest by the procuratorate remains open.[31]

Even after all the restrictions noted there is a further caveat: that each jurisdiction may refuse an application for recognition and enforcement where it is contrary to "social and public interests" (PRC) or contrary to "public policy" (HKSAR).

12.2.2 Mutual recognition of arbitral awards

It is an irony that, in some respects, "reunification" has made the legal interface between the PRC and the Hong Kong SAR more difficult. In no area is that more true than in respect of the mutual recognition and enforcement of arbitral awards. Prior to 1997, mutual enforcement was on the basis that both "parties" were signatories to the New York Convention (NYC)[32] which provides for the enforcement of an arbitral award determined in one signatory "state" in any other signatory state (subject to minor exceptions). Article 1(1) of the NYC provides for:

> The recognition and enforcement of arbitral awards made in the territory of a State other than the State where the recognition and enforcement of such awards are sought.

This part of the NYC was given statutory force in Hong Kong by section 42(1) of the Arbitration Ordinance[33] which states:

> A Convention award shall, subject to this Part, be enforceable either by action or in the same manner as the award of an arbitrator is enforceable by virtue of section 2GG.[34]

---

30. [2016] 3 HKLRD 7.
31. Ibid para 51.
32. See Chapter 10 at 10.2.
33. Cap 341.
34. Essentially, s 2GG provides for enforcement subject to leave of the court.

Fu[35] writes that:

> According to one commentator, awards made on the Mainland constituted between one half to two thirds of the total convention awards made in Hong Kong between 1990 and 1994, indicating that the mutual enforcement of convention awards had worked reasonably well before the transition.[36]

Post-1997, the New York Convention could no longer provide a solution to the mutual enforcement problem since, clearly, the PRC could not treat the Hong Kong SAR as another signatory "state". Any solution would have to be by means of a mutual agreement between the PRC and the Hong Kong SAR. Such an agreement was established in 1999 via the "Memorandum of Understanding on the Arrangement Concerning Mutual Enforcement of Arbitral Awards between the Mainland and Hong Kong".[37] The Arrangement made "in accordance with the provisions of Article 95 of the Basic Law" provides for enforcement, in Hong Kong, of awards made "pursuant to the Arbitration Law of the PRC" and for enforcement, in the PRC, of awards made in the Hong Kong SAR "pursuant to the Arbitration Ordinance of the HKSAR".

As regards the enforcement of mainland awards in Hong Kong the Arrangement came into operation in February 2000 via an amendment to the Arbitration Ordinance.[38] The rules are now set down in the revised Arbitration Ordinance.[39] The Agreement was given force in the PRC (so as to provide for mainland enforcement of Hong Kong awards) by a "judicial interpretation" in January 2000.[40]

It may also be noted that a similar problem arose in terms of enforcement with regard to Hong Kong and Macau after Macau ceased to be "foreign" with the resulting loss of NYC recourse. This was resolved by the "Arrangement Concerning Reciprocal Recognition and Enforcement of Arbitral Awards between the Hong Kong SAR and the Macao SAR", signed on 7 January 2013.[41]

The timing of the Hong Kong–PRC Agreement meant that it could not provide for enforcement, in Hong Kong, of arbitral awards made in the PRC between 1 July 1997 (when the NYC became inapplicable) and February 2000 (when the

---

35. HL Fu, 'The Form and Substance of Legal Interaction Between Hong Kong and Mainland China' (n 20).
36. Ibid 119.
37. Signed on 21 June 1999.
38. The Arbitration (Amendment) Ordinance of 2000 added a new Part IIIA and section 2GG(2).
39. Cap 609. Sections 92 and 94 explain the principle of enforcement and ss 93 and 95 explain the restrictions on enforcement and grounds for refusal.
40. 'Notice Concerning the Arrangement for Mutual Enforcement of Arbitral Awards between the Mainland China and the Hong Kong SAR' (Supreme People's Court (SPC) 24 January 2000) and see SPC Interpretation [2000] No 3.
41. Macau and the PRC had signed a similar agreement in 2007. See also 'Regulations Concerning Recognition by People's Courts of Civil Judgments of Taiwan Courts (1998) and Supplementary Regulations Concerning Recognition by People's Courts of Civil Judgments of Taiwan Courts' (2009).

Arrangement came into effect).[42] The "lacuna" had been predicted by academics[43] and lamented by judges[44] so the delay should have been avoided. Be that as it may, the enforcement regime (for PRC arbitral awards) has worked well in Hong Kong from 2000. In the first four years (2000 to 2003) following the Arrangement, 56 applications for enforcement of mainland awards were made in Hong Kong, of which 53 were successful.[45] Of these applications, the majority (42) were made in 2000,[46] reflecting the backlog caused by the lack of an enforcement mechanism between 1997 and 2000.[47]

The enforcement procedure is, put simply, that where a party refuses to perform an arbitral award made in Hong Kong or the PRC, application may be made to the "relevant courts" for enforcement in the "other jurisdiction". In Hong Kong the relevant court is the High Court; in the PRC the relevant court is the Intermediate People's Court in the place of domicile of the party against whom enforcement is sought, or the place where the property of such party is located. Applicants for enforcement need to submit an application for enforcement, details of the arbitral award and sight of the arbitration agreement itself. If the enforcement is sought in the PRC, the application must be made in Chinese. The application must be within the time limits of the jurisdiction in which enforcement is sought.

As regards the enforcement of Hong Kong arbitral awards on the mainland (from February 2000), the Arrangement seemed to have effected a satisfactory solution though certain doubts remained. The reason for the uncertainty was that the PRC tended to recognise only those "domestic" arbitrations (ie, PRC arbitrations) which have been conducted by a recognised arbitral institution.[48] Most commonly this will involve arbitrations conducted under CIETAC rules but will include other recognised institutions. As mentioned previously,[49] the requirement of conformity to established procedures has some advantages in the PRC and no doubt helps to foster confidence in the international business community. However, the formal requirements have produced difficulties in respect of the recognition and enforcement of Hong Kong "ad hoc" arbitrations.[50] The "ad hoc" procedure is frequently chosen by Hong Kong parties to arbitration and there had, before 1997, been little problem with mainland enforcement by virtue of the NYC. Post-1997, there seemed to be a question mark over recognition and enforcement of this type of arbitration which

---

42. See *Shandong Textiles Import and Export Corporation v A Hua Non-Ferrous Metals Co Ltd* [2002] 2 HKC 122.
43. Eg, R Mushkat, *One Country, Two International Legal Personalities: The Case of Hong Kong* (Hong Kong University Press 1997).
44. See Findlay J in *Ng Fung Hong Ltd v ABC* [1998] 1 HKC 213, 216.
45. See Department of Justice (Legal Policy Division), *Report*, March 2004.
46. Hong Kong International Arbitration Centre statistics.
47. Applicants caught by the "lacuna" were permitted to lodge fresh applications for enforcement post-2000.
48. See Chapter 11.
49. See Chapter 11.
50. See Chapter 10.

does not conform to the PRC's own domestic requirements. In January 2005, an interesting dialogue took place in LegCo between Margaret Ng ("legal functional constituency" representative) and Elsie Leung, then Secretary for Justice. Ng asked for figures on the applications for enforcement of Hong Kong arbitral awards on the mainland. Leung replied that her department had approached the Supreme People's Court on the issue and been told that no applications for the enforcement (on the mainland) of Hong Kong arbitral awards had been received. Leung added:

> This was not satisfactory. I therefore followed up with the Supreme People's Court during my visit to Beijing in summer 2004 and again when the President of the Supreme People's Court . . . visited Hong Kong in November 2004. I was informed that [there would be] a 'field study' by visiting the courts in Guangdong province responsible for the enforcement of Hong Kong awards to study the reason why there is no record of any application for enforcement of Hong Kong arbitral awards.[51]

Doubts as to mainland enforcement remained in the legal and business community. An "update" from leading law firm, Allen & Overy, in August 2008 concluded:

> A reciprocal enforcement regime . . . has been in place since 2000 . . . Nonetheless, in the mainland, delay and problems with the execution of arbitral awards persist in practice. It remains to be seen whether, following the introduction of the new reciprocal enforcement regime for court judgments,[52] it will be quicker and easier to enforce a Hong Kong court judgment or a Hong Kong arbitral award in the mainland.[53]

Concerns such as these prompted further action in the PRC, anxious to attract foreign business and allay "enforceability" fears. The Chinese Supreme People's Court (SPC) issued, on 31 December 2009, a "Notice Concerning Questions Related to the Enforcement of Hong Kong Arbitral Awards in the Mainland". The "Notice" states that:

> Ad hoc arbitral awards made in Hong Kong and arbitral awards made in Hong Kong by the ICC (International Chamber of Commerce) and other foreign arbitration institutions are enforceable in the PRC in accordance with the Arrangement concerning Mutual Enforcement of Arbitral Awards between Mainland China and Hong Kong signed in 1999, except where grounds of refusal of enforcement under Article 7 of the Arrangement exist.

The "caveat" in respect of Article 7 is not significant, given that it essentially reflects the grounds for refusal of enforcement which previously obtained under the NYC. These grounds are very limited and do not include disputing the merits of the arbitral decision.

---

51. LegCo, 26 January 2005 (oral reply).
52. See 12.2.1 above.
53. Allen and Overy (Review), 'Reciprocal Enforcement of Judgments between Hong Kong and the Mainland' (August 2008).

More significant is the fact that this latest "Notice" is not the first "clarification" issued by the SPC on the issue since 2000. In the *Wei Mao International* case,[54] that court had issued a reply to the Higher People's Court of Shanxi Province in respect of the "non-enforcement" of an International Chamber of Commerce (ICC) award arising from an arbitration conducted in Hong Kong. The SPC, in that case, treated the case as a "foreign" award, enforceable under the NYC, on the basis that the ICC is a foreign institution established in France. This did not assist the general question of enforcement of Hong Kong awards, since it merely treated the award in question as a foreign (NYC-governed) one, applying the "nationality of the conducting Institution" test rather than the generally-accepted "nationality of the seat of award" one.

Some development on this issue was made by the SPC's 2006 "Interpretation on Several Issues Concerning the Application of the PRC Arbitration Law" which stated that the "place of arbitration" would be the governing law for an arbitration where the parties have failed to specify the governing law.

A further confirmation of the position of ad hoc Hong Kong arbitral awards had been issued in response to a request for clarification from the Hong Kong Secretary for Justice in 2007. This affirmed[55] that such awards would be enforceable in the mainland (subject to the Article 7 caveats) but left open the question of whether, for example, ICC arbitrations conducted in Hong Kong would be subject to "the Arrangement" or the NYC rules.[56]

The December 2009 "Notice" is significant, therefore, in confirming not only that both Hong Kong "institutional" *and* ad hoc awards made in Hong Kong are enforceable in the mainland but that they are both enforceable on the same basis: the terms of the 1999 "Arrangement". This *appears* to indicate that the Supreme People's Court is now prepared to accept the "seat of arbitral award" test as opposed to the "conducting institution" test (such that, for example, ICC awards made in Hong Kong are no longer regarded as "French"). Arbitration professionals seem to be optimistic that the issue has now been laid to rest. Ng and Chan,[57] for example, write that:

> The Notice is likely to mean that parties can now select Hong Kong as a seat for international arbitrations with confidence that an eventual award can be enforced against counterparties in mainland China.[58]

---

54. *Wei Mao International (Hong Kong) Co Ltd v Shanxi Tianli Industrial Co Ltd* (SPC reply, 5 June 2004).
55. By means of a letter of reply, dated 25 October 2007.
56. There is little difference in "form" but enforcement via the Agreement is "procedurally easier": M Ng and K Chan, 'Chinese Court Confirms Enforceability of Hong Kong Arbitral Awards on Mainland' DLA Piper Publications (24 February 2010).
57. Ibid.
58. Ibid.

Such optimism is echoed by Ow,[59] who writes:

> The awards to which the Notification [Notice] applies specifically include those rendered under the auspices of the International Court of Arbitration of the ICC. Any doubt over the enforceability of such awards in Mainland China should now be removed.
>
> The Notification is a welcome step forward. It is likely to boost Hong Kong's development as a seat for international dispute resolution.[60]

It should be pointed out that the uncertainty over "jurisdiction" obtained not only in the mainland. In *Shenzhen Kai Long Investment & Development Co Ltd v CEC Electrical Manufacturing (International) Co Ltd*,[61] a Hong Kong court refused to enforce an arbitral award of the Shenzhen division of CIETAC in 1994. The refusal was on the ground that, since the PRC Arbitration Law did not take effect until 1 January 1995, the Shenzhen award could not have been made under it. It may have been under PRC arbitration law, but not under the Arbitration Law.

12.2.2.1 Grounds for non-enforcement

Whether under the (old) NYC rules applicable to the Hong Kong/mainland China relationship, or the current "Arrangement" procedures, similar (limited) grounds have existed for the refusal to enforce an arbitral award made in the "other jurisdiction" and these apply equally in both jurisdictions. The grounds for non-enforcement in Hong Kong under section 95 of the Arbitration Ordinance[62] are that:

(2) (a) a party to the arbitration is under some incapacity;
   (b) the arbitration agreement was not valid under the relevant law chosen by the parties or, absent such, the law of the place of arbitration;
   (c) the party against whom the application for enforcement has been filed was not given proper notice at the original hearing or was unable reasonably to present his case;
   (d) the award exceeds the terms of the original submission to arbitration, though partial enforcement (of the non "ultra vires" part of the award) may be permitted;
   (e) the composition of the arbitral "court" was not in accordance with the agreement of the parties or, absent such, not in accordance with Mainland law;
   (f) the award has not yet become binding on the parties or has been set aside on the Mainland.
(3) (a) the award is a matter not capable of settlement by arbitration;
   (b) the award is contrary to Hong Kong public policy public interest of the PRC.

---

59. KK Ow, 'Enforcement in Mainland China of ICC Arbitral Awards Rendered in Hong Kong' ICC Asia (News) February 2010.
60. Ibid.
61. [2003] 3 HKLRD 774.
62. Cap 609.

Essentially these grounds for non-enforcement mirror those of the NYC but a further is added under the Agreement in that applications for enforcement cannot be filed in Hong Kong and the PRC at the same time.[63] Broadly the same limitations on enforcement apply *pari passu* in the mainland with minor differences such as the words "public interest of the PRC" replacing the Hong Kong "public policy" of 95(3) (b).

Most commentators opine that both the relevant PRC courts and those of Hong Kong have applied a "pro-enforcement" approach, refusing enforcement only on a sound basis.[64] To take just one example from each jurisdiction, a Hong Kong court in *Kunming Factory of Prestressed Vibrohydropressed Concrete Pipe v True Stand Investment Ltd & Another*[65] recognised and enforced an arbitral award made by CIETAC even though the relevant arbitration agreement called for arbitration before the "China International Economic & Trade Promotion [*sic*] Arbitration Commission". Since no such body existed, the court determined that CIETAC must, in fact, have been intended. The court *could*, of course, have refused enforcement under reason (iv) but this would have been very harsh in the circumstances.

Similarly, in *Xinggang Ouya Technology Co Ltd v Xinjiang Pijiuhua Inc*[66] the Supreme People's Court overturned a lower court refusal to enforce an arbitration award involving a subsidiary contract on the grounds that there was no arbitration clause therein. The SPC found that the *main* contract had an arbitration clause which could be extended to the subsidiary contract by implication.

It might be assumed that the PRC would reject regularly on "public policy" grounds (ground vi). In practice, such rejections have been rare and not involving Hong Kong. From 2000 to June 2008 no award was unenforced[67] on public policy grounds.[68] Since that date the only clear case of refusal to enforce an arbitral award on the grounds (*inter alia*) of public policy was in *Hemofarm DD, MAG International Trade Holding DD, Suram Media Ltd v Jinan Yongning Pharmaceutical Co Ltd*[69] where the Supreme People's Court upheld a refusal to enforce an ICC award which was seen as "violating China's judicial sovereignty" and therefore contrary to China's public policy.

---

63. Section 93(1), Arbitration Ordinance. Where enforcement in one place does not fully satisfy the "loser's" liabilities, enforcement for "the balance" may then be sought in the other jurisdiction (in Hong Kong, s 93(2)).
64. One key difference is that the limitation period in Hong Kong (six years) is far more generous than that in the PRC (usually two years).
65. [2006] 4 HKLRD.
66. *Supreme People's Court Reply to Civil Court Ruling No 48* (2006), issued 28 November 2007.
67. In some cases, refusal to enforce had been urged by lower courts but rejected by the Supreme People's Court.
68. See speech by Wan E'xiang, Deputy Chief Justice of the Supreme People's Court, 6 June 2008.
69. [2008] Min Si Ta Zi No 11.

In short, given the significant differences between the PRC and HKSAR systems, the system for mutual recognition and enforcement is working well.[70] It remains to be seen, however, what effect the "breakaway" of the Shanghai and Shenzhen sub-commissions, in 2012, might have on recognition.

12.2.3 Service of judicial documents

A clear example of juridical co-operation is indicated by the procedures on the service of judicial documents. Under the principle of mutual "juridical" assistance, as provided for in Article 95 of the Basic Law, one of the first mutual agreements between Hong Kong and the PRC was the "Arrangement for Mutual Service of Judicial Documents in Civil and Commercial Proceedings between the Mainland and Hong Kong Courts" (the Arrangement), signed, in Shenzhen, on 14 January 1999 and in force from 30 March 1999.[71] Such an arrangement was necessary, by analogy with the position of arbitral awards, because the previous "international" rules were no longer politically acceptable post-reunification. The previous practice had been to serve documents between Hong Kong and the PRC as "service abroad", as provided for by the Hague Convention.[72] Hong Kong remained a party to the Hague Convention post-1997 but service on the mainland could no longer be treated as "service abroad".

The key principles of the Arrangement, in respect of Hong Kong judicial documents being served in the PRC, may be explained briefly. First, "the Mainland and Hong Kong courts may entrust to each other the service of judicial documents in civil and commercial proceedings."[73] It can be seen, then, that the Arrangement does not extend to documents in respect of criminal proceedings. The procedure is that a request for service is made through the appropriate Higher People's Court (in the Mainland), and the High Court (in Hong Kong). The Supreme People's Court may make a direct application to the Hong Kong High Court for service.[74] The requests for service are made by means of a sealed "letter of entrustment" (written in, or translated into, Chinese) from the "entrusting" court to the "entrusted" court.[75] The letter of entrustment must state the name of the entrusting party, the name and details of the party to be served and the nature of the proceedings. The entrusted court will comply with the request for service and serve the documents(s) unless the request

---

70. See L Fei, 'Enforcement of Arbitral Awards between Hong Kong and Mainland China: A Successful Model?' *Chinese Journal of International Law*, 10 March 2009.
71. Prior to this there had been an informal (limited) arrangement for the service of documents between Hong Kong (the Hong Kong Supreme Court) and Guangdong province (the Higher People's Court of Guangdong). This operated from 1988 with the approval of the Supreme People's Court until reunification in 1997.
72. *Convention on the Service Abroad of Judicial and Extrajudicial Documents in Civil or Commercial Matters* (signed at The Hague on 15 November 1965).
73. The Agreement, para 1.
74. Ibid para 2.
75. Ibid para 3.

is deemed to be invalid.[76] The entrusted party must serve the document(s) promptly and, in any event, no later than two months after receipt.[77] Once service has been effected, a return form will be issued by the relevant mainland people's court and the Hong Kong court will issue a certificate of service. In the event of a failure to serve or a refusal to accept service, the "entrusted party" will state on the form the reason for non-service and promptly return the documents.[78] A wide range of "judicial documents" is included within the ambit of the Arrangement including (in the case of the Hong Kong SAR) a copy of the originating process, copy of notice of appeal, summons, pleading, affidavit, judgment, decision or ruling, notice, court order, certificate of service or non-service.[79]

12.2.4 Extradition and rendition

Extradition for alleged criminal offences is a far more controversial political issue than mutual recognition and enforcement in the civil field, at least in so far as the relationship between Hong Kong and the mainland PRC is concerned. While extradition to "foreign" jurisdictions is relatively unproblematic, the problems involved in "rendition" of suspects from Hong Kong to the mainland have yet to be resolved.

12.2.4.1 Extradition from Hong Kong (and mainland China) to foreign states

As regards extradition between Hong Kong and other countries (strictly "surrender of fugitive offenders" since Hong Kong as a "non-state" has no extradition powers), or mainland China and other countries, the history has been of the signing of bi-lateral or multilateral agreements. A number of states have bi-lateral extradition agreements with the PRC while many others have entered into such agreements with Hong Kong. Even where the latter were entered into prior to 1997, under colonial rule, the PRC has raised no serious objection to their continuation. Indeed, Article 96 of the Basic Law specifically permits the Hong Kong SAR government (with the support of the PRC Central Government) "to make appropriate arrangements with foreign states for reciprocal juridical assistance".

A general legislative basis for the mutual surrender of allegedly fugitive offenders was provided, immediately on the return of Hong Kong's sovereignty to China on 1 July 1997, by the Fugitive Offenders Ordinance (FOO),[80] an enabling Ordinance which permits the Chief Executive, essentially, to add to the list of foreign states

---

76. In such case the "entrusted party" may seek supplementary information.
77. The Arrangement, para 4.
78. Ibid para 5.
79. Ibid para 9.
80. Cap 503.

with whom Hong Kong may have reciprocal extradition arrangements,[81] subject to the safeguards laid down in the Ordinance.[82]

Various safeguards exist as to Hong Kong's obligation to return alleged offenders. These involve, for example, the issue of whether the alleged offence is "political"; whether the offence would be regarded as such in Hong Kong; whether trial is likely for the named offence rather than for another; whether the "subject's" trial was held in his/her absence; and whether there is a risk of re-extradition to a third party state.

What, broadly, characterises the states which have agreements with the PRC is that they are communist/socialist (or only recently democratised) while, in general, those states which have signed agreements with Hong Kong (currently 19) have a considerable history of western-style democracy (Indonesia represents a notable exception).

What is significant is that states have *not* entered into agreements with *both* Hong Kong and the PRC. The two basic concerns of those lacking an extradition agreement with the PRC are the lack of "due process" in PRC criminal cases (in particular the absence of an independent judiciary and impartial hearings) and the draconian sentences in existence. The latter is highlighted by the extensive use of capital punishment for a variety of offences not limited to homicide.

Since, as mentioned, Hong Kong has agreements with different states than has the mainland, there is potential for embarrassment. United States NSA whistleblower Edward Snowden initially sought refuge in Hong Kong, praising its liberal society and free speech. Hong Kong had, however, concluded an extradition treaty with the USA in 1996,[83] under the aegis of which the USA sought Snowden's extradition. This placed Hong Kong in difficulties since mainland China has no extradition with the USA (and clearly relished the embarrassment to the USA caused by Snowden's outpourings, which included claims that the US had hacked Hong Kong SAR sites). Given that the mainland Central Government is ultimately responsible for China's foreign relations and defence issues, Hong Kong's position was a delicate one.[84] The situation was finessed by Hong Kong's claim to defer extradition

---

81. Section 3, Fugitive Offenders Ordinance (FOO).
82. The key safeguards, imposed by s 5, FOO are the need to ensure a fair trial and the refusal to extradite for political offences. Section 13 adds the important safeguard, commonly found worldwide, that extradition will be refused where there is a risk of the extradited person suffering the death penalty. All these caveats are relevant to the failure to agree on rendition from Hong Kong to the PRC. However, not all the states with which Hong Kog has FOO agreements are fully "abolitionist" (eg, USA, Indonesia and Malaysia).
83. *Agreement for the Surrender of Fugitive Offenders* signed 20 December 1996 but ratified (post-handover) by the US 28 July 1998. See also *Chong Bing Keung Peter v Government of USA & Another* [2000] 2 HKC 137.
84. Brabyn writes that the CPG *does* have power to veto a proposed surrender from Hong Kong to a foreign state (J Brabyn, 'Inter-Jurisdictional Co-operation in Criminal Matters' in Wacks (ed), *The New Legal Order in Hong Kong* (n 20) 144.

The Legal Interface between Hong Kong and Mainland China 505

because of defects in the documents provided by the US.[85] Pending a re-application, Snowden was allowed to move on to Russia, much to the USA's annoyance.

12.2.4.2 Cross-border crimes and jurisdiction

The issue of jurisdiction for "cross-border" crimes, in this context the border[86] between the PRC mainland and the Hong Kong SAR, is an extremely controversial one involving, as it does, the fundamentals of Hong Kong's legal autonomy and the concept of "one country two systems". The key issue has become the extent to which, if at all, the PRC should have jurisdiction over offences committed primarily by Hong Kong citizens in Hong Kong. Several causes célèbres have underlined the controversy. One important case was that of Cheung Tze-keung ("Big Spender") shortly after the return of Hong Kong's sovereignty to China. Cheung and others were tried and ultimately executed in the PRC for (kidnapping) offences committed "primarily" in Hong Kong. While there was little sympathy in Hong Kong for Cheung's plight *per se*, the case raised the spectre of Hong Kong citizens being tried on the mainland for offences committed in Hong Kong even, potentially, where their activities do not constitute a crime in Hong Kong. A subsequent case of concern, that of the "Telford Gardens murderer", concerned an alleged murder of five persons, in Hong Kong, by a *mainland* resident, Li Yuhui. The Big Spender and Telford Gardens cases prompted Margaret Ng, (then) LegCo representative for the legal functional constituency, to ask:[87]

(i) Whether, where an SAR criminal court has jurisdiction, the jurisdiction of the mainland courts is precluded by virtue of Article 22 of the Basic Law;
(ii) If mainland jurisdiction is not precluded, what principles govern the appropriate criminal forum?
(iii) Whether the Hong Kong SAR government had discussed the issue with Mainland authorities.

In the same forum (Hong Kong Lawyer)[88] Elsie Leung, the then Secretary for Justice, "explained" the principles involved in the mainland trial of Big Spender. The basic foundation of Leung's explanation was that Hong Kong has a "concurrent" but not "exclusive" jurisdiction over crimes committed within its borders.[89] Such crimes might be subject to criminal proceedings elsewhere if they were partly

---

85. Not all commentators were convinced by Hong Kong's "official" explanation.
86. Strictly, since 1 July 1997, a "boundary" rather than a border.
87. Margaret Ng, 'The Protection of Justice under Hong Kong's System of Laws' *Hong Kong Lawyer* ("From LegCo") (December 1998).
88. E. Leung SJ, 'Viewing the Jurisdictional Issue from a Proper Perspective' *Hong Kong Lawyer* ("Focus") (January 1999).
89. "[T]here is no country or region in the world that has an exclusive jurisdiction over crimes committed within its boundaries" (Elsie Leung, speech in LegCo motion debate, "the HKSAR's judicial jurisdiction", 9 December 1998.

committed, or planned,[90] there or if the relevant crime was "extraterritorial" (triable in a national's home country, though committed abroad). As an example of the latter situation, Leung referred to section 4 of the Prevention of Bribery Ordinance,[91] offences against which can be committed "in Hong Kong or elsewhere".

In essence, then, Leung defended the Big Spender trial in the PRC on the basis that much of the "preparation" for the kidnappings was done in the PRC *and* that other, firearms and explosives, crimes were committed in the PRC. Indeed:

> whereas Cheung Tze-keung was sentenced to life imprisonment in respect of the kidnapping offences and the smuggling offence, it was only in relation to the explosives offence that he received the death penalty.[92]

While concerns were expressed by Margaret Ng and others for the reasons explained above, Leung had her supporters. Fu[93] writes:

> The Criminal Law of the PRC . . . confers wide personality jurisdiction over PRC citizens . . .
> . . . The Big Spender was not wanted by the police in Hong Kong when he left Hong Kong for the mainland through the legal channel at the beginning of 1998 . . .
> The Big Spender and other gang members apparently planned a series of serious criminal offences in the mainland to be carried out in Hong Kong . . . The link between those crimes and the mainland is substantial.[94]

Conversely, the Telford trial in the PRC was justified on the basis that the perpetrator was a *mainland* resident.[95] Leung conceded that Hong Kong had jurisdiction over both cases but added that, in the absence of a "rendition" agreement with the PRC, had no legal basis to seek the return of the suspects.

While the arguments of the former Secretary for Justice might be compelling in respect of an "ordinary" inter-state relationship, the relationship between Hong Kong and the PRC is anything but ordinary. "One country, two systems" represents a unique legal and constitutional framework, involving a relationship between two very different systems, requiring the greatest sensitivity and good will if it is to

---

90. The SJ cited the case of Cheung Wai-ming, convicted and sentenced in Hong Kong for conspiracy to commit a murder *in Singapore*.
91. Cap 201.
92. Speech by Elsie Leung, SJ, in LegCo motion debate, op cit. It appears clear, however, that there were "extra-judicial" factors. "Big Spender" had kidnapped the son of Hong Kong tycoon, Li Ka-shing, who spoke to then PRC President, Jiang Zemin, personally. It is also alleged that Big Spender's explosives were obtained from corrupt PRC military sources (disclosure of which in a Hong Kong court would not have been welcome to the Central Government).
93. HL Fu, 'The Battle of Criminal Jurisdictions' (1998) HKLJ ("Comment") 274–281.
94. Ibid 275 and 279–280.
95. The same was true of Yang Wen, a PLA veteran executed on the mainland for the murder of Hong Kong businessman, Harry Lam, in the Luk Yu teahouse, Hong Kong. This despite Hong Kong's apparent jurisdiction over crimes committed in Hong Kong via Article 19(2) of the Basic Law. James To of the Democratic Party described the PRC trials as "a serious breach of 'one country, two systems'": see J Cheng, 'Trial Starts for Murder Plot' *The Standard* (Hong Kong, 26 October 2006).

flourish. Concerns remain that Hong Kong citizens may be prosecuted on the China mainland for alleged "offences" committed solely in Hong Kong.[96] It is concern as to the procedures in such PRC courts, and the sentencing powers with which they are vested, which has, thus far, prevented the institution of a formal "rendition" system between Hong Kong and the PRC. It must be emphasised, however, that no Hong Kong citizen has (yet) been tried on the mainland for an offence committed solely in Hong Kong. Even in the most controversial recent case, the "Bossini kidnap", that particular principle was not undermined. The case concerned the robbery of a residence in Clearwater Bay (Hong Kong) and the kidnapping, for ransom, of Bossini heiress, Queenie Rosita Law. Eight of the alleged kidnappers were arrested in Guangdong (PRC) and tried/convicted in Shenzhen. A ninth suspect was arrested in Hong Kong and tried there. While Hong Kong authorities were entitled to ask for the return of the suspects (since the crimes were committed in Hong Kong) it appears that no such request was made. This is in spite of the fact that the offences "appear" to be entirely Hong Kong based. The offences of robbery and kidnap were committed in Hong Kong and the suspects did not go to the mainland until the offences were concluded.[97] Again, the rationale for a mainland trial appears to be an assertion that a criminal "conspiracy" to commit the crimes was formed on the mainland.[98]

It should be noted that, while many Hong Kong people are anxious as to the possibility of mainland "incursions" in this area, there is also some sentiment that serious criminals "deserve" the harsher penalties meted out across the "border". Fu writes:

> One may blame the victims for not reporting the case to Hong Kong police and for paying ransom . . . But ultimately it is the victim who decides which jurisdiction he has faith in.
>
> For many, including the victims, Hong Kong appears to be a weak prosecutor and its criminal justice is not tough enough to handle the Big Spender case.[99]

12.2.4.3 "Regional surrender" of fugitive offenders

"Extradition" from Hong Kong to the mainland (and vice versa) is legally impossible since, technically:

---

96. Especially where the conduct concerned is not illegal in Hong Kong, as in the case of the "Causeway Bay booksellers", mysteriously spirited away from Hong Kong and Thailand after distributing books critical of the PRC leadership.
97. It is asserted, however, that the criminal "mastermind" never, in fact, left the PRC.
98. See S Lau, 'Chance of Rendition to Hong Kong for Kidnap Suspects Slim, Expert Says' *South China Morning Post* (Hong Kong, 15 May 2015).
99. HL Fu, 'The Battle of Criminal Jurisdictions' (n 93) 279–280.

Mainland China and Hong Kong are parts of the same country, their mutual 'extradition of fugitive offenders' should be regarded as regional surrender of fugitive offenders and should be treated as such.[100]

Of course, before 1997 extradition *was* possible; given Hong Kong's status as a British Colony. Indeed, one of the Colonial Government's first pieces of legislation provided for the rendition for trial of "criminals, subjects of China, who may take refuge in Hong Kong.[101]

The return of "fugitive offenders" between Hong Kong and the mainland must now be regarded as "regional surrender".[102] The *formalisation* of such surrender would require the completion of a formal "rendition" agreement, thus far lacking.

12.2.4.4 The "rendition agreement" debate

Even before "rendition" became associated in the public consciousness with a system whereby the USA sent suspects abroad to be tortured, free from interference from its own domestic courts, rendition was an issue of great significance in Hong Kong. With a relatively porous border between Hong Kong and the PRC, the potential has long existed for criminals to commit crimes in one place and flee to the other. In the absence of a formal agreement between the two sides for the return of such offenders, and given the prevailing uncertainty over jurisdictional issues,[103] there exists an obvious lacuna in the area of law enforcement. The *South China Morning Post*, in a 2017 editorial, highlighted the problem:

> Little progress has been made on criminal matters, such as the striking of a much-needed rendition agreement to provide a sound legal basis for the transfer of suspects.[104]

Given such a background why is it that no rendition agreement has been concluded between Hong Kong and the PRC? The main reason is highlighted in the following quotation from former Secretary for Justice, Elsie Leung:[105]

> The two cases [Big Spender and Li Yuhui] have highlighted the need for putting in place a formal rendition agreement with the Mainland. The Administration has already engaged in discussions with the Mainland authorities and both sides

---

100. LegCo Secretariat (Research and Library Services Division): *Research Study on the Agreement between Hong Kong and the Mainland concerning Surrender of Fugitive Offenders: The Issue of Re-extradition* at p 2.
101. No 2 of 1850. This was "clarified" by Rendition of Chinese Criminals Ordinance (No 2 of 1871) which was itself repealed by Ordinance No 26 of 1889.
102. For the avoidance of all doubt, s 2 of the Fugitive Offenders Ordinance is stated not to apply to extraditions from one part of China to another.
103. See 13.2.4.2.
104. Editorial, 'Reconcile One Country, Two Legal Systems' *South China Morning Post* (Hong Kong, 19 May 2017).
105. Elsie Leung, SJ, 'Viewing the Jurisdictional Issue from a Proper Perspective' *Hong Kong Lawyer* (January 1999) 56–57.

recognise the importance of the issues . . . The presence of capital punishment in the Mainland, but not in Hong Kong, is one of the important factors that has to be considered . . . we have to give full weight to the need to prevent criminals from escaping justice and the need to safeguard the rights of individuals.[106]

The capital punishment issue is one of great concern. Hong Kong itself abolished capital punishment only relatively recently, in April 1993,[107] and the last execution in Hong Kong occurred on 16 November 1966.[108] All surveys on the issue showed a majority in Hong Kong in favour of capital punishment for murder.[109] Abolition was effected chiefly on the basis that Britain, the colonial power, had itself abolished capital punishment for murder some years earlier[110] and prompted by the fear that, with the imminent "handover" in 1997, the PRC would insist on the implementation of capital punishment in Hong Kong, not just for murder.[111]

It is a common practice for abolitionist states to refuse requests for extradition from states where capital punishment is practised or, at the least, to refuse extradition where there exists the possibility of the extradited suspect being executed.

A significant consideration, to which Elsie Leung, SJ, made only implicit reference is the issue of "due process" and the right to a fair trial. There are legitimate concerns in Hong Kong about the quality of the judicial process in the PRC—not to mention that the judicial process is not the final determinant, in the PRC, of the fate of the accused.[112] While the plight of Big Spender and the Telford Gardens killer is unlikely to elicit sympathy, the right of all accused to a fair trial is worthy of protection.[113]

Moreover, in this context, the absence of judicial independence and autonomy on the mainland is crucial. It is, for example, far more likely, in the PRC, that a request for rendition would be based on "political" grounds. Even more importantly, there is every likelihood of a returned suspect being executed after a (probably unsatisfactory) trial.

---

106. Ibid 57.
107. Though between 1966 and 1993 all death sentences passed had been suspended given the *de facto* then *de jure* abolition in Britain which would practically have required the commutation of death sentences in colonial Hong Kong.
108. At Stanley Prison.
109. See, eg, Kang-Chung Ng, '84% Call for Death Penalty Restoration' *South China Morning Post* (Hong Kong, 12 May 1992).
110. In 1969. The penalty remained "on the books" for treason and piracy until 1998.
111. The PRC has an extensive list of capital offences and is the world's leading "practitioner" in the implementation of capital punishment. Some legislators who support capital punishment in principle, voted for its abolition in Hong Kong because of mainland-related fears.
112. See Chapter 11.
113. There are also genuine fears that PRC police (or similar) may "swoop" on Hong Kong suspects and convey them to the mainland for trial. Given that five Hong Kong booksellers who displeased Beijing were spirited away to the mainland "for questioning" (without completing any boundary formalities), the fears appear justified (and see n 179).

One further important concern, highlighted by the LegCo Secretariat,[114] is the potential, were Hong Kong and the PRC to exercise a formal and extensive policy of mutual surrender of fugitive offenders, for those extradited to Hong Kong to be "re-extradited" to the PRC.[115] Fears of such an eventuality would be likely to lead to the cancellation of bi-lateral treaties between foreign states and Hong Kong, were the latter to conclude a rendition agreement with the PRC.

The present impasse is best summarised by Margaret Ng, previously LegCo (Functional) Representative for the Legal Constituency, who has said:

> There are strong objections against rendition altogether by the SAR to the Mainland. This is on the ground that, at the present stage, the concept of a fair trial as understood by the SAR does not exist in the Mainland. The practical chances of a fair trial together with the same safeguards for the rights of the accused are too small. Conviction is too inevitable to invite confidence. The SAR owes an obligation to people residing under its system of law not to hand them over to a place where their rights might be jeopardised, with dire consequences to themselves. At the moment there is no reason for confidence.[116]

The LegCo Research Study[117] previously alluded to summarises the problem as follows:

> 1.1 ... Some Members noted that certain countries might be concerned with the future arrangement on the surrender of fugitive offenders between Hong Kong and mainland China, because of the possibility that fugitive offenders extradited from other countries to Hong Kong may be re-surrendered to mainland China ...
>
> ...
>
> 2.1 Generally, re-extradition refers to the surrender of a fugitive offender to a third state for trial or the enforcement of sentence after the offender has been extradited to a requesting state for trial or the enforcement of sentence.
>
> ...
>
> 2.3 Mainland China and Hong Kong are parts of the same country, their mutual 'extradition of fugitive offenders' should be regarded as regional surrender of fugitive offenders and treated as such. Because of the 'One Country, Two Systems' principle, each has, on its own, entered into extradition treaties and agreement on the surrender of fugitive offenders with other countries. After the re-unification, Hong Kong continues to negotiate with foreign countries and enter into agreements on the surrender of

---

114. LegCo Research Study (op cit, supra, para 2.5 and post).
115. Of course the converse would be true; that those extradited to the PRC could be handed over to Hong Kong. However, this has not been regarded as a major concern.
116. M Ng, 'Jurisdiction and Rendition: Fundamental Questions Raised by the Trial of Cheung Tze Keung and Others' Hong Kong Policy Research Institute, Bulletin 9.
117. Legislative Council Secretariat, *Research Study on the Agreement between Hong Kong and the Mainland Concerning Surrender of Fugitive Offenders: The Issue of Re-extradition.*

fugitive offenders according to the authorization of the Central Government pursuant to the *Basic Law*. In addition, Hong Kong enjoys the independence of the judiciary and the right of final adjudication. At the moment, mainland China and Hong Kong have respectively entered into extradition agreements with different countries. Yet, there is not a single country which has entered into an extradition agreement with both mainland China and Hong Kong.

. . .

4.2 . . . In August of 1996, the English Divisional Court quashed an order for the extradition of a Hong Kong fugitive offender, Ewan Launder, on the ground that the offender's rights might be violated after Hong Kong's return to China.[118]

4.3 The decision was subsequently reversed by the House of Lords.[119] One of the issues was whether the relator, Ewan Launder, would be re-extradited to China after his extradition to Hong Kong. The House of Lords was aware of the fact that there was no arrangement for the surrender of fugitive offenders between China and Hong Kong, and the extradition agreement soon to be reached between Hong Kong and the UK would contain speciality[120] protection. In addition, the *Basic Law* protects personal freedoms and the rights of parties to proceedings. Therefore the court considered that the relator would enjoy the right not to be surrendered to mainland China.

4.4 In December, 1997, The Chief Executive of Hong Kong gave an undertaking to the UK Government not to surrender [Launder] to mainland China. The relator applied for judicial review on the ground that the Chief Executive did not have the authority to give the undertaking. The court finally held that the undertaking . . . was consistent with the requirements of the UK Extradition Act.[121]

. . .

5.9 Since there is not a single country which has entered into a bilateral extradition agreement with both mainland China and Hong Kong, this [potential Agreement between Hong Kong and the PRC] arrangement may serve as a channel through which either mainland China or Hong Kong may extradite a fugitive offender to a country with which no extradition agreement has been signed.

Comment

The Research Paper stresses the distinct nature of the states with which Hong Kong and China have made arrangements. The potential for abuse via a mutual agreement between Hong Kong and the mainland is clear. The Paper also looked at cases from the United States in which courts had permitted extradition to Hong Kong despite

---

118. See *R v Secretary of State for the Home Department, ex parte Launder*, The Times, 29 October 1996.
119. See *R v Secretary of State for the Home Department, ex parte Launder* [1997] 3 All ER 961.
120. The "speciality" principle involves an assurance from the requesting state that a returned fugitive will stand trial only for those offences described in the extradition request.
121. See *R v Secretary of State for the Home Department, ex parte Launder (No 2)* [1998] 3 WLR 221.

concerns, pre-1997, as to possible "re-extradition", to China post-1997 or interference by China with the "speciality" principle.[122] The situation, in reverse, potentially arose in the Edward Snowden case, because Hong Kong (whereto Snowden had fled) has an extradition arrangement with the United States, while mainland China does not.

The concerns described have served to prevent, thus far, any concluded agreement between Hong Kong and the PRC.

Of further concern is a proposed mutual extradition agreement between Hong Kong and Macau (the two SARS). While there would be welcome opportunity for each SAR to recover alleged fugitives from their justice systems, there is the fear, unless a "double criminality" provision is included, *that a Hong Kong citizen could be extradited to Macau (and thence to the PRC?) for breaches of Macau's form of Article 23 (anti-sedition) laws*,[123] despite the fact that Hong Kong has yet to enact such laws.[124]

For the first time, following the "five booksellers" case, the issue is being considered of Hong Kong citizens claiming refugee status abroad; on the grounds that, on return to Hong Kong, they could be in danger of being taken to the mainland against their will.[125]

The result of the continued lack of any "rendition" agreement between Hong Kong and the Mainland is that no suspects have been *formally* returned from Hong Kong to the PRC.[126] "Informally", some Hong Kong suspects have been returned from the PRC to Hong Kong by the process of "informed deportation" whereby, on request by the Hong Kong police, they have been expelled from the PRC as "undesirables" and then been picked up by Hong Kong police on crossing the border.

12.2.6 Cross-border insolvency[127]

It is trite to say that whenever there are economic crises in the world community, insolvency issues, and international approaches thereto, come to the fore. While Hong Kong is not a signatory to the increasingly popular United Nations Commission on International Trade Law (UNCITRAL) Model Law on Cross-Border Insolvency,

---

122. Eg, *United States v Lui Kin Hong* 110 F 3d 103 (1st Circuit 1997).
123. See K Cheng, 'Hongkongers Could Be Extradited to Macau for Exposing State Secrets under Upcoming Treaty' *Hong Kong Free Press* (Hong Kong, 11 September 2015).
124. See Chapter 2.
125. R Carvalho, 'Seeking Safety Abroad' *South China Morning Post* (Hong Kong, 10 July 2016).
126. Though it is believed that mainland officials may, on occasion, have taken suspects from Hong Kong to the PRC against their will. The spiriting away (from Hong Kong and Thailand) of five Hong Kong sellers of books critical of the Chinese Communist Party, has gained worldwide prominence.
127. Insolvency may be corporate or individual. Consequences may vary (from voluntary arrangements, administration, liquidation (winding up) or personal bankruptcy). It is not possible to deal with these in detail and the key focus will be how Hong Kong interfaces with other jurisdictions (especially that of the PRC) in recognising and helping to enforce relevant orders.

it has co-operated consistently and successfully with international courts in the enforcement of overseas insolvency orders. Since this chapter is concerned with the Hong Kong/PRC interface, however, it must be admitted that there are problems with the recognition and enforcement of cross-border insolvency vis à vis Hong Kong and the mainland, because of a reluctance on the part of the PRC (which like Hong Kong is not an UNCITRAL signatory) to recognise, and assist in the enforcement of, insolvency orders made outside the PRC. The problem, as will be seen, is largely a "one-sided" one.

Unlike some other problems, the difficulty with "mutuality" in respect of the Hong Kong/mainland winding-up enforcement does *not* arise from the post-1997 change of relationship between Hong Kong and the mainland. Although relevant legislation, such as the PRC Enterprise Insolvency Law,[128] does talk about the impact of "foreign courts' decisions",[129] the distinction in this context (for the Hong Kong courts at least) is between "Hong Kong" and "non-Hong Kong" companies. Moreover, mutual agreement between Hong Kong and the PRC over the enforcement of civil judgments has the potential to make cross-border collaboration a relatively easier proposition as regards the PRC and Hong Kong than as between the PRC and "everywhere else". One suggestion is that the civil judgments approach could be explicitly extended to cross-border (ie, "cross boundary") insolvency.[130]

As well as the obvious jurisdiction to wind up Hong Kong companies, the Hong Kong courts have a limited *statutory* jurisdiction (under section 327 of the Companies (Winding Up and Miscellaneous Provisions) Ordinance)[131] to liquidate an insolvent *non*-Hong Kong company, *provided that* such company has a sufficient Hong Kong connection.[132] It should be borne in mind that the majority of companies operating in Hong Kong are incorporated elsewhere.[133] The current "favourite" location for overseas incorporation is the Cayman Islands; and only 10% of non-Hong Kong companies operating here are incorporated on the mainland.

An early example of *statutory* enforcement occurs in *Re Irish Shipping Ltd*.[134] Here, a winding-up order on a company had been made by the Irish courts. The Hong Kong High Court agreed to a petition from the official liquidator to wind up

---

128. In force from 2007 and also known as the Enterprise Bankruptcy Law.
129. "Foreign courts" appears not to be used in a technical, "political" sense.
130. See E Lee, 'Problems of Judicial Recognition and Enforcement in Cross-Border Insolvency Matters Between Hong Kong and Mainland China' (2015) 63(2) *American Journal of Comparative Law* 439–465.
131. Cap 32.
132. The lack of a sufficient Hong Kong connection was key to the refusal to grant a winding-up order in *Re Insigma Technology Co Ltd* [2014] HKCFI 1839 though the fact that the company concerned was incorporated in the PRC where liquidation had been refused was also a significant "practical" consideration for Harris J.
133. HSBC started the trend for overseas incorporation, based on "1997" fears. Overseas incorporation tends now to be for "other reasons".
134. [1985] HKLR 437.

the company in Hong Kong, on the basis that, although unregistered in Hong Kong, the company had assets in the jurisdiction.[135]

The statutory requirements (predominantly the need for a Hong Kong *nexus*) have been restated in *Re Pioneer Iron and Steel Group Co Ltd*[136] and subsequent cases[137] where the requirements for Hong Kong enforcement have been clarified (primarily) by Hong Kong's brilliant company law judge, Jonathan Harris, in the Court of First Instance. The approach is that Hong Kong courts have "discretion" as to whether to enforce non-Hong Kong windings-up of insolvent companies.[138] In exercising that discretion the court needs to be satisfied that: the company concerned has a sufficient connection[139] to Hong Kong; the winding-up order will be of substantial benefit to the petitioner; and that the court has the power to exercise jurisdiction over one or more persons who have an interest in the distribution of assets.[140] Of course, provided that these three criteria exist, jurisdiction would equally apply to a mainland company.

In terms of a *purely* "foreign" insolvency, however, Hong Kong has no *statutory* power to recognise and enforce insolvencies because it is not a UNCITRAL signatory. There *is*, however, some potential at *common law*. In the common law context, two major international approaches to insolvency can be identified: the "universalist" approach and the "territorial" one. In the former, broadly, a court in one jurisdiction seeks to administer all the property of the insolvent party worldwide and asks for the support of courts in other jurisdictions to assist in the enterprise. In the territorial approach, courts in each jurisdiction where the insolvent has property seek to administer such property on an independent, "local" basis. It is possible to have insolvency claims being made both on an international basis and a territorial one and the UNCITRAL Model Law provides for reconciliation between the two approaches.

The dominant legal view, in the *common law* world, is increasingly a "universalist" one, which requires *recognition* of the determination of the "dominant" foreign court and a decision to assist in the enforcement of that court's determination. The leading "British"[141] case adopting a "modified" universalist approach is *Cambridge Gas Transportation Corporation v Official Committee of Unsecured Creditors of*

---

135. The Hong Kong court's (obiter) view that it was enough if assets existed at the time of the hearing (rather than at the time the petition was made) has been criticised: see P Smart, 'Cross-Border Insolvency' *Law Lectures for Practitioners* (1991]].
136. [2013] HKCFI 324.
137. Eg, *Re China Medical Technologies* [2014] 2 HKLRD 997.
138. The jurisdiction to order a "just and equitable" winding up for "unfair prejudice" is outside the scope of this book.
139. This "core requirement" is more important than the other two, such that a *very* strong connection might be enough even absent requirement 3.
140. Counsel have argued that these three "core requirements" go to jurisdiction, but Harris J's view that they go to "discretion" has been upheld in the CFA: see *Re Yung Kee Holdings* (2015) 18 HKCFAR 501.
141. In the sense that it was ultimately determined in the Judicial Committee of the Privy Council.

Navigator Holdings plc.[142] In this case, a group of insolvent Isle of Man companies (Navigator Holdings) went into voluntary liquidation ("Chapter 11") in America. Through a "Letter of Request" the American court asked the Manx (Isle of Man) High Court to assist in the Chapter 11 plan. A Navigator shareholder (Cambridge Gas) objected on the grounds that it had not personally submitted to the jurisdiction of the American court. Although the Cambridge Gas complaint was upheld in the Manx High Court, it failed, ultimately, on appeal to the Privy Council. Highly significantly, Lord Hoffman stated that:

> The important point is that bankruptcy, whether personal or corporate, is a collective proceeding to enforce rights and not to establish them.[143]

The universalist approach is based on a two-stage test of, first, *recognising* the foreign award and then, where its effect is intended to extend overseas, assisting in its *enforcement*.

Of course the case is not binding on Hong Kong courts, though it will be treated with great respect.[144] In practice, Hong Kong has generally adopted a "modified universalist" approach despite not being a signatory to the UNCITRAL Model Law. Since Hong Kong has not adopted the Model Law and has no relevant legislation, its capacity to render assistance to a foreign court in an insolvency matter is based on the common law. In *Joint Official Liquidators of A Co and B*,[145] it was held that the Hong Kong court could recognise and assist in respect of foreign insolvencies where the law of the foreign insolvency was similar to that of Hong Kong and where the order sought would be available in Hong Kong.[146]

Similarly, Hong Kong courts have recognised PRC insolvencies. By implication this was the effect of *Ku Chia Chun & Others v Ting Lei Miao & Others*.[147] In that, potentially "political", case the Hong Kong courts had to determine whether to support and enforce in Hong Kong a Taiwanese bankruptcy order. At first instance Chan J (as he then was) refused to enforce an order from a court in part of China under the administration of a "usurper government". However, that view was overturned on appeal,[148] both by the Court of Appeal and the Court of Final Appeal (CFA) though the "usurping" status of the Taiwanese government was accepted by all judges. The majority view was that there was nothing inimical to the interests of the legitimate government in enforcing private rights and that, on the contrary, it

---

142. [2007] 1 AC 508.
143. Ibid para 15.
144. See Chapter 5.
145. [2014] 4 HKLRD 374.
146. A slightly more restrictive approach, adopted by the Privy Council in *Re Singularis Holdings* [2014] UKPC 36, nonetheless appears to support such an approach at "common law".
147. Reported in Court of Final Appeal (in re the same matter) as *Chen Li Hung & Another v Ting Lei Miao & Others* [2000] 1 HKC 461.
148. In fairness to Chan J, his was the unenviable task of delivering judgment only three days before the 1997 "handover", a politically sensitive time.

was in the sovereign power's interest to have law and order upheld in all parts of the jurisdiction. In the CFA Bokhary PJ stated:

> I hold that the Taiwanese Bankruptcy Order extends to Mr Ting's assets situated in Hong Kong ...
>
> ... The Taiwanese Bankruptcy Order is to be given effect by the Hong Kong courts. The rights thereunder are plainly private. By the general nature and particular circumstances of those rights, giving effect to them accords with the interests of justice, the dictates of common sense and the needs of law and order.[149]

Given the desirability, as the courts saw it, of enforcing orders from one part of the PRC in another, *a fortiori*, PRC insolvency orders should be upheld and enforced in Hong Kong unless they impinge on Hong Kong's common law system and the requirements of "one country, two systems". This view was given further support by the decision in *CCIC Finance Ltd v Guangdong International Trust & Investment Corporation*.[150] Here, the plaintiff was a bank operating in Hong Kong. The defendant, GITIC, was a PRC company registered in Hong Kong as an overseas company. GITIC HK was a wholly owned subsidiary of GITIC. The plaintiff sought a "garnishee" order[151] and the central issue of the case was whether bankruptcy proceedings in the PRC should "stay" local proceedings in Hong Kong pending the outcome. It was held that they should, that the PRC proceedings should be recognised and assisted, and the garnishee order should be rejected so as to prevent an individual creditor "jumping the queue".

Recognition of PRC insolvencies in Hong Kong should be further enhanced by the introduction of broader, clearer rules on corporate insolvency in China via the PRC Enterprise Insolvency Law,[152] promulgated in 2006 and in force from 1 June 2007. The law extends PRC legislative control of insolvency to most enterprises,[153] rather than merely state-owned ones (as was the previous case) and provides for recognition of an "Administrator's System".

What is clear, however, is that recognition and enforcement has not been, so far, readily *reciprocated*. There has been a reluctance in the PRC to uphold "foreign" (which in this context includes Hong Kong) insolvency orders which appears to stem from a more "territorial" approach to insolvency on the (civil law-based) mainland rather than from any concern over Hong Kong's "foreign" status. Even post the PRC Enterprise Insolvency Law:

> it will remain difficult to obtain enforcement in China of an insolvency judgment or ruling made by a foreign court.

---

149. [2000] 1 HKC 461 at 470–474.
150. [2005] 2 HKC 589.
151. Essentially an order transferring a debtor's assets to his creditor.
152. Or Enterprise Bankruptcy Law.
153. The PRC still has no personal bankruptcy laws. This has been noted as a deficiency following the personal property losses of many citizens in the Sichuan earthquake: see C Berube and P Pu, 'Bankruptcy and Insolvency in the PRC: A Myth' *IPBA Journal* (March 2009).

For inbound cross-border insolvency cases, the PRC Enterprise Insolvency Law sets out onerous conditions that will make it extremely difficult for a foreign insolvency officer to obtain recognition and enforcement in China.[154]

Amongst the "onerous conditions" are the requirement of reciprocal relations ("relevant treaties or reciprocal relations") between the country of the foreign court and the PRC; the condition that state sovereignty, national security and public interest must not be compromised; and the requirement that the foreign proceedings do not harm the lawful rights of PRC creditors.

The fear, of course, is that the PRC courts (or at least many of them)[155] will continue to adopt a local "territorial" approach. If the "relevant relations" rule is narrowly interpreted, this alone could preclude PRC recognition of awards/decisions made elsewhere, since the PRC does not have mutual relations relating specifically to insolvency. However, the hope has been expressed that with the formal accord between Hong Kong and the PRC on the mutual enforcement of civil judgments, recognition and enforcement of Hong Kong insolvency orders will become more likely for "psychological" reasons. There is no doubt that the scope of the "mutual enforcement" legislation precludes insolvency[156] so that there will be no direct, "causal" result. However, from a "purposive" standpoint, the agreement and resulting legislation evidence an increased level of trust and co-operation between both "sides", in the spirit of Article 95 of the Basic Law. Just as Lord Hoffman stated in *Navigator*, insolvency proceedings are about *enforcing* private rights rather than *determining* them, so the mutual recognition agreement, similarly, seeks cross-border enforcement of rights already established in court.

12.2.7 Admissibility of mainland documents

The admissibility of legal documents is yet another area of cross-border co-operation which has actually been rendered more problematic post-1997. Prior to the reunification, written evidence from the PRC was admissible in Hong Kong courts in the same way as any other "foreign" documentary evidence. The statutory authority is section 37 of the Evidence Ordinance[157] which is as follows:

> Admissibility of document filed in foreign court or consulate
>
> All documents whatsoever legally and properly filed or recorded in any foreign court of justice or consulate according to the law and practice of such court or consulate, and all copies of such documents, shall be admissible in evidence in the courts of Hong Kong on being proved in like manner as any documents filed or recorded in any foreign court are provable under this or any other Ordinance; and

---

154. Norton Rose, 'Cross-Border Insolvencies: China Assets at Risk?' China insight.
155. The courts of the PRC are not a homogeneous, consistently trained unit (see Chapter 11).
156. *Inter alia*, the agreement is restricted to "money judgments on disputes arising from commercial contracts".
157. Cap 8.

all documents whatsoever so filed or recorded in any foreign court or consulate, and all copies of such documents, shall, when so proved or admitted, be held authentic and effectual for all purposes of evidence as the same would be held in such foreign court or consulate.

Post-1997, once again, rules for "foreign" court or consulate documents should not be applicable in the Hong Kong/PRC context. It appears that the previous practice of PRC documents being authenticated in the PRC[158] and then sent to Hong Kong is continuing in practice though, absent new legislation, this may be open to legal challenge.[159]

12.2.8 Mutual investigation and evidence-taking in Hong Kong and the PRC

A key aspect of the mutual assistance envisaged by Article 95 of the Basic Law involves the taking of evidence by one "side" in the jurisdiction of the other. The matter is of particular significance in the criminal sphere; where a perceived increase in cross-border crime is of particular public importance, but where "due process" concerns have also been expressed, especially in relation to the taking of evidence by mainland authorities in Hong Kong.

The mutual taking of evidence is also of limited importance in the civil (non-criminal) law arena where, just as with the criminal law position, "international" approaches can no longer, post-1997, assist in solving Hong Kong/PRC problems. However, this issue is essentially that obtaining in respect of the admissibility of documents, discussed above.[160]

12.2.8.1 Mutual investigation and evidence-taking in criminal matters

A key public concern, even before 1997, was the increase in "cross-border" crime; especially drug-trafficking, smuggling and, with the increasingly "capitalist" PRC, cross-border corruption. It was obviously beneficial to have a scheme which would allow the taking of evidence by police (and, especially as regards Hong Kong, the Independent Commission Against Corruption) from one jurisdiction in the other. With the advent of reunification in 1997, once again, a solution could no longer be found in any international conventions, since Hong Kong and the PRC were now officially part of "one country".[161] The solution, therefore, had to lie in mutual co-operation. Indeed, as early as 1988 the Hong Kong Independent Commission Against

---

158. By the PRC Ministry of Foreign Affairs.
159. As long ago as December 1998, the Secretary for Justice was questioned on the issue in LegCo and new legislation was advocated.
160. See 12.2.7.
161. In 1997, the ICAC established the "J4" section to deal with "operational liaison". One part of J4 deals with international liaison and the other part deals with the PRC and Macau.

Corruption (ICAC) had agreed a Mutual Case Assistance Scheme (the Scheme) with authorities in Guangdong Province. The taking of evidence by ICAC officers in the PRC appears to have been relatively unproblematic. In the first 20 years of the Scheme:

> the ICAC has interviewed over 530 witnesses on the Mainland, leading to the successful investigation of many graft cases involving Mainland citizens or companies.[162]

However, the "reverse visits" (PRC authorities taking evidence in Hong Kong) have been more problematic,[163] as the following LegCo question and answer details make clear. The key words of the (supplementary) question, from the Honourable Emily Lau, were:

> Please give more details of the Mutual Case Assistance Scheme:– when it was put in place; whether there is an agreement or memorandum signed with the Mainland, if so what is the content; details of the guidelines issued to ICAC officers to remind them about the rights of Hong Kong people invited to be interviewed by Mainland officials and the number of Hong Kong residents who have refused to be interviewed since 1998.[164]

The gist of the reply (from the "Controlling Officer" (ICAC Commissioner)) was as follows:

> The Mutual Case Assistance Scheme has been put in place since 1988 as a result of an understanding between the ICAC and Guangdong People's Procuratorate to facilitate interview of witnesses in each other's jurisdiction in relation to corruption investigations.
>
> Since 1990, this arrangement . . . has been set out in the form of an agreed minute. The agreed minute outlines the broad areas of cooperation [sic] between the ICAC and the Guangdong People's Procuratorate on investigation, prevention and education . . .
>
> . . . our working procedures are set down as follows:–
>
> All requests for interview in Hong Kong will be personally approved by a directorate officer. They must contain full justification and must be corruption related.
>
> When the Mainland authorities made [sic] a request to ICAC . . . An interview will only be arranged with the witness's consent and such interviews will be made by

---

162. Hong Kong Government website, *Law and Order*, 18 December 2007, quoting ICAC Commissioner, Timothy Tong.
163. Annually there are somewhat more visits from the PRC to Hong Kong than vice versa.
164. Like lawyers, politicians should not ask a question unless they already know the answer! It is safe to assume that Ms Lau knew many of the answers before they were formally rendered.

> appointment, at ICAC premises and in the presence of ICAC officers. The witness will
> be clearly informed that he/she will be treated as a witness only...
>
> Before the interview... ICAC officers will inform the witness of his/her rights
> again...
>
> A witness... has a right to have a lawyer present during the interview.
>
> During the interview, if a witness does not wish to continue... he/she has the full
> right to discontinue the interview or refuse to give information.
>
> In normal practice, only Putonghua [sic] and Cantonese are used in interviewing
> witnesses. The ICAC has now proposed to tighten up the use of language in all future
> interviews.
>
> Since 1998, out of 173 requests, 14 Hong Kong residents have declined interviews with Mainland officials.

The question and response is significant in several respects. The first is that the dialogue took place in 2001, more than 12 years after the Assistance Scheme commenced. Even allowing for a measure of disingenuousness from Lau, it is remarkable that the Scheme should have remained relatively informal, and unofficially "recognised" (other than by the "agreed minute")[165] for so long. Anna Wu,[166] writing in 2006, states that:

> Co-operation with the mainland began in 1988 with the mutual case assistance scheme. This provides reciprocal aid in gathering evidence and securing witnesses. Significant cases have been cracked through co-operative efforts on this basis. However, this is an administrative measure and not a legal or juridical framework. Hopefully it will not be too long before this arrangement is formalized and put on a proper legal footing.[167]

The second and more important point relates to the "subtext" of the question which refers to a disturbing case involving the interviewing of a "witness" (Ng) by Guangdong People's Procuratorate officers on ICAC premises, in which the "witness",[168] who had no lawyer present at the time, alleged that he was abused, treated like a suspect and threatened "in the Chiu Chow dialect" which the ICAC officers present could not understand. The ICAC Commissioner subsequently confirmed, to LegCo, that the "dialect" had been used, that ICAC officers had not been informed in advance, and that the ICAC had conveyed its "grave concern" about

---

165. In fact a more formal agreement was signed by the respective parties in February 1996 and this was subsequently endorsed by the Supreme People's Procuratorate. The 1996 agreement was more streamlined and eliminated previous "red tape" requirements.
166. A Wu, 'Hong Kong's Fight Against Corruption Has Lessons for Others' *Hong Kong Journal* (Spring 2006).
167. Ibid 3. The desired formalisation has yet to be realised.
168. The crux of the scheme is that interviews are to be of "witnesses" only, on a voluntary basis, and (as regards interviews in Hong Kong by PRC Procuratorate staff) in the presence of ICAC officers.

the incident to the Guangdong People's Procuratorate. Ng's case, and the ensuing controversy represents a classic example of the tension between "due process" and "crime control" criteria and reflects, it seems, differing priorities in the two jurisdictions. That said, it is important to remember that, as 1997 approached, grave concerns were being expressed about the potential growth of corruption in Hong Kong, post-reunification. In 1996, for example, then ICAC Commissioner, Michael Leung, reporting on the increasing levels of corruption between 1992 and 1996,[169] expressed his fears for judicial independence post-1997, adding that:

> The ICAC cannot function alone . . .
> . . . Once we arrest people and send them to the courts, if the courts are not reliable then that is the end of the matter. Without strong legal backing, without a good strong judiciary independent of the administration we can't expect justice to be done.
> The ICAC's concern with the viability of Hong Kong's judicial system after 1997 is partly due to the fact that it is one essential link in the anti-corruption process which is beyond the ICAC's control.[170]

Fourteen years on, Leung's fears for the judiciary appear unfounded and many would feel that the "politicisation" of the ICAC[171] has been a greater factor in the failure to prosecute corrupt "big fish".[172]

12.2.8.2 Cross-border policing

The Mutual Case Assistance Scheme is limited, in that it only involves the interviewing of witnesses, the collecting of evidence and the exchange of intelligence. Moreover, it is restricted (from the Hong Kong side) to the ICAC. This means that requests by Hong Kong police to interview on the mainland are on an "ad hoc, informal" basis. Hufnagel[173] writes:

> In 1998, Mainland China and Hong Kong also signed a Memorandum of Understanding (MOU) on cross-border policing, which stipulated in very general terms the independence of both sides, and the aim of mutual contacts and communications. This MOU can, due to its lack of clear provisions concerning operational co-operation, only be considered a declaration of intent.[174]

---

169. Reported in "Law News" *Hong Kong Lawyer* (September 1996).
170. Ibid 6.
171. Referred to in A Wu (n 166).
172. That said, Hong Kong remains an international leader in the fight against increasingly sophisticated and "global" corruption. As an example, HKUSPACE established the first post-graduate certificate course in (global) "Corruption Studies" as long ago as 2003.
173. S Hufnagel, 'Transnational Organized Crime: Police Co-operation in China and the EU' (2014) 2(1) *Griffith Asia Quarterly*.
174. Ibid 80.

Nonetheless, co-operation between the Hong Kong and Guangdong police began as early as 1981. By 2000 a liaison officer system and a 24-hour hotline had been established. Key cross-border areas of concern were, and remain, drug-trafficking, smuggling, organised illegal immigration, robbery, kidnapping and prostitution. In the earliest days of the liaison a huge concern was the theft and smuggling out of Hong Kong of luxury cars, allegedly "to order"; this despite the fact that smuggled cars from Hong Kong (with right-hand drive) must have been very conspicuous on the mainland. Liaison (on land and water) had a significant effect and the problem has been largely eradicated. It was reported that in July 2000, Guangdong police had transferred, to their Hong Kong counterparts, 138 criminal suspects, 199 stolen cars, 10 yachts, 1,178 computer printers, 14 containers, 58,838 square feet of Italian leather and 15,485 tons of steel! In addition another $1.5 million US worth of stolen currency and other goods had also been returned.[175] Rather more controversially the two police forces had collaborated in the apprehension of Cheung Tze-keung ("Big Spender") discussed elsewhere.[176]

Much of the "request for assistance" procedure, as regards Hong Kong and the PRC, pre-1997, was effected via Interpol. While Hong Kong remains a member of Interpol, co-operation with the mainland can no longer, legalistically, be seen as an "international" issue, for previously explained political reasons. Indeed, even before 1997, Hong Kong and neighbouring regions of the PRC were operating increasingly through bi-lateral ties.[177] As regards the collecting of evidence or the conducting of interviews by police from one jurisdiction in the other, it is scarcely surprising that this has been viewed with some concern in Hong Kong. Nonetheless, Fu[178] has written:

> The police have gone even further (than the ICAC) in cross-border co-operation with the Mainland. After his high profile first trip to Beijing in August 1994, the Commissioner of Police, Mr Eddie Hui, reached an agreement with the Mainland counterpart to strengthen co-operation in the areas of exchange of information, direct contact of related police departments, training and research. Mainland police were also granted the power to interview suspects in Hong Kong with the approval, and under the supervision, of the Hong Kong police. But the police ruled out the possibility of setting up a Mainland police office in Hong Kong and any direct exchange of police officers. There was speculation at that time that both parties might agree that police officers could cross the border to conduct investigation of selected offences on the other side . . . the Commissioner categorically rules out the

---

175. Reported in *People's Daily* (English edition) (Beijing, 11 August 2000).
176. See 12.2.4.2 above.
177. See reference to Guangdong–Hong Kong police collaboration from 1981 above.
178. HL Fu, 'The Form and Substance of Legal Interaction Between Hong Kong and Mainland China' (n 20).

possibility that Mainland officers could come to Hong Kong to conduct their own investigations.[179]

Despite the limitations, it appears that Hong Kong police officers have been allowed to conduct investigations and interview suspects in the Mainland.

Mainland witnesses have been *invited* to testify in Hong Kong courts.[180] [emphasis added]

Despite the occasional problem, police co-operation between Hong Kong and the mainland has continued to work well, post-1997, as it did for some years before. Police and governments on both sides of the border have recognised the value of co-operation and the need to combat growing and increasingly sophisticated cross-border crime. KC Wong[181] writes:

> Between 1984 and 1993, the gross crime rate [in the PRC] rose from 510,000 reported cases to 1,618,000 reported cases . . . with major crimes rising from 63,000 cases to 539,000 cases . . . in 2002, Ministry of Public Security (MPS) reported investigating 509,000 criminal cases and clearing 221,000 of them . . . The crimes were also getting more serious, violent, sophisticated and organized.[182]

A typical headline relates that "Police Hit Cross-border Prostitution" as:

> Shenzhen and Hong Kong police combined on Wednesday night to smash four crime rings, rounding up more than 100 suspects in a blitz on crime.
>
> Hong Kong police arrested seven alleged fugitives and 58 prostitutes from the mainland.
>
> The raids also saw the arrest of 27 suspects in a cross-border prostitution ring.[183]

---

179. Despite the Commissioner's assurance, there have been some "aberrations". In 2004, following complaints from residents in Mt Davis Road, seven men, "acting suspiciously" and apparently "staking out" the area over several nights, were arrested by Hong Kong police. Having claimed to be PRC police (public security officers) and showing their IDs, they were released on bail: see 'PRC "Police" Arrested after Complaints of Espionage' *Taipei Times* (Taipei, 19 June 2004)]. The incident was hushed up officially, as was the "incursion" into Hong Kong by plain clothes PRC police to apprehend (and detain in the PRC for three hours) four protesters, complaining about the imprisonment of dissident Liu Xiaobo, and two (Hong Kong) *Ming Pao* journalists. Hong Kong police claimed not to have seen any mainlanders crossing the border despite photographic evidence provided by Hong Kong media: see *China Digital Times*, 18 June 2010. The most egregious incident has been the 2016 "abduction" of five Hong Kong booksellers, taken to the PRC ("unofficially") to assist with enquiries. Their "crime" appears to be the publication of works critical of the PRC leadership. As with the Mt Davis Road case, Hong Kong police seem to have been taken by surprise. The latest "mystery" concerns the "escorting" of mainland businessman, Xiao Jianhua, from the Four Seasons Hotel in Hong Kong to "help with enquiries" on the mainland. Requests for information by Hong Kong police have been ignored by mainland authorities. It has been reported that a "deal on faster notification of detentions [is] near" following the "booksellers" case: see *South China Morning Post* (Hong Kong, 14 December 2017).
180. See H Fu (n 20 above) op cit, supra, 110.
181. KC Wong, 'Policing Cross-Border Crimes between China and Hong Kong: A Preliminary Assessment' (2004) 2(1) Asian Policing.
182. Ibid 4.
183. S Chu (ed), 'Police Hit Cross-border Prostitution' Life of Guangzhou (website), 15 January 2010. Similar stories tell of cross-border co-operation in the detection of illegal football ("soccer") betting

The key problem is the tension between the need, in an increasingly globalised criminal world (involving drug, tobacco and people smuggling, etc) for cross-boundary liaison and the desire to maintain "one country, two systems". It appears that this tension will be exacerbated when, as is now certain, PRC officers will be permitted to police the imminent Hong Kong–Guangzhou train link within Hong Kong's territory. Without PRC officers operating within Hong Kong, speed of travel (the project's raison d'être) would be lost, but such is the widespread public mistrust of PRC intentions towards Hong Kong that such policing is widely resisted.[184] On 24 May 2017, it was announced that agreement had been reached for PRC authorities to have a police presence on the rail link within Hong Kong territory and to enforce mainland law.[185] While there seems little legal justification for this move, on a proper interpretation of the Basic Law, it should be remembered that mainland-bound Hong Kong travellers affected will have already decided willingly to submit themselves imminently to the law of the PRC.[186] However, justifiable fears have been expressed as to the legal implications of this apparent breach of Article 18 of the Basic Law.[187]

It seems that while the police themselves see merit in, and accept, a measure of "cross border policing", the criminal fraternity regards mainland China as a very distinct entity from Hong Kong, Taiwan, and Macau. Sonny Lo[188] writes:

> It is noteworthy that some of the law enforcement agents in the PRC have regarded the return of sovereignty over Hong Kong and Macao to the mainland as legitimate justification for the cross-border implementation of mainland laws. At the same time, law enforcement authorities in both Hong Kong and Macao have appeared to be tolerant of such cross-border implementation of mainland laws . . . However, ironically, the criminal elements in Greater China have viewed the varying legal systems within it as providing a golden opportunity for them to enrich themselves by illicit means.[189]

Somewhat strangely the favoured *locus* of the crime may vary. Violent criminals, for example, may favour Hong Kong's more lenient sentencing and lack of

---

especially during the summer 2010 World Cup.
184. Even pro-establishment writers have expressed concern: see Alex Lo, 'Right to Worry about Joint Rail Checkpoint' *South China Morning Post* (Hong Kong, 5 January 2016). The contrary view is expressed by legislator Bernard Chan: B Chan, 'Joint Checkpoint Best for Express Rail Convenience' *South China Morning Post* (Hong Kong, 9 June 2017). Full agreement appears to have been reached on terms whereby the PRC authorities will have jurisdiction *beyond* immigration matters only, despite concerns that this infringes Basic Law rules on application of PRC laws in Hong Kong: see 'Michael Tien Speaks out on Railway Checkpoint' *South China Morning Post* (Hong Kong, 19 June 2017).
185. Though this had already been conceded in principle by Secretary for Justice, Rimsky Yuen: see S Lau, 'Mainland Security to Police Kowloon Railway Terminus' *South China Morning Post* (Hong Kong, 22 November 2015).
186. Hong Kong–bound passengers will, of course, already have so subjected themselves.
187. Discussed in chapter 2.
188. Sonny Shiu Hing Lo, *The Politics of Cross-border Crime in Greater China: Case Studies of Mainland China, Hong Kong and Macao* (M E Sharpe 2009).
189. Ibid 196.

capital punishment, while some well-connected professional criminals may favour commission in the Mainland, where it is seen as easier to "buy off" the police.

12.3 Conflicts between the two systems

The syllabus for "Hong Kong Legal System" for the pre-PCLL "conversion" examinations refers to "conflicts between the systems". Obviously, this could be used in the context of the differing approaches to law in Hong Kong and the PRC. This would be within the notion of "conflict of laws", otherwise known as "private international law" which recognises differences between rules and approaches in different jurisdictions and seeks to provide a workable solution. So, for example, Smart and Zhang,[190] in writing about arrangements for mutual recognition and enforcement of judgments in Hong Kong and the PRC, refer to the development of a "regional conflict of laws".

Alternatively, "conflict" between systems may refer to those differences which have not been reconciled and over which the parties have failed to find a solution acceptable to both sides. In this context, the amount of genuine "conflict" between the systems is very limited, largely because the Basic Law spells out the rights and obligations on both sides. Of course, the legal systems of Hong Kong and the PRC differ markedly,[191] but the Basic Law clearly recognises this and guarantees that the differences will be respected and preserved (at least until 2047).

Where "conflict" in the "antagonism" sense occurs this will be only where either of the "parties" feel that the other has not kept its side of the Basic Law "bargain". So, for example, the Standing Committee of the National People's Congress (NPCSC) has indicated its view that the Hong Kong courts exceeded their powers of interpretation of the Basic Law in the "right of abode" cases[192] while, in the same scenario, others will have seen the NCPSC "intervention" as an incursion against Hong Kong's promised "high degree of autonomy"[193] and "right of final adjudication".[194]

Similarly, on the issue of democratic progress, many saw the NCPSC Interpretation on the method of appointment of the Hong Kong Chief Executive[195] as calculated to frustrate the Basic Law's statement that:

---

190. X Zhang and P Smart, 'Development of Regional Conflict of Laws: On the Arrangement of Mutual Recognition and Enforcement of Judgments in Civil and Commercial Matters between Mainland China and Hong Kong SAR' (2006) 36 HKLJ 553–584.
191. See Chapter 11.
192. See (for further discussion) Chapter 4 at 4.4.
193. Article 2, Basic Law.
194. Article 19, Basic Law.
195. NPC Standing Committee, *The Interpretation by the Standing Committee of the NPC of Article 7 of Annex I and Article III of Annex II to the Basic Law of the Hong Kong SAR of the PRC* (6 April 2004).

The ultimate aim is the selection of the Chief Executive by universal suffrage upon nomination by a *broadly representative* nominating committee in accordance with democratic procedures.[196] [emphasis added]

In August 2014, it became abundantly clear that Beijing's expectations of this "ultimate aim" differed from that of most Hong Kong people (and from all international standards) when the mainland produced its universal suffrage "model" for Hong Kong.[197] This, indeed, provided the right to vote to all Hong Kong citizens *but* only for one of "two or three" candidates pre-selected by a Beijing-friendly small circle "nominating committee" (in fact the old Beijing-friendly "election committee" wearing a different hat). In short everyone would be allowed to vote, but only for one of two or three candidates with little popular support. To limit the "nature" of the nominated candidates, a further requirement was added that they must "love Hong Kong and China".[198] This "fake democracy" model was clearly at odds with pre-1997 Beijing assurances that post-1997 democratic development would be a matter for Hong Kong.[199] The model, which caused widespread street protests,[200] was ultimately resoundingly rejected by LegCo.[201]

The "Beijing side" can also, with justification, point to Hong Kong's failure to implement Article 23 of the Basic Law,[202] which *requires* Hong Kong, on its own, to implement laws to prohibit treason, secession, sedition, subversion against the Central People's Government as well as theft of state secrets and "establishing ties" with foreign political organizations. Efforts by the Tung Chee Hwa administration to enact such laws (seen by many as excessive) were thwarted following massive street protests.[203]

---

196. Article 45, Basic Law.
197. NPC Standing Committee, *Decision on Universal Suffrage on Hong Kong.*
198. "Loving China" is equated, in the Beijing mind, with loving the CCP. HKSAR Chief Secretary, Carrie Lam, argued that this would not be necessary since the candidates would merely have to take the oath of office, yet were this the case the "love" requirement would be redundant since taking the oath is axiomatic.
199. In 1994 the PRC Ministry of Foreign Affairs stated that, "The democratic election of all LegCo members by universal suffrage is a question to be decided by the HKSAR itself and needs no guarantee by the Chinese Government." This reinforced even broader promises as to Hong Kong autonomy, with respect to democratic development, by Hong Kong and Macau Affairs csar, Lu Ping, in March 1993.
200. Hong Kong's lengthiest ever street protest, "Occupy Central", lasted for 79 days. For much fuller detail of "Occupy", see J Chan, 'Hong Kong's Umbrella Movement' (2014) 103(6) *Commonwealth Journal of International Affairs.*
201. The vote was 28:8 against (a two-thirds majority *in favour* was required to adopt the model). The "anti" vote was boosted by the incompetence of the pro-Beijing side, many of whom quit the LegCo Chamber in a vain attempt to stall the vote on grounds on inquoracy.
202. This is contrasted with Macau's "laudably" speedy introduction of such legislation, post-reunification in 1999: see T Cheung, 'NPC Chief's Praise for Macau not Lost on HK' *South China Morning Post* (Hong Kong, 10 May 2017).
203. *Inter alia*, it was felt that the legislation would be used to extend the vicious PRC suppression of the Falun Gong movement to Hong Kong. For further discussion of Article 23 see Chapter 1. Since the decision of CY Leung not to seek "re-election" as Chief Executive, PRC spokespersons have

Conflict can also be seen in the areas of policing and criminal procedure as, while co-operation is essential, there is a significant tension between the avowedly "crime control" approach to crime in the PRC and the more "due process" approach in Hong Kong. This philosophical conflict, outlined above, best explains the failure to reach agreement on a rendition agreement between Hong Kong and the PRC despite a realisation that both sides must compromise in "forging consensus instead of accentuating differences and fostering co-operation instead of creating alienation between two drastically different criminal justice systems that are not only forced to live with each other under one roof . . . but also compelled to work with each other to deal with common concerns".[204]

These (exceptional) examples of true "conflict" have, of course been dealt with elsewhere.[205] It should be stressed that they are, indeed, exceptional, while expressing the hope that this will continue to be the case.

---

dropped heavy hints that Leung's successor, Carrie Lam, will be expected to enact Article 23. See S Lau, 'Beijing Signals Tighter Grip' *South China Morning Post* (Hong Kong, 28 May 2017).
204. KC Wong (n 181) 16.
205. On "interpretation" of the Basic Law, see, in particular, Chapters 2 and 4.

13
Policing and the Decision to Prosecute

Overview

Hong Kong police are regularly described as "Asia's finest". Given the quality of the opposition, this is probably a deserved epithet, but one involving "faint praise". Hong Kong police have, indeed, been generally well regarded by the public (at least in the past 30 years), approachable and non-confrontational. Despite frequent complaints of police misconduct in respect of detention and interrogation, the public has generally seen the police as doing a reasonable job, with any abuses of power directed towards the criminal elements rather than law-abiding citizens. Much of this confidence was shattered during "Occupy Central" by shocking scenes of unnecessary and excessive use of tear gas by the police employed as a first, rather than a last, resort and the filmed beating of an arrested (and defenceless) Occupy demonstrator by police officers.

It has become clear that the police force has been increasingly politicised, with strategic decisions taken at a supra-police level. Such strategy can be seen not only in police response to public demonstrations (use of force and deliberate under-counting of anti-government protesters) but in more minor (in)actions such as refusal to enforce parking regulations against the rich or well-connected. Conversely, minor infractions, which cause offence only to the well-connected (hawking or open-air dining), tend to be "policed" vigorously (though not always by the police as such).

Given the deterioration in relations between police and public, one amendment which is desperately needed is a Hong Kong "codifying" equivalent of Britain's Police and Criminal Evidence Act (PACE); mooted for many years but, like so many much-needed legal reforms, never legislated.

Moreover, it is highly desirable that complaints against police are handled in a far more independent and transparent way than at present. In this context it should be noted that the post of "Ombudsman", often occupied by independent and efficient men (and especially women!), is precluded from investigating all but a small part of the work of police.

The decision to prosecute in Hong Kong has, traditionally, been handled in a very thorough and efficient way in all serious cases. The very high conviction rate in the superior courts bears testimony to the efficiency of the screening process employed in the relevant department, the Department of Justice. Some have argued that the high conviction rate in District Courts reflects a pro-prosecution bias, but the high correlation between conviction rates without and *with* juries indicates that the main reason for high conviction rates is that those charged with offences in Hong Kong are generally guilty of having committed them.

The main concerns in relation to the prosecution determinations of the Department of Justice have tended to be in relation to "non-prosecutions"; seen, in some notable cases, as examples of the well-connected being treated more favourably than the "man in the street". Political interference is strongly suspected and has much to do with the fact that the ultimate power, to decide whether or not to prosecute, resides with the Secretary for Justice (a politician and head of the Department of Justice) rather than the Director of Public Prosecutions. More recent, and analogous, concern has been raised as to the allegedly "political" decision to seek a "review of sentence" for "Occupy Central"-supporting legislators; initially given a non-custodial sentence.

13.1 Policing in Hong Kong[1]

While "policing" in Hong Kong is practised by other agencies (ICAC, Immigration Department, etc) as well as the Hong Kong Police Force, the main focus here will be on the Hong Kong police.[2]

The current policing ideal in Hong Kong is essentially one of policing with consent.[3] It has not always been so. Having been established in 1842 with 32 officers recruited from the army garrison considered unsuitable for regular army service,[4] the force was, for many years, ill-regarded and inefficient. Governor Macdonnell (1866–1872) is reported to have said that he could not remember seeing a body of men so corrupt or inefficient as the Hong Kong police force. Even after efficiency was increased with the recruitment of Sikh officers, the police role was seen, essentially, as one of *control* of the local population for the benefit of the colonial master. Even up to the 1970s:

> the people were afraid of the police and usually stayed away from them. The police were perceived as 'licensed rascals' and took bribes from street hawkers, gambling

---

1. For a dedicated text on this topic, see Kam C Wong, *Policing in Hong Kong: Research and Practice* (Palgrave MacMillan London 2015).
2. For an interesting historical study of *private* policing, see S Hamilton, *Watching Over Hong Kong: Private Policing 1841–1941* (Hong Kong University Press 2009).
3. But is this changing? A quick study of police recruitment posters will show that only a few years ago the force was seeking to recruit those wishing to "help others". Current posters, in contrast, show a paramilitary force looking "armed-up and dangerous". It is clear that the force is now looking for a different sort of recruit.
4. They were under the command of the Chief Magistrate, William Caine. Their role was primarily protection of the British quarters.

dens and vice organisations. The public was coerced to comply with police operations such as stop-and-search, entry, seizure and arrest.[5]

Not until the ICAC-led anti-corruption purge in the 1970s did the Hong Kong police earn their title of "Asia's Finest", with a perception of the police as honest, efficient and working for the common good. The police force's relatively new motto is (the grammatically dubious) "We Serve with Pride and Care" and, while it is not always clear *who*, primarily, the police are "serving", in major respects it must be said that the police function efficiently in protecting Hong Kong society. Most Hong Kong residents would agree that Hong Kong is a safe place and almost all oversees visitors attest to the safety of Hong Kong. Of course, education, family influence, peer pressure and other societal factors play their part in contributing to a low crime rate, but Hong Kong's police deserve their share of credit. Police numbers are also a factor since Hong Kong has almost the highest ratio of police to general community in the world.[6] However, sheer numbers alone would not be effective without a reasonable level of efficiency in terms of crime prevention and detection.

"Reputationally" the Hong Kong police force has been affected by two major events: the 1967 riots and, far more recently, "Occupy Central".[7] The force's reputation was enhanced by its strong stand against communist-inspired riots and bombing during the mainland's "Cultural Revolution".[8] While the riots began with justifiable complaints about working conditions in one of Li Ka-shing's plastics factories, the trade unionists involved were supported by mainland revolutionaries; and almost all public support for the rioters evaporated as they resorted to the tactics of bombing, with schools a major target.

"Occupy Central" (dealt with in more detail below)[9] was very different. The eventually futile attempt to persuade China to bestow a measure of genuine democracy in Hong Kong was, initially, treated with scepticism by many in Hong Kong. A massive increase in support for the movement (and a corresponding decline in the police's reputation) followed the over-zealous use of tear gas and pepper spray by

---

5. Y-N Pang, 'An Analysis of the Legitimization of Police Powers in Hong Kong' (The University of Hong Kong: HKU Scholars Hub, 1999).
6. Hong Kong's seven million residents are policed by over 28,000 front-line police, supported by over 4,000 civilian support staff and 3,500 (voluntary) Auxiliary Police. For a more detailed (if not entirely objective) history of the latter, see Royal Hong Kong Auxiliary Police Force, *A Pearl in the British Treasury*, 30 June 1997.
7. Initially envisaged as "Occupy Central with Love and Peace", the latter part of the epithet is generally discarded.
8. See K Sinclair, *Asia's Finest: An Illustrated Account of the Royal Hong Kong Police* (Unicorn Books, Hong Kong 1983). It is much to be regretted that an increasingly politicised Hong Kong Police has now seen fit to "amend" its website and delete references to the communist inspiration for the riots (some comments have been reinstated after public protest). "Politicisation" can also be seen in the consistent "under-counting" by the police of anti-government protests and the refusal to allow peaceful protest near the Central Liaison Office: see P Siu, 'Abuse of Police Powers Claimed in Protest' *The Standard* (Hong Kong, 14 May 2012).
9. See 13.1.4 below.

the police on "day one" of Occupy. Although the initial "show of force" was almost certainly ordered from above, citizens in Hong Kong and around the world were able to witness the enthusiasm with which the police responded. It must, however, be recognised that responses to the police's "get tough" approach varied, largely on "generational" lines. The older generation tended to be more supportive of the police while young people were largely appalled by the police actions. This polarisation was well illustrated by responses to the imprisonment of the seven policemen (unwittingly) filmed beating up a defenceless arrested suspect. Many saw the imprisonment as a long overdue recognition that all (including policemen) are subject to the law, while others (mainly from the pro-establishment camp) felt that the police should be immune to punishment, even when caught red-handed.

As with many societies, concerns about policing tend to revolve around alleged abuses of power (stop and search, arrest, search and seizure, etc), the *selective* use of powers against specific "targets", and corruption. Criticisms of the police have increased dramatically post-"Occupy Central" and much of this is attributed to Hong Kong's confrontational police chief from 2011 to 2015, Andy Tsang.[10]

Various pieces of legislation prescribe in detail police powers in Hong Kong, notably the Police Force Ordinance[11] and the Dangerous Drugs Ordinance.[12] Moreover, other pieces of legislation affect the relationship of such powers with the rights of the individual; in particular, the Bill of Rights Ordinance and the Basic Law itself. However, no modern, dedicated "code", such as the English Police and Criminal Evidence Act (PACE), exists in Hong Kong.

Before considering Hong Kong police powers *in Hong Kong*, brief mention should be made of the police's "international" role. As regards Hong Kong's policing interface with the rest of the world, this has remained essentially unchanged "post-1997", with Hong Kong's continuance as a member of Interpol, valued by the rest of the world for its efficient and co-operative police force. Writing shortly after reunification, Police Deputy Commissioner, Tsang Yam Pui, delivered the following "business as usual" message:

> As regards to our status, we are a separate police force from the Chinese mainland police organisation . . . The relationship between the Hong Kong police force and the Police organisation in mainland China is built on the agreement of the following three simple principles: our Commissioner is responsible to the Chief Executive of the Hong Kong SAR; There should be mutual co-operation and; There should be mutual support.

---

10. See, eg, 'The Decline of Hong Kong's Police' *Wall Street Journal* (New York, 7 May 2015). *The Standard* newspaper reported in December 2014, that Hong Kong police's popularity had fallen to its lowest level since 1997: '"Asia's Finest" Take Poll Fall' *The Standard* (10 December 2014).
11. Cap 232.
12. Cap 134.

Liaison . . . is being conducted on a well-practised framework, which existed for 12 years prior to the changeover of sovereignty. The only change is that the Hong Kong Police Force is now a sub-bureau of NCB China in the Interpol network.[13]

13.1.1 Stop and question, stop and search

Despite various *prima facie* protections of the liberty of the individual in Hong Kong, police here have considerable powers to stop, question and, to a lesser extent, search individuals. Though these are hedged around by restrictions such as "reasonable cause", in practice such restrictions are imprecise and unlikely to limit police activity significantly. Criticisms of the exercise of stop/question, or stop/search powers tend to be based either on excessive or selective use of such powers.

The Basic Law appears to be relevant here by virtue of Articles 28 and 31. Article 28 states that:

> The freedom of the person of Hong Kong residents[14] shall be inviolable.
>
> No Hong Kong resident shall be subjected to arbitrary or unlawful arrest, detention or imprisonment. *Arbitrary or unlawful search of the body of any resident or deprivation or restriction of the freedom of the person shall be prohibited.* [emphasis added]

Article 31 adds that residents shall have freedom of movement within the HKSAR.

Moreover, the Bill of Rights Ordinance (BORO)[15] establishes that the citizen has the "right to silence" and may refuse to answer questions put to him.

The "inviolability" pronouncement of paragraph one must be read in the light of paragraph two which states that residents must not be subjected to "arbitrary or unlawful" arrest, detention or imprisonment nor to "arbitrary or unlawful" search of the body or restriction of the freedom of the person. In short, there are powers of the police to arrest, detain, question and search residents, but they must be exercised lawfully.

The right of police to stop and question is governed primarily by section 54(1) of the Police Force Ordinance[16] which states that a police officer may stop a person who is "acting in a suspicious manner" and require proof of identity. The stopped person may be detained for a "reasonable period" to determine whether or not he is suspected of commission of a crime.

It is clear that the words "suspicious manner" and "reasonable period" are open to interpretation and may be abused. The power is undoubtedly used selectively; such that young Chinese males, for example, are far more likely to be stopped than middle-aged Westerners. On the other hand, police would argue that it is part of their

---

13. Y Tsang, 'State of The Reunion' (*Offbeat*, Hong Kong Government Police website).
14. Article 41 essentially extends these rights to non-resident visitors.
15. Cap 383.
16. Cap 232.

job to investigate illegal immigration which is far more likely to be relevant to the former group. Indeed, section 17(C)(2) of the Immigration Ordinance[17] permitting police to require production of proof of identity (without a requirement of suspicion), excludes from its ambit temporary overseas visitors.

A tension clearly exists between the policemen's power to ask questions of a person detained under the above provisions and the citizen's "right to silence" as guaranteed by the Bill of Rights Ordinance (BORO).[18] BORO gives legislative force to the common law "presumption of innocence" and the rule against self-incrimination. The rule, originating in Britain and made famous in the United States via the Fifth Amendment to the Constitution, permits the citizen, under investigation or charge, to remain silent and insist on the prosecution proving his guilt. While some small inroads have been made on the right to silence in Britain, via section 34 of the Criminal Justice and Public Order Act 1994 (permitting, in limited circumstances, a court to draw adverse inferences from a suspect's silence when questioned),[19] Hong Kong has not followed this lead. The principle remains in Hong Kong that, in *almost every case*,[20] a suspect may choose to remain silent when questioned without adverse inferences being drawn.[21] In practice, of course, the exercise of the right to silence and the refusal to answer questions is likely to extend the period of any police "stop" and may, in the event of subsequent arrest and charge, be regarded as suspicious by a jury of laymen, despite appropriate advice having been given by the judge.

In practice, Hong Kong police have considerable powers to search, as well as stop, residents. Indeed, the main grounds for instituting a "stop" (the stopped person acting suspiciously,[22] or the stopped person being "reasonably" suspected of having committed or being about to commit an offence)[23] also permit search for the purpose of discovering any object posing a danger to the police officer or, in the latter case, providing supporting evidence of the alleged crime.

In Hong Kong, as in Britain, criticisms of stop and search tend to be based on "selectivity", as indicated above, and on the ineffectiveness of stops. Police tend to support stops by stating that they are effective both in detecting *and* in avoiding crime. It is difficult to be precise about how effective stops are in the context of crime *prevention* since this involves "what if" issues. However, a critical *South China Morning Post* (*SCMP*) article in 2013[24] cast serious doubt on the effectiveness of Hong Kong stop and search practices. The *SCMP* stated that:

---

17. Cap 115.
18. BORO s 8 (The Hong Kong Bill of Rights), Article 11.
19. Given the limited nature of the legislative change, it has been upheld as reasonable by the European Court of Human Rights (see *Condron v UK* [2001] 31 EHRR 1).
20. A limited exception exists in relation to the *duty* of disclosure of the owner of a motor vehicle involved in an offence and the SFC and ICAC have greater rights to *require* a response (see below).
21. See, eg, *Lee Fuk Hing v HKSAR* [2004] 7 HKCFAR 600.
22. Section 54(1), Police Force Ordinance.
23. Section 54(2), Police Force Ordinance.
24. 'Hong Kong Police Stop-and-Search Tactics Questioned after 1.6 Million Spot Checks Last Year' *South China Morning Post* (Hong Kong, 24 November 2013).

Hong Kong police carry out four times as many identity checks and on-the spot searches as their counterparts in New York and London, official figures show, even though the effectiveness of the procedure appears to be in sharp decline.

The article pointed out that the relatively high number of searches took place despite the fact that Hong Kong is a much safer place (with far less crime) than New York and London.[25] It added that excessive and selective stops tend to promote disrespect of the police and referred to the targeting of "ethnic minorities, especially South Asians". The *SCMP* stated that (unlike New York and London) police in Hong Kong do not record the ethnicity of those stopped.[26] The key premise of the *SCMP* article was that the stops were ineffective in that "only one in 113 searches resulted in the detection of a crime." However, by way of counter-argument, the *SCMP* quoted a "retired senior police officer" who said that:

> You have to remember that Hong Kong is a very easy place to get into for many people, from many different places. Illegal immigration has been and will continue to be a problem.

It should also be noted that the *SCMP* article generated a great deal of online response from readers; much of it supportive of the police. Typically, respondents referred to the much greater safety of Hong Kong (as opposed to the two overseas cities cited) and suggested that the extensive use of stop and search was a contributory factor in the low level of crime in Hong Kong.

13.1.2 Search and seizure of property

In addition to restrictions on stopping/searching the individual, the Basic Law restricts the right of police to search the homes of residents. Article 29 states that:

> The homes and other premises of Hong Kong residents shall be inviolable. Arbitrary or unlawful search of, or intrusion into, a resident's home or other premises shall be prohibited.

As a consequence, there is no *general* right to search premises, without the consent of the occupier, *unless* a warrant is issued. A warrant can be issued by a magistrate for police to enter premises and search for/seize any items "of value to the investigation of an offence committed or likely to be committed".[27]

There are also limited rights to enter and search premises *without* warrant. For example, a policeman intending to arrest a suspect may enter premises to do so where entry into such premises has been refused or where waiting for a warrant

---

25. The *SCMP* sources included the US Census Bureau, Home Office (UK), Hong Kong census, and Hong Kong Police Force.
26. Online respondents have disputed the accuracy of this *SCMP* assertion.
27. Section 50(7), Police Force Ordinance. Other powers of search/seizure with warrant apply under s 28 of the Theft Ordinance (Cap 210) (regarding stolen goods) and s 104 Criminal Procedure Ordinance (Cap 221) (regarding items used to prepare for commission of crime).

may provide the suspect with an opportunity to escape.[28] A significant expansion of the power to enter and search premises was envisaged for the proposed Article 23 legislation,[29] abandoned, in 2003, after enormous public opposition.[30]

13.1.3 Arrest/detention

In addition to the restrictions on arrest stipulated by the Basic Law, stated above, the Bill of Rights Ordinance[31] states that:

> No one shall be subjected to arbitrary arrest or detention. No one shall be deprived of his liberty except on such grounds and in accordance with such procedure as are established by law.
> ... Anyone who is arrested shall be informed, at the time of the arrest, of the reasons for his arrest and shall be promptly informed of any charges against him.
> ... Anyone arrested ... shall be promptly before a judge or other officer authorized by law to exercise judicial power and shall be entitled to trial within a reasonable time or to release. It shall not be the general rule that awaiting trial shall be detained in custody, but release may be subject to guarantees to appear for trial ...[32]

Police powers of arrest in Hong Kong are regulated, primarily, by the Police Force Ordinance (PFO). Under the PFO there is a power of arrest under warrant (under section 53) and powers to arrest *without* warrant (under section 50). The section 50 powers relate, essentially, to the power to arrest on reasonable suspicion of the commission of a serious[33] offence *or* in relation to such suspicion with regard to *any* offence where the service of a summons (for arrest) is impracticable because the name or address of the suspect is unknown or may have been given falsely.

Once arrested, a suspect should be speedily brought to a police station. Maximum limits are placed on the amount of time a suspect may be detained before a charge is made against him/her. Once a charge is made, the suspect must be brought promptly before a magistrate. At this stage he will either be "bailed" (with or without "surety") to appear in court to face the charge at a later date or remanded in custody (where bail is opposed and the magistrate upholds the objection). Since the Bill of Rights Ordinance, there is in Hong Kong (as in Britain) a presumption in favour of bail after charge in that Article 5 states that: "It shall not be the general rule that persons awaiting trial shall be detained in custody". If bail is to be refused, therefore, reasons for objection/rejection must be given.

---

28. Section 50, Police Force Ordinance.
29. See Simon NM Young, "'Knock, Knock. Who's There?" Warrantless Searches for Article 23 Offences', Centre for Comparative and Public Law (HKU), Occasional Paper No 10 (June 2003).
30. See Chapter 1.
31. Cap 383.
32. Ibid s 8 (The Hong Kong Bill of Rights), Article 5.
33. Where the sentence is "fixed by law" (essentially murder) or where the offence is imprisonable.

13.1.4 Abuse of police power

There is no modern liberal society in which there are not at least some complaints about police excessive use (or abuse) of their powers. It should be said that, *comparatively*, Hong Kong's police are far more restrained and non-confrontational than many others. To take just one example, *The Guardian* newspaper (UK) is maintaining records of all citizens killed by police in the United States.[34] By the end of November 2015, the figure for that year stood at 1,046.[35]

Serious concerns have been raised in Hong Kong (and elsewhere) in relation to the excessive use of tear gas against demonstrators in the early days of "Occupy Central" in 2014. There is little doubt that the well-publicised use of tear gas encouraged support for Occupy. Before the use of tear gas many supported Occupy's aims but not its methods; after the tear gas the government and police were far more clearly seen as the "bad guys". The hard-line attitude of police boss, Commissioner Andy Tsang,[36] added to the feeling that the days of policing by consent in Hong Kong were over. University of Hong Kong legal academic Simon Young has written that, to be lawful, the force used by the police (including the use of tear gas) must be only that "reasonably necessary" to disperse any gathering reasonably believed (by a senior officer) to be likely to cause a breach of the peace. Young concludes that the televised coverage showed:

> no clear acts of violence or rioting that necessitated the use of tear gas . . . repeated use of the tear gas (to protesters' surprise) suggesting that either an inadequate warning was given or insufficient time was allowed for protesters to comply . . . throwing of tear gas canisters directly at protesters . . . suggesting that not the minimum of force was used and quick regathering of protesters . . . suggesting that the tear gas achieved very little and certainly nothing that less intrusive means could not have achieved.[37]

Young's conclusion was that the police had at least a case to answer to justify their considerable use of tear gas. It is now very unlikely, however, that any action will be taken and, again, it must be said that other citizens (especially older ones) had greater sympathy towards the police actions.

Complaints of police mistreatment in Hong Kong are often made by those arrested but rarely substantiated. Ken Tsang, for example, the "Occupy" demonstrator filmed being beaten by police officers in what they thought to be a hidden

---

34. 'The Counted' *The Guardian* (London, 2015 et seq).
35. The records are not necessarily accurate as they rely on "crowdfunding" and include some deaths which police have recorded as suicides. In any event, the figure is appallingly high. By 2016 the US Justice Department will have established a formal recording system operated by the Bureau of Justice Statistics (BJS). Meanwhile the *Washington Post* has given a figure of 965 such killings by 24 December 2015 while the *New York Times* recorded 1,134 for the whole of 2015.
36. Tsang was succeeded as Commissioner of Police by Stephen Lo Wai-chung.
37. Simon N M Young, 'Was it Lawful for the Police to Use Tear Gas on Protesters in Hong Kong?' HKU Legal Scholarship Blog, 29 September 2014.

spot,[38] claimed to have been further beaten while at the police station. Away from the cameras, and alone, the word of a suspect is unlikely to be corroborated. Similar claims of mistreatment were legion in Britain but became far less common after the introduction of the Police and Criminal Evidence Act (PACE) 1984, which, in addition to establishing rules on arrest, stop, search seizure and detention, created the role of "custody officer", an officer charged with maintaining a strict custody "log", detailing time of arrest, cautions, length of detention, meal breaks, confession warnings, etc. Despite some criticisms from "all sides" (and legislative reform in some areas), it is generally thought that PACE was an improvement on the previous position. The Law Reform Commission of Hong Kong considered the importation of PACE-like reforms and issued a report in 1992 on arrest. By 2015 only around half of the report's LegCo-endorsed recommendations had been implemented via legislation.

13.1.5 Complaints against the police[39]

Hong Kong is far from unique in having a mechanism for complaints against the police which is perceived as insufficiently independent. The position in Hong Kong, under the so-called "two tier" system, is that all complaints against police must originally be made to the Complaints Against Police Office (CAPO), a unit of the police force and thus clearly not independent. While it is true that CAPO's work is monitored by an Independent Police Complaints Council (IPCC), it is widely believed that IPCC's supervisory powers are too constrained. A typical concern is evidenced by the following LegCo question in 2009:

> Question: (Hon Joseph Lee Kok-long)
> There are quite a number of comments that ... CAPO of the Hong Kong Police Force lacks credibility and transparency in handling complaints against the Police, for example, the investigations are conducted by police officers, and it has also been claimed that the ... IPCC has limited monitoring power ... will the Government inform this Council:
>
> a) of the number of police officers who were disciplined in each of the past three years after the complaints against them had been substantiated, together with a breakdown by the type of penalties imposed on them; and

---

38. The seven officers (immediately identified and suspended from duty) were finally charged, convicted and sentenced to imprisonment 18 months later (as was Tsang, for assault via the pouring of an unidentified liquid over policemen).
39. For further detail, cf KC Wong, 'Police Powers & Control in Hong Kong' (2010) 34(1) International Journal of Comparative & Applied Criminal Justice.

> b) whether it has considered further strengthening IPCC's power on monitoring the day-to-day investigation of CAPO (such as appointing full-time observers) to ensure that the investigations are conducted in a fair and impartial manner; if so, of the details, if not, the reasons for that?

The response to the question both indicated the validity of concerns and promised improvement via newly introduced legislation:

> Reply:
>
> President,
>
> a) In 2006–2008, 325 officers were disciplined on substantiation of the complaints against them. Of these, 292 were given advice, 12 given warnings, 12 cautioned, two reprimanded, six severely reprimanded and one dismissed subsequent to criminal conviction.
>
> ... The Independent Police Complaints Council (IPCC) Ordinance[40] ... enacted in July 2008 puts the IPCC on a statutory basis while maintaining the two-tier police complaints system ...
>
> The enactment of the IPCC Ordinance is conducive to enhancing and reinforcing the independent status as well as the monitoring function of the IPCC. It also enhances the transparency and creditability of the police complaints system ...
>
> ... the Ordinance empowers IPCC members and observers to attend any interviews to be conducted by the Police and to observe the collection of evidence undertaken by the Police in respect of reportable complaints ...

Despite the response and the improvements noted therein, concerns remain, especially as to the fact that initial investigation of complaints against police must *always* be conducted by CAPO.[41] It is striking that such a high proportion of initial complaints to CAPO are "withdrawn" or "unsubstantiated". Of 323 complaints of police assaults in 2012–2013, for example, only *one* was "substantiated in part" and *none* in full. Depending on one's perspective, this is either extremely impressive or "too good to be true". Similar concerns are highlighted in the following extract from Hong Kong Human Rights Commission, presented in surprisingly poor English.

---

40. Cap 604.
41. See LCQ6 *Complaints Against Police System* (LegCo question from Hon Kenneth Leung with regard to the Ken Tsang case [see 13.1.4 supra] 29 October 2014).

Hong Kong Human Rights Commission
Society for Community Organization
Report to the United Nations[42]
CHAPTER III
POLICE POWER AND POLICE BRUTALITY

Strong Police Power brings serious Police Brutality

19. The Hong Kong SAR Government is one of the cities with the highest police ratio (1 police offer to 221 citizens) with more than 31,500 police officers (increased from 27,314 in 1994 to 31,688 in 2006) keeping public order in a city of six million people. Police officers are vested with great power to maintain social order. They can stop people to check their identity cards, detain people, search and seize premises. They are also empowered by the existing laws to control public assemblies and associations. Unfortunately, police always [sic] abuse their power, by torturing and threatening the safety of citizens. According to a survey by the Hong Kong University, the public generally think that police abuse their power. This general belief implies that the problem of police abusive use of power has become more and more serious. Judging from the observations of social workers, most abuse of police powers fall on the grassroots and marginal groups.

20. The Complaint Against Police Officer [sic] (CAPO), which is part of the police system dealing with the complaints against police, regularly receives more than 500 cases concerning police assault, which has continuously been the top three among various complaints . . . The number of complaints presented cannot reflect the real situation. It is just the tip of the iceberg. There are speculations that the number of the unreported cases is three to four times more as the complainants may be threatened, intimidated by the police or have already lost confidence in the complaint mechanism. Many cases have been hidden up [sic]. The hidden situation has become more serious in the past three years, which can be explained by the change of police complaint mechanism at the operational level. Some victims give up complaining after police persuasion or their apathy towards an ineffective complaint mechanism. However, the Hong Kong SAR Government has not carried out any study to uncover the problem, nor has it set up any competent and independent complaint mechanism or monitoring body to handle these complaints.

. . .

Lack of Independent and Credible Police Complaint Mechanism

35. Although a huge sum has been spent on advertisements boosting the image of the Hong Kong Police Force, the problem of police brutality and its abusive use of power remain serious in the entire society. As mentioned earlier, in the past years there

---

42. Full title, *Report to the United Nations Committee Against Torture on the Second Report by the HKSAR under Article 19 of the Convention Against Torture and Other Cruel, Inhuman or Degrading Treatment or Punishment* (April 2008).

have been many cases, where the Hong Kong Police Force has brutally and barbarically interference [sic] into peaceful public processions and meetings.

36. Unfortunately, this unfavourable condition has not been resolved by the current complaint mechanism. Indeed, as a part of the police system, CAPO has long been criticized for its lack of credibility. It functions within the Police Complaints and Internal Investigations Branch. The whole branch is commanded by a Chief Superintendent of Police who reports directly to the Director of Management and Inspection Services in Police Headquarters. Officers working in CAPO came from the police force and will return to their posts in future. A conflict of interest is obvious and thus the fairness of the judgment is questionable.

37. The number of allegations against police officers has decreased in the past two years ... which the Police Force may explain by improvements in police conduct and behaviour. However, a more plausible explanation might be that the general public distrust the complaint mechanism and has given up lodging complaints even though the Police Force continues its malpractices and misconduct.

38. The complaints about abusive use of power by the police remain common and an independent complaint mechanism to investigate the complaints has been urged by various sectors of the community. Indeed, the Complaints against Police Office (CAPO) have long been criticized for lack of credibility because it is a part of the police system. The independence and fairness of officers working in CAPO is questionable, as they come from the police force and will return to their posts in future. In fact, many complaints have been dropped due to the lack of evidence.

39. ... The figures reveal that the general public is reluctant to use the present complaint system and that institutional reform is necessary to create legitimacy and enhance public confidence.

40. The decreasing trend in the number of allegations can be explained by the ineffective complaint investigation mechanism. Thus the institutional defect of the current police complaint monitoring mechanism remain serious.

41. Until now, all cases investigated by CAPO have to be scrutinized and recorded by the Independent Police Complaints Council (IPCC). The IPCC has commented that police employed excessive power in the above mentioned cases, and it has raised a number of suggestions, such as asking the police "to avoid tactics which may reasonably give rise to the perception that the rights of freedom of expression and of assembly and demonstration are being unnecessarily curtailed". However, the IPCC is not a statutory organization, so the recommendations are not binding and they have not been followed up the by the Police Force.

42. In June 2007, the Security Bureau of the Government proposed an Independent Police Complaints Council Bill, which turns the IPCC into a statutory body. The proposed Bill does not delegate the IPCC any investigative powers for complaints. As a result, the monitoring function of the IPCC is not substantial, which makes the mechanism ineffective ...

> 43. Lastly, in the proposed Bill, the implementation of the recommendations of the IPCC to the police force cannot be guaranteed as they are still not legally binding. Thus it is not compulsory for the Police Force to comply with the recommendations. Thus, even though the IPCC is proposed to be a statutory body, in the absence of the power of investigation, the monitoring mechanism is still handicapped.

Comment

The Report highlights the case for independent oversight (though at times poorly expressed). The Report seems also unduly polemic. The statement, for example, that "police always [sic] abuse their power, by torturing and threatening the safety of citizens", with little supporting evidence, seems out of place in a Report to the United Nations. Similarly, with the assertion that the "number of complaints presented cannot reflect the real situation. It is just the tip of the iceberg". It is noteworthy that this statement is followed by the words "There are speculations . . ." Nonetheless, it is to be regretted that complaints against the police cannot be dealt with in a unified system within the ambit of the "Ombudsman".[43]

13.1.6 Other policing institutions

Brief mention should also be made of the other institutions in Hong Kong which exercise a policing role. These include the Tobacco Control Inspectors (TCIs); the Food and Environmental Hygiene Department (FEHD); the Securities and Futures Commission (SFC); the Independent Commission Against Corruption (ICAC) and the Immigration Department.

13.1.6.1 Tobacco Control Inspectors (TCIs)

The role of enforcing anti-smoking laws in Hong Kong is given both to police and TCIs. Both are largely ineffectual and laws banning smoking in public places are largely ignored. One problem is that the relevant legislation places the primary obligation on smokers rather than the management of establishments where smoking occurs. Such management invariably state that, should the customer refuse to stop smoking, there is little they can do. This "defence" overlooks the fact that many of such establishments sell smoking products on site (clearly "aiding and abetting" offences). As with illegal parking, police are rarely interested in enforcement and it is rumoured that TCIs only work 9–5! The latter deficiency was implicitly mentioned in the following LegCo question (though denied in response):

---

43. See 13.1.6.6.

> Question (Hon Christopher Chung):
>
> I have recently received complaints from members of the public about the ineffective enforcement of the tobacco control legislation by the Tobacco Control Office (TCO) under the Department of Health. Regarding the enforcement of the tobacco control legislation, will the Government inform this Council:
>
> a) Of the number of fixed penalty notices/summonses issued to smoking offenders in each of the past five years, broken down by law enforcement agency;
>
> b) Whether there is any difference between TCO's procedure for handling complaints about smoking offences received during office hours and outside office hours ...
>
> ...
>
> Reply
>
> ... Tobacco Control Inspectors (TCIs) of TCO are mainly responsible for front-line enforcement work, which includes handling enquiries and complaints against smoking, and inspections and prosecutions under the Smoking (Public Health) Ordinance. As the act of smoking usually lasts for a short period of time,[44] and given the larger number of public areas and indoor workplaces designated as no smoking areas ... it is impossible for TCIs to inspect the concerned venues immediately upon receiving reports of smoking offences. TCO follows up on all complaints about smoking offences ...
>
> ... Besides during office hours, TCIs also conduct inspections on Saturdays, Sundays and public holidays as well as at night time and in the early morning. In premises where offences are prevalent, TCO takes vigorous enforcement actions.

Comment

If the respondent, Secretary for Food and Health, Dr Ko Wing-man, genuinely believes the last statement, he needs to get out more!

13.1.6.2 Food and Environmental Hygiene Department (FEHD)

The work of the FEHD is often controversial since it involves, primarily, anti-"hawking" operations and the restriction of outside dining. Anti-hawking tends to be perceived, as so much of Hong Kong law enforcement, as "picking on the little man" (while bigger offenders remain undisturbed). As an example, *The Standard* reported, in February 2015,[45] that several protest groups had protested outside the home of

---

44. This does not explain why there is a problem in respect of venues where smoking is constant (and encouraged).
45. Staff Reporter, 'Rally at Ko Home over Anti-hawker Drive' *The Standard* (Hong Kong, 23 February 2015).

the Secretary for Food and Health, against an anti-hawker operation in Mong Kok during Chinese New Year.[46] The newspaper quoted community organiser, Lee Tai-shing, as saying:

> It is unreasonable for the government to step up anti-hawker operations during the Lunar New Year holiday.
> It is a tradition for hawkers to sell cooked food or other festival items in celebration in the territory.

Similarly, the refusal to issue "outdoor licences" and restrict "al fresco dining" arouses much anger at what is perceived as unnecessary bureaucracy. Here, however, it must be said that many "outdoor restaurants" have been found to be operating on what has been designated "public space" and, in the worst cases, to be charging citizens for the right to enter such public space.[47] In this context, it is fair to say that FEHD "intervention" is often welcomed by the public.[48]

13.1.6.3 The Securities and Futures Commission (SFC)

The SFC was founded in 1989, shortly after the stock market crash of 1987. While the SFC has an important advisory role, in the context of this chapter, the focus will be on "policing" (investigation and prosecution). The SFC's powers of investigation were increased by the Securities and Futures Ordinance (SFO),[49] section 182 of which gives SFC employees permission to investigate alleged offences committed by companies listed on the Stock Exchange or firms licensed by or registered with the SFC. Section 183 of the Ordinance empowers investigators to "require a person" to:

1. produce to the investigator at a required time and place any record or document requested which is in his/her possession and relevant to the investigation;
2. attend at a specified time and place and answer any relevant questions asked by the investigator;
3. render any assistance to the investigator reasonably required.

It is clear that the powers/duties described above exceed, in certain respects, those of the police, since there is a greater duty to answer questions on the part

---

46. At Chinese New Year, 2016, what seems to have started as a similar protest escalated into a "riot" in Mong Kok (over 30, mostly young, people were charged with riot over the incident and some have been imprisoned for up to three years). Given the events of 2015, it is barely credible that the police were taken by surprise in 2016.
47. See, in particular, Legislative Council (Panel on Food Safety and Environmental Hygiene), 'Regulatory Control on Outside Seating Accommodation of and Unauthorized Extension of Business Area by Restaurants', LC Paper No CB (2) 1461/13-14(08) (13 May 2014).
48. In 2012 FEHD received 4,955 complaints against illegal extensions of food premises, with 198 licence suspensions resulting (Advisory Council on Food and Environmental Hygiene: Paper 8/2013).
49. Cap 571, in effect from 1 April 2003.

of those "assisting the investigation".[50] In practice, the public generally seems not disturbed by the extensive powers of the SFC, as long as it operates efficiently. The draconian powers of the SFC *do* have their critics, however, especially those "in the business", whose views are summed up in an article by Jake Van der Kamp criticising both the extent of SFC intervention *and* perceived gross over-spending. Van der Kamp comments on a 71% increase in "requests" for trading and account records from brokers and fund managers for surveillance purposes by the SFC in the period April 2014–March 2015 (over the same period the previous year).[51] He writes:[52]

> Yes Big Brother will extend his reach right into your living room soon, but the real news here is that the SFC now employs 793 people and pays them an average of $1.25 million a year each . . .
>
> The plain fact is that the SFC has spun out of control with a tame chairman and a tame board that cannot or will not restrain the executive.

The tone of other articles also suggests that a "visit" from the SFC tends to be viewed as a cause for concern.[53] Moreover, no less a figure than the then Director of Public Prosecutions, Kevin Zervos (now Judge Zervos),[54] has questioned the SFC's dual investigation *and* prosecution role. Zervos writes:

> I note that the SFC is a regulatory and investigatory agency with extensive coercive powers . . . But it also has prosecutorial responsibility and in this regard there has been tension between us . . .
>
> Unlike the ICAC, there appears with the SFC to be a lack of appropriate internal regulation and policing as well as effective oversight . . .
>
> There is cause for concern and it would be preferable if the SFC did not have any prosecutorial responsibility.[55]

Zervos's concerns were publicised again in summer 2013 in article in the *South China Morning Post*,[56] referring specifically to the risk of the SFC becoming a "judge in its own cause" (unlike the Justice Department promise of neutrality). Zervos contrasted the SFC dual role with the position of the ICAC, in respect of which prosecution decisions must be approved by an Operations Review Committee (comprising

---

50. The SFC officers also have similar powers to those of the police to search for relevant materials where a search warrant has been issued.
51. Reported by *South China Morning Post* (Hong Kong, 18 June 2015).
52. J Van der Kamp (Jake's View), 'It's Time to Shake Things Up as SFC Has Spun out of Control' *South China Morning Post* (Hong Kong, 21 June 2015).
53. See, eg, J McBride and R Yip, 'How Ready Are You for the SFC's Routine Inspection Call?' *Hong Kong Lawyer* (February 2015). See also T Loh and G Cumming, 'Dawn Raids: What to Do When the SFC Appears at Your Premises with a Search Warrant' Timothy Loh Solicitors (12 December 2012).
54. Zervos was succeeded as DPP in September 2013 by Mr Keith Yeung.
55. Prosecutions Hong Kong Report, 2012. The Report prompted a LegCo question as to the "*rather unique*" position of the SFC in this regard (see *Question LCQ 10 from Mr Dennis Kwok*: 8 May 2013).
56. C Buddle, 'Top Prosecutor Kevin Zervos Calls for Curb on Legal Powers of SFC' *South China Morning Post* (Hong Kong, 17 August 2013).

Policing and the Decision to Prosecute 545

members of the public). The SFC issued a "rebuttal" Statement on Prosecutorial Responsibility two weeks later.[57]

Importantly, unlike its British counterpart, the SFC appears to be investigating efficiently, and with success. The Commission's 2014–2015 Annual Report states that 71 criminal charges were brought in the reporting year and that convictions had been secured against 12 individuals and three corporations (including 26 counts of market manipulation).[58]

13.1.6.4 The Independent Commission Against Corruption (ICAC)

One institution which truly has extensive (even "draconian") investigatory powers but has retained a large measure of public confidence is the ICAC, founded in February 1974. The establishment of the "independent" commission was the result, almost entirely, of public concern over police corruption in general, and the individual corruption of one senior officer, Chief Superintendent Peter Godber, in particular. The origins of the ICAC are recounted in the institution's own official history,[59] extracts from which follow:

> *Corruption on the Rampage*
>
> Hong Kong was in a state of rapid change in the 1960s and 70s. The massive growth in population and fast expansion of the manufacturing industry accelerated the pace of social and economic development. The Government . . . was unable to meet the insatiable needs of the swelling population. This provided fertile ground for the unscrupulous. Many people had to take the 'backdoor route' simply to earn a living and secure other than basic services. 'Tea money', 'black money', 'hell money'—whatever its name—became not only familiar to many Hong Kong people, but accepted with resignation as a necessary way of life.
>
> *The Victims*
>
> Corruption was rampant in the public sector. Ambulance crews would demand tea money before picking up a sick person . . . Offering bribes to the right officials was also necessary when applying for public housing, schooling and other public services. Corruption was particularly serious in the Police Force. Corrupt police officers offered protection to vice, gambling and drug activities. Law and order was under threat. Many in the community had fallen victim to corruption.[60] And yet, they swallowed their anger.

---

57. 30 August 2013.
58. SFC Annual Report 2014–2015, 53.
59. 'About ICAC: Brief History', Hong Kong ICAC website (last review date: 17 February 2014).
60. It has been estimated that triads and police connived to extort HK$10 billion in payoffs between 1963 and 1973.

Community Backlash

Corruption had become a major social problem in Hong Kong, but the Government at the time seemed powerless to deal with it ... In the early 70s, a new and potent force of public opinion emerged. Public resentment escalated to new heights when a corrupt expatriate police officer under investigation was able to flee Hong Kong ...

Last Straw

Controlling assets of over HK$4.3 million,[61] Peter Godber, a Chief Police Superintendent, was under investigation in 1973 ... But Godber managed to slip out of the territory undetected during the week given to him by the Attorney General to explain the source of his assets ... Demanding prompt government action, protesters with slogans like 'Fight Corruption, Arrest Godber'[62] insisted that Godber be extradited to stand trial.

Answering the Call

... the Government was quick to take action ... Sir Alistair Blair-Kerr ... was appointed to form a Commission of Inquiry ... He compiled two reports ...

In the waked of the Blair-Kerr reports, the then Governor Sir Murray MacLehose[63] articulated for an independent anti-corruption organisation in a speech delivered to LegCo in October 1973.

...

The Birth of the ICAC

The ICAC was established in February 1974.[64] Since its inception, the Commission has been committed to fighting corruption using a three-pronged approach of law enforcement, prevention and education. The ICAC's first important task was to bring Godber to justice. In early 1975, Godber was extradited from England to stand trial. The charges were a conspiracy offence and one of accepting bribes.[65] Godber was found guilty on both counts and sentenced to four years' imprisonment. Godber's extradition and prosecution were an unmistakable statement of ICAC's determination and resolve to eradicate corruption. It was this landmark case that kicked off a new start against corruption and the beginning of a quiet revolution.

---

61. Now worth at least ten times that amount.
62. A leading figure in the anti-corruption movement was Mrs Elsie Tu (née Elliot), a British-born fierce opponent of the colonial government (her particular bête noire was last Governor, Chris Patten). Mrs Tu's view was that many of the most corrupt survived despite the foundation of the ICAC. (Note: Mrs Tu's death, at age 102, was announced on 9 December 2015 during the preparation of this book. The widespread praise of her life, and efforts for Hong Kong's disadvantaged, from all sides, bore witness to the affection in which she was held by many in Hong Kong.)
63. See A Craig-Bennett, 'Sir Murray MacLehose and the End of Fragrant Grease' (*Gwulo: Old Hong Kong*, 20 August 2010).
64. By the Independent Commission Against Corruption Ordinance (Cap 204).
65. Godber was convicted largely on the evidence of an informant.

Comment

There is no doubt that the founding of ICAC led to a sharp downturn in corruption in Hong Kong, nor that the institution is well-respected, with corruption levels far lower in Hong Kong than on the mainland.[66] *The institution's very extensive investigative power does lead to occasional calls for increased oversight ('quis custodiet ipsos custodes?')*[67] *but generally it is accepted that such power is an acceptable price to pay for a Commission that has been prepared to investigate even "big fish".*[68]

In its early years the ICAC encountered significant opposition, primarily from police officers. Indeed, in order to avoid a police strike and a breakdown of law and order,[69] a partial amnesty for minor police corruption had to be agreed.[70] However, the ICAC has contributed significantly to reduction in corruption in Hong Kong; not least amongst the police themselves,[71] whose efforts at "self-regulation" have often been found wanting.[72] There has been anti-corruption legislation in Hong Kong since 1898[73] and the current Prevention of Bribery Ordinance[74] enacted in 1971, existed before the establishment of the ICAC. However, crucially, investigation prior to the ICAC's foundation was entirely a matter for the "Anti-Corruption Unit" of the police, themselves a major fount of corruption. The need for an ICAC in Hong Kong (to continue post-1997) is recognised in the Basic Law, Article 57 of which states that:

> A Commission Against Corruption shall be established in the Hong Kong SAR. It shall function independently[75] and be accountable to the Chief Executive.

---

66. Of particular note is the Hong Kong offence (useful to the ICAC) of "possessing financial assets disproportionate to an official emolument": s 10, Prevention of Bribery Ordinance. This was the initial case against Godber but could not be used in support of an application for extradition because there was no equivalent offence in Britain.
67. Former DPP, Grenville Cross, has, for example, stated that the investigation of former ICAC officer, Timothy Tong, should have been handled by the police rather than the ICAC themselves.
68. The Ombudsman received only six complaints against the ICAC in 2014/2015.
69. Police officers actually attacked the ICAC offices and assaulted staff in October 1977.
70. See Independent Commission Against Corruption Ordinance (Cap 204) s 18A.
71. In the early days, many police were forced to leave under "Colonial Regulation 55" which did not require proof of cause.
72. While the initial investigation which caused Godber to flee was by the police anti-corruption unit, the ICAC uncovered huge swathes of further police corruption such that 118 police officers were asked to leave and another 24 charged with conspiracy.
73. See Misdemeanours Punishment Ordinance (No 1 of 1898).
74. Cap 201.
75. On the issue of "independence", serious concerns have been raised with regard to the sacking of Rebecca Li, ICAC chief investigator who was investigating an "undeclared" $50 million payment made to Chief Executive CY Leung post-"election". Leung claimed not to be responsible and ICAC Chief, Simon Peh, later declared the decision to be his alone. Given that Li had been in post only one year and had an unblemished record the explanation is barely credible. ICAC morale is said to be low as a result and Peh's own reputation is clearly not enhanced: see S Lau, 'Leung Denies Any Part in Removal of Top Graft-Buster' *South China Morning Post* (Hong Kong, 10 July 2016); J Ng, 'ICAC Chief Claims He Alone & Not CY Leung Made Decision to Remove Deputy' *South China Morning*

The fact that the ICAC is accountable directly to the Chief Executive (and previously to the Governor) is crucial to its role as a truly independent body not, for example, under police supervision. Unfortunately, when the Chief Executive is *himself* the target of investigation, difficulties arise.[76] Since the "demise" of Senior Investigator Rebecca Li (sacked while investigating an "undeclared" payment to Chief Executive CY Leung) it is rumoured that the ICAC has unsuccessfully requested documents relating to CY Leung's undeclared payment. Democratic legislators have *again* unsuccessfully tried to impeach Leung over the Li affair (they first did this over Leung's undeclared "illegal structures" which, ironically, had been a major reason for the failure of his Chief Executive election rival, Henry Tang). The morale-weakening removal of Rebecca Li can be seen in a wider assault on "watchdogs" during the CY Leung regime. Winn points out that Department of Justice manpower has been reduced (especially at the senior level); that the "status" of judges has been undermined; that environmentalists have been replaced by civil servants in the "environmental protection" area to reduce opposition to the government's many environmentally damaging infrastructure projects (welcomed only by the tycoons and the Beijing government); and that Government Archives have been taken over by civil servants happily presiding over the destruction of valuable (but perhaps "unwanted") records.[77]

While the ICAC is best known for its investigative role, it is divided into three units: Operations, Corruption Prevention, and Community Relations.[78] The first unit (Operations), involving corruption investigation is the largest and best known. It investigates, primarily,[79] allegations of offences under the Prevention of Bribery Ordinance,[80] the Elections (Corrupt and Illegal Conduct) Ordinance[81] and the Independent Commission Against Corruption Ordinance.[82] In 2014, the ICAC prosecuted 115 cases, involving 223 persons (175 of whom were convicted).[83]

Speaking of the current position, ICAC's Steven Lam[84] has stated that:

Post (Hong Kong, 9 July 2016); and Hong Kong Free Press, 'Ex-civil Service Chief Says CY Leung Lacks Ethics & Integrity, Urges Corruption Probe into UGL Payment' (Hong Kong, 5 June 2017).

76. It will be a supreme test of the power and independence of the ICAC if they are able to properly investigate the CY Leung case. It is, no doubt, far easier to investigate and bring down a former Chief Executive (and a former Chief Secretary) with links to the colonial government than a (former) Chief Executive with "close links" to the Chinese Communist Party.
77. H Winn, 'Weakening of Watchdogs May Be No Accident' *South China Morning Post* (Hong Kong, 10 May 2012).
78. A particular brief of the Community Relations Department is the commitment to "clean" elections (for District Councils 2015, LegCo 2016 and Chief Executive 2017). In the latter case, the electoral base is so small (and the outcome sufficiently pre-determined) for ICAC scrutiny to be unnecessary.
79. ICAC officers may arrest for some other offences where evidence comes to light in respect of the three stated Ordinances.
80. Cap 201.
81. Cap 554 (amended 2012).
82. Cap 204.
83. Sources: Information Services Department, HKSAR (August 2015).
84. Then acting assistant director, ICAC, Hong Kong SAR.

Hong Kong has transformed itself from a graft-plagued city into a place distinguished by its strong anti-corruption regime. To quote the Secretary General of Interpol . . . Hong Kong has become the "anti-corruption capital of the world".

. . .

In the space of three decades, a new culture—a culture of probity—has evolved and taken root in our community . . .

The local community now fully appreciates the benefits of freedom from corruption. From the Annual Surveys conducted in the last 10 years, each year up to 98% to 99% of the respondents expressed support for the anti-corruption cause.[85]

Finally, it should be noted that the ICAC (with the full support of the mainland authorities) plays an important *international* role; in particular with its involvement in the United Nations Convention against Corruption (UNCAC) and the United Nations Convention against Transnational Organized Crime (UNTOC).

13.1.6.5 The Immigration Department

The Immigration Department (ID) of Hong Kong is a large and generally well-respected organisation. The scope of ID's role and its powers are laid down primarily in the Immigration Ordinance.[86] ID has a significant role in non-policing activities, such as the issuance of identity cards, dealing with applications for permanent residence, employment visa issuance etc. In terms of "policing", though, the ID's main functions are immigration control, "removal assessment" and "enforcement". While the "control" branch seeks to prevent illegal entry (or the entry of "undesirables") into Hong Kong, the enforcement branch is responsible for investigation as to illegal presence in Hong Kong and, where necessary, deportation. Illegal immigration is, of course, big business throughout the world though, in Hong Kong, a major focus is illegal immigration from the mainland. In 2014, the ID intercepted 736 illegal immigrants from the mainland, a decrease of 23% from the previous year.[87] Related to such immigration is illegal employment in Hong Kong and the ID is active in investigating the problem. In 2014, over 6,000 illegal workers were arrested, two thirds of these involved in prostitution.[88] Since illegal immigration, especially by air, tends to involve forged documents, the ID's "Anti-Illegal Migration Agency" has operated since the opening of the new airport in 1998; with a major focus on anti-forgery. ID's activities have also included the prosecution of mainland women illegally over-staying to give birth in Hong Kong[89] and the investigation of bogus marriages.

---

85. S Lam, 'Tackling Corruption: The Hong Kong Experience' Visiting Experts' Papers (13th International Training Course on the Criminal Justice Response to Corruption) 108–109.
86. Cap 115.
87. Source: Immigration Department, Annual Report 2014.
88. Ibid.
89. This phenomenon previously led to calls for an amendment of the Basic Law (which confers rights on all those born in Hong Kong) while it is now clear that the issue can be handled by administrative

A major task of the ID is the handling of the increasing number of "non-refoulement" claims, involving claims by those without right of entry into Hong Kong, that they are the victims of torture,[90] persecution, or inhuman and degrading treatment (or face the risk of such should they be returned to their place of origin). Hong Kong's official line is that it does not grant "asylum" but will assess claims with the possibility of successful claimants being resettled elsewhere. Whereas, previously, different sorts of claims were handled under discrete mechanisms, Hong Kong has initiated, since March 2014, a "Unified Screening Mechanism" for all non-refoulement claims.

13.1.6.6 The Ombudsman

The office of the "Ombudsman" was established in Hong Kong in 1989 by the Ombudsman Ordinance.[91] The Ordinance confers powers to investigate complaints from those affected by government "maladministration". Crucially, the Ombudsman's role is limited to looking into complaints against public bodies, *not* individuals. The Ombudsman has power to investigate complaints into those areas which appear to be of public concern. In addition, the Ombudsman has specific power to investigate complaints against public bodies for non-compliance with the Code on Access to Information (the Code).

The powers of the Ombudsman are significantly restricted because, although there is a power to "investigate", such investigation cannot proceed, in particular, where:

1. the complainant has had knowledge of the issue of complaint for more than 2 years;
2. the complaint is anonymous;
3. the complainant cannot be traced;
4. the complaint is not made by the aggrieved party personally; or
5. a complaint is ostensibly made on behalf of a corporate body which the Ombudsman believes did not authorise the complaint.[92]

Moreover, the Ombudsman has no power to look into complaints against the police in terms of "policing" *per se*. However, there *is* power to investigate complaints regarding non-compliance with the Code.[93]

On receipt of a complaint, the Ombudsman may decide to take no action where the case appears frivolous or trivial, or where it appears to have been investigated

---

means.
90. The rules on torture claims are to be found in Part VIIC of the Immigration Ordinance (Cap 115).
91. Cap 397.
92. See Cap 397 s 10(1).
93. In 2014/2015 the Ombudsman found inadequacies or deficiencies in three cases against the police for non-compliance.

previously.[94] Where there is action this may take the form of reference to mediation,[95] inquiry, or full investigation. Of 6,241 complaints received in 2014/2015 only 314 merited full investigation as possibly evidencing serious maladministration.[96] Of these only 23% were found to be "substantiated" or "partly substantiated".

Most important of the restraints on the ombudsman's powers, however, is the fact that there may be investigation but not *enforcement*. The Ombudsman can, and does, make recommendations to government departments for improvement, but no direct sanction exists in the absence of resulting action. However, of 283 recommendations made in 2013/2014, 248 had been accepted by the relevant bodies for implementation by 31 March 2014.

13.2 The decision to prosecute

Effectively, all prosecutions in Hong Kong are brought by the "state" despite the theoretical option of the private prosecution. Ho[97] writes:

> The Department of Justice is vested with the power to control criminal prosecutions, but every citizen in Hong Kong can exercise the right to initiate proceedings in courts by way of private prosecution. The Secretary for Justice, however, is empowered to terminate the proceedings by the entry of a 'nolle prosequi'.[98]

Ho may have added that the time and expense of instituting proceedings would deter most citizens even without the Secretary for Justice's power of intervention.

The ultimate responsibility for the decision whether or not to prosecute lies with the Secretary for Justice (SJ), who is a member of the Executive Council and Head of the Department of Justice. In practice, many decisions in lesser cases are taken by the police or other enforcement agency (eg, the ICAC) with *or without* the advice of the Department of Justice. Former Director of Public Prosecutions, Grenville Cross, has suggested that the "shockingly low" conviction rate in Magistrates' Courts[99] is partly due to the failure to ask for advice in too many cases. Cross states that:

> Magistrates' Courts need to review their habit of acting without seeking advice from the Department of Justice.[100]

In more serious cases, or where advice is sought, most decisions will be taken by prosecutors working for the Director of Public Prosecutions (DPP).

---

94. Ibid s 10(2).
95. Current Ombudsman, Connie Lau (appointed in 2014), has indicated in her Annual Report (2015), that she favours an increase in mediation (in line with current judicial trends in Hong Kong).
96. Under Cap 397 s 12.
97. Victor W-K Ho, *Criminal Law in Hong Kong* (Kluwer Law International 2011).
98. Ibid 185.
99. Stated to be around 50% (for contested cases) in 2014; this compares with over 70% in the District Court; Department of Justice, Annual Report 2015.
100. Quoted in Hong Kong Free Press, 8 July 2015.

13.2.1 The Director of Public Prosecutions

The Director of Public Prosecutions (DPP) is Head of the Prosecutions Division, the largest office in the Department of Justice. The role of the DPP is, primarily, to exercise the discretion whether or not to prosecute alleged criminal offences, to oversee the conduct of trials, and to give advice to government on any proposed changes to Hong Kong's criminal law. Since, post-1997, legal reform in Hong Kong is almost at a standstill, the latter function may be seen as very much a secondary one.

The DPP has a large prosecutorial staff (around 250 in number) comprising Deputy Directors, Public Prosecutors and lay prosecutors.[101] All are required to observe the Prosecution Code[102] in determining whether or not to proceed to prosecution. The key elements of the Code are as follows:

> Prosecution Code
>
> The prosecution Code seeks to:
>
> a. promote consistency in prosecution practice, eliminating unwarranted disparity between cases;
>
> b. promote regularity, without regimentation;
>
> c. facilitate the exercise of discretion in a flexible and principled manner;
>
> d. ensure the fair and effective exercise of prosecutorial responsibility;
>
> e. promote confidence in the community and with accused persons that decisions will be made rationally and objectively on the merits of each case;
>
> f. provide reference points and guidance for prosecutors;
>
> g. assist in training prosecutors;
>
> h. ensure the accountability of prosecution decision making;
>
> i. enhance understanding between agencies and therefore better coordination;
>
> j. inform the public of the processes and standards being applied;
>
> k. demonstrate internationally the standards and principles applied in Hong Kong.
>
> 1. *Independence of the Prosecutor*
>
> Independence Generally
>
> 1.1. A prosecutor is required to act in the general public interest, but independently as a "minister of justice". In making decisions and exercising discretion a prosecutor must act fairly and dispassionately on the basis of the law, the facts provable

---

101. The latter role is controversial (see Chapter 8).
102. Introduced in 2013 to replace the previous *Statement of Prosecution Policy and Practice* (2009). DPP Keith Yeung described the innovation as a "major criminal justice initiative" (DOJ Press Release, 30 December 2013).

by the admissible evidence, other relevant information known to the prosecution and any applicable policy or guidelines.

1.2 ...

Department of Justice

1.3 Articles 63 of the Basic Law of the Hong Kong Special Administrative Region provides that the Department of Justice "shall control criminal prosecutions, free from any interference". That constitutional guarantee of independence ensures that prosecutors within the Department may act independently without political or other improper or undue influence.

Secretary for Justice

1.4 The Secretary for Justice is head of the Department of Justice. The Court of Appeal stated in *In Re C (A Bankrupt)* [2006] 4 HKC 582 at 590:

"The prosecutorial independence of the Secretary for Justice is a linchpin of the rule of law . . . 'the decision whether any citizen should be prosecuted or whether any prosecution should be discontinued, should be a matter for the prosecuting authorities to decide on the merits of the case without political or other pressure.' [Sir Robert Finlay, 1903] . . . these statements . . . reflect accepted and applied fundamental principle in this jurisdiction the continuation of which is preserved by the entire theme of the Basic Law as well, specifically, as by article 63."

1.5 The Secretary for Justice is responsible for applying the criminal law, formulating prosecution policy, and superintending the Director of Public Prosecutions and prosecutors in the Prosecutions Division of the Department. The Secretary is accountable for decisions made by prosecutors, to whom various powers are delegated.

1. *Director of Public Prosecutions*

1.1 The Director of Public Prosecutions is head of the Prosecutions Division of the Department of Justice and responsible for the conduct of the Prosecutions Division.

1.2 The Director initiates and conducts the prosecution of cases on behalf of the Hong Kong Special Administrative Region. The Director is responsible to the Secretary for Justice for:

a. directing public prosecutions;

b. advising the Secretary on criminal law related matters, except in specific matters in which the Secretary has authorised the Director to determine the matter on his or her own;

c. advising law enforcement agencies in respect of prosecutions generally or in respect of a particular investigation that may lead to a prosecution;

d. developing and promoting prosecution policy;

e. advising the government on the development, enforcement and implementation of the criminal law.

2. Role and Duties of the Prosecutor

Role and Functions

3.1 A prosecutor is required to comply with and promote the rule of law. A prosecutor acts on behalf of the community in an impartial manner and as a "minister of justice". To this end, a prosecutor must fairly and objectively assist the court to arrive at the truth and to do justice between the community and the accused according to law.

...

1.3 A prosecutor works in an adversarial and accusatorial litigation system.

The prosecutor's advocacy role must be conducted temperately and with restraint; nevertheless, a prosecutor is entitled to advocate firmly and courteously the prosecution's position on an issue and to test and, if necessary, attack the position adopted or evidence advanced on behalf of an accused.

1.4 Prosecutors carry out their roles as an integral part of a criminal justice process that includes investigation, prosecution, defence, adjudication and punishment. Their contribution to the criminal justice process and the outcomes achieved must be made professionally and to the highest standards reasonably achievable. Prosecutors should not seek to step beyond the proper roles of the prosecution in the criminal justice process.

...

3.8 A prosecutor must at all times assist the court to avoid appealable error and must strive to correct any error of law or fact that becomes apparent in the course of the trial and sentence proceedings.

Fairness

3.9 A prosecutor should prepare and assemble all relevant evidence available to the prosecution well in advance of trial. The prosecution should, as a general rule, offer all its evidence during the presentation of its case. It should inform the court and defence of authorities, warnings and directions that may be appropriate, even if unfavourable to the prosecution case.

...

5. Decision to Prosecute

5.1 Section 15(1) of the Criminal Procedure Ordinance, Cap 221 states:

"The Secretary for Justice shall not be bound to prosecute an accused person in any case in which he may be of opinion that the interest of public justice do not require his interference."

1.2 That provision applies such discretion equally to the Director of Public Prosecutions and to prosecutors acting on behalf of the Secretary for Justice pursuant to delegations.

5.3 The effect of the provision is to endorse generally accepted and longstanding international practice under the common law – that the decision to prosecute includes two required components. The first is that the admissible evidence available is sufficient to justify instituting or continuing proceedings. The second is that the general public interest must require that the prosecution be conducted.

Sufficiency of Evidence

5.4 There must be legally sufficient evidence to support a prosecution; that is, evidence that is admissible and reliable and, together with any reasonable inferences able to be drawn from it, likely to prove the offence.

5.5 The test is whether the evidence demonstrates a reasonable prospect of conviction.

Public Interest

5.8 Even where the first component of the prosecution test is satisfied, a prosecutor must consider the second component, the requirements of the public interest . . .

6.1 The Secretary for Justice must give his/her consent before certain kinds of prosecutions can be undertaken. This is safeguard to ensure that an appropriate level of scrutiny is exercised in particular cases. Accordingly, a prosecutor should consider if consent is required by law. The power to consent has been delegated to the Director of Public Prosecutions and senior prosecutors in some cases.

7. *Private Prosecution*

7.1. Under the common law a person has the right to commence a criminal prosecution in the public interest.

. . .

7.3 The Secretary for Justice is entitled to intervene in a private prosecution and assume its conduct, becoming a party to the proceedings at that time and displacing the original prosecutor.

. . .

19. *Public Order Events*

19.1 Article 27 of the Basic Law guarantees Hong Kong residents "freedom of speech, of the press and of publication; freedom of association, of assembly, of procession and of demonstration . . ." Articles 16, 17 and 18 of the Hong Kong Bill of Rights give the same protections to other persons who are in Hong Kong . . .

19.3 . . . Cases in relation to public order events require the striking of a balance between the interest of society in maintaining public order and the right of a person lawfully and peacefully to exercise his or her rights.

Comment

Fundamental to the operation of the Code is the underlying principle, stipulated in Article 63 of the Basic Law, that "the Department of Justice shall control criminal prosecutions, free from any interference". In this regard there have been, as will be noted below, concerns expressed, especially with regard to the role and status of the Secretary for Justice.

13.2.2 The DPP's relationship with the Secretary for Justice

The DPP is a senior civil servant who is likely to have had long experience at the Hong Kong criminal bar. Conversely, the Secretary for Justice (SJ), though certain to have a legal background, is a political appointee, a member of the Executive Council, and the interface between the government and the Department of Justice. The SJ's political role has caused some concerns, outlined in a paper delivered at the University of Hong Kong[103] by Grenville Cross, Hong Kong's longest-serving post-1997 DPP (prior to his retirement in 2010). In his speech Cross focused on the perceived disadvantage of the DPP not being in control of all prosecutions in Hong Kong[104] and on the "problem" of Hong Kong's SJ having both a political *and* a judicial role. Cross pointed out, for example, that in Britain the DPP had assumed responsibility for most prosecution decisions in England and Wales. He added that, were the Hong Kong Secretary for Justice to cede the decision whether or not to prosecute to the DPP, public confidence in the administration of justice in Hong Kong would increase. Expanding on this theme in an article in *Hong Kong Lawyer*[105] Cross states:

> Since Article 13 of the United Nations Guidelines on the Role of Prosecutors (1990) requires the prosecutor to 'protect the public interest' and to 'act with objectivity', the chief prosecutor must be genuinely free of political interference, in whatever guise, and should not have to keep looking over his or her shoulder at a political master every time an important decision is to be made.
>
> The fiction that a member of the government . . . can legitimately wear two hats, one as a politician and the other as prosecutor, is now largely discredited, and has been discarded in many places.[106]

The Cross views raise not merely a "theoretical" issue. The situation would be less problematic were it possible to say that *in practice* no problems had arisen from the SJ's conflict of interest situation. Alas this is not so and serious concerns have been raised in a number of cases discussed in the following LegCo paper.

---

103. G Cross, 'Prosecutorial Freedom: Why Hong Kong Needs an Independent Director of Public Prosecutions' Seminar Centre for Comparative & Public Law, HKU, 29 May 2012. This followed G Cross, 'Let the Public Prosecutor Decide, Not the Political Appointee' *Hong Kong Lawyer* (March 2011).
104. Mr Cross's particular complaint seems to lie with the Magistrates' Courts, which he believes fail to seek DPP advice far too often; one of the causes of what he describes as a "shockingly low" conviction rate.
105. *Hong Kong Lawyer* (March 2011).
106. Ibid 57–58.

Legislative Council

LC Paper No. CB(2)2201/10-11(01)

Panel on Administration of Justice and Legal Services

Background brief prepared by the Legislative Council Secretariat

for the meeting on 27 June 2011

An independent Director of Public Prosecutions and

prosecution policy and practice

Background

The role of the Secretary for Justice ("SJ") and the Director of Public Prosecutions ("DPP")

2. SJ is appointed by the Central People's Government ("CPG") upon the nomination by the Chief Executive ("CE") of the Hong Kong Special Administrative Region ("HKSAR"). SJ is the principal legal adviser to CE, to the Government and to individual government bureaux, departments and agencies. SJ is also a Member of the Executive Council ("ExCo").

3. SJ is the head of the Department of Justice ("DoJ") which is responsible for the conduct of criminal proceedings in Hong Kong. Article 63 of the Basic Law ("BL") provides that "the Department of Justice of the Hong Kong Special Administrative Region shall control criminal prosecutions, free form any interference". The decision to prosecute criminal offences is the sole responsibility of SJ. SJ is also the defendant in all civil actions brought against the Government and represents both the Government and the public interest in the courts.

...

SJ's role under the Accountability System for Principal Officials ("POs")

8. When the Panel on Constitutional Affairs ("the CA Panel") and the former Subcommittee on the Proposed System of Accountability for Principal Officials and Related Issues discussed the new Accountability System for POs initially outlined in the CE's Policy Address in 2001 and presented by CE to LegCo on 17 April 2002, some members had expressed strong opposition to the inclusion of the post of SJ in the proposed system under which POs were held accountable to CE and would be appointed on terms different to those in the civil service.

9. In its written submission to the CA Panel in November 2001, the Hong Kong Bar Association ("the Bar Association") had raised questions as to whether it was appropriate to include the post of SJ as a political appointee under the proposed Accountability System ...

...

The case of Ms AW Sian in 1998

21. In the wake of public concern over the decision of the then SJ not to prosecute Ms AW Sian after the trial of the *Hong Kong Standard* case in which three accused were

convicted of the offence of conspiracy to defraud by, among other charges, inflating the circulation figures of the *Hong Kong Standard* and *Sunday Standard* newspapers over some three years from 1994, the AJLS Panel held two meetings on 23 March 1998 and 4 February 1999 respectively to follow up on the matter.

22. In her statement to the Panel in respect of the decision not to prosecute Ms AW following the delivery of judgment on the case on 20 January 1999, the then SJ explained that she had reached her decision not to prosecute Ms AW on the basis of insufficient evidence. After the careful evaluation of the evidence, the advice of her advisers and the representations from Ms AW's lawyers, she concluded that there was no reasonable prospect of securing a conviction. She also considered that if Ms AW was prosecuted, it would be a serious obstacle to the restructuring of the Sing Tao Group of which Ms AW was the Chairman. Should a well-established and important media group collapse, it would send a very bad message to the international community, not to mention about the interests of about 1,900 local and overseas employees of the Group at a time when unemployment was on the rise. In light of the circumstances, it was not in the public interest to initiate a prosecution of Ms AW.

23. Some members queried whether it was necessary for SJ to consider public interest at all in the case if it had been decided that there was insufficient evidence to bring a prosecution against Ms AW. They did not agree with the SJ's understanding of public interest, and pointed out that in deciding whether or not to prosecute a person, it would be irrelevant and grossly unfair to have regard to factors such as the person's financial position, the nature of his/her business or the number of people under his/her employment. The then SJ explained that her decision was not based on consideration of a person's status and financial position. The consideration of the interests of the employees concerned was within the broad parameters of public interest considerations specified in the Prosecution Policy of DoJ. She further assured members that she had acted in good faith at all times and no pressure of any sort was brought to bear upon her to take the decision. Her decision was not based on considerations of any personal connections or political status.

24. Some members also asked whether SJ had sought legal advice outside DoJ in the case. SJ replied in the negative explaining that it was normally only for cases of exceptional complexity, or for cases where the required expertise was not available within DoJ, or for cases involving members of DoJ, that outside legal advice would be sought.

...

The case of Mr Anthony LEUNG Kam-chung in 2003

26. A special meeting of the AJLS Panel was held in response to the formal announcement made by the then SJ on 15 December 2003 of the decision not to prosecute Mr Antony LEUNG Kam-chung, the former Financial Secretary, for his conduct in respect of a car purchase by him in January 2003, several weeks before an increase in Motor Vehicles First Registration Tax in the 2003–2004 Budget.

27. The Administration briefed the AJLS Panel on the facts of the case and the legal reasoning behind the decision not to prosecute Mr LEUNG for the criminal offence of misconduct in public office. According to the Administration, the decision was made after consideration of the reports of the Independent Commission Against Corruption ("ICAC"), the evidence, the law, the prosecution policy and the legal advice provided by two leading counsel at the private Bar.

29. ... In view of the sensitivity of the case and that Mr LEUNG was a former colleague of SJ, SJ had delegated to [the DPP] the full authority of deciding whether or not to prosecute Mr LEUNG so as to avoid any possible perception of bias.

30. Members welcomed the SJ's decision to explain openly the approach and the process that had been adopted in handling the case and deciding not to prosecute Mr LEUNG. They also supported her decision to delegate to DPP the authority of deciding whether or not to prosecute Mr LEUNG and to seek independent legal advice on the case from outside counsel.

...

36. The AJLS panel held another meeting on 15 July 2009 to discuss SJ's decision not to institute a prosecution of the bodyguards of Miss Bona Mugabe, the daughter of the President of the Republic of Zimbabwe, in relation to an alleged assault of two journalists on 13 February 2009 outside a house in Tai Po occupied by Miss Mugabe. Members expressed concern that the incident raised the question as to whether bodyguards, in particular those protecting well-known personalities and the rich, had special privileges that they could use force against journalists and ordinary citizens without being prosecuted. Members also noted that the Hong Kong Journalists Association had expressed concern that the alleged assault was against journalists who were performing no more that their ordinary journalistic duties.

37. The incumbent SJ explained that the crux of the matter was whether the bodyguards had a genuine concern for the safety of Miss Mugabe and considered it necessary to take actions to minimize the danger posed. If the evidence showed that the bodyguards had genuine concern for Miss Mugabe's safety, a potential defense of justification would be open to them. He stressed that the decision not to prosecute was reached after full consideration of all the evidence and circumstances of the case, including the fact that the complainants were journalists.

Recent developments

38. In his articles published on the *South China Morning Post* on 10 February 2011 and in the March 20011 edition of Hong Kong Lawyer respectively, Mr Grenville Cross, the former DPP, suggested that control of prosecutions should rest with an independent DPP and SJ should step back from the prosecution process in order to promote prosecutorial independence ...

39. At the meeting on 28 March 2011, members agreed that the Panel should invite the SJ (Mr Wong Yan Lung), Mr Kevin Zervos, the newly appointed DPP, Mr Cross,

the former DPP, legal profession and academics to join the future discussion of the issue relating to and independent DPP.

Comment

It is difficult to be convinced by statements that the cases referred to were dealt with "non-politically". In the case of Aw, a pro-Beijing personality and friend of the then CE, the SJ's arguments for non-prosecution were extremely weak.[107] *Leung was a senior Exco Member who, even were his plea of inadvertence to have been ultimately accepted, should have, as an experienced politician, had this tested in court.*[108] *The Mugabes are, of course, "friends of China" (and almost no one else!) and while no one doubts that the Mugabes themselves were diplomatically "immune", no such protection extended to their bodyguards.*[109] *Conversely, a decision to prosecute was made in the case of Donald Tsang (who served, perhaps significantly, the colonial government) accused of accepting (and not declaring) favours from tycoons. The decision to prosecute Tsang for "misconduct in public office" was finally taken after three and a half years of ICAC investigation.*[110]

In a response to the LegCo background brief, the Department of Justice stated,[111] *inter alia*, that:

> Prosecutorial independence is constitutionally guaranteed under the Basic Law. BL63 provides that the Department of Justice shall control criminal prosecutions, free from any interference. To this end, the SJ exercises his prosecutorial responsibilities bearing in mind the public interest and the independence of the prosecution function. As head of the department of Justice under the constitution, the SJ cannot

---

107. Post his retirement then DPP, Grenville Cross, suggested that he was unhappy with the decision not to prosecute: see C Buddle, 'Former DPP Grenville Cross Reveals Split over Sally Aw Sian Prosecution' *South China Morning Post* (Hong Kong, 17 June 2014).
108. Even more implausible was the excuse by new Secretary for Justice, Teresa Cheng, for a multitude of illegal structures in her (company-owned) home. Cheng, an expert on housing law, was "too busy" to notice!
109. Then DPP, Grenville Cross, denies that political considerations were involved.
110. The decision to prosecute was finally taken in 2015 despite an assurance from then DPP, Kevin Zervos, in 2013, that a decision would be made "soon"! Tsang's major offence was the acceptance of a luxury flat in Shenzhen from a grateful recipient of a television licence; authorised by Tsang when Chief Executive. See K Cheung, 'Donald Tsang Corruption Investigation Sluggish Progress "Could Make Guinness World Records"—Former Prosecutions Director' *Hong Kong Free Press* (Hong Kong, 11 November 2015). It has also taken three years to prosecute former police superintendent Franklyn Chu, accused of hitting a protester with a baton. In this case however, the delay was caused by CAPO's (see 13.1.5) obstructionism: see K Lau, 'Leung May Get Report in Case of Baton Cop' *The Standard* (Hong Kong, 3 December 2015). Chu was finally convicted in December 2017.
111. LegCo Panel on Administration of Justice and Legal Services, 'Response to the Background Brief Provided by the LegCo Secretariat Entitled "An Independent Director of Public prosecutions"' (LC Paper No CB(2)2154/10-11 (01) (June 2011)).

abdicate from his constitutional duty by a complete transfer of his prosecution responsibilities to the DPP[112] or otherwise.[113]

Minutes of the resulting LegCo meeting show that the Administration maintained its stance that the "abdication" of the Secretary for Justice's (SJ's) power of prosecutorial determination to the DPP would be contrary to Article 63 of the Basic Law since the SJ is Head of the Department of Justice (DOJ) and the DOJ "shall control criminal prosecutions free from interference".[114]

Secretary for Justice "political independence" has again been to the fore with the decision by the DOJ to seek a review of sentences for those legislators supporting "Occupy Central" (Joshua Wong, Nathan Law, and Alex Chow) who had previously been given non-custodial sentences for public order offences. It was strongly rumoured that then SJ, Rimsky Yuen, had personally supported the review against the advice of his staff. If true, it is an egregious conflict with the principle of "natural justice" that one should not be a judge in one's own cause. Despite Yuen's strong avowal that "proper procedures" were followed[115] this overlooks the fact that the government, of which Yuen is a member, had a strong "interest" in custodial sentences resulting in LegCo disqualifications (and a reduction in LegCo "opposition" ranks). Similarly overlooked in the "proper procedures" justification is the fact that Yuen had been *personally* rebuffed by the "Occupy" movement which resisted Beijing's offer of "fake democracy" for Hong Kong; an offer which Yuen had been tasked with "selling" to Hong Kong. No clearer example could exist of a situation in which delegation to the DPP should have occurred.[116] Most tellingly (despite initial support for the sentence review in the Court of Appeal) the Court of Final Appeal largely supported the sentencing decisions of the initial trial judge and confirmed that the applications for review "should have been refused."[117] Moreover, irrespective of who actually made the decision:

"One can only wonder what the Department of Justice was thinking in pushing the courts to lock up so far 16 of Hong Kong's dedicated young men and women, over moments of excessive zeal."[118]

---

112. Conversely, Grenville Cross's view is that Article 63 of the Basic Law permits reform, since it confers the power to control criminal prosecutions on the *Department of Justice* rather than on the *Secretary for Justice*.
113. LegCo Response, 27 June 2011 at para 5.
114. LegCo Minutes (Panel on Administration of Justice and Legal Services), 27 June 2011 (LC Paper No CB (2) 515/11-12). Grenville Cross has pointed out that the prosecution decision is stated to lie with "The Department" not necessarily the SJ. However, with the ranks of LegCo opposition now thinned (see below) change is extremely unlikely (see J Lam, "Call to reform prosecuting role rejected" *South China Morning Post* [Hong Kong 25 January 2018]).
115. R Yuen, "Facts of the case" *South China Morning Post* (Hong Kong, 24 August 2017).
116. One counter-argument is that the DPP, as an officer on "contract terms", may be just as susceptible to political pressure.
117. [2018] HKCFA 4 at para 106.
118. M Davis, "Civil society is now in jail, along with young activists" *South China Morning Post* (Hong Kong, 24 August 2017).

It has also been pointed out that the enthusiasm with which youthful "Occupiers" have been prosecuted is in contrast to prosecutorial inertia over calls to "kill" pro-independence supporters by "loyalist" Junius Ho.[119]

The other side of the coin in respect of alleged "partiality" is the decision to prosecute the "little man", a situation illustrated by the following LegCo question from the then representative of the Legal functional constituency and response:

> LEGISLATIVE COUNCIL[120]
>
> ORAL ANSWERS TO QUESTIONS
>
> ...
>
> Prosecution Policy
>
> Dr MARGARET NG
>
> President it has been reported that on 19 December last year, a physically disabled hawker holding a valid ... [ice-cream seller] Licence ... was alleged to have caused obstruction when hawking in the vicinity of the Star Ferry Pier ... as well as engaged in selling candies named "lollipop" and he was subsequently charged with causing street obstruction and hawking a commodity not specified in the licence. The prosecutor withdrew the [obstruction] charge ... while retaining the second charge. The magistrate stated clearly in court that the case was of a minor nature and prosecution was unnecessary. He questioned the enforcement standards of the law enforcement officers as well as the prosecution principles of the prosecutor ... It has also been reported that some members of the public were dissatisfied with the authorities indiscriminately enforcing the law ... will the Government inform this Council:
>
> a) ... in respect of the aforesaid case, of the public interest grounds based on which the DoJ decided to institute prosecution;
>
> b) whether [continuing with the minor charge of selling contrary to licence would result in] loss of confidence in the administration of justice; and
>
> c) whether DoJ will conduct a comprehensive review in the light of the case, with a view to improving the prosecution policy?
>
> SECRETARY FOR JUSTICE
>
> President, the DOJ is responsible for discharging the prosecution function ... based on a consideration of two matters. Firstly whether there is sufficient evidence to justify the institution or continuation of proceedings ... secondly whether the public interest requires a prosecution to be pursued ... Before issuing the summons the FEHD [the relevant enforcement body] sought legal advice ... the FEHD did not seek further advice before making that decision [to continue with just one charge]. Minor though this offence was, we understand that the FEHD had made every effort to inform the defendant that he was breaking the law.

---

119. A Cheng, "Get tough with the pro-Beijing radicals, too" *South China Morning Post* (Hong Kong, 22 September 2017).
120. Legislative Council, 14 July 2010 at 11342–11345.

Comment

Ms Ng asked further questions emphasising the hardship inflicted on the disabled defendant and making clear that she was far from convinced by the SJ's response which, she felt, had not properly addressed the issue of public interest. It has been suggested earlier that the rigour of the FEHD in respect of hawker control is often controversial.[121]

One discretionary power in which the prosecution plays a significant role in Hong Kong is the determination as to *which court* a case will be heard (trial venue).[122] This may affect not only the perceived "seriousness" of the offence, but also the accused's access to jury trial. Briefly, the situation in Hong Kong is that many "non-magistrates" criminal cases, other than the most serious, involve a decision by the *prosecution* as to whether a case should be tried in District Court, by a judge with no jury, or in the Court of First Instance, before a judge and jury. While conviction rates in contested cases are similar in the two courts, there is sometimes a *perception* that District Court judges are more pro-prosecution than Court of First Instance juries. The concept that a case may be tried in either of two courts is not unique to Hong Kong, but in other jurisdictions the accused has a greater say. In Britain, for example, in "either way" cases where the accused could be tried *either* before magistrates *or* before a judge and jury, the accused *almost always* has the final say.[123] A clear example of the difference in approach can be seen in the case of Lili Chiang, whose applications for Judicial Review against the refusal to grant her a jury trial went all the way to the Court of Final Appeal (CFA). Ms Chiang faced five charges relating to commercial crimes. The Secretary for Justice had successfully applied for the "indictable" case to be transferred to the District Court pursuant to section 88 of the Magistrates' Ordinance.[124] Ms Chiang's applications were based on two contentions: that the SJ's decision to transfer was "unreasonable" since it failed to give due consideration to the principle of trial by jury (JR1); and that section 88 was unconstitutional since, merging the SJ's political *and* judicial power, it infringed the principle of "separation of powers" enshrined, claimed Ms Chiang, in the Basic Law (JR2). On the first issue, the CFA held that Ms Chiang was unable to suggest that she would not have a fair trial in the District Court without a jury. The case sparked fresh calls for the extension of the jury system to the District Court (dealt with elsewhere).[125]

On the second issue, the CFA rejected the JR2 application as an abuse of process; involving an issue which could have been dealt with in JR1 *and* had been conceded by the applicant in JR1. Overriding any "separation of powers" argument

---

121. See 13.1.6.2 above.
122. "An Issue of *Prosecutorial Choice*" *Basic Law Bulletin* Issue 13 (Hong Kong, December 2011).
123. The choice was, formerly, *entirely* a matter for the accused, but limited scope for the refusal of a jury now exists in cases where there is a clear threat of "jury tampering".
124. Cap 227.
125. See Chapter 8.

was the *clear* statement in Article 63 of the Basic Law that the Secretary for Justice should control prosecutions free from any external interference.

13.2.3 Other prosecution agencies

It should be remembered that while the majority of prosecutions proceed under the aegis of the Department of Justice, significant (if limited) prosecution roles are played by the Securities and Futures Commission and the Hong Kong Monetary Authority. The former's prosecutorial role is to regulate the securities and futures market by prosecuting "insider dealing" has already been discussed.[126] The latter's role is, essentially, limited to combatting money-laundering. The existence of these "alternative" prosecutorial agencies has been criticised, as previously noted, on various grounds; primarily the potential for these agencies to have an "interest" in the outcome of prosecutions as opposed to the avowed neutrality of the Department of Justice. It should, perhaps, be noted that the Monetary Fund's main activities in this area involve "disciplining" financial institutions for failure to observe strict protocols intended to prevent money-laundering. The fines involved, however, are significant, even for financial institutions.[127]

---

126. See 13.1.6.3 above.
127. To take just two examples, Coutts & Co were fined HK$7 million while the State Bank of India was fined HK$7.5 million.

14
An Introduction to Legal Research in Hong Kong

Overview

One reviewer of this work believes that this chapter is "out of place" or out of keeping with the rest of the book. It is included, very simply, because I have set out to cover the *whole of* the required Hong Kong syllabus for Hong Kong Legal System, and legal research is included.

Most Hong Kong Law students will have had classes on how to do research. Those coming to the subject from outside Hong Kong will, again, almost certainly have done some work on legal research. The purpose of this chapter is, therefore, to give a brief introduction to the topic for those coming to the subject for the first time and, more significantly, to provide some guidance to those whose expertise in research has been formed in another jurisdiction; especially those intending to sit the PCLL "conversion examination" in Hong Kong Legal System for which legal research is included in the syllabus.

There are two major works on doing legal research in Hong Kong, both of which will be referred to throughout this brief chapter. The first is by Jill Cottrell,[1] previously of the University of Hong Kong's Faculty of Law. Cottrell's work is a scholarly and highly Hong Kong–focused text on how to do legal research, written from the viewpoint of a legal academic.

The second important work is by John Bahrij.[2] This useful, but rather more succinct, text is written from the perspective of a law librarian[3] and its primary focus is on the practicalities of *finding* and *citing* legal sources.

Since, as noted in Chapter 2, English law continues, at least indirectly, to be a significant source of Hong Kong law, this chapter will look at researching English as well as Hong Kong law. The focus will be primarily on researching through cases and statutory law but there will also be mention of secondary sources, such as textbooks and journals. For "traditionalists" (like the author!) research is still regarded as a library, book-based endeavour, while for most students, electronic research is

---

1. J Cottrell, *Legal Research: A Guide for Students* (Hong Kong University Press 1997, reprinted 2003).
2. J Bahrij, *Hong Kong Legal Research: Methods and Skills* (Sweet & Maxwell Asia 2007).
3. Mr Bahrij is currently law librarian at the Chinese University of Hong Kong.

the norm. Hard copy research still has its place, however, especially with regard to older cases.

14.1 Sources of Hong Kong law

The major sources of Hong Kong law are those described in Chapter 2. They are:

(i) The Basic Law;
(ii) Hong Kong legislation (including delegated legislation);
(iii) laws of the People's Republic of China (PRC);
(iv) the common law (including equity);
(v) Chinese customary law;
(vi) academic/secondary sources.

These sources of law in Hong Kong may be conveniently classified as "primary", "secondary" or "tertiary". "Primary" sources are the legal rules themselves; whether made via legislation or by "common" (in the sense of non-statutory, case-derived) law. The Basic Law, English and Hong Kong legislation, relevant PRC legislation and decided cases all constitute "primary" sources.

"Secondary" sources consist of commentaries on the law in the form of textbooks, academic journals, government reports, speeches, newspaper articles, etc. Primary sources are the most important ones and students (and the courts) should always refer first to primary sources before considering secondary ones. Moreover, in cases of conflict, primary sources take precedence. By way of clear example, many English academics wrote, in textbooks and articles, disagreeing with the so-called "fiction of fraud" in relation to the judicial interpretation of section 1(2) of the Misrepresentation Act, 1967.[4] The Court of Appeal judges in the case of *Royscot Trust Ltd v Rogerson*[5] held that the writers had avoided the clear meaning of the words of the subsection. *Royscot*, not the learned writers, represents the law, in England, on the matter.[6] That said, the English courts themselves now seem to be having second thoughts on the issue and may, eventually, overrule *Royscot*. At that point, *but not before*, the law will have been changed.

It is sometimes said that there is a third category of sources, described as "tertiary". These take the forms of documents such as encyclopaedias of forms and precedents, much valued by practitioners as drafting models. These sources do not represent the substantive law, as such, but the form in which such law is pleaded in the courts.

---

4. The same wording is to be found in s 3(1) of the Hong Kong Misrepresentation Ordinance (Cap 284).
5. [1991] 3 All ER 294.
6. A similar interpretation had already been applied in Hong Kong in *Pepsi-Cola International Ltd v Charles Lee* [1974] HKLR 13 (per Cons J).

14.2 Researching English law

Research into English law is crucial in Hong Kong for several reasons. First, some decisions of English courts will still have *direct* effect in Hong Kong. While, pedantically, it could be argued that the Judicial Committee of the Privy Council (the Privy Council) is not an "English" court (and it does not, technically, deliver "judgments" but, rather, advice to the sovereign), in practice the "judgments" of the Privy Council are to be found in the English "Appeal Cases" volumes. It has been confirmed that this court's decisions, on issues of Appeal from Hong Kong before 1997, are binding on all Hong Kong courts, *except the Court of Final Appeal* (CFA), unless and until they are overturned by the CFA[7] (or by Hong Kong legislation).

Other decisions of English courts will *indirectly* affect Hong Kong law. As made clear in Chapter 2, the laws in force as at 30 June 1997 will continue in force, provided that they do not conflict with the Basic Law, have not been superseded by Hong Kong legislation[8] or overturned by a Hong Kong appellate court.[9] The law in force as at 30 June 1997 was, *generally*, the English common law, provided that it was not inconsistent with local conditions.[10] As a result, English case-law decisions, especially those of the highest court, the Judicial Committee of the House of Lords (House of Lords), would represent the English common law position and, indirectly therefore, the current Hong Kong position in the absence of local inconsistency or amendment. It is, therefore, essential for Hong Kong students to be able to research English cases.

There are other major sources of English law. These include *legislation* generally, the Human Rights Act 1998 specifically, and, given the United Kingdom's membership of the European Union (only recently ended), European Union (EU) Law. For the purposes of doing Hong Kong legal research, other than from a comparative perspective, these sources are of far less importance than the study of English cases. The Human Rights Act has no application to Hong Kong and the continuance of the "common law" system in Hong Kong, post-1997, as guaranteed by the Basic Law, makes no provision for EU Law, which is, in any event, essentially a civil law system. There is some irony, of course, in the fact that English law, the foundation for the common law in Hong Kong as well as in so many other jurisdictions, is itself no longer a purely common law system. English *legislation* is also of far less significance than its case law since, as was explained in Chapter 2, it was not *generally* applicable in Hong Kong, even before 1997. Post-1997 English legislation, of course, is never applicable in Hong Kong. Only brief mention, therefore, will be made of researching English legislation.

---

7. *A Solicitor v Law Society of Hong Kong* [2008] 2 HKC 1.
8. Article 8, Basic Law.
9. This last exception is not expressed in the Basic Law but is implicit in the Basic Law's assertion that Hong Kong courts have the right of final adjudication.
10. See Chapter 2 for fuller discussion.

14.2.1 English case law

Law reporting in the English legal system goes back many hundreds of years and early reports are regarded as highly unreliable. "Year books" were produced from 1285 to 1535 and then replaced by private reports or "nominate reports" named after the individual law reporters who wrote the reports until 1865. Important cases from the nominate reports period are consolidated and replicated in the English Reports series. An extremely useful tool for researching these old cases, at least in hard copy, is the Index to the English Reports, without which finding an individual case is an extremely difficult task.

Because, in the "private reporter" times, the same case could be reported by a number of different individuals, there are often significant discrepancies. A well-known example, and one where interpretation has modern significance, occurred in the contract case of *Stilk v Myrick*.[11] The case involved the relatively simple question of whether sailors could claim extra wages promised to them to continue sailing a ship after it had lost some crew members. The English court determined that the extra wages were not recoverable. However, the reports differ as to the reason for the decision. The "Campbell" report[12] emphasises the "lack of consideration" for the additional promise. Thus:

> I doubt whether the ground of public policy . . . be the true principle on which the decision is to be supported. Here, I say, the agreement is void for want of consideration.[13]

However, the "Espinasse" Report[14] reflects the "public policy" principle, previously established in *Harris v Watson*,[15] emphasising the dangerous potential for allowing crew to "blackmail" their employers in difficult situations. Thus:

> Lord Ellenborough ruled, That [*sic*] the plaintiff could not recover this part of his demand. His Lordship said, that he recognized the principle of the case of *Harris v Watson* as founded on just and proper policy.

This discrepancy had much to do with the capacity of the English Court of Appeal, in *Williams v Roffey Bros & Nicholls (Contractors) Ltd*,[16] to overturn the *Stilk* decision while claiming to "approve" it! The "story" has relevance to Hong Kong in that *Roffey* was later applied, albeit incorrectly, in *UBC (Construction) Ltd v Sung Foo Kee Ltd*.[17]

---

11. (1809) 2 Camp 317, (1809) 6 esp 129.
12. Note 11.
13. Per Lord Ellenborough CJ.
14. Note 11.
15. (1791) Peake 102.
16. [1990] 1 All ER 512.
17. See M Fisher and D Greenwood, *Contract Law in Hong Kong* (3nd edn, Hong Kong University Press 2018) 159–163.

From 1865 onwards, a series known as The Law Reports, produced by the Incorporated Council of Law Reporting for England and Wales (ICLR), has been recognised as the most authoritative source of law English law reports. The series comprises four major parts:

i. Appeal Cases (AC)

This series contains decisions of the Judicial Committee of the House of Lords (House of Lords), Judicial Committee of the Privy Council (Privy Council) and the new Supreme Court of the United Kingdom which has replaced the House of Lords as the final appellate court in Britain. Although the newest court, the Supreme Court is of less significance for Hong Kong since, as a post-1997 court, its decisions have little impact on Hong Kong except in so far as Hong Kong courts are permitted to consider precedents of "other common law jurisdictions" and, in practice, tend to pay more attention to English decisions than those from elsewhere in the common law world.[18]

ii. Chancery (Ch)

The Chancery or Chancellor's Court(s) were the foundation for that branch of law known as "equity", specifically retained as a source of law in Hong Kong by Article 8 of the Basic Law. Before the fusion of common law and equity courts by the Judicature Acts of 1873–1875, Chancery administered, effectively, a separate system of law, albeit one based on the notion of "filling the gaps" in the common law. Chancery had its own appeal court, the Court of Appeal in Chancery for which, briefly, there were separate reports to be found under Ch App. With the statutory fusion of common law and equity,[19] by 1875, via the Judicature Acts, Chancery ceased to be a separate court. Its appeal court was fused with the common law appeal court, the Court of Exchequer Chamber, to become the new Court of Appeal.[20] The first instance part of Chancery became a Division of the then newly-formed High Court of Judiciary. From 1875 to 1890, therefore, reports are to be found under the heading Ch D. Thereafter, Chancery Reports are, officially, just Ch. Under the Ch label are to be found reports of Chancery Division cases in the High Court and on subsequent appeal to the Court of Appeal.

iii. Queen's Bench (QB)

The Queen's Bench (or King's Bench as appropriate) was an important common law court in its own right with a very long history, far pre-dating the Judicature Acts. With the setting up of the High Court of Judicature in 1875, Queen's Bench became

---

18. See Chapters 5 and 6 for suggestions as to why this might be so.
19. The Judicature Acts provided that in cases of conflict between common law and equity post-1875, the rule of equity should prevail.
20. It was envisaged that the new Court of Appeal should replace the (Judicial Committee of the) House of Lords as the final appeal court but political opposition (fear that the political role of the House of Lords would also be abolished) delayed the abolition of the Judicial Committee by over 130 years.

a Division of the High Court; the only Division exercising both a civil and criminal jurisdiction.[21] Briefly,[22] therefore, the court's Reports were labelled QBD but are now, simply, QB. Under the QB label are to be found decisions of the Queen's Bench Division in the High Court and, where applicable, decisions on appeal from the Queen's Bench Division to the Court of Appeal.

iv. Family (Fam)

The Family Division is the "newest" of the full Divisions of the High Court. It replaced the old "Probate, Divorce and Admiralty" (PDA) Division[23] in 1972.[24] Under the label Fam are to be found reports of proceedings in the Family Division of the High Court as well as those relating to appeals therefrom to the Court of Appeal.

Outside the "Incorporated" (ICLR) reports there are two major *general* series of reports: Weekly Law Reports (WLR) and All England Reports (All ER). The Weekly Law Reports date from 1953 and, as their name suggests, they are produced weekly, which means very fast reporting with, often, full regard to arguments raised by counsel to the court. These reports are subsequently revised by the judges and published within the "Incorporated" series. The All England Law Reports, reliable[25] and user-friendly, have been produced since 1936. In small law libraries with only one set of English law reports, the likelihood is that this will be the All England Reports.

Other specialist reports such as Human Rights Law Reports (HRLR), Criminal Appeal Reports (Cr App R), Construction Law Reports, Industrial Cases Reports (ICR), Butterworths Company Law Cases (BCLC), Reports of Patents, Design and Trade Mark Cases (RPC) and Family Law Reports (FLR) are widely available, in hard copy or online. From a Hong Kong student perspective, the most important and relevant of these would be the Criminal Appeal Reports since they would cover important comparative material. Human rights issues, on the other hand, differ so much in Hong Kong and the UK that the English-produced material is of little practical relevance.[26]

14.2.1.1 Finding and citing English cases

A case can most easily be found by its name and full citation but sometimes the information available is incomplete.

In civil cases the names reflect the individual parties in the case—for example, *Carlill v The Carbolic Smoke Ball Company* [1893] 1 QB 256—whereas in criminal

---

21. There were briefly seven, then five, Divisions of the High Court but the jurisdiction of the Common Pleas and Exchequer Divisions was soon subsumed under that of the Queen's Bench Division.
22. From 1875 to 1890.
23. Known affectionately as "wills, wives and wrecks".
24. Some PDA functions were distributed elsewhere: notably, the Admiralty function was transferred to the Queen's Bench Division and contentious probate to Chancery.
25. They are judicially approved.
26. For further information on specialist reports see Chapter 3 of Bahrij J, op cit.

cases one party represents the Prosecution (the "Crown" in serious cases)—ie, *R (Regina) v Shivpuri* [1986] 2 All ER 334. The citation is made up of the elements below:

**YEAR VOLUME NUMBER REPORT SERIES PAGE
[2006] 2 ALL ER 334**

The citation comprises: the case name; the year in round brackets ( ) or square brackets [ ]; the volume number; the abbreviation of law report series; and the page number at which the case begins.

Remember that square brackets are to be used if the year forms an essential part of the citation (without which you will be unable to locate the case), otherwise round brackets are used (see the Hong Kong cases section below). The following are examples:

- *Fisher v Bell* [1961] 1 QB 394
- *Union Eagle Ltd v Golden Achievement Ltd* [1997] 2 All ER 215
- *R v Meyrick* (1929) 21 Cr App R 523

In a written submission it is usual to put the case name (only) in italics, thus:

- *Fisher v Bell*

The [1961] 1 QB 394 reference would then be put in a footnote. Less commonly, case names may be underlined. This is a useful practice in examinations (which will earn the marker's gratitude!).

If the full citation or name is not known, reference may be made to: the Current Law Service (published by Sweet & Maxwell UK); Monthly Digest (monthly updates on case law, legislation and government materials); Yearbooks (annually consolidated, with updates in the Monthly Digest); Case Citator (citation references for primary and secondary judicial consideration (ie, cited in other cases) of cases), or The Digest (a LexisNexis publication). While many libraries would have these reference aids in hard copy, electronic search is increasingly common. When such electronic searches can be accessed remotely, they are of particular value to non-full-time students.[27]

Similarly, when case references need updating, current law case citators or electronic sources can be used.

Electronic sources now proliferate[28] and mean that research is no longer library-bound. Decisions of the Supreme Court, House of Lords, Privy Council and

---

27. For a very detailed coverage of the citation of English authorities see D French, *How to Cite Legal Authorities* (Blackstone Press, London 1996).
28. To take just one example, the Chinese University of Hong Kong's Lee Quo Wei Law Library provides access to around 70 electronic sites, 3,000 electronic journals and over 22,000 electronic law books. Electronic or "computer-assisted" legal research is crucial enough now to be offered in some law schools as a separate elective.

(English) Court of Appeal from 1996 are available online on www.bailii.org. You should refer also to www.lawreports.co.uk, www.parliament.uk/judicial_work and the new Supreme Court website, www.supremecourt.gov.uk (as well as WestLaw, LawTel and LexisNexis). A useful, newer and expanding website is AustLII. Old-fashioned "hard-copy" research remains important in the case of *old* cases (which are often reported electronically in truncated form) and *very old* cases (for which there may still be no electronic report). A *crucial* advantage of online search engines (especially for cases) is the opportunity for *Boolean* research; essentially the method of limiting *or expanding* searches by combining concepts. For example, by the use of "and", two apparently unconnected subjects (eg, negligence/snails) may be combined to find cases in which a link exists. Conversely, by the use of "not" a subject may be excluded to narrow a search. All search engines provide for some form of Boolean search.

The increase in the number of cases being reported electronically had led to the problem that there is no common method in presenting the case in electronic form. The response of the judiciary was a "Practice Direction" on neutral citation, issued by the Lord Chief Justice (Practice Direction [Judgments: Form and Citation], *The Times*, 16 January 2001) whereby the Court of Appeal (followed by the House of Lords, High Court and Privy Council) took up the "neutral" form of citation. Under the "neutral" system, whether a case is subsequently reported or not, each case is given a specific reference number and paragraph numbers which will appear in both the printed form and electronic forms of the report. The numbered paragraphs do not stop at the end of each judgment but continue sequentially. The neutral reports are as follows:–

> UKSC (for United Kingdom Supreme Court) (added since Oct 2009)
> UKHL (for United Kingdom House of Lords)
> UKPC (for United Kingdom Privy Council)
> EWCA Civ (for England and Wales Court of Appeal, Civil Division)
> EWCA Crim (for England and Wales Court of Appeal, Criminal divisions)
> EWHC (Ch) (for England and Wales High Court, Chancery Division)
> EWHC (Pat) (for England and Wales High Court, Patents Court)
> EWHC (QB) (for England and Wales High Court, Queen's Bench)
> EWHC (Admin) (for England and Wales High Court, Administrative Court)
> EWHC (Comm) (for England and Wales High Court, Commercial Court)
> EWHC (Fam) (for England and Wales High Court, Family Division)

When citing a neutral report, or referring to an extract therefrom, this formula is used, together with paragraph numbers as appropriate. For example, one would refer to

- *Smith v Jones* [2003] EWCA Civ 10 at [1], [5], and [30]–[35].

While the system has obvious advantages, the cases are far less "user-friendly", especially for the student new to law. A typical All England report, for example, would have a "headnote" outlining the main features of a case. This would briefly explain, in the case of an appeal, the previous history of the case, the cases that had been considered, whether these had been "applied", "not followed", "distinguished", etc. The determination of the court and its reasons would be explained and, especially in older cases, the location of specific points within the judgments would be made. In the neutral system no introductory guidance is given to the reader as to the outcome of the case, its relationship to previous precedents, etc. Some assistance could be derived in an electronic search where, for example, the researcher searches via the name of a relevant previous case or a particular phrase. This would be highlighted on screen wherever referred to by the court. Nonetheless, assessing the significance, history and impact of a case *quickly* is far easier with All England reports than with the neutral ones.

14.2.2 Researching English legislation

Legislation, whether from Britain or Hong Kong, may be "primary" or "delegated" legislation. Primary legislation in Britain is referred to as an "Act of Parliament". Acts of Parliament go through a lengthy process of Parliamentary debate and scrutiny, the detail of which can be found in any English (British) work on constitutional or "public" law but those studying Hong Kong law need, rather, to concern themselves with the Hong Kong legislative process, dealt with in Chapter 3. A key feature of legislation, again whether in Britain or Hong Kong, is that it is *superior to* judge-made case law and can overturn or amend it. One traditional feature of the English constitution was always that Parliament was "sovereign" (supreme). This meant that Parliament could pass any law to affect the United Kingdom, which could not be challenged on the grounds of unreasonableness, unfairness, unconstitutionality[29] or even retrospectiveness.[30] Britain's membership of the European Union has meant that Parliamentary sovereignty is now a thing of the past.[31]

Much legislation, in Britain and Hong Kong, is "delegated". This means that the legislature has passed a broad "enabling" statute which describes generally the powers conferred by the enabling legislation but gives the power to a body or minister to carry out, via subsequent rules and regulations, the essential tasks and

---

29. By way of contrast to the United States where the Supreme Court may declare legislation "unconstitutional".
30. There was a strong presumption against retrospective legislation but if Parliament clearly enacted such legislation it could not be struck down by the courts.
31. There is an argument that EU membership is only a voluntary suspension and that the United Kingdom Parliament has the power to give up EU membership and restore its sovereignty. Given the Conservative government's introduction of a referendum in which a majority voted to leave the EU, this premise is now being tested to the full. Having lost the vote, anti-"Brexiters" now seek to challenge the validity of the referendum on "constitutional" grounds.

purposes of the original legislation. The curb on the power of the designated body is that it must not exceed the powers granted by the enabling legislation. Should it do so, the "excesses" may be challenged on the grounds that they are "ultra vires" (beyond the body's powers).

It is unlikely that Hong Kong students will need much in the way of researching English legislation except by way of comparison. Some pre-1997 statutes were said to apply to Hong Kong but, with the resumption of sovereignty by the PRC, these are of little significance. Other statutes, copied or amended only slightly in local Hong Kong legislation, were passed after significant Parliamentary debate, the content of which is useful in determining the "purpose" of such legislation. Still other legislation had the effect, it is argued, of amending the common law, thus *indirectly* affecting the "laws in force" in Hong Kong as at 30 June, 1997. Overall, however, English legislation is of much less significance to Hong Kong students, especially when of the "delegated" variety, and there will be only a brief coverage of how to find it.

14.2.2.1 Finding and citing English legislation

Statutes (Acts of Parliament) are cited as follows:

[short title] [year]; or
[Year] [chapter number (abbreviated as c.)]

- For example, Unfair Contract Terms Act 1977

or (less commonly)

- Act of 1977, c. 50.

"Delegated" legislation is cited as follows:
[Title] [year/number]
For example:

- The Supplementary Benefit (Single Payments) Regulations 1980/985 s 4.
- Water Pollution Control (Appeal Board) Regulations 1995/817 s 2.

Or simply, S.I. [year/number], for example:

- S.I. 1980/985

To find legislation, bills and records of Parliamentary debates recourse may be had to both hard copy and online sources.

English legislation is available via the UK Government's printer, The Stationery Office (www.tso.co.uk) or online (for Acts from 1988 onwards) through the Office of Public Sector Information or OPSI (www.opsi.gov.uk/legislation) as well as in traditional hard copy form (orders to The Stationery Office can be made online) or via the London Gazette (www.gazettes-online.co.uk). The leading sources are:

i. Law Reports: Statutes

This collection is published by the Incorporated Council of Law Reporting. The contents are not annotated or revised.

ii. Halsbury's Statutes of England

This series provides an annotated version of legislation currently in force organised by subject. Therefore, it is very useful for discovering whether there is legislation in any given subject area. The most efficient way to search here is to start with the General Index. This gives a wide range of "key words", each of which will refer you to a volume and paragraph number within the main collection. However, if the name of the statute is known then go to the **Alphabetical List of Statutes** at the beginning of the Table of Statutes and General Index.

Any revisions which post-date the publication of the work can be updated using the Cumulative Supplement or, for more recent amendments, the Noter-up binder.

iii. Current Law Statutes Annotated

All statutes are published in loose-leaf form (unannotated) after coming into force but some will be chosen by legal publishers to annotate on the basis of their overall importance. Over the course of a year bound volumes of Current Law Statutes Annotated are published in order according to their chapter numbers. The Annotations do not form any part of the statute and do not have any legal effect. However, the series is very useful for those seeking to know the background to legislation and its operation. The Annotations provide a very helpful overview of the legislation, its history and its significance, generally, or of specific sections. It is far more helpful to use this series, where applicable, than to read legislation without guidance.

For updating statutes, a very useful resource is the Current Law Statute Citator. This is part of the Current Law Service published by Sweet & Maxwell and contains information on all legislation passed from 1947 to 1971 (Vol 1); 1972 to 1988 (Vol 2); 1989 to 1995 (Vol 3); with a soft-back copy for 1996 onwards. Each volume of the Citator is organised chronologically by year and by chapter number (and the short title). Any changes to the statute are listed section by section but when looking at whether any case law exists in relation to a statutory provision it may still be useful to look at Halsbury's Laws[32] as this will refer to both statute and case law on any proposition.

Current Law Legislation Citator also lists the prominent cases dealing with particular legislative provisions. Note that in later citators cases appear by name but for the period 1947–1971 they are identified only by their reference to Current Law Yearbooks (year/paragraph number, eg, 55/588). The yearbook will need to be checked for the full citation.

---

32. See 14.4.2.1, infra.

Hansard is an official record of Proceedings in the Westminster (English) Parliament. This represents an indirect "source" of rules in so far as Parliament's "intention" is relevant to the interpretation of a piece of legislation.[33] Following the decision by the House of Lords in *Pepper v Hart*[34] courts are able to refer to Hansard, in order to aid statutory interpretation where the language of the legislation is unclear.[35] *Pepper v Hart* affects *all* "Acts in force" (statutes), not just those passed since 1993.

14.2.2.1.1 Electronic sources

Legislation, delegated legislation, bills, etc, are all available via commercial information retrieval systems such as LexisNexis, Lawtel and Westlaw. They are also accessible via UK public sector websites such as www.opsi.gov.uk or www.parliament.uk or more generalist search engines such as "Google". Special mention should be made of www.bailii.org (British & Irish Legal Information Institute), a charitable trust based in England[36] at the Institute for Advanced Studies in London. Like its Hong Kong counterpart Hklii, Bailii is somewhat underfunded and has been rather overtaken by the commercial sites listed above.

14.3 Researching PRC law

As the legal system of the People's Republic of China (PRC) becomes increasingly developed and the interface between the Hong Kong SAR and PRC systems increases, the study of PRC law will become increasingly important. As a civil law/socialist law system, the key sources of PRC law are *statutory*. The most important statutes are:

(i) statutes enacted by the National People's Congress (NPC);
(ii) administrative regulations of the State Council;
(iii) local laws and regulations enacted by provincial legislatures.

Judicial interpretations of statutes are not official sources of law, as they are in common law systems. However, as with legal systems everywhere, courts will *tend to* follow past practice (even if they are not required so to do) especially where the previous decision was from a leading court in the judicial hierarchy. The main courts in the PRC structure are:

(i) the Supreme People's Court (in Beijing) which hears first instance/appeal and protest cases;
(ii) the Higher People's Court (at Provincial level);

---

33. See Chapter 4.
34. [1993] 1 All ER 42.
35. See Steyn Johan, 'Pepper v Hart; A Re-examination' (2001) 21(1) *Oxford Journal of Legal Studies* 59, 72.
36. There are also centres in Ireland and Northern Ireland.

(iii) the Intermediate People's Court (at Prefecture level);
(iv) the Basic People's Courts (sometimes referred to as "grassroots" courts and operating at the county, administrative district or small city level); and
(v) specialised People's Courts (such as military, maritime and "railway transportation" courts).

There are useful hard copy subscription sources produced by CCH Asia, notably the "China Law Reference Service". Moreover, given the Supreme People's Court's (SPC's) position at the top of the court hierarchy, the SPC "Gazette" is a useful work of reference. However, at the same time as the amount of written China law materials has rapidly expanded, so, too, has the development of online sites. The following are probably the most useful websites and all provide information in both English and Chinese (traditional and simplified text):

(i) www.isinolaw.com which was the first site to establish a bilingual China law website. It has sections on "latest laws and regulations" and "legal news". Almost all of its information is available via subscription only.
(ii) www.lawinfochina.com has both a section open to the public and one available to subscribers only. Within the public site there is a useful overview of the "legal system of China" as well as reference to the "main laws" and "legal news". The subscriber section has a wealth of material on "laws and regulations", tax treaties, World Trade Organization (WTO)-related information and a number of journals and gazettes. Much of the information on this site is now bilingual.
(iii) www.lawyee.net is another useful site which focuses primarily on business-related issues of PRC law, especially arbitration, WTO-related matters and commercial cases. It has close connections with the prestigious Peking (Beijing) University and, again, most of its data are available only to subscribers.
(iv) www.en.pkulaw.com established by the Legal Information Centre of Peking University, this site provides useful bilingual legal information for researchers and businesses.
(v) the more recent ChinaLaw and ChinaOnline are useful research sites for PRC law; the latter focused on PRC laws and regulations.

The study of PRC cases, especially those in the higher courts, is likely to become increasingly important as the PRC system moves towards a sort of "de facto" precedent system. The Chinese Supreme People's Curt has issued "Detailed Rules on Implementing Guiding Cases", a move towards standardisation of approach. Essentially, a court is required to cite "Guiding Cases" where these deal with the same principle as the court's instant case. If the Guiding Case is not to be followed the court must explain why not. This appears to indicate a "presumption in favour" of following superior precedents.

For further information on China law resources refer to Chapter 6 of Bahrij.[37] Note that some sites described by Bharij as in "Chinese only" are now available bilingually.

14.4 Researching Hong Kong law

Despite the (diminishing) importance of English law and the increasing significance of PRC law, clearly the most important research task for the Hong Kong student is to research Hong Kong primary and secondary sources. As regards the "primary" category there is a need, in this common law-based jurisdiction, to research both legislation (statutory law) *and* case law (judge-made law). In the "secondary" category are included a large number of books, journals and articles relating to the law in Hong Kong.

14.4.1 Researching Hong Kong legislation

Ordinances and subordinate or delegated legislation are all enacted via the Legislative Council of Hong Kong (LegCo). The legislative process itself has been dealt with in Chapter 4.

Since 1989, statutes and subordinate legislation have been enacted with English and Chinese texts side by side. Both the Chinese and English are authentic texts of the laws.[38] Hong Kong's Ordinances have chapter (Cap) numbers. New public Ordinances are either allocated a chapter number formerly used by a repealed Ordinance, or one in sequence after the most recent highest allocation, for example Sale of Goods Ordinance (Cap 26), Money Lenders Ordinance (Cap 163).

Hong Kong Ordinances are published in Legal Supplement No 1 to the Hong Kong Government Gazette. They are also issued in the form of a loose-leaf edition called the Laws of Hong Kong which contains all the Ordinances (except the Appropriation Ordinance, ie, the budget) enacted in Hong Kong (together with subsidiary legislation).

One problem with using this source is that, where statutes are repealed or amended, this is easy to miss, especially where library material is not kept constantly up-to-date. Where legislation is amended, this may be done by amendment legislation or amendment "subsidiary" legislation. After the commencement of the amendment it is inserted into the "principal" (original) Ordinance. The practical problem, then, is to find the commencement date of the amendment and the proper version of the (amended) legislation. For legislation printed in the Laws of Hong Kong (loose-leaf edition print copy) a check can be made for the date of the commencement (printed below the long title). If no date is there, then a check can be made of the

---

37. J Bahrij (n 2).
38. The Department of Justice also publishes a glossary of English-Chinese legal terms.

Index to Regulations and Notices of commencement dates in Hong Kong Gazette's Legal Supplement No 2.

For new legislation not yet printed in the Laws of Hong Kong (loose-leaf) again the Index to Regulations and Notices of commencement dates in Hong Kong Gazette's Legal Supplement No 2 (as above) can be used.

However, in this context, it is far simpler, and more efficient, to use an "electronic" (online) source. Special statutory recognition of the importance of electronic research in this context is provided by the Legislation Publication Ordinance.[39] Traditionally, the two best-known and useful sources are the Bilingual Laws Information Service (BLIS) or Hong Legal Information Institute (HKLII).[40] A useful download facility is to seek either the part of the legislation currently in force *or* the whole original legislation. This is useful in several respects. If a student were asked to research how a particular piece of legislation had evolved, a comparison of the "before and after" would be very useful. Alternatively, in the original version, those sections no longer in force would be so described together with a date for their repeal or amendment. Cottrell[41] gives the example of giving advice on a contract entered into some years previously and needing to know the relevant legislation *at the time of the contract's formation*.[42] Poorly funded (and in the case of BLIS almost extinct) these two sites have been largely superseded by better-funded "commercial sites" such as LexisNexis and Westlaw; which are international "subscription" sites but with large sections devoted to Hong Kong including much journal information. For comparative research WestlawAsia is supplemented by WestlawNext which is US focused. Similarly, extensive for American research is Heinonline. The government-funded Hong Kong e-Legislation (HKeL) is rapidly expanding its sources of Hong Kong legislation; including all new laws and gradually including all earlier legislation. The site:

> will ultimately contain verified copies (within the meaning of the Legislation Publication Ordinance [Cap 614] of all Hong Kong legislation.[43]

It should also be noted that Hong Kong judges have a similar scope as their English counterparts to search for "legislative intent" to assist their *interpretation* of legislation.[44] As such, debates in LegCo are an important source. These are available via Hong Kong Hansard which can, again, be found in both hard copy and online. The source is: www.legco.gov.hk.

---

39. Cap 614.
40. The author finds HKLII more user-friendly. Tragically, at the time of going to press, HKLII (established jointly at HKU by the Department of Computer Science and the Law Faculty in 2003) is seriously under-funded and the quality of its product is at risk.
41. J Cottrell (n 1).
42. Ibid 135.
43. Hong Kong e-Legislation website, "What is Hong Kong e-Legislation".
44. See Chapter 4.

14.4.1.1 Citing Hong Kong legislation

There are two major forms of citation for Hong Kong legislation. The first, and more usual, is simply to cite the "Cap" (chapter) number. The second, generally used *until* the legislation is published in the Laws of Hong Kong and assigned a chapter number, is to give the chronological order of the legislation in its relevant year. For example, reference may be made to:

(i) Toys and Children's Products Safety Ordinance (Cap 424); or
(ii) Toys and Children's Products Safety Ordinance (No 80 of 1982)

As before, an online search would be simple. Reference would be made to "Toys and Children's Products" and the icon for "find all these words" should be used. When citing the legislation, it is then preferable to refer to the "Cap" number, once one has been assigned.

14.4.2 Researching Hong Kong case law

We have already recognised, especially in Chapter 2, the special place that case law (judge-made law) occupies in common law systems. Decisions, especially of the highest courts, serve as sources of law second only, in hierarchical terms, to legislative rules. Moreover, in a common law system like Hong Kong's, much of the law in many areas can be ascertained only by reference to previously decided cases. Hong Kong's law of tort or law of contract may contain important pieces of legislation but they are additions or amendments to the common law. It is the latter which provides the overall framework of the subject. Even where legislation exists it may only partially deal with an area of law. The Misrepresentation Ordinance,[45] for example, explains the *effects* of misrepresentation but it does not *define* the term. Even in cases of detailed, "codified" areas, such as the law relation to sale of goods,[46] the cases need to be studied to discover the *interpretation* which the courts have applied to particular words, phrases or sections. The cases are thus of crucial importance to the study of Hong Kong law.

14.4.2.1 Citing and finding Hong Kong cases

Cases may be "reported" or "unreported". At one time in Hong Kong, with only the Hong Kong Law Reports available, there was a large number of important, yet unreported, cases. With the expansion of law reporting following the introduction of the Hong Kong Cases series, most important cases are *eventually* reported, though very recent important cases (the sort that examiners like to make use of!) will, of course, not yet be reported in the "official" reports. Unreported Hong Kong cases

---
45. Cap 284.
46. See Sale of Goods Ordinance (Cap 26) (SOGO).

are given a unique reference number by the judiciary (referring to court level and court type). This is the official court reference number and can be seen in the top right hand corner of the front page of the case judgment. These decisions are now readily available online on http://legalref.judicary.gov.hk and on the Hong Kong Legal Information Institute (HKLII) website.

Once a case has become reported, its reported citation is used. The case will be assigned a unique citation by the legal publisher to indicate where it can be found in that law report series. Typically, there will be reference to the year (in square brackets) in which the case was reported, the volume number of the law report series, the abbreviation for the law report series and the page number of the title page of the case report. The main (general) hard copy reports are:

(i) Hong Kong Law Reports and Digest (HKLRD) and its predecessor Hong Kong Law Reports (HKLR);
(ii) Hong Kong Cases (HKC).

Hong Kong Law Reports & Digest (HKLRD) (1997–present) is a monthly publication by Sweet & Maxwell Asia. At the end of the year, the 12 monthly parts are put together to form a Yearbook, Hong Kong Law Reports & Digest Yearbook (HKLRD Yrbk). Although the HKLRD is comparatively recent, note that its predecessor, Hong Kong Law Reports (HKLR), operated between 1905 and 1996. HKLR, as its title suggests, offered law reports but without the notes, comments, etc, to be found in the Digest. HKLR and HKLRD citations are as follows:

(i) *Eastweek Publisher Ltd and another v Cheung Ng Sheong, Steven* [1995] HKLR 1453 [for pre-1997 decisions];
(ii) *HKSAR v Tse Ka Wah* [1998] 1 HKLRD 925 [for post-1996 decisions].

Hong Kong Cases, though established comparatively recently, has "retroactively" produced a series of law reports dating from 1842. This widely-available series, though not as accurately reported as the HKLRD series, is rather more extensive and generally easier to read. Hong Kong Cases are cited as follows:

- *Susanto-Wing Sun Co Ltd v Yung Chi Hardware Machinery Co Ltd* [1989] 2 HKC 504

There are, in addition, a number of "specialised" reports which may focus on one particular subject or a particular court. For example, decisions of the Court of Final Appeal (CFA) have been reported since 1997, when the court first began sitting, in the Hong Kong Court of Final Appeal Reports (HKCFAR). Likewise, the Hong Kong Law Reports series has a separate section for Hong Kong District Court Law Reports (HKDCLR) which operated, like the Hong Kong Law Reports themselves, until 1996. On a "topic" basis, cases involving tax disputes are reported in Hong Kong Tax Cases (HKTC). Other specialist law reports include:

(i) Hong Kong Conveyancing and Property Reports (CPR) (1980–present)
(ii) Hong Kong Family Law Reports (2005–present)
(iii) Hong Kong Inland Revenue Board of Review Decisions (IRBRD) (1974–present)
(iv) Hong Kong Public Law Reports (HKPLR) (1989–present)
(v) Hong Kong Revenue Cases (HKRC) (1989–present)[47]

As access to computers has mushroomed, case research via electronic sources has become far more widespread and is generally more convenient. Most online access can be effected "remotely" (away from a library) though sometimes subscription charges apply. Moreover, the electronic sites are much easier to use for unreported cases (and where someone else is using the volume of law reports you want!). The most popular sites for Hong Kong case research are HKLII (for the Hong Kong Legal Information Institute), Westlaw International and LexisNexis. Mention should also be made of AustLII which is rapidly expanding its database. The electronic sources use their own "neutral" form of citation which lists the case name, court and a reference number. A HKLII reference would be like this:

- *Eastweek Publisher Ltd & Another v Cheung Ng Sheong, Steven* [1995] HKCA 547

In Westlaw, unreported case *Chinachem Charitable Foundation Ltd v Chan Chun Chuen* would be cited as:

- *Chinachem Charitable Foundation Ltd v Chan Chun Chuen* [2009] HKEC 798 (CFI) [HKEC meaning "Hong Kong Electronic Cases"; CFI meaning "Court of First Instance"]

Using LexisNexis, unreported case *Leung Lai Fong v Ho Sin Ying* is cited as:

- *Leung Lai Fong v Ho Sin Ying* [2009] HKCU 1080 (CFA) [meaning "Hong Kong Cases Unreported" in the Court of Final Appeal)]

There is no pagination in electronic case reports so if, for example, reference is made to a specific section of a judgment there needs to be reference to a paragraph number (the modern style is that all the paragraphs in a judgment are numbered).

It can be seen from the above that it is extremely likely that a case, certainly any important one, will be reported in more than one publication. In such cases it is normal to cite all, or at least all *major*, references. For example, the leading case on judicial precedent in Hong Kong is cited in the Hong Kong Court of Final Appeal Reports (HKCFAR) as:

- *A Solicitor v The Law Society of Hong Kong* (2008) 11 HKCFAR 117;

---

47. For a list of law report citation abbreviations (for Hong Kong and elsewhere), see J Bahrij (n 2) Appendix 2.

The same case is cited in Hong Kong Cases as:

- *A Solicitor v The Law Society of Hong Kong* [2008] 2 HKC 1

To assist in research into such cases of multiple or "parallel" citations, those arising post-1905 can be found in the Hong Kong Case Citator (with similar tools available online via Westlaw as "KeyCite" and via LexisNexis as "CaseBase"). Alternatively, recourse may be had to the Consolidated Index to All Reported Hong Kong Decisions (a service index of all the major Hong Kong case series and 25 other major case report series around the world) published since 2007 with Cumulative Supplements issued periodically. Given the "relatively" recent nature of Hong Kong case reporting, most cases can be located electronically; this contrasts with the position for English-law research based on more "venerable" jurisprudence.

When writing an essay or delivering a paper or presentation on such parallel cases, the "student" should first cite the name of the case in the main text (possibly with the year though practice varies) and then list all (full) references as a footnote. Thereafter reference may be made to the case name, or even just "in the *A Solicitor* case", with a footnote reading "loc cit" together with a page and/or paragraph number where appropriate. Some referencing styles eschew Latin and references would be to "see footnote (number) above".

The use of brackets is sometimes confusing for students. Should the brackets surrounding the year of a case be "( )" or [ ]? The simple answer is that it depends on whether the year is *part of* the reference or merely informative as to the year of the case. For example, the reference [1989] 2 HKC 321 involves finding the case via the second volume of Hong Kong cases for 1989. Armed with this, it is necessary merely to turn to the page number listed. Conversely in some reports (especially older English ones) the year would be given merely as (non-necessary) information. For example:

- *Derry v Peek* (1889) 14 App Cas 337

can be found in the 14th volume of the series "Appeal Cases" at page 337. There is no need to know the year but it may well be, of course, of interest. For a Hong Kong example note that Court of Final Appeal Cases Reports (HKCFAR), similarly, use *round* brackets because the year is not essential to the finding of the case. The volume numbering of the law report series dates back to the beginning of the series (in the case of HKCFAR, volume 1 was published in 1997 and covered a period July 1997–December 1998; by 2017, 20 volumes had been published). This elementary point seems to have been lost on a website "JustCite" aimed, supposedly, at assisting correct citation but failing miserably. For example, JustCite gives the citation for the famous *Jumbo King* case as [1999] 2 HKCFAR 279. It should, of course, be (1999) 2 HKCFAR 279 as explained above.

When searching for a new case (especially if there is a need to access its significance in a hurry) case digests are especially useful. Since it can take some time for an unreported case to be selected for its significance and then officially reported, some legal publishers will produce an intermediately available case digest on, for example, a fortnightly or monthly basis. The case digest will provide a short case summary and/or headnotes of the unreported decision within, for example, the current month. The unreported decision remains "unreported" until it is formally reported in a law report series. In addition, many law firms provide website synopses of recent cases and their significance.

A valuable starting point for more detailed research of an already familiar area is Halsbury's Laws of Hong Kong (or Halsbury's Laws of England if dealing with a relevant/comparative English law issue). This text is available in hard copy or online. The first step would be to search the index volumes of Halsbury's for "key words", which should identify the legal problem or issue involved. The key word will provide a set of references (paragraph numbers) to a main volume within the series. The next step is to search the text (in the main volume). Then, from the searched text in the main volume, it is necessary to move on to the "Current Service" to update the material previously located. Updates in the Current Service will appear under the same paragraph number. As before, the Current Service is available in hard copy or online.

14.4.3 Researching Hong Kong secondary sources

For any student, especially one coming new to a subject, guidance is essential. In very traditional law schools this might take the form of simply "directing" students to original sources (law reports, cases, etc) and leaving them to their own devices. Very few courses are now taught in that way, although "independent research" remains one of the ultimate avowed aims of most programmes. Guidance, of course, may come from the direction of the law teacher indicating the key areas of a topic but, almost certainly, many "gaps" remain to be filled and textbooks are the first port of call. A useful "labour saving device" is the casebook and, where this also includes learned commentary and reference to relevant articles on a particular case or topic, it is especially helpful. Textbooks, dictionaries, journals, legal encyclopaedias, government reports, newspaper articles, speeches, conference, etc, are all useful research materials and regarded as "secondary" (or "literary") sources of law.

14.4.3.1 Textbooks

When researching Hong Kong law, as indeed the law of any jurisdiction, a good textbook with its detailed commentary and footnote references will be a great resource and a good starting point. The bad news about Hong Kong textbooks is that there is a relatively small variety of them. In criminal law, for example, there is no textbook of significance other than Michael Jackson's text in the Hong Kong

University Press series.[48] The book was published in 2003 and, while reprinted, has not been revised.[49] With no "competition" in Hong Kong's small market place, different/alternative perspectives on important topics are in short supply. Much of the problem stems from the obsession, in academia, with "Research Assessment Exercises" whereby the reputation of an institution and its staff derives largely from their research output (and textbooks are not regarded as "research"!) and their "international impact" ("local", Hong Kong, research rates poorly on this criterion). Related to this issue is the fact that from the short list of major Hong Kong texts it is also unfortunate that many are out-of-date (law is a dynamic area, and books need constant updating but the market is small and there is no "research" incentive). For example, Peter Wesley-Smith's *Introduction to the Hong Kong Legal System*[50] is now 20 years out of date. The good news, on the other hand, is that students are rarely spoiled for choice unlike their English or American counterparts.

Textbooks in Hong Kong may be of the "academic" type, such as Michael Jackson's book noted above,[51] intended primarily for a student readership, or "practitioner" volumes such as *Chitty on Contract*, or *Archbold Hong Kong* (on Hong Kong criminal law and procedure), intended primarily for those in legal practice.

When *citing* textbooks there are different styles but the full citation is usually via surname of author, first name(s) or initial(s), *title*, (edition, publisher location year). For example:

> Glofcheski, R. A. *Tort Law in Hong Kong* (4nd edn, Sweet & Maxwell/Thomson Reuters Asia 2012).

This full reference needs only to be cited once. Thereafter reference may be made to:

> Glofcheski R. A., see footnote [number].

Confusingly, in the now widely-adopted "OSCOLA" system the initials come first in footnotes (R A Glofcheski) but as above in a bibliography.

As with so much legal research today, many "books" may be accessed online and Hong Kong law students based at a university will have ready access to these under "their" university's licensing system.

---

48. M Jackson, *Criminal Law in Hong Kong* (Hong Kong University Press 2003).
49. Some law schools in Hong Kong use an English criminal law text as their essential reading; despite the wide (and widening) differences between the two systems.
50. P Wesley-Smith, *An Introduction to the Hong Kong Legal System* (3rd edn, Oxford University Press 1998).
51. M Jackson (n 47).

14.4.3.2 Journals

Journals, bulletins, reviews, newsletters, etc (known collectively as legal periodicals) take a wide variety of forms but will generally appeal to either practitioners or an academic audience. High "status" law journals will usually focus on a new, significant or controversial legal case or statute and analyse its merits and significance. Ironically, the higher the status of a law journal, the longer the waiting time for peer review and publication, with consequent loss of "topicality".

In Hong Kong the most common journals are:

(i) Hong Kong Law Journal;
(ii) Hong Kong Lawyer
(iii) Hong Kong Journal of Legal Studies (previously Student Law Review)
(iv) Asia Pacific Law Review

The Hong Kong Law Journal has been traditionally associated with the Law Faculty of the University of Hong Kong (HKU). The Hong Kong Lawyer is the journal of the Law Society of Hong Kong. The Hong Kong Journal of Legal Studies is "Hong Kong's only law journal that is fully written, edited and managed by students".[52] Finally, the Asia Pacific Law Review is, essentially, a City University of Hong Kong publication. For "electronic" journal access, in addition to the "usual suspects" Westlaw and LexisNexis, special mention should be made of HeinOnline.

14.4.3.3 Legal encyclopaedias

Encyclopaedias, usually practitioner guides in loose-leaf form, are designed to give a comprehensive statement of the law, usually in limited or specific areas and written very concisely. Examples from Hong Kong and the surrounding region include "Law of the Internet",[53] "Arbitration in Asia",[54] and "Employment Law in Hong Kong".[55]

14.4.3.4 Other secondary sources

Speeches, conference papers, Government Reports and newspaper articles can usually be located online and contain much useful information, especially in the "socio-legal" area. The Hong Kong Judiciary website www.judiciary.gov.hk will provide, for example, the text of the more recent speeches of the Chief Justice.[56]

For those studying public/constitutional Law generally (or the Basic Law specifically) the following are extremely useful: www.info.gov.hk for connection to all

---

52. Hong Kong Journal of Legal Studies, "homepage".
53. FL Street and MP Grant (LexisNexis 2002, with regular updates).
54. MJ Moser (ed) (2nd edn, Juris Publishing 2008 with updates).
55. P Walsh (2nd edn, CCH Publications Hong Kong 2008).
56. For further information on researching secondary sources, research techniques and methods, see J Bahrij, (n 2), Chapters 4 and 5.

government bureaux; www.legco.gov.hk for explanation of LegCo procedures and details of debates, and www.info.gov.hk/basic_law for Basic Law text and related cases.

All government departments have their own websites and particularly useful are those for the ICAC, Department of Justice, Legal Aid Department and the Law Reform Commission of Hong Kong.[57]

---

57. The latter provides details on recommendations and follow up which dramatically illustrate the lack of prompt legislative response.

Postscript

It is some time since this text was originally submitted. In the meantime, there have been significant developments. While specific changes have been flagged in individual chapters, it is the *mood* in Hong Kong engendered by such changes which is most noteworthy.

Completing the circle, if we look back to Chapter 1 and the interface between "optimistic" and "pessimistic" expectations for 2047, what is most striking is how unrealistically optimistic the "optimistic" forecasts were. Few now seriously believe in "two systems" *post*-2047. Optimists now hope for some semblance of two systems to survive *until* 2047.

The chilling tone of the CPG's 2014 White Paper, "explaining" the PRC's "comprehensive jurisdiction" over Hong Kong and the description of our once proud judiciary as civil servants required to be "patriotic" and love China, has set the framework for the end of two systems; the pieces are now being rapidly put into place.

Examples abound of PRC interference with Hong Kong's promised "high degree of autonomy". No one seriously believes, for example, that the road bridge to Zhuhai was a "local" Hong Kong idea; merely one disproportionately financed by Hong Kong taxpayers. We now have the spectre of a convenient road link between Macau and Zhuhai being financed largely by Hong Kong, but to which most Hong Kong people will be denied access.

What is sometimes termed "mainlandisation", but (barrister and former Democratic Party leader) Martin Lee has called "Tibetanisation", increases apace. Over two million mainland citizens will have settled in Hong Kong between 1997 and 2047 via the so-called "family reunion" system, administered entirely by the PRC. This does not include the thousands of mainland business employees in banking, trade, policing (unofficially) and the armed forces. Only mass protest has, thus far, prevented the introduction of so-called "national education", intended to buttress "patriotism" and "love of China". However, with the imminent introduction of compulsory "Chinese history" (no doubt highly selective) for schools, only the *label* will actually be different.[1]

---

1. See below. The *SCMP* has reported that, in a clear affront to two systems, the PRC's education minister has called on Hong Kong teachers to do "a better job of instilling patriotism in the city's

No end is in sight for Hong Kong's chronic housing problem. This is presented as a shortage of land but is actually a shortage of *affordable* housing. Since only mainland buyers can afford good quality housing in Hong Kong, a legislative curb on "external" purchasing could solve the problem at a stroke. Since this would upset the government's friends in the property industry (on either side of the boundary) the political will is lacking. Nor will the government use "agricultural" land for public housing in the New Territories, since this would involve confronting the vested interests of the Heung Yee Kuk whose soi-disant "indigenous" villagers demand the retention of their "small house" rights on the spurious ground that these are protected by the Basic Law.[2] Instead, the government via its so-called "Citizens Task Force on Land Resources" offers Hong Kong people the calamitous choice of building on country parks or yet more unnecessary land reclamation at the taxpayer's huge expense.[3] Yet while over-priced housing remains as before, the "beneficiaries" have changed. The once despised "local" property barons are now rapidly giving way to those from the mainland. Once regal Lee Ka-shing rationalised his property and business empire and re-located much of it prior to retirement.

There have been other examples of the erosion of "two systems", many involving assaults on the Basic Law itself. It now appears that the joint checkpoint ("co-location") arrangement, whereby PRC officers will apply *all* mainland law in a specially designated part of the check-in area for the new Hong Kong–Guangzhou high speed train, is a fait accompli. This despite its apparent conflict with Article 18. This Article *clearly* states that mainland laws will *not* be enforced in Hong Kong *unless* listed in Annex III and locally enacted. While the PRC's right to *add to* the Annex III list of applicable laws is recognised in Article 18, there is *no* provision for the application of *all* mainland laws in one area of Hong Kong rather than another. The insistence on *all* mainland laws being enforced at the checkpoint area (rather than merely immigration ones) is legally dubious and unnecessary, given that those about to board will subject themselves to PRC law as soon as they arrive on the mainland. Co-location supporters have been unable to produce a convincing and

---

youth": V Zhou, 'Love Country First, HK Teachers Told' *South China Morning Post* (Hong Kong, 24 February 2017)].
2. See Chapter 2.
3. The government's latest choice appears to be the environmentally disastrous creation of an artificial island and the consequent destruction of most of Lantau. Chief Executive Carrie Lam has already shown her contempt for public opinion by stating, while the "consultation" process is ongoing, her preference for the awful artificial island option; despite its inevitable environmental destruction and cost/completion date overruns. For a succinct academic destruction of the artificial island plan see T Yam, 'Next white elephant' *South China Morning Post* (Hong Kong, 21 August 2018) showing that the sole beneficiaries of the plan will be the government's business friends. Lest this critique be considered "anti-government" note agreement with the sentiment by a normally pro-government journalist: A Lo, 'Just forget any East Lantau mega project' *South China Morning Post* (Hong Kong, 23 August 2018). Predictably, and without waiting for the Task Force's Report, Carrie Lam has announced plans for a huge "East Lantau" reclamation.

consistent legal argument[4] and the Hong Kong Bar has expressed serious concern. While the effects of co-location are not *per se* worrying, there is a fear that this cession of Hong Kong jurisdiction to the mainland may be the "thin edge of the wedge". Should we next expect mainland laws to be applied in the "Lok Ma Chau Loop", on the basis that most businesses actually operating there will be Shenzhen ones?

Further, Article 27's guarantee of freedom of speech and publication sits uneasily with the abduction from Hong Kong and elsewhere of those publishing or distributing material critical of the PRC leadership,[5] and the same may be said of Article 28's rejection of "arbitrary arrest".[6] Moreover, as newspaper publication becomes increasingly "mainlandised", *freedom of the press*, except in online form, is rapidly eroding. To take just one example, Alibaba's Jack Ma now owns Hong Kong's main English-language newspaper, the *South China Morning Post* (*SCMP*). This journal has campaigned to amend the "one share, one vote" company law regime which saw Ma (who insists on power without financial risk) unable to list on the Hong Kong Stock Exchange. Legal change to introduce Ma's preferred variable voting rights has now been effected.[7] To his credit, *SCMP* writer Jake Van der Kamp has opposed the legislative change and maintained an independent stance. However, editorial "influence" is evident in a change of tone by other *SCMP* writers. Alex Lo, for example, who not long ago wrote that Hong Kong people were right to be concerned about the joint rail checkpoint,[8] now supports it and asks what all the fuss is about. The excellent Philip Bowring, often critical of the government, has been marginalised and, with notable exceptions,[9] coverage has become increasingly pro-establishment.

Most disheartening of all, especially for young people, has been China's refusal to honour its Article 45 pledge to (ultimately) introduce genuine universal suffrage in Hong Kong. China's version of universal suffrage offered to Hong Kong for the 2017 Chief Executive "election" involved the selection of two or three candidates (by a Committee of 1,200) who, with the blessing of at least half of the Committee, could then be voted on by all. LegCo rejected China's offer and prospects for genuine democracy in Hong Kong now appear dim.

This cynical version of universal suffrage saw thousands on the streets as part of the brave but doomed "Occupy Central" movement. Numbers swelled rapidly as scenes of police excesses were witnessed. After 79 days no concessions on the "fake democracy" package were obtained. Official retribution has been slow but harsh;

---

4. Li Fei, head of the Basic Law Committee, has said there is "no single Basic Law Article justifying the move", and leftist academic, Professor Albert Chen, has admitted this is a "grey area".
5. See Chapter 12.
6. Ibid.
7. On 2 January 2018 the *SCMP* proclaimed that there had been an IPO boost based partly on the introduction of two-class shares. [cf L He, 'After a Poor Year, HK Set for IPO Boost' *South China Morning Post* (Hong Kong, 2 January 2018)].
8. See Chapter 12.
9. To the name of Vanderkamp may be added some others, notably special projects editor, Cliff Buddle.

with democracy supporters imprisoned and elected democrats removed from the Legislative Council on various legal grounds.[10] At the time of going to press, the additionally vindictive step of reclaiming LegCo salaries (to bankrupt the former members and thereby render them ineligible to stand) has just been abandoned by the Hong Kong government; not for altruistic reasons but on legal advice that the claim was likely to fail.

International support for Hong Kong's democracy movement has been muted; China is a powerful country and a wealthy potential trading partner. Such support for Hong Kong as has been voiced has been distressingly ill-informed. Former Governor, Chris Patten, has urged China to honour its Joint Declaration promises on democracy. In fact, none exist; the promise of an ultimate universal suffrage is to be found in the Basic Law *not* the Joint Declaration. Foolishly, "external" pro-democrats have also questioned Hong Kong's *judicial* independence in the light of the imprisonment of LegCo members involved in the Occupy protests. The jailing, effected via a successful Department of Justice appeal to the Court of Appeal against the non-custodial sentences initially imposed, was controversial. However, while some judicial comments in the Court of Appeal were undoubtedly intemperate,[11] it is too soon to assert that the judiciary has become politicised.[12] What *is* undeniable is that the decision of then Secretary for Justice, Rimsky Yuen, to seek a review of sentence was an egregious affront to the principles of natural justice.[13] Proper procedures may have been followed[14] but there can be no denying that Yuen, as a member of the government, had a professional interest in the imprisonment of the members; which reduced opposition to the government in LegCo. Moreover, Yuen had a *personal* interest, given "Occupy's" rejection of the "fake democracy" package which he had been (jointly) tasked with "selling" to Hong Kong.[15] No clearer example could be seen of the need for a genuinely independent prosecutorial body.[16] Implicit criticism of Yuen's professional judgement (though not his political motivation) is to be found in the Court of Final Appeal's determination that the application for sentence review should have been refused.[17]

The developments outlined above have had a significant effect on morale in Hong Kong; especially among the young. "Localism" has been a desperate response

---

10. By-elections to fill the now vacated seats have yet to be held and the government has made hay in the meantime; with its supporters changing LegCo rules of procedure to prevent the slowing up of unpopular legislation by the "opposition".
11. In particular, those of Wally Yeung JA.
12. See, in strong defence of the judges, G Cross, 'A Just decision' *South China Morning Post* (Hong Kong 30 August 2017).
13. Which dictate that no one should be a judge in his own cause (see chapter 13).
14. See R Yuen, 'Facts of the Case' *South China Morning Post* (Hong Kong, 24 August 2017).
15. Along with current Chief Executive, Carrie Lam and Raymond Tam, Secretary for Constitutional and Mainland Affairs.
16. See Chapter 13. It remains to be seen whether Yuen's successor, Teresa Cheng, will adopt a more independent approach.
17. [2018] HKCFA 4 at para 106.

to what is perceived as a desperate situation. The booing of the Chinese national anthem by localists at football matches has led to the introduction of the mainland anthem law into Hong Kong law (implemented by local legislation). While this need not be, in itself, an issue of great concern, more worrying has been the call from some in the establishment camp to give this legislation retrospective effect. This would conflict with both Hong Kong's Bill of Rights and Article 39 of the Basic Law.[18] While the retrospective proposal is likely to be resisted, its very suggestion indicates the scant regard for the rule of law held by its proponents.

"Optimists" may hope that the views expressed here are merely jaundiced and anti-establishment. Note, then, the views of establishment journalist Alex Lo who writes:[19]

> mainlandisation is going full steam ahead with cross-border integration. We are in the midst of an infrastructure-building boom with showcase projects . . . joint customs and immigration clearance anyone?
>
> In education, Chinese history is being made mandatory again, and versions of national education are being revived. In the legislature, a loyalist majority in being entrenched. The list goes on.
>
> Xi really does deserve full credit for a policy towards Hong Kong that is comprehensive, total and inevitable.

Not to be outdone in the "being realistic" stakes, Michael Chugani concludes an article on Hong's future[20] with the words:

> As we head into the future, your choices are limited. Stand up for the national anthem, recognise Hong Kong as part of red China, and kiss genuine democracy goodbye . . .
>
> If you can't bring yourself to do that, there is just one other alternative: pack up and leave.

Is it any wonder that our young people are losing hope, especially those for whom to "pack up and leave" is not an option?

MJF April 2018

---

18. See C Buddle, 'Beware the Ills of Retroactive Punishment' *South China Morning Post* (Hong Kong, 2 November 2017).
19. A Lo, 'Give Xi Credit for an Inevitable HK Policy' *South China Morning Post* (Hong Kong, 18 October 2017).
20. M Chugani, 'HK's Democracy Dream Is Dead under Red China' *South China Morning Post* (Hong Kong, 14 December 2017).

Illustration Credits/Acknowledgements

The author acknowledges the following sources of extracts:

pp 39–40	Martin Lee, 'Courting Disaster' (*South China Morning Post* 14 June 1995)
pp 40–41	Albert Chen, 'Crown, State and Adaptation of Laws' (*The Other Hong Kong Report* Chinese University Press pp 29–48)
pp 42–43	Department of Justice, 'Act of State' LC Paper No CB (2) 86/02-03 (02)
page 47	(Illustration) Peter Wesley-Smith, *An Introduction to the Hong Kong Legal System* 3rd edn Oxford University Press p 45)
pp 51–52	Danny Gittings, *An Introduction to the Hong Kong Basic Law* (2nd edn Hong Kong University Press pp 318–321)
pp 72–78	Hong Kong Bar Association, 'Response to the Consultation Document on the Proposals to Implement Article 23 of the Basic Law (9 December 2002)
pp 80–81	Bob Allcock (then Solicitor General), 'Letter to Hong Kong' (Department of Justice 15 December 2002)
pp 87–88	Chen Lei, *Legal Culture and Legal Transplants* (International Academy of Comparative Law
pp 90–93	Christine Loh, *Inheritance Rights of Indigenous Women of the New Territories* (Seminar Address 22 May 2004)
pp 106–108	Peter Wesley-Smith, 'The Content of the Common Law in Hong Kong in R Wacks (ed) *The New Legal Order in Hong Kong* (Hong Kong University Press)
page 125	Ludwig Ng, 'Law for the times' (*South China Morning Post* 29 September 2010)
pp 157–159	Anne Cheung, 'Language Rights and the Hong Kong Courts *(Hong Kong Journal of Applied Linguistics* (December 1997)
page 189	(Illustration) Legislative Council, 'How Laws Are Made' and see www.legco.hk
pp 196–198	Hong Kong Judiciary, *Guido Karl Wenk v Alan Lee Goldstein* [1998] HKCFI 252

pp 207–210	Law Reform Commission of Hong Kong, 'Extrinsic Materials as an Aid to Statutory Interpretation' (Report March 1997)
pp 241–249	Hong Kong Judiciary, *A Solicitor v Law Society of Hong Kong* [2008] 2 HKC 1
pp 272–275	Legislative Council, LC Paper No CB(4) 822/13-14 (04)
pp 276–277	Malcolm Merry, 'Not Entirely Legal' (Blog part 55)
pp 326–327	Steering Committee on the Review of Legal Education and Training in Hong Kong, 'Preliminary Review (Report of the Consultants)' August 2001
pp 349–353	Law Reform Commission of Hong Kong, 'Criteria for Jury Service' (Report June 2010)
page 392	Law Reform Commission of Hong Kong, 'Release of report on conditional fees' (Press Release 9 July 2007)
pp 393–394	Legislative Council (Proceedings) 26 March 2014
pp 435–436	Paul Shieh (Chairman HKBA) Speech at Opening of the Legal Year (2015)
pp 453–454	Cary Huang, 'Party faces Catch 22 with attempts at Judicial Reform (*South China Morning Post* 5 April 2015)
pp 472–473	Chen Youxi, 'A Tale of Two Cities: The Legal Profession in China' (IBA Human Rights Institute, March 2013)
pp 510–511	Legislative Council Secretariat, *Research Study on the Agreement between Hong Kong and the Mainland Concerning Surrender of Fugitive Offenders: The Issue of Re-extradition*
pp 539–540	Hong Kong Human Rights Commission: Society for Community Organization, *Report to the United Nations April 2008*
pp 552–555	Department of Justice, 'Prosecution Code 2013'
pp 557–559	Legislative Council, LC Paper No CB(2) 2201/10-11 (01)

Index

Access to Justice, 367–372, 394–400, 469–474
Act of State, 38–43, 60, 67, 69, 134–136, 170, 223, 232
Alternative Dispute Resolution, 401–431, 476–482
  Adjudication, 430, 431
  Arbitration, 405–415, 476–480, 495–502
  Mediation and Conciliation, 416–430, 477–482
Aw, Sally, 94, 440, 449, 557–560

Basic Law (Hong Kong)
  Amendment of, 46, 99, 100
  Article, 1 57
  Article 2, 45, 60, 70, 137, 490, 525
  Article 5, 43, 55, 56, 61, 62
  Article 8, 43–46, 59–62, 64, 70, 100–109, 112, 113, 116, 173, 174, 176, 212, 239, 240, 242, 250, 432, 490, 567, 569
  Article 9, 70, 157–161
  Article 12, 60, 137
  Article 13, 230
  Article 17 25, 67, 173, 185
  Article 18, 10, 25, 46, 49, 60, 62, 68–70, 173, 177, 212, 240, 242, 260, 432, 524, 589
  Article 19, 38, 42, 69, 137, 170, 230, 231, 236, 260, 506, 525
  Article 22, 41, 84, 98, 225, 226, 296, 505
  Article 23, 26, 42, 43, 71–83, 377, 446, 512, 526, 527, 535
  Article 24, 84, 85, 98, 171, 224–226, 232–234, 296, 297
  Article 25, 439
  Article 26, 85
  Article 27, 83, 84, 86, 555, 590
  Article 28, 532
  Article 29, 534
  Article 31, 532
  Article 35, 309, 370
  Article 39, 35, 36, 83, 592
  Article 40, 54, 83, 86, 88–93, 115, 117
  Article 44, 85
  Article 45, 54, 57, 85, 173, 526, 590
  Article 46, 137, 227, 485, 486
  Article 48, 225
  Article 57, 547
  Article 63, 553, 555, 557, 561, 564
  Article 64, 212
  Article 66, 65, 176–178
  Article 68, 178
  Article 73, 179, 194
  Article 74, 190
  Article 80, 103
  Article 81, 45, 60
  Article 82, 60, 102, 103, 109, 280, 300
  Article 84, 95, 118, 121, 131, 244, 260, 269, 291, 432, 438
  Article 85, 95, 285, 296, 449
  Article 86, 339, 355, 360, 362–364
  Article 87, 486
  Article 88, 279, 284
  Article 89, 285, 449
  Article 90, 279, 282, 449
  Article 92, 285, 300

Article 93, 160, 449
Article 95, 489, 490, 492, 493, 496, 502, 518
Article 96, 503
Article 158, 97–99, 170, 171, 223–235, 250, 295, 299, 438
Article 159, 2, 46, 97, 99, 100, 490
Article 160, 44, 62, 63, 65, 66, 212, 222, 446
Enactment 27
Interpretation of, 30, 41, 45, 69, 84, 85, 97–99, 122, 137, 138, 154, 170–172, 174, 175, 194, 223–235, 250, 295–299, 360, 438, 459, 483–486, 524, 525
(as a) Source of Hong Kong Law, 60, 70–100
Status, 36, 63, 66, 67, 70
"Big Spender", 458, 464, 505–509, 522
Bill of Rights (Ordinance), 23, 36, 63, 66, 67, 70, 104, 147, 211, 219, 221–224, 266, 295, 363, 370, 378, 383, 387, 409, 446, 458, 467, 531–533, 535, 555, 592
Bokhary, Amina, 165, 166, 169, 440–442
Bokhary J, 38, 156, 171, 172, 203, 224, 225, 230, 231, 258, 262, 293, 298, 299, 310, 409, 516
(The) **"Booksellers"**, 86, 507, 509, 512, 523

Cantonese (use of in the courts), 45, 145, 146, 157–161, 346–348, 366
Capital Punishment, 130, 163, 164, 443, 461, 465–470, 489, 504, 509, 525
Captain Elliot, 2–7, 113, 115
Proclamations, 3–7, 113, 115
Chancery (*see* **Equity**)
Chek Lap Kok Airport, 23, 31, 425, 430
Chief Executive (Hong Kong)
Appointment, 14, 16, 21, 28, 51, 71, 93, 100, 173, 179, 182, 525, 526
(S) Election Committee/Nominating Committee, 28, 29, 51, 54, 85, 446, 526, 590
Eligibility, 26, 29, 48, 85, 153
Lam, Carrie, 26, 54, 341, 526, 527, 589, 591

Leung, C Y, 96, 341, 387, 526, 547, 548
Role and Functions, 27, 34, 38, 65, 67, 99, 124, 134–136, 149, 150, 170, 174, 179, 180, 183–187, 189–191, 225, 233, 268, 279–282, 284–286, 294, 372, 446, 503, 511, 531, 547, 548, 557
Status, 455
Term of Office, 53–55, 137, 138, 227, 485, 486
Tsang, Donald, 89, 182, 194, 355, 485, 560
Tung Chee Hwa, 46, 72, 82, 86, 137, 227, 296, 305, 440, 485, 526
Chief Judge of the High Court, 32, 33, 160, 214, 242, 245, 272, 274, 279, 280–285, 287, 293, 353
Chief Justice (Hong Kong)
Eligibility, Appointment and Removal, 33, 93, 335, 336
Li, Andrew, 121, 161, 162, 166, 167, 171, 172, 214, 241–251, 260, 268, 271, 282, 284, 298, 300, 337, 369, 398, 404, 417, 435, 449, 457, 477
Ma, Geoffrey, 49, 56, 120, 230, 234, 261, 282–284, 293, 298, 300, 418, 419, 436–439, 456, 477
Role and Functions, 105, 124, 134–136, 146, 155, 158, 161, 179, 278–280, 285, 286, 295, 332, 355, 388, 395, 446
Chief Secretary for Administration
Chan, Anson, 28
Hui, Rafael, 340, 361, 548
Lam, Carrie, 82, 233, 298, 526
Role and Functions, 374, 485
Tsang, Donald, 137
Chinese (PRC) Law
As a Source of Hong Kong Law, 60, 63, 68, 69, 175, 177, 566, 576, 577, 589
"Co-location" (Collocation), 69, 94, 142, 177, 589, 590
Not Generally Applicable in Hong Kong, 49, 52, 60, 62, 68, 69, 71, 83, 177, 490, 589

Index 597

Chinese (PRC) Legal System
  Contrasted with Hong Kong System, 432–488
  Interface with Hong Kong System, 489–527
Civil Law
  (In) China (PRC), 434, 447, 459, 486, 488, 489
  Civil and Criminal Law Contrasted, 102, 129, 130
  (And) Common Law (see Common Law), 100, 101
Common Law
  (And) Civil Law, 100, 101
  Declaratory Theory of, 8, 103–109, 116, 131, 259, 289, 290
  Equity Contrasted, 100, 101
  Meaning(s), 100–103
  Preservation post-1997, 10, 46, 47, 60–62, 100–103, 105–109, 567
  (As a) Source of Hong Kong Law, 59, 60, 100–109
  (And) Statute Law, 101
  System(s), 105–109
Communist Party (PRC)
  Supremacy, 296, 434, 438, 439, 447, 451, 453, 454
Conditional and Contingency Fee, 337, 338, 368, 369, 390–392, 398
Confucius/Confucianism, 477, 478
"Congo" Case (see **Basic Law Interpretation**), 41, 97, 171, 228–231, 283, 438
Convention of Peking (1860), 2, 12
Convention of Peking (1898), 2, 3, 12
Court of Appeal (England), 111, 123, 217, 240, 249, 253, 256–259, 262, 291, 341, 348, 409, 483, 566, 568, 570, 572
Court of Appeal (Hong Kong), 5, 25, 34, 44, 98, 131–133, 138, 143, 152–155, 160, 165–167, 213, 214, 229, 230, 240–243, 245–252, 259–261, 268, 269, 273–275, 278, 283, 293, 300, 301, 308, 317, 320–322, 324, 341, 375, 382, 394, 495, 515, 561, 591

Court of Final Appeal, 25, 30, 32, 33, 37, 38, 41, 45, 46, 49, 50, 60, 68, 95, 97–99, 102, 103, 105, 108, 109, 118, 122, 123, 129, 133–137, 153, 155, 156, 160, 165, 170, 171, 174, 203, 214, 215, 219, 223–234, 236, 239–241, 244, 245, 247–251, 254, 258, 259, 261, 264, 268–271, 276, 278–282, 291, 293, 295–297, 299, 300, 308, 310, 320, 321, 324, 336, 341, 376, 381, 386, 394, 395, 409, 411, 412, 438, 440, 446, 450, 457, 486, 490, 493, 495, 515, 561, 563, 567, 581–583, 591
  Appointment, Removal, Retirement of Judges, 32, 33, 134–136, 172, 179, 262, 271, 278–286, 300
  Autonomy (and Limits), 30, 45, 99, 135, 155, 156, 170–172, 224–235, 260, 290, 296–301, 450–451, 525
  Final Adjudication, 45, 49, 60, 95, 97, 102, 103, 105, 108, 133, 136, 137, 170, 174, 250, 409, 446, 490, 567
  Interpretation of Basic Law, 45, 97–99, 137, 170–175, 223–235, 250, 295–297, 438, 525
  Overseas Judges, 55, 122, 123, 156, 161, 165, 269–271, 274, 280–282, 293, 300
  Role and Powers, 25, 37, 129, 133–138
Court of First Instance
  And Jury Trials, 138–140, 340, 363, 464, 563
  Language of the Court, 160, 344, 345, 363
  Precedent Status, 251, 252
  Role and Functions, 138–141, 145–147, 150–155, 199, 213, 220, 221, 229, 241, 275, 293, 386, 394, 408, 409, 420, 423, 458, 495, 514, 563
Cross-Border Crime, 458, 505–512, 518–525
Cross-Border Insolvency, 490, 512–517
Cultural Revolution, 364, 433, 465, 478, 530
Customary Law, 1, 48, 59–61, 63, 87–93, 113–118, 240, 266, 566

Delegated Legislation
  Creation of, 191–193
  Definition, 191–193
  Researching and Citing, 573, 574, 576, 578
  As a Source of Law, 92, 122, 175, 566
Deng Xiaoping, vi, 15, 20, 51, 441, 442, 489
Department of Justice
  Independence, 41, 456, 529, 551–562, 564, 591
  (Application for) Review of Sentence, 138, 165–167, 300, 301, 529, 561, 591
  Role and Functions, 42, 81, 93, 163, 183, 185–188, 190, 269, 293, 299, 305, 354, 407, 414, 440, 456, 498
Director of Public Prosecutions
  Cross, Grenville, 162, 163, 165, 167, 168, 440, 459, 547, 551, 556, 559–561
  Zervos, Kevin, 299, 314, 395, 544, 559, 560
Due Process
  (And) Crime Control, 356, 464, 521, 527
  Meaning, 408, 413
  (In) PRC, 460, 464, 504, 509, 518, 527
Durkheim, E, 169, 465, 466, 468

Elliot, Elsie
  (*see* Tu, Elsie)
English Law
  (Continuing) Influence, 60, 120, 121, 261
  Reception of, 4–10
  Researching, 567–576
English Legislation
  Amending English Common Law, 9, 10, 63, 64
  Researching, 573–576
  (as a) Source of Hong Kong Law, 5–10, 29, 44, 63–66
  Status, 63–66
Equity
  History, 109–112
  Jury, 358, 359, 361
  Meaning, 100, 101, 109, 110, 569
  Practice and Procedure, 109, 110
  (As a) Source of Hong Kong Law,

8–10, 46, 59, 61–63, 92, 100, 102, 109–114, 240, 566
Executive Council (ExCo), 7, 27, 48, 173, 179, 183, 184, 186, 294, 445

Falun Gong, 42, 72, 77, 82, 83, 172, 293, 460, 468, 526
Functional Constituencies, 31, 96, 174, 178, 179, 181, 189, 294, 445

Genn (Hazel, Dame, Professor), 130, 402–404, 418, 419, 477
"Golden Rule" (*see* **Statutory Interpretation**), 201, 202, 208, 218

"High Degree of Autonomy" (for Hong Kong), 16, 21, 37, 50, 52, 53, 60, 70, 71, 137, 138, 155, 170, 173, 177, 296, 490, 525, 588
Hong Kong Courts
  Precedent Status, 236–252
  Structure, 129–133, 152–155
Hong Kong Government
  Executive-led, 27, 64, 65, 174, 179, 287, 294, 444, 445, 455, 456
Hong Kong Judiciary
  Appointment, Removal, Retirement, 32, 33, 93, 94, 135, 179, 271–274, 277–287, 296, 300, 446, 449
  Background, 261, 265, 271, 280, 282, 286–290, 292, 293, 444
  Independence and Autonomy, 45, 49, 155, 294–301
  Manpower Shortage, 272–278, 282
Hong Kong Legislation
  Adaptation and Localisation, 28–31
  Amendment of Law via, 8–10, 46, 47, 49, 61, 63–67, 103, 105, 113, 117
  Legislative Process, 180–191, 194
  Limits on Autonomy, 25, 69, 70, 109
  Researching and Citing, 578–580
  (as a) Source of Hong Kong Law, 64–67, 177–180, 566
House of Lords (Judicial Committee of the)
  Precedent Position, 50, 103, 104,

Index 599

107–109, 123, 131, 132, 237, 239,
240, 243–245, 249, 250, 253, 259,
260, 263, 264, 288, 290, 291
(And) Purposive Interpretation, 203–215
Replacement by Supreme Court, 131,
241, 569

**Independent Commission Against
Corruption (ICAC)**, 14, 28, 93, 309,
318, 393, 394, 456, 518–522, 529, 530,
533, 541, 544–549, 551, 559, 560, 587
**International Covenant on Civil and
Political Rights (ICCPR)**, 26, 35, 36,
66, 73, 81, 83, 222, 378, 470
**International Covenant on Economic,
Social and Cultural Rights
(ICESCR)**, 35, 73, 83
(Court) **Interpreters**, 45, 161, 346, 366
Ip, Regina, 26, 71, 78, 79, 82, 95

**Joint Declaration (On the Hong Kong
Question)**, 12, 15–29, 31, 32, 34, 35,
38, 39, 44, 48, 52, 53, 61, 72, 73, 86,
135, 157, 193, 279, 489, 591
Joint Liaison Group (Sino-British), 18, 21,
29, 37, 135, 226, 280, 300
Judicial Precedent
Binding (Stare Decisis), 236–243, 248,
249, 251, 252, 263–266
Hierarchy of the Courts, 236, 239–250,
252, 411
Law Reporting and, 237, 266, 267
Obiter Dicta, 103, 237, 238, 261
Persuasive (Non-binding), 244–247,
259–261
Ratio Decidendi, 103, 236, 237, 245, 252,
254–258
(The) **Jury**
Basic Law and, 95, 339, 355, 360,
362–364
Criticisms of, 162, 360–362
Eligibility for Service, 343–346
"Equity", 358, 359
Limited Use, 340, 341
Representativeness, 347–354
Research on, 356–358

Role and Function, 342–343

Kowloon Walled City, 11, 12, 142, 143

Law Reform Commission of Hong Kong,
123–128
Lack of Prompt Statutory Response to,
127, 188, 212, 354
"Laws Previously in Force" (*see* **Article 8
Basic Law**)
**Lay Participation in the Hong Kong Legal
System**
(The) Jury, 339–364
Lay (Special) Magistrates, 366
Lay Prosecutors, 365, 366
Lee, Martin, 39–41, 55, 57, 71, 231, 467,
588
Legal Aid and Advice
(and) Access to Justice, 337, 338,
367–372, 385–401, 469–477
Administration, 368, 372–374
Civil Legal Aid, 367, 377–381
Criminal Legal Aid, 367, 374–377
Duty Lawyer Service, 383–385
Eligibility for, 163, 237, 337, 367, 369
Supplementary, 367, 381–382
Legal Profession (Hong Kong), 302–338
Barriers to Entry, 302, 305–307, 326, 330,
331
Barristers, 312–320
Discipline and Regulation of, 320–324
"Fusion" Debate, 334–337
Legal Education and Training, 325–334
Legal Executives, 338
Rights of Audience
Solicitors, 303–312
Legal Research (Introduction to), 565–587
Online, 565, 566, 571–573, 576, 577, 579,
581, 582, 587
Researching English Law, 567–576
Researching Hong Kong Law, 578–587
Researching PRC Law, 576–578
Legislative Council (LegCo)
Constitution, 94, 113, 177–180
Eligibility and Ineligibility (for), 48, 69,
85, 234, 561, 590, 591

Limited Role, 27, 64, 65, 173–175, 178, 180, 190, 194
Members' Bills, 188–191
(the) "Through Train" (Abandoned), 25, 31
Legislative Process (Hong Kong), 180–191
Letters Patent (and Royal Instructions), 7, 44, 64, 176
Li, Rebecca, 547, 548
"Literal Rule" (*see* **Statutory Interpretation**)
Litigants in Person (Unrepresented Litigants), 367, 369, 384, 388–390, 397, 399, 477
"Localisation" (and Adaptation) of Previous Laws, 28–31
Lord Chancellor (United Kingdom), 110, 444, 449

Macau
  Basic Law, 26, 484
  Court of Final Appeal (TUI), 257, 300, 450, 457
  National Security Law, 26, 82, 512, 526
  Sovereignty, 15, 18
Mao Zedong, 14, 434, 463, 471, 478, 487
"Mischief Rule" (*see* **Statutory Interpretation**)
Mutual Legal Assistance, 492, 502, 503
  Arbitration Awards, 495–502
  Cross-border Collaboration, 517–524
  Cross-border Insolvency, 512–517
  Enforcement of Judgments, 492–495
  Rendition Debate, 503–512

National People's Congress
  Constitution, Role, Powers, 25, 26, 46, 60, 69, 70, 93, 99, 100, 173, 452, 491
  Standing Committee of, 65–67, 70, 84, 85, 97–99, 137, 170, 171, 175, 177, 185, 194, 223–228, 230–235, 250, 292, 296–299, 360, 438, 446, 447, 457, 483–486, 491, 494, 525, 526
Natural Justice, 151, 222, 295, 321, 408, 409, 456, 561, 591

New Territories
  Customary Law, 54, 61, 83, 86–96, 115–118
  (1898) Lease, 1, 2, 11, 14–16, 19
  Sovereignty, 11, 12, 21
New York Convention (re Arbitral Awards), 409, 410, 479, 495, 496

"One Country, Two Systems", vi, 20, 21, 30, 43, 48, 49, 51–56, 60, 61, 76, 78, 83, 99, 175, 177, 227, 229, 287, 293, 296–298, 336, 432, 450, 489–491, 505, 506, 508, 510, 516, 524, 589

Palmerston (Lord), 1–3, 113
Parliamentary Sovereignty, 104, 208, 445, 573
Patten (Last Governor), 22, 25, 29, 31, 32, 39, 40, 66, 98, 135, 445, 546, 591
Pepper v Hart (*see* **Statutory Interpretation**)
Plea Bargaining, 167, 168, 316, 464
PRC Constitution, 69, 70, 122, 434, 441, 447, 448, 451, 452, 459–461, 463, 480
PRC Judiciary, 296, 448, 450–455, 461, 464, 489, 491, 494, 504
PRC Legislation
  Interpretation of, 85, 97–99, 223–235, 482–486
  Limited Application to Hong Kong, 46, 49, 62, 63, 173, 177
  Researching, 576–578
  (As a) Source of Hong Kong Law, 22, 32, 49, 60, 61, 68–100, 175, 177, 566
Privy Council (Judicial Committee)
  Replacement by Court of Final Appeal, 25, 33, 45, 46, 105, 118, 129, 133, 136, 137
  Role and Precedent Position, 49, 50, 131, 132, 138, 156, 237, 239–245, 247, 249–251, 257, 259, 260, 267–269, 299, 514, 567
Provisional Legislative Council, 25, 31–33, 40, 98, 224, 446
"Purposive" Approaches (to **Statutory Interpretation**)

Index

Qing (Ch'ing) Law, 92, 116, 117, 433, 442

Retrospective (Retroactive) Legislation, 104, 219, 221–223, 290, 573, 592
Right of Abode (Hong Kong), 15, 20, 23, 24, 26, 29–31, 84, 85, 98–100, 171, 219, 224–227, 232–234, 278, 279, 282, 283, 296–299, 360, 446, 483, 525
"Rule of Law"
  Hong Kong/PRC comparison, vii, 57, 336, 432, 438–465, 483, 486, 488
  Meaning, 39, 41, 233, 278, 295, 297, 298, 373, 435–465, 553, 554, 592

Secretary for Justice
  Cheng, Teresa, 94, 228, 560, 591
  Leung, Elsie, 30, 33, 39, 44, 84, 94, 137, 155, 165, 171, 225, 227, 228, 233, 296–298, 440, 459, 485, 498, 505, 506, 508
  Role and Functions, 124, 138, 166, 180, 183, 185–187, 232, 268, 284, 333, 342, 365, 499, 529, 551, 553–557, 561–564, 591
  Wong Yan Lung, 68, 94, 125, 126, 228, 362, 364, 372, 382, 399, 406, 418, 419, 428–430, 477
  Yuen, Rimsky, 69, 94, 186, 187, 228, 233, 301, 406, 414, 436, 456, 524, 561, 591
Separation of Powers, 179, 203, 227, 293–296, 373, 442–456, 482, 563
Sources of Hong Kong Law, 59–128
State of Emergency, 25, 69, 71
State Secrets, 71, 72, 75, 76, 81, 460, 461, 463, 473, 474, 512, 526

Statutory Interpretation, 173–235
  (Of) Basic Law 30, 32, 41, 45, 69, 84, 97–99, 122, 137, 138, 154, 170–175, 223–235, 250, 295–297, 438, 459, 483–486, 525
  "Ejusdem Generis" Rule, 217, 218
  "Golden Rule", 201–202
  "Literal Rule", 195–201
  "Mischief Rule", 202
  Pepper v Hart, 205–216, 576
  "Purposive" Approaches, 195, 202–216
Supreme People's Court, 434, 447, 451–454, 461–463, 471, 484, 493, 495, 496, 498, 499, 501, 502, 576, 577
Supreme People's Procuratorate, 484, 520

Thatcher, Margaret, 15, 18, 347, 444
Tiananmen Square, 20, 23, 24, 31, 434, 487
Treaty of Nanking, 2–4, 11, 12, 113
Tribunals
  Generally, 32, 33, 130, 131, 133, 138, 141–151
  Labour, 144, 145
  Land, 141–143
  Legal Representation at, 141, 320, 377
  Obscene Articles, 146–148
Tu, Elsie, 546

Unequal Treaties, 12–15, 20

Weber, M, 288, 358, 359, 464, 465
Woolf (Lord), 130, 168, 398, 399, 402, 403, 418, 477
Writ System, 102, 109, 110